France

A HANDBOOK FOR NEW RESIDENTS

More related titles from How To Books

A French Restoration
*The story of two people who bought and restored
their own mini chateau*

Starting a Business in France
*A step by step guide to turning your dream of self-employment
in France into successful reality*

Starting & Running a B & B in France
*How to make money and enjoy a new lifestyle running
your own chambres d'hôtes*

Going to Live on the French Riviera
*Whether you are going to the Cote d'Azur to study, retire or work
this book will tell you all you need to know*

howtobooks

Please send for a free copy of the latest catalogue:
How To Books
Spring Hill House, Spring Hill Road,
Begbroke, Oxford OX5 1RX, United Kingdom
info@howtobooks.co.uk
www.howtobooks.co.uk

France

A HANDBOOK FOR NEW RESIDENTS

—M. MICHAEL BRADY—

howtobooks

Published by How To Books Ltd,
Spring Hill House, Spring Hill Road,
Begbroke, Oxford OX5 1RX, United Kingdom
Tel: (01865) 375794 Fax: (01865) 379162
email: info@howtobooks.co.uk
http://www.howtobooks.co.uk

First published 2007

British Library Cataloguing in Publication Data
A catalogue record for this book is available from
the British Library.

ISBN 13: 978 1 84528 132 8

Produced for How To Books by Deer Park Productions, Tavistock
Typeset by *specialist* publishing services ltd, Montgomery
Printed and bound by Bell & Bain Ltd, Glasgow

NOTE: The material contained in this book is set out in good
faith for general guidance and no liability can be accepted
for loss or expense incurred as a result of relying in particular
circumstances on statements made in the book. The laws and
regulations are complex and liable to change, and readers should
check the current with the relevant authorities before taking action.

Contents

France: a handbook for new residents

Preface

This book is a window through which you can view a selection of the enormous amount of information available on France, arranged as a ready reference for new residents or long-term visitors. It's not a narrative, so it's not a book to be read cover-to-cover. It is a collection of the bits and pieces of information needed in everyday life and work, but it is not a tourist guidebook (though tourists may find it useful). It's intended to be read before you depart for France as well as after you arrive and settle there.

The approach is bottom-up. This is a book about France and the French as they are, not as they might be seen from somewhere else. So, save for international statistical rankings, there are no comparisons of the country or its inhabitants with other countries or peoples. Yet, even facts need context. So, each of the 47 chapters begins with an introduction to set it in perspective. From automobiles to cross-borders initiatives, French contributions are greater than realised by the world at large.

The topics are arranged in alphabetical order, grouped by subject into 47 chapters, which also are in alphabetical order. All facts presented are available in France from the organisations and the printed and online sources mentioned. So this book is also a starting point for finding further information.

As its title indicates, the aim is to ease and speed your access to essential information, whether your search is triggered by thinking of a topic in English or by encountering a term in French. Consequently, there are two indexes, one in English and one in French.

British English is the language of this book, because it best suits the majority of new residents from other countries, many of whom have English as a second if not first language. A glossary of British English – American English is included for the convenience of American readers.

I compiled this book at the suggestion of colleague Nick Hutchins, who, like me, is a long-time Francophile. I am grateful to him for that suggestion and for his vetting of the manuscript as I compiled it. And to Olivia Ney, a young, polyglot native French speaker, I am grateful for the meticulous yet sensitive editing of the French terms and expressions in the book. Finally, I am grateful to colleague Michael Rogers for his assistance with many illustrations.

M. Michael Brady

How to use this book

If possible, read the Checklist before you depart for France. Then you may find information by reading the chapters or by reading individual entries, in alphabetical order in the chapters. Public and private sector organisations are mentioned by their names in English. You may locate a specific entry among those of the chapter to which it relates or by its page number as listed in the English or French indexes.

Most entries and many principal terms are in English and are followed by their French equivalents, italicised in brackets: English word(s) [*Mot(s) français*]. The French names in brackets are written in the style of encyclopaedias, such as *Larousse*, without the definite articles, *le, la* and *les*, that otherwise usually appear in French. There are two exceptions to that rule: names that always appear with a definite article in French, such as that of the French social security system (Chapter 22) and words for which the omission of the definite article changes meaning, as happens with the French word for kiss, *le baiser* (Chapter 5) that without the definite article *le* becomes *baiser*, a rude word. Words in French that have no direct equivalents and consequently usually are not translated into English, such as the motto *Liberté, Egalité, Fraternité*, appear in French only. Moreover, following the convention of official French texts in English, to preserve their specific meanings, four French words spelled almost as they are in English are not translated: the administrative divisions of *Département, Région* and *Provence* and the historical event of the *Révolution*, but the Republic [*République*] is translated.

All multiword names are written in title case in English, with the first letter of each principal word capitalised, and in sentence case in French, with only the first letter of the first word capitalised, save for the name of the country, which always is capitalised.

Cross-references to other topics in the same chapter are indicated by the name of a topic in **bold**, whilst cross-references to topics in other chapters are suffixed with the chapter number in parentheses: **topic** (Chapter number).

The names and postal addresses of organisations are written as they are by the organisations themselves, though in compliance with present addressing standards, without the comma between the number and the name of a street. Except for emergency numbers and four-digit service numbers, all mainland French telecommunications numbers are eight digits long plus a two-digit destination code that begins with a zero. Traditionally they are written in groups of two with intervening spaces, but some organisations write them with other groupings. So, for consistency, numbers are written without intervening spaces, save for a single space between the initial destination code and the eight-digit number. All numbers are written as they are to be dialled in France. If you dial a number from abroad, add the international access indicator (00 in Europe) and the country code for France (33), but delete the initial zero of the destination code, to dial the numbers. The country codes for numbers in other countries are given, prefixed by the international standard plus sign, such as +44 for a number in the United Kingdom, which from France would be dialled 0044.

For private individuals, email and interactive communication via websites now is more commonplace than electronic communication using physical telefax terminals [*télécopieurs physiques*]. Moreover, organisations with facsimile numbers often have several numbers, one for each department or person to be contacted. So facsimile numbers are not listed with addresses unless an organisation lists a facsimile number as its only telecommunications number. If you wish to communicate via facsimile, visit the website listed to find the facsimile number(s).

All websites are listed in italics without the http:// prefix, such as *www.howtobooks.co.uk*, whilst email addresses are listed in italics in full, such as *info@howtobooks.co.uk*. Most of the websites listed are French, so:

- for French websites (most with a .fr suffix), language is not stated if the site is in French only, but languages in addition to French are stated, such as "with pages in English and in Spanish".

- for international organisations and organisations based in other countries (usually with .org, .com or country suffix), all site languages are stated, such as "pages in English, French, German and Spanish".

Relevant books and periodicals are referenced, not least because they are lasting, while websites, particularly commercial websites, may change by the day, if not faster.

For organisations with local offices, there are references to the White Pages [*Pages Blanches*] or Yellow Pages [*Pages Jaunes*] of telephone directories. The Yellow Pages are available online at *www.pagesjaunes.fr* with alphabetical indexing and search in French and in English. However, *Pages Jaunes* is a commercial enterprise, owned 54% by France Telecom, and there are other directory publishers, such as Elitel with directories for cities in the southern and western parts of the country. These directories have yellow and white pages, but under different names, such as Elitel's *Les pages elite* for the yellow pages and *Les pages alpha* for the white pages. So in this book, the terms "yellow pages" and "white pages" refer only to the colours on which the pages are printed and are not to proprietary names.

Prices vary over time by location. So, typical prices valid at press time are included in Chapter 37 on Prices, but elsewhere prices are stated only when they refer to specific dates or are likely to stay fixed for many years.

The metric system of measurement is used throughout this book, not least because it originated in France. If you are accustomed to the English system of measurement, as used in the USA and some areas of life in the UK, you may wish to convert.

- In length, there are about two and a half centimetres to the inch, so ten centimetres is about four inches, and one metre is a little less than 40 inches. A person two metres tall (6 ft. 7 in.) is very tall, but a car with a length of 2.5 metres (the length of the Smart coupé made in France) is very short.

- In weight, there are 454 grammes to a pound and 2.2 pounds to a kilogramme. So to convert from kilogrammes to pounds, divide by two then subtract 10%. To convert from kilogrammes to pounds, multiply by two and add 10%.

- For liquid volumes, as for dairy products and petrol, there are two conversions, because Imperial (UK) units are 20% larger than US units. There are 3.785 litres in a US gallon, and a US quart is equivalent to 0.95 litre. There are 4.546 litres in an Imperial gallon, and a UK quart is equivalent to 1.14 litre.

- For temperature, convert from Fahrenheit to Celsius by first subtracting 32, then dividing by 2 and finally adding 10%. Example: what is 50°F, a typical spring or autumn temperature, in Celsius degrees?

$50° - 32° = 18°$ above freezing
$18°/2 = 9°$
$9° + 10%$ of $9° = 9.9°C$

To convert from Celsius to Fahrenheit degrees, multiply by 2 and subtract 10%, then add 32. Example: what is −10°C, a chilly winter temperature, in Fahrenheit degrees?

$-10° \times 2 = -20°$
$-20° - 10%$ of $-20° = -18°$ below freezing
$-18° + 32° = 24°F$

Remembering a few temperature equivalents also helps mental conversions between the two scales. A comfortable indoor temperature is 20°C (68°F); the body temperature is 37°C (98.6°F); water freezes at 0°C (32°F).

Glossary of British English – American English words

The spelling conventions of British English and American English differ, most famously in the s-z differences in spellings, as in *recognise* (British) and *recognize* (American). Moreover, American English tends to be more phonetic – *esthetic* (American) is spelled more closely to the way it is spoken than is *aesthetic* (British). These and other differences in spelling are minor; they often escape reader notice, though word processing spell checkers highlight them. However, some words are problematic, because their meanings differ. So, for the benefit of American readers, here's a list of the principal everyday words that differ between the UK and the USA, the British word first in **bold**, followed by the American word.

aerial: antenna

anti-clockwise: counterclockwise

baby's dummy: pacifier

banknote: bill

caravan: house trailer

cashpoint: ATM

cheque: check

chips: French fries

cooker: stove

crisps: chips

current account: checking account

curtains: drapes

district: neighborhood

doctor: physician

driving licence: driver's license

estate agent: real-estate agent

estate car: station wagon

flat: apartment

football: soccer
garden: yard
gearbox: transmission
greengrocer: vegetable market
grill: broil
ground floor: first floor
handbrake: emergency brake
high street: main street
motorway: freeway
nappy: diaper
number plates: license plates
pavement: sidewalk
petrol: gasoline
petrol station: gas station
pitch (football): field
post (verb): mail
refuse / rubbish: garbage
railway: railroad
ring road: beltway
road surface: pavement
spanner: wrench
shareholder: stockholder
spirits: liquor
sweets: candy
terraced house: row house
toilet: bathroom, restroom
transport: transportation
trousers: pants or slacks
trunk call: long-distance call
tyre: tire
underground: subway
walk: hike
wardrobe: closet

Check list (*Check-list*)

Before you leave for France, check the following. Except for passports, identification cards, driving licences and credit cards, which must be originals, you may bring photocopies of all documents. In alphabetical order, the principal details and documents are:

- Apostille affixed to give international validity to any legally valid document that you believe you may need, such as a copy of your professional certificate.
- Bank account number, bank branch address and international transfer number.
- Baptism certificate if you have been baptised in a Christian church and wish to join a congregation in France.
- Birth certificate(s) for yourself and all members of your family, as needed to apply for a national identity number.
- Car ownership records, including purchase receipt, if you will import the car to France.
- Car insurance policies and records.
- Credit card(s) and credit details.
- Curriculum vitae (*CV*) or résumé of your qualifications and experience.
- Customs: Make a list, in French, of the belongings you will bring into France as removal goods, principally for clearing French customs but also in case outgoing customs clearance is required in your country of departure.
- Divorce papers, including any agreement on alimony payments by or to yourself.
- Driving licence(s).
- Educational certificates, including school, college or university diplomas, transcripts of marks if you intend to continue your education, trade certifications, professional organisation and union membership details. If possible, have these documents translated into French.
- Embassy registration: Check whether your home country requires or does not require registration at its embassy in France. Most countries do not require registration, but some strongly encourage it.
- French language capability is essential to getting on well in the country. If you are reasonably proficient or wish to refresh your capability in the language, watch TV5, the second most extensive international TV channel available via 59

satellite links or on cable on all five continents. If you don't speak or read French, start learning as soon as possible.

- Health insurance: If you are a national of and a member of the National Insurance of one of the 25 EEA countries, you should have a valid European Health Insurance Card, which entitles you to treatment on a par with residents of France. If you are a national of a country outside the EEA, you may need private health insurance.

- Home country matters: The embassies of most countries offer advice to citizens on their rights in France, on tax and other home country matters when living abroad, and on aspects of life in France that differ from the home country. For example, services for Britons are offered by the Consulate-General, 18bis rue d'Anjou, 75008 Paris, Tel 01 44513100, including forms and information sheets downloadable from its website at *www.britishembassy.gov.uk*, and the American Embassy has an Office of American Services at 2, rue Saint-Florentin, 75001 Paris Cedex 08 and a website at *www.amb-usa.fr* that offers numerous fact sheets as well as a 202-page "Blue Book Guide for U.S. Citizens residing in France".

- Insurance policies that may remain in force and for which you may need to continue paying premiums, as with life assurance.

- Internet familiarity, as public sector information increasingly is electronic only.

- Mail redirection: Notify all correspondents and business connections of your change of address. Check with the post office that serves your home to ensure that post will be redirected.

- Marriage certificate if you are married and particularly if your spouse moves with you; needed in public registrations and tax matters.

- Medical record, particularly if you are disabled or depend on a prescription drug and wish to transfer your medical status to France.

- Medicine: You will need a Schengen certificate if you take a prescription medicine that may be classified as a narcotic, as are many hypnotics, sedatives and painkillers. If you wish to know if a specific medicine is classified as a narcotic, ask at a pharmacy or your home country medicines agency.

- National service record, particularly if you are a young man or woman intending to apply for French military service (conscription was suspended in 1997).

- Passport for yourself and all members of your family; citizens of EU/EEA countries (except the UK) may bring a National ID card instead of a passport.

- Pet passport or Veterinary Certificate for all pets imported.

- Professional certification, such as that of a medical doctor or dentist, should you wish to practise in France. Have these documents translated into French, with an Apostille affixed to prove authenticity and accuracy of translation.

- Proof of purchase including amount and date of purchase of expensive items, such as cars and professional equipment, upon which duty might be charged when you bring them into the country.

- Social security details, which may be necessary if you wish to have income in France credited to your social security account in your home country.

- Unemployment benefits: If you are a citizen of an EU or EEA country and are entitled to unemployment benefits in your home country, the benefits may be paid out in France for a period of three months. The relevant authority in your home country will issue the proper form.

- Vaccination records or certificates, particularly for children, for filling in health records, as needed by health services and schools. Ask for records to be transferred to international standard vaccination cards, which are recognised world-wide.

- Visa if required from your own country to enter France.

Beware, be French

More is written in English about France than about any other country not having English as its national language. The travel sections of bookshops have shelves lined with books and the Internet has innumerable websites offering advice on France and French topics. At best, most of this information is second-hand: it originates in France and percolates over time in the minds of myriad writers, many with something to sell. Moreover, France changes continuously, so no compilation of information – including this book – can be completely up-to-date.

The best rule, then, is to rely first and foremost on information from French sources, such as those mentioned in this book. Among them, three stand out in the accuracy, quality and scope of information offered in print and online, as well as from offices in France and abroad:

- Label France, a quarterly printed and online magazine in ten languages, with a website at *www.diplomatie.gouv.fr/label_france*
- Égide with a website at *www.egide.asso.fr* in French and in English
- Invest in France Agency with a website at *www.investinfrance.org* in French and in English.

Moreover, four governmental public-service websites offer comprehensive information:

- The online Public service portal at *www.service-public.fr*, in French and key pages in English.
- The Foreign Service website at *www.diplomatie.gouv.fr*, in French, English, German, Spanish, Arabic and Japanese, offers succinct overviews of the country and its place in Europe.
- The Ministry of the Interior website at *www.interieur.gouv.fr*, in French, English, German, and Spanish has a service sections on a wide range of topics relevant to everyday life.
- The Ministry for infrastructure, transport, spatial planning, tourism and the sea website at *www.equipement.gouv.fr*, in French, English and Spanish, offers overviews of travel, transport, city planning and tourism.

If France will be your first experience of living abroad, prepare to cope with the challenges you may meet by considering how a newly-arrived foreigner may experience your own country. Start with a familiar procedure, such as opening a bank account with a payment card. Then seek out the additional requirements for an applicant from another country. In so doing, you will become familiar with the full requirements of your country. The requirements in France probably will be similar, though different in some respects, as no two countries are alike. Then you can cope as easily as you do, say, in accommodating to the new version of a familiar software application by realising that everything you seek is there, but in different places and with different appearances.

Frequently Asked Questions – FAQs

Some FAQs on the country and its population*:

Adult literacy? 99.0%.

Airports? 27.

Area? mainland 549,000 sq km.

Biggest company? Total (energy), 10th biggest in world.

Border? total 2868.5 km; with Spain 650 km, with Belgium 620 km, with Switzerland 572 km, with Italy 515 km, with Germany 450 km, with Andorra 57 km and with Monaco 4.5 km.

Coast line? 2962 km.

Constitution? 1st Republic 24 June 1793, 2nd Republic 4 November 1848, 3rd Republic 4 September 1870, 4th Republic 13 October 1946, and 5th Republic 4 October 1958.

Currency? €, Euro.

Divorces per 1000 population? 2.1.

Farms? 10% of land area.

Favourite holiday country? France, 89.2% on holiday.

Fertility rate (per woman)? 1.91.

Forests? 27.1% of land area.

Healthcare spending? 9.7% of GDP.

Highest mountain? Mt. Blanc, 4807 m.

Highest waterfall? Gavarnie, 442 m.

Home ownership? 53%.

Households? 24.7 million.

Housing? 57% houses, 43% apartments.

Immigrant population? 22%; 7% born abroad, 9% 1st generation born in France, 6% 2nd generation born in France.

Largest urban population? Paris, 9.8 million.

Largest glacier? Mer de Glace, 40 sq km.

Largest lake? Berre, 156 sq km.

Life expectancy? men 75.9 years, women 82.9 years.

Longest river? Loire, 1020 km.

Marriages per 1000 population? 4.6.

National animal? cock (rooster).

National anthem? La Marseillaise.

National flower? iris.

National parks? 7.

National symbol? Marianne.

Nobel laureates? 49: Literature 13, Physics 11, Peace 9, Physiology and Medicine 8, Chemistry 7, Economics 1.

Number of men per 100 women? 95.

Population? 60.7 million metropolitan (mainland), 2.5 million overseas.

Population in urban areas? 76.3%.

Population per sq km? 110.5.

Population over 60? 20.7%.

Population under 20? 25.1%.

Principal exports? raw materials, semifinished goods, food and drink, motor vehicles.

Principal imports? raw materials, semifinished goods, consumer goods, motor vehicles, energy.

Social security spending? 29% of GDP.

Tallest building? Eiffel Tower, Paris, 312.3 m original, 320.7 m with TV antenna.

Unemployment? 9.5%.

* Figures quoted from *Annuaire statistique de la France 2006*.

Take more of your money with you

If you're planning a move to France it's likely that the last thing on your mind is foreign exchange. However, at some point you will have to change your hard earned money into euros. Unfortunately, exchange rates are constantly moving and as a result can have a big impact on the amount of money you have to create your dream home.

For example, if you look at the euro during 2005 you can see how this movement can affect your capital. Sterling against the euro was as high as 1.5124 and as low as 1.4086. This meant that if you had £200,000 you could have ended up with as much as €302,480 or as little as €281,720, a difference of over €20,000.

It is possible to avoid this pitfall by fixing a rate through a **forward contract**. A small deposit will secure you a rate for anywhere up to 2 years in advance and by doing so provides the security of having the currency you need at a guaranteed cost.

Another option if you have time on your side is a **limit order**. This is used when you want to achieve a rate that is currently not available. You set the rate that you want and the market is then monitored. As soon as that rate is achieved the currency is purchased for you.

If you need to act swiftly and your capital is readily available then it is most likely that you will use a **spot transaction**. This is the *Buy now, Pay now* option where you get the most competitive rate on the day.

To ensure you get the most for your money it's a good idea to use a foreign exchange specialist such as Currencies Direct. As an alternative to your bank, Currencies Direct is able to offer you extremely competitive exchange rates, no commission charges and free transfers*. This can mean considerable savings on your transfer when compared to using a bank.

*Over £5,000

Information provided by Currencies Direct.
Website: *www.currenciesdirect.com*
Email: *info@currenciesdirect.com*
Tel: 0845 389 1729

1
Arriving and settling

When you go to France with the intent of staying, you are following in the footsteps of many who have gone before you. Since the early 19th century, France has been a country that has taken in and been shaped by immigrants, so much so that an ambitious project, the **National Centre for Immigration History** (Chapter 20) in Paris now commemorates and documents the impact of new residents on the country and its culture.

Like a tourist, you may visit France and stay there for up to three months, provided you have a visa or are a citizen of an EEA (EU and EFTA) country or one of the 33 other countries for which a visa is not required. Thereafter, your permission to stay depends on your nationality. If you are a citizen of an EEA country or Switzerland, you may stay and work with no further formalities, but if you are a citizen of another country, you will need a residence permit to live in the country and a work permit to take employment. There are varieties of residence and work permits that depend on the reason for your stay and on your nationality. Likewise, for a visit of up to three months, you may bring and use personal belongings, including a car. But for longer stays, you will be required to import belongings and in some cases pay duty, particularly on a car. The complete details of any of these matters would fill this book, so only brief summaries are given here along with addresses, telecommunications numbers and Internet websites where you can find further information.

ANAEM – National Agency for the Reception of Foreigners and Migration [*Agence Nationale de l'Accueil des Étrangers et des Migrations (ANAEM)*]

In April 2005, the Office of International Migration [*Office des migrations internationals (OMI)*] and the Social Service Assistance for Emigrants [*Service social d'aide aux émigrants (SSAE)*] merged to the ANAEM to ease the integration of new residents into the society and to coordinate administrative, health and social services for:

- foreigners staying three months or less
- asylum seekers

1

- foreigners who are citizens of countries outside the EU/EEA
- **Medical examination** of applicants for a **Residence permit**
- foreigners returning to their countries of origin
- French citizens employed abroad.

Extensive services are offered, including the **CAI** programmes of orientation and language teaching.

Simply put, for its services within France, the ANAEM exists to provide opportunities to persons who do not enjoy the free access to work and living prevailing within the EU/EEA. Consequently, its services are not offered to EU/EEA or Swiss citizens and their immediate families. However, as this book goes to press, the ten new countries that became members of the EU in May 2004 – Cyprus, Czech Republic, Estonia, Hungary, Latvia, Lithuania, Malta, Poland, Slovakia and Slovenia – have yet to be fully integrated into the EU social security programmes, so ANAEM still offers its services to their citizens.

For further details, contact the nearest local office of ANAEM or the head office at 44 rue Bargue, 75732 Paris Cedex 15, Tel: 01 53695370, *www.anaem.social.fr*, in French and in English, with an interactive locator map of the offices in France and abroad.

Asylum [*Asile*]

In accordance with the UN Refugee Convention of 1951, asylum may be granted to persons having a well-founded fear of persecution because of their race, religion, nationality, membership of a particular social group or political opinion. If you are a refugee newly arrived at the border and wish to apply for asylum, tell the immigration officials at your point of arrival. After checking and making a record of your papers, the officials most likely will put you in contact with the Association for Assistance at Borders for Foreigners [*Association Nationale d'Assistance aux Frontières pour les Étrangers (ANAFÉ)*], 21 ter rue Voltaire, 75001 Paris, Tel: 01 43672752, *www.anafe.org*, *contact@anafe.org* or a cooperating organisation that will arrange further aid, including temporary lodging.

Next, you must apply for asylum at one of the **Prefectures** (Chapter 21). If you have a visa, you should apply at the Prefecture before it expires. The Prefecture will require several documents with your application, principally four passport-type photos, the details of your name, date of birth, marital status, etc., and the details of how you entered France and the itinerary of your travels from your home country. When your application has been approved, you will be issued a provisional stay authorisation [*Autorisation Provisoire de Séjour (APS)*] and be given an asylum application form [*formulaire de demande d'asile*] that you must fill in and within 21 days submit to the Office for the Protection of Refugees and Stateless Persons

[*Office Français de Protection des Réfugiés et Apatrides (OFPRA)*], 201, rue Carnot, 94136 Fontenay-sous-Bois Cedex, *www.ofpra.gouv.fr*.

Once you have an APS, you may apply for accommodation at one of the 217 asylum seeker reception centres [*Centres d'Accueil pour Demandeurs d'Asile (CADA)*] or one of the 27 provisional accommodation centres [*Centres Provisoires d'Hébergement (CPH)*] across the country that together have places for nearly 16,000 asylum seekers (19,500 by the end of 2007). If the national asylum seeker reception centre system has no place for you and cannot offer temporary accommodation elsewhere, you most likely must find other accommodation. Depending on where you are in the country, there are many varieties of temporary accommodation, including centres for the homeless [*centres pour sans-abri*]. For accommodation in an emergency, call 115 from any telephone box, and you will be housed in an emergency centre for the night.

The Refugee Forum [*Forum des réfugiés*] is the best single source of information for asylum seekers; head office BP 1054, 69612 Villeurbanne, Tel: 04 78037445, *www.forumrefugies.org*, *direction@forumrefugies.org*. It does not provide advice to individual asylum seekers, but it offers many publications including two booklets that may be downloaded free from its website and which contain all the information an asylum seeker may need: *The Asylum Seeker's Welcome Book* (2004 edition, 32 pages, available in 6 language editions: French, English, Albanian, Arabic, Russian and Serbo-Croatian) and the *Guide for Asylum Seekers* (2005 edition, 32 pages, available in 3 language editions: French, English and Russian). Another organisation, **GISTI** (Chapter 33), is a clearing house for all information relevant to immigration.

AVF

AVF is the abbreviation for *Accueil des Villes Françaises,* a non-profit national network of associations dedicated to assisting relocating professionals and their families to adapt to France. The first AVF associations were created in 1963, in response to decentralisation. Today across the country, there are 350 AVF associations that together each year help some 300,000 people adapt to new living and working environments. The typical AVF association has 10 to 100 volunteer members, depending on the size of the town or city. Upon being contacted, an AVF association acts as a welcome service, providing information, assisting with contacts and helping newcomers meet local people. Typically, an AVF association cooperates with the town council, other associations and public as well as private organisations. For further information, contact UNAVF, 3 rue de Paradis, 75010 Paris, Tel: 01 47704585, *www.avf.asso.fr* selectable in French, English, German, Spanish or Italian and with an interactive association locator map.

CAI – Reception and Integration Contract
[*Contrat d'Accueil et d'Intégration (CAI)*]

If you are a foreign national or a refugee intending to apply for a **Residence permit** to live and work permanently in France, you may be eligible for CAI, the Reception and Integration Contract offered by **ANAEM** at its orientation sessions for newly-arrived immigrants. CAI is not offered to citizens of EEA (EU & EFTA) countries or to people applying for a temporary residence permit valid for less than one year.

At an orientation session, which lasts half a day, you will be introduced to the essentials of life and work in the country, be shown a film, "Living in France" [*Vivre en France*] and be given a language placement test. You then will be offered the Reception and Integration Contract, which is optional and free. It includes a day of civics classes, in your native language, as well as language classes, depending on your fluency in French. If the language placement test showed that you already are sufficiently fluent in French, you will be given a "Ministerial Language Skills Certificate" [*Attestation ministérielle de compétence linguistique (AMCL)*]. If you are insufficiently fluent in French, you will be assigned to a language course, of 200 to 500 hours duration, divided into weekly modules of six to 30 hours. Your progress in the course will be monitored every three months, and when you have attained sufficient fluency, you will be awarded the AMCL.

In addition to permanent workers, CAI is offered to spouses and adult children eligible for family reunification, immediate families of French citizens, refugees and their immediate families and some holders of temporary visas designated "private and family life" [*vie privée et familiale*]. For further details, contact ANAEM, 44 Rue Bargue, 75732 Paris Cedex 15, Tel: 01 53695370, *www.anaem.social.fr*, in French and in English, with a locator map of the offices in France and abroad.

Customs duties [*Droits de douane*]

Within a year of moving to France, you may import your personal effects and household goods free of duty and value added tax (VAT) [*taxe à valeur ajoutée (TVA)*] provided you have resided abroad continuously for six months or more and can prove that all the items imported have been used and will continue to be used by yourself and your family. Your household effects must be accompanied by a signed and dated detailed inventory list, with estimated values [*inventaire détaillé, estimatif, daté et signé*] that is submitted to the Customs Service [*Douane*], if you wish by the removal company working on your behalf. If you bring in personal effects and household goods from a third country outside the EU/EEA where you have lived for 12 months or more, you must submit a declaration on CERFA form No. 10070*01, *Déclaration d'entrée en France en Franchise de biens personnels en provenance de pays tiers à la C.E.*, that can be downloaded from the **Forms online** (Chapter 31) website at *www.service-public.fr/formulaires/*.

4

New articles and consumer goods (household effects, spirits, wine, beer and tobacco) may be subject to VAT and import duty. If you are a citizen of an EU/EEA country and can provide receipts proving that VAT has been paid in another EU/EEA country, neither VAT nor duty will be charged. However, VAT will be charged on new items for which you cannot prove that it has been paid in another EU/EEA country. If you are a citizen of a country outside the EU/EEA, duty and VAT may be charged on new goods.

Special regulations apply to **car import** (Chapter 4) and to **pet import** (Chapter 35). If you bring in a TV, you must register it and pay a **TV licence** (Chapter 44). Just as in ordinary international travel, all international airports have red and green channels. You enter through the green channel if the goods you are carrying are bought duty and tax-free, the amount of spirits, wine and tobacco allowed depends on your nationality and your point of departure. If you have more than the specified **duty-free quota** (Chapter 46), you should enter through the red channel.

For further information on import regulations, duties and the like, contact the nearest **Customs** (Chapter 43) office as listed online at *www.douane.gouv.fr*, or, if you live in the UK or the USA, the French Customs service offices at the Embassies:

- Kingsgate House, 5th floor, 115 High Holborn, London WC1V 6JJ, UK, Tel: +44 20 78310142, *frenchcustoms@onetel.net.uk*
- Bureau B-254, 4101 Reservoir Road N.W., Washington D.C. 20007-2169, USA, Tel: +1 202 9446394, *washington.douane@missioneco.org*.

Employment and Professional Training Directorate [*Délégation générale de l'emploi et à la formation professionnelle*]

As its name indicates, the Employment and Professional Training Directorate [*Délégation générale de l'emploi et à la formation professionnelle*] is the principal government agency concerned with the administration of employment and vocational training. Across the country, it has offices in the Regions (DRTEFP) and the Departments (DDTEFP), as well as a head office at 7 square Max Hymans, 75741 Paris Cedex 15, Tel: 01 44383838. The *Direction Départementale du Travail de l'Emploi et de la Formation Professionnelle (DDTEFP)* are the principal public service points of contact and have services for foreigners, *Service de la Main d'Œuvre Etrangère*, that deal with work permits. You can find the nearest DDTEFP on the interactive office locator map on the website at *www.travail.gouv.fr*.

French citizenship [*Nationalité française*]

Each year, 90,000 to 150,000 foreigners obtain French citizenship in one of three principal ways:

- marriage to a French citizen: acquisition is by decree [*acquisition de la nationalité française par décret*], and application may be made after one year of marriage.

- naturalisation: acquisition is by declaration [*acquisition de la nationalité française par déclaration*], and application may be made after five years of residence.

- birth in and residence in France: acquisition is by legal right [*acquisition de la nationalité française à raison de la naissance et de la résidence en France*], and acquisition is automatic at age 18 for persons born in France, regardless of the nationality of their parents, and resident in France for at least five years between ages 11 and 18.

The procedures involved and documentation required depend on the way of acquisition and are set out in brochures published by the Social Measures, Integration and Equality Section [*Espace Action sociale, intégration et Parité*] of Ministry of Employment, Social Cohesion and Housing, available in print from its offices and online on its website at *www.social.gouv.fr*; navigate to the locator map to find the addresses and telecoms numbers of the offices across the country and click on *Dossiers thématiques* to bring up links to download the online versions.

Applications based on marriage or birth are made at one of the 181 civil courts, either a magistrate's court [*Tribunal d'instance*] or a county court [*Tribunal de grande instance*], that can be found in the Yellow pages or in the online locator map at *www.justice.gouv.fr/region/mapjurid.php*.

Applications for naturalisation are made at the nearest *Préfecture*. The naturalisation procedure includes a language test and a 200-question civics examination, for which applicants may prepare by reading the *Guide des droits et devoirs du citoyen français* ("Guide to the Rights and Duties of a French Citizen"), published April 2005 and available at the *Préfectures*, listed in the Yellow Pages or in the online locator map at *www.interieur.gouv.fr/rubriques/c/c4_les_prefectures/c46_votre_prefecture*.

If you are a hardy young man interested in the military, there's an alternative route to naturalisation: after three years of service in the **Foreign Legion** (Chapter 11), you may request French citizenship.

France is signatory to the European Convention on Nationality [*Convention européenne sur la nationalité*], in force since 1 March 2000 and available online from the Council of Europe [*Conseil de l'Europe*] on its website at *www.conventions.coe.int*; scroll to and click on no. 166 in the Full list [*Liste complète*] to download the text or extracts of it; Chapter III, Articles 6-9 concern the acquisition, loss and recovery of nationality. The relevant national rules are increasingly uniform across Europe, but some differ from country to country. For instance, in Europe, France, the UK and most other countries permit multiple nationality, while some countries do not. So, if you wish to retain your home country citizenship, before applying for French citizenship, ask your country's embassy in Paris if dual citizenship is permitted.

Identity spot checks [*Contrôles d'identité*]

Police officers, and customs officers within their jurisdiction, are empowered to conduct spot checks of identity by asking to see the identity papers of any person in any public place, including streets, public buildings, transport stations, airports and the like. So you should always carry one or more documents that prove your identity, such as your passport, **National Identification Card** (Chapter 38), **Residence Permit** or student card if you are enrolled at a college or university. It's wise not to carry the originals that may be difficult to replace if lost or stolen, but carry photocopies stamped as certified copies [*copies conformes*] at the nearest town hall [*mairie*]. If you don't produce identity papers upon being checked, you may be taken to a police station to verify your identity [*vérification d'identité*]. The police can detain you no more than four hours, and you are allowed to make one telephone call. The relevant laws, last updated in 2001, are the code of penal procedure [*Code de procédure pénale*] articles 78-1 to 78-6 and the customs code [*Code des douanes*] article 67.

Medical examination [*Visite médicale*]

All foreigners applying for a **Residence permit** are required to have a medical examination arranged by **ANAEM**, either in France or by one of the ANAEM facilities abroad. The examination includes a general clinical examination, a chest X-Ray, diabetes screening by measuring capillary blood glucose level and verification of vaccinations, which must comply with current regulations.

If the examination identifies a health problem, the examinee will be referred to a relevant specialist. Four instances are cause for failing a medical examination:

- illness specified in Part V of the World Health Organisation's *International Health Regulations*, which, according to the third annotated edition* are cholera, plague and yellow fever.
- active pulmonary tuberculosis if the person refuses medical treatment.
- addiction to substances or plants classified as narcotics.
- mental illness likely to disrupt law and order or endanger the person's health.

If the examination is successfully passed, ANAEM issues a medical certificate [*certificat médical*] that can be used in applying for a Residence permit.

* *International Health Regulations (1969)*, Geneva, WHO, third annotated edition updated 1995, ISBN 92-4-158007-0.

Relocation services [*Services de relocalisation*]

As elsewhere, relocation services provide assistance in moving to and settling in France. The professional services offered vary from local orientation and contacts to comprehensive packages of familiarisation, training, guiding and housing location services, as suits companies relocating executives. Typically, services are offered by specialist companies, usually with offices in major international business cities. They range in size from global networks to local bureaux. Two networks of agencies, one European and one French, offer online lists of member agencies on their websites:

- European Relocation Association (EuRA) with 250 member agencies operating in 46 countries, including 26 agencies in France; head office: PO Box 189, Diss IP22 1PE, UK, Tel: +44 08700 726727, *www.eura-relocation.com*, *enquiries@eura-relocation.com*.

- *Syndicat National des Professionnels de la Relocation et de la Mobilité (SNPRM)* with member agencies across the country, 3 rue Léon Bonnat, 75016 Paris, *www.relocation-france.org*.

Removals [*Déménagements*]

The removal business is competitive, so you can shop around for both prices and services offered. In moving to France, be sure to engage a company that has a liaison agreement with a French removals company. Likewise, in moving from France, engage a company that has a liaison agreement with a company in your destination country. Most international liaison agreements are between removals companies belonging to international removal company associations, of which the two largest are:

- FIDI, the abbreviation for *Fédération Internationale des Déménageurs Internationaux*, the "International Federation of International Furniture Removers", 69 Rue Picard B5, 1080 Brussels, Belgium, Tel: +32 2 4265160, *www.fidi.com*, *fidi@fidi.com*. The website has an interactive map for locating the more than 500 affiliated removal companies, including 18 in France. FIDI supports a quality standard, FAIM, the abbreviation for FIDI Accredited International Mover, now the *de facto* standard of the removals trade.

- OMNI, the abbreviation for Overseas Moving Network International, Priory House, 45-51 High Street, Reigate, Surrey RH2 9AE, UK, Tel: +44 1737 222022, *www.omnimoving.com*, *omnihq@omnimoving.com*. The website has a locator for finding more than 260 companies in 70 countries, including five in France.

In France, you can find a removals company by looking under *Déménagements* in the Yellow pages, by visiting the FIDI or OMNI websites mentioned above, or by using the interactive locator map for the more than 800 removals companies in France, at *www.csdemenagement.fr*, the website of the national movers association, *Chambre Syndicale du Déménagement*, 73 avenue Jean Lolive, 93108 Montreuil Cedex, Tel: 01 49886140 or 08 00010020 freephone [*N° vert*].

Most removal companies with international trade now standardise on **Containers** (Chapter 46), particularly when sea transport is involved. The contents of a typical house will fill a 20-foot container, though the 40-foot size may be needed for the contents of a large house. The removal company will bring the container to your house, most often on a truck fitted with a hydraulic lifter that can place the container alongside the truck bed, on the ground, and lift it back again when it is filled. The standard container is about 2.5 m wide, so the truck will need a width of at least 6 m to drive in and manoeuvre the container.

Residence permit [*Permis de séjour*]

Depending on your citizenship, you may or may not need a *Titre de séjour*, also known as a *Carte de séjour* because it is issued on a card. According to the "Sarkozy Act" [*loi Sarkozy*] passed 26 November 2003, if you are a citizen of a country belonging to the EEA (EU and EFTA) or of Switzerland, you no longer need a residence permit provided that you have official identification from your home country, such as a passport or a national identity card.

If you are a citizen of a country other than those of the EEA or Switzerland, you will need a residence permit to live in the country. There are two types of residence permit:

- temporary [*Carte de séjour temporaire*] valid for one year and renewable within the last two months of that year.
- permanent residence [*Carte de résident*] valid for ten years and automatically renewed, provided you have committed no serious offence.

The initial application procedure is the same for both types of residence permit.

Within three months of arriving in the country, you may apply for a residence permit at the registry office [*bureau d'état civil*] at the local town hall [*Mairie*], a police station or the *Service des étrangers* at the **Prefecture** (Chapter 21). You apply by obtaining and filling in an application for a residence permit [*Demande de titre de séjour, CERFA no. 20 3243*], supported by the following documentation – take originals and two photocopies of each:

- identification [*pièces d'identité*]: your passport [*passeport*], birth certificate [*certificate de naissance*], and if applicable, your marriage certificate [*extrait d'acte de mariage*] and birth certificates of your children.
- proof of residence [*justificatif de domicile*]: a recent (last 3 months) EDF/GDF electricity/gas or fixed-line telephone [*téléphone fixe*] bill if you own your residence, a deed of sale [*acte de vente*] if you have just bought a residence, or, if renting, a signed lease agreement [*bail à loyer*] or receipt for rent paid [*quittance de loyer*].
- proof of financial resources [*justificatif de ressources*] and health insurance [*assurance maladie*], depending on whether you work [*actif*] or do not work [*non-actif*].

Status	Proof of finances	Proof of health insurance
Working [*actif*]		
Contractually employed	Contract of employment	Contract of employment
Self-employed	**Liberal profession** (Chapter 3) registration with a **Chamber of tradesmen and artisans** (Chapter 3), a **Chamber of commerce and industry** (Chapter 3) or an agency of **URSSAF** (Chapter 22)	Proof of registration with health services or health insurance contract
Not working [*non-actif*]		
Independent means	Proof of income	EEA: Health insurance or social security certificate; Others: proof of private health insurance
Retired	Proof of pension received	as above
Student	Certificate of enrolment at an educational institution and bank statement showing monthly income	Certificate of enrolment or proof of private health insurance

Other than your passport, all documents should be in French or accompanied by a translation [*avec traduction*] made by a registered translator [*traducteur agréé*]. You may have a translation made by a registered translator in your home country, as may be advisable if its language is not common among registered translators in France. If so, be sure that the translation has an affixed **Apostille** (Chapter 38) to certify its authenticity. You also may have a translation made by a registered translator selected from a list [*La liste des traducteurs agréés*] posted in town halls or by any of the authorised **Translators** (Chapter 28) in the country.

When you have satisfactorily completed your application, you will be issued a temporary permit [*récépissé*] valid for three months. If your application is approved, you will be notified by post. Take the notice and your *récépissé* to the office where you applied, and you will be issued the laminated plastic *Permis de séjour*.

Temporary work permit [*Autorisation provisoire de travail*]

Citizens of countries outside the EU/EEA who wish to work temporarily but not permanently, such as students, performers or staff on short-term assignment to the French subsidiary of a foreign company, need a temporary work permit [*Autorisation provisoire de travail (APT)*].

An APT may be issued for a period of up to one year, or up to nine months for students, for whom it is renewable. You may apply for an APT by filling in an application [*Demande d'autorisation provisoire de travail*] that you submit to the *Service de la Main d'Œuvre Etrangère* at the nearest DDTEFP office of the **Employment and Professional Training Directorate**. Upon application at the office, you should show a promise of work [*engagement de travail*] signed by the employer, a temporary residence permit [*carte de séjour temporaire*] and, if you are a student, your student's card [*carte d'étudiant*].

Visa requirements [*Obligation du visa*]

Visas are issued by French Consulates abroad. They are of two categories:

- short-stay visa [*visa de court séjour*] is valid for three months and is intended for visitors.

- long-stay visa [*visa de long séjour*] is valid for three to six months, or up to nine months in some cases. A long-stay visa may grant temporary permission to reside in France pending the issuing of **Residence permit**, in which case it includes a statement of that purpose: *voire carte de séjour*. There are special long-stay visas for students [*visa de long séjour mention étudiant*].

Visas are not required for citizens of:

- the 25 countries of the European Union (EU)

- the three countries of the European Free Trade Area (EFTA) that together with the EU make up the European Economic Area (EEA)

- 33 other countries: Andorra, Argentina, Australia, Bolivia, Brasil, Brunei, Bulgaria, Canada, Chile, Costa Rica, Croatia, El Salvador, Ecuador, Guatemala, Honduras, Israel, Japan, Malaysia, Mexico, Monaco, New Zealand, Nicaragua, Panama, Paraguay, Romania, San Marino, Singapore, South Korea, Switzerland, United States, Uruguay, Vatican and Venezuela. But visas are required for citizens of these countries for stays of more than three months.

Visa requirements may change; for updated information, contact a French Consulate or visit the Ministry of Foreign Affairs visa site at *www.diplomatie.gouv.fr/venir/visas* with interactive "Do you need a visa?" [*Avez-vous besoin d'un visa?*] pages in French, English and Spanish.

Work permit [*Permis de travail*]

As for the **Residence permit**, if you are a citizen of a country belonging to the EEA (EU and EFTA) or of Switzerland, you need no permit to work in France, but if you are a citizen of a country other than those of the EEA or Switzerland, you will need a permit to work in the country.

The principal rule is that a work permit is granted only if you have a work contract from a French employer who has successfully applied for it. There are seven steps in the application procedure:

1. From your country of residence (not France), you negotiate an offer of employment with an employer.

2. The employer then applies for a permit on your behalf to the **Employment and Professional Training Directorate**, which processes the application and, if it's accepted, sends it to **ANAEM**.

3. ANAEM records the application on its database and forwards it to the Ministry of the Interior, which then returns it to ANAEM.

4. ANAEM then sends the approved application to the French Consulate in your country of residence.

5 The Consulate notifies you of the success of your application and, if necessary, issues a long-stay visa [*visa de long séjour*].

6. You arrange with ANAEM for a medical examination.

7. After passing the medical examination, you take your collected papers to the Prefecture, which will issue the work permit.

There are exceptions to this procedure, principally for executives, students, au pairs and seasonal agricultural workers; contact the Consulate in your country of residence for the most recent details.

Otherwise, for further information, contact the Foreign workers department [*Service de la main d'œuvre étrangère*] of the **Employment and Professional Training Directorate** office in the *Département* where you will live.

2
Banking, insurance and money matters

France is the world's fifth largest economic power and Europe's largest exporter of agricultural products. France is a leader in banking and insurance, and two French banks are among the top ten in the world in assets. The French Interbank Teleclearing System is the largest retail system in Europe, both in volume and in value. Understandably, banking, insurance and related matters are high profile sectors. They rest on tradition. The Franc, the erstwhile currency of France and one of Europe's oldest continuously issued currencies in the pre-Euro days, derived its name from the inscription *Francorum Rex*, Latin for "King of the Franks", on gold coins first minted during the reign of Jean II le Bon (1319-1364), King of France 1350-1364. One of the great economists of all time is Jean-Baptiste Say, remembered for the Law of Markets. And today, the average French household saving rate in percentage of disposable income is second among 30 OECD countries.

ATA Carnet [*Carnet ATA*]

The ATA Carnet is a customs document that eases the temporary importation of goods, such as commercial samples for trade shows, professional equipment to be used for shorter time periods and vehicles and horses used in international competition. An ATA Carnet is valid for one year and for the goods covered exempts the holder from paying import duties and VAT, simplifies customs procedures and eases re-entry of the goods to the originating country.

ATA is an abbreviation of the French and English names of the purpose of the Carnet: "*Admission Temporaire*/Temporary Admission", and was adopted in 1961 by the predecessor of the World Customs Organisation (WCO) [*Organisation Mondiale des Douanes (OMD)*], head office at 30 Rue du Marché, 1210 Brussels, Belgium, Tel: +32 22099211, *www.wcoomd.org*. More than 50 countries, including all those in the EU/EEA and all English and French speaking countries, recognise the ATA Carnet. Worldwide, ATA Carnets are arranged by Chambers of Commerce;

in France, by the Chamber of Commerce and Industry in Paris [*Chambre de Commerce et d'Industrie de Paris (CCIP)*], International Services Department [*Direction des Actions et de la Coopération Internationale (DIACI)*] at 2 rue Adolphe-Jullien, 75001 Paris, Tel: 01 55653140, *www.formint.ccip.fr*.

Banks [*Banques*]

Banking is strong in France: two banks, BNP Paribas and the Crédit Agricole Group are among the top ten in the world in terms of total assets, and there are more than 26,000 permanent bank branches. In alphabetical order, the six main banking groups are:

- Banque Populaire, a mutual bank with more than three million members and one of the largest networks in the country, *www.banquepopulaire.fr*.
- BNP Paribas, the largest commercial bank in the country, *www.bnpparibas.net*.
- Caisse d'Epargne Group, the principal savings institution that offers the **Livret A** passbook as well as other services, *www.groupe.caisse-epargne.com*.
- Crédit Agricole Group, a mutual institution that now has numerous subsidiaries, including the Crédit Lyonnais retail bank group, *www.creditagricole.fr*.
- Crédit Mutuel, a mutual credit bank with the second largest network in the country, *www.creditmutuel.com*.
- Société Générale, a commercial bank that is the country's seventh largest company and a leader in financial services in the Euro zone, *www.socgen.com*.

You can locate a bank branch by looking under *Banques* in the Yellow pages or by visiting the bank group websites, as all have branch locators and most have pages in English as well as in French.

From 1 January 2006, the **Postal services** (Chapter 36), which long has offered financial services through 17,000 post offices across the country, joined the banking sector by establishing *Banque Postale*, *www.labanquepostale.fr*.

Dexia of Belgium and France is the world's largest municipal credit group, offering services to the public sector including the financing of sustainable development across the country, *www.dexia-creditlocal.com*.

Bank Account Numbers [*Identifiants de compte bancaire*]

Across Europe, bank account numbers have a uniform structure, in compliance with the standards set forth by The European Committee for Banking Standards (ECBS). In France, the structure for the Basic Bank Account Number (BBAN) is a 23-digit number in the format:

BBBBBGGGGGNNNNNNNNNNNCC

where BBBBB is the five-digit bank code [*code banque*], GGGGG is the five-digit branch code [*code guichet*], NNNNNNNNNNN is the eleven-digit account number [*numéro de compte*] and CC comprise two check digits [*clé de contrôle*]. In daily transactions within the country, this number is called the *Relève d'Identité Bancaire (RIB)*. The RIB of an account is used by banks to process payment transactions, and account customers are given slips stating the RIBs of their accounts, so they may certify the accounts in paying invoices.

For cross-border transactions, the BBAN is extended by four alphanumeric characters to an International Bank Account Number (IBAN). Even if you know little about another country's banking system and are puzzled by its bank account numbers, you need only know the IBAN and the **Bank Identifier Code** to pay an invoice or otherwise transfer funds. For France, the first two characters of an IBAN are FR, the International Standards Organisation (ISO) Country Code for France, and the second two are check digits. The BBAN (*RIB*) follows. So the IBAN of an account with a RIB is:

FRKKBBBBBGGGGGNNNNNNNNNNNCC

where KK are the check digits for the IBAN. On paper, an IBAN is written in groups of four characters:

FRKK BBBB BGGG GGNN NNNN NNNN NCC

For further information on account numbers in France, contact *Comité français d'organisation et de normalisation bancaires (CFONB)*, 18, rue la Fayette, 75009 Paris, Tel: 01 48005184, *www.cfonb.org*. For comprehensive information on IBAN across Europe as well as for a downloadable overview brochure on the IBAN, contact the European Committee for Banking Standards (ECBS), Avenue de Tervueren 12, B-1040 Brussels, Belgium, Tel: +32 27333533, Fax: +32 27364988, *www.ecbs.org*.

Bank Identifier Code [*Code bancaire international*]

In all international transfers, banks round the world identify themselves using the Bank Identifier Code (BIC), also known as the "SWIFT code", because it was originated by **SWIFT**, the organisation that issues and keeps a register of the codes.

The BIC is an eight-character sequence of letters and sometimes numbers that identifies the bank head office, or 11 characters if the bank is a branch of the head office. For the full 11 characters, the meanings of the letters are:

BANKCCLLOOO

Where BANK a four-character code for the bank, CC is the two-character ISO country code (FR for France), LL is a locator code within the country and OOO is the bank's designation of a branch office. If the BIC is for a head office, the last three characters are XXX, to preserve the eleven-character format. For instance, the BIC for the ABC International Bank Paris Branch, alphabetically the first of more than 3300 BICs in France, is:

ABCOFRPPXXX

For further information on BICs, contact SWIFT, Avenue Adéle 1, B-1310 La Hulpe, Belgium *www.swift.com*, with a BIC finder for banks by country and by name.

Banking Commission [*Commission bancaire*]

The Banking Commission is a collegial body of seven members chaired by the Governor of the **Central bank**. Its purpose is to protect depositors as well as to be the watchdog over the country's banking and financial system. Its everyday activities are conducted by a Secretariat [*Secrétariat Général de la Commission Bancaire (SGCB)*] that cooperates with other regulatory agencies, including the **Insurance regulator**, the **Securities regulator** and the Credit Institutions and Investment Firms Committee [*Comité des etablissements de crédit et des entreprises d'inversement (CECEI)*], a part of the Central bank. For a comprehensive overview of the Commission, request or download a copy of "The Commission Bancaire", Fact Sheet No. 132, December 2004, from the Communication Department of the Central bank, *www.banque-france.fr*.

Cashpoints [*Points argent*]

There now are nearly 50,000 cashpoints in the country, implemented with automatic teller machines (ATMs). Technically, they are of two sorts: open access ATMs [*Guichet Automatique de Banque (GAB)*] that dispense banknotes and provide access to account details, and limited access ATMs [*Distributeur Automatique de Billets (DAB)*] that only dispense banknotes. GABs are by far the most prevalent, so much so that statistics on the number of DABs in the country no longer are available, though the name survives.

Points argent usually are identified by graphic signs of various designs, showing a right hand holding a card between thumb and forefinger. Most are located outdoors at bank branches, while many are located indoors at banks, airports, railway stations and shopping malls as well as in outdoor and indoor self-service walk-in kiosks. The operating banks determine the cards acceptable at their *Points argent*. All *Points argent* in the country accept the French *Carte Bleue* and most also accept Visa and Mastercard international cards as well as other cards specified on the ATM faceplate, including Maestro and Cirrus.

Many *Points argent* offer choices of foreign languages, principally English, German, Italian and Spanish, and some at gateway airports and city banks with international trade also offer foreign exchange services in several languages.

Central Bank [*Banque de France*]

The Banque de France (its name is not translated) was set up in 1800. As one of the members of the European System or Central Banks (ESCB) and since 1999 the Eurosystem, it contributes to supporting the common polices of the Euro area. Each year, it sorts some six billion banknotes, puts 1.6 billion banknotes and eight billion coins into circulation and prints 1.5 billion Euro banknotes, including those of other countries in the Eurosystem. It regulates and monitors banks and other financial institutions in the country, supervises monetary policy, compiles statistics and performs analyses, interacts with international banking and financial agencies and supports consumer protection activities. Head office: 31 rue Croix des Petits Champs, 75001 Paris, Tel: 01 42924292, *www.banque-france.fr*, with pages in French and in English and an interactive map locator for offices across the country, *infos@banque-france.fr*.

Cheques [*Chèques*]

As late as the mid 1990s, cheques were the most common form of payment. Though **payment cards** are increasingly favoured, cheques remain popular, accounting for about 28% of payments. In that respect, France is unique in Europe, as cheque usage in the country accounts for more than three-quarters of all cheques exchanged in the Euro area. So banks almost always offer cheque books with current accounts, and it's wise to carry both a chequebook and a **payment card**, because some shops and services do not have **point of sale terminals**. Moreover, a chequebook provides payment backup should you come to a shop with a terminal that is offline.

You can issue a cheque [*émettre un cheque*] by filling it in as shown below. As in English, you may also be said to draw a cheque [*tirer un chèque*] or write a cheque [*faire un cheque* or *écrire un chèque*] on your account. A cheque with two oblique parallel lines [*deux barres parallèles obliques*] across its face is a crossed cheque that cannot be cashed and is valid only if deposited in a bank account. This feature provides protection both for the person writing a cheque and for the recipient who endorses it, such as in a point of sale terminal fitted with a cheque printer, as it is then valid only for the account stated in the endorsement. Consequently, most banks issue cheques pre-printed with the two lines. In general, a cheque is valid for one year from its date of issue.

17

Counterfeiting [*Contrefaçon*]

Counterfeiting probably started soon after money was first introduced, is widespread, and persists, with counterfeit coins and banknotes appearing following new issues. In 2002, soon after the **Euro** became the official currency of 12 European countries, counterfeit Euro coins and banknotes appeared.

Counterfeit coins are produced in clandestine mints by stamping and by casting. By the end of 2004 across the Euro area, more than 100,000 counterfeit 50 cent, 1 Euro and 2 Euro coins had been detected in and withdrawn from circulation and more than 160,000 seized before they were put into circulation. The European Technical and Scientific Centre [*Le Centre technique et scientifique européen*] at the **Mint** in Paris is responsible for monitoring coin counterfeiting and implementing measures to combat it.

Counterfeit banknotes are a more serious problem, most likely because the potential gain for a counterfeiter is greater than for coins and because copying machines, scanners and colour printers are increasingly commonplace. Starting in 2003, more than half a million counterfeit banknotes are detected and withdrawn from circulation each year. The €50 denomination is the most often counterfeited, comprising 56% of all counterfeited banknotes seized. The gains to the counterfeiter and the corresponding losses to users are great, more than 16 million Euros for the €50 banknote in 2005 alone. Consequently, shops increasingly are fitted with counterfeit banknote detectors and announce their use to ward off attempts to pass counterfeits; a typical sign on a shop in France reads: *Magasin muni d'un détecteur de faux billets*. Moreover, Euro banknotes are printed so they may easily be distinguished from counterfeits, without special equipment, simply by feeling, looking and touching, as outlined in the European Central Bank (ECB) brochure, "Feel, Look, Tilt" [*Toucher-Regarder-Incliner*], available at banks and downloadable in 20 languages from the ECB website at *www.ecb.int* along with other counterfeit watchfulness publications, including a credit-card sized pocket guide and animated video sequences.

For an overview of counterfeiting and the measures enacted to combat it, contact the **European Anti-Fraud Office** (Chapter 10).

Credit [*Crédit*]

The many credit offerings sort into five principal categories:

- credit cards [*cartes de crédit*], as offered by domestic and international companies offering **payment cards**.
- overdraft facilities [*découverts*] on bank accounts, by agreement with the bank providing a current account against which overdraft is permitted by cheque or payment card debiting.
- permanent credit [*crédit permanent*], also called revolving credit, usually connected to a current account.

- assigned credit [*achat à crédit*], also called instalment credit, as offered by various consumer goods shops.

- personal loans [*prêts*], as offered by **banks** and **insurance companies**.

With minor modifications, the procedures for and rules concerning credit are similar to those elsewhere in Europe. As this book goes to press, the Committee on Economic and Monetary Affairs of the European Parliament is drafting but has yet to enact a directive on the harmonisation of laws, regulations and administrative provisions of the Member States concerning consumer credit [reference: 2002/0222(COD)].

Direct debit [*Prélèvement automatique*]

Direct debit offers a convenient means of paying regular bills, such as for electricity and gas, particularly when you are away from your residence. First, you must authorise direct debit, usually by signing a form provided by a supplier. Then, whenever an invoice is near due, you will receive a notice of imminent direct debit. If you wish, you may stop the payment by notifying your bank. Otherwise, the payment will be made automatically and will be shown as a debit on your next bank account statement. Direct debit schemes vary among **banks**; most do not charge for debits, but do charge for debits stopped.

Due date [*Date d'échéance*]

Bills and invoices almost always have a stated due date, which is the last date on which the amount stated may be paid without incurring late-payment penalties [*pénalités de retard de paiement*]. There is no standard statement of due date; three common statements are *Montant à régler avant le* ("To be paid by"), *Net à régler au plus tard le* ("To be settled no later than") and *Somme totale à payer pour le* ("Total sum to be paid by"). Late payment penalties usually are stipulated in contracts or purchase agreements and typically entail interest on the overdue payment at rates of 1.5% a month or 1.5 times the prevailing interest rate per year.

Euro

Since 1 January 2002, the Euro is the official currency of France and 11 other European Union countries – Austria, Belgium, Finland, Germany, Greece, Ireland, Italy, Luxembourg, the Netherlands, Portugal and Spain. The graphic symbol for the euro was inspired by the Greek letter epsilon and looks like an upper-case letter "e" with two horizontal, parallel lines across it, €. The official abbreviation is EUR on the International Standards Organisation (ISO) currency designation list. The predecessor of the EUR, the European Currency Unit (ECU) computed from a basket of national currencies of the EU countries, was used in transactions and listed in tables of exchange rates up to 31 December 1998. The exchange rates on that date remain the official rates for computation between present Euro figures and former national currency figures, which still are quoted in most Euro currency countries. The exchange rate for France is 6.55957 French francs (FRF) to the Euro (EUR).

There are seven Euro banknotes [*Les billets en euros*] of the same design for all 12 Euro currency countries and in seven denominations: 5, 10, 20, 50, 100, 200 and 500 Euros. On the fronts of the banknotes, gateways and windows symbolise openness, whilst the reverse sides show bridges that symbolise cooperation between countries. The Euro is divided into 100 cents, and there are eight Euro coins [*Les pieces en euros* or *centimes d'euro*]: 1 and 2 Euros and 1, 2, 5, 10, 20 and 50 cents. The fronts of the coins have the same designs for all 12 countries, while the reverse sides are in specific designs for each country. French Euro coins are identified on their reverse sides by the letters 'RF', the abbreviation for the French Republic [*République Française*]. Two coins feature the motto of the Republic, *Liberté, Egalité, Fraternité*, three feature the sower [*Semeuse*], and three feature Marianne, an allegory for the French Republic that also appears on the former French franc coins and on postage stamps as well as in art, including a sculpture at *Place de la Nation* in Paris.

For further information on the Euro, contact the **Central Bank** concerning banknotes or the **Mint** concerning coins, or visit the European Central Bank website at *www.euro.ecb.int* for complete overviews in 11 languages.

Exchange rates [*Cours de change*]

The European Central Bank (ECB) sets daily Euro foreign exchange reference rates that in turn are used by banks across the Euro area to calculate buying and selling rates for cash and electronic exchanges to and from other currencies. In France, the **Central bank** makes the ECB daily reference rates available online at *www.banque-france.fr*; click on *Cours de change de l'Euro*.

Franc

In the pre-Euro days, the French Franc was one of Europe's oldest continuously issued currencies. Francs were first issued from 1360 to 1641 and then again in decimal form from 1795 on. In modern times, the symbol for the Franc was an F with a line through it, and in banking it had the three-letter abbreviation FRF. In 1960, the Franc was revalued, with one new Franc [*nouveau franc*] equal to 100 old Francs [*anciens francs*]. Accordingly, the abbreviation NF was used for a few years on banknotes to distinguish the new from the old. On 1 January 1999, the **Euro** replaced the Franc for non-cash transactions, and on 1 January 2002 Euro currency replaced Franc banknotes and coins for cash transactions, and prices were converted from Francs to Euros at the exchange rate of 6.55957 Francs to the Euro valid on 31

December 1998. Nonetheless, as people adjust to changes less rapidly than computers, prices in shops were, and still often are, stated both in Euros and in Francs. The transition has had some odd outcomes, such as fees to be paid using **Revenue stamps** (Chapter 43) being stated in amounts impossible to pay exactly. Moreover, people often talk about prices of high-value items, such as houses, in old Francs. An apartment costing a hundred thousand Euros is worth 655,957 Francs or nearly 66 million old Francs.

Herfindahl-Hirschman Index [*Index d'Herfindahl-Hirschman*]

The Herfindahl-Hirschman Index (HHI) is used to measure market concentration, on a scale of 0 (zero) for perfect competition to 1 for complete monopoly. The French bank system* is relatively competitive in assets, with an HHI of 0.133, but less competitive in private deposits, with an HHI of 0.2103, reflecting the large proportion of savings in the **Livret A** and other passbook schemes offered by a limited number of financial organisations. The HHI itself has a strong French connection. It was originally known as the Herfindahl index, after environmental economist Orris Clement Herfindahl. But later it was found to have been used earlier by another economist, Albert O. Hirschman, born in 1915 in Berlin and educated at the Sorbonne in Paris. Hence it now is known by the hyphenated name.

* Figures for 2004, the last year reported as this book goes to press, extracted from *the French banking and financial system in 2004*, published by the **Central bank**.

Holiday savings [*Chèques-Vacances*]

Across the country, many employers contribute to a holiday savings scheme supported jointly by private sector businesses and public sector agencies, including the **National Family Allowance Fund** (Chapter 22). The scheme aims to enable everyone, particularly families with school-age children, to afford holidays and leisure pursuits. In practice, it entails issuing vouchers that may be used to pay for holiday services, such as air, boat and train travel, restaurants, sports, theatre and theme parks. The *Agence Nationale pour les Chèques-Vacances (ANCV)* coordinates the activities of public and private sector organisations involved in the scheme and publishes information for users, including an annual guide. For further details, contact ANCV, 36 bd Henri Bergson, 95201 Sarcelles Cedex, Tel: 08 25844344, *www.ancv.com*.

Home loans [*Prêts immobilier*]

Home loans comprise the greatest sector of lending to the economy, amounting in all to more than €466 billion in metropolitan France.* The home loan market is accordingly competitive, with **banks** and **insurance companies** offering loans. Traditional home loans [*prêts immobiliers classiques*] and mortgages [*hypothèques*]

remain, but there are innumerable other plans tailored to individual needs and financial circumstances. Describing them all would be beyond the scope of this book. Fortunately, there is an excellent overview of the principal home loan plans presently available and including a comprehensive glossary of home loan terms, provided in French, English, Dutch and Italian by *Crédit Foncier de France*, *www.creditfoncier.fr*, part of the Caisse d'Epargne Group, *www.groupe.caisse-epargne.com*.

* As at 31 December 2004, as reported by the **Banking commission**.

Insurance [*Assurance*]

Insurance functions as it does elsewhere in Europe, and indeed many **insurance companies** are affiliated with international groups or have trans-border alliances. Likewise, insurance is classified by client category as being for private persons [*particuliers*] or for professionals and businesses [*professionnels et enterprises*] and within the private sector as being life insurance [*assurance vie*] or non-life insurance [*assurance*].

Life insurance often is associated with investment and accordingly termed *placements et assurance vie*. About 60% of the population hold life insurance policies. Many life insurance policies also provide benefits for retirement [*retraite*], though retirement insurance may be separate.

Many types of non-life insurance are available, of which four are compulsory:

- **Car insurance** (Chapter 4) if you own a car.
- Home insurance [*Assurance habitation*] if you own or rent your home. Many home insurance policies are comprehensive [*multi-risques*], providing coverage of theft and natural disasters.
- Civil liability [*Assurance responsabilité civile*] to cover any accidental damages you may cause to another person or their property.
- School insurance [*Assurance scolaire*] if you have children of school age, to cover injuries sustained by or damage caused by a child. A school will request a certificate of insurance [*attestation d'assurance scolaire*] upon enrolling a child.

Insurance companies [*Entreprises d'assurance*]

Some 500 insurance companies, from smaller local enterprises to larger national and international companies, offer insurance in a competitive market. All insurance companies operating in the country are monitored by the **Insurance regulator,** and the *Ministre de l'Économie des Finances et de l'Industrie* publishes an updated list of all approved companies [*les enterprises d'assurance agréées*] on its website at *www.minefi.gouv.fr*. The seven largest insurance companies, all with offices and agencies across the country, are, in alphabetical order:

- AGF, head office at 87 rue de Richelieu, 75002 Paris, *www.agf.fr*.

- AXA, head office at 26 rue Drouot, 75009 Paris, *www.axa.fr*.
- AZUR, head office at 7 avenue Marcel Proust, 28392 Chartres Cedex 9, *www.azur-assurances.fr*.
- GMF, head office at 76 rue de Prony, 75017 Paris, *www.gmf.fr*.
- MAAF, head office at Chauray, 79036 Niort Cedex 9, *www.maaf.fr*.
- MACIF, head office at 2 and 4 rue Pied de Fond, 79037 Niort Cedex 9, *www.macif.fr*.
- MAE, head office at 62 rue Louis Bouilhet, 76044 Rlouen Cedex, *www.mae.fr*.

You can find the telephone numbers and addresses of local offices and agents in the Yellow pages or by using the online locators on the websites mentioned above.

As elsewhere in Europe, there are crossovers between the banking and insurance sectors: some **banks** now offer insurance and some insurance companies now offer banking services. Moreover, insurance now is offered at competitive rates by some major hypermarket chains, including:

- Auchan, *www.auchan.fr/services/assurances*.
- Carrefour, *www.carrefourassurances.com*.

Insurance ombudsman [*Médiation dans l'assurance*]

If you are dissatisfied with an insurance company's service, you should first send a complaint to the company. If that fails, you may contact the ombudsman of the Insurance sector organisation with which your insurance company is associated:

- Ombudsman of the French Federation of Insurance Companies [*Médiateur de la Fédération Française des Sociétés d'Assurances*], 26 Bd. Haussmann, 75009 Paris, Tel: 01 42479131
- Ombudsman of the Association of Mutual Insurers [*Médiateur du Groupement des Entreprises Mutuelles d'Assurances*], 9 rue de Saint Petersbourg, 75008 Paris, Tel: 01 53042139.

Or, if you wish, you may contact the central insurance ombudsman agency by registered letter: Médiation Assurance, 11 rue de la Rouchefoucauld, 75009 Paris, Tel: 01 53322448.

Insurance regulator [*Commission de Contrôle des Assurances, des Mutuelles et des Institutions de Prévoyance*]

The Insurance regulator [*Commission de Contrôle des Assurances, des Mutuelles et des Institutions de Prévoyance (CCAMIP)*] is an independent public agency that monitors the insurance sector that includes 394 insurance companies [*sociétés d'assurance*], 31 reassurance companies [*sociétés de réassurance*], 17 group assurance companies [*groupes d'assurance*], about 2400 mutual insurance companies [*mutuelles*], 79 vested pension benefit schemes [*institutions de prévoyance*] and 95 supplementary retirement schemes [*institutions de retraite supplémentaire*] that together comprise a market of more than 170 billion Euros a year. For further information, contact the head office, CCAMIP, 54 rue de Châteaudun, 75346 Paris Cedex 09, Tel: 01 55074141, *www.ccamip.fr*.

Insurance sector organisations
[*Organisations du secteur d'assurance*]

Almost all insurance companies are members of an insurance sector organisation, of which there are two, both with extensive information services for the public as well as **Insurance ombudsman** services:

- French Federation of Insurance Companies [*Fédération Française des Sociétés d'Assurance (FFSA)*], 26 boulevard Haussmann, 75009 Paris, Tel: 01 42479000, *www.ffsa.fr*.

- Association of Mutual Insurers [*Groupement des Entreprises Mutuelles d'Assurances (GEMA)*], 9 rue de Saint Petersbourg, 75008 Paris, Tel: 01 53042139, *www.gema.fr*.

Interbank payment order [*Titre Interbancaire de Paiement (TIP)*]

A TIP is convenient means for cashless payment of invoices, such as those regularly sent by utility companies. Typically, invoices have detachable TIP slips that you sign and return to initiate payment by transfer from your bank account via the Interbank Teleclearing System. Typically, after you open an account with a utility company or other supplier, the TIP on the first invoice sent will have a request, *RIB Merci*, which means that you should enclose one of the *Relève d'Identité Bancaire (RIB)* slips for your bank account, as well as sign and return the TIP. Thereafter, the TIPs on invoices will be imprinted with your bank account number, so you need send no more RIBs. Most suppliers send postage-free TIP return envelopes with invoices, imprinted with a reminder that they are to be used for TIP return only. For further information on how TIPs are processed, contact *Groupement pour un Système Interbancaire de Télécompensation (GSIT)*, 31 rue de Berri, 75408 Paris Cedex 08, Tel: 01 53893535, *www.gsit.fr*.

Interbank payment systems
[*Systèmes interbancaires de paiement*]

France has three interbank payment systems, two for large-value payments and one for mass retail transfers.

- The *Transferts Banque de France (TBF)* system, a part of the Trans-European Automated Real-time Gross settlement Express Transfer (TARGET) system, started up in October 1997. It is operated by *Banque de France* and is a Real-Time Gross Settlement (RTGS) system that provides continuous transaction-by-transaction settlement.

- The Paris Net Settlement (PNS) system started up in April 1999 as a successor of the Protected Net Settlement system [*Système Net Protégé (SNP)*] that had operated since 1997. It is operated by CRI, a joint venture of *Banque de France* and nine credit institutions, and is a real-time system operating on a net basis to provide final and continuous settlement for transfer operations in central bank money accounts held by participants.

- The Interbank Teleclearing System [*Système Interbancaire de Télécompensation (SIT)*] handles retail payments and clearing of interbank exchanges of cashless payments. It started up in 1992 and in July 2002 became the sole system in the country. It processes some 45 million transactions a day, with a value of 19 billion Euros, and consequently is the largest retail system in Europe, both in volume and in value.

Contact the **Central bank** for further information on TBF and PNS, the European Central Bank, Kaiserstrasse 29, 60311 Frankfurt am Main, Germany, Fax: +49 6913447407, *www.ecb.int* for further information on TARGET, and *Groupement pour un Système Interbancaire de Télécompensation (GSIT)*, 31 rue de Berri, 75408 Paris Cedex 08, Tel: 01 53893535, *www.gsit.fr* for further information on SIT.

Livret A

The *Livret A* is the country's most popular savings plan, held by three-quarters of all residents and accounting for about a fifth of all savings. Its popularity is due in part to it being fully accessible, paying a guaranteed interest of 2.25% set by the government and being tax exempt on a balance of up to € 15,300. Its roots go back to 1818, when the first savings banks [*caisses d'épargne*] were established with the purpose of making private savings [*épargne populaire*] available to finance public-sector projects. As this book goes to press, *Livret A* is offered only by the *Caisse d'Epargne* mutual savings banks and by *La Banque Postale*, part of **La Poste** (Chapter 36), but after more than ten years of protesting that monopoly, other **Banks** may be allowed to offer it, in step with the ongoing liberalisation of the banking sector.

The Mint [*Monnaie de Paris*]

The French Mint traces its history back to the year 864, when Emperor Charles II or Charles the Bald (823-877) issued a decree "forbidding the striking of coinage in any other location than the Palace" [*fait défense de fabriquer des monnaies en nul lieu si ce n'est au Palais*]. Today, *Monnaie de Paris* is one of the largest mints in the world. Its factory at Pessac (Gironde) handles all processes in coin manufacture, from casting metals in its foundry to the final packaging of finished coins for circulation in France as well as in other countries. Accordingly, it is a major producer of the eight **Euro** coins. It also produces commemorative coins, pendants, medals and other collectables that are sold in its shop as well as by authorised distributors. It has a numismatic museum open to the public and an extensive numismatic research library and archives. Its principal facility is at 11 quai de Conti, 75270 Paris Cedex 06, Tel: 01 40465656; the museum is at the same address; the numismatic shop is at 2 rue Guénégaud, 75006 Paris, Tel: 01 40465855; the website at *www.monnaiedeparis.com* has pages in French and in English and a locator of the Mint's distributors across the country as well as elsewhere in Europe.

Moneo

Launched in 2000, Moneo is an electronic purse [*porte-monnaie électronique*] system for small daily transactions. The basic Moneo card may be preloaded with up to € 100 at a Moneo terminal and thereafter used to settle cash payments of up to € 30. The card does not require a bank account, so it may be used by children or tourists. Like cash, it is anonymous, which is why its content limit is € 100. The Moneo function also may be integrated into a **payment card** on an account. In use, the Moneo card is inserted into a hand-held terminal in which the seller has keyed in the cash amount due. The customer then confirms the purchase by pushing a button on the terminal, and the Moneo card is debited. Moneo cards are available from almost all **banks**, and terminal use is widespread. For complete details, contact a bank or visit *www.moneo.net*.

Money transfer [*Transfère d'argent*]

Money transfer is convenient as neither the sender nor the recipient need have a bank account. *La Banque Postale*, available at *La Poste* offices across the country, offers two types of money transfer:

*   Postal money orders [*Les mandats*] are available with ordinary delivery to 150 countries of transfers up to € 3500 in four to 10 days or with express delivery to 12 EU countries of transfers up to € 3500 in two days. Further information is available at all post offices.

*   Western Union electronic transfer of up to € 7600 within minutes to more than 225,000 agents in 195 countries. For further information, pick up a Western Union brochure at a post office or visit the French website at *www.westernunion.fr*.

Novice investor training [*École de la Bourse*]

The *École de la Bourse* offers short courses and correspondence courses as well as publications to help ordinary people – small savers, students, wage-earners – understand the stockmarket and the financial details published by listed companies and the media and thereby become sufficiently skilled to manage their own portfolios. A typical novice investor course, held at one of 50 centres across the country, comprises seven two-hour evening sessions and costs € 107, with discounts in certain cases, and there are advanced courses for derivatives and warrants. Part of the Euronext consortium of stock exchanges, *École de la Bourse* is located at the **Stock exchange,** Palais Brongniart, 75002 Paris, Tel: 01 49275536, *www.ecolebourse.com*, with an interactive locator map of facilities across the country as well as copious free online information, including a dictionary of stockmarket and investment terminology.

Online banking [*Banque à distance*]

Almost all **banks** offer online banking services via fixed or mobile telephone, Minitel or Internet. The Internet option is the most comprehensive, as it supports access to and management of accounts, transfers between accounts in France, printout of *RIB* bank account identifiers and ordering of other bank services. Contact your bank for further details.

Opening a bank account in France
[*Pour ouvrir un compte en France*]

You may open an account with a bank by post from abroad. However, it's best to open an account in person, because it's quicker and because you then establish a personal contact at the bank.

You will need to provide [*Il faudra vous munir*]:

- an official identity document or valid passport [*de votre carte nationale d'identité ou passeport en cours de validité*]
- proof of your address in France, such as a telephone or electricity bill less than three months old [*d'un justificatif de domicile – facture de téléphone fixe ou d'électricité de moins de 3 mois par exemple*]
- recent written proof of income, if you wish to domicile your revenues in France [*d'un justificatif de revenus récent – si vous souhaitez domicilier vos revenus*]
- a deposit to start your account [*d'un dépôt pour activer le compte*].

A bank account is considered to be a contract, so the bank must explain the conditions of it, including all relevant charges. If you open a current account [*compte courant*] you most likely will want a cheque book [*chéquier*], because **cheques** are a much-used means of non-cash payment. Note that an overdraft facility [*découvert*] requires prior approval. If you issue a cheque on insufficient funds, you risk loss of the right to use cheques for five years.

Payment cards [*Cartes de paiement*]

Though **cheques** remain more popular than elsewhere in Europe, payment cards now account for more non-cash transactions, about four in ten across the country. There are three principal varieties of cards: debit cards, credit cards and charge cards.

Debit cards [*cartes de débit*], also called bank cards [*cartes bancaire*], are used at **cashpoints** to withdraw money and in **point of sale (POS)** terminals in shops and professional offices to pay for goods and services. A debit card is the electronic equivalent of a paper cheque: it identifies the holder of an account with a bank, which must have sufficient balance to cover the amount debited when the card is used. If the balance is insufficient, a card debiting will be refused, just as an overdrawn cheque is returned. Likewise, like paper cheques, debit cards usually are valid only within their country of issue unless special provisions have been made by their issuing banks.

Credit cards [*cartes de crédit*] are used in the same way as debit cards, but provide an overdraft or credit facility. Most credit cards are issued by banks in various plans that combine debit to a current account with a credit extension to it.

Charge cards [*cartes de charge*] are valid at the outlets of specific retailers and require regular monthly settlement, usually against an invoice sent on a specified day of the month. Most petrol station companies and larger hypermarkets issue charge cards valid for purchases at their outlets across the country and, in some cases, elsewhere in Europe.

All debit and charge cards issued in France can be used at all cashpoints and in all shop point of sale terminals, as can most international cards issued abroad. All payment cards physically conform to the international **Identification cards** (Chapter 30) standard ID-1 size, an 85.6×53.98 mm rectangle with rounded corners. Most have a black magnetic stripe on the reverse side that is read out when the card is swiped through the slot of a terminal, but smart cards with embedded microprocessors are now almost as numerous and are read by inserting into a slot in a terminal. The two leading French credit card entities are *Carte Bleue* and *Cartes Bancaires*, which, as they have the same two initials, are sometimes confused with each other.

Carte Bleue was founded in 1967 when six banks (BNP, CCF, CIC, Crédit du Nord, Crédit Lyonais and Société Génénerale] launched the country's first payment card. In 1973, *Carte Bleue* joined Bank Americard, then the world's largest payment card network, in a joint network that later became Visa. By 1984, the *Carte Bleue* group included the 200 largest banks, groups of banks and financial institutions in the country. In 1986, France became the first country to issue smart cards, used in the Visa Premier cards issued by *Carte Bleue* member banks. *Carte Bleue* grew to be a leader in the French electronic payment sector and now comprises two companies, *GIE Carte Bleue (Groupement Carte Bleue)* that is the French representative of Visa at the international level and accordingly attends to Visa matters in France, and *SAS Carte Bleue* that offers a broad range of Visa system credit cards to its 40 member banks and financial institutions. Newest is the *e-Carte Bleue*, a card for transactions over the Internet that hinders fraud or theft of a card number, as instead of using the physical card number, you receive a new e-number for each transaction. For further information, visit the *Carte Bleue* website at *www.carte-bleue.fr*, with pages in English as well as in French.

Cartes Bancaires, abbreviated CB, was founded in 1984 by *Carte Bleue* members and other principal banks in order to promote the use of bank cards by arranging for interoperability, so all bank cards would be accepted by all cashpoints and point of sale terminals affiliated with the CB network. Today, the CB network covers almost all terminals in the country, and almost all banks will issue CB cards for debiting current accounts. As the name implies, the basic CB card is a bank card, another name for a debit card. It can be used only within the CB system. As in other countries, issuing banks offer various international add-ons to the domestic CB card through agreements with *Carte Bleue*, *MasterCard* or *Visa*. For further information, visit the *Cartes Bancaires* website at *www.cartes-bancaires.com*, with pages in English as well as in French.

In summary, like a French chequebook, a payment card with the stylised CB logo and no other logos is a debit card valid only at CB terminals in France. If it also has the logos of one or more international payment card organisations, it may be used in other countries as well. For instance, the *Carte Bleue Visa* card has three logos – CB, *Carte Bleue* and Visa – and consequently is valid worldwide.

Carte Bleue logo, on credit and debit cards valid internationally, usually appears with Visa logo.

Cartes Bancaires logo; when appearing alone, designates a debit card valid in France only.

Point of Sale Terminals (POS)
[*Terminales de Pointe de Vente (TPV)*]

Point of Sale Terminals (POS) are commonplace; there now is one POS Terminal for every 60 residents in the country. Magnetic-stripe card readers, in which you swipe your card through a slot in the terminal, are common, but most shops now also have smart-card readers in which you insert the card for reading of its microchip. Supermarkets and most volume retailers have POS Terminals fitted with combined receipt and cheque printers [*imprimante pointe de vente*], so if you pay by cheque, the Terminal writes the cheque correctly for the amount due, ready for your signature.

Say's law [*Loi de Say*]

One of the great economists of the late 18th and early 19th centuries was Jean-Bapiste Say (1767-1832). Early influenced by Adam Smith during a visit to the UK, in 1789 he published a brochure entitled Freedom of the Media [*la Liberté de la presse*] and in 1792 took part in the Revolution. He wrote *Traite d'Economie Politique*, a text that inspired the neoclassical economists of the 19th century. But he is most remembered for "Say's Law", or the "Law of Markets", which states that supply creates demand. This is the diametrical opposite of the principle espoused by British economist John Maynard Keynes (1883-1946) in what has become known as Keynes's Law, that demand creates supply. To this day, economists debate Say vs. Keynes.

Securities regulator [*Autorité des Marches Financiers*]

The Securities regulator [*Autorité des Marches Financiers (AMF)*] provides investor protection, information and transparency, both within the country and in international matters according to the rules of the European Commission. The AMF is a member of the Committee of European Securities Regulators (CESR) and works bilaterally with more than 30 European and international regulatory agencies under cooperative and information sharing agreements. It has an ombudsman to answer investor queries and organise mediation in the event of a dispute. For further information, contact AMF, 17 place de la Bourse, 75082 Paris Cedex 02, Tel: 01 53456000, *www.amf-france.org*, or for the ombudsman, Tel 01 53456464 Tuesdays and Thursdays 14:00 -16:00.

Social security ceiling [*Plafond de sécurité sociale*]

The central reference point in the calculations of social security contributions to unemployment and health insurance and to retirement funds is called the "Social security ceiling" [*Plafond de sécurité sociale*], often abbreviated P. It is set once a year, effective 1st January, and for 2006, is €2,589 a month, or €31,068 a year. Contributions are calculated in brackets [*tranches*], each of which has a ceiling that is a multiple of P:

Bracket	Gross income (2006)	
[*Tranche*]	monthly	annual
Tranche A, 1P	€2,589	€31,068
Tranche B, 4P	€10,356	€124,272
Tranche C, 8P	€20,712	€248,544

There also are intermediate brackets used in calculating retirement contributions: *Tranche 1* has a ceiling of 3P, and *Tranche 2* has a ceiling of 2P. **CLEISS** (Chapter 22) regularly updates and publishes the rates and ceilings on its website at *www.cleiss.fr*.

Stock exchange [*Bourse de Paris*]

Founded in 1724, *Bourse de Paris* is the world's second oldest stock exchange, after the Amsterdam exchange, founded in 1602. In terms of market capitalisation, the French stockmarket is the world's fourth largest, after the USA, Japan and the UK. The *Bourse de Paris* is accordingly busy and large; its head office is in the Brongniart Palace [*Palais Brongniart*], commissioned by Napoleon and named after its designer, architect Alexandre Théodore Brongniart (1739-1813). It is located at Place de la Bourse, 75002 Paris, Tel: 01 49271470.

In September 2000, the *Bourse de Paris* and the exchanges in Amsterdam and Brussels merged to form Euronext NV, the first cross-border exchange in Europe. In January 2002, Euronext expanded by acquiring the London International Financial Futures and Options Exchange (LIFFE), and a month later it merged with the Portuguese exchange. Today, Euronext has facilities in Amsterdam, Brussels, Lisbon, London and Paris and operates in four languages: English, French, Dutch and Portuguese. For further information on the merging of the exchanges and on present operations, see two brochures, "From Amsterdam, Brussels and Paris exchanges to Euronext" and "Euronext: organisation and procedures", downloadable from the website at *www.euronext.com*. The Paris office of Euronext is at 39 rue Cambon, 75039 Paris Cedex 01, Tel: 01 49271000.

Stockmarket indices [*Indices boursiers*]

Several indices are used on the stockmarket, including the major indices used in other countries, such as the Dow Jones, the NASDAQ, the Nikkei 225 and Standard & Poor's 500. The four most used indices in France are:

- CAC 40: CAC is an abbreviation for *Cotation Assistée en Continu* ("Continuous-time Computer-Assisted Quotation) and is the benchmark index on the Paris **Stock exchange**. It lists the 40 biggest companies on the exchange to a base value of 1000 starting 31 December 1987.

- SBF 120: SBF is an abbreviation for *Société de Bourses Françaises*; the SBF 120 includes 120 market capitalisations and consequently is broader than CAC

40 and arguably a better indicator of the market in general. It is calculated every 30 seconds to a base value of 1000 starting 31 December 1990.

- SBF 80 is a truncated version of SBF 120 that excludes the CAC 40 companies. It is calculated every 30 seconds to a base value of 1000 starting 31 December 1990.

- SBF 250: An indicator of the market in general that is based on 250 capitalisations listed by Euronext Paris.

Surety [*Cautionnement*]

Surety is a contractual document, such as a bond or a guarantee, that provides security to a beneficiary against the default of the principal. It is most often used in connection with larger transactions, such as by a government department against the failure of an organisation to pay taxes or duties. However, surety is also used in everyday matters, such as by landlords to ensure payment of rent and in the temporary importation of goods not covered by an **ATA Carnet**. Many banks offer surety bonds.

Vocabulary of banking [*Vocabulaire bancaire*]

The terminology of banking, insurance and the like is extensive. The commonplace terms are listed below, alphabetically by their names in English.

English	*French*	
balance	*solde*	
bank charges	*frais bancaires*	
bank fees	*tarification*	
bank identity details	*relevé d'identité bancaire (RIB)*	
bank statement	*relevé de compte*	
card	*carte*	
change	*monnaie*	
cheque	*chèque*	
chequebook	*chéquier*	
currency	*devise*	
current account	*compte courant*	
customer help / service	*service d'assistance*	
deposit	*dépôt*	
exchange rates	*taux de change*	
expiry date	*date d'expiration*	
guarantee payment	*caution*	
insurance	*assurances*	
investment	*placement*	
loan	*prêt*	
mortgage	*crédit immobilier*	
overdraft	*découvert*	
partner	*allié*	
PIN code	*code confidentiel, code PIN*	
profitability	*rentabilité*	
proof of your home address	*justificatif de domicile*	
repayment	*remboursement*	
savings account	*compte épargne*	
share	*action*	
stop cheque or payment	*faire opposition*	
tax	*impôt*	
transfer	*virement*	

Youth savings [*Livret jeune*]

Youth savings [*Livret jeune*] is a passbook savings scheme created in 1996 and now offered by most **banks** to people from age 12, until 31 December of the year of their 25th birthday, to encourage saving for larger expenses, such as holidays or courses of instruction for driving licences. The minimum deposit is € 15, the accumulated maximum is € 1600, and accounts earn interest at a guaranteed rate of 4% per year.

3
Business and work

France has the world's fifth-largest gross domestic product (GDP) per person and is the world's sixth largest trader. The economy is diversified: most companies are private, but many national services, including health care and education are provided principally by public sector organisations.

As elsewhere in Europe, many nationalised business monopolies have recently been privatised and their markets opened to competition. However, the public sector employs one person in four in the civil service, the police, health care, education, post and telecoms, electricity and gas and the armed forces.

Agriculture and the food industries account for a greater share of overall economic activity than in most other western European countries, employing 5% of the workforce and contributing 3.4% of the GDP. The industrial sector's share of the GDP is slightly less than 20%, but manufacturing accounts for three-quarters of the overall export of goods and services. The services sector is big and accounts for 72% of the GDP. Tourism is one of the more visible sectors of the country's business: France is the world's leading holiday destination country, and tourism accounts for more than 6% of the GDP.

Business is large and visible as well as old. Total, an energy company, is the tenth biggest business in the world, in terms of annual turnover. One motor vehicle in six in the world is made by a French company. The European Aeronautic Defence and Space Company (EADS), with joint headquarters in Paris and in Munich, arguably is the world's leading aerospace company: in 2005, Airbus, its commercial aircraft sector, delivered more planes than Boeing of the USA, and the Ariane 5 rocket now is the world's most powerful for launching satellites into orbit. The Carrefour retailing group is the world's sixth largest company in number of employees. Unsurprisingly, the oldest company in Europe and third oldest in the world is a French vineyard, Château du Goulaine, founded in 1000, and the world's eighth oldest company is a French papermaker, Richard de Bas, founded in 1326.

With few exceptions, all jobs are open to all persons qualified for them, regardless of sex, ethnic background or religious beliefs. Foreigners from EU/EEA countries are treated equally with French citizens in applying for work. Foreigners from countries outside the EU/EEA must have **Work permits** (Chapter 1) and may be hired only for jobs for which no local or national hires have been found. Women and men have equal rights in work, education and care for children in the home. Increasingly, women work outside the home and now account for 80% of all part-time workers.

The unemployment rate of 9.5% is high but only slightly above the average for the EU (25 countries). Steps are being taken to lower unemployment, particularly among the young, and the rate is falling.

Compared to many other countries, annual vacations are long, five for all full-time employees. The legal working week is 35 hours, though with overtime, the average working week is 38.5 hours.

Agricultural sector employment agency [*APECITA*]

If your vocation is in farming or the agricultural and food processing sector, you may benefit from the services of the Agricultural Sector Employment Agency [*Association pour l'emploi des cadres, ingénieurs et techniciens de l'agriculture (APECITA)*]. APECITA has 16 regional offices, keeps updated lists of vacancies for job seekers and the CVs of persons seeking work and publishes job offers in its magazine, *Tribune Verte*. For further information and the locations of the regional offices, visit the website at *www.apecita.fr*.

Chambers of Commerce and Industry [*Assemblée des chambres française de commerce et d'industrie*]

The French chambers of commerce and industry (ACFCI) is a panoply organisation for 155 metropolitan and overseas chambers of commerce, as well as 20 regional chambers of commerce, together representing 1.8 million companies. The ACFCI is the intermediary between the chambers of commerce and national as well as international authorities. It has a head office in Paris at 45 avenue d'Iéna, BP 3003, 75773 Paris Cedex 16, Tel: 01 40693700, *www.acfci.cci.fr* in French and in English, with an interactive locator map to bring up addresses and telecoms numbers of the chambers of commerce across the country.

Chambers of Tradesmen and Artisans [*Chambres des métiers et de l'artisanat*]

Across the country, chambers of tradesmen and artisans in all *Départements* act to further the interests of their member organisations as well as to fulfil quasi-public functions, such as registration of new trade and craft enterprises. A national panoply association, *Assemblée permanente des chambres de métiers et de l'artisanat (APCMA)* is the coordinating body, with a head office in Paris at 12 avenue Marceau, 75008 Paris, Tel: 01 44431000, and a website at *www.apcm.com* with an interactive locator map of all the Chambers across the country.

Company forms [*Types des sociétés*]

As elsewhere in Europe, there are three general types of company organisation, sole proprietorships, corporate ownerships and **Cooperative societies**.

In a sole proprietorship [*Entreprise unipersonnelle à responsabilité limitée (EURL)*], one person provides all the capital and bears all the risk. Typically, craftsmen have EURLs.

There are many forms of corporate ownership, of which six apply to most businesses:

- SA, the abbreviation for *Société Anonyme*, the most common form for big businesses; may be set up by seven or more shareholders.

- SAS, the abbreviation for *Société Actions Simplifiée*, a simplified version of SA available since 1994 and intended principally for joint ventures; may be set up by a sole shareholder.

- SARL, the abbreviation for *Société A Responsabilité Limitée*, the most prevalent form for smaller businesses; may be set up by one to 50 people.

- SCA, the abbreviation for *Société en Commandite par Actions*, a limited partnership, usually involved in financing.

- SCI, the abbreviation for *Société Civile Immobilière*, a property holding company set up by the owners of a business, such as an SA or SARL.

- SCS, the abbreviation for *Société en Commandite Simple*, a limited partnership, usually of two dissimilar companies; requires no share capital.

Cooperative societies [*Sociétés coopératives*]

There are innumerable cooperative societies in the country. Many vineyards are amalgamated in cooperatives [*caves coopératives*] as are stove and fireplace artisans. There are two large associations of cooperatives, CUMA and SCOP.

CUMA, the abbreviation for *Coopératives d'utilisation de matériel agricole*, is the big agricultural sector cooperative with more than 230,000 members in 13,000 cooperative organisations. It has offices across the country and a head office in Paris: 49 avenue de la Grande Armée, 75116 Paris, Tel: 01 44175800, *www.cuma.fr*, *fncuma@cuma.fr*.

SCOP, the abbreviation for *Société coopérative de production*, is a type of cooperative business in which the employees hold most of the share capital. SCOPs are considered to be an attractive form of company for participatory management and are organised in almost all business sectors. The typical SCOP is a small to medium-sized company with two to a thousand participant employees. A central organisation, *SCOP Entreprises* promotes the concept, provides information in French, English and Spanish, and assists in founding new ventures: *Confédération générale des Scop*, 37 rue Jean leclaire, 75017 Paris, Tel: 01 44854700, *www.scop.coop*, *scopreprises@scop.coop*.

Discrimination [*Discrimination*]

By law, in employment, housing and services, people shall not be subjected to discrimination because of their age, handicap, their sex or their sexual orientation, their origin, their physical appearance, their religion, their political beliefs or their labour union activities [*en raison de leur âge, de leur handicap, de leur sexe or de leur orientation sexuelle, de leur origine, de leur apparence physique, de leur religion, de leurs opinions politiques, de leurs activités syndicales*].

Nonetheless, discrimination exists. If you feel that you are subjected to discrimination at work, you should notify your immediate superior. If your supervisor does not act, you may seek advice by calling the **Equality and Anti-Discrimination Authority** (Chapter 27) help line at 08 10005000, 09:00-19:00, Monday-Friday.

If you feel that you are subject to discrimination because of your sex – in most cases, because you are a woman – you also may contact one of the 119 public information Centres on Women's Rights [*Centres d'Information sur les Droits des Femmes (CIDF)*], which you can find using the locator map on the CIDF website at *www.infofemmes.com*. Not all perceived unfairness toward women is intentional, as much of it arises because workplaces have yet to adjust to the stresses imposed on women who combine careers and work with domestic duties and children. CNIDFF, the administrative parent of the CIDF centres, has published a guideline brochure aimed at overcoming the difficulties involved, *Guide pratique: Entreprises et articulation des temps familiaux et professionnels* (ANDCP, CJD, CFE and CGC, 2002, 48 pages, A4 format). Simple, straightforward and illustrated with comic strips, it is available free (plus postage) on company order from CNIDFF, 7 rue du Jura, 75013 Paris, Fax: 01 43311581 .

Employer organisation [*Mouvement des Entreprises*]

Most employers in the private sector are represented by the French business confederation, *Mouvement des entreprises de France (MEDF)*, a panoply organisation previously, until 1998, known as the *Conseil national du patronat français (CNPF)*. MEDF represents some 700,000 large and small enterprises in the country that together employ 15 million people. Administratively, it is divided into 155 sections representing the departments and regions of the mainland and abroad. For further information, contact the head office, MEDF, 55 avenue Bosquet, 75330 Paris Cedex 07, Tel: 01 53591919, Fax: 01 45512044, *www.medef.fr*.

Employment agency [*ANPE*]

If you need help to find a job, seek courses or other measures to improve your skills, wish to apply for unemployment or disability benefits, or are handicapped and seeking work, your best single contact is the local office of the National Employment Agency [*Agence nationale pour l'emploi (ANPE)*].

Created in 1967 as an amalgamation of services to job seekers and to employers as well as of the compilation of statistics concerning the workforce, ANPE now has more than a thousand public-service offices across the country. It coordinates activities related to work, employment and vocational training with the regional departments of Labour, Employment and Vocational Training (**DRTEFP**) and the Adult Vocational and Professional Training and Education Association (**AFPA**). It has an extensive website at *www.anpe.fr*, with an online interactive locator map for finding offices, descriptions of all services offered and continuously updated lists of positions available to job seekers [*Candidat*] and, for employers [*Employeurs*], of the CVs of job seekers. It coordinates activities with separate websites dedicated to the aerospace sector, *emploi-aviation.anpe.fr* and to the entertainment sector, *www.culture-spectacle.anpe.fr*.

In addition to ANPE, the **Executive Employment Agency**, the **Agricultural Sector Employment Agency** and the **Office of International Migration** offer employment services. ANPE is a partner in the **EURES** network, and there are EURES advisers at many ANPE offices. If you are a citizen of another EEA country, contact EURES by visiting the European website at *europa.eu.int* and click on "Working" to navigating to the EURES job mobility portal, where you can navigate to a list of EURES advisers in your home country as well as in France.

Employment contracts [*Contrats de travail*]

There are more than 20 different forms of employment contract; for a complete list with links to summaries of each, visit the Ministry of Social Affairs, Labour and Solidarity website at *www.travail.gouv.fr* and click on *Fiches pratiques* on the opening page. The **Employment agency (ANPE)** provides guidelines, and **EURES** offers updated overviews for France as well as for all other EU/EEA countries.

The five most used forms of contract are the permanent contract [*Contrat à durée indéterminée (CDI)*], the fixed-term contract [*Contrat à durée déterminée (CDD)*], the temporary contract [*Contrat de travail temporaire*], the part-time contract [*Contrat de travail à temps partiel*] and the intermittent contract [*Contrat de travail intermittent*]. All contracts must be written, save for the permanent contract, which may be oral.

- The permanent contract [*Contrat à durée indéterminée (CDI)*] also is called an open-ended contract because its date of termination is not specified at the outset, though it may be terminated by either party. The contract will set forth a description of the position, the date for starting work, the details of social security provisions, the company specifics, the place of work, the salary, the notice period and the duration of the probationary period, usually one to three months. An employee insufficiently fluent in French to understand the contract may request that it be translated.

- The fixed-term contract [*Contrat à durée déterminée (CDD)*] is used for a temporary task of specified duration, such as being a substitute for an employee on leave, filling out staff for a short-term increase in company activity and for seasonal work. The reason for the short duration of the task must be specified. A CDD may be valid for no more than 18 months, or no more than 24 months if the workplace is abroad, and may be renewed for a period equal to that of the initial contract. The probationary period of a CDD may be no more than two weeks for a six-month contract and no more than one month for a contract of longer duration.

- The temporary contract [*Contrat de travail temporaire*] is entered under the same conditions as a CDD, principally for short-term employees provided by **Temping agencies**. Consequently the contract involves three parties: the employee, the temping agency who contractually is the employer, and the agency's client who allots the workplace. A temporary contract may be renewed once, provided the total length of employment is no more than 18 months.

- The part-time contract [*Contrat de travail à temps partiel*] is similar to a CDI or a CDD for full-time work, except that it specifies fewer working hours, up to 80% of full-time in the private sector and 50% to 80% of full-time in the public sector. No minimums are specified, though employees wishing to benefit from social security coverage must work at least 60 hours a month.

- The intermittent contract [*Contrat de travail intermittent*] is similar to a CDI or a CDD and usually is entered for full-time work in a specified season.

Employment Research Centre [*Centre d'études de l'emploi*]

The Employment Research Centre [*Centre d'Etudes de l'Emploi (CEE)*] is a public research institute connected with the Ministries of Employment and of Education. It is principally concerned with guiding public authorities, in probing the impact of market and technical changes on employment, contributing to public and private sector polices and on studying various aspects of the labour market. It has a permanent research group of 40 sociologists, economists and statisticians who publish their findings mostly in French but also in English. Consequently, it probably is the best single source of information on and analyses of the labour market. Head facility: 29 Promenade Michel Simon, 93166 Noisy-le-Grand Cedex, Tel: 01 45926800, *www.cee-recherche.fr* with pages in French and in English.

EURES [*EURES*]

The European Employment Services (EURES) is an agency of the European Commission (EC) that comprises a network of partners, each of which is a national employment agency. In France, there are two EURES partners, APNE and APEC. The principal purpose of EURES is to aid workers and employers as well as individuals wishing to avail themselves of the free movement of persons in Europe. It accomplishes this through more than 500 advisers in the various partner agencies across Europe. For further information, contact the employment agency in your home country, APNE or APEC in France or visit the EURES European Job Mobility Portal at *europa.eu.int/eures*; select one of the 20 languages on the opening page to enter the site.

Euro info centre network [*Réseau des euro info centres*]

Across 45 countries, there are more than 300 Euro Info Centres (EICs) that advise and assist in all matters of internationalisation across Europe. Each EIC is integrated into the local and regional business environment and can provide it with expertise on practices in other countries. In France, there are EICs across the country, under the auspices of the *Ministre de l'économie, des finances et de l'industrie*; for locations and addresses, use the interactive map on the EIC website at *www.eic.minefi.gouv.fr*, with pages in French, English, German and Spanish.

European Agency for Safety and Health at Work [*Agence européenne pour la sécurité et la santé au travail*]

The European Agency for Safety and Health at Work is an organisation of the European Union that brings together representatives from governments, employers' organisations and labour organisations to deal with occupational safety and health (OSH) [*santé et sécurité au travail*] issues. At the national level, it acts principally through a network of national focal points [*points focal national*], the national focal point in France is the Labour Relations Directorate [*Direction des relations du travail (DRT)*] of the Ministry for Employment, Labour and Social Cohesion [*Ministère de l'emploi, de la cohésion sociale et du logement*], 39-44 quai André Citroën, 75739 Paris Cedex 15, Tel: 01 44383838, *www.travail.gouv.fr*, as well as its panoply OSH public information website at *www.sante-securite.travail.gouv.fr* with pages in English, German, Italian and Spanish. In French texts on OSH matters the Agency occasionally is referred to as "BILBAO", because its head office is in that city: Gran Via 33, E-48009 Bilbao, Spain, Tel: +34 944794360, *osha.eu.int*, *information@osha.eu.int*.

Executive employment agency [*APEC*]

If you are of managerial level or are a young university or college graduate seeking employment, you may benefit from the services of the Executive Employment Agency [*Association pour l'emploi des cadres (APEC)*]. APEC has offices in most cities and larger towns, keeps updated lists of vacancies for degreed job seekers, has an online *Candidathèque* database where you may post your CV, and publishes a weekly magazine, *Courier Cadres*. For further information and the locations of the offices, visit the website at *www.apec.fr*.

Fayolism [*Fayolisme*]

One of the great management thinkers of the 20th century was Henri Fayol (1841-1925). Originally educated at the St. Etienne School of Mines [*École des Mines de Saint-Étienne*], he started his career at a mining company, *Compagnie de Commentry-Fourchambeau-Decazeville*. As CEO from 1888 to 1918, he made the company one of the most successful in France. In so doing, he evolved what became known as the Administration School of Management, detailed in a book, *Administration industrielle et générale*, published in 1916. The book had unprecedented impact, and "Fayolism" revolutionised business in France. In contrast to Frederick Winslow Taylor (1856-1915), the American engineer who evolved the principles of scientific management that influenced industries in America as well as in other counties, including the USSR, Fayol set forth general principles that were useful in a broad range of organisations as well as in government. Fayolism remained little known outside France until 1949 when his book was translated into English and published under the title "General and Industrial Management". The book, which still is in print, became one of the most influential management books of the 20th century.

The Federation of European Employers [*La Fédération des Employeurs Européens*]

The Federation of European Employers (FedEE) is a service organisation for international employers operating across Europe. It was founded in 1989 with funding from the European Commission, and now acts as a resource centre, supports an employment law programme, human resources (HR) certification, a European HR newswire and provides online advice. Particularly for companies setting up operations in a country for the first time, it is an essential resource. Several large French companies are members. Head office: Adam House, 7-10 Adam Street, The Strand, London WC2N 6AA, UK, Tel: +44 2075209264, *www.fedee.com*.

Franchising [*Franchise*]

Individuals and companies increasingly enter business sectors through a franchise in which a parent company, the franchisor [*franchiseur*] grants a licence to another, the franchisee [*franchisé*] that permits conducting business under the trade name of the franchisor and to make use of all the support necessary to establish, maintain and promote business. The outlets and shops of many international chains, particularly in fast food services, actually are franchised and are owned and operated as local businesses. In France, there are more than 800 franchised trade name chains and nearly 40,000 franchisees, nearly one in five in the EEA, making France the leader in franchising. For information on franchising, contact the French franchise federation [*Fédéderation française de la franchise*], 60 rue La Boetie, 75008 Paris, Tel: 01 53752225, *www.franchise-fff.com*, *info@franchise-fff.com*. For an A-Z list of available franchises, visit the *www.infofranchise.fr* website.

Holiday Entitlement [*Congés payés*]

A full-time employee is entitled to five weeks paid leave [*congés payés*] each year, exclusive of public holidays. The five weeks may include days when the employing company traditionally shuts down, such as during the peak holiday period in August or at Christmas. Holiday entitlement is built up at the rate of 2.5 days per month worked usually starting after an employee has worked one month. Part-time employees accumulate holiday entitlement in proportion to the time worked compared to full-time.

Invest in France Agency [*Agence française pour les investissements internationaux*]

The Invest in France Agency (IFA) [*Agence française pour les investissements internationaux (AFII)*] was set up and is maintained by the government to attract business from other countries to France. From 17 offices round the globe, it offers a broad range of services and information and provides access to various incentives.

Its services are customised to company needs and include providing industry sector contacts, aiding in site selection, accessing regulatory information and assisting in identifying potential partners and acquisition opportunities. It offers copious information, in print and online, on all aspects of conducting business in France, from setting up businesses to labour law and corporate taxation. Its websites are continuously updated and accordingly are excellent starting points for authoritative information.

Head office: AFII, 2 avenue Vélasquez, 75008 Paris, Tel: 01 40747440; London office: IFA, 21 Grosvenor Place, London SW1X 7HU, Tel: +44 2078230900, *www.afii.fr*, *www.investinfrance.org* with a locator map of offices.

Jobs [*Emplois*]

The ways you seek, apply for and start a job are similar to those elsewhere in Europe. First, you should be prepared with an updated curriculum vitae (CV) and letter of application and a recent passport-sized portrait photo, because most organisations prefer written applications and many wish to see photos of applicants. Then you can learn about vacancies from several sources:

- local and national newspaper advertisements; the Monday edition of *Le Figaro* has the greatest selection.

- recruitment advertising sections of international magazines, such as The Economist and New Scientist.

- the public **Employment agency** (ANPE) that lists all available jobs or, in their sectors, the **Agricultural sector employment agency** (APECITA) or the **Executive employment agency** (APEC).

- **Recruitment agencies**, particularly for professional positions.
- **Temping agencies**, if you wish to take on short-term or part-time work.
- **EURES** office in your home country.
- if you are studying, word of mouth, notices and other ways of finding **Student jobs**.

By law, access to job offers is free to job seekers [*candidats*]. Application procedures vary; the office contacted will tell you what is required. As a rule, your CV and letter of application should be in French, but some international organisations may request applications in English.

Aside from your professional qualifications for a position, your ability to function in French is decisive. Be honest about it; avoid the word fluency [*couramment*], which can be interpreted to mean that you speak the language as well as a native.

Labour code [*Code du travail*]

In all, there are more than 3700 laws, rules and regulations dealing with work, social security and human rights. Of these, the Labour code [*Code du travail*] is most relevant to conditions of employment, including working hours, health, working environment, safety, hiring and dismissal, union rights and other aspects of life at work. There are four principal sources of information on the Code:

- The entire code may be downloaded from the governmental Legifrance website at *www.legifrance.gouv.fr*.
- The International Labour Organisation's National Labour Legislation (NATLEX) online database lists links to the Code and all other relevant documents now in force: visit *www.ilo.org*, click on "Standards and Fundamental Principals and Rights at Work", then on the NATLEX link, then on "Browse by Country" and finally on France to bring up the list of links.
- *VO editions*, the book publishing section of the **General Confederation of Labour**, offers several books on the Code and related topics, usually updated once a year, *www.librairie-nvo.com*.
- Several private-sector publishers offer transcripts and interpretations of the Code and related topics in books sold in bookshops and online, as by *www.amazon.fr*.

Labour inspectorate [*Inspection du travail*]

The Labour inspectorate monitors and enforces employment laws and regulations. It also monitors provisions derived from collective agreements, advises employers and employees and is empowered to make some decisions, particularly in matters in which administrative authorisation is required prior to a private action. These tasks are performed by inspectors based at the Labour inspectorate offices in the Regions and Departments, and there are special inspectors for transport and agriculture. To find the closest office, visit the principal website at *www.travail.gouv.fr*, click on *Services en régions* to bring up an interactive map of the Regions, and then click on the relevant Region to bring up a list of offices. The similar function concerning safety and health regulations is the responsibility of the **Occupational safety and health** watchdog agency.

Liberal profession [*Profession libérale*]

In the workforce, 80% of persons are employed, and the remaining 20% work for themselves in private practice or other forms of self-employment. From doctors to taxi drivers, the occupations of the smaller group are called the liberal professions [*professions libérale*] in publications concerning work, healthcare and social security. The **ILO Thesaurus** (Chapter 28) is the authoritative listing of all the names of the occupations in English, French and Spanish.

Maternity and parental leave
[*Congé de maternité et congé parental*]

A working woman is entitled to 16 weeks of paid maternity leave, six antenatal and ten postnatal. The antenatal period can be extended to eight weeks in case of a complicated pregnancy, a multiple pregnancy or the third child. Paid paternity leave is 11 days, or 18 days in case of a multiple pregnancy.

McJob

In his 1991 novel "Generation X", Canadian author Douglas Coupland (1961-) coined the word "McJob" as a term applicable to "a low-pay, low-prestige, low-dignity, low-benefit, no-future job in the service sector". The term was quickly adopted by the youth of the day and entered the slang of other languages, including French ca. 1995. In 2003, it was included in English dictionaries, and by 2005 it was in international use, as by *The Economist* and by the *OECD*. Understandably, McDonalds was perturbed; its chairman protested inclusion of McJob in dictionaries, and in November 2005, McDonalds France argued against its negative connotation in a video on the company website at *www.mcdonalds.fr*. Nonetheless, McJob now is part of the everyday lingo of the youth of the land and in media descriptions of them. In May 2006, *Le Monde diplomatique* lamented the precarious situations of the "McJob generation" in which young, university-educated people could not find jobs for which they were qualified and accordingly were becoming an intellectual underclass.

Minimum wage [*SMIC*]

The minimum wage [*Salaire minimum interprofessionnel de croissance (SMIC)*] is set once a year, effective 1 July. Its annual increase is automatically based on price levels and the real value of average earnings and is occasionally supplemented as needed by decree. The SMIC is fair and stable, more so than in most European countries where the worth of the minimum wage relative to earnings has declined over the years. The SMIC effective 1 July 2006 is €8.27 an hour, corresponding to a monthly gross minimum wage of €1254.28*.

* *Source: Service-Public*

Mutual insurance [*Mutualité*]

Many federations and unions as well as companies arrange complementary insurance in addition to that provided through **Social security contributions**. As the name implies, this private insurance is almost always provided through a mutual benefit fund built up from premiums paid in by its members, so employees who contribute to the fund are both the insurers and the insured.

Occupational health and safety [*Santé et sécurité au travail*]

Occupational health and safety, also known as occupational risk prevention, is extensive: four governmental agencies are concerned with it, and ten websites are dedicated to it. Two organisations provide expertise and extensive services on the everyday aspects of occupational health and safety (OSH):

* National Agency for the Improvement of Working Conditions [*Agence pour l'amélioration des conditions de travail (ANACT)*] conducts research on working conditions and accordingly disseminates relevant information intended to aid employers in preventing occupational hazards. Head office: 4 quai des Etroits, 69623 Lyon Cedex, Tel: 04 72561313, *www.anact.fr*.

* Occupational Risk Prevention Organisation for the Building and Civil Engineering Industries [*Organisme professionnel de prévention du bâtiment et des travaux publics (OPPBTP)*] contributes to preventing occupational hazards in the building trades, in part by publishing printed and online booklets and fact sheets aimed at workers. National committee: 204 round-point du Pont-de-Sèvres, 92516 Boulogne-Billiancourt Cedex, Tel: 01 46092700, *www.oppbtp.fr*.

The National Research and Safety Institute [*Institut national de recherche et de sécurité*] liaises with all the relevant public and private sector organisations, conducts research and makes printed and online publications available from two centres: Paris Centre: 30 rue Oliver Noyer, 75680 Paris Cedex 14, Tel: 01 40443000, and Lorraine Centre: Avenue de Bourgone, BP 27, 54501 Vandoeuvre Cedex, Tel: 03 83502000; website for both: *www.inrs.fr*.

Part-time work [*Travail à mi-temps*]

Though modest compared to other European countries, the part-time employment sector is growing, and one employee in six in France works part time. Of the part-time workers, some four million people, 80% are women and nearly half are young people. Part-time work is most common in services, health, education, retail shops and agriculture.

By definition, part-time work is employment for fewer than 35 hours per week. Wages vary as they do for full-time work, but in all cases, a part-time employee must be paid at the same rate as a full-time employee in the same job. Numerous other rules apply, such as the requirement that students in higher-education institutions work no more than 19.5 hours a week during the academic year and no more than 884 hours in the course of a calendar year. For a complete overview of the rules for and practices of part-time work, contact the **Employment agency** (*ANPE*).

Permanent workers [*Salariés permanents*]

A citizen of a country other than those of the EU/EEA or Switzerland who settles in France to work is considered a permanent worker who must have a **Work permit** (Chapter 1). The administrative procedures for recruiting as well as for working depend on the worker's residence status and the conditions of employment. For the complete details of working and employing workers in French and in English, contact **ANAEM** (Chapter 1).

Recruitment agencies [*Conseils en recrutement*]

Recruitment agencies are private-sector employment organisations that offer services in recruiting [*conseils*] and counselling [*cabinets*]. Sometimes they are called head-hunters [*chasseurs de têtes*] because they principally are concerned with finding and placing selected professionals, though specialist agencies deal with workers in all sectors. You can find agencies listed in the Yellow pages under *Recrutement (cabinets, conseils)* as well is an annual national directory, *Guides des Conseils en Recrutement* (Paris, Cercomm Publications, 2005 edition, 344 pages paperback, ISBN 2905737085). There are two large chains of agencies, each with websites offering extensive advice to job seekers:

- APR-JOB, 9 rue de Lens, 92000 Nanterre, Tel: 08 25802424, *www.apr-job.com*

- SYNTEC Conseil en Recrutement, with 140 agencies and a head office at 72 avenue de Victor Hugo, 75016 Paris, Tel: 01 40679593, *www.syntec-recrutement.org*.

Regional departments of labour, employment and vocational training [*Direction régionale du travail, de l'emploi et de la formation professionnelle (DRTEFP)*]

In 1995, departments of labour, employment and vocational training (DRTEFP) were set up in each Region, in part to decentralise the Ministry of Labour and in part to improve and enhance public access to vocational training. Each DRTEFP evolves strategies related to work, employment and vocational training and consequently liaises with the **Employment agency (ANPA)** and with the **Adult vocational and professional training and education association** (Chapter 13) to meet the needs of the public of the Region. Moreover, each DRTEFP includes administrative functions such as the **Labour inspectorate**. For further information, visit the Ministry of Labour website at *www.travail.gouv.fr*, click on "Services en régions" to bring up an interactive map of the Regions, then click on a Region to bring up a list of its DRTEFP as well as of the departmental offices and the regional labour inspectorate.

Seasonal workers [*Travailleurs saisonniers*]

Seasonal work, as in the agricultural or tourist sectors, is a form of temporary employment that occurs at the same time each year for a period of limited duration. Each year, French employers hire some 16,000 foreign seasonal workers, principally from Morocco, Poland and Tunisia. In general, the maximum length of stay is six of 12 consecutive months, but for agricultural jobs, the stay may be eight months. For the complete details of working and recruiting workers in French or in English, contact **ANAEM** (Chapter 1).

Setting up a business [*Monter une affaire*]

Setting up a business anywhere, even in your own country, entails risk and involves paperwork. The challenges multiply whenever you set up a business in a new country, including France, even though the seven procedures involved are fewer and take less time than in most European countries. Books larger than this one have been written on the topic, some regrettably outdated, as business practices, rules and regulations change with time.

Fortunately, the governmental Business start-up agency [*Agence pour la création d'entreprises (APCE)*] provides updated information and consultation on setting up a business, in four languages: French, English, German and Spanish; contact for further information: APCE, 14 rue Delambere, 75682 Paris Cedex 14, Tel: 01 42185858, *www.apce.com*, *info@apce.com*. There's an authoritative, first-hand reference in English covering all forms of incorporations, published under the aegis of the **Invest in France Agency**: *Setting up a Business in France* (London, the French Chamber of Commerce in Great Britain, 2004, 224 pages, softcover, A5 format, ISBN 0-9541776-6-5). The SCOP production cooperative association publishes a 16-page brochure (French only) that covers the equivalent details of setting up a cooperative venture, downloadable from the website at *www.scop.coop*. Moreover, **Starting a Business in France** (Chapter 47), published in July 2006, provides a comprehensive guide.

Sick leave [*Congé maladie*]

Absence from work due to illness results in suspension of the employment contract. Legally, the employer then need not pay wages, but the employee can claim social security daily allowances [*indemnités journalières*], usually against a sick note [*certificat médical*] provided by the doctor treating the illness. However, in most cases, the allowances are lower than the earnings lost while away from work, so collective agreements and contracts often may include provisions for compensation for loss of earnings caused by illness [*indemnité compensatrice de perte de salaire pour cause de maladie*]. Time away from work due to illness is not deducted from the **Holiday entitlement**.

Social security contributions [*Cotisations sociales*]

Employees contribute a certain percentage of their pay to the social security scheme. Social security contributions are deducted from an employee's pay [*cotisations salariales*] or are paid by the employer as part of the overall wage cost [*cotisations patronales*]. There are more than 20 categories of contributions, of which some are general and apply to all employees, and some are specific to business sector or company size. The six principal contributions paid by all employees are:

* *Contribution Social Généralisée (CSG)*, Supplementary social security contribution in aid of the underprivileged
* *Contribution pour le Remboursement de la Dette Social (CRDS)*, Levy introduced in 1996 to help pay off the deficit in the social security scheme
* *Assurance maladie*, Health insurance
* *Vieillesse plafonnée*, Old-age ceiling
* *Assurance chômage*, Unemployment insurance
* *Retraite complémentairee*, Retirement contribution.

The contribution rates, set 1 January each year, are available in French, English and other languages on the **CLEISS** (Chapter 22) website at *www.cleiss.fr*.

Strikes [*Grèves*]

Save for vital public sector employees, such as the police, employees have the right to strike. Though labour disputes and strikes sometimes are international news, they are no more common than in many other European countries. With the present average of 16 working days lost per year per 1000 employees*, France actually is median among European countries, as 13 are less strike prone and 13 – including the ostensibly more stable Scandinavian countries – are more strike prone. Strikes in France arguably attract attention because of the national penchant for airing grievances in public that started with the storming of the Bastille in 1789, a fete now commemorated in **Bastille Day** [Chapter 5) that marks the founding of the Republic.

* According to the most recent **Federation of European Employers** *table of strikes and lockouts*.

Student jobs [*Jobs étudiant*]

Most students have part-time or occasional jobs. French students may work freely, as do native students in any country, but foreign students who wish to work must be enrolled at an institution of higher education and be covered by the students' health insurance scheme [*régime étudiant de la sécurité sociale*]. Moreover, just as for work in general, students from EU/EEA countries need no special authorisation or permit, while students from other countries must have a **Temporary work permit** (Chapter 1).

Many students take a **McJob**. But there are many other options. The **Youth information centres** (Chapter 31) across the country are helpful in finding jobs and offer a comprehensive booklet with more than a thousand leads to jobs, *1000 pistes de jobs étudiants*, that also may be ordered online at *www.cidj.com*. The *Phosphore* youth magazine publishes a job-seekers guide, *Le Guide des Stages et Jobs*, that can be ordered online from its website at *www.phosphore.com*. **Égide** (Chapter 13) suggest six favourite student jobs:

- Babysitting [*garde d'enfants*]; most jobs are found by word-of-mouth, but there are agencies that act as intermediaries between parents and students.
- Language teaching [*cours de langue*] is a classic student job, particularly for native speakers of English, German and Spanish. Language teachers and their pupils usually contact each other via notices on school or local shop notice boards.
- Nude models [*modèles nus*], women or men, slim or portly, for *croquis* drawing classes at art schools. To find a modelling job, contact the art schools or look for advertisements in local newspapers.
- Delivering advertising material [*distributeur de prospectus*] door-to-door. Companies likely to hire students for such tasks can be found under *Distribution d'imprimés* in the Yellow pages.
- Beta testers for video games or other software packages [*Bêta-testeur de jeux vidéos ou de logiciels*]. Direct queries to software houses are the usual way to find testing jobs.

- Internet hot-line operators [*hot-liner*] to solve customer problems. Direct queries to Internet access providers, such as Orange, are the usual way to find operator jobs.

Temping agencies [*Agences d'intérim*]

Across the country, nearly 70 agencies and agency groups offer employment for and placement of temps [*Intérimaires*]; look for them under the *Agences intérim* in the **Yellow pages** (Chapter 31).

Some agencies are specialised, as in health services or high-tech, while many are organised in chains of agencies. The largest chain in France is Adecco France, part of the Swiss-based group that is the world leader in human resources, with 1383 offices in France and an average temps placement of 135,000 people a day in 40 job categories. For further information, contact the head office at 4 rue Louis Guérin, 69626 Villeurbanne Cedex, Tel: 04 72822828, *www.adecco.fr* with an online agency finder and forms for both people seeking work as temps and for companies wishing to employ temps. Adecco also funds the Adecco Foundation [*Fondation Adecco*], set up in 2002 under the aegis of **Fondation de France** (Chapter 33) to promote vocational and professional training in programmes for young people at the local level across the country.

Contractually, a temping agency is an employer that enters three-party **Employment contracts**, usually temporary contracts [*Contrats de travail temporaire*], with its clients and the temporary employees it places.

Tourism [*Tourisme*]

France is the world's leading holiday destination country, with more than 75 million visits a year, of which 80% are from other countries in Europe. Understandably, tourism is a major sector, involving some 180,000 businesses, directly employing more than 700,000 people and accounting for more than 6% of the Gross Domestic Product (GDP). Starting December 2005, the **National Institute of Statistics and Economic Studies** (Chapter 42) publishes *Le Tourisme en France*, a comprehensive annual reference book of statistics and overviews of various aspects of tourism in France and abroad.

Maison de la France (MDLF), the official tourism agency, promotes France as a holiday destination, both within the country and abroad. It has 33 offices in 28 countries as well as a head office in Paris, 20 avenue de l'Opéra, 75041 Paris Cedex 01, Tel: 01 42967000. Its tourism portal at *www.franceguide.com* links to 39 portals in almost as many languages and provides a broad range of information and online access to publications of interest to tourists.

Unemployment [*Chômage*]

The unemployment rate, as calculated by **EUROSTAT** (Chapter 42), now is 9.5%*, which means that nearly one person in ten in the workforce is unemployed. As elsewhere in Europe, the unemployment rate is high, principally because overall growth in the economy has been low, unemployment benefits are so generous that the unemployed often postpone seeking work, and because the **minimum wage** plus social security and other taxes results in a high direct cost of labour that discourages hiring people with few or no qualifications.

* February 2005 figure.

Unemployment benefit [*Allocation d'assurance chômage*]

A person may be unemployed due to involuntary loss of work or due to illness or disability. Consequently, unemployment benefits lie between the employment sector and the social security sector. The governmental agencies involved are organised accordingly. In the employment sector are:

- ANPE, the National Employment Agency [*Agence Nationale pour l'Emploi*]
- DGEFP, the General Delegation for Employment and Vocational Training [*Délégation à l'Emploi et à la Formation Professionnelle*]
- DDTEFP, the Departmental Agencies for Work, Employment and Vocational Training [*Directions Départementales du Travail, de l'Emploi et de la Formation Professionnelle*].

And in the social security sector are:

- CNAM, the National Health Insurance Fund [*Caisse Nationale d'Assurance Maladie*]
- CNAVTS, the National Retirement Insurance Fund for Salaried Workers [*Caisse Nationale d'Assurance Vieillesse des Travailleurs Salariés*]
- CAF, the Family Allowances Fund [*Caisse des Allocations Familiales*].

As illustrated in the diagram, the two sectors can be envisioned as overlapping in a region where unemployment benefits are paid. The principal organisations are:

- UNEDIC, the National organisation managing unemployment benefit schemes [*Union nationale pour l'emploi dans l'industrie et le commerce*]
- ASSEDIC, the Organisation managing unemployment insurance payments [*Association pour l'emploi dan l'industrie et le commerce*].

Simply put, UNEDIC administers all benefit schemes and coordinates the work of ASSEDIC, which has agencies across the country that work with employers, collect contributions, register and assist job seekers, and pay out unemployment benefits.

Employment   Social Security

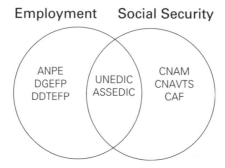

If you are an employed resident and lose your job you may qualify for unemployment benefit provided that you are under age 60, have worked at least three months within the last 12 and for two of the last three years, and are registered with the **National employment agency** (ANPE) as a job seeker. You then will be registered for unemployment benefits with the nearest ASSEDIC office, of which there are 30 across the country; in the Paris area, the four ASSEDIC offices are combined in a single organisation, GARP. Further details are on the ASSEDIC website at *www.assedic.fr*.

If you are a resident of and receiving unemployment benefits from another EEA country, upon moving to France, you may transfer the right to receive those payments via ASSEDIC. To do that, before you depart for France, you should fill out and submit a "Certificate concerning retention of the right to unemployment benefits" [*Attestation concernant le maintien du droit aux présentations de chômage*], EU form E303, to the employment or unemployment office in your home country. The form consists of six copies, the first of which, E303/0, is kept by the employment or unemployment office of your home country. You should take the other five copies with you and within seven days of arriving in France, submit them to a local ANPE office. Their purposes are:

- E303/1 reference copy kept by ANPE
- E303/2 returned to the issuing agency in your home country once payments begin
- E303/3 used if unemployment is due to health problems or disability
- E303/4 for accounting; sent to issuing agency when payments terminate
- E303/5 instructions to the unemployed person and overview of payments.

The various rules concerning unemployment benefit in France, including the amounts paid, are summarised in a comprehensive pamphlet entitled "Unemployment insurance: A scheme for social protection within the dynamics of employment" downloadable in French (no. DAJ 265), English (DAJ 266), German (DAJ 267) and Spanish (DAJ 268) from the ASSEDIC website at *www.assedic.fr*.

The employment and/or unemployment agencies of most EEA countries have compiled leaflets explaining the rules for transfer of social security and unemployment benefits between countries. In Britain, the two relevant leaflets are:

*   "Your Social Security Insurance Benefits (Pensions) and Healthcare in the EU", no. SA29
*   "Unemployment Benefit in the EU", no. UBL22.

Both forms are available from:

Department for Work and Pensions
Pensions & Overseas Benefits Directorate
Tyneview Park, Whitley Road
Newcastle Upon Tyne
NE98 1BA
UK

Website: *www.dwp.gov.uk*.

Unions [*Syndicats*]

Together, the many unions count some six million members, or 31% of the workforce, about the same percentage as in Canada (30%) or the UK (29%)*. Most unions are associated with one of six confederations of unions:

*   General Confederation of Labour [*Confédération générale du travail (CGT)*], founded in 1895, is the oldest confederation. In the 1920s, it linked with the Communist Party, which led in 1948 to a split, with discontented members forming *Force ouvière*. In the mid 1990s, CGT severed its link with the Party and in 1999 joined the European Trade Union Confederation. CGT publishes a labour weekly, *La Nouvelle vie ouvrière* ("The Working Life News") as well as other periodicals and books in its *VO Editions* ("Working Life Publications") series, *www.librairie-nvo.com*. Head office: 263 rue de Paris, 93516 Montreuil, Tel: 01 48188000, *www.cgt.fr*.

*   The General Confederation of Labour – Workers' Force [*Confédération Générale du Travail – Force Ouvière (CGT-FO)*] was founded in 1948 by former CGT members. Head office: 114 avenue du Maine, 75680 Paris Cedex 14, Tel: 01 40528200, *www.force-ouvriere.fr*.

*   French Confederation of Christian Workers [*Confédération française des travailleurs chrétiens (CFTC)*] was founded in 1919. In 1964, it split, with the majority of members founding CFDT, a secular confederation. Head office: 13 rue des Ecluses-St-Martin, 75010 Paris, Tel: 01 44524900, *www.cftc.fr*.

*   French Democratic Confederation of Labour [*Confédération Française Démocratique du Travail (CFDT)*] was founded in 1964 as a secular split-off from the CFTC. Head office: 78 rue de Crimée, 75109 Paris, Tel: 01 42038900, *www.cfdt.fr*.

- French Confederation of Management – General Confederation of Executives [*Confédération française de l'encadrement – Confédération générale des cadres (CFE-CGC)*] was amalgamated in 1945 from former unions of engineers. Head office: 59/63 rue du Rocher, 75008 Paris, Tel: 01 55301212, *www.cfecgc.org*.
- Solidarity Union Democratic [*Solidaires unitaires démocratiques (SUD)*], also known as the Group of 10, or G10, was formed on 10 December 1981 by unions holding progressive views. Head office: 93 bis rue de Montreuil, 75001 Paris, Tel: 01 58393020, *www.xolidaires.org*.

*International Labour Organisation statistics

Upper level management [*Cadres de haut niveau*]

Multinational and foreign companies often assign upper level executives to their facilities in France. Accordingly, in 2004 the administrative formalities involved in bringing executives and their families into the country were eased, and special tax and social provisions were implemented. The new rules distinguish between two categories of assignments to France:

- Secondment [*Détachement*] is a temporary assignment typically of no more than 18 months, usually for a specific task, such as a technical project or financial control. Seconded staff members remain the employees of the company abroad and are not subject to French labour law, though they are subject to rules on working hours and minimum wage.
- Transfer [*Introduction*] entails long-term assignment. Transferred staff members become contractual employees of the facility in France and are subject to French labour law. A transferred staff member may maintain legal links to the company abroad to ease return once the assignment in France terminates.

For complete information, in French or in English, contact **ANAEM** (Chapter 1) and request circulars numbered 143 of 26 March 2004, 212 of 7 May 2004 and 2000/14 of 7 July 2004.

Women in the workplace [*Femmes au travail*]

Women have always worked in France. A century ago, women made up more than a third of the workforce and more than half of all women of working age had jobs outside the home. The overall employment of women dropped from 1920 to 1945, but then soared from the 1960s on. Lifestyle changes triggered the upswing. Before then, women who worked either were childless or were mothers who returned to work after their children were grown. That situation had long been substantiated by the Civil Code, under which a husband ruled the household, and his wife could not work without his consent. But in 1965, the law changed to make women full legal persons on a par with men. The effects were immediate: from 1968 to 1975, three in four new workers were women.

Today, women combine careers with having children. In the 25 to 49 prime working age group, eight women in ten work. Overall, women make up more than 45% of the workforce and 80% of the part-time sector. The high proportion of women in the part-time workforce underscores a higher rate of employment in the less skilled trades. Nonetheless, women have become more upwardly mobile than men. More women than men born after 1950 attain the baccalaureate level of schooling, and as many women as men born after 1970 attain the master's degree level of higher education. Today more than half of all students pursuing higher-level education are women, and across the workforce, women tend to have higher levels of education than men.

Nonetheless, inequalities persist, as they do in most countries. Women are more likely to be unemployed than men and more likely to work below their education level at unskilled trades. In numbers, women are less likely to be promoted than men and at all levels are paid less than men.

Legal steps have been taken to correct the imbalance, most notably the "Roudy Act", no. 83-635 of 13 July 1983, *Loi portent modification du code du travail et du code pénal en ce qui concerne l'égalité professionnelle entre les femmes et les hommes* ("Law modifying the labour code and the penal code regarding professional equality of women and men") and the "parity law", Act no. 2000-493 of 6 June 2000, *Loi tendant à favoriser l'égal accès des femmes et des hommes aux mandates électoraux et fonctions électives*, stipulating that there must be equal numbers of men and women on party candidate lists in municipal and various other elections.

These laws reflect a society in change. Although only one Member of Parliament in eight is a woman, there have been remarkable firsts. In 1979, the year that Margaret Thatcher became the first woman Prime Minister of the UK, Simone Weil became the first woman President of the European Parliament, and in 1991, Edith Cresson became the first woman Prime Minister. And according to a survey conducted in February 2005, 85% of all women and men are ready to elect a woman as President of the Republic. Today, in the private sector, two of the country's leading executives are women: Anne Lauvergeon, CEO of Areva, the energy giant, and Laurence Parisot, the head of MEDF, the **Employer organisation**.

Workers with temporary work permits
[*Travailleurs au titre de l'autorisation provisoire de travail*]

A foreigner holding a **Temporary work permit** (Chapter 1) may work in the country for up to one year at a job of limited duration, such as in entertainment, research, training and temporary staff of the subsidiary of a foreign company. For complete details in French or in English, contact **ANAEM** (Chapter 1).

Working day [*Jour ouvrable*]

As elsewhere, the working day varies, though the French tradition of closing down at midday persists. The working day is generally taken to be the same as the relevant business day, though in administration a distinction is made between days on which work can be done [*jours ouvrables*], as opposed to public holidays [*jours fériés*], and days on which work is performed or business is conducted [*jour ouvré*]. Whenever stated, the specification of opening days and hours, *jours et heures d'ouverture*, is more precise.

Working hours [*Heures de travail*]

The government has long been the guardian of working hours. In 1841, the number of hours that children could work per week was limited. At the time, other countries also had limits set by the State, but in France, legislators of all political persuasions continued to limit working hours. In 1919 the working day was limited to eight hours; in 1936 the working week was limited to 40 hours and then reduced to 39 hours in 1982. In 1998 and 2000, two new laws, called the "Aubry Acts" after Martine Aubry, the Minister of Employment and Solidarity at the time, further reduced the working week to 35 hours, principally to increase employment. The reduction went into effect in stages, and from 1 January 2002, the 35 hour week is mandatory for all employers.

The 35 hours week, or 1600 hours a year for employees whose salaries are fixed to an annual figure, is not an absolute ceiling on working. Companies are free to pay overtime, from the 36th hour per week or from 1601 hours per year. Consequently, time put in at work averages more than 38 hours. Moreover, some employees, as well as their employers, opt for complying with the limit of 35 hours a week, yet have workdays of eight or more hours. The disparity is accommodated in a system known as *Réduction du Temps de Travail (RTT)*, in which the employee takes time off for accumulated extra hours. As the employee recuperates a loss of legal free hours, RTT is sometimes called *Récupération de Temps Travaillé*.

At the outset, the reduction of the working week with no corresponding cut in wages was expected to meet with widespread approval among employees. Though most employees appreciate the change, many have difficulty coping with it. In many cases, workers must do in 35 hours what they previously did in 39, and in an effort to comply with the law yet get work done, many employers shift working hours about, which results in irregular hours for their employees. These drawbacks, along with the increase in employment being less than anticipated and the complications of accommodating to changes in social security contributions greater than feared, have made the 35 hour week a subject of continued debate. Reports and books have been written on it, and the **Employment Research Centre** has studied it extensively. One of the best overviews in English is a monograph published by the Centre, *Working Time Policy in France* by Pierre Boisard, Publication No. 34, October 2004, ISBN 2-11-094585-0.

Works council [*Comité d'entreprise*]

All companies with 50 or more employees are required to have a works council [*comité d'entreprise (CE)*] made up of representatives of labour and management who are elected for two years. The size of a CE depends on the number of employees, from three representatives for 50 to 74 employees up to 15 representatives for 10,000 employees. Aside from dealing with issues of concern to labour and management, the typical CE also arranges social activities, discounts on merchandise, holiday travel and other employee benefits. The CEs have amalgamated into common-interest networks, such as comitedentreprise.com with a comprehensive website of the same name, *www.comitedentreprise.com*.

4
Cars, roads and traffic

Car ownership in France ranks high, 12th in the world, ahead of the USA (14th) and the UK (24th). Yet its roads are less crowded than those of 35 other countries, principally because it has Europe's longest and the world's seventh longest road network, including nearly 10,000 kilometres of major highways and motorways*. Moreover, driving is increasingly safe: the accident rate is less than average for the EU countries and is falling fast, in part because of widespread concern, from the office of the President down.

Many aspects of modern motoring have French roots, not least driving on the right side of the road. The Romans and other peoples of centuries past rode or drove carriages on the left, evidently to leave the right arm free for defence. However, in the late 18th century, French farmers began hauling produce in large wagons drawn by teams of horses in pairs. The team was managed not by a coachman on the wagon, but by a postillion** mounted on the left horse of the rearmost pair. The postillions preferred to pass left-to-left, so they drove their wagons on the right, which was the side of the road traditionally used by the peasantry, as the nobility adhered to the left, in the Roman tradition. After the Revolution, keep right became the custom that was first made law in 1794 in Paris. Napoleon's conquests spread the keep-right rule to Belgium, Germany, Luxembourg, the Netherlands, Poland and Russia as well as parts of Italy and Spain. The countries that Napoleon did not conquer – the Austro-Hungarian Empire, Great Britain and Portugal – kept to the left. The division of left driving and right driving countries remained until the early 1920s. Thereafter, left-hand driving countries on the Continent changed to right-hand driving, one by one, the last being Sweden, in 1967. Today, 163 of the 221 countries and territories of the world drive on the right, while 58, most prominently Great Britain and its former colonies, drive on the left. That said, the norm for on-the-right did not affect French railways, as trains run on the left.

The French influence in automotive technologies is long standing. In 1884, Edouard Delmare-Debouteville (1856-1901) patented the world's first car. In 1898, car manufacturing pioneer Albert de Dion (1856-1946) founded the world's first automobile show. In 1909, the World Road Association was founded in Paris. In 1934, gear-maker André Citroën brought out the first mass-produced, front-wheel drive car. Motor racing originated in France, and Formula 1 still has its headquarters in Paris. These technical breakthroughs rested on a solid foundation in science, starting with the theories of Sadi Carnot (1796-1832) that enabled development of the internal combustion engine.

Today, the French automobile industry is gigantic, making one in ten of the nearly 60 million motor vehicles sold worldwide each year. French intelligent motorway technologies are being adopted elsewhere, and the Paris Motor Show is the largest and most famed of its kind. Even away from the automotive sector there's a reminder of it: the Michelin Guide, considered an authority on cuisine, is published by a tyre-maker.

* Comparative rankings from The Economist Pocket World in Figures, 2006 edition.

** *Postillion* is a loanword from French, first used in English in 1616 and, according to Frédéric Godefroy's *Dictionnaire de l'ancienne langue française* (1902) first used in print in France in 1538.

Automatic traffic control [*Contrôle automatique*]

There are more than a thousand automatic traffic control zones, principally implemented with radar speed cameras along highways and motorways, 70% fixed and the remainder mobile units. Each zone is signed, and the locations of the zones is made public in an interactive map on the Road safety agency website at *www.securiteroutiere.gouv.fr/data/radars/index.html*. For further details, see the *Le control automatisé* brochure, available in print at road safety training centres and police stations and online on the **Road safety agency** website.

Automobile associations [*Clubs automobile*]

In 1895, the world's first automobile association, *Automobile Club de France*, was founded in Paris. Through the years, it has grown to be a panoply organisation with a central administration and nine regional groups of automobile clubs in all *Départements* across the country: Fédération Française des Automobile-Clubs et des Usagers de la Route, 76 avenue Marceau, 75008 Paris, Tel: 01 56892070, *www.automobileclub.org.*, with an interactive map for locating local clubs and organisations.

The *Fédération Internationale de l'Automobile (FIA)*, most widely known as the governing body for Formula One and other major automobile racing events, was founded in 1904 in Paris and now has 207 national member organisations in 122 countries. Head office: 8 Place de la Concorde, 75008 Paris, Tel. 01 43124455, *www.fia.com*.

The *Automobile Club de l'Ouest* is now most known as the organiser of the annual le Mans 24-hour race, but also lobbies on automobile and road matters, driver education and the like. Head office: 72019 Le Mans Cedex 2, Tel: 02 43402424, *www.lemans.org*.

The International Touring Alliance [*Alliance Internationale de Tourisme (AIT)*] is a worldwide organisation of touring clubs and automobile associations. Though it does not deal directly with the public, it supports reciprocal agreements between clubs and associations in its 102 member countries, which, in turn, benefit members travelling abroad. For complete information on the AIT, contact the head office: Chemin de Blandonnet 2, PO Box 111, 1215 Geneva 15, Switzerland, Tel: +41 225444500, *www.aitgva.ch*, *ait@aitfia.ch*. The AIT affiliate in France is *Union des groupes du touring club de France (UGTCF)*, 9 Port Des Champs-Elysées, 75008 Paris, Tel: 01 42659070.

Automotive trade [*Distribution automobile*]

The independent automotive aftermarket comprises all aspects of the automotive sector not associated with new car sales and service. It includes businesses dealing in parts, accessories, supplies and repairs as well as affiliated activities such as technical training. Accordingly, it is large, with a total annual turnover approaching five billion Euros a year. The panoply trade association, the Automotive Distribution Federation [*Fédération des syndicats de la distribution automobile (FEDA)*] is correspondingly extensive, with activities across the country, interaction with private organisations and public agencies and liaison with organisations in other countries. It probably is the best single starting point for statistics and other information on the automotive sector. Head office: 10 rue Pergolese, 75016 Paris, Tel: 01 45003971, *www.feda.fr*, *infos@feda.fr*.

Biofuels [*Pétrole vert*]

Biofuels that burn more cleanly than pure petroleum products have long been produced and promoted; as early as the mid 1980s, biofuels were encouraged by granting tax breaks to their producers. The two principal ingredients of biofuels are:

- ethanol, both in its pure form and in Ethyl Tertiary Butyl Ether (ETBE), an oxygenated fuel blended with gasoline. In Europe, France is the third largest producer of both ethanol and ETBE.

- vegetable oil methyl esters (VOME) [*esters méthyliques d'huile végétale (EMVH)*], mixed in diesel fuels. Germany is the world's largest producer, but France is second, with more than a fifth of world production.

For complete information on biofuels, in French and in English, contact the **French Petroleum Institute** (Chapter 7).

Car accident reporting
[*Constat à l'amiable d'accident automobile*]

If you are involved in a car accident in which people are injured, you should immediately call the Police national number 12 or the police emergency number 17 and, if necessary, the ambulance number 15 or fire number 18. If nobody is injured and you only collided with another car, you and the driver of the other car should file reports to your insurance companies if the damage is sufficient for an insurance claim. All **Car insurance** companies support telephone and online reporting of accidents. For accuracy of reporting, it's best to fill in an Accident Statement form at the site of the accident, using the English or French [*Constat à l'amiable d'accident automobile*] version of the international form compiled by the European Federation of National Insurance Association (CEA), available from your insurance company or **Automobile association**. The form is A4 size and folds conveniently to A5 to tuck in with your registration documents, so you'll always have one on hand. The Automobile Club's legal service [*guide juridique*] has an online guide to the form with brief instructions on how to fill it in properly, *www.automobileclub. org/site/juridique/assurance_accident/index_constat_amiable.php*.

Car import [*Importation des véhicules*]

Car import is an effort, no matter how and where the car is sold. In buying a new car made in another country and taking delivery of it with number plates attached, you are at the end of a scenario of car import in which others took care of the financial, technical and administrative details. The car importer, often a subsidiary of the automaker, took care of customs formalities, paid duties and VAT, and arranged for type approval that certifies compliance with safety standards. The dealer who sold you the car took care of registration formalities. The people who performed these tasks were familiar with the procedures and handled them easily. As in most endeavours, car import is simple and straightforward, provided you are practised at it.

But for most people, that is hardly the case: car import is a one-off, do-it-yourself (DIY) effort. You are bound to err, so you may have to repeat some tasks. That said, the following is a DIY guide to car import, which, like all DIY guides, doesn't explain everything and probably can be misread.

Just as in the scenario for an imported new car delivered with number plates affixed, there are three principal steps: financial, technical and administrative. Financial outlays are involved throughout, the most decisive upfront, at customs. So your first step is to go to the nearest customs centre [*Centre des impôts* or *Hôtel des impôts*], listed in the Yellow pages under *Administrations de l'économie et des finances*. At the customs centre you will need four documents:

- personal identification, such as your passport or *carte de séjour*
- proof of residence, such as a recent utility bill

- your car's registration documents
- a copy of the bill of sale for the car, with specification of VAT paid if the car was bought new.

If the car is being imported from an EU/EEA country, there is no import duty and no VAT to be paid, and the customs centre will issue a certificate of fiscal conformity [*certificat de régularité fiscale*]. If the car is being imported from a country outside the EU/EEA, duty and VAT, together usually about 30% of the car's assessed value upon import, will be charged. Once payment has been made, the customs centre will issue a customs clearance certificate [*certificat de dédouanement*] no. 846A.

Your next step initiates the administrative procedure and attends to the technical details. Two agencies are involved:

- the **Prefecture** (Chapter 21) for the administrative details
- the *Directions Régionales de l'Industrie, de la Recherche et de l'Environnement (DRIRE)*, for the technical details. Locate the nearest DRIRE facility in the Yellow pages or by using the interactive map on the website at *www.drire.gouv.fr*.

In addition to the certificate issued by the customs centre and the four documents listed above, you may need:

- the type approval certificate [*attestation de conformité*] for the make and model of car that ensures its compliance with safety regulations. Type approval requirements have been harmonised across the EU/EEA for passenger cars, but national differences remain. For makes and models of cars that are or recently have been sold in France, the certificate may not be required. But it's best to have one should it be needed. As a rule, type approval certificates are kept on file in the head offices of automakers or their principal distributors in most countries.

You will need to fill in two forms:

- the application form for a registration document [*Demande de certificat d'immatriculation d'un véhicule*] Cerfa no. 10672, available at the Prefecture or downloadable from government's public service website at *www2. equipement.gouv.fr/formulaires/formdomaines.htm*, click on the *Cartes grises et immatriculation* link under the *Sécurité Routière* heading. Deliver the filled-in form at the *Préfecture* to initiate the file on your registration. Some minor fees are involved.
- the application for certification of specifications [*Demande d'identification*], with explanatory texts in French and in English, available from a DRIRE facility or downloadable from *www.drire.gouv.fr*, click on *Missions*, then on *Véhicules*, then on *La réception des véhicules routiers*, then in the *Véhicules importés* scroll list on *Voiture importée*, then on the *dossier de demande d'identification* link, and, finally, on the *imprimé de demande d'attestation d'identification* link to print out the form. Fill in the form and take with the car to a DRIRE facility, where an inspector will verify it against the car, and against a minor fee, issue

62

an approval. If the car is more than four years old, DRIRE will require that it be submitted to **Periodic vehicle inspection** before it is approved.

Procedures vary slightly across the country, so it's best to inquire at the *Préfectures* as to whether you should go to DRIRE first.

Finally, with your registration file initiated and the DRIRE approval in hand, return to the *Préfecture* to complete registration. You then will be given your *Carte grise* and can have **Number plates** made.

Car insurance [*Assurance automobile*]

As elsewhere in Europe, car insurance is of two types, mandatory and optional:

• Mandatory liability insurance covers third parties, that is, persons other than the insured and the insurer. It is the minimum insurance required by law for valid car registration and is certified by a sticker affixed to the windscreen. It also is the minimum insurance required by the **Green card systems** across Europe.

Insurance sticker.

Driving without liability insurance is an offence subject to a fine of €3500 and suspension of driving licence for three years (according to 2005 edition of *Welcome on France's Roads* published by the **Road safety agency**).

• Optional insurance covering supplementary risks, including comprehensive damage to own vehicle however caused [*dommages tous accidents*], collision damage to own vehicle [*dommages collision*], theft and fire [*vol et incendie*], glass breakage [*bris de glaces*], common accessories [*options les plus courantes*], subsidiary damage to accessories [*attachées obligatoirement*], natural disasters [*catastrophes naturelles*], infrastructure failures [*catastrophes technologiques*], storms [*tempête*] and violence or terrorism [*attentats et actes de terrorisme*].

Likewise, as elsewhere in Europe, car insurance premiums [*tarifications*] depend on the car and on its driver:

• Car [*véhicule*]: size and power, price category and age.

• Drivers [*conducteurs*]: age and how long licensed [*âge du conducteur et ancienneté du permis*], occasional drivers [*conduite occasionnelle*], sole driver [*conduite exclusive*], past driving record [*le "passé" du conducteur*], learner drivers [*les antécédents*], preferential rates [*tarifs préférentiels*], business use [*usage de la voiture*], kilometres driven a year [*assurance au kilometre*] and place usually garaged [*lieu de garage habituel*].

Moreover, premiums vary according to the insurance claims made or likely to be made: there is reward of a discount [*bonus*] for no-claims driving and a surcharge [*malus*] for unsafe driving:

- *Bonus*: after a no-claim year, the premium goes down by 5% to 95% of the preceding year, with a minimum of 50% of the basic rate, or 50% bonus.

- *Malus*: after a year with one or more claims, the premium goes up by 25% to 125% of the preceding year, with a maximum of 3.5 times the basic premium. If you have had a 50% bonus for three or more years, there is no surcharge following one claim in a year.

In 2004, the European Commission took the view that the *Bonus-malus* systems of France and Luxembourg violated the freedom of setting premiums according to the motor insurance Directive of 1992 and consequently brought infringement proceedings against the two countries before the Court of Justice of the European Communities. On 7 September 2004, the Court found that the *Bonus-malus* systems were not unlawful and consequently refuted the Commission's argument (Cases C-346/02 and C-347/02).

Car insurance is specialised and ever changing. So for comprehensive, up-to-date information, contact the French Federation of Insurance Companies [*Fédération Française des Sociétés d'Assurances*], 26 bd Haussmann, 75311 Paris Cedex 09, Tel: 01 42479000, *www.ffsa.fr*, with downloadable PDF brochures providing complete information on the matters summarised above.

Car parts and accessories [*Accessoires et pièces détachées*]

Across the country, there are more than 1500 car parts shops as well as more than 800 specialist workshops, such as motor rebuilders, that offer parts. Moreover, most hypermarkets and many supermarkets sell car accessories, and car repair workshops sell parts and accessories, as do new car dealers for their marques. In the Yellow pages, look for the car parts shops listed under *Automobiles, pièces de rechange et accessoires* and for the other outlets in their categories. There are several chains of car parts shops; the two largest are *France Auto Pièces (FAP)* and *France Pièces Automobiles (FPA)*.

Car rental [*Location de voitures*]

As in other countries, cars may be rented from agencies at airports, railway stations and other locations in cities and towns. All the major international car rental firms have agencies, and Europcar is the leader, as it is across Europe. In the market of some six million rentals a year, two French rental companies, both with franchised agencies, are highly competitive:

- ADA car rentals, now fourth largest in the country with more than 480 agencies, Tel: 0825169169, *www.ada.fr*.

- UCAR utility vehicle rentals, with 250 agencies, Tel: 0892881010, *www.ucar.fr*.

As elsewhere, rental prices vary by size and type of vehicle, company, season, duration of rental and location. The legal minimum age for rental is 18, but many companies require a minimum age of 21 or 23, and a renter must have a driving licence valid in the EU/EEA and have held it for at least one year. Otherwise, car rental particulars are like those elsewhere in Europe; for further information, contact any car rental company or visit its website and read the *conditions de vente* or *conditions générales de location*.

Car repair [*Réparation automobile*]

Hardly a village or town is without one or more car repair workshops; according to *Union Nationale des Indépendants de la Rechange et de la Réparation Automobile (UNIRRA)*, there are some 45,000 in the country. Many workshops also sell parts, accessories and tyres, and there are specialist shops for painting [*peinture*] and body work [*carrosserie*]. As elsewhere, chains of rapid repair and parts centres, often located near hypermarket malls, are expanding rapidly. The two largest are Norauto with 350 centres and a head office at Rue du Fort, BP 25, 59812 Lesquin Cedex, Tel: 03 20607474, *www.norauto.fr* and FeuVert with more than 300 centres and a customer service centre at 5 route du Paisy, BP 19, 69571 Dardilly, *www.feuvert.fr*. In the Yellow pages, the car repair workshops are listed under *garages d'automobiles, réparation*, and the rapid repair centres under *centres autos, entretien rapide*.

Cars, new [*Véhicules neufs*]

New cars are sold by dealers listed under *Agents, concessionnaires et distributeurs automobiles* in the Yellow pages. Almost all makes of cars and light utility vehicles made round the world are on the market. Makes not regularly marketed are imported by specialist dealers, listed under *Automobiles, construction, importation*. A new car dealer will take care of registration formalities and deliver a car with its **Registration documents**.

Copious information on new cars is available in French and foreign magazines, not least in connection with the **Paris Motor Show** (Chapter 32). The three French automakers have extensive websites in several languages, Citroën at *www.citroen.com*, Peugeot at *www.peugeot.com* and Renault at *www.renault.com*.

Cars, used [*Voitures d'occasion*]

Used cars are sold both by car dealers and by private persons. Car dealers, listed in the Yellow pages include new car dealers, listed under *Agents, concessionnaires et distributeurs d'automobiles* and used car dealers, listed under *Automobiles d'occasion*. There are numerous vehicle auctions; arguably the largest is part of the

Anaf group that also includes assessing and art auctions: *Anaf Auto Auction*, 6 rue Pierre et Marie Curie, 69802 St-Priest Cedex, Tel: 04 72791919, *www.anaf.com*. There are magazines and websites dedicated to used vehicle advertising; the largest is *Auto-Occasion*, with a large, A3 format monthly magazine sold by newsagents and by subscription and a more frequently updated website, head office at 1 Bd de l'Oise, 95030 Cergy Pontoise Cedex, Tel: 01 34223000, *www.auto-occasion.fr*, *annonces@auto-occasion.fr*.

Most car dealers will take care of registration formalities and deliver a car with its **Registration documents**. If you buy a used car on the private market, you may register it yourself at the nearest **Prefecture** (Chapter 21). Several documents, principally the *Certificat de cession d'un véhicule* ("Transfer of vehicle ownership form"), are involved. As this book goes to press, the procedures are changing. So for the latest instructions on re-registration, visit the *Automobile Club* website at *www.automobileclub.org* and navigate to *Acheter une voiture d'occasion*. In all cases, it's best to have an independent assessment of a car before you buy. The *Automobile Club* website has an online calculator, *Cote de vente*, for the maximum market price based on make, model, year and kilometres driven. A more comprehensive service is available online from *Autocote*, *www.autocote.com*.

Categories of vehicles [*Catégories de véhicules*]

In France, as across the EEA, a **Driving licence** is valid for specific categories of vehicles, as defined in Directive 91/439/EEC, updated last in 2000. There are five principal categories:

Specification of vehicle category, as in an EU-standard driving licence.

A Motorcycles with or without a sidecar.

B Vehicles other than those of category A, with a maximum weight of 3500 kg. Most private cars are in this category.

C Vehicles used principally for transport of goods and weighing 3500–7500 kg. Many sport utility vehicles (SUVs) and all-terrain vehicles are in this category.

D Buses and similar vehicles for carrying more than eight people.

E Combinations of vehicles, such as articulated lorries and cars towing trailers.

Within each category, there are sub-categories, for instance, A1 is a light motorcycle with a motor of less than 125 cubic centimetres and a power of less than 11 kW, and B1 is a motor-powered tricycle or quadricycle.

Diesel engines [*Motorisations diesel*]

More than half of all registered motor vehicles and 70% of new cars have diesel motors. That proportion, the highest in Europe, is due to lower cost and increasingly better technology.

Though a new diesel car usually costs more than a petrol model of the same specifications, diesel (usually called *gazole*) is cheaper at the pump, and per kilometre, a car consumes about 20% less diesel than petrol. Moreover, with proper care, a diesel motor may last half as long again as a petrol motor. The life-cycle economy of keeping a car favours diesel.

The diesel motor was invented in Germany, and Mercedes was the first automaker to produce diesel cars. But French engineers early contributed to diesel car development, starting in 1921, when a diesel-powered prototype of the Peugeot 156 car averaged 48 km/h in the Paris-Bordeaux rally. In 1936, both Peugeot and Citroën built diesel-powered taxis and commercial vehicles, and by 1959 Peugeot rivalled Mercedes in producing diesel passenger cars. More recently, in 1998 PSA Peugeot-Citroën developed the high-pressure, direct injection (HDi) technology that reduced motor noise and cut particulate emission by 60%, and in 2000 combined HDi with a particulate filter – *Filtre à particules (FAP)* – that traps particles for burning in the motor. Today, more than half a million Peugeot-Citroën vehicles are fitted with HDi-FAP motors, and automakers in other countries have licensed the technology. In France, "HDi FAP" has become so much a part of the vocabulary of cars that an advertisement for a new car with a 110 horsepower motor might mention that alone – such as "HDi FAP 110" – without a word that it's diesel-powered.

Drink driving [*Conduite en état d'ivresse*]

As across Europe, drink driving is a leading cause of accidents in which people are injured or killed. The risks are well known: a blood alcohol level (AL) of 0.5 mg/ml doubles the risk of causing an accident, an AL of 0.8 mg/ml multiplies the risk by 10, and an AL of 2.0 mg/ml multiplies the risk by 80. Moreover, the risks are even greater whenever a driver has consumed both alcohol and narcotics. Consequently, police and gendarmes may perform roadside breathalyser tests, either at random [*contrôles intempestifs*] or at the scene of an accident and may arrange drug tests if need be.

All drink driving offences result in an endorsement of 6 points on a licence and penalties that vary from a fine of € 135 and suspension of licence for three years for driving with an AL of 0.5 mg/ml to 0.8 mg/ml up to a fine of € 75,000, suspension of licence for ten years, impounding of the vehicle and a prison sentence of five years for drink driving resulting in disabling injury or death. For the graduated penalties and the equivalents between blood alcohol levels and breathalyser levels, see the *L'alcool et La Conduite* brochure published by the **Road safety agency**.

Driving licences [*Permis de conduire*]

The requirements for and issuing of driving licences comply with EU directives. The first step for any licence is to go through training and successfully pass a test for a road safety certificate [*brevet de sécurité routière – BSR*]. There are two schemes of training for the BSR test:

- in schools, there are classes for *attestation scolaires de sécurité routière (ASSR)* in two levels. The fist level [*1er niveau*] usually is given in the fifth year of school and is required for being allowed to ride a moped [*cyclomoteur*] at age 14. The second level (*2^d niveau*) usually is given in the third year of secondary school and is required for all licences for driving cars and other motor vehicles. Pupils outside the national school system or coming in from abroad may take the ASSR classes at the National centre for distance learning (CNED). For further details, see the *L'attestation Scolaire De Sécurité Routière* brochure published by the **Road safety agency**.

- for people who have not attended public schools, such as those schooled in other countries, the **Adult education centres (GRETA)** (Chapter 13) offer the *attestation de sécurité routière (ASR)*, which is equivalent to ASSR but takes place outside the school system. For further details, see *L'attestation De Sécurité Routière* brochure published by the **Road safety agency**.

At age 16, a young person holding a BSR may begin as a learner driver in a scheme called *L'apprentissage anticipé de la conduite (AAC)*. The first step is to register with the *Service des permis de conduire* at the nearest **Préfecture** (Chapter 21), have permission for AAC from the car's insurer and enrol in a driving school [*école de conduite*] that offers AAC. Then, the learner driver may drive in a car fitted with two inside rear-view mirrors, accompanied by a qualified driver who is at least 28 years old and has held a licence for at least three years with no point endorsements and is named in the AAC agreement with the driving school. A learner driver may not exceed 100 km/h on a motorway, and an accompanied driver vignette [*Conduite accompagnée*] must be affixed on the boot or rear door of the car. After driving 3000 km, the learner may take the final practical training at the driving school in preparation for the theoretical and practical tests for a licence given at the Préfecture. For further details, see the *La conduite accompagnée* brochure published by the **Road safety agency**.

The AAC vignette, 15 cm diameter, black on white.

Upon passing the driving licence test, the new driver is issued a provisional licence [*permis probatoire*] that has a maximum of six penalty points, compared to 12 for the regular licence. A car driven by a provisional licensee must have a red letter A vignette affixed on the boot, rear door or rear window. For further details, see the *Le permis probatoire* brochure published by the **Road safety agency**.

The provisional driver vignette, 15 cm diameter, red on white.

After driving 3000 km or more over three years, or two years if AAC training was successfully completed, a driver wither fewer than six penalty points is eligible for a regular licence. The present licence is the paper version first issued 1 March 1999, black printing on pink background, 10.6 × 22.2 cm, folded twice to 7.4 × 10.6 cm. As this book goes to press, details have yet to be released on a new, more secure, plastic, credit-card size licence scheduled for introduction in 2007. For further information on the regular licence, see *Le permis conduire* brochure published by the **Road safety agency**.

Each year, about 700,000 people come of age and are eligible to go through proper training and take the driving licence test. However, some cannot afford the expense of training, and some choose to drive unlicensed, which is a threat to safety on the roads. Consequently, starting in July 2005, 16 to 25 year-olds are eligible for interest-free loans to support training for the driving licence. After a licence has been granted, a loan is repaid at a rate of one Euro per day, so the scheme is called *Permis 1€ par jour*. For further details, see the *N'Attendez plus pour apprendre* ("Don't wait to learn") brochure published by the **Road safety agency.**

Driving schools [*Auto-écoles*]

Coordination with or training in a driving school are required for all classes of **Driving licences**, not least because the schools are approved and kept up-to-date on the latest rules and regulations. Moreover, driving school cars are fitted with dual controls, have four doors and an *Auto École* sign on the roof, as required for professional training as well as for taking the driving licence examination.

According to the **National Association for Training in the Automotive Sector** (Chapter 13), there are more than 10,500 driving schools in the country, increasingly organised in chains of two types:

* alliances of independents; the largest is the *auto-école organisation* with nearly 5000 members that can be located using the interactive map on its website at *www.auto-ecole.org*.

- franchises with agencies operating under the same name; the largest is *l'École de Conduite Française (ECF)*, with 1180 driving school agencies and 17 professional training institutes [*Instituts de Formation Professionnelle (IFP*] that can be located using the interactive fields on its website at *www.ecf.asso.fr*.

You also can find a driving school in the Yellow pages, as on the *Pages jaunes* website, *www.pagesjaunes.fr*, by keying *Auto-écoles* (but not its synonym, *Écoles de conduite*) into the *Activité* searchword field. Most driving schools offer a variety of courses tailored to the requirements of the various driving licences, and some offer instruction in other languages for people who do not speak French well.

Driving with an EU/EEA licence [*Conduire en France avec un permis d'un Etat de l'Union européenne*]

A valid driving licence issued by an EU or EEA country is equally valid for driving in France. If you reside in the country, you may, but are not required to, exchange your licence for a French driving licence. However, if you commit a traffic offence, you must exchange your driving licence, so points may be endorsed to it.

The exchange procedure is straightforward. First, fill in the driving licence application form [*Demande de délivrance de permis de conduire*], Cerfa no. 11247*02, obtainable from the *Service des permis de conduire* at the **Prefecture** (Chapter 21) having jurisdiction over your place of residence. Take it to the Prefecture, along with the originals as well as photocopies of your driving licence, your residence permit, proof of residence (a recent EDF/GDF utilities bill), and, if you are a student, your registration certificate, as well as two passport portrait photos, 3.5 cm square. When your French driving licence is issued, you must hand in your original licence, which will be returned to the relevant authority in its country of issuance. For further details, contact the Prefecture.

Driving with a licence issued outside the EU/EEA [*Conduire en France avec un permis hors de l'Union européenne*]

A valid driving licence issued by a country other than those of the EU or EEA may be valid for driving in France or may be exchanged for a French driving licence, depending on the reciprocal agreements in force at the time, as summarised in the *Le permis délivré hors de l'union européenne* brochure published by the **Road safety agency**. For further information on licence validity, contact the French embassy or the automobile association in your home country, which may recommend that you supplement your national licence with an International driving licence [*Le permis international*], described in a brochure of that name, also published by the Road safety agency.

Electric cars [*Véhicules électriques*]

There are nearly 9000 pure electric cars on the road in France, more than in any other European country. That standing is due principally to decades of involvement, from the late 1970s on. Today, electric cars are encouraged by a governmental subsidy of up to €3810 per vehicle, substantial vehicle tax relief and the increasingly widespread availability of public parking and charging facilities. Moreover, the big three automakers, Citroën, Peugeot and Renault, all have electric models of their smaller vehicles, sold in France and round the world. For further information, including listings of electric cars on the market, contact *Association pour le développement des véhicules électriques (AVERE)*, 24 rue de la Rochefoucauld, 75009 Paris, Tel: 01 53250060, *www.avere-france.org*, or the head office of The European Association for Battery, Hybrid and Fuel Cell Electric Vehicles (AVERE), c/o VUB-TW-ETEC, Bd. de la Plaine 2, 1050 Brussels, Belgium, *www.avere.org*.

Electronic toll collection [*Télépéage*]

The **Tolled motorways** are fitted with an Electronic Tagging System (ETS) implemented at all toll plazas. The system is tradenamed *liber-t*, because a single electronic tag stuck to the windscreen of a car or a light utility vehicle is valid on all motorways in the country, and the electronic toll collection lanes at plazas are uniformly identified by the *liber-t* logo, an orange lower-case letter t on a black background. Nearly 1.2 million electronic tags are now in use, and in 2006-2007, ETS services will be expanded and made available to lorries and other large vehicles.

You may subscribe to *liber-t* by filling in a subscription form at any tolled motorway company toll plaza or online at the company's website. A deposit of €30 (refunded upon termination of contract), an annual fee of €20 and toll charges accumulated are charged to your bank account (which must be with a bank in France) against monthly invoices. You can start using the system as soon as you stick the electronic tag to your windscreen. The tags work well on almost any windscreen. But they may work poorly on an athermic (heat reflecting) windscreen, so the athermic windscreens of cars made in France have a small area, marked in black, where the tag is to be stuck.

To use your tag to pay toll at a plaza, slow down and drive into one of the *liber-t* lanes, usually marked *réservé*. The system in the lane reads your tag and debits your account, and the barrier swings up so you may drive on.

liber-t logo, orange on black.

The *liber-t* system was developed and implemented by the CS Group, an Information Technology company that is the European leader in road toll systems; for technical details and further information, contact the head office: CS Communications & Systems, 22 avenue Galilée, 92350 Le Plessis Robinson, Tel: 01 41284000, *www.c-s.fr*.

Emission label [*Étiquette-énergie*]

All new cars sold in France after 10 May 2006 must have an emission label that states the **fuel consumption** and the carbon dioxide emission in grams per kilometre driven, in an A-to-G coloured bar chart diagram similar to that mandatory across Europe for **electrical goods marking** (Chapter 14).

End of life vehicles [*Véhicules hors d'usage*]

According to EU Directives, an End of life vehicle (ELV) classifies as waste that its owner either discards or intends to discard. Consequently, ELVs are of environmental concern, principally because they can be recycled and because they contain materials that are hazardous if not disposed of properly.

The relevant laws are accordingly strict but straightforward. Abandoning an ELV is a criminal offence, so the only legal way to discard an ELV is to take it along with its **Registration document** [*Carte grise*] to one of the 1300 **Vehicle dismantlers** in the country. The dismantler may buy the car if it is relatively new and has parts that can be sold or just take it in if it's older and can only be recycled. In either case, the dismantler fills in a notice of dismantling of the vehicle and within 15 days returns a copy of it and the *carte grise* to the owner. Each year in France, some 1.5 million *véhicules hors d'usage (VHU)* are discarded, and by weight, more than 80% of the materials they contain are recycled or resold. Car manufacturers bear a share of the costs involved, in part by designing and building cars so they may be recycled. For further information on ELV requirements and recycling, contact the recycling association, Prorecyclage, 49 avenue Georges Pompidou, 92593 Levallois-Perret Cedex, *www.prorecyclage.com*.

European Community automobile regulations
[*Réglementation automobile communauté européenne (RACE)*]

If you are involved with automobiles or simply wish to verify technical details upon taking a car to another country, your best reference is the EC automobile regulations that increasingly are reflected in the national standards of countries across the EU and EFTA. For instance, national type approval standards and **Periodic vehicle inspection** now are nearly uniform, which eases moving with a car from one country to another. However, the regulations are extensive, complex and dynamic in the sense that most are continuously updated. Fortunately, they now are collected and updated several times a year on a CD with dedicated software, entitled *Réglementation automobile communauté européenne (RACE)*, published in a bilingual edition (French and English) by **UTAC** (Chapter 30). For details, contact UTAC r.a.c.e., BP 20212, 91311 Montlhery Cedex, Tel: 01 69801711, *www.utac.com*, *marie.govi@utac.com*.

Filling stations [*Stations service*]

There are more than 13,800 filling stations in the country, of three types:

* operated by and usually attached to hypermarkets [*Grandes Moyennes Surfaces (GMS)*], more than 4600 stations commanding 55% of the overall market.

* bearing the names of and often owned by oil companies [*compagnies pétrolières*], more than 6200 stations commanding 42% of the overall market.

* independent and miscellaneous [*indépendantes et autres*], nearly 3000 stations commanding 3% of the market.

Retailing giant Carrefour, *www.carrefour.fr*, leads in the hypermarket group, with nearly 1200 stations, and Total, *www.total.fr*, leads in the oil company group, with 2700 stations. Along the **Tolled motorways** [*Autoroutes*], there are 67 stations, of which 50 are in the oil company group, and 17 are owned by Carrefour in the hypermarket group. Almost all stations are automatic, with payment via bank debit card or operating company charge card, or semi-automatic, with payment at a cashier. Except for those along the *Autoroutes*, many stations are closed on Sundays and only accept French payment cards for self-service automatic payments. Many stations are active day-round, year-round, and most stations with cashiers are automatic after hours.

French automakers [*Constructeurs Français d'Automobiles*]

Each year, the French automakers – Alpine, Automobiles Citroën, Heuliez, Panhard & Levassor, Automobiles Peugeot, Renault and Renault Trucks – make nearly one in ten of the more than 60 million motor vehicles sold worldwide, and in Europe, more than one in three new heavy vehicles, over 3.5 tons, is of French manufacture.

With an annual production of more than 3.3 million vehicles, PSA Peugeot-Citroën is the largest automaker in France and the sixth largest in the world. The company was formed in 1976 when Peugeot and Citroën merged, but the two makes have retained their individual identities and production facilities. Head office: 75 avenue de la Grand Armée, 75116 Paris, *www.psa-peugeot-citroen.com*.

Renault manufactures about two-thirds as many vehicles as PSA Peugeot-Citroën, but is one of Europe's leading makers of heavy trucks and is involved in Formula 1 racing. Head office: 13-15 quai Le Gallo, 92513 Boulogne-Billancourt Cedex, Tel: 01 76845050, *www.renault.com*.

Though it is not a French automaker, Smart GmbH, a wholly-owned subsidiary of Diamler-Chrysler AG, manufactures more than 150,000 Smart micro-cars a year at Hambach, in north-eastern France and consequently is a significant automaker in the country. Head office: Leibnitzstraße 2, PO Box 2060, 71010 Böblingen, Germany, Tel: +49 810803803, *www.smart.com*.

French Car Manufacturers' Association
[*Comité des Constructeurs Français d'Automobiles*]

The French Car Manufacturers' Association furthers the interests of **French automakers**, compiles sales and other statistics, publishes national reports and international comparisons and acts as a clearing house for administrative, commercial and technical information relevant to motor vehicle production and use, though parts and ancillary services are dealt with by other organisations. Head office: Comité des Constructeurs Français d'Automobiles, 2, rue de Presbourg, 75008 Paris, Tel: 01 49525100, *www.ccfa.fr*.

Fuel consumption [*Consommation de carburant*]

The fuel consumed by a motor vehicle is stated in litres per 100 km. For example, a 2006 model of a fuel-efficient small car advertises its consumption as *3,8 litres/100 km Consommation Extra-Urbaine*, which means that it uses 3.8 litres per 100 km driven aside from the start-and-stop driving in urban areas. If you are accustomed to thinking in terms of miles per gallon, you may wish to convert. The UK and US gallons differ, so there are two conversion factors:

- 1 mile per UK gallon = 0.354 km/litre
- 1 mile per US gallon = 0.425 km/litre

Conversions to typical figures are:

consumption	litres/100 km	miles/UK gallon	miles/US gallon
low	5 or less	56	48
average	about 10	28	24
high	15 or more	19	16

Green Card System [*Système carte verte*]

A green card extends the validity of minimum compulsory third-party insurance on a vehicle to other countries. Green Cards are issued by almost all European countries west of the Urals and the Caspian Sea as well as by countries bordering the Mediterranean Sea. The Green Card System was implemented in 1953 and is managed by the Council of Bureaux, a body established in London in 1949 by 12 countries, including France. Today, 44 countries participate in the System, and a Green Card signifies its issuing country's compliance with the relevant EU Motor

Insurance Directives in force: the Fourth Directive 2000/26/EC of 16 May 2000 and the Fifth Directive 2005/14/EC of 11 May 2005.

In practice, if you have car insurance in one of the 44 countries, a Green Card fulfils the minimum insurance requirements in any of the other countries. Likewise, if you are injured in your country of residence, say France, in an accident caused by a motorist with a car registered in one of the other 43 countries, its Green Card will ensure that you are entitled to compensation according to French third-party insurance law.

For the 25 countries of the European Union as well as Croatia, Iceland, Norway and Switzerland, a Green Card is not required, as an insurance certificate issued by any of these countries provides the same proof of insurance as a Green Card. Nonetheless, before driving abroad, you should check with your insurance company to see if a Green Card is advisable or if other coverage might be recommended.

For further information on the Green Card System, including lists of the bureaux of the member countries, contact Council of Bureaux (CoB), Sardina House, 52 Lincoln's Inn Fields, London WC2A 3LZ, UK, Tel: +44 1714041515, *www.cobx.org*.

In France, the CoB is Bureau central Français des Sociétés d'Assurances contre les accidents automobiles, 11 rue de la Rochefoucauld, 75431 Paris Cedex 09, Tel: 01 53322450, *www.bcf.asso.fr*, and the compensation body is Fonds de Garantie des Assurances Obligatoires de dommages, (FGAO), 64 rue Defrance, 94682 Vincennes Cedex, Tel: 01 43987700, and 39 Boulevard Vincent Delpuech, 13255 Marseille Cedex 06, Tel: 04 91832727, *www.fga.fr*, *contact@fga.fr*.

Guarantee Fund of Compulsory Damage Insurance [*Fonds de Garantie des Assurances Obligatoires de dommages (FGAO)*]

The FGAO ensures that a victim of a vehicle accident will be compensated, regardless of whether the person causing the accident is unknown, the vehicle causing the accident is uninsured or the responsible insurance company is insolvent. Its area of responsibility includes vehicles registered in France or in countries outside the **Green card system**. It is financed by a 0.1% levy on mandatory liability insurance policies, and it is similar to and manages the funds of but is separate from the **Guarantee Fund for Victims of Acts of Terrorism and Other Offences** (Chapter 10). For further information, contact FGAO at 64 rue Defrance, 94682 Vincennes Cedex, Tel: 01 43987700, or 39 Boulevard Vincent Delpuech, 13255 Marseille Cedex 06, Tel: 04 91832727, *www.fga.fr*, *contact@fga.fr*.

Headlights [*Phares*]

At night, from 1936 on, cars registered in France were easily distinguished by their yellow headlights. No more; in 1993, the yellow headlight requirement was repealed in accordance with a **UNECE** (Chapter 21) directive applying across the EU/EEA. From 1995 on, new cars have been delivered with white headlights. Yellow headlights are still to be seen on older cars, but with time they will disappear, as white is mandatory from June 2005 on.

The "French headlamp yellow" actually was not pure yellow, but rather "selective yellow", which is white light with its blue component removed. Today it's also called "corporate yellow" (RGB colour coordinates 255, 186, 9) because it is a yellow frequently used in colour laser printing.

In 1936, selective yellow was made the required headlight colour, principally to aid identification of French-registered cars at night. That it did, because no other country made selective yellow headlights mandatory. Selective yellow also was thought to improve night driving vision by reducing glare. That it did to an extent still debated by scientists, because two visual reactions were involved. First, removing blue light cut the overall intensity of a headlight beam by about 12%, so there was less light to produce glare. Second, blue and violet light, at the upper end of the visual spectrum, are difficult for the human eye to perceive and process as well as colours at longer wavelengths, such as orange and red. Moreover, an intense blue light brings forth a reaction perceived as glare, so cutting out blue further reduces the glare seen.

Highway code [*Code de la route*]

The Highway code [*Code de la route*] applies to everyone using the roads, including drivers, motorcyclists, cyclists and pedestrians. Much of it is advisory, but many of its rules are legally binding and, if disobeyed, amount to criminal offence. As in other countries, the code is extensive; even the abstract and guide to it, on the Road safety agency website at *www.securiteroutiere.gouv.fr/infos-ref/education/code/index.html*, is long.

Fortunately for young people and others learning to drive in France, there are innumerable multimedia DVD sets and downloadable interactive programs as well as books on the code. Arguably the best of the lot is a straightforward, easily-understood book used in driver training: *Code de la route Rousseau* (2006 edition, ISBN 2-7095-09091-1), published by Codes Rousseau, part of the Springer Science + Business Media Group and a speciality publisher in printed and multimedia learning materials for drivers; head office: Codes Rousseau, BP 80093, 85109 Les Sables d'Olonne Cedex, Tel: 02 51231100, *www.codes-rousseau.com*.

Level crossings [*Passages à niveau*]

Crossing a railway line on a level crossing is not like crossing a road. A car travelling at 90 km/h may stop in 70 m, but a mainline train, travelling at 160 km/h, takes at least 800 m to stop and unlike a car, cannot swerve to avoid collision. A level crossing is a hazard, as a collision between a train and a car not only can injure or kill the people in the car, but also can derail the train and injure or kill its passengers and staff.

There are some 19,400 level crossings in France, of which some 13,500 are on municipal roads, nearly 5500 on departmental roads and the remainder, fewer than 400, on national roads. In numbers, nearly 80% of level crossings are unprotected, though most of these, some 60%, are fitted with automatic warning signals, and the remaining marked with the Saint Andrew's cross. The most heavily-trafficked level crossings are protected, either with manually-operated gates or automatic barriers.

Nonetheless, each year at level crossings there are about 200 accidents that seriously injure 20 and kill 50 people. The majority of the accidents are caused by crossing users, often local people, either vehicle drivers or pedestrians who disobey crossing rules or ignore warnings. The penalties for crossing violations are accordingly strict: a fine of €750 and, for a driving licence-holder, an endorsement of 4 penalty points and a suspension for 3 years. Likewise, the **Railway infrastructure manager** (Chapter 46) has a works programme to eliminate at least half of the more dangerous level crossings by the year 2012.

For further information, see the illustrated *Les passages à niveau* brochure published by the **Road Safety Agency**.

Medicines that affect driving
[Médicaments et conduite automobile]

Many medicines, including tranquillisers [*tranquillisants*], sleeping pills [*somnifères*], painkillers [*medicament contre la douleur*] and analgesics [*analgésiques*] as well as many preparations taken in treating temporary or chronic conditions may affect your ability to drive. They are marked with a triangle, with its apex up, on the package, so you easily can identify and refrain from driving if you must take them, or avoid them if you must drive. There are three levels of severity, indicated by the wording and background colour of the triangle:

Level 1, yellow triangle:

Be careful!

Level 2, orange triangle:

Be very careful!

Level 3, red triangle:

Don't drive!

77

Even small amounts of alcohol usually will amplify the effects of many of these medicines and further degrade the ability to drive or perform any other activities requiring coordination and judgement. Depending on the person, other medicines also may affect driving; consult your doctor and your pharmacist if in doubt. Further details are available from the French Health Products Safety Agency [*Agence française de sécurité sanitaire des produits de santé (AFSSAPS)*], 143/147, bd Anatole France, 93285 Saint-Denis Cedex, Tel: 01 55873000, *www.afssaps.sante.fr*. A brochure on medications and driving is available free at pharmacies and in a complete version online at *www.agmed.sante.gouv.fr/htm/10/picauto/mapauto.pdf*. The **Road safety association** publishes a free printed and online brochure, *Infections hivernales, Gare à la somnolence au Volant* ("Winter illness, beware drowsiness at the wheel") on the dangers incurred in driving while taking cough syrups, anti-flu preparations, decongestants and other medications for respiratory maladies.

Mobile telephone ban [*Interdiction du téléphone portable*]

Using a hand-held mobile telephone while driving is a recognised cause of accidents and accordingly is banned as it is in many other European countries. The penalty for using a hand-held mobile while driving is an endorsement of 2 penalty points on a driving licence and a fine of €35 or more. However, the use of hands-free kits is permitted. Nonetheless, driver organisations and mobile phone operators advise that the only safe use while driving is no use: if you receive a call while driving, pull over and stop before answering. For further details, see the *Mobile et voiture: sécurité en route* brochure published by the **Road safety agency**.

Motor vehicle fuels [*Carburants routiers*]

All motor vehicle fuel [*carburant*] meets the EU requirements for quality and low sulphur content and consequently is at least of "Eurograde". Most **Filling stations** [*Stations-service*] offer three varieties:

- 98 octane petrol (gasoline) with lubricating additives [*98 super*], with blue signs and hose nozzle collars on pumps.

- 95 and 98 octane petrol [gasoline] with no additives [*sans plomb*, abbreviated *s. plomb* or *SP*], with green signs and hose nozzle collars on pumps.

- Diesel [*diesel* or *gazole*], with black signs and hose nozzle collars on pumps.

As elsewhere in Europe, the octane rating [*indice d'octane*] is the Research Octane Number (RON), so fuels sometimes are so designated. The RON is determined by running a Cooperative Fuel Research (CFR) test engine on a fuel to see how resistant it is to premature ignition ("knocking"), compared to pure isooctane. A 95 octane fuel has the same resistance to premature ignition as does a mixture of 95% isooctane and 5% n-heptane.

The equivalent rating for diesel fuels is the cetane number [*indice de cétane*], abbreviated CN. As for the octane rating, it is measured by running a CFR test engine on a fuel to see how readily it ignites compared to pure cetane.

Sale of leaded petrol (gasoline) ceased across the EU on 31 December 1999. So the unleaded [*sans plomb*] designation is outdated. But it persists, both in everyday language and in signs on pumps in filling stations. So when you see *sans plomb*, regard it to mean "no additives".

As across Europe since 1999, more diesel than petrol is sold. Accordingly, filling stations offer varieties of it, including:

* Eurograde diesel, usually with a CN of 40-46.
* Biodiesel, a **Biofuel** containing vegetable oil methyl esters (VOME).
* High-performance fuels for cars, under various trade names, usually with a CN of 45-50.

Liquid Petroleum Gas, abbreviated LPG (*Gepel*, abbreviated *GPL*) is available at some stations, particularly along motorways.

For further information as well as for the latest developments in motor fuels, contact the **French Petroleum Institute** (Chapter 7).

National Institute for Transport and Safety Research [*Institut national de recherche sur les transports et leur sécurité (INRETS)*]

Founded in 1985, INRETS is the national think tank for transportation and traffic matters, including safety and socioeconomic impact. At its headquarters near Paris as well as at three other facilities in the country, it conducts research and studies and provides expertise to policy-makers. It publishes extensively, in English as well as in French, and maintains four libraries and documentation centres in cooperation with the National Library. Head office: 2 av Général Malleret-joinville, 94114 Arcueil, Tel: 01 47407000, *www.inrets.fr*.

New car registrations by make [*Voitures particulières neuves immatriculées selon le constructeur*]

Slightly more than two million cars are sold each year, according to the **National institute of statistics and economic studies** (Chapter 42) and the **French car manufacturers' association**. The **French automakers** lead with 58% of the market. The foreign makes now account for 42% of the market and are gaining about a percentage point a year; Volkswagen leads, followed by Opel, Ford, Toyota-Lexus, Mercedes, Fiat, Nissan, BMW, Audi, Seat and Hyundai. About seven new cars out of ten are diesels, and diesel car sales are increasing by nearly three percentage points a year. Saloon cars [*berlines*] remain most popular, but sales are declining rapidly, by four percentage points a year. Though less popular in France than elsewhere, sales of Sport Utility Vehicles (SUVs) are on the upswing and now account for more than 5% of the cars sold in the country.

Number plates [*Plaques d'immatriculation*]

All registered motor vehicles have number plates. The present series of plates are made of reflecting metal foil affixed to stamped 1 mm gauge aluminium backing plates, a white [*blanche*] plate for the front, a yellow [*jaune*] plate for the rear of the vehicle, each with a 4.3 cm wide blue strip at the left showing the EU ring of stars in yellow and the letter F for France in white. Most prevalent is the 11 × 52 cm size with a three or four digit number, followed by two or three letters and then by the two-digit number of the *Département* or three-digit number of the overseas *Département* in which the vehicle is registered. The plates are made at shops in hypermarket malls as well as at hardware and auto parts shops. There are several exceptions to the most prevalent normal series plates, including trade and provisional plates, official vehicle plates, military vehicle plates and temporary plates that are for vehicles imported temporarily or bought tax free for subsequent export that are red with silver characters consisting of up to three numbers followed by three letters, TAA to TZZ designating manufacturers, and the two-digit *Département* code, with no blue field at the left but with the month and year of expiry in the MM YY format at the right.

Sample front and rear plates of present design.

If you take your car with you in a move to another *Département*, you must re-register and buy new number plates for it. Aside from inconveniencing car owners, with an increasingly mobile population, registration by *Département* grew to overburden the registry offices. Moreover, it complicated tracing stolen cars. Consequently, a new registry system [*Système d'immatriculation des véhicules (SIV)*] with a single, centralised database register is being implemented and will be effective 1 January 2008. It will have a uniform new series of number plates, yellow front and rear, with a sequence of one or two letters, followed by up to two or three figures and then one or two letters. The alphanumeric sequences will be chronologically assigned, and there will be no characters indicating the *Département* or *Région* of registry. A number plate will be assigned to a car and kept on it throughout its useful life, regardless of whether the owner moves or the car is sold. The basic plate design, with the blue strip at the left, is similar to that of the rear plate of the present series. As an option, owners who so wish may have a local reference added at the right of the plate in a blue strip with a local logo in a white hexagon and the *Département* number in white. For the full details of the present and future series of plates as well as of valid and discontinued past plates, visit the **Francoplaque** (Chapter 41) website at *www.plaque.free.fr* in French and in English.

Sample SIV series plate issued after 1 January 2008.

Sample SIV series plate with local identifier at right.

Offences and penalties [*Infractions et pénalités*]

Aside from the endorsement of a driving licence with **Penalty points**, offences can be penalised with fines, bans on driving in France, disabling or impounding a vehicle, or, for more serious offences, be indictable. The principal offences, adapted from the *Welcome on France's Roads* brochure published by the **Road safety agency** are listed over the page.

For more detailed lists of the graduated, fixed penalties for speeding, see the *La Vitesse* brochure, and for drink driving, the *L'alcool et La Conduite* brochure, both published by the **Road safety agency.**

Penalty points [*Permis à points*]

Driving offences are penalised by endorsing your driving licence with one to 12 penalty points, depending on the severity of the offence. The points endorsed on your licence last three years from the date of conviction. If you accumulate 12 or more points within three years, or 6 or more if you hold a provisional licence, your driving licence will be revoked and you must start anew and take further examination before regaining your licence. You may apply to have up to four expired endorsements removed by contacting the nearest Training centre [*Centre de formation*]; an interactive locator map of the centres is on the Road safety agency website at *www1.securiteroutiere.gouv.fr/pap/pap_carte.asp*. For further details, see *Le permis à points*, available in print at the Training centres and police stations and online on the **Road safety agency** website.

Offence	Fine	Driving in France banned	Disable-ment or impound-ing vehicle	Prison sentence
Failure to wear a seatbelt or helmet	€135[1]	–	yes	–
Use of a hand-held mobile phone by the driver while driving	€35[2]	–	–	–
Failure to keep a safe distance from the preceding vehicle	€135	3 years	–	–
Exceeding the posted speed limit by 20–49 km/h	€135	3 years	–	–
Exceeding the posted speed limit by more than 50 km/hr	€1500	3 years	–	–
Driving with a blood alcohol level more than 0.5 g/l but less than 0.8 g/l (or more than 0.25 mg/l but less than 0.4 mg/l in exhaled breath)	€135	3 years	–	–
Driving without a licence	€15,000	–	yes	1 year
Driving without insurance	€3750	3 years	yes	–
Driving with a blood alcohol level of more than 8 g/l (or more than 4 mg/l in exhaled breath), or refusing to submit to a breathalyser	€4500	3 years	yes	2 years
Driving while under the influence of drugs, or refusing to take a drug test	€4500	3 years	yes	2 years
Exceeding the posted speed limit by more than 50 km/h and causing injury resulting in inability to work for 3 or more months	€75,000	10 years	yes	5 years
(1) Standard-rate, reduced to €90 if paid on the spot.				
(2) Standard-rate, reduced to €22 if paid on the spot.				

Periodic vehicle inspection [*Contrôle technique*]

In accordance with international directives administered by **UNECE** (Chapter 21), almost all registered motor vehicles must be periodically inspected for roadworthiness and emissions. Private cars and light commercial vehicles up to 3500 kg kerb weight are inspected first within six months of being four years old and thereafter every other year. Light commercial vehicles are also subject to an annual additional inspection of vehicle identification and emission level. Buses and taxis, regardless of weight, and all other motor vehicles and trailers over 3500 kg are inspected once a year. **Classic vehicles**, diplomatic corps vehicles and vehicles used by French forces in Germany are exempt from inspection. However, an inspection may be required of a classic vehicle to verify its status on its registration document. An inspection may be conducted at any of the nearly 5000 **Vehicle testing centres** and normally takes no more than an hour. It comprises 125 checks, of which 68 are considered to be crucial to roadworthiness, so failure of any of them require remedial repairs.

Upon completing a test, the testing centre will affix an inspection certificate (CT) in the **Registration document** [*Carte grise*], with a letter A indicating a successful test and a letter S indicating that the car must be retested within two months. A car that passes the test will be issued a vignette that includes the deadline date for the next inspection. If your car fails the test, you are allowed two months to repair the faults and present the car for reinspection of those items. If you return later, the car will be subject to a full test. If you don't return and don't have the car retested, you may be fined, as police can verify testing status by looking at the vignette attached to the windscreen.

Visit the **UTAC** (Chapter 30) website at *www.utac.com* for the full details of testing in French and, in summary, in English.

Priority at crossroads [*Priorité à carrefour*]

Priority is the right to proceed before other traffic and depends on road classification and traffic direction. On **Roundabouts and gyratories** priority depends on the classification of the circular traffic. There are five main classes of priority:

Sign(s) Road classification and traffic priority at crossroads

150m

Crossings of two no-priority roads may be unmarked, or there may be a triangular advance warning sign ahead of the crossing on one or both roads. The priority to the right [*la priorité à droite*] rule applies, so traffic on one road must give way to traffic from the right on the other road. This rule also applies to traditional roundabouts.

83

Priority roads [*routes prioritaires*] have priority over all crossing roads and are marked with a sign showing a yellow diamond on a white background. Upon passing a priority sign on a road, you have priority until you see an end of priority sign, which is the same yellow diamond with a diagonal black slash and usually is at the edge of a town. After you pass an end-of-priority sign, the priority to the right rule applies.

CÉDEZ LE
PASSAGE

No-priority roads [*routes non prioritaires*] are marked with signs before junctions with priority roads. The signs may be either the triangular Give Way [*Cédez le passage*] sign, or the hexagonal Stop sign.

VOUS N'AVEZ PAS
LA PRIORITÉ

A gyratory has priority over all entering roads, regardless of their priority status. Accordingly, before a gyratory there are one or more warning signs, often with a panel underneath with a reminder that "You have no priority" [*Vous n'avez pas la priorité*], as the traffic on the gyratory comes from the left. At the gyratory, there will be a Give Way sign.

Traffic lights take precedence over all other indications of priority: red for stop, yellow for slow and stop if possible, and green for go, usually in a vertical array, with red on top. When traffic lights are not operating, the priority to the right rule applies.

Registration document [*Carte grise*]

The vehicle registration document [*carte grise*] is of a new design and content, in conformance with the EU directive of 1999. Because the information it contains is coded by letters, it eases verification of ownership in other countries. It also simplifies changes of address or ownership, as it has a detachable slip that can be filled in and posted. From 1 June 2004 on, the new *carte grise* is issued with new vehicles, to new owners of used vehicles and to owners who change address.

The format is slightly smaller than the EU maximum of A4, so as to be closer to the old *carte grise*. It has three sections and is printed in a blue design, a country road on the front and a bridge deck on the back. Car dealers, both new and used, usually take care of registration formalities and deliver a car with its *carte grise*. If you buy a used car on the private market, you may register it yourself at the nearest **Prefecture** (Chapter 21). All relevant application forms are available online at *www2.equipement.gouv.fr/formulaires/formdomaines.htm*, click on the *Cartes grises et immatriculation* link under the *Sécurité Routière* heading. The most comprehensive and continually updated overview of the particulars of registration is available online at the *Préfecture de Police de Paris* website at *www.prefecture-police-paris.interieur.gouv.fr*; in the pull-down list under the *Délivrance de documents* heading on the opening page, scroll down to and click on *Carte grise*.

Ring roads [*Périphériques*]

Paris, Lyon, Toulouse and other larger cities are encircled by ring roads [*périphériques*], which are bypasses that connect to intercity motorways. The ring roads are built to motorway standard [*voie rapide urbaine (VRU)*] and have two or more lanes in each direction. Nonetheless, most of them suffer congestion in peak hours [*heures de pointe*]. In most cases, access priority is like that of intercity motorways: vehicles on the motorway have priority over vehicles entering it. However, the Paris ring road – the country's oldest, opened in 1973 – has the same priority rule as that of a traditional roundabout, so markings and radar controls have been implemented to ease traffic flow.

Roads [*Routes*]

There are more than a million kilometres of public roads, of four types:

- Motorways [*Autoroutes*]: more than 10,000 km of limited-access roads for fast traffic, with two or more lanes in each direction. More than 8000 km are **Tolled motorways** and more than 2500 km are municipal motorways, most around larger cities; designated by the letter A followed by a one to three digit number, in white on a red background on road signs.
- National roads [*Routes nationales*]: more than 27,000 km of main roads, many of motorway standard, designated by the letter N followed by a one to three digit number, white on a red background on road signs.
- Departmental roads [*Routes départementales*]: more than 360,000 km of surfaced roads, most with one but some with two lanes in each direction, designated by the letter D followed by a one to three digit number, in black on a yellow background on road signs.
- Municipal ways [*Voies communales*]: more than 600,000 km of streets and roads having various surfaces and numbers of lanes.

For further information on roads, contact the Directorate of Roads [*Direction générale des routes*], la Grande Arche, 92055 La Défense Cedex, Tel: 01 40812122, *www.route.equipement.gouv.fr*.

Many of the motorways and national roads also are in the European E Route system and are designated with the letter E followed by a two to three digit number, in white on a green background on road signs. The numbering follows a defined hierarchy. For example, principal north–south roads have two-digit odd numbers terminating in 5, such as E15, which starts at Inverness in Scotland, crosses the English channel from Dover to Calais, continues through Paris and Lyon into Spain, via Barcelona to its southern end at Algeciras. The E Route system was initiated by the United Nations Economic Commission for Europe (UNECE) in 1975, was modified in 1992 and has been continuously updated since. For further details, visit the UNECE website at *www.unece.org*.

Road safety agency [*Sécurité routière*]

The Road safety agency [*Sécurité routière*] is an amalgamation of the road safety activities of seven Ministries and interacts at national and local levels with the police and other governmental agencies, insurance companies and other enterprises concerned with roads and traffic. It supports extensive information services for the general public, such as in publishing and regularly updating more than 40 printed and online brochures for the A-to-Z of cars and driving. The printed brochures are available at the agency's offices and at police stations, and the online versions are downloadable from links at *www.securiteroutiere.gouv.fr/ressources/les-depliants-thematiques.html*.

For further information, contact Délégation interministérielle à la sécurité routière (DISR), Arche de la Défense, Paroi Sud, 92055 La-Défense Cedex, Tel: 01 40812122, *www.securiteroutiere.gouv.fr* with interactive locator maps of its offices and associated services.

Liberté • Égalité • Fraternité
RÉPUBLIQUE FRANÇAISE
Ministère de l'Équipement,
des transports et du Logement
sécurité
routière

Road safety agency logo appearing on all publications.

Road safety association [*Association prévention routière*]

The *Association prévention routière* is a private foundation dedicated to heightening public awareness of road safety. Many of its initiatives are directed toward children, such as its "Tom and Lila" animation films on DVDs and its teaching aids for use in schools. It has awareness programmes for all age groups in the population, and it publishes printed and online brochures and other information on the everyday aspects of road safety. It interacts with several Ministries, and lobbies for safety measures. It carries on its work from a head office in Paris and through committees across the country: 6 avenue Hoche, 75008 Paris, Tel: 01 44152753, *www.preventionroutiere.asso.fr* with an interactive committee finder map of the country. It is a member of the Main Council of the European Transport Safety Council (ETSC), which focuses on road safety across Europe and consequently conducts studies and compiles national and international comparative statistics; head office: ETSC, Rue du Cornet 22, 1040 Brussels, Belgium, Tel: +32 22304106, *www.etsc.be*.

Road safety houses [*Maisons de la sécurité routière*]

Starting in 2004, the **Road safety agency** and the prefectures and regions are jointly setting up Road safety houses [*Maisons de la sécurité routière*] across the country. The typical Road safety house offers support to the victims of traffic accidents and their families, works with local volunteer groups, interacts with schools and other educational institutions, makes statistics and other information available to the public and acts as a local focal point for all matters of road safety. As this book goes to press, Road safety houses are being opened, so contact the nearest **Prefecture** (Chapter 21) to see if there is one nearby.

Road signs [*Signalisation routière*]

Though some national signs remain, road signs increasingly are uniform across Europe, in accordance with the UN Economic Commission for Europe "Convention on Road Signs and Signals" of 1968, last amended in 1995, available online at the UNECE website at *www.unece.org/trans/conventn/signalse.pdf*. Road signs in France are divided into 13 international categories:

- Danger warning signs [*Les signaux de danger*], equilateral triangle, apex up, red border, black or red on white background.
- Priority signs [*Les signaux d'intersection et de priorité*], equilateral triangles, apex up or down with red borders, diamonds with white borders, red hexagonal STOP sign.
- Prohibitive or restrictive signs [*Les signaux d'interdiction*], circular, most with red border and black on white background.
- Zone signs [*Les signaux de zone*], squares and rectangles, white background, most indicating cessation or limits of other signage.
- Mandatory signs [*Les signaux d'obligation*], round, most white on blue background.
- Markers [*Les balises*], various shapes and colours.
- Direction signs [*La signalisation de direction*], mostly rectangles, various geometries and colours.
- Tourism signs [*La signalisation touristique*], rectangular, white on brown background.
- Location signs [*La signalisation de localisation*], rectangular, most black on white background.
- Informative signs [*Les signaux d'indication*], squares and rectangles, most white on blue background.

- Temporary signs [*Les signaux temporaires*], equilateral rectangles with red borders and rectangular signs, all with black on yellow background.

- Symbols [*La signalisation des services*], squares with blue borders, most with black on white background.

- Supplementary panels [*Les panonceaux*], small rectangles under other signs, most black on white background.

For an overview in colour of the most common signs in these categories, see the *La signalisation routière* brochure published in print and online by the **Road safety agency**.

Road traffic accidents [*Accidents de la circulation routière*]

Until the early 1970s, France had one of the highest road traffic accident rates in Europe. No more. Measures enacted starting in 1973, including lower speed limits, stricter definitions of drink driving and the penalty points system halved the accident rate by the mid 1990s. Yet rates were dropping faster in other countries, and in 2002, President Jacques Chirac remarked that "The violence on our roads, which strikes the French so cruelly, is unworthy of a great, modern country." Made on the eve of the first Road Safety Conference, that remark signalled top-level concern and helped win public acceptance of further safety measures, including a provisional licence for new drivers, automatic penalties and harsher fines and sentences. As this book goes to press, the accident rate in France is lower than the average across the EU and is falling more rapidly than in any other country. For further information on accidents in France, see the *Les grandes données de l'accidentologie* brochure published by the **Road safety agency.** For the most recent accident statistics and safety programmes across Europe, contact the European Transport Safety Council (ETSC), Rue du Cornet 22, 1040 Brussels, Belgium, Tel: +32 22304106, *www.etsc.be*. Comprehensive statistics are made available on the European Commission road transport website under the name CARE, an acronym for the Community database on Accidents on the Roads in Europe, at *europa.eu.int/comm/transport/care*.

Roundabouts and gyratories [*Rond-point et carrefour giratoire*]

Roundabouts and gyratories are road junctions in which traffic moves in a circular direction, anticlockwise around a central island to go between convergent roads. The meanings of the two words vary from country to country, and there are synonyms for both. That said, the words are used here in the meanings that they have today in France.

The roundabout [*rond-point*] is the oldest circular traffic junction. In 1906, Eugène Hénard (1848-1923), architect of the city of Paris (1900-1914) proposed roundabouts for principal junctions. In 1907, the first was built at Place de l'Étoile (renamed Place Charles De Gaulle in 1970), site of the Arc de Triomphe, where 12 roads converge. Architect Hénard is regarded to be the inventor of the roundabout in Europe, though American architect William Eno designed the Columbus Circle roundabout built in 1905 in New York. The two architects were unaware of each other's works, so the roundabout is an example of independent invention at about the same time. With a diameter of just under 241 metres and a distance around its outer lane of more than 750 metres, the roundabout at Place Charles De Gaulle is the world's largest. However, the residents of Port of Spain, the capital of Trinidad and Tobago, claim that the one-way traffic on their city's 3.7 km ring road around the Queen's Park Savannah recreational and cultural park classifies it as the world's largest roundabout. If so, the roundabout in Paris is the largest in an urban environment.

Though simple in concept, with today's traffic, the traditional roundabout has several drawbacks. Entering traffic has the right-of-way over traffic on the roundabout, so congestion is common at higher volumes. Access regulation by traffic lights or policemen helps somewhat, but can slow traffic flow. In peak traffic periods, the roundabout at Place Charles De Gaulle can be the most congested in France, if not the world.

The gyratory [Carrefour giratoire] resembles a roundabout but differs in one vital way: the circular traffic on it has priority over entering traffic, and there are yield signs on all entry roads. When first implemented in 1984, this change to what traffic engineers call "off-side priority" brought forth many humorous remarks about "English roundabouts". Nonetheless, the "left-of-way" rule triggered new designs that eased traffic flow, including deflection upon entry so no traffic can speed straight through and entry flares to added lanes at the give-way line to increase flow. There now are nearly 20,000 new-design gyratories in the country, and the design concept has spread across Europe.

Roundabouts and gyratories are so prevalent in the landscape that there's a website, *Sens giratoire* ("Traffic circle"), dedicated to their aesthetic aspects, with a comprehensive online news and information centre at *www.sens-giratorie.com*. For a comprehensive overview and history of circular plazas and junctions, from Roman times to today, see architect Éric Alonzo' beautifully-illustrated book, *Du rond-point au giratoire* (Marseille, Editions Parenthèses, 2005, 23 × 27 cm, p.168 hardcover, ISBN 2-86364-127-1).

Seat belts and child restraints
[*Ceintures de sécurité et systèmes de retenue*]

All occupants of passenger cars and light utility vehicles are required to use seat belts, and children up to 10 years old are required to use approved child restraints. The driver is responsible and risks a penalty of €135 and driving licence endorsement of 2 points for any occupant's failure to comply with the rule. For further details, see the *La ceinture* and *Le siège enfant* brochures published by the

Road safety agency. For comprehensive details and international comparisons, see the Fact Sheets and the Belt Monitor published by the European Transport Safety Council, *www.etsc.be*.

Speed limits [*Limitations de vitesse*]

Posted speed limits in kilometres per hour, adapted from the *Welcome on France's Roads* brochure published by the **Road safety agency** are listed below.

	Motorway	Urban motorway or dual carriage-way with a central barrier	Other roads	Built-up areas COURPIÈRE
Normal, dry	130	110	90	50
Rain or other precipitation	110	100	80	50
Visibility less than 50 metres	50	50	50	50

The graduated, fixed penalties for violations of speed limits vary from a fine of €68 and a licence endorsement of 1 point for driving up to 20 km over the posted limit on open road up to a fine of €75,000, a licence endorsement of 6 points, disabling the vehicle and a prison sentence of 5 years for driving more than 50 km/h over the posted limit and causing an accident in which people are seriously injured. For the graduated penalties, see the *La Vitesse* brochure published by the **Road safety agency**.

Tax horsepower [*Puissance administrative*]

As in many European countries, tax on cars is assessed on the basis of motor power as calculated according to a formula. The earliest version of the formula expressed the *Cheval-vapeur* ("Horsepower") of the motor, abbreviated CV:

$$CV = 18[C/3.15]$$

where C is the motor capacity in litres and 3.15 is π (pi) rounded off. The model names of cars often stated their CV, most famously the Citroën 2CV, which had a 0.325 litre motor and of which some five million were produced from 1948 to 1990. CV came into the language as a descriptive term for cars and is still used in a car's registration document [*carte grise*] and in advertisements.

Early on, the CV of a car was close to its actual horsepower, but with developments in motors, actual horsepower outstripped CV by as much as ten times. Consequently, starting in the mid 1950s, the formula was changed to more accurately represent the actual horsepower and to take account of the differences between diesel and petrol engines. Then, with increasing environmental concern, the formula was changed again to include carbon dioxide emission. The present formula, valid from July 1998, is:

$$Pa = [CO_2/45] + [P/40]^{1.6}$$

where Pa stands for the precise technical term of *Puissance fiscale* ("Fiscal horsepower"), CO_2 is the emission of carbon dioxide in grams per kilometre and P is the power of the motor in kilowatts (1 kW = 1.36 metric horsepower = 1.34 UK horsepower). Power and CO_2 emission figures for all cars sold in France are kept in a database maintained by **UTAC** (Chapter 30) and published each year by **ADEME** (Chapter 7). A calculator for the formula is available online at *www.auto-innovations.com*, click on *Glossarie* and then on the letter P; select *Puissance fiscale* and then click on the link for *Téléchargez le programme de calcul* to bring up the calculator dialogue window. An example given to explain the calculation is for a Renault diesel car having a motor rated at 130 kW (180 HP) and emitting 232 g/km carbon dioxide. The result of the calculation is 11.75, which is rounded of to 12, so the car is a 12CV.

Tolled motorways [*Autoroutes à péage*]

No road is free, motorways even less so, as their high standards entail high construction, maintenance and operating costs. Across Europe, the costs of motorways are met either through taxes or through tolls paid by users. Tax-funded motorways benefit their users but penalise people who don't use them, as the tax burden is shared by all. France favours tolled motorways paid for only by their users, not least because funding motorways through taxes would entail raising income taxes by 8%. The system of tolled motorways is fair, particularly in France, where many motorway users, such as tourists and international truckers, pay no tax.

Nonetheless, some motorways are free to users, particularly in urban areas, where they are supported by local taxes, and in areas where they are essential in the economic development of an infrastructure that will support present and attract new industries.

Most motorways, more than 8000 km in all, are operated by companies joined in an alliance, *Association des Sociétés Françaises d'Autoroutes et d'Ouvrages à Péage (ASFA)* ("Federation of French motorway and toll facility companies"). There are 11 principal motorway operating companies and several smaller companies that operate tunnels, bridges and viaducts. The motorways are intelligent in the modern information technology sense, as they are implemented with **Electronic toll collection** at all toll plazas, real-time information display on Variable Message Signs (VMS), a single FM radio channel at 107.7 MHz that features a Traffic Message Channel (TMC) available in several languages, real-time traffic information via WAP, I-Mode, GSM and GRPS mobiles, information terminals at service areas and Internet as well as TV traffic information services.

The tolls charged are not uniform but vary, principally because the costs of building and maintaining motorways vary: per kilometre, a motorway in the mountains costs three times as much and one in a tunnel ten times as much as one on level ground.

For further information, including route locators, toll calculators and weather reports, visit the ASFA website at, *www.autoroutes.fr*. For specific motorway information as well as for the *liber-t* electronic toll collection stickers, contact the motorway operating companies, most of which also have extensive web services on their websites.

Name, address, website / length of motorway operated / location in country

APRR (Autoroutes Paris-Rhin-Rhône)
148 rue de l'Université 75343 PARIS Cedex 07
www.parisrhinrhone.fr / 1810 km / Southeast from Paris

AREA (Les Autoroutes Rhône-Alpes)
148 rue de l'Université 75343 PARIS cedex 07
www.area-autoroutes.fr / 384 km / Alps south of Chamonix

ASF (Autoroutes du Sud de la France)
100 avenue de Suffren 75725 PARIS Cedex 15
www.asf.fr / 2,551 km / Southern, north of Spanish border

ATMB (Autoroutes et Tunnel du Mont Blanc)
100 avenue de Suffren 75015 PARIS
www.atmb.net / 106 km / Tunnel under Alps, from Chamonix to Courmayeur, Italy

COFIROUTE (Compagnie Financière et Industrielle des Autoroutes)
6/10 rue Troyon 92316 SEVRES Cedex
www.cofiroute.fr / 928 km / Southwest from Paris

ESCOTA (Société des Autoroutes Estérel, Côte d'Azur, Provence, Alpes)
100 avenue de Suffren 75015 PARIS
www.escota.com / 460 km / Southeast, Mediterranean coast

SANEF (Société des Autoroutes du Nord et de l'Est de la France)
100 avenue de Suffren 75015 PARIS
www.sanef.com / 1,316 km / Northern, south of border to Belgium and Luxembourg

SAPN (Société des Autoroutes Paris-Normandie)
100 avenue de Suffren 75015 PARIS
www.sapn.fr / 368 km / Northwest from Paris

SFTRF (Société Française du Tunnel Routier du Fréjus)
3 rue Edmond Valentin 75007 PARIS
www.tunneldufrejus.com / 68 km / Tunnel under Alps, from Modane to Bardonècchia, Italy

CCI du Havre (Chambre de Commerce et d'Industrie du Havre)
Place Jules Ferry 76067 – LE HAVRE CEDEX
www.ma-cci.com / 6.6 km / Le Havre

SMTPC (Société Marseillaise du Tunnel du Prado Carénage)
B.P. 40, 13448 MARSEILLE CANTINI CEDEX
www.tunnelprado.com / 2.5 km / Marseille

Traffic information service [*Information Routière*]

The national traffic information centre [*Centre national d'information routière*] offers the *Bison Futé* (literally "Crafty bison") service that reports on continuously updated traffic conditions across the country, particularly during peak holidays. Road and weather conditions, road works and the like are reported across the media, on radio and TV, in newspapers and online, on the Internet and via Minitel. A key feature of the website is an interactive map that upon clicking brings up detailed road maps of parts of the country, with roads marked in colours – green, red, yellow and black – to indicate traffic intensity. Bison Futé has seven regional centres and a head office in Paris: Ministère de l'Equipement, du Logement et des Transports, Direction de la Sécurité et de la Circulation Routières, La Grande Arche, Paroi Sud, 92055 Paris la Défense Cedex, Tel: 01 40812122, *www.bison-fute.equipement. gouv.fr*.

BiSON-FUTÉ
sur tous vos trajets, du départ à l'arrivée

Traffic jams [*Bouchons, embouteillages*]

Traffic jams happen as they do elsewhere. You can minimise the annoyance of being caught in them by not driving in peak hours or on stretches of road marked with triangular signs warning of frequent congestion. Two traffic jam avoidance strategies are uniquely French. First, avoid driving in August, the peak holiday month. Second, in congested areas, such as shopping districts, drive between 12 noon and 2 pm, the traditional lunchtime when many drivers are eating, not driving.

Warning sign along road stretch prone to congestion.

Vehicle dismantlers [*Démolisseurs*]

There are more than 1300 vehicle dismantlers in the country, listed under *Démolition autos* ("Car dismantlers") on Internet websites and in directories and under *Casses automobiles* ("Car breakers") in the Yellow pages. Most dismantlers offer services including sales of damaged and second-hand vehicles [*véhicules accidents et d'occasions*] and used parts [*pièces d'occasion*] and repairs in workshops [*ateliers*]. Many dismantlers have websites listing cars and parts for sale, and there is a country-wide trade portal at *www.casseauto.fr*. Some dismantlers have formed alliances, principally to sell parts salvaged from newer cars; the leading alliance is *La Déconstruction Automobile (LDA)*, with extensive renovation and export activities located in Normandy: 177 route de Paris, 76920 Amfreville La Mivoie, Tel: 02 32762222, *www.lda-france.com*. For further information on dismantlers across the country, contact *Fédération nationale de déconstruction automobile,* 101 rue de Prony, 75017 Paris, Tel: 01 40547654, *www.fnda.org*.

Vehicle testing centres [*Centres de contrôle technique*]

A vehicle testing centre [*centre de contrôle technique*] performs **Periodic vehicle inspection** and offers other services related to the technical condition of cars, classified as "light vehicles" [*véhicules légers*] and heavier vehicles [*véhicules lourds*]. There are nearly 5000 centres for testing cars across the country, each identified by a sign indicating its authorisation.

The central testing agency (OTC) of **UTAC** (Chapter 30) supports an online vehicle testing centre finder at *www.utac-otc.com*, click on the car icon to bring up the centre finder map. Some 97% of the centres are in five chains, each with a centre locator on its website:

Auto Sécurité France (800 centres)
1 Avenue du Maréchal Juin
B. P. : 249, 92504 Rueil Malmaison Cedex
Tel: 01 41420505 *www.autosecurite.com*

Secta / Autossur (700 centres)
3 Rue Sainte Marie, 92415 Courvevoie Cedex
Tel. : 01 49041500 *www.autosur.com*

Vivauto / Autovision (900 centres)
7 Avenue du Bel Air, 75012 PARIS
Tel: 01 53024343 *www.autovision.tm.fr*

Norisko Auto (formerly Dekra Veritas Automobile) (1500 centres)
11-13 Avenue Georges Politzer
B. P. 152, 78196 Trappes Cedex
Tel: 01 30695200 *www.dekra-veritas.fr*

Securitest (840 centres)
1 Place du Gué de Maulny, 72019 Le Mans Cedex 2
Tel: 02 43414141 *www.securitest.fr*

Vocabulary [*Vocabulaire*]

The vocabulary of cars, roads and traffic is large in any language. Below are the more commonplace words in French and English.

French	English		French	English
accident	accident		*pneu neige*	studded tyres
aire de repos	layby		*pont*	bridge
arrêt	stop		*ralentir*	slow down
autoroute	motorway		*rappel*	remember
bande d'arrêt			*rond-point*	roundabout
d'urgence	emergency lane		*route*	road
bouchon,			*sens interdit*	no entry
embouteillage	traffic jam		*sens unique*	one way
carambolage	pile-up		*tomber en panne*	breakdown
cédez le passage	give way		*vous n'avez pas*	you do not have
chaînes	snow chains		*la priorité*	priority
chaussée déformée	deformed road			
chaussée glissante	slippery road		**véhicules**	**vehicles**
circulation	traffic		*auto*	car
conducteur /			*autobus, bus*	bus
conductrice	driver		*berline*	saloon
dépassement	overtake		*berlinette*	concept car
déviation	diversion		*break*	estate car
douane	customs		*cabriolet*	convertible
feu de signalisation	traffic light		*camion*	lorry, truck
fin de chantier	end of roadwork		*coupé*	coupe
limitation de vitesse	speed limit		*limousine*	limousine
panne	broken down		*ludospace*	multi-purpose
panneau de				vehicle (MPV)
signalisation	road sign		*monospace*	people carrier,
passage piétons	zebra crossing			minivan
péage	toll		*pickup*	pickup
piéton	pedestrian		*spider*	roadster
pneu	tyres		*tout terrain*	all-terrain
			véhicule utilitaire	utility vehicle

World Road Association [*Association mondiale de la Route*]

The World Road Association [*Association mondiale de la Route*] is concerned with the planning, building, operating and maintaining of roads and road networks and cooperates with major international organisations, including the United Nations and the World Bank. Its services are mainly for professionals in the road sector, and through World Interchange Network (WIN) for transfer of road expertise between countries. However, it also provides more general information on all aspects of roads, such as nine multilingual dictionaries of road terminology.

France has been involved in the Association from its founding in 1909 in Paris, as the *Association Internationale Permanente des Congrès de la route (AIPCR)*, or in English, the Permanent International Association of Road Congresses (PIARC). Though the name has changed, the original abbreviations have been retained. Moreover, aside from being the host of the 23rd international congress in 2007 in Paris, France has always been a leading contributor, such as at a conference held in October 2005 in Beijing, with a presentation of 50 years of motorway building that documented the successful involvement of the private sector in national road networks. For further information, contact the French national committee at Laboratoire Centrale des Ponts et Chaussées, Point de distribution 33, 58 boulevard Lefèbvre, 75732 Paris Cedex 15, Tel: 01 40435031, or visit the Association website at *www.piarc.org*, with pages in French, English and Spanish.

French national committee logo.

5

Character, customs and country

Arguably more is written in English about France than about any other country not having English as its native language. Moreover, as reflected by its history, France is diverse; although there are many common aspects across the country, the experience of living and working varies as much as it might between four or five unrelated countries. Paris is a subject in itself, and parts of the country – Brittany, Catalonia, Haute Savoie and others – differ markedly from each other, so much so that local identity is strong, such as in towns in Pyrénées-Orientales *Département*, which covers most of French Catalonia and whose flag is derived from the yellow and red striped Catalonian flag and is flown along with the French flag on public buildings, and though unofficial, Catalonian identity signs can be seen on cars. Covering all such matters in a book the size of this one would be impossible, so closer views of the character, customs and country are left to other books on French topics, some of which are listed in Chapter 47.

Anglo-French rivalry [*Rivalité franco-britannique*]

In 1904, France and Britain signed an *Entente Cordiale* that ended the conflict of centuries. But rivalry remains, in part due to the ballast of shared history that most likely started at Agincourt, now Azincourt, a village in the Pas-de-Calais Department (No. 62) in northern France. There, on 25 October 1415, longbowmen under King Henry V beat the superior forces of heavily-armoured French knights, forever changing the tactics of land combat as well as providing real-life precedent for later drama, most famously Shakespeare's Henry V. Likewise, naval engagements that peaked during the Napoleonic Wars advanced military tactics and thereafter triggered a genre of literature, the novel of the age of sail. To this day, the legend lingers, in books and films, as in the film version of Patrick O'Brian's

"Master and Commander, The Far Side of the World" that won two Academy Awards in 2004. Moreover, Anglo-French conflict affected other countries, such as Norway, that owes the start of its modern history to having been on the losing side in 1814.

The swords have been turned into ploughshares, but sharp remarks still are aimed across the Channel. *Les rosbifs* are as much the butt of jokes in France as "The Frogs" are of jokes in Britain. Criticism goes both ways: what the British say about the French is matched by what the French say about the British. Humour at the expense of the other country goes both ways: in 2005, "A Year in the Merde" by Stephen Clarke (London, Black Swan, ISBN 0-522-77296-8) and *Les Nouveaux Anglais: Clichés revisités* by Agnès-Catherine Poirer (Paris, Alvik Editions, ISBN 2-914833-29-6) were best sellers. Even politicians occasionally risk critical remarks: in July 2005, at a meeting with German and Russian leaders, President Jacques Chirac cracked jokes about British food, to the amusement of Gerhard Schröder of Germany and Vladimir Putin of Russia. Unsurprisingly, the banter was picked up by French and British newspapers, and diplomatic spokesmen were queried but declined comment.

One reason for rivalry is, of course, that Britain and France are different. Hence an attraction, that these days goes both ways. Today, some 300,000 French people live in Britain, making it the largest French expatriate community in Europe. For each British family settling in France, there's a French family settling in Britain. There's at least one surprising outcome of that statistic: two French entrepreneurs living in London set up a company, France in London, Tel: +44 (0)2085637804, *www.franceinlondon.com*, *customer-relations@franceinlondon.com*, with the intent of supplying British Francophiles with French products. But French customers were soon as numerous as the British, and the website is now in French as well as in English.

Basques

The Basques are a people that have lived since the dawn of European history in a region now known as Basque Country [*Pays basque*] that covers an area of more than 20,000 square kilometres, about two-thirds the size of Belgium, partly in France and partly in Spain. The largest city in the French part of the region [*le Pays basque français*] is Bayonne in the *Pyrénées-Atlantiques Département* (no. 64). Each year, a carnival is held there, featuring Basque cultural events, including bull fighting. Today, there are about 2.1 million people of Basque extraction in the region. Their language, *Euskara*, is believed to be one of the first languages of Europe, and in it, the name of the region is *Euskadi*. The Basques have long sought autonomy, but have yet to be recognised as separate from France and Spain. In France, the *Euskara* language is taught in schools in the region, and in Spain, the Basques have some administrative independence. For further information, contact

Institut France Euskadi, 16, avenue Friedland, 75008 Paris, Tel: 01 53772044, *www.france-euskadi.org*, or visit the region's official website at *www.euskadi.net* or the tourist office website at *www.tourisme-pays-basque.fr*.

Bastille Day [*Fête nationale* or *14 juillet*]

On 14 July 1789, as Paris was close to insurrection, a band of some 600 men attached the Bastille Prison, principally not to free the prisoners – there were only seven at the time – but to gain access to quantities of arms and ammunition stored there. Negotiations failed, and the *vainqueurs de la Bastille* stormed the fortress, forcing the garrison to surrender. One odd fact of the day underscores the cause of the unrest that triggered its events: the king, Louis XVI, was so out of touch with the people that the entry in his diary for that day read *Rien* ("Nothing").

The storming of the Bastille triggered open rebellion and since 1790, its anniversary is celebrated as a national holiday [*fête nationale*]. In everyday French, it's known simply by its date, *14 juillet*, while in English it usually is called Bastille Day. Modern celebrations include military parades in the morning, the largest on Champs Élysées in Paris, in front of the **President**, and across the country, most cities and towns put on firework displays.

BCBG

BCBG is an abbreviation of *Bon Chic Bon Genre*, the Parisian slang term for a specific well-to-do class that sets itself apart by lifestyle, dress and language, and is the equivalent of the Sloane Ranger of London or the Preppie of the Northeastern United States. It has come to connote someone who is *bourgeois* and consequently isn't always a complement. Nonetheless, the abbreviation and the full term have entered the mainstream in France and in other countries, in titles and names. There's a *Bon Chic Bon Genre* audio CD, a BCBG brand of shoes, a BCBG fashion house and, unsurprisingly, a *Bon Chic Bon Genre* escort service.

Bureaucracy [*Bureaucratie*]

Bureaucracy sometimes is said to be a French invention and consequently fiercer in France than elsewhere. The first contention is etymological record, the second is debatable.

The root of the word bureaucracy is the word bureau, long used in Europe to designate an office, particularly one involved in public administration. In the mid 18th century in France, the suffix -cratie, from the Greek -kratia, meaning "power" was added to create the word *bureaucratie*. The concept of "office power" then spread to other countries and other languages, including English. With time, bureaucracy grew in most countries and was studied by scientists, most notably by

German social economist Max Weber (1864-1920), who pointed to its advantages as well as its drawbacks.

After the Second World War in France, the advantages of bureaucracy became evident, as a dedicated corps of civil servants led the rebuilding and modernisation of the country and laid the foundations for its rise to economic power. But by the late 1950s, the drawbacks of bureaucracy had become apparent, and one of the first measures enacted in the Fifth Republic was to extend the remit of a ministry to create the Ministry for the Civil Service and Government Reform [*Ministère de la Fonction Publique et de la Réforme de l'Etat*]. Today, the results are obvious. For example, a business may be started more rapidly at lower cost in France than is average for OECD countries.* For individuals, the ready access to online information and downloadable forms of all sorts has vastly simplified everyday dealings with officialdom. The public sector remains large, employing a fifth of the workforce, so bureaucracy remains. But through ongoing reorganisation and privatisation, it is slenderising apace.

* According to the 2005 "Starting a Business" tabulation of the Doing Business sector of the World Bank Group, *www.doingbusiness.org/ExploreTopics/StartingBusiness*.

Corruption [*Corruption*]

France suffers corruption to about the same extent as in many other countries in Europe, according to the annual Corruption Perceptions Index (CPI) compiled by Transparency International (TI), the coalition against corruption based in Berlin. The CPI defines corruption as the misuse of public funds for private gain. It averages the results of several different polls of businessmen, risk analysts and the general public to arrive at a score ranging from ten (very clean) to zero (highly corrupt). In the 2005 ranking of 159 countries, France was in 18th place with a score of 7.5, behind first-place Iceland, with a score of 9.7. The CPI indicates that corruption is declining: in 2004, France ranked 22nd with a score of 7.1, and in 2003 France ranked 23rd with a score of 6.9. The complete CPI and other publications on corruption are available online from TI at *www.transparency.org* in English, French, German, Russian, Spanish, Arabic and Chinese.

de Gaulle

He was born, registered, married and buried Charles André Joseph Marie de Gaulle (1890-1970), but otherwise known today only by his first name and surname, Charles de Gaulle, as well as half a dozen other names, such as *le Général*, that refer to him as one of the towering figures of the 20th century. Educated at *École Spéciale Militaire de Saint-Cyr*, he fought, was wounded and imprisoned in the First World War and went on to a military career that included serving on the French military mission to Poland in the 1919-20 Polish-Soviet war. He was one of the first to propose that mechanised armoured divisions replace tactics based on fixed emplacements, a bold view that set him apart from the military establishment of the time. In June 1940, he took an equally bold stand and refused to surrender to the invading Germans, but instead fled to London to continue rebellion. From there, he led the Free French forces, and ultimately returned victorious to Paris in 1944.

It was then that he entered politics, as President of the provisional government until January 1946. He remained active in politics until 1953, and then retired to write his war memoirs. His retirement was short-lived: in 1958, the Fourth Republic collapsed, a new constitution was drafted to form the Fifth Republic, and de Gaulle was elected President in December. He continued for eleven turbulent years, supporting the EEC that became the EU that reshaped Europe, and initiating state support of industry and commerce, which laid the foundations for the economic power that France enjoys today. He resigned the Presidency in April 1969 and died just a year and a half later, while writing his memoirs.

de Tocqueville

To this day, Alexis-Charles-Henri Clérel de Tocqueville (1805-1859) remains one of the most studied and quoted political thinkers of all time. His two best-known works, *De la démocratie en Amérique* ("Democracy in America"), published in two volumes in 1835 and 1840 and *L'Ancien Régime et la Révolution* ("The Old Regime and the Revolution") published in 1856, are still in print and are references for university studies. Of his own country, France, he remarked that it constituted "… the most brilliant and the most dangerous nation in Europe and the best qualified in turn to become an object of admiration, hatred, pity or terror but never indifference". [*…la plus brillante et la plus dangereuse des nations de l'Europe et la mieux faite pour y devenir tour à tour un objet d'admiration, de pitié, de terreur, mais jamais d'indifférence.*]*

* Political essays [*Essai politique*], complete works [*Ouvres Complètes*], Volume IV, p. 310.

Dreyfus affair [*Affaire Dreyfus*]

In 1894, army artillery officer Alfred Dreyfus (1859-1935) was accused of passing military secrets to the German Embassy in Paris, court-martialled and sentenced to life imprisonment on Devil's Island, a penal colony in French Guiana. In truth, Dreyfus was innocent. But he was Jewish, and the strong anti-Semitism of the time had focused in part on criticising Jews in the army. The accusation against him and his conviction had been based on fabricated documents. When this became apparent, the army attempted to cover up the case. Writer Émile Zola exposed the affair in an open letter to the President, entitled *J'accuse!*, published in *L'Aurore*, a literary newspaper.

The affair split the country, most noticeably because it reflected opposing strong sentiments of the time, to an extent between the left wing and the right wing. The left wing supported the principles of the Revolution and consequently Dreyfus. Indeed, for the first time in Europe, the Revolution had given Jews full equality, and Dreyfus had been educated in the country's best schools and had been made an officer in the army. The right wing leaned the other way, toward a return to monarchy and greater involvement of the Catholic Church in public policy.

Notwithstanding opposition from the army, the Catholic Church and right-wing politicians, the case was re-opened. In 1899, Dreyfus was pardoned and re-admitted to the army. The affair dishonoured the army and the Catholic Church and precipitated the legal separation of Church and State in 1905.

Records of and documents relating to the Dreyfus affair are kept and displayed by the *Musée d'art et d'historie du Judaïsme*, Hôtel de Saint-Aignan, 71 rue du Temple, 75013 Paris, Tel: 01 53018660, *www.mahj.org* with pages in French and in English.

Economy [*Économie*]

The national economy [*l'économie du pays*] is the world's fourth largest in terms of Gross Domestic Product (GDP). France is the world's fourth largest exporter of goods and the world's second largest in services and agriculture. It is Europe's largest producer and exporter of farm products. In goods, the farm products and foodstuffs sector is larger than any other, in fact 15% larger than motor vehicles, the sector that produces about a tenth of the world's needs. Yet in services, France ranks higher still: the insurance sector is the world's fourth largest, and market capitalisation on the stock exchange is the seventh highest in the world. For comprehensive, updated details on the national economy, visit the Ministry of Foreign Affairs website at *www.diplomatie.gouv.fr*.

Elitism [*Élitisme*]

Elitism, the notion that society is best run by people considered superior, is said to be a French trait, worthy both of criticism and praise. Indeed, both views are justified, as in France, elitism is regarded to be of two sorts, distinguished from each other as is the country's history, by the Revolution.

In its most widely understood sense, elitism implies rule by favoured groups set apart by inheritance, language, religion, class, social status or wealth. The elite ensure their privilege by preserving status quo and consequently tend to be conservative. The Revolution overthrew an aristocracy, the most conservative form of inherited elitism. Consequently, in French this form of elitism is called *élitisme au sens péjoratif* ("elitism in the pejorative sense").

The second sort is *élitisme républicain* ("Republican elitism"). It is a form of egalitarian meritocracy, in which all citizens have an equal opportunity to ascend to the elite through exercising their capabilities and gaining education. The concept is attributed to Jules François Camille Ferry (1832-1893), the statesman and minister under whose administration public education was made secular [*laïque*], obligatory and free, and the number of professors doubled.

Though clear in concept, the distinction between the two sorts of elitism is less clear in practice, as pointed out by two neo-Marxist sociologists, Pierre Bourdieu (1930-2002) and Jean-Claude Passeron (1930-), in a landmark book, *Les Héritiers: Les étudiants et la culture* (Paris, Les Editions de Minuit, 1964, ISBN 2-7073008-1-0), translated into English as "The Inheritors: French Students and Their Relation to Culture" (Chicago, University of Chicago Press, 1999, ISBN 0-2260673-9-4). Based on a sociological study made in the 1960s, the principal finding was that the educational system reinforced traditional class distinctions and cultural differences. Understandably, it was much quoted during the **May 68** student insurrections.

Flag [*Drapeau*]

The tricolour blue, white and red flag was designed in 1790, initially with the order of colours the reverse of today's flag, with red at the hoist, and revised in 1794 to the modern form, with blue at the hoist. The present Constitution of 1958 states that "The national emblem is the tricolour flag, blue, white, red." [*L'emblème national est le drapeau tricolore, bleu, blanc, rouge.*] The colours are historically significant. Blue is the colour of Saint Martin, the Gallo-Roman officer who cut off half of his blue coat to give it to an impoverished beggar in the snow; it is a symbol of care and of the duty of the rich to aid the poor. White is the colour of the Joan of Arc, under whose banner the English were driven out of the Kingdom in the 15th century as well as the colour of the Virgin Mary, to whom King Louis XII concentrated the Kingdom in the 17th century. Red is the colour of Saint Denis, the patron saint of Paris. In the modern Pantone colour system, the approximate specifications of the blue and red are:

- Blue: Pantone 282c / CMYK (%) C 100 – M 70 – Y 0 – K 50
- Red: Pantone 186 c / CMYK (%) C 0 – M 90 – Y 80 – K5

The proportions of the flag are 2 vertical to 3 horizontal. There are two flags, differing in the proportions of Blue, White and Red across the flag. Most seen on land is the civil and state flag, in which each colour extends over one-third of the width. The naval ensign used at sea is intended to be visually effective when flying and has optical proportions: 30% blue, 33% white and 37% red. For full details on French flags, visit the Flags Of The World (FOTW) website at *www.crwflags.com/fotw/flags/fr.html*.

Gallic Cock [*Coq Gaulois*]

Artisans have long used the cock in motifs on ceramics, carvings on furniture and ornaments on church bell towers, as a symbol of vigilance. During the **Revolution**, the *Coq Gaulois* appeared on flags and thereby became a symbol of the people, in part because its name is a play on words in Latin: *gallus* means both Gaul, the country, and cock, the male bird. From 1848 on, *Coq Gaulois* has appeared on the seal of the Republic, and it occasionally has appeared on coins and on stamps. It now is the emblem of French sports teams in international competition.

Coq Gaulois on a stamp.

Hello Laziness [*Bonjour Paresse*]

In France as elsewhere, the corporate world is a mystery to those on the outside and a struggle to many on the inside. Corinne Maier (1964 -), an economist with the privatised electricity giant EDF, the world's biggest generator of nuclear power, reasoned that the underlying cause was a glaring gap between the theories of business schools and the practices of everyday survival at work. Indeed the root of *travail*, the word in French for work and in English for oppressive toil, is the Latin *trepalium*, meaning an instrument of torture. The key to getting ahead, she found, was not to do more, but to do less. She chronicled her observations in *Bonjour Paresse* ("Hello Laziness"), a book that jumped to the top of Amazon France's best seller list after it was published in 2004.

Subtitled *De l'art et de la nécessité d'en faire le moins possible en entreprise* ("The art and the importance of doing the least possible in the workplace"), *Bonjour Paresse* is both a parody of the corporate jungle and a slacker's guidebook to work in a large company. It concludes with the author's ten counter-commandments:

1. Salaried work is the new slavery. You work for your pay cheque at the end of the month, 'full stop'.

2. It's pointless trying to change the system. By opposing it, you merely reinforce it, entrench it further.

3. The work you do is fundamentally pointless. So do as little work as possible and spend some time… 'networking' so that you have some back-up with which to protect yourself next time the company restructures.

4. You will not be judged on the way you do your work, but on your ability to conform. The more jargon you speak, the more people will think you are in the loop.

5. Never, under any circumstances, accept positions of responsibility. You will be obliged to work more for no other reward than a bit more dosh.

6. In the larger companies, seek out the most useless jobs; adviser, consultant, researcher. The more useless they are, the harder it is to quantify your 'contribution to the wealth-creation of the company'.

7. Once you've hidden yourself away, try to stay that way: only those who are most exposed are meddled with.

8. Learn how to read the subtle clues... that identify those who, like you, doubt the system and have realised how absurd the whole business is.

9. When you recruit temporary staff for the company, treat them well: remember, they are the only ones who actually do any work.

10. Tell yourself that this whole ridiculous ideology promulgated by business is no more 'true' than the dialectical materialism that the communist system raised to the status of official dogma.

The book has been a bestseller in Germany, Italy, Spain and the UK, and has been translated and sold in more than 20 other countries. The UK edition (from which the 10 counter-commandments are extracted) is *Hello Laziness*, London, Orion Books, 2005, 130 pages 14 × 22 cm hardcover, ISBN 0752871862.

Homeless [*Sans domicile fixe*]

According to counts by the **National Institute of Statistics and Economic Studies** (Chapter 42), across the country, there are some 86,000 permanently homeless people [*Sans Domicile Fixe (SDF)*]. In Paris alone, there are an estimated 10,000 to 15,000 permanently homeless people plus twice as many on the streets temporarily. Municipal authorities in Paris and other cities provide dormitories where SDFs may spend the night, but capacities are limited, so SDFs often sleep in public transport stations. Two NGOs, **Les restos du cœur** and **Samisocial** (Chapter 33) are dedicated to helping SDFs and other equally unfortunate people.

Intellectuals [*Intellectuels*]

The intellectual has long been prominent in the French cultural landscape, and indeed the word intellectual came from Latin via French into other languages. In recent years, the French intellectual has been declared dead several times. Such declarations have been premature. Although some intellectuals of recent renown are no longer alive, the ethos of the French intellectual is alive and active. A sample of four French intellectuals of world renown in the 21st century, in alphabetical order:

- Henri Cartier-Bresson (1909-2004), one of the greatest photographers of the 20th century, who defined it in searching black-and-white.

- Jacques Derrida (1930-2004), the philosopher who invented deconstruction and triggered controversy at home and abroad, including in the UK, where he was awarded an honorary doctorate at Cambridge.

- Françoise Giroud (1917-2003), who mastered the language, worked in films, edited two magazines new to France, *Elle* and *L'Express* and served as a government minister.

- Roger-Pol Droit (1949-), the philosopher who broadened philosophy and popularised it, as in *101 Expériences de philosophie quotidienne* (Paris, Odile Jacob, 2003, ISBN 2-738-11218-8), translated into 22 languages including English: "101 Experiments in the Philosophy of Everyday Life" (London, Faber & Faber, 2003, ISBN 0-571-21206-9).

Inventions [*Inventions*]

Numerous devices and methods now commonplace worldwide were invented in France, among them:

1642: first digital calculator, Blaise Pascal

1748: first electroscope to sense electrical charge, Jean Nollet

1783: first hot-air balloon, Joseph and Étienne Montgolfier

1783: first practical parachute, Louis Lenormand

1795: first practical process to make pencils, Nicolas Conte

1821: dynamometer to measure motor power, Gaspard de Prony

1829: first pressure gauge, Eugene Bourdon

1829: printed language for the blind, Louis Braille

1830: first practical sewing machine, Barthelemy Thimonnier

1850: first gyroscope, Jean Foucault

1869: margarine, Mège Mouriés

1888: Pasteurisation, Louis Pasteur

1910: first stethoscope, René Laënnec

1910: first successful seaplane, Henri Fabre

1934: first front-wheel drive suitable for mass production, André Citroën

1946: bikini bathing suit, Jacques Heim and Louis Reard

1974: smart cards with computer chip memories, Roland Moreno

1980: first interactive public data communications network, Minitel

Kiss [*Le baiser*]

In continental Europe, particularly in France, kisses are of three sorts: salutatory, symbolic and amorous.

The salutatory kiss is a brushing of cheeks [*baiser sur la joue*] between two people of the same or opposite sex, as an affectionate greeting. There are no fixed rules for its conduct, but in general the kiss is not an introduction, but rather an exchange between people who know each other. Women kiss women, women kiss men and men kiss women, but men kiss men only when they are relatives or close friends. A kiss may be just one brush of the cheeks, two brushes on alternate cheeks, or several brushes, alternating right and left. The custom of which cheek to brush first and how many times to brush varies across the country. Your best guide then is to watch what the natives do and mimic their style.

The symbolic kiss entails a token touch of the lips to the back of the hand [*le baise-main*]. In higher society of days gone by, it was a chivalrous greeting extended by a man, on bent knee, to a woman. To this day, it still is practised in circles that cling to past ways, as well as in some orders, as a symbol of subservience.

The amorous kiss [*baiser amoureux*], lips-to-lips as well as lips to other parts of the body, is a romantic exchange intended to stimulate. The deep kiss [*le patin*], lips-to-lips with tongues interlocking, is called a "French kiss" in English, even though there's no evidence that it originated in France. Most likely, it originated in another country, as it has been a widespread western custom since the 18th century.

Liberté, Egalité, Fraternité

Liberté, Egalité, Fraternité, ou la mort! ("Freedom, equality, fraternity, or death!") was the motto of the Revolution of 1789. The motto outlived the Revolution and subsequently was shortened to *Liberté, Egalité, Fraternité*, which became the slogan of the French Republic and a capsule summary of the principles of French society. Today, it is most often seen emblazoned on the facades of public buildings and schools, and it appears on the reverse of the two largest denomination **Euro** (Chapter 2) coins minted in France.

Marianne

The ethereal figure that embodies the spirit of the French Republic [*la République française*] is a woman known only as Marianne. Drawings of her in profile appear in the logo of the Republic, on stamps and on the reverse side of three smaller denomination Euro coins, and there are statutes of her in public places across the country, most famously at Place de la Nation in Paris. Often she is depicted wearing a Phrygian bonnet, one of the symbols of the Revolution of 1789. Contemporary beauties have been models for busts of Marianne, among them actress Brigitte Bardot.

Liberté • Égalité • Fraternité
RÉPUBLIQUE FRANÇAISE

Marianne on the logo of the Republic; from the website of the office of the Prime Minister at www.premier-ministre.gouv.fr.

107

The Marseillaise [*La Marseillaise*]

The national anthem, *La Marseillaise*, is a product of the Revolution. It was written in one night of April 1792 by Claude-Joseph Rouget l'Isle (1760-1836) as a marching song for the army of the Rhine led by Marshal Lukner and consequently was first published in Strasbourg under the title *Chant de guerre pour l'armée du Rhin*. It became popular under its present name after a battalion of volunteers from Marseilles sang it as they entered Paris in July 1792. It was adopted unofficially in 1795 and officially made the national anthem in 1946. The English translation of the first line below is by Percy Bysshe Shelley (1792-1822). The full details of the anthem in French and English are available online at *www.adminet.com/marseillaise.html*.

Al-lons en - fants de la pa - tri – e, Le jour de gloire est ar - ri - vé.

"Ye sons of France, a – wake to glo – ry, Hark, hark, what my – raids bid you rise"

May 68 [*Mai 68*]

In the spring months of 1968, students at the University of Paris clashed with the university administration, which responded by closing down the university on 2 May. That precipitated student strikes at universities and high schools elsewhere in Paris, to which the government responded with police action that led to battles in the streets. In turn, that led to a countrywide strike by students and strikes by ten million workers across the country. The unrest rose to the level of insurrection, and led to dissolution of Parliament and President de Gaulle's call for new elections on 23 June 1968.

The events of May 1968 were not uniquely French, as there were student protests elsewhere, most notably in the USA, Germany, Italy and South America. To this day, their causes are debated by historians and philosophers, some of whom argue that *mai 68* was the pre-eminent revolutionary event of the 20th century, because it was a popular uprising that crossed class and cultural boundaries. A more moderate view is that though most of the protesters held left-wing views and opposed the war in Vietnam, the common cause was the dissatisfaction of the younger generation with the established society. Whatever the causes might have been, *mai 68* triggered a wave of slogans and graffiti, at least five films and tens of books.

May 68 protest poster reading "Be young and shut up".

Nobel Prizes [*Prix Nobel*]

The Nobel Prizes are awards given each year since 1901, for achievements in chemistry, literature, medicine, peace and physics. In 1968, the Swedish Central Bank established the Prize in Economic Sciences in memory of Alfred Nobel, the Swedish industrialist who founded the Prizes. The Prizes are awarded on 10 December, the anniversary of Alfred Nobel's death, and are announced in advance, in October. Of the 776 Prizes awarded from 1901 to 2005, 49 have been to French citizens: 7 in chemistry, 13 in literature, 8 in medicine, 9 in peace, 11 in physics and 1 in economics. The unofficial record for Prizes awarded to one family is held by a French family: Marie Curie (née Skiodowska) and her husband Pierre Curie (physics, 1903), their daughter, Irène Joliot-Curie and her husband Frédéric Joliot (chemistry, 1935). Of the two winners to decline the Prize, one was French: Jean-Paul Sartre, awarded the 1964 Prize in Literature, declined it as he did all official honours. For further details on the Prizes, visit the Nobel Prize website at *www.nobelprize.org*.

Racism [*Racisme*]

Racism involves personal opinion, which may or may not result in action. So it may remain unseen. **Discrimination** (Chapter 3), on the other hand, involves action, which can be seen, such as refusing to employ an otherwise qualified person because of his or her race.

As in many countries, racism has long been an issue in France. Until the 20th century, anti-Semitism [*antisémitisme*] was its most common form, prompted in part by the theory of an Aryan master race put forth by aristocrat and diplomat Joseph Arthur Comte de Gobineau (1816-1882) in his book, *Essai sur l'inégalité des races humaines* ("An Essay on the Inequality of the Human Races") published in 1855. Anti-Semitism was the key issue on the **Dreyfus affair** of 1894, and during the Second World War, the puppet Vichy regime was fervently anti-Semitic. In the late 20th and early 21st centuries, under the leadership of Jean-Marie Le Pen, *Le Front National* has been openly anti-Semitic and xenophobic.

Since the 1980s, inter-racial friction has increased, in step with the increasing numbers of immigrants in the country. It was one of the triggers of the riots that erupted in the *banlieues* (Chapter 9) across the country in 2005. Race relations, immigration, assimilation and integration have been in the forefront of public debate in recent years. Accordingly, the government has addressed the underlying issues, such as by enacting laws forbidding discrimination. And there are anti-racist movements; the largest is *SOS Racisme*, 51 av Flandre, 75019 Paris, Tel: 01 40353655, *www.sos-racisme.org*, *presse@sos-racisme.org*.

Rentrée

The start of the new school year in September is called *la rentrée des classes*, usually shortened to *rentrée* and now applied to the resumption of social and political life after the long holiday in August. So *la rentrée scolaire* applies to the school and academic year, *la rentrée littéraire* to the start of the literary year, and *la rentrée parlementaire* to the resumption of parliament after summer recess. In the preceding weeks, shops take advantage of the comeback (the literal translation of *rentrée*) with intensive advertising and innumerable sales of school supplies, books, clothing and sports equipment, as well as items not directly associated with schooling.

Secularism [*Laïcité*]

Secularism [*laïcité*] has been a cornerstone of society since the *Révolution*, when the functions of religion and government were separated, though Church and State were formally separated later, in 1905. The concept of *laïcité* is antithetical to that of a theocracy, because it holds that people shall not be bound by religious rule. But it recognises free expression of religion and consequently is a broader concept than laicism, which means to deprive of clerical character.

The balance between secularism and the free expression of religion has long been an issue of public debate, and arguably no other aspect of contemporary life in the country has been more thoroughly studied. In February 2002, philosopher and writer Régis Debray submitted a report on the matter, compiled at the request of the Minister of Education and entitled *L'enseignement du fait religieux dans l'École laïque* ("Teaching about religion in secular schools"). The two most visible responses to the report were the founding in June 2002 of the **European Institute of Religious Studies** (Chapter 6) and increased teaching of the history of religions in State schools.

In July 2003, a top-level commission was set up to study the related question of open display of religious symbols in secular schools. Chaired by Bernard Stasi, the mediator for the Republic, and comprising 18 members, including philosopher Debray, the commission worked for six months and elicited opinion from all sectors of society. In its final report of December 2003, it recommended legislation to prohibit conspicuous religious symbols in schools and to ensure secularism in the health sector and in other public services. It also recommended two new school holidays, for *Yom Kippur*, the Jewish festival, and for *Eid al'Adhra*, the Muslim festival. The recommendations were incorporated in the law of 15 March 2004 that specifically prohibited the wearing in State schools of conspicuous symbols or dress exhibiting religious affiliation. Since then, there have been incidents when the law has been applied, but their numbers are declining and most are resolved through dialogue, as recommended by the law. Apparently schoolchildren favour the law and the support it provides for shared values and equal treatment of all, girls and boys, of all faiths.

The centennial of the legal separation of Church and State heightened interest in *laïcité*, and several books about it were published after the turn of the 21st century, including:

* *Laïcité 1905-2005, entre passion et raison*, by Jean Baubérot, Paris, Éditions du Seuil, 2005, 280 pages, ISBN 2-02-063741-3.
* *La laïcité, textes choisis et présentées par Henri Pena-Ruiz*, Paris, Éditions Flammarion, Corpus series, 2003, 254 pages, ISBN 2-08-073067-3.

Sexual relations [*Relations sexuelle*]

According to the 2005 Global Sex Survey conducted for Durex, a manufacturer of condoms, the average French couple has sex 120 times a year, sixth most of the 41 countries surveyed and more often than the global average of 103 times; the average age for first sex is 17.2, compared to the global average of 17.3; and the average number of sex partners per person is 8.1, compared with the global average of 9. For the further details of the latest survey, visit the Durex website at *www.durex.com*.

Though statistically average according to the Durex survey, arguably France is distinguished by openness in behaviour and language. The term for a late afternoon tryst, *cinq à sept* ("five to seven") now also applies to other fleeting joys, and a small overnight bag is called a *baise-en-ville*, literally "screw in town".

Terroir

A fondness for *terroir* is a subtle French characteristic. For peoples elsewhere, the word is synonymous with *territory*, which has the same Latin root and designates land subject to a specific jurisdiction, as of a city or national government. Not so simple in France, where *terroir* is a strong thread in the fabric of life. From the 15th century on, *terroir* contextually designated the country itself, the land of France, as well as its farmlands and the people who tended them. More recently, from the end of the 19th century on, *terroir* also came to mean the districts renowned for their wines, as defined from 1935 on by the **Appellation d'Origine Contrôle (AOC)** (Chapter 13). From 1990 on, the AOC designations were extended to dairy products and other foods. Today, the expression *Goût du terroir* is a synonym for the best of regional delicacies and consequently the title for TV Channel and magazine reporting on cuisine across the country. Indeed, the national predilection for good wines and foods rests on an appreciation of their distinctive regions of origin, of the *terroirs* that nurtured them, which explains why one of the more popular, recent culinary books has the simple title "The taste of origin": *Le goût de l'origine* (Paris, INAO, Hachette, October 2005, 255 pages paperback, ISBN 2-01-23-7070-5).

Tipping and charges [*Pourboire et service*]

A 15% service charge is automatically added in restaurant bills and so stated by *service compris* often abbreviated *SC*. Other services may be offered *SC*, or exclusive of service charge, *service non compris (SNC)*. If you believe that you have had superior service in a restaurant, you may leave a modest tip of a few Euro coins. Taxi drivers, barbers and hair dressers will also appreciate modest tips, even if the bill is only rounded up to the next Euro.

Tourism [*Tourisme*]

France is a major tourist destination, first in the world in number of arrivals, 77 million tourists a year, and third in the world in total turnover in the tourist sector. For statistics, analyses and studies on tourism in France as well as links to all organisations concerned, visit the *Geotourisme* website at *www.geotourweb.com*; the principal clearing house for tourism and the 3600 tourist offices and information centres in the country is *Fédération National des offices de Tourisme*, 280, Bld St Germain, 75007 Paris, Tel: 01 44101130, *www.tourisme.fr* with pages in French, Chinese, English and Japanese.

6
Church, religion and belief

Modern France is secular, yet historically the country is Catholic. Some 87 Gothic and Roman cathedrals and 45,000 churches bear evidence of the Catholic heritage, but today the religious landscape includes many other faiths. Most notable is Islam, now the second largest faith: nearly a tenth of the population is Muslim, and there are 1555 Mosques in the country. In order of number of places of worship, the Protestant denominations have 2021 churches and meeting halls, the Jews have 280 Synagogues, Shuls and houses of prayer, the Buddhists nave 128 Pagodas and places of prayer, the Orthodox have 128 churches and the Armenian Catholics have 5 churches.

In keeping with the secular principles of the Revolution, humanism, secularism and freethought are firm and widespread. Astrology is popular, most likely for historical reasons: Michel de Nostradam, known as Nostradamus (1503-1566), astrologer and physician to the French court, was said to have effected cures during the plague years in southern France and in 1555 published *Les Prophéties*, a book of prophecies covering ten centuries, that is discussed to this day. The principal religions and beliefs practiced in the country are summarised in the brief, factual entries of this chapter. Discussion of the social strife ascribed to clashes between religions is beyond the scope of this book.

Astrology [*Astrologie*]

Astrologers practise across the country; you can find one listed in the Yellow pages under *Astrologie*, or by contacting the *Fédération Des Astrologues Francophones (FDAF)*, 41-43 rue de Cronstadt, 75015 Paris, Tel: 01 42501228, *www.fdaf.org*, with a locator map of astrologer members. The University Centre for Astrological Research [*Centre Universitaire de Recherche en Astrologie (CURA)*] supports an online magazine at *cura.free.fr*, with pages in French, English and Spanish.

The French names of the zodiac signs of astrology are similar to those in English, as listed below. However, in describing people, French does not use the derived adjectival form as does English, but uses the noun: *Je suis Bélier* = I'm an Arian.

English	Dates	French
Aries	21 March-20 April	*Bélier*
Taurus	21 April-21 May	*Taureau*
Gemini	22 May-21 June	*Gémeaux*
Cancer	22 June-23 July	*Cancer*
Leo	24 July-23 August	*Lion*
Virgo	24 August-23 September	*Vierge*
Libra	24 September-23 October	*Balance*
Scorpio	24 October-22 November	*Scorpion*
Sagittarius	23 November-21 December	*Sagittaire*
Capricorn	22 December-20 January	*Capricorne*
Aquarius	21 January-19 February	*Verseau*
Pisces	20 February-20 March	*Poissons*

Bible

Translations of the Bible into French have been made from the original manuscripts as well as from the fourth-century Vulgate Latin translation. Two were made before the age of printing, in 1250 and in 1377, and more than 50 have been made thereafter, the first in 1476 and the most recent in 2003. For further information, contact the French Bible Society [*Société biblique française et aliance biblique française*] 5 avenue des Erables, 95400 Villiers-le-Bel, Tel: 01 39945051, *www.la-bible.net*.

There are several versions of the Catholic Bible [*Bible Catholique*] and the Protestant Bible [*Bible Protestante*] The Books of the New Testament are identical in most versions, but the Books of the Old Testament differ among them, depending principally on the sources from which the translations into French originally were taken. The Books that the Catholic and Protestant French Bibles have in common with the King James Version of the English Bible are listed below.

Old Testament	Ancien testament		
Genesis	*Genèse*	I Kings	*1 Rois*
Exodus	*Exode*	II Kings	*2 Rois*
Leviticus	*Lévitique*	I Chronicles	*1 Chroniques*
Numbers	*Nombres*	II Chronicles	*2 Chroniques*
Deuteronomy	*Deutéronome*	Ezra	*Esdras*
Joshua	*Josué*	Nehemiah	*Néhémie*
Judges	*Juges*	Esther	*Esther*
Ruth	*Ruth*	Job	*Job*
I Samuel	*1 Samuel*	Psalms	*Psaumes*
II Samuel	*2 Samuel*	Proverbs	*Proverbes*
		Ecclesiastes	*Ecclésiaste*

Song of Songs	*Cantique des cantiques*	**New Testament**	*Nouveau testament*
		Matthew	*Matthieu*
Isaiah	*Eaïe*	Mark	*Marc*
Jeremiah	*Jérémie*	Luke	*Luc*
Lamentations	*Lamentations*	John	*Jean*
Ezekiel	*Ézéchiel*	The Acts	*Actes des Apôtres*
Daniel	*Daniel*	Romans	*Romains*
Hosea	*Osée*	I Corinthians	*1 Corinthiens*
Joel	*Jöel*	II Corinthians	*2 Corinthiens*
Amos	*Amos*	Galatians	*Galates*
Obadiah	*Abdias*	Ephesians	*Éphésiens*
Jonah	*Jonas*	Philippians	*Philippiens*
Micah	*Michée*	Colossians	*Colossiens*
Nahum	*Nahum*	I Thessalonians	*1 Thessaloniciens*
Habakkuk	*Habacuc*	II Thessalonians	*2 Thessaloniciens*
Zephaniah	*Sophonie*	I Timothy	*1 Timothée*
Haggai	*Aggée*	II Timothy	*2 Timothée*
Zechariah	*Zacharie*	Titus	*Tite*
Malachi	*Malachie*	Philemon	*Philémon*
		Hebrews	*Hébreux*
		James	*Jacques*
		I Peter	*1 Pierre*
		II Peter	*2 Pierre*
		I John	*1 Jean*
		II John	*2 Jean*
		III John	*3 Jean*
		Jude	*Jude*
		Revelation	*Apocalypse*

Catholicism [*Catholicisme*]

Historically and culturally the faith of France, Catholicism remains prominent in society, despite the legal separation of Church and State in 1905. Metropolitan France is divided into 93 dioceses [*diocèses*], and there are 9 dioceses in the overseas departments and territories. Accordingly, there are 102 bishops [*évêques*], as well as seven cardinals [*cardinaux*]. Almost all Catholic orders are active as are orders and associations unique to France. Across the country, there are 45,000 churches and 87 cathedrals. For further information on the Catholic Church in France, visit the official website set up by the Conference of Bishops in France [*Conférence des évêques de France*], 106 rue du Bac, 75007 Paris, Tel: 01 45496990, *www.cef.fr*, or buy the inexpensive (€ 11.50 in 2006) annual *Guide de l'Église catholique en France* (Paris, Bayard, 288 pages softcover, ISBN 2-7289-1172-X) published in February and sold by bookshops.

Ecumenism [*Œcuménisme*]

The Christian churches in the country cooperate in the ecumenical movement [*mouvement œcuménique*], principally through the World Council of Churches [*Conseil œcuménique des Eglises*], with information and news published in *Unité des Chrétiens*, a magazine published three to five times a year by the Catholic Church of France. For further information, contact the World Council of Churches, 150 route de Ferney, Case Postale 2100, 1211 Genève, Switzerland, *www2.wcc-coe.org*.

European Institute of Religious Studies
[*L'institut Européen en Sciences des Religions (IESR)*]

Established in 2002 in response to the recommendations of the Debray report on **Secularism** (Chapter 5) in schools, the European Institute of Religious Studies (IESR) is located at *Ecole Pratique des Hautes Etudes (EPHE)* in Paris and is backed by its religious studies department. The principal remit of IESR is to work with institutions at home and abroad and to serve as a clearing house for expertise on matters relevant to religion in society. For further information, contact IESR, 134 rue Ernest Cresson, 75014 Paris, Tel: 01 40521000, *www.iesr.ephe.sorbonne.fr* with pages in French and in English.

Humanism and secularism [*Humanisme et Laïcité*]

The philosophy of humanism is attributed to Protagoras (490-421 BC), a Greek philosopher of Abdera. The roots of humanism in France can be traced to 1847, when philosophers Jules Simon (1814-1906) and Amédée Jacques (1813-1865) founded *La Liberté de Penser* to forward the principles of free thought and secular philosophy. **Secularism** (Chapter 5) has been a key principle in French society since the Revolution. Today, there are humanist, secular and freethought groups and organisations across the country, most affiliated with one or more of five national organisations:

* *Fédération National de la Libre Pensée Athéisme Laïcité Rational*, descended from *La Liberté de Penser* founded in 1847; head office of *La Libre Pensée (LP)* at 10-12 rue des Fossés St Jacques, 75005 Paris, Tel: 01 46342150, *librepenseefrance.ouvaton.org*, with an interactive locator map of 84 organisations and groups across the country.

* *La ligue de l'enseignement*, a popular educational movement founded in 1866 and now having some two million members in 102 departmental federations, 22 unions and more than 30,000 organisations. Head office: 3 rue Récamier, 75341 Paris Cedex 07, Tel: 01 43589733, *www.laligue.org*.

* *Mouvement Europe & Laïcité* that promotes secularism and the separation of Church from State and education in France, in Europe and elsewhere. The

President's office: 11 rue des Huguenots, 94420 Le Plessis Trévise, Tel: 01 45764263, *www.europe-et-laicite.org*.

- *Union des familles laïques (UFAL)*, founded in 1988 to promote secular family life; head office: 27 rue de la Réunion, 75020 Paris, Fax: 01 46272366, *www.ufal.org*, with an interactive locator map of contacts across the country.

- *Union Rationaliste (UR)*, founded in 1930 by physicist Paul Langevin (1872-1946) and other prominent scientists and intellectuals, to promote independent, rational thought. Today, UR is based in Paris, has sections elsewhere in the country and offers an extensive selection of publications, including a bi-monthly journal, *La Cahiers Rationalistes*. Head office: 14 rue de l'école Polytechnique, 75005 Paris, Tel: 01 46330350, *www.union-rationaliste.org*, *union.rationaliste@wanadoo.fr*.

These five national organisations liaise with or are members of two organisations at the European level:

- European Humanist Federation [*Fédération Humaniste Européenne*], Bâtiment du Centre d'Action Laïque, Campus de la Plaine ULB, CP-237, Accès 2, Avenue Arnaud Fraiteur, 1050 Brussels, Belgium, +32 2 6276890, *www.humanism.be*.

- International Humanist and Ethical Union, 1 Gower Street, London WC1E 6HD, UK, Tel: + 44 20 76313170, *www.iheu.org*

Islam

There are more than 1555 Mosques in the country, listed under *culte musulman* in the Yellow pages. The representative Muslim body is *Conseil français du culte musulman (CFCM)*, established in 2003 at the initiative of the government, with a head office in Paris at 270 rue Lecourbe, 75015 Paris, Tel: 01 45572435. The CFCM is composed of representatives leading Muslim organisations, of which the three largest are, in alphabetical order:

- *La fédération nationale des musulmans de France (FNMF)*, linked to Morocco, with a head office at 9 rue Petits Hôtels. 75010 Paris, Tel : 01 42021769, *www.lnmf.net*.

- *La grande mosquée de Paris (GMP)*, was built in the 5th *Arrondissement* the early 1920s in Moorish style and is one of the Europe's largest Mosques, 2 bis Place du Puits de l'Ermite, 75005 Paris, Tel: 01 45359733, *www.mosque-de-paris.net*.

- *L'Union des organisations islamiques de France (UOIF)*, a subsidiary of the Union of Islamic Organisations in Europe [*l'Union des organisations islamistes en Europe*], 20 rue de la Prévôté, 93120 La Courneuve, Tel. 01 43111060, *www.uoif-online.com*.

The Koran in French translation [*Coran*] is available in several editions in bookshops. French translations of the 114 Suras, in text and audio recordings, are

117

online at *islamfrance.free.fr*, linked from the principal IslamFrance website at *www.islamfrance.com*, a leading source of online information on Islam in French.

Judaism [*Judaïsme*]

There are 280 synagogues and other places of worship in the country, listed under *culte israélite* in the Yellow pages. The three principal Jewish organisations based in France are:

- *Akadem*, a project on Jewish studies and documentation, 39 rue Broca, 75005 Paris, Tel: 08 73052626, *www.akadem.org*.

- *Lamed.fr*, a website named for the 12th letter of the Hebrew alphabet, is a central online clearing house for information on Judaism in France; head office: 65 rue Bayen, 75017 Paris, Tel: 01 47301525, *www.lamed.fr*. Lamed is part of Aish Ha Torah, the network of Jewish educational centres based in Israel at One Western Wall Plaza, POB 14149 Old City, Jerusalem 91141, Israel, Tel: +972 2 6285666, *www.aish.com*.

- *Fondation du Judaïsme Français (FDJF)*, founded in 1980 to enrich Jewish culture in France as well as to promote contemplation of the place of Judaism in history. Head office: 72 rue de Bellechasse, 75007 Paris, Tel: 01 53594747, *www.fdjf.org*.

Protestantism [*Protestantisme*]

About 2.2% of the population adhere to a Protestant faith, and there are 1268 Protestant parishes across the country. There are two associations of Protestant churches:

- French Protestant Federation [*Fédéderation Portestante de France*], 47 rue de Clichy, 75311 Paris Cedex 09, *www.protestants.org* with a 24 page list of all member Protestant churches and organisations.

- French Evangelical Federation [*Fédéderation évangélique de France*9, c/o Secrétaire general Dominique Ferret, BP 18. 65290 Juillan, Tel: 05 62329816, *www.lafef.com*, with a list of 21 regional delegations, each of which maintains contacts with member organisations.

7
Climate, environment and physical geography

France is the largest country in Western Europe and after Russia, the second largest in Europe. It has coasts on both the Atlantic and the Mediterranean, and most of its landscape is flat or rolling. But it also has parts of the two major mountain ranges of Europe, the Alps and the Pyrenees, and nearly 7% of its area lies above 1000 metres elevation. It is home to more species of animals than any other country in Europe. Although it claims no meteorological records, its climate, like its topography, is the most varied in Europe.

Against this natural backdrop, France is the world's fifth largest economy and the leading agricultural country in Europe. It has Europe's largest road network and nearly half as many cars as people. Its airports are among the busiest in the world, and each year, it has more tourist arrivals than any other country. Understandably, it has environmental problems, which are addressed by national and local agencies as well as by networks of conservation organisations.

ADEME

ADEME is an acronym for *Agence de l'Environnement et de la Maîtrise de l'Énergie* ("Environment and Energy Management Agency"). It is a commercial public institution under the Ministries of the Environment, Energy and Research and deals with almost all environmental problems as well as with energy management. It offers a wide range of publications, including consumer advice brochures on topics from composting and car efficiency to refuse disposal and wood burning. Accordingly, it has a large staff, some 850 in three principal offices, 26 regional branches, three representatives in overseas territories and an office at the EU in Brussels. For further information, contact ADEME, 27 rue Louis-Vicat, 75737 Paris Cedex 15, Tel: 01 47652000, *www.ademe.fr*.

Alps [*Alpes*]

The Alps comprise the principal mountain range of Europe that extends from the region north of Monaco, between the Alpes-Maritimes *Département* in south-eastern France and Savona in north-western Italy, north-eastward in a great arc, 1000 km long, along the national borders, through Switzerland, Germany and Austria, to Slovenia. The name "Alp" is of Celtic origin, meaning either "high mountain", from the Gaelic *alp* or "white", from the Latin *albus*.

Indeed, the Alps are both high and often white. There are more than 60 summits higher than 4000 m elevation, or there may be as many as 80, depending on the definition of a separate summit. In 1900, Austrian mountaineer Karl Blodig (1859-1956) became the first to climb all of the "4000'ers", some 62 by his definition, including Mt. Blanc in France, at 4807 m, the highest point in Europe. There are many glaciers, and the Alps are home to innumerable ski trails, slopes and resorts. One of the more famed resorts is Chamonix in the Haute-Savoie *Département*, venue in 1924 of the first Olympic Winter Games and then as now, a centre for year-round mountaineering. It was here that Maurice Herzog (1919-), a Chamonix guide and later mayor (1968-1977), honed skills for the ascent in 1950 of Annapurna, the first 8000 m peak ever climbed. Today, the word alpinism is a synonym for mountaineering, and Alpine skiing, a discipline in the Olympic Winter Games from 1936 on, is a major winter sport worldwide. For comprehensive information on the Alps, contact the Secretariat of the Alpine Convention, Herzog-Friedrich-Strasse 15, 6020 Innsbruck, Austria, Tel: +43 512 5885890, *www.alpenkonvention.org*.

Avalanches [*Avalanches*]

An avalanche is the descent of a large mass of snow, often mixed with ice and earth, down a mountainside. It is an awesome spectacle, not least because avalanches occur every year, most often in winter, and frequently claim lives. In France, avalanches are one of the principal **natural hazards**, because roads, railways and towns in mountain valleys are at risk as are off-piste skiers at resorts. For instance, in 1999, an avalanche buried the village of Montroc, near Chamonix in Haute-Savoie, and killed 12 people. Understandably, avalanches have long been of concern in the mountainous areas of the country. The word avalanche reflects that: its root goes back to the Old French *à val*, meaning to the valley, from the verb *avaler*, meaning to swallow or gulp down. The *Association nationale pour l'étude de la neige et des avalanches (ANENA)* is the principal research centre and clearing house for information on avalanches, including research, monitoring, training and publication. For further information, contact ANENA, 15 rue Ernest Calvat, 38000 Grenoble, Tel: 04 76513939, *www.anena.org*.

Carbon Sequestration Leadership Forum
[*Forum directif pour la séquestration du carbone*]

Founded in 2003, the Carbon Sequestration Leadership Forum (CSLF) is an international climate change initiative of 21 countries that together account for three-quarters of the global man-made emissions of carbon dioxide. The principal aim of the CSLF is to work through coordinated research and development to evolve carbon capture and storage technologies that will accomplish long-term stabilisation of greenhouse gas levels. France is a member, as are Australia, Brazil, Canada, China, Columbia, Denmark, Germany, India, Italy, Japan, Korea, Mexico, the Netherlands, Norway, Russia, Saudi Arabia, South Africa, the UK and the USA, as well as other countries of the EU via the EC. CSLF activities in France are conducted by the **French Petroleum Institute**. The CSLF Secretariat is in the USA, at the US Department of Energy, FE-27, 1000 Independence Ave., S.W., Washington, DC 20585, USA, Tel: +1 3019033820, *www.cslforum.org*

Climate [*Climat*]

The climate of the country is affected by its being midway between the equator and the North Pole and is a collage of four distinct types of climate:

- Atlantic, or moderate maritime, between the Cotentin, the peninsula that juts into the English channel with Cherbourg at its northern tip, and the **Pyrenees**. It is further subdivided into the Armoricain (wet, foggy and colder) and the Aquitain (warmer, clearer).
- Continental, or more benign, between the Cotentin peninsula and the Rhone valley, further subdivided into Parisian (like the Atlantic climate, with less rain), the Auvergnat (harsh and cold), Lorraine (cold and wet in winter) and Alsatian (typically continental, dry with thunderstorms in summer).
- Mediterranean, along the southern coast and on Corsica.
- Alpine, in the **Alps** and the **Pyrenees**.

Precipitation is greatest in the south central part of the country; a record of 4017 mm per year was set in 1913 at the Mont Aigoual observatory. In 2003, the record high temperature of 44.1°C was set at Conquerac, and in 1985, the record low of minus 41°C was set at Mouthe near the Swiss border. The highest wind speed of 320 km/h was recorded in February 1967 at Mont Ventoux in the south-eastern part of the country.

Coastal Protection Agency [*Conservatoire du littoral*]

The Coastal Protection Agency is responsible for monitoring and managing land use along the Atlantic and Mediterranean coasts of the mainland, along the shores of all lakes, and on the islands of Guadeloupe, Guyane, Martinique, Mayotte, Réunion and St. Pierre et Miquelon. One of its principal activities is to acquire land that is threatened, has deteriorated or is closed to the public when it should be open to all. As at 1 January 2006, it had acquired 300 sites that together are visited each year by more than 15 million people. The *Conservatoire* is funded in part by private donations, which are tax deductible. For further information, contact the head office at 36 quai d'Austerlitz, 75013 Paris, Tel: 01 44068900, *www.conservatoire-du-littoral.fr*, with pages in French and in English.

Conservation organisations [*Organisations de conservation*]

There are several thousand environmental and conservation groups and organisations in the country. Three thousand of them are affiliated with France Nature Environment (FNE), a federation that was started in 1968 and became a public agency in 1976 and now is involved in almost all environmental matters and offers a wide range of publications to the public. Its happy porcupine logo is widely recognised as a symbol of environmental awareness. For further information, contact FNE, 6 rue Dupanloup, 45000 Orleans, Tel: 02 38624448, *www.fne.asso.fr*.

FRANCE NATURE
ENVIRONNEMENT

Three French affiliates of international organisations are active in conservation matters:

- Friends of the Earth International, *Les Amis de la Terre France*, 2b rue Jules Ferry, 93100 Montreuil, Tel: 01 48513222, *www.amisdelaterre.org*.
- Friends of Nature International, *Union Touristique Les Amis de la Nature (UTAN)*, 197 rue Championnet, 75018 Paris, Tel: 01 46275356, *www.utan.asso.fr* with a locator map of sections across the country.
- Greenpeace France, 22 rue des Rasselins, 75020 Paris, Tel: 01 44640202, *www.greenpeace.org/france*, with a locator map of sections across the country.

Energy [*Energie*]

France imports more than half of the energy it consumes, but the difference between production and consumption varies by primary energy source:

- Coal accounts for about 5% of overall energy consumption. The coal reserves of the country are so small that in April 2004 domestic production was abandoned, and thereafter all coal has been imported, principally from Australia, South Africa and the USA.

- Electricity is the only form of energy export, as France is the world's eighth largest producer, in step with being the third largest consumer and producer in Europe, behind Russia and Germany. More than three-quarters of electricity is generated in nuclear power plants, and France exports electricity to Germany, Italy, Switzerland and the UK.

- Natural gas accounts for about 15% of all energy consumed in the country, ranking France 13th in the world in consumption. More than 95% of the natural gas is imported by pipeline from Algeria, the Netherlands, Norway and Russia. About a quarter of the natural gas consumption is liquefied natural gas (LNG), imported from Algeria, Nigeria and Egypt.

- Petroleum is found only in small reserves in Aquitaine and the Paris basin, so the country imports more than 95% of the oil it consumes, mostly from Norway and Saudi Arabia, with smaller amounts coming from Iran, Iraq, Nigeria, Russia and the UK. Overall, France is the world's fifth largest oil importer, behind the USA, Japan, Germany and Korea.

For further details on energy production and consumption in France, as well as in other countries, see the country overviews compiled by the **Carbon Sequestration Leadership Forum**.

Environmental labelling [*Éco label*]

Products meeting environmental requirements usually are labelled. The four most common labels are the NF Environment, the EU flower, the Green Dot and AB.

The *NF Environnement* label is the official French environmental label, administered by **AFNOR** (Chapter 30) and applied to a range of consumer products and services, as well as to school and office furniture and to plastic shopping bags.

The NF Environment label.

The European Eco-label is an EU initiative aimed at encouraging compliance with environmental guidelines and promote sustainable consumption. The EU Eco-label organisation publishes the free "The Flower News" newsletter on environmental labelling, in English, French, Spanish, Italian and Greek. For further details, contact the Eco-label Helpdesk, c/o Bio Intelligence Service, 1 rue Berthelot, 94200 Ivry-sur Seine, Tel: 01 56202898, Fax: 01 58460995, *www.europa.eu.int/comm/ environment/ecolabel*, *ecolabel@biois.com*.

The European Eco label.

The Green Dot label on packaging indicates that recycling fees for it have been paid so it may be collected and recycled free of charge to the user. It is one of the most widely used logos in the world, appearing on more than 470 billion packaged items. The responsible organisation in France is *Eco-Emballages,* 44 avenue Georges Pompidou, BP 306, 92302 Levallois-Perret Cedex, Tel: 01 40899999, Fax: 01 40899988, *www.ecoemballages.fr*.

The Green Dot.

The AB label on a food product indicates that its production fulfils the environmental and organic agriculture criteria of *La Fédération Nationale d'Agriculture Biologique (FNAB)*. Further information on the organisation as well as on organic agriculture is available in all departments, both on the mainland and overseas; addresses and contact information are on online at *www.agriculturebio.org*.

AB certification label.

European Environment Agency
[*Agence européenne pour l'environnement*]

France is one of the 31 members of the European Environment Agency (EEA), an EU advisory body that gathers and distributes data on environmental topics and advises the European Commission and other policy-making EU organisations. For further information, contact the EEA head office, Kongens Nytorv 6, DK-1050 Copenhagen K, Denmark, Tel: +45 33367100, Fax: +45 33367199, *www.eea.eu.int*, in 24 languages. The principal EEA tool is the European Environment Information and Observation Network (EIONET), *www.eionet.eu.int*, which brings together 300 environmentally oriented organisations across Europe, 16 of them French. For further information on EIONET in France, contact the French Environmental Institute [*Institut français de l'environnement (IFEN)*], 61 boulevard Alexandre Martin, 45058 Orleans Cedex 1, Tel: 02 38797878, Fax: 02 38797870, *www.ifen.fr* with pages in English, *ifen@ifen.fr*.

French Environmental Research Institute [*Institut Français de l'Environnement (IFEN)*]

The Environmental Research Institute is a national competence centre under the Ministry of Ecology and Sustainable Development [*Ministère de l'écologie et du développement durable*]. It is the central clearing house and repository for environmental data, including the *Ensemble Intégré des Descripteurs de l'Environnement Régional (EIDER)* integrated regional environmental database, made available to the public on a CD-ROM. It is the French actor in several international programmes, including the European Environment Agency's inventory of nationally designated protected areas that began under the CORINE land cover programme. For further information, contact the Institute at 5 route d'Olivet, BP 16105, 45061 Orleans Cedex 2, Tel: 02 38797878, *www.ifen.fr*.

French Institute for Exploration of the Sea [*Institut Français de Recherche pour l'exploration de la Mer (IFREMER)*]

IFREMER is a research and development institute of world rank in the marine sciences, with activities in six principal fields: oceanography, monitoring and use of coastal seas, monitoring and optimising of aquaculture, fisheries, exploration and exploitation of ocean floors and ocean circulation and ecosystems. It has 25 research departments in five centres and 21 stations along the coast of Metropolitan France and overseas, and it is one of the nine organisations supporting the polar activities of the **French Polar Institute**. For further information, contact the principal facility at 155 rue Jean-Jacques Rousseau, 92138 Issy-les-Moulineaux Cedex, Tel: 01 46482100, *www.ifremer.fr*, with pages in French and in English.

French National Meteorological Service [*Météo-France*]

Météo-France is most known as the source of data for weather forecasts. But it also compiles extensive meteorological data from round the world and conducts related activities including:

- The National Centre for Meteorological Research [*Centre National de Recherches Météorologiques*] at Toulouse
- The National School of Meteorology [*Ecole Nationale de la Météorologie*] at Toulouse.

- The Meteorological Satellite Data Acquisition and Processing Service [*Service d'Archivage et de Traitement Météorologique des Observations Spatiales*] at Lannion.
- Supporting the thunderstorm monitoring network operated by **Météorage**.
- Operating online weather information service online at *www.meteo.fr* and by telephone for the country at 3250 and for the Departments at 08 926802NN where NN is the Department number.

The head office is at 1 Quay Branly, 75340 Paris Cedex 07, Tel: 01 45567171, Fax: 01 45567005, *www.meteo.fr*.

French Petroleum Institute [*Institut Français du Pétrole (IFP)*]

The French Petroleum Institute is a research and development centre active in the oil, gas, sustainable development and new energy technology sectors. Jointly with *Ecole nationale supérieure du pétrole et des moteurs (ENSPM)*, IFP offers an academic-level training programme for oil, gas and petrochemical professionals that each year draw some 12,000 participants from round the world. IFP supports one of Europe's largest databases and programme of publications in its fields of interest. It is the contact organisation in France for the **Carbon Sequestration Leadership Forum** and other international organisations concerned with climate change and environmental impact. For further information contact the head office: 1 and 4 avenue de Bois-Préau, 92852 Rueil-Malmaison Cedex, Tel: 01 47526000, *www.ifp.fr*.

French Polar Institute [*Institut Polaire Français*]

The full name of the institute is *Institut Polaire Français Paul-Émile Victor (IPEV)*, in honour of ethnographer and explorer Paul-Émile Victor (1907-1995), famed for his expeditions in southern and northern extremes, including a walk across Greenland in 1936. Administratively, it is a public service group [*Groupement d'Intérêt Public (GIP)*] that combines the polar interests of nine national agencies. It has a staff of 50 and six permanent bases in polar regions: five in the Antarctic region, including Crozet on the continent, and one at Ny Ålesund in the Svalbard archipelago close to the North Pole. For further information contact IPEV, Technopôle Brest-Iroise, BP 75, 29280 Plouzané, Tel: 02 98056500, *www.ipev.fr,infoipev@ipev.fr*.

Geography [*Géographie*]

Geographically, France consists of a hexagonal-shaped country of continental Europe, Metropolitan France [*France métropolitaine*] and ten areas overseas.

The geographical features of Metropolitan France are:

- Area: 551,602 km^2 plus 1260 km^2 coastal islands and Corsica, 8747 km^2

- Border: with Spain 650 km, with Belgium 620 km, with Switzerland 572 km, with Italy 515 km, with Germany 450 km, with Andorra 57 km and with Monaco 4.5 km

- Coast line: 2962 km

- Delimitation of the mainland: 42°20' to 51°5' N and 5°56' to 7°9' E

- Highest mountain: Mt. Blanc, 4807 m

- Highest waterfall: Gavarnie, 442 m

- Largest glacier: Mer de Glace, 40 km^2

- Largest lake: Berre, 156 km^2

- Longest river: Loire, 1020 km

- Maximum distances: 973 km north-south, Dunkerque to Prats-de-Mollo, 945.5 km east-west, Lauterbourg to Pointe de Corsen, 1082 km north-west to south-east, Pointe de Corsen to Menton.

The ten overseas areas together are designated *DOM-TOM*, originally an acronym for *Département d'outre-mer – Territoire d'outre-mer*, but by constitutional amendment of 28 March 2003, *Territoire d'outre-mer (TOM)* was revoked as an official designation, so it is not used separately. The overseas areas that are not *Départements* now are called Overseas communities [*Collectivités d'outre-mer*].

Département d'outre-mer (DOM):

- Guadeloupe, 1780 km^2 island in the Caribbean

- Guyane, called French Guiana in English, 91,000 km^2 country on north coast of South America

- Martinique, 1100 km^2 island off north coast of South America

- Réunion, 2511 km^2 island in Indian Ocean, off south-east coast of Africa

Overseas communities [*Collectivités d'outre-mer*]:

- Mayotte, 374 km^2 island in Indian Ocean, off south-east coast of Africa

- Nouvelle Calédonie, 19,103 km^2 archipelago in south-west Pacific Ocean

- Polynésie Française, 4000 km^2 island in south-west Pacific Ocean, east of Australia

- Territories in the Antarctic and the Arctic [*Terres australes et antarctiques*]

- Saint Pierre et Miquelon, 242 km^2 island in North Atlantic Ocean, south of Newfoundland

- Wallis et Futuna, 225 km^2 islands in south-west Pacific Ocean, east of Australia

Geological Society of France
[*Société géologique de France (SGF)*]

The geology of the country is as varied as its topography. Accordingly, geology is among the strongest of scientific fields, and the Geological Society of France one of the oldest scientific organisations, founded in 1830. Today, SGF is concerned with geology in its broadest sense and is involved in various aspects of earth and planetary sciences, principally through organising conferences and expeditions as well as through advising governmental agencies. It offers numerous periodicals and publications, most recently *Guide de la Géologie en France* (Paris, Éditions Belin, 2004, 816 pages hardcover, ISBN 2-7011-2680-0), with more than 2000 entries and 425 colour photos, one of the more impressive guides to the country. For further information, contact the head office at 77 rue Claude Bernard, 75007 Paris, Tel: 01 43317735, *sgfr.free.fr*, with pages in French, English and Spanish.

Hazard symbols [*Symboles de danger*]

Dangerous chemicals must be clearly marked with the European danger symbols, each comprising a black pictogram on an orange square, accompanied by a letter. For further information, contact one of the **Poison Control Centres** (Chapter 15).

See chart on the next page.

International Office for Water
[*Office International de l'Eau (OIEAU)*]

The International Office for Water is a non-profit association dedicated to serving and coordinating the activities of public and private organisations involved in water resources management and protection in France, in Europe and round the world. It is affiliated with four water resources databanks, five international networks and six research communities. For further information, contact the head office at 21 rue de Madrid, 75008 Paris, Tel: 01 44908860, *www.oieau.fr*, with pages in French, English, Italian and Spanish.

Management and Impacts of Climate Change
[*Gestion et Impacts des Changements du Climat (GICC)*]

GICC is a joint effort of the Ministry of Ecology and Sustainable Development [*Ministère de l'Ecologie et du Développement Durable (MEDD)*], *www.ecologie.gouv.fr* and the Inter-Ministerial Mission on Greenhouse Effect [*Mission Interministérielle de l'Effet de Serre, (MIES)*], *www.effet-de-serre.gouv.fr*.

Its remit is to promote and develop French scientific research on the impacts of climate change and associated physical mechanisms. The principal goal is to provide scientific grounds for implementing means and methods as well as to advise policy and decision makers. It works in accordance with the United Nations Framework Convention on Climate Change (UNFCCC) *unfccc.int* and the Kyoto Protocol of December 1997, *unfccc.int/resource/convkp.html*. For further information, contact

	O Oxidising [*Comburant*]	Chemicals that react exothermically with other chemicals.
	E Explosive [*Explosif*]	Chemicals that explode.
	F Highly flammable [*Inflammable*] **F+** Extremely flammable [*Très inflammable*]	Chemicals that may catch fire in contact with air, only need brief contact with an ignition source, have a very low flash point or evolve highly flammable gases in contact with water. Chemicals that have an extremely low flash point and boiling point, and gases that catch fire in contact with air.
	T Toxic [*Toxique*] **T+** Very toxic [*Très toxique*]	Chemicals that at low levels cause damage to health. Chemicals that at very low levels cause damage to health.
	Xn Harmful [*Nocif*] **Xi** Irritant [*Irritant*]	Chemicals that may cause damage to health. Chemicals that may cause inflammation to the skin or other mucous membranes.
	C Corrosive [*Corrosif*]	Chemicals that may destroy living tissue on contact.
	N Dangerous for the environment [*Dangereux pour l'environnement*]	Chemicals that may present an immediate or delayed danger to one or more components of the environment.

Hazard symbols. The wordings of these descriptions are the same as those of Health & Safety Executive (HSE), UK.

the secretariat at MIES/MEDD, 20 Avenue de Ségur, 75007 Paris, Tel: 01 421915559, *medias.obs-mip.fr/gicc*, in French, with some pages in English.

Météorage

Météorage – the name is a portmanteau word formed from *météorologique* ("meteorology") and *orage* ("thunderstorm") – is the operator of the thunderstorm monitoring network for the **French National Meteorological Service**. Founded in 1987, the company has developed the proprietary Computer Aided Thunderstorm Surveillance System (CATS) and in addition to France has installed thunderstorm monitoring networks in several countries, including Austria, Italy, Spain, Switzerland and Tunisia. It is associated with the European Cooperation for Lightning Detection (EUCLID) and is active in the Euromediterranean thunderstorm monitoring network. For further information, contact the head office at Helioparc, 2 avenue Pierre A ngot, 64053 Pau Cedex 9, Tel: 05 59807730, Fax: 05 59807731, *www.meteorage.com* with pages in English, *commercial@ meteorage.com*.

National Forest Office [*Office National des Forêts (ONF)*]

Forests cover 27.1% of the land area of Metropolitan France, so the protection and management of forests is a principal concern. The National Forest Office oversees all relevant activities, including the forest inventory [*Inventaire Forestier National (IFN)*] and the national RENECOFOR forest health surveillance system. For further information, contact the head office, ONF, 2 av. de Saint-Mandé, 75570 Paris Cedex 12, Tel: 01 40195800, *www.onf.fr*, with an interactive locator map of ONF facilities across the country.

National Geographic Institute
[*Institute Géographique National (IGN)*]

Originally founded in 1887 as the Army Map Service [*Service géographique des armées*], IGN now is one of the world's leading geographic institutes. It maintains two public service repositories, the national cartographic library [*Cartothèque Nationale*] and the national geographical photo archives [*Photothèque Nationale*] with more than 3.5 million photos from 1921 to the present day. It has two shops for sale of **maps and guides** (Chapter 31) and its activities include an academic-level school of geographical sciences, *Ecole Nationale des Sciences Géographiques* and liaison with geographic organisations round the world. For further information, contact the headquarters at 136 bis, rue de Grenelle, 75700 Paris 07 SP, Tel: 01 43988000, *www.ign.fr*, with pages in French, English and German.

Natural hazards [*Dangers naturels*]

The natural hazards of the country are as varied as its terrain and weather and include*:

- **avalanches**, with 400 municipalities at risk.
- drought [*sécheresse*], the record long being 97 days in Marseille in 1906, though the 55 day Paris drought of 1897 affected more people.
- floods [*inondations*], with 2000 municipalities and a population of 2 million at risk.
- forest fires [*incendie de forêt*] in 15 *Départements* in the south-eastern part of the country.
- land slides [*mouvements de terrain*], with 3000 municipalities at risk.
- windstorms in winter [*vent de tempête*] at higher elevations in the south-eastern part of the country.

*Reference: *QUID 2006*.

Noise [*Bruit*]

The word noise comes from the Latin *nausea*, which means seasickness. Indeed, noise causes illness, including loss of hearing, stress, and high blood pressure, as well as loss of sleep at home and reduced productivity at workplaces. As in most industrialised countries, noise is the most widespread form of pollution. Across the country, people are subjected to traffic noise that is higher than the recommended limit of 55 decibels. Aircraft noise is a major problem, affecting 300,000 people in the Ile-de-France region and half a million in the country as a whole. Construction works, industries and railways also create noise that bothers those who live nearby. Moreover, noise from neighbours, such as from high-power audio systems, bothers many people. Consequently, the national agency, *Centre d'information et de Documentation sur le Bruit (CIDB)* monitors noise, conducts research on noise abatement and publishes information for professionals and the public. For further information, contact the CIDB head office at 12-14 rue Jules-Bourdais, 75017 Paris, Tel: 01 47646464, *www.infobruit.org*.

Nuclear energy [*Energie nucléaire*]

The 58 nuclear plants in France produce about 78% of the country's electrical energy, far more than the global average of 17%*. EDF, the principal electricity supplier, estimates that 83.4% of the electrical energy it sells comes from nuclear plants**. Understandably, nuclear power is a topic of public debate. According to a survey conducted for the European Commission in January 2006 on public attitudes on meeting future energy needs, only 8% of the population in France support the development of nuclear power, compared to 12% of all Europeans. As this book

goes to press, debate is ever more furious, in step with the scheduled 2007 completion of the European Pressurised water Reactor (EPR) being built at Flamanville in Normandy.

** Source: Energie, mai 2005, **Science & Décision** (Chapter 31).*

** Source: EDF La letrre d'information, mai-octobre 2005.

Poisonous plants [*Plantes toxiques*]

Each year, plant poisoning accounts for about 2.5% of all reported cases of poisoning but 90% of all cases of children being poisoned. Accordingly, **CEPR** (Chapter 33) publishes a public information leaflet advising people to contact one of the **Poison Control Centres** (Chapter 16) whenever ingestion of poisonous plants takes place. Nine commonplace poisonous plants are:

* House plants [*les plantes d'appartement*]: dieffenbachia [*diffenbachia*], ficus [*ficus*] and anthodium [*anthurium*].

* Decorative outdoor plants [*les plantes ornementales d'extérieur*]: pink laurel [*laurier rose*], aucuba [*aucuba*] and hydrangea [*hortensia*].

* Native plants [*les plantes indigènes*]: bush honeysuckle [*chèvrefeuille des bois*], digitalis [*digitale*] and holly [*houx*].

Prorecyclage

In 2000, ten organisations active in recycling created *Prorecyclage*, an expertise centre and cooperative network for exchange of ecological and recycling information. The network now has 28 members, varying from companies that produce chemicals and packaging to recycling specialists. For further information, contact the head office at 49 avenue Georges Pompidou, 92593 Levallois-Perret Cedex, Fax: 01 49645275, *www.prorecyclage.com*.

Pyrenees [*Pyrénées*]

The Pyrenees are the mountains of the range that extends 450 km from the Mediterranean Sea westward to the Bay of Biscay, separating the Iberian Peninsula from the rest of Continental Europe and consequently including the border between France and Spain. The peaks are second only to the Alps; the highest is Pic de Aneto, 3404 m, in Spain. There are many caves and grottos, including Grotte Casteret, the highest ice cave in Europe, and there are glaciers, in all covering 33 km^2. The name of the range comes from Pyrène of Greek mythology, said to be buried there after being killed by wild animals. In 218 BC, Hannibal made his famed crossing on the way to Italy. The range includes the sources of the Adour, Aude and Garonne rivers in France.

Snakes [*Serpents*]

The two principal species of snakes in France are the grass snake [*couleuvre*] and the viper [*vipère*]. Only the four species of viper are poisonous [*vénimeux*]: *Vipère aspic* (vipera aspis), *Vipère péliade* (vipera berus), *Vipère d'Orsini* (vipera ursinii) and *Vipère des Pyrénées* (Vipera seoanei). All have zig-zag patterns on their backs, and the adults average 45 cm in length, but may be up to 90 cm long. The principal habitats of the adders are meadows, grassy fields and rocky slopes, particularly in the southern part of the country. If you walk outdoors in these areas, it's wise to learn to recognise the snakes; one good reference with colour photos is *Guide des serpents de France et d'Europe* (Editions De Vecchi, 2005, 127 pages, ISBN 2-7328-3549-8).

The adders have been protected since 1980, because each year, they eat millions of rats and mice that otherwise destroy crops. Fortunately, they fear people and will flee if possible. Equally fortunate, their bites are seldom fatal: of the 1000 to 2000 bites registered each year, only one to three are fatal. The Institute for the Prevention of Accidents [*Institut Prévention Accidents*] advises that a person bitten should:

- rest, preferably in shade, to prevent the venom spreading in the body
- avoid alcoholic drink
- contact a doctor for treatment.

For further information, contact one of the 13 Poison Centres [*Centres AntiPoison*], as listed by *Association des Centres Antipoison et de Toxicovigilance (CAP-Tv)*, *www.centres-antipoison.net*, with a locator map and hotline numbers of the centres.

Water [*Eau*]

Water in cities, towns and villages across the country is safe to drink. However, safe water delivered to an older building with lead pipes can become polluted before it is drawn by residents, so the water agencies advise minimising risk of lead contamination by following five simple rules:

- Do not drink the first water out of the tap at the beginning of a day.
- Let water run until it is cool, which indicates that the pipes have been emptied of stagnant water.
- In an apartment building, draw drinking water at peak hours, when water flows so quickly that it doesn't stagnate in pipes.
- Do not use water from the hot tap for cooking or drinking, as heat increases lead dissolution in water.
- After being away for a few days or more, let water flow for a few minutes, to empty pipes of stagnant water.

Though water supplies are safe, even in older buildings if the above rules are followed, the custom of drinking **bottled water** (Chapter 19) persists, apparently because of taste, as much of the country's drinking water is chlorinated. Water that is unsafe to drink, as on trains or in public fountains, usually will have a caveat sign reading *Eau non potable*. Across the country, water is provided by six agencies joined in the *Agences de l'Eau* network, *www.lesagencesdeleau.fr*, with pages in French and in English and an interactive locator map of the six agencies. Water is supplied to customers by companies that specialise in outsourced services for local authorities in the water and waste management. In almost all municipalities, you will pay your water bill to one of these companies, of which the three largest are:

- *Groupe Saur*, a water engineering and services company, 1 avenue Eugène Freyssinet, 78064 Saint-Quentin-en-Yvelines Cedex, Tel: 01 30608400, *www.saur.com* in French and English.

- *Groupe Suez*, formerly *Lyonnaise des eaux*, the second oldest water services company, 16 rue de la Ville-l 'Evêque, 75383 Paris Cedex 08, Tel: 01 40066400, *www.suez.com* in French and English.

- *Veolia Eau – Compagnie Générale des Eaux*, the oldest and largest of the water services companies, 52 rue d'Anjou, 75008 Paris, Tel: 01 49244924, *www.veoliaeau.com* in French and English.

Weather forecasts [*Prévisions météorologiques*]

Weather forecasts are printed in newspapers and are part of radio and TV news programmes. The meteorological data on which they are based comes from the **French National Meteorological Service**, which makes it available online at *www.meteo.fr* and by telephone for the country at 3250 and for the Departments at 08 926802NN where NN is the Department number. There also are a number of private sector online and telephone weather information services, including *Météo-prévisions* at *www.meteo-previsions.com*, Tel: 08 92161212 and *Météo-Info* at *www.meteo-info.com*, Tel: 08 99700734.

World Conservation Union [*Union Mondiale Pour la Nature*]

The International Union for the Conservation of Nature and Natural Resources (IUCN) was founded in 1948 as the International Union for the Protection of Nature (IUPN), but since 1990 has been known as the World Conservation Union. It is the world's biggest and most important conservation network, bringing together 82 countries, 111 government agencies, more than 800 non-government organisations (NGOs) and some 10,000 scientists and experts from 181 countries. The regional office for Europe and the permanent representation to the European Union is in Belgium at Boulevard Louis Schmidt 64, 1040 Brussels, Belgium, Tel: +32 2 7328299, *www.iucn.org* and the French committee is at the *Muséum national d'Historie Naturelle*, 36, rue Geoffry saint-Hilaire, 75005 Paris, Tel: 01 47077858.

8
Clothing, footwear and fashion

Although France is a major producer of clothing and footwear, shops attest to the globalisation of the clothing, footwear and fashion industries, particularly since 1 January 2005 when textile quotas were abandoned in accordance with World Trade Organisation (WTO) agreements and imports from China and other Asian countries grew apace. If you are new to the country, you may find this an advantage, as walking into clothing, footwear or fashion shops in France is much like walking into similar shops elsewhere in Europe. Nonetheless, differences exist. French sizes are uniformly to European norms, which differ from those of the UK or the USA. Clothing for men [*vêtements pour hommes*], women [*vêtements pour femmes*] and children [*vêtements pour enfants*] is mostly of French or European design and labelling, as are shoes and footwear [*chaussures*].

Care symbols [*Symboles d'entretien*]

Care symbols on garment labels [*étiquettes des vêtements*] indicate the recommended washing, bleaching, drying, ironing and dry cleaning. If you heed the symbols on a garment, it should not shrink, stretch or change colour unduly.

Now used on garments and textiles round the world, the symbols are registered trademarks developed starting in 1958 and now maintained by the International Association for Textile Care Labelling [*Groupement international de l'étiquetage pour l'entretien des textiles (GINTEX)*], BP 121, 92113 Clichy Cedex, *www.ginetex.org* with pages in English, *contact@gintetex.org* and its member association in France, *Comité français de l'etiquetage pour l'entretien des textiles (COFREET)*, 37 rue de Neuillly, BP 121, 92582 Clichy Cedex, *www.cofreet.com*. The most frequently used symbols are listed on the next page; for other symbols and further details, visit the GINTEX and COFREET websites.

Basic symbol	Label symbol	Care	Warning
Wash	95	Hot (95°C) Normal setting, normal rinse, normal spin	Do not wash
	60	Warm (60°C) Normal setting, normal rinse, normal spin	
	60	Warm (60°C) Reduced agitation, cooling rinse, gentle spin	
	40	Lukewarm (40°C) Normal setting, normal rinse, normal spin	
	40	Lukewarm (40°C) Reduced agitation, cooling rinse, gentle spin	
	40	Lukewarm (40°C) Little agitation, normal rinse, normal spin, do not hand wring	
	30	Cool (30°C) Little agitation, normal rinse, gentle spin	
		Lukewarm (40°C) hand wash	
Bleach	Cl	Can use chlorine bleach	Do not bleach
Dry		Hot (60°C) tumble dry	Do not tumble dry
		Warm (40°C) tumble dry	
Iron		High (200°C)	Do not iron
		Medium (150°C)	
		Low (100°C)	
Dry clean	A	Any solvent	Do not dry clean
	P	Any solvent except trichloroethylene	
	P	Any solvent except trichloroethylene, gentle programme	
	F	Petroleum solvent only	
	F	Petroleum solvent only, gentle programme	

Care symbols.

Children's clothing [*Vêtements pour enfants*]

As elsewhere in Continental Europe, children's clothing sizes are in centimetres length/height up to two years, and by age in years thereafter: 56 cm (newborn to 2 months old), 62 cm (2-4 months), 68 cm (4-6 months), 74 cm (6-9 months), 80 cm (9-12 months), 90 cm (2 years), 3 years, 4 years, 5 years, 6 years, 7 years, 8 years, 9 years, 10 years. So for children under two years old, use a measuring tape [*mètre ruban*] and the child's age to select sizes.

Clothing sizes [*Tailles des vêtements*]

Clothing labels carry French sizes and increasingly also other European and American/British sizes; the principal equivalents are listed below. Stocking sizes are the same as **shoe sizes**.

Men's sizes

French number	waist cm	European	American/ British numerical	American/ British name
T2	71–78 cm	46	36	Small
		48	38	
T3	79–86 cm	50	40	Medium
T4	87–94 cm	52	42	Large
		54	44	
T5	95–102 cm	56	46	Extra Large
T6	103–110 cm	58	48	

Men's shirt sizes

French number	chest cm	European	American/ British, by collar in inches	American/ British name
T2	83–90 cm	36	14	Small
		37	14 ½	Small
T3	91–98 cm	38	15	Medium
		39	15 ½	Medium
T4	99–106 cm	41	16	Large
		42	16 ½	Large
T5	107–114 cm	43	17	Extra Large
		44–45	17 ½	Extra Large
		46	18	Extra Large

Women's sizes

French number	trouser waist cm	blouse bust cm	European	American numerical	British numerical	American/ British name
T1	61–64	83–86	36		6	Extra Small
T2	65–68	87–90	38		8	Small
	69–72	91–94	40		10	Medium
T3	73–76	95–98	42	34	12	
	77–80	99–102	44	36	14	Large
T4	81–84	103–106	46	38	16	
	85–88	107–110	48	40	18	Extra Large
T5	89–92	111–114	50	42	20	
	95–98	115–118	52	44		

Children's sizes

European (height in cm)	American numerical	British (height in inches)
125	4	43
135	6	48
150	8	55
155	10	58
160	12	60
165	14	62

The above comparisons of size systems are at best approximate. Moreover, the systems themselves are flawed, because they relate to items of clothing and not to the wearers and because many of their designations have changed with time: a "Large" shirt of the 1970s might only be "Medium" today. These difficulties, exacerbated by the increasing internationalisation of the clothing trade, led in 2001 to a new inter-European standard for clothing sizes. Known by its standard number, EN 13402, it specifies three-digit size numbers related to body dimensions in centimetres, as shown on pictograms, of the sort already in use in France and other European countries. From 2006 on, across Europe, clothing will be labelled according to EN 13402, and the older national size systems will be phased out.

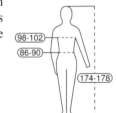

Clothing label size pictogram.

Haute couture

The high fashion of France, *haute couture*, has an English connection. In the 18th century, French art, architecture, fashions and music became popular across Europe. With advances in transport, wealthy women travelled by steamship and railway to Paris to shop, particularly for clothing and accessories, and Parisian creations were considered to be the best available. In 1846, an English couturier, Charles Frédéric Worth (1826-1895) went to Paris and set up a fashion house that soon gained international renown. In the late 19th century, wealthy women from as far as New York travelled to Paris to order Worth's creations. Worth set the stage for the great international names of fashion that followed, including Chanel, Yves Saint-Laurent, Pierre Cardin, Christian Dior, Christian Lacroix, Givenchy, Paco Rabanne, Guy Laroche and Ungaro.

Today, the designation *haute couture* is protected by law, and "only those companies on the list drawn up each year by a commission domiciled at the Ministry for Industry are entitled to avail themselves thereof" (*dont ne peuvent se prévaloir que les entreprises figurant sur la liste établie chaque année par une commission siégeant au ministère de l'Industrie*). The principal organisation dealing with *haute couture* is the *Fédération française de la couture du prêt à porter des couturiers et des créateurs de mode*, 100 rue du Faubourg Saint-Honoré, 75008 Paris, Tel: 01 42666444, *www.modeaparis.com* with pages in French and English. As indicated by the name of the organisation, the clothing sector now is divided into three parts: *haute couture* fashions for women, ready-to-wear [*prêt-à-porter*] and men's fashions [*mode masculine*].

Professional associations [*Fédérations professionnelles*]

The principal clothing and footwear professional associations are:

* Union of Textile Industries [*Union des Industries Textiles (UIT)*], whose members comprise most of the 1100 textile and clothing manufacturers in the country that together have some 100,000 employees. Head office: UIT, 37-39 rue de Neuilly, BP 121, 92110 Clichy, Tel: 01 47563100, *www.textile.fr*, with pages in French and summary pages in English.

* French Trade Association for the Shoe Industry [*Fédération Française de la Chaussure (FFC)*], whose members are the 173 small and medium-sized companies that together have some 17,500 employees. Head office: 51 rue de Miromesnil, 75008 Paris, Tel: 01 44717171, *www.chaussuredefrance.com*, with pages in French and summary pages in English.

Second-hand clothing [*Vêtements d'occasion*]

There are many second-hand clothing shops, listed in the **Yellow pages** (Chapter 31) in three categories:

- *Friperies*: second-hand clothing speciality shops, often offering specific clothing sectors, such as retro, women's fashions, children's clothing, etc.

- *Dépôts-vente: vêtements*: second-hand shops offering clothing, sometimes for specific sectors.

- *Discount, stocks, dégriffés*: Discount, stocks and off-labels, usually new clothing at low prices.

There's an online second-hand clothing shop at *www.vetements-occasion.com*, in which private individuals and smaller companies place advertisements with email addresses for buyer responses.

Shoe sizes [*Pointures*]

European size	Mondopoint size	UK size	US men's size	US women's size	US children's size
33	225	1			1.5
34	228	2		3.5	2.5
35	231	2.5		4	3
36	235	3.5		5	4
37	238	4		5.5	4.5
38	245	5	6	6.5	5.5
39	251	6	7	7.5	6.5
40	254	6.5	7.5	8	7
41	257	7.5	8.5	9	
42	260	8	9	9.5	
43	267	9	10	10.5	
44	273	9.5	10.5	11	
45	279	10.5	11.5		
46	285	11.5	12.5		
47	291	12	13		

Most shoes and footwear, as well as stockings, are sized according to the European system, in which sizes are 1.5 times the inside length in centimetres of a shoe. For instance, a shoe with an inside length of 28 cm is a size 42. The system originated in France [*pointure française*], where it also is known as the Paris Point System [*le point de Paris*], after the custom of old-time bootmakers of using three stitches for each two centimetres of welt, which is why each increment in size is equal to 2/3 cm. Starting in the early 1990s, the sizes of shoes and other footwear, particularly those sold internationally, also are designated in the *Mondopoint* system according to international standard ISO 9701. In Mondopoint, a size is the length in millimetres of the foot it best fits; widths also may be stated, so a 280/110 shoe fits a foot that is 280 mm long and 110 mm wide at the instep. Some shoes and boots, particularly those made by multinational athletic shoe makers, are sized in American, English, European and Mondopoint systems. Equivalents of the most sold sizes are listed above.

Testing for harmful substances in textiles
[*Contrôle de substances indésirables à textile*]

Chemicals are used in dyeing, preserving, softening and in other ways to alter the basic properties of textiles, as used in clothing. Many of the chemicals used are toxic, principally formaldehyde and the Azo dyes. Consequently, minimising the content of harmful substances is one of the measures of textile quality, as promoted by *Association pour la promotion de l'assurance qualité dans la filière du textile et de l'habillement (ASQUAL)*, 14, rue des Reculettes, 75013 Paris, *www.asqual.com*. ASQUAL is the authority in France for issuing certificates of conformance with one of two European textile product requirements: Oeko-Tex 100 for maximum content of chemicals hazardous to health, and Oeko-Tex 1000 for maximum content of compounds posing environmental hazard, and products so certified may carry Oeko-Tex labels. For further details, visit the international Oeko-Tex website at *www.oeko-tex.com*, with pages in English, French and German.

Oeko-Tex 100 label.

9
Concise gazetteer

France was long the most centralised yet most rural country in Europe. The power of the monarchy and then of the Republic was centred in Paris, which was the only large city until 1945, when, of the country's population of 40 million, a third lived on farms and only half in urban areas. The France of today differs, both because the population is half again as large, around 60 million, and because three-quarters of all residents live in cities, towns and villages. Across the country, medium-sized cities are growing and becoming economic and cultural capitals of their surroundings. Any of them, as well as the large cities of Paris, Lille, Lyons and Marseilles, could be the topic of a book larger than this one. Moreover, more has been written about Paris than any other city in the world.

Consequently, this Chapter is an A-Z of the human geography of the country, exclusive of its principal cities that are worthy of more extensive description.

Administrative divisions [*Divisions principales*]

For administrative purposes, the country is divided into **Départements**, which are an outcome of the *Révolution*, as in 1790 they replaced the former **Provences** that originally were territories of the Roman Empire. From 1972 on, the *Départements* are grouped into **Régions**. Each Département is divided into **Arrondissements**. In turn, the *Arrondissements* are subdivided into **Cantons**, and the *Cantons* into **Communes**. Moreover, nine of ten *communes* are members of *Établissements Publics de Coopération Intercommunale (EPCI)*.

So, as many as six names may be associated with the place where you live: the *commune* and often the EPCI of which it is a member, the *Canton*, the *Département* (and its number), the *Région* and the ancient *Provence*. Moreover, if you live on a coast, the name of the *Canton* may be applied to it, such as Côte Vermeille, the southern part of the coast of the Pyrénées-Orientales Département, or the wine you buy may carry the name of the ancient *Provence*, such as Côte Roussillion.

Alsace

Alsace is a **Région** in the north-eastern part of the country, bordering on Germany to the east and Switzerland to the south, and consisting of two **Départements**, Bas-Rhin (no. 67) and Haut-Rhin (no. 68). Its ancient name is *Alsatia*, the root of the word Alsatian in English, which is both an adjective and the name of the local language of Alsace.

Alsace was long subject to territorial dispute between France and Germany. Originally, it was part of Lorraine before it was absorbed by the German Empire, though in 1648 it was mostly returned to France. But in 1871, after the Franco-Prussian War, it was again ceded to Germany as part of the Imperial territory of Alsace-Lorraine, the location of some of the bloodiest battles of the First World War, after which, in 1918, it was returned to France. It has been part of France since, though France was occupied by Germany in 1940. Its capital city is Strasbourg, since 1949 the seat of the Council of Europe [*Conseil de l'Europe*], and today it is one of the more international areas of Europe, with residents crossing the Rhine daily to work in another country. Alsatian wines, particularly white wines, are regarded highly, and its traditional cabbage dish, *choucroute*, or *sürkrüt* in German, is widely known under its name in Alsacian, *sauerkraut*.

Arc de Triomphe

The Arc de Triomphe stands in Paris at the centre of Place Charles De Gaulle (named Place de l'Étoile until 1970), now the world's largest roundabout and the meeting point of 12 radiating avenues. In 1806, it was commissioned by Napoléon in commemoration of his victories, and was completed 30 years later, in 1836. In 1921, it was made a war memorial and the tomb of the Unknown Soldier [*Soldat Inconnu*]; every evening, at 18:30, a flame is lit in honour of all who have fallen in battle.

Arrondissements

The *Arrondissements* are subdivisions of the **Départements**, created in 1800 to replace the districts of 1789. An *Arrondissement* usually comprises a number of **Communes**, though in Lyon, Marseilles and Paris, the *Arrondissements* are subdivisions of the *Communes*. The principal function is implicit in the word, which comes from *arrondiss*, the lengthened stem of the verb *arrondir*, meaning to fill out or round off. In each *Arrondissement*, there is a *Sous-préfecture*, which is its **Administrative centre** (Chapter 21). As at 31 December 2005, there are 342 *Arrondissements* in the country, of which 13 are abroad.

143

Avignon

Avignon, the relatively small Administrative Centre of the *Département* of Vaucluse (No. 84), has played a key role in the history of Europe. Established by the Romans in the first century BC on the east bank of the Rhone River, it briefly was the capital of the Medieval western world. In 1309, Pope Clemet V chose to reside at Avignon, not Rome, and initiated a period of 70 years in which all the Popes were French and all resided at Avignon. Since, Avignon has been nicknamed "The other Rome" [*Altera Roma*] and the "City of the Popes" [*Cité des Papes*]. The grandiose Popes' Palace [*Palais des Papes*] remains, as do remnants of the Saint Bénezet Bridge [*Point Saint Bénezet*] built in the 12th century and the city walls [*Remparts d'Avignon*] built in the 17th century. Today, Avignon is renowned for its annual theatre festival as well as for its museums and cultural monuments. For further information, visit the Avignon and Provence website at *www.avignon-et-provence.com*, with pages in French and in English.

Banlieues

The *banlieues* are the outlying residential areas around city centres. Originally, in the Middle Ages, a *banlieu* was an area under the jurisdiction of a city, extending about 4 km outside its fortified wall; the word comes from the Germanic *bann* ("authority") and the Latin *leuca* ("league", about 4 km). The people of the early *banlieues* were farmers, tradesmen and artisans essential to the economy of the city. By the mid 17th century, city authority over their surrounding *banlieues* declined, and the word *banlieue* came to mean an outlying residential district. Some *banlieues*, such as Saint-Cloud, Sceaux and Versailles, became aristocratic suburbs. Others became working-class districts, starting in the 19th century, when industrialisation triggered the migrations from rural areas that swelled the populations of urban centres. In the early 20th century, the working-class *banlieues* grew in step with the influx of immigrant workers, mainly from Italy, Poland and Spain, who came to fill jobs in the burgeoning industrial sector. In the 1920s and 1930s, these *banlieues* became home to a large industrial working class, with its own social and cultural identity as well as collective spirit to improve its lot. In the mid 1930s, the *banlieues rouges* became a political factor, with the success of *Le Front Populaire*, a left-wing coalition.

The character of the *banlieues* changed markedly during *Les Trente glorieuses*, the name given by economist Jean Fourastié (1907-1990) to the period of prosperity from the end of the Second World War in 1945 until the oil crisis of 1973. From 1955 to 1975, some three million *logements sociaux* – local authority social housing units similar to the Council Flats of the UK – were built in the *banlieues* to alleviate the post-war housing shortage, made more acute by the new influx of immigrants from the African continent. Most of the new housing built was in high-rise estates that became known as *grands ensembles*.

Les Trente glorieuses came to an abrupt end in 1973, when the oil crisis triggered a recession that in turn brought about factory closures, layoffs and unemployment. The *banlieues* suffered an exodus of their more affluent residents – managers and skilled workers – to jobs elsewhere, and thereby an upswing in the proportions of their residents on low incomes, particularly in estates that had been built to house the workers in the factories that had closed down. As the low income residents predominantly were immigrants, the *grands ensembles* became ethnic ghettos. That problem was first recognised and addressed in 1976, with the enactment of the *Habitat et vie sociales* initiative to improve living conditions in the *banlieues*. There have been numerous similar initiatives since, some at the European level, such as *Banlieues d'Europe*, 13a, rue du Hohwald, 67000 Strasbourg, Tel: 03 88222443, *www.banlieues-europe.com*, with pages in French and in English, an initiative dedicated to combating cultural exclusion in the *banlieues* of 14 countries.

Nonetheless, the problems of the *banlieues* persist and have precipitated widespread disaffection that has led to violence, most recently the riots of October and November 2005. The roots of the problems are painfully apparent in the lower standards of living and high rates of unemployment, particularly among the predominantly Muslim youth of the banlieues. As this book goes to press, measures are being enacted to address the problems, including strict controls of unemployment benefits, tax breaks for businesses locating in the *banlieues*, apprenticeships for teenagers and support for local associations.

Bercy

Bercy, a district in the 12th *Arrondissement* bordering the Seine, may be the oldest settlement in Paris, as archaeological excavations there have uncovered artefacts dating from 4000 BC. Today, Bercy is the home of a large entertainment and sports complex, *Palais Omnisports de Paris-Bercy (POPB)*, the railway terminal for the SNCF *auto-trains*, *Gare de Bercy*, and the Ministry of Finance (*Ministère des finances*), with which it is so closely associated that in everyday usage, Bercy is synonymous with the Ministry.

Bordeaux

The city of Bordeaux is an inland port and the **Administrative centre** (Chapter 21) of the *Département* of Gironde (No. 33) as well as of the *Région* of Aquitaine. It is one of the principal ports of France and the commercial and cultural centre of the south-western part of the country. Around the world, it is perhaps best known for its wines. For further information, visit the city website at *www.ville-bordeaux.com*.

Bretagne

Known as Brittany in English, Bretagne is the north-west peninsula of the country and a former Province, most of which now is the *Région* of Bretagne, encompassing four *Départements*: Côtes d'Armor (No. 22), Finistère (29), Ille-et-Vilaine (35) and Morbihan (56). The principal cities are Brest, Lorient, Nantes, Quimper and Rennes. Bretagne is known for its many megalithic monuments and for the history of the Celtic Bretons that link it with Great Britain. For further information, visit the Bretagne *Région* website at *www.region-bretagne.fr*. Bretagne has its own minority language, *le Breton* and its own group espousing independence, *Armée révolutionnaire bretonne (ARB)*.

Camargue

Camargue is an alluvial island between two arms of the Rhône River where it meets the Mediterranean Sea in the *Département* of Bouches-du-Rhône (No. 13) east of the city of Montpellier. About a third of its area of 930 km^2 comprises lakes and marshlands, and about 85,000 hectares are a natural reserve. Its indigenous species include pink flamingos, white Camaguais horses and black fighting bulls, raised for export to Spain. There is an equestrian school, and there are numerous facilities for boating and riding. The traditional gathering in May of each year of Gypsies at its principal town, the port of Saintes-Maries de la Mer, has become *Festival de la Camargue*, offering cultural and culinary events. For further information, visit the Camargue website at *www.camargue.fr*.

Cantons

A *Canton* is a subdivision of an **Arrondissement** that contains several **Communes.** The *Cantons* of a **Département** elect one member each to its governing *Conseil Général*. In neighbouring Switzerland, a *Canton* is one of the 26 sovereign states that together form the Swiss Confederation (*Confédération Suisse*).

Caves [*Grottes*]

There are more subterranean caves [*grottes*] in France than in any other European country. Many of the caves bear traces of occupation by prehistoric peoples, most famously the *Grotte Chauvet* in the *Département* of Ardèche (No. 07), known for its engravings and paintings from the Palaeolithic era, some 30,000 years ago. The *Grotte de Massabielle at Lourdes* in the *Département* of Hautes-Pyrénées (No. 65) is a Christian pilgrimage site; in 1858, a local shepherd girl, Bernadette Soubirous (1844-1879) was several times led by a vision of the Virgin Mary to its healing springs. In 1933, the Catholic Church canonised her to St. Bernadette. Austrian novelist Franz Werfel (1890-1945) was so moved by a visit to Lourdes in the late

146

1930s that in 1941, in exile in the USA, he wrote "The song of Bernadette", which in 1943 was made into a film starring Jennifer Jones that won four Academy Awards (Oscars) in 1944.

The caves open to the public are listed by *L'Association National des Cavernes Aménagées pour le tourisme (ANECAT)*, 38390 Balme les Grottes, Tel: 04 74906049, *www.grottes.net*, with pages in French and in English.

Champs-Élysées

Among the most famed avenues in the world, Avenue des Champs-Élysées in the 8th *Arrondissement* of Paris extends 3 km straight, from Place de la Concorde to the **Arc de Triomphe** at Place Charles de Gaulle. The name, which means "Elysian Fields", originally designated fields and parklands, through which a grand avenue was built in the mid 18th century. Today, the Avenue is lined with cafés, cinemas, hotels and luxury shops and is a major tourist attraction as well as a principal thoroughfare of the city.

Chartres Cathedral

The Cathedral of Our Lady of Chartres [*Cathédrale Notre-Dame de Chartres*] in high gothic style [*apogée époque gothique*] is often said to be the greatest human artefact of the western world. Located at Chartres, now the **Administrative centre** (Chapter 21) of the *Département* of Eure-et-Loir (No. 28), it was built in 1164-1220 to replace a Romanesque cathedral that had burned down in 1020. Since 876, the Cathedral has housed the *Sancta Camisia*, believed to be the cloak of the Virgin Mary, and to this day, faithful from round the world come to the Cathedral to honour the relic. For further information, visit the City of Chartres website at *www.ville-chartres.com*.

Château

Across the country, there are magnificent *Châteaux*, castles, palaces and mansions built from the middle ages on. Though they vary widely in size and style, all were built to house a Lord and symbolise his power over the surrounding lands that made the château self-sufficient. The earliest *châteaux* were fortified [*châteaux forts*], but later, particularly from the Renaissance on, the *châteaux* were unfortified. By definition, a *château* is in a rural setting; its urban equivalent is a palace [*palais*], and indeed some palaces, such as the Louvre in Paris, originally were built as *châteaux* but became palaces as they were enveloped by growing cities. Three famed large *châteaux* are Fontainebleau, Pierrefonds and Versailles.

Communes

A *commune* is the smallest administrative division governed by a mayor [*Maire*] and a municipal council [*Conseil municipal*] and is equivalent to a "municipality" in English. As a rule, a *commune* is a subdivision of a **Canton**, though save for Paris, cities and towns consist of a single *commune*. As at 31 December 2005, there are 36,568 *communes* in the country. Nine out of ten *communes* are members of *Établissements Publics de Coopération Intercommunale (EPCI)*, of three sorts:

* 14 urban municipalities [*Communautés urbaines*]
* 156 agglomerations [*Communautés d'agglomération*]
* 2,333 communities of municipalities [*Communautés de communes*].

Corse

La Corse – the name means "scented isle" – is an island south of the mainland, the country's largest and the fourth largest in the Mediterranean Sea. In 1767, it was bought by France after having been Italian for several centuries. Administratively, it is organised in two **Départements** (Nos. 2A and 2B) with their **Administrative centres** at the principal towns of Ajaccio and Bastia. It has its own minority language and its own group espousing independence. Topographically, it is mountainous; the summit of the highest peak, Mont Cinto, is at 2710 m. Agriculture, fishing and tourism are its principal activities. For further information, visit the official Corse website at *www.corse.fr*, with pages in French and English.

Côte d'Azur

The Côte d'Azur ("Azure Coast") is the French part of the Riviera, the coastal strip of south-eastern France and northern Italy that has a subtropical climate and vegetation. It extends westward to just south of Marseilles and includes the luxury resort towns of Cannes, Monte Carlo and Nice, made famous in the 1920s by wealthy foreigners, particularly the English gentry, who stayed there. For further information, visit the official website at *www.cote.azur.fr*, with pages in French, English, German, Italian, Russian and Spanish.

Départements

The 96 *Départements* are numbered mostly alphabetically by name from 01 to 95, with Corsica, number 20 in the listing, having two *Départements*, 2A and 2B. The numbers are according to the **Official geographic code** and appear in the first two digits of **Postcodes** (Chapter 36) and until 1 January 2008, in the last two digits of **Car number plates** (Chapter 4) and as well in many private-sector listings of entities across the country, such as in the listings of outlets in the catalogues or advertisements of **Chain stores** (Chapter 40). In each *Département*, there is a

Préfecture, which is its **Administrative centre** (Chapter 21). So the *Départements* are the most visible evidence of administration in everyday life. The map of the *Départements* on the next page is reproduced by permission from the Flags of the World (FOTW) website at *www.crwflags.com/fotw/flags*, where it is in colour and supports clickable linking between the map and text descriptions.

Please see the next page for key to *départements*.

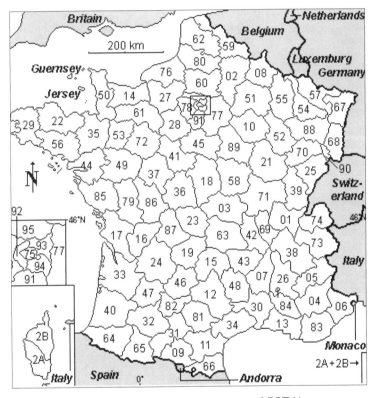

The Departments; map courtesy of FOTW.

Département names:

01 Ain	35 Ille-et-Vilaine	71 Saône-et-Loire
02 Aisne	36 Indre	72 Sarthe
03 Allier	37 Indre-et-Loire	73 Savoie
04 Alpes-de-Haute-Provence	38 Isère	74 Haute-Savoie
05 Hautes-Alpes	39 Jura	75 Paris
06 Alpes-Maritimes	40 Landes	76 Seine-Maritime
07 Ardèche	41 Loir-et-Cher	77 Seine-et-Marne
08 Ardennes	42 Loire	78 Yvelines
09 Ariège	43 Haute-Loire	79 Deux-Sèvres
10 Aube	44 Loire-Atlantique	80 Somme
11 Aude	45 Loiret	81 Tarn
12 Aveyron	46 Lot	82 Tarn-et-Garonne
13 Bouches-du-Rhône	47 Lot-et-Garonne	83 Var
14 Calvados	48 Lozère	84 Vaucluse
15 Cantal	49 Maine-et-Loire	85 Vendée
16 Charente	50 Manche	86 Vienne
17 Charente-Maritime	51 Marne	87 Haute-Vienne
18 Cher	52 Haute-Marne	88 Vosges
19 Corrèze	53 Mayenne	89 Yonne
2A Corse-du-Sud	54 Meurthe-et-Moselle	90 Territoire de Belfort
2B Haute-Corse	55 Meuse	91 Essonne
21 Côte d'Or	56 Morbihan	92 Hauts-de-Seine
22 Côtes d'Armor	57 Moselle	93 Seine-Saint-Denis
23 Creuse	58 Nièvre	94 Val-de-Marne
24 Dordogne	59 Nord	95 Val-d'Oise
25 Doubs	60 Oise	
26 Drôme	61 Orne	The four overseas *Départements* [*Départements d'outre mer (DOM)*] have three-digit numbers:
27 Eure	62 Pas-de-Calais	
28 Eure-et-Loir	63 Puy-de-Dôme	
29 Finistère	64 Pyrénées-Atlantiques	
30 Gard	65 Hautes-Pyrénées	971 Guadeloupe
31 Haute-Garonne	66 Pyrénées-Orientales	972 Martinque
32 Gers	67 Bas-Rhin	973 Guyane
33 Gironde	68 Haut-Rhin	974 Réunion
34 Hérault	69 Rhône	
	70 Haute-Saône	

DOM-TOM

The ten overseas areas together are designated *DOM-TOM*, originally an acronym for *Département d'outre-mer – Territoire d'outre-mer*, but by constitutional amendment of 28 March 2003, *Territoire d'outre-mer (TOM)* was revoked as an official designation, so it is not used separately. The overseas areas that are not *Départements* now are called Overseas communities [*Collectivités d'outre-mer*]. Nonetheless, the designation TOM persists in unofficial uses, perhaps by force of habit.

The four DOMs each have an **Administrative centre** (Chapter 21) and function as do the *Départements* of Metropolitan France. Three of the DOM are grouped by location in the designation *Départements français d'Amérique (DFA)*:

* Guadeloupe, *Département* No. 971, an island in the Caribbean

* Guyane, called French Guiana in English, *Département* No. 973, a country on north coast of South America

* Martinique, *Département* No. 972, an island off north coast of South America

The fourth DOM, Réunion, Déparatement No. 974, is an island in Indian Ocean, off south-east coast of Africa

The six Overseas communities [*Collectivités d'outre-mer*] have differing legal status, which is why the TOM collective designation was revoked.

* Mayotte, an island in Indian Ocean, off south-east coast of Africa, is an overseas local community [*collectivité départementale d'outre-mer*).

* Nouvelle Calédonie, an archipelago in south-west Pacific Ocean, has unique legal status (*sui generis*) and is designated by its name only.

* Polynésie Française, an island in south-west Pacific Ocean, east of Australia, is an overseas country [*pay d'outre-mer*].

* Territories in the Antarctic and the Arctic [*Terres australes et antarctiques françaises (TAAF)*] are protectorates administered from Saint-Pierre on Réunion.

* Saint Pierre et Miquelon, an island in North Atlantic Ocean, south of Newfoundland, is an overseas community.

* Wallis et Futuna, islands in south-west Pacific Ocean, east of Australia, comprise an overseas community.

For further information on the individual DOM-TOMs, visit the collective website at *www.domtomfr.com*.

Eiffel Tower [*Tour Eiffel*]

The Eiffel Tower in Paris is among the world's most-known landmarks. Each year it draws some six million visitors and thereby is the country's leading tourist attraction. The concept for the tower was born in 1884, when Émile Nouguier and Maurice Koechlin, the principal engineers in the company founded by engineer Alexandre Gustave Eiffel (1832-1923) joined with architect Stephen Sauvestre to present their vision of a tall tower at the *Exposition des Arts Décoratifs*. The immediate result was a competition for a 300-metre-high tower to be built for the Paris World Exhibition of 1889. Some 700 proposed designs came in, and the Eiffel-Nouguier-Koechlin-Sauvestre design won. Construction began in 1887, and the tower was completed for the opening of the Exhibition in May 1889, held to celebrate the Centennial of the *Révolution*. When completed in March 1889, the tower was 312 m high and thereby the world's tallest structure, a record it retained until 1930. When built, Mr. Eiffel was granted a permit to let it stand for 20 years, to recoup his investment. But with the advent of radio, it was found useful and kept after its original permit expired.

France Congrès

France Congrès is an organisation of the offices of the Mayor of 49 cities and towns across the country that have facilities for conferences, exhibitions. It works with various national tourist organisations, the French Caterers' Association [*Traiteurs de France*] and the railways to enable its members to offer venues to national and international organisers. For further information, contact its permanent head office at 19 rue Penthièvre, 75008 Paris, Tel: 01 42651001, *www.france-congres.org* with a locator map of all member cities and towns and with pages in French and English.

Hexagon [*Hexagone*]

The map of mainland France [*France métropolitaine*] resembles a hexagon (six-sided geometric figure). Consequently, *L'Hexagone* is an everyday synonym for *France métropolitaine*.

Llíva

The town of Llíva in the *Département* of Pyrénées-Orientales (No. 66) is one of the two foreign enclaves in the country; the other is **Monaco**. Llíva, once the capital of the ancient Catalan kingdom of Cerdagne, was not included in the lands ceded in 1659 by Spain to the French crown by the Treaty of the Pyrnees and consequently remained Spanish. Today, though small, just 12 km^2, Llíva is a tourist attraction, known for its annual music festival held since 1908. For further information, visit the official website at *www.lliva.com*.

Maghreb

The Maghreb takes its name from Arabic and designates the region of North Africa west of the Nile and north of the Sahara Desert. It includes Algeria, Libya, Mauritania, Morocco and Tunisia, though in France the name often is applied collectively to the former French colonies of Algeria, Morocco and Tunisia that have been sources of immigration since the 1960s. For further information on the Maghreb, visit the official website of the *Union du Maghreb arabe* at *www.maghrebarabe.org/fr*.

Metropolitan France [*France métropolitaine*]

Metropolitan France designates the principal part of the country on the mainland of Europe, including the island of **Corse** (Corsica in English) and excluding the overseas areas of the **DOM-TOM**. Without Corsica, *France métropolitaine* is referred to as *France continentale*.

Monaco

The Principality of Monaco [*Principauté de Monaco*] on the Mediterranean coast, near the Italian border and surrounded by the *Département* of Alpes-Maritimes (No. 06), is one of the two foreign enclaves in the country; the other is **Llíva**. Though under the protection of France, Monaco is an independent principality, that with an area of 1.95 km^2, is the second smallest independent State in the world, after the Vatican City. It has been ruled since 1419 by the House of Grimaldi and today is a constitutional monarchy. Its economy is based strongly on tourism, including gambling at the casino at Monte Carlo, but it also has a small cosmetics industry. For further information, visit the official visitors website at *www.visitmonaco.com* in French and English.

Newer architecture [*Architecture plus récente*]

Since the 1970s, the government has supported numerous major architectural projects, principally in Paris. Five of note, in chronological order of their date of completion:

* Centre Pompidou of the arts, at Beauborg in Paris, designed by Italian architect Renzo Piano and British architect Richard Rogers, completed in 1977. Website at *www.cnac-gp.fr* with pages in French, English and Spanish.

* Institut du Monde Arabe, at Place Mohammed-V in Paris, designed by French architects Jean Nouvel and Pierre Soria, completed in 1987. Website at *www.imarabe.org* with pages in French, Arabic and English.

* The glass pyramid at the Louvre museum in Paris, designed by American architect Ioeh Ming Pei, completed in 1989. Website at *www.louvre.fr*, with pages in French and English.

* Grande Arche de la Défense centre in Paris, designed by Danish architect Otto Von Spreckelsen, opened in 1989. Website at *www.grandearche.com* with pages in French and English.

* Millau Viaduct, a cable-stayed bridge on the River Tarn valley on the motorway between Paris and Barcelona; it spans 2.5 km and its tallest piers are 240 m high, the highest in the world; designed by British architect Norman Foster, opened in 2004-2005.

Notre Dame

The Cathedral of Notre Dame de Paris in high gothic style [*apogée de l'époque gothique*] stands on Île de la Cité, an island in the River Seine in Paris. It was built in 1163-1345 on the site of the first Christian church in the city, Saint-Étienne Basilica, in a style that departed markedly from the earlier Romanesque. It has been the venue of significant events throughout history, including the crowning of Henry VI of England as King of France in 1431, the crowning of Napoleon Bonaparte as Emperor of France in 1804 and the Beautification of Joan of Arc in 1909. Today, it is a major tourist attraction, offering concerts of sacred music and tours for scholars as well as the public. For further information, visit the Notre Dame website at *www.cathedraledeparis.com*, with pages in French, English, German and Spanish.

Préfecture

A *Préfecture* is the ***Chef-lieu*** (Chapter 21) of a ***Département*** and usually is located in its principal city.

Provences

In 1790, the *Provences* were replaced by the ***Départements***, and many of their names remain, perhaps most famously in Provence in the southeastern part of the country that now extends over all or parts of the Departments of Alpes-de-Haute-Provence (04), Alpes-Maritimes (06), Bouches-du-Rhône (13), Var (83) and Vaucluse (84). Some of the Province names have been incorporated in modern administrative names, including those of some of the *Régions*. Though they no longer are administrative entities, the *Provences* still reflect the basic geographic, economic and cultural divisions of the country. The map of the ancient *Provences* below is reproduced by permission from the Flags of the World (FOTW) website at *www.crwflags.com/fotw/flags*, where it is in colour and supports clickable linking between the map and text descriptions.

The ancient Provinces, map courtesy of FOTW.

Régions

There are 22 *Régions*, each consisting of two to nine *Départements*. Each *Région* has a chief administrative officer, the *Préfet de region*, who is the *Préfet* of the **Département** in which the **Chef-lieu** (Chapter 21) of the *Région* is located. The map of the *Régions* below is reproduced by permission from the Flags of the World (FOTW) website at *www.crwflags.com/fotw/flags*, where it is in colour and supports clickable linking between the map and text descriptions.

The Régions, map courtesy of FOTW.

The *Régions* with constituent *Département* numbers in parentheses:

Alsace (67, 68)
Aquitaine (24, 33, 40, 47, 64)
Auvergne (3, 15, 43, 63)
Basse-Normandie (14, 50, 61)
Bourgogne (21, 58, 71, 89)
Bretagne (22, 29, 35, 56)
Centre (18, 28, 36, 37, 41, 45)
Champagne-Ardenne (8, 10, 51, 52)
Corse (2A, 2B)
Franche-Comté (25, 39, 70)
Haute-Normandie (27, 76)
Île-de-France (75, 77, 78, 91, 92, 93, 94, 95)
Languedoc-Roussillon (11, 30, 34, 48, 66)
Limousin (19, 25, 87)
Lorraine (54, 55, 57, 88)
Midi-Pyrénées (9, 12, 31, 32, 46, 65, 81, 82)
Nord-Pas-de-Calais (59, 62)
Pays de la Loire (44, 49, 85)

Picardie (2, 60, 80)
Poitou-Charentes (16, 17, 79, 86)
Provence-Alpes-Côte d'Azur (4, 6, 13, 83, 84)
Rhône-Alpes (1, 5, 7, 26, 38, 42, 69, 73, 74)

Sous-préfecture

A *Sous-préfecture* is the **Administrative centre** (Chapter 21) of an *Arrondissement* and usually is located in its principal city or town.

Valréas

Valréas, a *Canton* comprising four *Communes* located in the *Département* of Drôme (No. 26) is the country's sole *Canton enclave*, because it is part of the *Département* of Vaucluse (No. 84), not Drôme. The reason is connected with the residence of the Popes at **Avignon**. Originally part of the Province of Dauphiné, Valréas became part of the County of Venaissin [*Comtat Venaissin*] that passed to the King in 1271 and then to the papacy in 1274. In 1791, the citizens of the County chose by plebiscite to rejoin France. In 1793, when the borders between *Départements* were set, Valréas was not included in the part of the County in Vaucluse. Though the citizens of the neighbouring *Canton* of St-Paul-Trios-Châteaux were pleased to be in Drôme, the citizens of Valréas were not. They wished to preserve their history as a former papal enclave, and that they have done to this day. For further information, visit the Valréas website at *www.ot-valreas.info*, with pages in French and English.

10
Crimes, wrongs and countermeasures

Security ranks among the greater worries of the citizenry, and it was a key topic in the 2002 presidential and parliamentary election. As this book goes to press, Interior Minister Nicolas Sarkozy is one of the country's more popular politicians, in part because of his hard line on crime.

Yet, international comparisons imply that crime is less of a problem in France than in many other countries: in proportion to its population, France is not in the top 20 in the world in numbers of police, reported crimes or people imprisoned*. In part that enviable standing may be due to having well-organised police forces with traditions that imbue *esprit de corps*. But it's also due to widespread concern, from the grassroots up: in 1987, Gilbert Bonnemaison, a Member of Parliament, founded the European Forum for Urban Safety, now a pre-eminent Non-Governmental Organisation (NGO) dedicated to combating crime across Europe.

Many of the principles of law enforcement have French roots. Historically most famous, perhaps, is the Guillotine, devised in 1789 by Paris doctor Joseph Ignace Guillotin (1738-1814) and used for capital punishment by beheading from 1792 to 1977. In 1981, capital punishment was abolished, but the Guillotine survives, not least in English, as a synonym for set termination of parliamentary debate.

The Economist, Pocket World in Figures, 2006 edition, p.99.

Arrests [*Arrestations*]

The police make arrests of persons suspected of **infractions** but usually are not involved in matters of Civil law [*Droit civil*]. If you are arrested by the police, you normally can be detained for no more than 24 hours, or at the most 48 hours, before initiation of an indictment [*la mise en examen*], except in cases involving narcotics [*stupéfiants*] or terrorism [*terrorisme*] for which the detention limit is four days. The custody officer [*L'officier de police judiciaire*] is responsible for notifying the Public prosecutor's office [*Le Parquet*] and for informing you of the grounds for detention and your rights, which include:

157

- Speak with a lawyer, at the start of and after the 20th and 36th hour of detention, save for narcotics and terrorism cases when special rules apply.
- Notify a relative or an employer, unless opposed by the Prosecutor.
- Be examined by a doctor.

Within three hours of the start of your detention, the police must notify your family and if required, summon a doctor. If required by the investigation, an intimate body search may be performed only by a doctor.

Upon being indicted, you may be subject to temporary detention [*La détention provisoire*] in only three instances:

- the indictment is for a crime punishable by imprisonment for 10 years or more
- the indictment is for an offence punishable by correctional imprisonment for three years or more
- you defy or fail to respect judicial authority.

The duration of Temporary detention depend on the severity of the infraction and on whether the indictment is for a crime [*crime*] or for an offence [*délit*]. For further details of **your rights**, see the brochure on the Rights of suspects [*Les fiches de la justice; Les droits des personnes mises en cause pénalement*] published by the Ministry of Justice.

Companies for Republican Security
[*Compagnies Républicaines de Sécurité (CRS)*]

The CRS is an elite police force of mobile units that comprise the general reserve of the **National police**. Created in 1944 after the liberation, its initial task was to ensure restoration of public order and government in the country. Since then, the CRS remit has expanded to include everyday security, policing ports, airports and motorways and escorting high-ranking national and international executives, legislators and diplomats. These tasks are similar to those of the mobile units of the **Gendarmerie**, so CRS officers sometimes are mistaken for Gendarmerie officers. The two are easily distinguished from each other: CRS officers have blue uniforms with red CRS badges, and the *Gendarmerie Mobile* officers have black uniforms with stylised flaming grenade badges. The head office of the CRS is at Place Beauvau, 75008 Paris Cedex 08, unofficial website: *www-crs.policenationale.com*.

Domestic violence [*Violence conjugale*]

Domestic violence [*violence conjugale*], also called family violence [*violence familiale*], takes place whenever a person tries to control their partner or other family members by aberrant means including assault, rape and sexual abuse, threats, humiliation, financial exploitation and social isolation, as in forbidding contact with family or friends. Victims of domestic violence may live in fear, both for themselves and for their children, even after they have left an abusive relationship. As in most countries, domestic violence is the most frequent human rights violation in France: on average, it causes the death of a woman every four days and of a man every 16 days; one death in ten is caused by battering without the intent to kill; 31% of all crimes involving domestic violence are connected with separation; 95% of the premeditated murders by ex-partners are committed by men, most in rural environments.*

Accordingly, many public and private organisations deal with the problems of domestic and workplace violence; the eight largest are:

• *Association européenne contre les violences faites aux femmes au travail (AVFT)*, an organisation that is an advisor to the United Nations and is concerned with the problems of physical and psychological abuse of women in the workplace, BP 60108, 75561 Paris Cedex 12, Tel: 01 45842424, *www.avft.org*.

• *Association nationale contre les abus sexuels commis par les professionnels de santé (ANCAS – CPPS)*, an organisation dedicated to combating abuses of women by health sector professionals; head office at 9 villa d'Este, 75013 Paris, *perso.wanadoo.fr/ancas.cpps*

• *Centres d'Information sur les Droits des Femmes (CIDF)*, a national network of 119 centres offering expertise and counselling on all aspects of women's rights, *www.infofemmes.com* with an interactive locator map of the centres across the country.

• *Collectif Féministe Contre le Viol*, a Paris-based organisation that supports the national rape crisis hotline at freephone 08 00059595 and provides counselling to victims of assault, Tour Mantoue, 9 villa d'Este, 75013 Paris, *www.cfcv.asso.fr*.

• *Fédération Nationale Solidarité Femmes*, an extensive network that lobbies for women's rights and offers a broad range of support services, including a domestic violence information line at 01 40338060 with counsellors speaking Arabic, Berber, English, German and Spanish as well as French, Mondays to Saturdays, 07:30-23:30. Head office at 32-34 rue des Envierges, 75020 Paris, *www.solidaritefemmes.asso.fr*.

• *SOS Femmes*, a major initiative supporting women's shelters and counselling services and serving as an information clearing house, including a continuously updated interactive locator map for women's shelters; head office at Immeuble Vosges, 2 rue Saint-John Perse, 52100 Saint-Dizer, Tel: 03 25065070, *www.sosfemmes.com*, with pages in French and in English.

• *SOS Sexisme*, an organisation founded in 1988 to combat sexism in all its forms, including violence and religious fundamentalism, through lobbying and publishing to enhance public awareness; head office at 2 rue du Bel Air, 92190 Meudon, Tel: 01 46261482, *www.sos-sexisme.org* with pages in French, English, Spanish, Arabic and Farsi.

- *Women Against Violence Europe (WAVE)*, Europe's largest association of women's NGOs, with a head office in Vienna and a comprehensive database of organisations and initiatives dedicated to combatting violence against women at *www.wave-network.org*, with pages in English and selected pages in other languages.

* Figures from p. 7 of *Violences conjugales, Chiffres et mesures, Dossier de Presse,* Ministerial report, 23 November 2005, published by **Documentation française** (Chapter 31) and downloadable from website at *www.femmes-egalite.gouv.fr/ espace_presse/dossiers_2005/docs/violencesconjugales_231105.pdf*

École Nationale Supérieure des Officiers des Sapeurs-Pompiers (ENSOSP)

Founded in mid 2004, ENSOSP is the successor to the National Civil Security Research Institute (INESC) as well as being the national academy for training fire brigade and emergency management officers. As such, it conducts studies and research and compiles and publishes information on civil security matters. As this book goes to press, ENSOSP has two facilities: a school in Paris and its principal college at Nainville les Roches, and is building a new campus at Aix en Provence, scheduled to open in 2008. For further information, contact the main college: ENSOSP, BP 36, 91750 Nainville les Roches, Tel: 01 64982020, *www.ensosp.fr*.

Eurodac

Eurodac is the pan-European database of fingerprints, principally of asylum applicants and illegal immigrants. Instituted in compliance with the Dublin Convention of 1990, it now keeps fingerprints in a central register maintained by the European Commission and accessed from dedicated points in the EEA member countries. Technically, it is the first common Automated Fingerprint Identification System (AFIS) in the European Union. Aside from fulfilling its principal purpose of determining whether an asylum seeker has applied in and been rejected by another EEA country, the operation of Eurodac has revealed asylum trends and consequently is useful in demographic studies of immigration. Nonetheless, Eurodac has created controversy. Officials praise its efficiency; human rights organisations fear its potential intrusions: in 2004, the French branch of **Privacy International** (Chapter 33) gave the "Orwell EU Big Brother Award" jointly to Eurodac and the **Schengen Information System**. Full details of the Eurodac and the legislation behind it are on the "Summaries of legislation" part of the EU website at *www. europa.eu.int/scadplus/leg*. In France, the principal Eurodac facility is in Paris at the **Préfecture de Police**.

European Anti-Fraud Office
[*Office européen de Lutte Antifraude (OLAF)*]

The European Anti-Fraud Office is an independent agency established by the European Commission to combat fraud, corruption and misconduct in business. It works with and supports all EU countries and acts as a central repository of information on anti-fraud activities. It encourages the public to report observed fraud to freephone numbers in all member countries; the freephone number in France is 08 00917295. For further information, call that number or visit the website at *europa.eu.int/olaf*, with pages in 20 languages.

Europol

The European Police Office, contracted to Europol, is the EU agency that handles criminal intelligence. Its principal remit is to contribute to EU law enforcement actions against organised crime and terrorism. It does this in its own organisation at the headquarters in The Hague and in liaison with law enforcement organisations across Europe. It supports a pan-European computer system, TECS, that provides member police organisations with facilities for input, access and analyses of data. In France, the **National police** are the Europol contact. For further information, contact the head facility, PO Box 90850, 2509 LW The Hague, The Netherlands, Tel: +31 703025896, *www.europol.eu.int*.

French Forum for Urban Safety
[*Forum Français pour la Sécurité Urbaine (FFSU)*]

The French Forum for Urban Safety (FFSU) was created in 1992 by the **European Forum for Urban Safety** (Chapter 33), an NGO founded in 1987 by French parliamentarian Gilbert Bonnemaison. The FFSU brings together more than 130 local authorities across the country for mutual exchange of information on and experience in urban safety. Head office: FFSU, 38 rue Liancourt, 75014 Paris, Tel: 01 40644900, *www.ffsu.org*, *ffsu@urbansecurity.org*.

Gendarmerie

A *Gendarmerie* is a military unit that performs civilian police functions. Historically, the word *Gendarmerie* was first used in 1551 to describe a corps of cavalry of the old French army. With time, the *Gendarmerie*, mounted or on foot, were employed as civilian police, and from the late 19th century on, their duties were principally among civilian populations. More than 40 countries have similar forces, sometimes under other names, such as the *Carabinieri* of Italy, though *Gendarmerie* remains the most common name, particularly in countries once under French influence. Today in France, the *Gendarmerie nationale* is a police force of military status, subordinate to the Ministry of Defence as well as to the Ministry of the Interior. It is divided into:

- The *Gendarmerie Départementale*, the force in blue uniforms that provides local policing across the country in rural and semi-rural areas, patrols highways and motorways, supports search and rescue operations and assists local police forces in investigations.

- The *Gendarmerie Mobile*, the force in black uniforms that provides security at the national level, including riot and crowd control, building security, counter-terrorism and ensuring the safety of the President and his family.

- Special divisions including *Gendarmerie Maritime*, *Gendarmerie des Transports Aériens*, *Gendarmerie de l'Air* and *Gendarmerie de l'Armement*, as well as the ceremonial **Republican Guard**.

Head office: Direction générale de la gendarmerie nationale, 35 rue Saint-Didier, 75016 Paris Cedex, Tel: 01 56288999, *www.defense.gouv.fr/sites/gendarmerie*.

Guarantee Fund for Victims of Acts of Terrorism and other Offences [*Fonds de Garantie des Victimes des Actes de Terrorisme et d'autres Infractions (FGTI)*]

The FGTI is a unified scheme for compensating victims of terrorism and other offences, such as violence, assault and rape. It was created in 1990 by merging two separate schemes, one for victims of offences, set up in 1977 and expanded thereafter, and one for victims of terrorism, set up in 1986 and extended thereafter to grant victims the status of civilian war victims. It is financed by a levy on property insurance policies, and it is managed by but separate from the **Guarantee Fund of Compulsory Damage Insurance** (Chapter 4).

A victim of terrorism or other offence may put in a claim to the Compensation Commission for Victims of Offences [*Commission d'Indemnisation des Victimes d'Infractions (CIVI)*] at the nearest County Court (*Tribunal de Grande Instance*). For further information, contact the head office at 64 rue Defrance, 94682 Vincennes Cedex, Tel: 01 43987700, *www.fgti.fr* with a locator map of the CIVI offices across the country.

Infractions [*Infractions*]

French law distinguishes between three categories of infractions, in order of decreasing severity:

- Crime [*Crime*]: The most serious infractions, such as murder and rape, punishable by imprisonment [*pénalement*] or detention [*détention*] (for political crimes) for 10 years or more. Consequently, the word *crime* in French is not the overall term as it is in English, but rather a specific term with a meaning similar to that of the older designation of "felony" in English. Crimes are prosecuted before the *Cour d'assises*, which in the legal system is similar to the Crown Court in the UK.

- Offence [*Délit*]: The less serious infractions, such as theft, punishable by correctional imprisonment for less than 10 years or by fine and prosecuted before the Court of corrections [*Tribunal correctionnel*].

- Minor offence [*Contravention*]: Lesser infractions, such as traffic violations, punishable by fines or by limitation or suspension of privileges, such as of a driving licence, and tried before a police court [*Tribunaux de police*].

Interpol

Interpol is an abbreviation for the International Criminal Police Organisation [*L'Organisation Internationale de Police Criminelle*] and is the second largest international body in the world, after the United Nations. It was founded in 1923 to facilitate cross-border police cooperation, and now interacts with the National Central Bureaus (NCBs) of the police forces of 184 countries. Its principal aim is to support police cooperation, even between countries that do not have diplomatic relations with each other. In France, the NCB is at the headquarters of the **National Police**. Most Interpol activities are conducted by the General Secretariat at Lyon and by regional offices in Argentina, Côte d'Ivoire, El Salvador, Kenya, Thailand and Zimbabwe, as well as a liaison office at the United Nations in New York. For further information, contact Interpol, Communications and Public Relations, General Secretariat, 200 quai Charles de Gaulle, 69006 Lyon, Fax: 04 72447163, *www. interpol.int*, *cp@interpol.int* with pages in Arabic, English, French and Spanish.

Mobile Intervention and Protection Unit
[*Unité Mobile d'Intervention et de Protection (UMIP)*]

The UMIP is part of the Public order and traffic directorate [*Direction de l'Ordre Public et de la Circulation (DOPC)*], one of the six active police directorates of the **Préfecture de Police** in Paris. Established in November 2002, it essentially is the successor to the Surveillance and Protection Company [*Compagnie de Surveillance et de Protection (CSP)*] and is an elite force of some 280 volunteers that provide round-the-clock protection of governmental and diplomatic facilities and persons.

National Crime Observatory
[*Observatoire national de la délinquance (OND)*]

The National Crime Observatory (OND) is a division of the **National Institute for Security Studies** (Chapter 11) that is dedicated to the collection and analysis of data and statistics on crime with the goal of making information available to decision makers and to the public. Its Monthly bulletin [*Bulletin mensuel*] presents statistics and analyses for all crimes reported the previous month by police agencies across the country. It publishes annual reports as well as other periodic reports of trends over the years. For further information as well as for current and past reports, contact the head office at Les Borromées, 3 avenue du Stade de France, 93218 Saint-Denis-La-Plaine Cedex, Tel: 01 55845300, *www.ond.fr*.

National Police [*Police Nationale*]

The National Police are the country's largest and most comprehensive police force, with more than 2000 police headquarters, police stations, offices, barracks, quarters and centres, as well as 34 training colleges and centres. Combating crime is a major activity, but the National Police are also involved in road safety and other preventive measures. For further information, contact the nearest police unit listed in the Yellow pages or visit the Ministry of Interior website at *www.interieur.gouv.fr* and click on *La police nationale* to bring up the National Police pages.

Police [*Police*]

The police are organised in three main forces across the country as well as in many local forces. The three main forces are:

- **Companies for Republican Security** [*Compagnies Républicaines de Sécurité (CRS)*], an elite force of mobile units that comprise the general reserve of the National Police.
- **Gendarmerie** [*Gendarmerie nationale*], a police force of military status.
- **National Police** [*Police nationale*], the country's largest and most extensive force.

See the individual entries for further details.

Most cities and medium-sized towns have a local force known as *police municipal* or *corps urban* that deals with petty crime, traffic offences and road accidents. In Paris, the **Mobile Intervention and Protection Unit** [*Unité Mobile d'Intervention et de Protection (UMIP)*], an elite volunteer force, provides round-the-clock protection of governmental and diplomatic facilities and persons.

Préfecture de Police

The *Préfecture de Police* of Paris is a unique organisation, in step with the city's status as the largest city and capital of the country as well as being a *Département*. Consequently, it is a large organisation, which, as its name implies, fulfils the functions of a *Préfecture* as well as those of the Police of a major city. It has six active police directorates:

- Crime investigation [*Direction Régionale de la Police Judiciaire*]

- General information [*Direction Régionale des Renseignements Généraux*]
- Local urban police [*Direction de la Police Urbaine de Proximité*]
- Public order and traffic [*Direction de l'Ordre Public et de la Circulation*]
- Operations and logistics [*Direction Opérationnelle des Services Techniques et Logistiques*]
- General department inspectorate [*Inspection Générale des Services*]

and two administrative directorates:

- General police [*Direction de la Police Générale*]
- Transport and public protection [*Direction des Transports et de la Protection du Public*].

It supports extensive information services, online and in print, both in French and for new residents, in other languages. For further information, contact Préfecture de Police, 9 boulevard du Palais, 75195 Paris Cedex 04, Tel: 01 53735373, *www.prefecture-police-paris.interieur.gouv.fr*, with pages in French, English, Spanish, German, Dutch and Italian.

Prisons [*Pénitentiaires*]

France imprisons fewer people than median for the world, about 98 per 100,000 population, less than England and Wales (142) and less than one-seventh as many as the USA (714), the country with the highest prison population in the world*. Across the country, the French Prison Service [*Direction de l'administration pénitentiaire (DAP)*] has 118 prisons:

- 115 Remand prisons [*Maisons d'arrêt (MA)*] for pre-trial detainees and convicted prisoners with less than a year to serve
- 24 Detention centres [*Centres de détention (CD)*]
- 31 Penitentiary centres [*Centres pénitentiaires (CP)*] of which eight have high-security sections
- 8 High-security prisons [*Maisons centrales (MC)*]
- 13 Independent partial release centres [*Centres de semi-liberté (CSL)*].

DAP also has a National public health institute at Fresnes [*Établissement public de santé national à Fresnes (EPSNF)*], operational facilities to expand prison capacity and more than 100 probatory facilities. For further information, contact Direction de l'administration pénitentiaire (DAP), 13 place Vendôme, 75042 Paris Cedex 01, *www.justice.gouv.fr/minister/DAP/indexgb.htm* with pages in French and in English and interactive locator maps of all present and planned facilities.

* *World Prison Population List, Sixth Edition*, International Centre for Prison Studies, King's College, London – School of Law, 2005, *www.prisonstudies.org* with pages in English, French, Spanish, Russian and Portuguese.

Prostitution [*Prostitution*]

According to various estimates, there now are 15,000 to 20,000 prostitutes in the country, more than half of them in Paris and 60% believed to be foreigners. Finding a prostitute is relatively easy, as a stroll along Rue Saint-Denis in Paris or a visit to any one of innumerable websites touting sex services will confirm. But that situation may change, as recent debate and legislation may curtail the trade, in part in accordance with international human rights agreements to limit trafficking in and exploitation of women and children. Historically, the current mood is the outcome of more than a century of concern with the matter.

Public brothels [*maisons closes*] once were part of city life. In the mid 19th century, there were about 200 official brothels in Paris, some made famous, as by Henri de Toulouse-Lautrec's painting of 1894 of *Salon de la rue des Moulins*. The official brothels were under the supervision of the Police and doctors, who performed the medical examinations stipulated in a law of 1802 aimed to curtail the epidemic of syphilis of the time. But as elsewhere in Europe, opinion leaders opposed the practice, and prostitution became part of public debate, divided at the extremes between those for abolishing the practice and those for regulating it. A step between the extremes was taken through a law enacted in 1946 and known since by the name of the politician and former prostitute who had proposed it, Marthe Richard (1889-1980). Initially, the law closed the brothels and subsequently it repealed the regulatory arrangements that had been associated with them. In the years that followed, laws relevant to prostitution were enacted, the most recent in 2003 to forbid exploitation of a prostitute by a third party, effectively outlawing pimping.

Several human-rights organisations now are dedicated to bettering the lot of prostitutes; the most prominent is *Mouvement du nid*, an NGO and partner of the UN's **DPI-NGO** (Chapter 33). Its basic thesis is that prostitution is incompatible with human dignity, so its vision is a society without prostitution [*une société sans prostitution*]. It seeks that goal through enlightened social change, not through restrictive legal measures. Consequently, it supports public awareness campaigns and educational initiatives aimed particularly at younger persons and offers counselling and other services for prostitutes. Founded in France in 1946, it now has affiliates across the country in most *Départements* as well as in Belgium, Brazil, Côte d'Ivorie, Portugal and Switzerland. Head office: 8 bis rue Dagobert, BP 63, 92114 Clichy Cedex, Tel: 01 42709240, *www.mouvementdunid.org*, *nidnational@ mouvementdunid.org*.

Republican Guard [*Garde Républicaine*]

The Republican Guard is the country's ceremonial military unit and a part of the **Gendarmerie**. Founded in 1812, it comprises two infantry regiments, one with a motorcycle squadron, and a cavalry regiment, the last horsemen of the country's defence forces. It also has musical groups, an equestrian group and a motorcycle performing group. For further information, contact Section Communication de la Garde républicaine, Quartier des celestins, 18 Boulevard Henri IV, 75004 Paris, Tel: 01 58282072, *www.garderepublicaine.com*.

Schengen Information System
[*Système d'Information Schengen (SIS)*]

The Schengen Information System is an automatic data communications network that interconnects police agencies and consulates of the **Schengen space** (Chapter 21) to access data on wanted persons as well as on vehicles and objects that are lost or stolen. In France, SIS is accessed from about 15,000 terminals at facilities of the **National police**, the **Gendarmerie**, **Customs** (Chapter 43), the **Préfectures** (Chapter 9) and other offices of the Ministries of the Interior and Foreign Affairs. Starting in 2005, the second-generation system, SIS II, is being implemented. The Central SIS (C.SIS) is located in Strasbourg at 18 rue de la Faisanderie, BP 54, 67020 Strasbourg Cedex 01, Tel: 03 88407000.

Security services [*Sécurité privée*]

Private security services offer a range of services related to protecting people and property, from caretaking [*gardiennage*] to guarding and protection [*protection*] to surveillance [*surveillance*]. There are many security companies, listed in the **Yellow pages** (Chapter 31) under *Sécurité (Entreprises)*. The two largest companies are global operators:

* G4S Security Services, founded in 1951 in the UK and now with operations in more than 100 countries that together employ some 360,000 people; in France with a staff of 7000 and a head office at 11 rue Dumont d'Urville, 76000 Rouen, Tel: 02 32108210, *www.g4s.com*, *contact@fr.g4s.com*

* Securitas, founded in 1934 in Sweden and now with operations in 20 countries that together employ some 200,000 people; in France with 230 agencies and a head office at 2 bis rue Louis Armand, 75741 Paris Cedex 15, *www.securitas.fr*.

Victim support [*Aide aux victimes*]

Across the country, more than 150 organisations provide support to the victims of assault [*agression*], burglary [*cambriolage*], theft [*vol*] and violence [*violence*]. Each year, their 1500 permanent and voluntary staff members help some 150,000 victims. These activities are coordinated, documented and made known to the public by *L'Institut National d'Aide aux Victimes et de Médiation (INAVEM)*, 1 rue du Pré Saint Gervais, 93691 Pantin Cedex, Tel: 01 41834200, *www.inavem.org*. INAVEM supports a national victim support hotline, 08 10098609, Monday-Saturday, 10:00-22:00. The individual organisations can be found on the locator map online at *www.justice.gouv.fr/region/inavemc.htm*.

Women's shelters [*Centres d'hébergement*]

If you are a woman who has been beaten, raped or otherwise physically or psychologically abused, you can seek help by contacting *SOS Femmes*, *www.sosfemmes.com*, or, more directly, by:

- calling the national crisis number freephone 08 00059595 or the local numbers listed on the *SOS Femmes* website
- contacting one of the centres for the rights of women [*Centres d'Informations sur les Droits des Femmes*], as on the interactive locator map at *www.infofemmes.com/Adresses.html*.
- contacting one of the 1128 women's shelters [*Centres d'hébergement*] in the country, as on the locator map at *www.sosfemmes.com/ressources/contacts_chrs.htm*.

Your rights [*Vos droits*]

Your rights [*Vos droits*] according to French and international human rights acts are set forth in easily-understood brochures and guides published by the Ministry of Justice and available in print at courts or downloadable from the Ministry website page at *www.justice.gouv.fr/publicat/fiches1.htm*.

Basic right	Publication title and date
Brochures:	*Les fiches:*
Victims of domestic violence	*Victime de violences au sein du couple – 03/2005*
Parental responsibility	*L'autorité parentale – 01/2004*
Legal aid	*L'aide juridictionnelle – 01/2006*
Eligibility and application for legal aid	*La demande d'aide juridictionnelle – 01/2004*
Rights of suspects	*Les droits des personnes mises en cause pénalement – 09/2003*
Complaints about courts and legal services	*Vous portez plainte – 07/2003*
Rights of victims and witnesses	*Charte des droits et devoirs des victimes d'infraction – 05/2002*
Guides:	*Les guides :*
Born or becoming French	*Naître ou devenir français(e) – 10/2005*
Adults with special needs	*Les majeurs protégés – 06/2002*

11
Culture

Culture arguably is the most distinctive aspect of France. Other countries may claim comparable wines, cuisines, welfare systems and governments. But in France, culture is the national *élan*; it's what homesick French abroad miss from their native land and what tourists flock to experience.

The verve of French culture often is ascribed to a unique and pervasive policy of State involvement that began in the 17th century, during the reign of Louis XIV, when the State became the official patron of the arts by providing stipends and commissions to encourage and support artists and writers. The building of the Palace of Versailles, the royal residence from 1682, and the founding in 1680 of the Comédie Française company of actors are monuments to the cultural vision that became national policy.

Another significant trend was triggered by the *Révolution* of 1789. Starting in 1793, with the conversion of the Louvre Palace into a museum, culture ceased to be the province of the select few and became increasingly available to all. By the end of the 20th century, culture had broadened and become a commonplace aspect of everyday life, supported by the State, local authorities and innumerable organisations and businesses.

In numerical terms, culture stands high. The average household spends 3.5% of its income on culture, among the highest percentages in the world. France ranks fifth in the world in sales of recorded music, and a French entertainment company, Vivendi Universal, ranks second in the world, after Time Warner of the USA.

The arts [*Les arts*]

The arts, also called the fine arts [*beaux-arts*], are modes of expression in which imagination and skill are used to create aesthetic objects, milieux and experiences that can be shared with others. What they are has been a topic of philosophical debate since the term *beaux-arts* first appeared in 1752 in *l'Encyclopédie de Diderot et d'Alembert*. In "Philosophy of History and of Art" published posthumously, German philosopher Georg Wilhelm Friedrich Hegel (1770-1831) distinguished six arts, in order of importance: architecture, sculpture, painting, music, dance and poetry. Hegel's six designations are the classical categories of today, though debate continues as to whether painting should be expanded to include drawing, dance should be expanded to include theatre and poetry should be expanded to include literature. That debate aside, in modern times [*les temps modernes*] four newer modes of expression have been added to the classical list, two of them first defined in France.

The seventh art is the cinema, as first proposed in 1911 by Italian-born, pioneering film technician Ricciotto Canudo (1879-1923) in a manifesto entitled *La naissance du sixième art* ("The birth of the sixth art"), in which he argued that cinema combined the spatial arts of architecture, sculpture and painting and the temporal arts of music and dance. He later acknowledged the classical total of six arts and changed cinema to seventh, as published in 1923 in *Manifeste des Sept Arts* (facsimile reprinted 2003 by Seguier, Paris, 30 pages, ISBN 2-8404-9052-8).

The eighth art was first said in 1938 by American commercial photographer Victor Keppler (1904-1987) to be photography, but by 1962 it had become the designation for television, as reflected in "The Eighth Art, Twenty-Three Views on Television Today" the title of a book published in New York by Holt, Reinhart and Winston.

The ninth art, as proposed in 1971 in an essay, *Pour un neuvième art, la bande dessinée*, by French author and pop culture essayist Francis Lacassin (1931-), is the graphic novel.

The tenth art is said to be video in all its forms, including video games, though there's no agreement on who first used the term.

Book Fair, Paris [*Salon du Livre, Paris*]

The annual *Salon du Livre*, held over six days in late March in Paris, is the country's largest book fair, attracting some 185,000 visitors to the venue at Paris Expo, Porte de Versailles. The fair is for the public as well as for the book trade; admission is inexpensive, and discounts are given for children, pupils and students. For further information on the fair, contact the Publishers' Association [*Syndicat national de l'édition (SNE)*], 115 bd Saint Germain, 75006 Paris, Tel: 01 44414050, *www.sne.fr* or the Fair's dedicated website at *www.salondulivreparis.com* in French and in English.

Centre of National Monuments
[*Centre des Monuments Nationaux*]

The Centre of National Monuments [*Centre des Monuments Nationaux*] researches, registers, supports restoration, arranges events and publishes information for scholars and the public on buildings and other structures of value in the cultural history of the country. It keeps the **Inventory of historic monuments**, readily accessible via an interactive locator map on its website. For catalogues, brochures and other information, contact the head office at Hôtel de Béthune-Sully, 62 rue Saint-Antoine, 75186 Paris Cedex 04, Tel: 01 44612000, *www.monum.fr*, with pages in French and English.

Césars

The Césars are small golden statuettes, the French equivalent of the Oscars of Hollywood, that are awarded each year by the Academy of Cinematic Arts and Techniques [*L'Académie des Arts et Techniques du Cinéma*] at a ceremony held in late February or early March and televised live by Canal+. The statuettes are named after the sculptor who created them for the fist award ceremony in 1976, César Baldaccini (1921-1998), who worked with scrap iron and metal and was the first to use crushed motor vehicles as an art medium. For further details, contact the Academy at 19 rue Lauriston, 75116 Paris, Tel: 01 53640525, *www. lescesarducinema.com* with updated summaries of current nominations as well as lists of the annual winners in all categories since the first awards of 1976.

Chanson française

Chanson française is an increasingly popular genre of song also known as *chanson à textes*, as the lyrics of songs are meaningful. It first was popularised by famed singers Maurice Chevalier (1888-1972), Josephine Baker (1906-1975) and Edith Piaf (1915-1963), developed by other singers, including Georges Moustaki (1934-), Georges Brassens (1921-1981), Jacques Brel (1921-1978) and Johnny Hallyday (1943-). In the 21st century, it was taken further, by Renaud Séchan (1952-), rap singer MC Solaar (Claude M'Barali, 1969-) and soul singer Corneille (Cornelius Nyungura, 1977-). There's an annual contest for the genre in France, *Grand Prix de la chanson française* as well as abroad, *Grand Prix de la chanson française à l'étranger*. For further information, contact the Music Writers, Composers and Editors Society [*Société des auteurs, compositeurs et éditeurs de musique*], 225 av. Charles de Gaulle, 92528 Neuilly-sur-Seine Cedex, Tel: 01 47154715, *www.sacem.fr*.

Cinema [*Cinéma*]

Cinema is one of the more popular forms of entertainment: with more than 5200 cinemas, 97 of them multiplexes. On a per-capita basis, France ranks among the top cinema-going countries of the world. That lead is due in part to cinema being a French invention: on 28 December 1895, brothers August Lumière (1896-1954) and Louis Lumière (1864-1948) gave the first screening at Grand Café à Paris of a film entitled *La Sortie de l'usine Lumière à Lyon*. Accordingly, cinema became a popular medium that attracted many creative artists as well as the public.

By 1911, France had become the centre of film technology and art, and in that year Ricciotto Caudo defined cinema as the seventh of the **arts**. In the 1920s, Louis Delluc (1890-1924), Jean Cocteau (1889-1963) and others experimented with avant-garde films. In the 1930s, many films had political messages, such as *la Grande Illusion* of 1937, a cry for peace by Jean Renoir (1894-1979). In 1936, the *Cinémathèque française* was established as a repository for films and a centre for information on cinematic arts. In the 1950s and 1960s, *Cinémathèque française* became the cradle of the New wave [*Nouvelle vague*] movement that rejected classical cinematic form and was strongly influenced by youthful iconoclasm. Since 2005, *Cinémathèque française* is housed in a spacious, modern building designed in 1994 by American architect Frank Gehry, and conducts a broad range of cinematic activities, including maintaining the national film library [*Bibliothèque du film (BIFI)*], 51 rue de Bercy, 75012 Paris, Tel: 01 71193333, *www.cinematheque.fr*.

In 1946, the importance of cinema in national culture was recognised with the establishment of the National Centre for Cinematography [*Centre national de la cinématographie (CNC)*], 12 rue de Lübeck, 75784 Paris Cedex 16, Tel: 01 44343440, *www.cnc.fr*. In addition to its cinematic tasks, CNC keeps statistics on the film sector. From the 1980s on, new movements evolved to dominate French film, including *Cinéma Beur*, films by young directors of Maghrebi immigrant origin, and *Cinéma du look*, films emphasising beautiful albeit often simple scenes. Arguably the best known *Cinéma du look* film to date is *Le Fabuleux destin d'Amélie Poulain* a quirky romantic comedy directed by Jean-Pierre Jeunet (1953-) and released in 2001 to set box office records: it was seen by more than 32 million people round the world, including more than nine million in France and nearly six million in the USA.

Documentary [*documentaire*] is almost as old as cinema in France, and through the years, French documentary films have won acclaim round the world, such as those made in the 1950s by oceanographer Jacques-Yves Cousteau (1911-1997). Most recently, March of the Penguins [*La marche de l'empereur*], directed and in part filmed by Luc Jacquet, a biologist turned cameraman, was awarded an Oscar for the best Documentary Feature at the 78th Academy Awards Ceremony in 2006; further information at *www.luc-jacquet.com* in French and in English.

March of the Penguins poster.

172

Circus [*Cirque*]

Of the many circuses in the country, both travelling and fixed, five are large:

*   *Cirque Alexandro Klising*, *www.cirque-klising.com*
*   *Cirque Arlette Gruss*, *www.cirque-gruss.com* in French and in English
*   *Cirque d'hiver* in Paris, *www.cirquedhiver.com* in French and in English
*   *Cirque Plume*, *www.cirqueplume.com*
*   *Les Arrosés, www.lesarroses.com.*

The many schools of circus arts are organised into the *Fédération française des écoles du cirque*, 7 rue Taylor, 75010 Paris, *www.ffec.asso.fr*.

Comédie Française

Founded in August 1680 by King Louis XIV, *Comédie Française* is the oldest company of actors in the western world, also called *Théâtre-Français*, as it is the national theatre. It is located in an impressive building in the first *Arrondissement* of Paris and now has three theatres: *Salle Richelieu, Théâtre du Vieux-Colombier* and *Studio-Théâtre*. Its repertoire consists mostly of classical French drama; plays by Molière have been performed thousands of times, though plays by Shakespeare and other foreign playwrights also are performed regularly. For further information, contact the theatre at 2 rue de Richelieu, 75001 Paris, Tel: 08 25101680, *www.comedie-francaise.fr* with selected pages in English.

Conservatories and schools [*Conservatoires et écoles*]

Across the country, there are many conservatories and schools offering curricula in the arts, of which the most prestigious six are:

*   Two national music conservatories (*Les conservatoires nationaux supérieurs musique et danse*] in Paris, *www.cnsmd-paris.fr* and in Lyon *www.cnsmd-lyon.fr*.
*   The national fine arts school [*l'École nationale supérieure des beaux-arts (ENSBA)*], *www.ensba.fr*.
*   The national school of audiovisual arts [*Ecole nationale supérieure des métiers de l'image et du son*], *www.femis.fr*.
*   The national academy for dramatic art [*Le Conservatoire national supérieur d'art dramatique (CNSAD)*], *www.cnsad.fr*.
*   The national school of photography [*l'École nationale de la photographie (ENP)*], *www.enp-arles.com*.

Culture portal [*Le portail de la culture*]

The Culture portal is a continuously updated online clearing house for the details of all cultural events, from archaeology [*archéologie*] to shows [*spectacles*] across the country. Contact: Département de l'information et de la communication, Ministère de la Culture et de la Communication, 3 rue de Valois, 75033 Paris Cedex 01, Fax: 01 40158390, *www.culture.fr*, with pages in French, English and Spanish and an interactive locator map of cultural events across the country.

Dance [*La danse*]

As in music, the borders between classical and modern dance have become less distinct, though both genres thrive. The Paris National Opera Ballet is among the world's oldest, and its dance academy is regarded to be among the world's foremost. Choreographer Maurice Béjart (1927-) redefined dance, founding dance companies in France, Belgium and Switzerland, and dance schools in Brusels, Dakar and Lausanne, where he has lived since 1987. Paris has become a focal point for dance, regularly featuring performances of works by foreign choreographers, including Merce Cunningham (1919-) of the USA, Pina Bausch (1940-) of Germany and William Forsythe (1949-) of the USA, recognised in Europe for his works with the Royal Ballet of the UK and the Frankfurt Ballet in Germany. Starting in 1998, dance in France is coordinated by the National Dance Centre [*Centre national de la danse*], 1 rue Victor Hugo, 93507 Pantin Cedex, Tel: 01 41832727, *www.cnd.fr*.

Disneyland Resort Paris

In 1992, EuroDisney, now named Disneyland Resort Paris, opened at Marne la Vallée, 32 km east of Paris, amid controversy, as many feared that it would undermine French culture. Nonetheless, the resort drew increasing numbers of visitors, now more than 12 million a year, to a spectrum of entertainments similar to those of the original Disneyland at Anaheim near Los Angeles in the USA. For further information, contact Euro Disney Associés, BP 100, 77777 Marne la Vallée Cedex 04, Tel: 08 2530222, *www.disneylandparis.com* with complete sites in French, English, Dutch and German.

Ethnological heritage mission [*Mission Ethnologie*]

Mission Ethnologie aims to preserve the heritage of regional and local traditions across the country, in part through supporting the increasing number of museums and museum departments dedicated to folk arts and traditions, such as the recently-opened Camargue Museum between Provence and Languedoc and the Dauphiné Museum in the Alps. For further details and links to ethnological heritage entities, contact Mission Ethnologie, 182 rue Saint-Honoré, 75033 Paris Cedex 01, Tel: 01 40158739, *www.culture.gouv.fr/mpe*.

Eurovision Song Contest
[*Concours Eurovision de la Chanson*]

Each year in May, the European television broadcasting networks jointly host the Eurovision Song Contest (ESC). The first contest was held in 1956 – it was then called "The Eurovision Grand Prix" – and drew entries from seven countries. It now attracts more than five times as many and is Europe's most watched pan-European television programme. France has had an entry in the contest since its start, and French singers have been placed first five times, in 1958, 1960, 1962, 1969 and 1977. For further information, visit the official website at *www.eurovision.tv* with pages in English and in French. For further information on French participation in the contest, visit *www.eurovision-fr.net*.

Goncourt Prize [*Prix Goncourt*]

Each December since 1903, the *Académie Goncourt* awards the *Prix Goncourt*, the most prestigious prize in literature in French, awarded to the novel judged to be the best of the year. Famed writers who have received the *Prix Goncourt* include Marcel Proust (1919), Jean Fayard (1931) and Simone de Beauvoir (1954). Novelist, film director and diplomat Romain Gary won the prize twice, first in 1956 and, under the pseudonym Émile Ajar, again in 1975.

Writer, critic and publisher Edmond de Goncourt (1822-1896) founded the *Académie Goncourt* by bequest of his entire estate, in honour of his brother, Jules de Goncourt (1830-1870). Today, the *Académie* comprises ten members, and its archives are kept in the Municipal Archives of the city of Nancy (3 rue Henri Bazin, 54000 Nancy), where Edmond de Goncourt was born. Further details on the *Académie* and the Prize are available on the official website at *www.academie-goncourt.fr*.

Hard Rock Café [*Hard Rock Café*]

In 1971 in London, two Americans, Isaac Tigrett and Peter Morton, opened the first Hard Rock Café, featuring rock music, American food and low prices. The concept spread, and now there are 121 Hard Rock Cafés in 40 countries, including France, where the Hard Rock Café opened in Paris in November 1991. Located next to the Opera and the Grands Boulevards, the restaurant has regular events, such as the Friday evening Parisian DJ sessions. For further information, contact the Café at 14 Boulevard Montmartre, 75009 Paris, Tel: 01 53246000, *www.hardrock.com* in English with an interactive locator of Hard Rock Cafés round the world.

Inventory of historic monuments
[*Inventaire des monuments historiques*]

Started in 1980, the Inventory of historic monuments kept by the **Centre of national monuments** is a register of historically significant buildings that has been growing at a rate of several hundred a year. There now are more than 40,000 buildings on the list, most identified on site by a *Monument Historique* sign.

Literature [*Littérature*]

Literature in France has an enviably strong position, both in the culture of the country and in the literary world. The first Nobel Prize in literature was awarded to French poet and essayist René-François-Armand (Sully) Prudhomme (1839-1907) and since then the prize has been awarded 12 times to French writers, in all more than to the writers of any other country, though one writer, Jean-Paul Sartre declined the prize in 1964. For French writers, the **Goncourt Prize** is as prestigious as the Nobel Prize in Literature, but no writer has won both. All the greater, then, the challenge for contemporary writers to live up to the tradition of the modern classical writers before them, including Anouilh, Aragon, Beckett, Camus, Céline, Cohen, Genet, Gide, Malraux, Mauriac, Montherlant and Sartre. The novel remains the most popular form of literature, and though waning in popularity, poetry still has a respectable niche in the overall literary scene. The annual **Goncourt Prize** is an important cultural event of the year, as is the **Book Fair** in Paris.

Louvre Museum [*Musée du Louvre*]

With an area of more than 160,000 square metres, the Louvre is the largest museum in Paris and among the largest museums in the world. The original building on the site was erected in 1190 as a fortress, to defend Paris. Additions were built through the years, and it became a museum during the *Révolution*. Its displays include more than 3500 paintings, most famously Leonardo da Vinci's Mona Lisa, as well as Egyptian, Greek and Roman antiquities and artistic works that chronicle French history and culture. For further information, contact Musée du Louvre, 36 Quai du Louvre, 75008 Paris Cedex 01, Tel: 01 40205555, *www.louvre.fr* with entire site in French or in English.

Moulin Rouge

The Moulin Rouge was created in 1889 as a cabaret. Its banquets and balls soon became a hallmark of Paris nightlife, made famous by its can-can dancers the *Chahuteuses* ("unruly girls"), immortalised by Henri de Toulouse-Lautrec's 1891 poster painting of the most known of them, *La Goulue* (Louise Weber, 1866-1929). Many famed singers, including Joséphine Baker and Edith Piaf have sung at Moulin Rouge, and in 2001 the Australian-American musical film *Moulin Rouge* vividly portrayed the cabaret and the life of Paris in the 1890s. For further information contact Bal du Moulin Rouge, Montmartre, 82 boulevard de Clichy, 75018 Paris, Tel: 01 53098282, *www.moulinrouge.fr* with pages in French and in English and with online reservations.

Music [*La musique*]

Music often is said to be the international language, at least within western languages. Not completely so, according to recent scientific research on French and English music, which has shown that music echoes speech*.

The techno sector, led by Daft Punk, *www.daftpunk.com*, and Laurent Garnier, *www.thecloudmakingmachine.com* in French and in English, is internationally successful.

State encouragement as well as financial support is given to a wide range of organisations, including:

- The National Jazz Orchestra [*Orchestre national de jazz (ONJ)*], *www.onj.org/fr* in French and in English.
- The National Heritage Centre for Song, Variety and Contemporary Music [*Centre National du Patrimoine de la Chanson, des Variétés et des Musiques actuelles*], *www.lehall.com*,
- Rock and Popular Music Centre [*Centre d'information du rock et des variétés (CIR)*], *www.irma.asso.fr/cir*,
- The **Operas**.

Located at the Pompidou Centre in Paris, The Institute for Musical and Acoustic Research and Coordination [*L'institut de recherche et de coordination acoustique/musique (IRCAM)*] is developing a genre of contemporary classical music, *www.ircam.fr* in French and in English. The *Ensemble intercontemporain* orchestra promotes the new works in its tours of France and other countries, *www.ensembleinter.com*.

Of the many symphony orchestras in the country, five are considered of notable world rank:

- *Orchestre de Paris*, *www.orchestredeparis.com*.
- *Orchestre national de France*, the national broadcasting orchestra, *www.radiofrance.fr/chaines/orchestres/national/accueil*.
- *Orchestre national de Lille*, *www.onlille.com*.
- *Orchestre national du Capitole de Toulouse*, *www.onct.mairie-toulouse.fr*,
- *Orchestre philharmonique de Strasbourg*, *www.philharmonique-strasbourg.com*.

Music is considered a valuable national asset and, accordingly, an annual day of music, **Fête de la musique** (Chapter 32) takes place on 21 June each year.

*Concerto for mother tongue by Philip Ball, New Scientist, 9 July 2005, pp. 32-33.

National institute for research in preventive archaeology [*Institut national de recherches archéologiques préventives (INRAP)*]

Set up in 2002, INRAP now is the principal French archaeological organisation. As its name implies, it principally is concerned with preventive archaeology, the relatively new discipline that aims to prevent the destruction of archaeological remains and artefacts when land is developed for buildings, roads and the like. Consequently, archaeology now is integrated into development projects. The result has been a marked increase in the number of archaeological sites identified, now more than 300,000 across the country. For further information, contact the INRAP head office at 7 rue de Madrid, 75008 Paris, Tel: 01 40088000, *www.inrap.fr* with pages in French and English and a locator map of sites identified.

New media [*Nouveaux supports*]

The new media have become an integral part of the cultural landscape, worthy of preservation:

- Photography: more than five million negatives by great photographers are stored at the saint-Cyr Fort near Versailles, and the Photographic Heritage Mission [*Patrimoine photographique*] acquires and manages collections significant in the history of photography, many on display at Hôtel de Sully, 62 rue Saint-Antoine, 75004 Paris, Tel: 01 42744775, *www.patrimoine-photo.org*.

- Cinema: The National Centre for Cinematography [*Centre national de la cinématographie*] restores vintage films and now receives copies of films for preservation, 12 rue de Lübeck, 75874 Paris Cedex 16, Tel: 01 44343440, *www.cnc.fr*.

- Landscape photography: The National Photographic Observatory [*l'Observatoire photographique*] records environmental changes at sites characteristic of national geography. It is a mission of the Directorate of nature and landscapes [*Direction de la nature et des paysages*] of the Ministry of the Environment and Sustainable Development [*Ministère de l'écologie et du développement durable*], 20 avenue de Ségur, 75302 Paris Cedex 07 SP, Tel: 01 42191900, *www.ecologie.gouv.fr* with pages in French, English and German.

Oil painting framing [*Œuvres à l'huile – encadrement*]

Canvasses are stretched on frames that are called "stretchers" (*chassis*), because they permit tightening of the canvas. Most often, a painting on a stretched canvas is mounted in a frame (*cadre*), which usually is of wood but may be of metal or plastic. Most stretchers and frames are sized in the French system of 20 numerical point categories, each with three formats: portrait [*figure*], landscape [*paysage*] and seascape [*marine*].

N°	F – Figure Portrait	P – Paysage Landscape	M – Marine Seascape
0	18 x 14	18 x 12	18 x 10
1	22 x 16	22 x 14	22 x 12
2	24 x 19	24 x 16	24 x 14
3	27 x 22	27 x 19	27 x 16
4	33 x 24	33 x 22	33 x 19
5	35 x 27	35 x 24	35 x 22
6	41 x 33	41 x 27	41 x 24
8	46 x 38	46 x 33	46 x 27
10	55 x 46	55 x 38	55 x 33
12	61 x 50	61 x 46	61 x 38
15	65 x 54	65 x 50	65 x 46
20	73 x 60	73 x 54	73 x 50
25	81 x 65	81 x 60	81 x 54
30	92 x 73	92 x 65	92 x 60
40	100 x 81	100 x 73	100 x 65
50	116 x 89	116 x 81	116 x 73
60	130 x 97	130 x 89	130 x 81
80	146 x 114	146 x 97	146 x 89
100	162 x 130	162 x 114	162 x 97
120	195 x 130	195 x 114	195 x 97

Framing sizes.

A contemporary professional artists' rule-of-thumb relates the market price of a painting to its size in points. Based on professional art assessment or on prices attained over a period of two or three years, an artist's works will be evaluated at a number of Euros per point. For instance, a No. 10 painting in any of the three formats by an artist evaluated at € 100 per point will sell at € 1000.

Opera [*l'Opéra*]

French opera has Italian roots almost as old as those of Italian opera itself. The first operas in France were Italian ones imported by Cardinal Jules Mazarin (1602-1661) and given in 1644-1645. Jean-Baptiste Lully (1632-1687), the musician in the court of Louis XIV who wrote the first French operas and founded *l'école française d'opéra*, was born Giovanni Battista Lully in Florence and was brought to France at age 14.

In the late 17th century, other composers took up opera, and the first opera houses were built, among the first the *Salle d'Issy*, built in 1659 at Issy-les-Moulineaux southwest of Paris in the *Département* of Hauts-de-Seine. Today, the National Opera of Paris [*Opéra national de Paris*], Tel: 08 92899090, *www.operadeparis.fr*, has three opera houses:

- *Salle Favart* at Place Boieldieu, built in 1820-1821 and rebuilt in 1839 following a fire. It is the home of the *Opéra-Comique*, *www.opera-comique.com*.
- *Opéra Garnier*, built in 1875 in neo-baroque style at Place de l'Opéra, 8 rue Scribe, 75009 Paris.
- *Opéra Bastille*, built in 1990 at Place de la Bastille, 120 rue de Lyon, 75012 Paris.

Three other cities have significant opera houses and companies:

- *Opéra National de Bordeaux*, performing at *Le Grand-Théâtre*, built in 1756, as well as seven other venues in the city, BP 95, 33025 Bordeaux Cedex, Tel: 0556008595, *www.opera-bordeaux.com*.
- *Opéra National de Lyon*, performing at *Opéra Nouvel*, first built in 1831 and re-designed by architect Jean Nouvel (1945-) in 1985 and 1993, Place de la Comédie, 69001 Lyon, Tel: 08 26305325, *www.opera-lyon.com*.
- *Opéra de Marseille*, which first performed in 1685, making it one of the country's oldest operas, since 1924 housed in the *Opéra Municipal*, 2 rue Molière, 13001 Marseille, Tel: 04 91551140, *www.mairie-marseille. fr/vivre/culture/opera/contact.htm*.

Theatre [*Théâtre*]

The modern school of French theatre owes much to actor-manager André Antoine (1858-1943), who in 1897 in Paris founded the *Théâtre Libre* specifically to break with the teachings of the Paris Conservatory and to focus on more natural acting and stage setting and, consequently, was the first in France to stage works by the naturalist playwrights of other countries, including August Strindberg of Sweden, Henrik Ibsen of Norway and Leo Tolstoy of Russia. Across the country, there now are 44 national drama centres [*centres dramatiques*], 250 companies with State contracts [*compagnies conventionnées*] and 599 subsidised theatre companies [*compagnies subventionnées*]. In all, there now are more than a thousand independent theatre companies in the country. Moreover, many theatre buildings have been modernised or refurbished, such as the Théâtre National de la Colline in Paris, *www.colline.fr*, the Théâtre du Port de la Lune in Bordeaux, *www.tnba.org* and the Nouveau Théâtre in Nice, *www.nice.fr*.

Town centre protection [*Protection du centre-ville*]

Town centres have been accorded special cultural protection by a law enacted in 1962. Called the Malraux Law [*la loi Malraux*], after André Malraux (1901-1976), the Minister of Culture at the time, the law sets forth rehabilitation procedures that shall be followed in urban redevelopments. Age no longer is the sole criterion for preservation, as industrial and urban landscapes of the past two centuries also are preserved, such as the coal basins in the eastern and northern parts of the country.

Visual arts [*Les arts plastiques*]

From the late 19th century on, French artists have influenced modern painting. For example, Claude Monet (1840-1926) and other impressionists; Paul Gauguin (1848-1903), Paul Cézanne (1839-1906) and other post-impressionists; and Henri Matisse (1869-1954) and other fauvists inspired Georges Braque (1882-1963) and Pablo Picasso (1881-1973) in the evolution of the cubist movement. Over the years, artists from other countries, not least Picasso and Vincent Van Gogh (1853-1890) came to work in Paris.

In the latter half of the 20th century, as the focus of the avant-garde shifted from Paris to New York, French artists kept abreast: the works of all-media artist Christian Boltanski (1944-), conceptual artist Daniel Buren (1938-) and painter Pierre Soulages (1919-) are at the forefront of contemporary art. Galleries and art fairs have burgeoned accordingly, mostly in Paris, led since 1974 by the International Contemporary Art Fair [*Foire internationale d'art contemporain (FIAC)*], 11 rue du Colonel Pierre Avia, BP 571, 75526 Paris Cedex 15, Tel: 01 41904747, *www.fiacparis.com* that exhibits in many venues, principally the Louvre and the Grand Palais.

The State supports creative activities through programmes of grants and scholarships for studies, such as the Academy of France at the Villa Medici in Rome. Moreover, the Ministry of Culture's Fund for the Encouragement of Creativity [*Fonds d'incitation à la création (FIACRE) du ministère de la Culture*] encourages by offering support for first publication or first show by artists of all genres.

From the 1980s on, the State has commissioned works, as did wealthy patrons in the past. As a consequence, there are many new works in public places. Not unexpectedly, some have been controversial, most notably Daniel Buren's creation in 1986 of *Les Deux Plateaux*, a 3000 square-metre sculpture in the great courtyard of the Palais Royal in Paris that triggered debate reminiscent of that of a century earlier, when Rodin's statue of Balzac was put up in Paris.

World Heritage Sites [*Sites du patrimoine mondial*]

World-wide, the United Nations Educational, Scientific and Cultural Organization (UNESCO) promotes the protection of cultural and natural heritage. The 28 UNESCO World Heritage Sites in France are listed below. For descriptions of these and other sites round the world, contact the UNESCO World Heritage Centre, place de Fontenoy, 75352 Paris, Tel: 01 45681571, *www.unesco.org*, *wh-info@unesco.org* and request or download the most recent edition of the listing, available in two editions, "Properties Inscribed on the World Heritage List" in English and *Biens inscrits sur la liste du patrimoine mondial* in French.

Sites in France on the 2005 edition of the World Heritage List [*Liste du patrimoine mondial*] in wording and order of list with year of inscription in parentheses:

- Mont-Saint-Michel and its Bay (1979)
- Chartres Cathedral (1979)
- Palace and Park of Versailles (1979)
- Vézelay, Church and Hill (1979)
- Decorated Grottoes of the Vézère Valley (1979)
- Palace and Park of Fontainebleau (1981)
- Amiens Cathedral (1981)
- Roman Theatre and its Surroundings and the "Triumphal Arch" of Orange (1981)
- Roman and Romanesque Monuments of Arles (1981)
- Cistercian Abbey of Fontenay (1981)
- Royal Saltworks of Arc-et-Senans (1982)
- Place Stanislas, Place de la Carrière and Place d'Alliance in Nancy (1983)
- Church of Saint-Savin sur Gartempe (1983)
- Cape Girolata, Cape Porto, Scandola Nature Reserve and the Piana Calanches in Corsica (1983)
- Pont du Gard (Roman Aqueduct) (1985)
- Strasbourg – Grande île (1988)
- Paris, Banks of the Seine (1991)
- Cathedral of Notre-Dame, Former Abbey of Saint-Remi and Palace of Tau, Reims (1991)
- Bourges Cathedral (1992)
- Historic Centre of Avignon (1995)
- Canal du Midi (1996)
- Historic Fortified City of Carcassonne (1997)
- Routes of Santiago de Compostela in France (1998)
- Historic Site of Lyon (1998)
- Jurisdiction of Saint-Emilion (1999)
- Loire Valley between Sully-sur-Loire and Chalonnes (2000)
- Provins, Town of Medieval Fairs (2001)
- Le Havre, the City Rebuilt by Auguste Perret (2005)

12
Defence and security

France spends 2.5% of its GDP on defence, about the same level of expenditure as in the UK and many other member countries of NATO. Military spending has gone down in recent years, from an average of 3.7% of the GDP in 1985-1989 to the present level of 2.5%, fairly constant since 2001*. In part, the decline is due to modernisation of forces, in step with the country having one of the world's larger defence industries. The army, navy and air force are all high-tech forces, among the strongest in Europe.

Security within the country has top priority. Domestic and international intelligence agencies have long monitored terrorist groups as well as the radicals that hatch them. The criminal justice system was tough on terrorists well before terrorism hit the headlines round the world: laws enacted in the mid 1990s permit detention of terrorist suspects without indictment for four days, and radicals who incite violence can be and are deported.

Civil defence is consistent with the concern for security and recently has been updated to cope with more modern menaces as well as with traditional threats. The creation of a National Institute for Security Studies and a National Civil Security Council, comprising top-level public and private sector leaders, has brought security to the forefront of concern in all sectors of society.

*NATO-Russia Compendium of Financial and Economic Data Relating to Defence, Data Analysis Section, NATO International Staff, 8 December 2005, downloadable from *www.nato.int*.

Air Force [*Armée de l'air*]

The French Air Force [*Armée de l'air*] is considered to be the world's oldest military air unit, as it was established in 1910 as *Aviation Militaire*, then part of the Army. Historians also recognise it as the first Air Force to use a roundel insignia, which it painted on its aircraft in the First World War. Today, in addition the central command, it has seven major commands, two operational and five specialist functional. The operational commands are:

- The Air Strategic Force Command [*Commandement des forces aériennes stratégiques (CFAS)]*, with 2000 personnel, is the largest of the two operational commands. It controls the air component of the nuclear deterrence force, and its aircraft include Mirage 2000N fighters fitted with Air-to-Ground Medium-Range Missiles [*Air sol moyenne portée (ASMP)*] and C135FR supply aircraft.

- The Air Defence and Air Operations Command [*Commandement de la défense aérienne et des opérations aériennes (CDAOA)*], with 800 personnel, is tasked with air defence and the planning and conduct of air operations over national territory.

The specialist functional commands are:

- The Air Combat Command [*Commandement de la force aérienne de combat (CFAC)*], with 5300 personnel, comprises the conventional air combat assets including 300 combat aircraft in 16 squadrons.

- The Mobility Command [*Commandement de la force aérienne de projection (CFAP)*], with 4600 personnel, is responsible for deploying personnel and equipment for operations, making use of 230 aircraft based in France and overseas.

- The Air Surveillance, Communications and Information Command [*Commandement air des systèmes de surveillance, d'information et de communication (CASSIC)*], with 9000 personnel, is responsible for the operation and support of early warning, surveillance, control, ground-to-air defence and electronic support assets of all units, in 155 units in France, French overseas territories and in foreign countries.

- The Air Training Command [*Commandement des écoles de l'armée de l'air (CEAA)*], with 6000 personnel, delivers career education and training.

- The Force Protection and Security Command [*Commandement des forces de protection et de sécurité de l'armée de l'air (CFPSAA)*], with a staff of 3600 protection specialists and firemen, provides protection and ground defence missions at all sensitive sites. It has 34 protection units, 33 fire-fighting and rescue sections and three intervention paratrooper commandos.

For further information, contact the office of the Chief of Staff: Ministère de la défense, Armée de l'air, 26 bd Victor, 75015 Paris, Tel: 01 45524321, or 08 10715715 for recruitment, *www.defense.gouv.fr/sites/air*.

Tricolour blue, white and red roundel insignia, world's first on aircraft.

Army [*Armée de terre*]

The French Army [*Armée de terre*] is the country's largest defence force, with 134,000 military personnel, 15,500 reservists and 27,500 civilians. In 2005 it was reorganised and now comprises entities directly responsible to the Chief of Staff as well as the Commands, Forces and Services responsible to the General Staff.

The five entities directly responsible to the Chief of Staff [*Chef d'état-major de l'armée de Terre (CEMAT)*] are:

- Army Inspectorate [*Inspection de l'armée de Terre (IAT)*]

- Army Technical Section [*Section technique de l'armée de Terre (STAT)*]

- Command of Light Aviation [*Commandement de l'aviation légère de l'armée de Terre (COMALAT)*], principally helicopters

- Doctrine and Forces Employment Centre [*Centre de doctrine d'emploi des forces (CDEF)*]

- **Foreign Legion** Command [*Commandement de la légion étrangère (COMLE)*].

The eight principal entities responsible to the General Staff [*État-major de l'armée de Terre (EMAT)*] include two top-level commands, each with subordinate brigades and regiments that include armoured units and artillery:

- Command of the Terrestrial Fighting Forces [*Commandement de la force d'action terrestre (CFAT)*], with headquarters at Lille

- Command of the Terrestrial Logical Forces [*Commandement de la force logistique terrestre (CFLT)*], with headquarters at Montlhéry.

Four ancillary entities:

- Five Territorial Districts [*5 régions Terre (RT)*]

- Personnel Management Centre [*Direction du personnel militaire de l'armée de terre (DPMAT)*]

- Central Service Directorate [*Direction centrale de service*]

- Basic and Advanced Military Education Command [*Commandement de la formation de l'armée de terre (COFAT)*].

And two French contingents in multinational forces:

- French contingent of the **Eurofor** [*Eurofor (Fr)*]

- French contingent of the **Eurocorps** [*Corps européen (CE)(Fr)*].

For further information, contact the office of the Chief of Staff: Ministère de la défense, Armée de terre, 231 bd Saint-Germain, 75007 Paris, Tel: 01 42193011, *www.defense.gouv.fr/terre*, or for information and recruitment, one of the 102 *Centres d'Information et de recrutement de l'armée de terre (CIRAT)*, Tel: 3240, *www.recrutement.terre.defense.gouv.fr*.

Central Direction of General Intelligence
[*Direction centrale des renseignements généraux (DCRG)*]

The Central Direction of General Intelligence [*Direction Centrale des Renseignements Généraux (DCRG)*], often abbreviated *Renseignements Généraux (RG)*, is the intelligence service of the **National police** (Chapter 10). Originally founded in 1907, it now has extensive duties, from supervising gambling and horse racing to ensuring internal security and guarding against terrorism. It has a headquarters and four sub-directorates in Paris, seven *directions zonales*, 23 *directions régionales* and 99 *directions départementales*. For further information, contact the headquarters at 11 rue des Saussaies, 75008 Paris, Tel: 01 49274927, *www.interieur.gouv.fr/rubriques/c/c3_police_nationale*

Civil defence [*Sécurité civile*]

Civil defence is implemented in its modern sense in which civilian and military entities jointly perform a broad range of tasks, including search and rescue, fighting forest fires, locating and neutralising munitions from the world wars of the 20th century and providing aid in natural disasters, as well as supporting preparedness measures to protect life and property in the event of war or terrorist attack. Many governmental agencies and private organisations are involved. The two largest, which also act as portals for information from and contacts with other agencies and organisations, are:

* The Directorate of Defence and Civilian Security [*Direction de la Défense et de la Sécurité Civile (DDSC)*], 87-95 quai du Dr-Dervaux, 92600 Asnières, Tel: 01 49274927, *www.interieur.gouv.fr*, click on *Défense et sécurité civile*.

* The French High Committee for Civil Defence [*Haut Comité Français pour la Défense Civile (HCFDC)*], c/o **National Institute for Security Studies,** 3 avenue du Stade de France, 93210 Saint-Denis la Plaine, Tel: 01 49981020, *www.hcfdc.org*.

The Civil defence logo is a blue triangle in an orange circle.

Conscription

On 5 September 1798, Deputy Jean-Baptiste Jourdan (1762-1833) introduced a law that made defence of the country obligatory for all men of age 20; thereby France became the first country in the world to use conscription to raise military forces. Conscription remained in force for nearly 200 years and was suspended by a law enacted 8 November 1997. The last conscripts were called up in 2001, and from 2002 on, the armed forces consist only of professionals who enlist of their own volition. In place of conscription, for all young men and women ages 16-18 there now is an obligatory *rendez-vous citoyen* national defence preparedness day.

Defence industries [*Industries de défense*]

With 8% of the global arms transfer market, France is the world's third largest exporter, behind the USA (31%) and Russia (32%).* Understandably, two of Europe's largest defence industries are French: Thales, a group started in France a century ago and now with activities in more than 30 countries, *www. thalesgroup.com*, and EADS, an abbreviation of European Aeronautic Defence and Space, a joint French-German conglomerate, *www.eads.com*. For further information, visit *ixarm*, the French defence industries portal at *www.ixarm.com* supported by the *Délégation Générale pour l'Armement (DGA)* of the Ministry of Defence, 6, boulevard Victor, 00460 Armées, *www.defense.gouv.fr/dga*.

*SIPRI Yearbok 2005, Armaments, Disarmament and International Security, pocket-sized summary edition, page 15, Stockholm Peace Research Institute, Signalistgatan 9, 16970 Stockholm, Sweden, Tel: +46 8 6559700, downloadable in seven languages from *www.sipri.org*.

Directorate of Territorial Surveillance
[*Direction de la surveillance du territoire (DST)*]

Set up in 1944, the DST, a directorate of the **National Police** (Chapter 10), acts as the country's domestic intelligence agency. Its activities include counter-espionage, counter-terrorism and the general security of the country against threats from abroad. For further information including an overview of its missions, contact the head office at 7 rue Nélaton, 75015 Paris, Tel: 01 40579942, *www.interieur.gouv.fr/rubriques/c/c3_police_nationale/c335_dst/index_html*.

Emergency preparedness [*Organisation des secours*]

Emergency preparedness consists of precepts and plans to cope with natural or man-made disasters. The principal plans of France are:

* *Orsec*, an acronym for *Organisation des secours*, is an umbrella plan for coping with disasters for which local means are insufficient [*Catastrophe à moyens dépassés (CMD)*], such as floods, earthquakes, radioactive contamination (Orsec-Rad) or other widespread or long-lasting disasters. Each *Département* has an Orsec, administered by its **Administrative centre** (Chapter 21), and the office of the Prime Minister administers the national Orsec.

* Red plan [*Plan rouge*] for coping with a large number of casualties in a limited

area by organising and coordinating rescue resources. The Red plan is managed by the **Fire brigades** (Chapter 15).

- White plan [*Plan blanc*] for coping with a sudden influx of patients to hospitals, as the result of a natural disaster, epidemic or major accident, with patients arriving on their own or by red plan evacuation. Once initiated, the white plan is managed by **SAMU** (Chapter 15).

- Specific intervention plans [*Plans particuliers d'intervention (PPI)*] to cope with high-risk incidents. The PPI are managed by the relevant agencies; for instance, the Nuclear Safety Authority [*L'Autorité de Sûreté nucléaire*] manages the nuclear PPI.

- Special emergency plans [*Plans de secours spécialisés (PSS)*] to cope with specific incidents at defined places, including:

  - Accifer plan for railway accidents

  - Biotox plan for spread of biological agents

  - Piratair plan for aircraft hijacking

  - Piratome plan for spread of radioactive materials

  - Piratox plan for spread of toxic agents

  - Polmar plan for sea pollution

  - Samir plan for aviation accidents over water

  - Sater plan for aviation accidents on land

  - Accimada plan for hazardous material accidents.

The PSS are managed by the relevant national, departmental and local authorities as well as by the organisations involved, such as the railways for the Accifer plan.

Eurocorps [*Corps européen*]

The Eurocorps is a high-readiness force employed in the NATO framework. Upon founding in 1992, it initially was a French-German initiative that resulted from the Elysée Treaty of 1963 calling for strengthening French-German defence relationships. Spain joined in 1994, and Luxembourg joined in 1996. In 2002, Greece, Poland and Turkey integrated personnel into the Eurocorps headquarters staff. In 2003, Canada integrated personnel into the headquarters staff, and Austria, Finland, Italy, Great Britain and the Netherlands joined the staff. For further information, contact Eurocorps headquarters, BP 82E, 67020 Strasbourg Cedex 1, Tel: 03 88432002, *www.eurocorps.net*.

Eurofor

Eurofor, an acronym for European Operational Rapid Force, is a multinational entity comprising contingents from France, Italy, Portugal and Spain. Founded in

1995, it has a staff at its headquarters in Italy and a total force capability of a light division. In accordance with the Western European Union (WEU) Petersberg declaration of June 1992, Eurofor is principally involved in humanitarian, peacekeeping and peace enforcement tasks. After the EU members negotiated the Amsterdam Treaty of 1997, the WEU tasks essentially became part of the European Security and Defence Policy. For further information, contact Eurofor, Caserma Predieri via Arentia, 354 Florence, Italy, Tel: +39 055 6527312, *www.eurofor.it*.

Foreign Legion [*Légion étrangère*]

One of the famed military organisations of modern times, the French Foreign Legion [*Légion étrangère*] was founded in 1831 by King Louis Philippe, to support war in Algeria. Thereafter, Legions were raised to augment French forces in other engagements, including the Crimean War in 1855, the Italian campaign in 1859 and the expedition in Mexico in 1863. It was on 30 April 1863 at the battle of Camerone in Mexico that the Foreign Legion became a legend. An infantry unit of 62 soldiers and three officers, led by Captain Jean Danjou (1828-1863) was attacked by a far superior Mexican force of 1200 infantry and 300 cavalry. Despite the hopeless situation, the Legionnaires fought valiantly, losing 62 men, including the Captain. When the Mexican commander asked the last three soldiers to surrender, they insisted on keeping their flag and on being allowed safe passage home, taking their fallen Captain with them. The astonished Mexican commander agreed to their terms, commenting that "these are not men, but devils". Each year, the Legion now solemnly commemorates its fallen in ceremonies on the 30th of April, Camerone Day.

Today the Legion has a total strength of 411 officers, 1731 non-commissioned officers and 5513 Legionnaires, hailing from 136 different countries. Men of any nationality may join the Legion, as indeed although the Legion often serves abroad, "Foreign" applies to its personnel; if a Frenchman enlists, he does so under a "declared identity", and his nationality is changed to that of another French-speaking country.

In fact, all who enlist in the Legion must do so under a "declared identity". Even though most men who enlist have nothing to hide, and the Legion thoroughly investigates all applicants to weed out the undesirable, the declared identity ensures equal footing for all, regardless of whether they seek anonymity or not. After one year of service, a Legionnaire may apply for a "military regularisation of situation" and resume his real identity. After three years of honourable service, a Legionnaire serving under his real name may request French citizenship. The Legion is open to all who wish to start a new life as a Legionnaire. Previous military experience is an asset but is not required, as military skills are taught in basic training. Likewise, capability in French is an asset, but is not required, as French is taught during basic training.

For further information on the Foreign Legion, contact the Information and Recruitment headquarters at Fort de Nogent, 94120 Fontenay Sous Bois, Tel: 01 49745065, *www.legion-etrangere.com*. If you wish to enlist in the Legion, contact the Recruitment headquarters or any of the 11 enlistment centres in mainland France listed on the recruitment website at *www.legion-recrute.com*, with pages in French, English and 11 other languages. Note that you may enlist only in mainland France and that you must pay your own travel expenses and arrange for a visa if necessary. However, once enlisted, free board, lodging and clothing are immediately provided.

General Directorate for External Security
[*Direction générale de la sécurité extérieure (DGSE)*]

The DGSE is the country's external intelligence agency. It comprises five divisions:

- administration [*direction de l'administration*]
- operations [*direction des opérations*]
- intelligence [*direction du renseignement*]
- strategy [*direction de la stratégie*]
- technology [*direction technique*].

The DGSE headquarters are at 141 boulevard Mortier, 75020 Paris, Tel: 01 42193011, no website.

National Civil Security Council
[*Conseil national de sécurité civile (CNSC)*]

Established in February 2005 as part of the **National Institute for Security Studies**, the National Civil Security Council is a top-level group under the auspices of the Ministry of the Interior. It addresses all risks to life, property and the environment, and it consists of:

- Five colleges, each with 11 members, representing the State; Legislators and Representatives; Public protection, services, transport and utilities; Sector experts; and Expert organisations.
- 15 members of the elected administration.
- Selected consultants, called in as needed.
- An executive committee, with members of the executive, defence, emergency preparedness and securities studies entities.

The Council meets at least once a year and is empowered to recommend legislation and other measures to the Prime Minister. For further information, visit the National Institute for Security Studies website at *www.inhes.interieur.gouv.fr* and click on *Le CNSC*.

National Institute for Security Studies
[*Institut national des hautes études de sécurité (INHES)*]

Established in July 2004, the **National Institute for Security Studies** is the central agency for documentation, publication and studies related to all aspects of security, including:

* crime and crime statistics, the responsibility of one of its divisions, the **National Crime Observatory** (Chapter 10).

* top-level security matters, the responsibility of the **National Civil Security Council**

* economic security, including fair competition and financial practices

* information technology security, including matters of privacy and intrusion

* selected sectors, including the fight against hooliganism, video surveillance, public transport security, urban security and the impacts of technology on security.

It is the country's central repository for documentation concerning security, including books and other works, theses and compilations, research reports, educational materials and periodicals. All materials are catalogued in databases and are available at the Institute's documentation centre upon appointment, Tuesdays and Thursdays, 09:30-12:00 and 14:30-17:30. For further information, contact the Institute at 3 avenue du Stade de France, 93218 Saint-Denis-La-Plaine Cedex, Tel: 01 55845300, *www.inhes.interieur.gouv.fr*.

Navy [*Marine nationale*]

The French Navy [*Marine nationale*] is the second largest in Western Europe after the Royal Navy of the UK. It is organised in four branches:

* The Naval Action Force [*Force d'action navale (FAN)*], with 12,000 personnel, is the surface fleet of 115 ships. The largest ship is the 38,000 ton Charles de Gaulle nuclear-powered aircraft carrier; a planned second carrier is scheduled to enter service in 2014. The 12,000 ton Jean d'Arc is the fleet's helicopter carrier. The newest vessels are two Projection and Command Ships [*Bâtiments de Projection et de Commandement*], the Mistral and the Tonnerre, high-technology, multi-purpose ships for a wide range of missions including projection of force, command centres, population assistance, evacuation of citizens and hospitalisation.

* The submarine forces [*Force sous-marine (FSM)*], with 3300 personnel and ten boats, including nuclear deterrent submarines.

* The Naval Air Force [*Aviation navale (AVIA)*], with 7300 personnel and 147 combat and supply aircraft as well as helicopters.

* The Amphibious Assault and Ground Forces [*Fusiliers marins et commandos*], with 2020 personnel.

For further information, contact the office of the Chief of Staff: Ministère de la défense, Marine nationale, 1 place Saint-Thomas-d'Aquin, 75007 Paris, Tel: 01 42193110, or 08 10501501 for recruitment, *www.defense.gouv.fr/sites/marine*.

Vigipirate

Created in 1978, *Plan Vigipirate* is the national security alert system that entails reinforcing police and military security by increasing surveillance of and uniformed presence in public places whenever disorder threatens. It comprises four designated levels of threats, identified by colours:

- Yellow level [*Niveau jaune*]: raise security levels to deal with real yet uncertain risks with minimum disruption of everyday activities.

- Orange level [*Niveau orange*]: initiate measures against possible terrorist action, including means that partly disrupt everyday activities.

- Red level [*Niveau rouge*]: initiate measures against known risks of one or more terrorist attacks and authorise their resultant disruption of everyday activities.

- Scarlet level [*Niveau écarlate*]: prepare to deal with major attacks that may occur concurrently or separately and may cause extensive damage; prepare for rescue and response and authorise extensive disruptions of everyday activities.

For further details, visit the website of the office of the Prime Minister at *www.premier-ministre.gouv.fr/information/fiches_52/plan_vigipirate_50932.html*.

Volunteering [*Volontariat*]

After **conscription** was terminated and the last conscripts were called up in 2001, young people have been offered three principal options for volunteering:

- Volunteering in Civil Defence and Security [*Volontariat civil dans le domaine de le prévention, de la sécurité, et de la défense civil*], which for young men and woman, 18 to 26 years old, principally means enlisting in the **Army** or the **Gendarmerie** (Chapter 10).

- Volunteering for Social Cohesion and Solidarity in Mainland France [*Volontariat de cohésion sociale et de la solidarité en France Métropolitaine*] in most cases involves volunteer work for a Non-Government Organisation (NGO), such as the French Red Cross [*Croix-Rouge française*], 98 rue Didot, 75694 Paris Cedex 14, Tel: 01 44431100, *www.croix-rouge.fr*.

- Volunteering abroad [*Volontariat international*] for periods of up to two years in international development and humanitarian assistance initiatives; for further information, contact Civi, 30-34 rue La Pérouse, 75116 Paris, Tel: 08 10101828, *www.civiweb.com*.

13
Drink, drugs and tobacco

As elsewhere, people in France avidly consume mind-altering substances. Most stick to the legal ones – alcohol, caffeine and nicotine – but illegal drugs are sought-after. The reasons are as intractable as the human quest for intoxication is universal.

The result, as elsewhere, has been private and public dialogue on alcoholic drink, drugs and tobacco. Caffeine, the most popular substance, seems peripheral, perhaps because it is regarded as being the ingredient of a foodstuff, though it is included on the list of banned doping agents in sports.

The climate is a mix of permissiveness and prohibitionist, with good reason: mind-altering substances, legal and illegal, are known to harm individuals and families. Accordingly, many international as well as domestic French organisations address the health and social problems created by imprudent use of drink, drugs and tobacco. These efforts, along with more restrictive rules on smoking and stricter penalties for drink driving have had beneficial effects. Alcoholic drink consumption is declining: the per-capita consumption of wine is now about 60 litres a year, down from more than 103 litres a year in 1970. Smoking is dwindling, so much so that tobacconists now are diversifying into other goods.

Yet France remains the country where sales of drink and tobacco are less restricted than in many other countries. Almost all food shops, supermarkets and hypermarkets sell respectable selections of beers and wines, and vineyard outlets and roadside stands sell wines. And with some 31,000 shops across the country, most open 13 hours a day, the tobacconists are the country's most readily available local shop.

Absinthe

Absinthe, a high-alcohol, anise-flavoured liqueur, arguably is the most famed of French distilled drinks, linked to the lives of Parisian artists and writers of the late 19th and early 20th centuries. Its origin is not well documented, but according to the most accepted account, it was first made from wormwood [*absinthe*] around 1792 in Couvet, Switzerland by a French doctor, Pierre Ordinaire (1741-1821), a native of Quingey in the *Département* of Doubs (No. 25). In 1797, Henri-Louis Pernod

(1776-1851), a Swiss distiller, produced the first *absinthe* for sale. In 1805, Mr. Pernod opened *Maison Pernod Fils*, a distillery for *absinthe* in France, at Pontarlier in the *Département* of Doubs. From then on, the popularity of *absinthe* grew apace, and by the 1860s, cafés and cabarets across France served it, and by 1910, total sales of *absinthe* amounted to 36 million litres a year. It became too easy to drink too much, as depicted in 1876 in *L'absinthe*, a painting by Edgar Degas and described in 1877 in *L'Assommoir*, the seventh novel in Émile Zola's Rougon-Macquart cycle. *Absinthe* fell into disrepute and was claimed by many to be an addictive, dangerous drug. That led to it being banned in 1915. It became legal again in 1922, and today *spiritueux à base de plantes d'absinthe* are made in several varieties. They are not drunk straight, but are diluted, three to one or more, with ice water and sugar, and then take on a milky opalescence called *louche*. For further information, contact Pernod, 120 avenue du Maréchal Foch, 94015 Créteil Cedex, Tel: 01 49815151, *www.pernod.fr* with pages in French and English.

Pre-ban absinthe advertisement.

Alcoholics Anonymous [*Alcooliques Anonymes*]

Alcoholics Anonymous is the international organisation that helps alcoholics cure themselves. In France, there is a central AA office in Paris, seven regional sites and groups across the country. For further information, contact AA, 29 rue Campo Formio, 75013 Paris, Tel: 01 48064368 or helpline 08 20326883, *www.alcooliques-anonymes.fr*, with an interactive locator map for local groups.

Appellation d'Origine Contrôlee (AOC)

The *Appellation d'Origine Contrôlée (AOC)*, sometimes shortened to *Appellation Contrôlée (AC)*, is the designation of place of origin of wines and spirits in the highest of the four **wine categories.** By law enforced by the **Institut National des Appellations d'Origine (INAO)**, only registered products from the defined area of an appellation may carry its AOC designation. Some AOC names have become famous round the world, so much so that like some tradenames, they frequently, though incorrectly, are used as generic designations. Perhaps most known are champagne and cognac.

- Champagne is a sparkling white wine associated round the world with indulgence and celebration. It is produced in the appellation defined in four areas in the Region of Champagne-Ardenne, comprising the *Départements* of Ardennes (No. 8), Aube (No. 10), Marne (No. 51) and Haut-Marne (No. 52), and there are as many labels and varieties as there are wine producers in the Appellation. For further information on the Champaigne region, contact the Champagne-Ardenne tourist office at 15, avenue de Maréchal Leclerc, BP 319, 51013 Châlons-en-Champagne Cedex, Tel: 03 26218580, *www.tourisme-champagne-ardenne.com*, with pages in French, English, Dutch and German.

- Cognac is a double-distilled brandy made in the appellation defined around the *commune* of Cognac, in the *Département* of Charente (No. 16) in the west central part of the country. Considered a luxury brandy round the world, its five leading producers [*maisons de cognac*] are Camus, Hennessy, Martell, Otard and Remy-Martin. For further information on the Cognac area, contact Hôtel de Ville de Cognac, 68 boulevard Denfert Rochereau, BP 17, 16108 Cognac Cedex, Tel: 05 45365536 or freephone 08 00878889, *www.ville-cognac.fr*, with pages in French and English.

Beer [*Bière*]

Beer consumption is modest, amounting to 33.7 litres per capita per year, less than a quarter that of leading Ireland (118 litres), Germany (117 litres) and the UK (100.6 litres).* Nonetheless, 60% adults drink beer, and most supermarkets carry a wide selection of French and imported beers. As in other countries, French beers are classified according to percentage alcohol content by volume into five principal categories:

- *Sans alcool*, 0 – 1.2%
- *De table*, 2.0 – 2.2%
- *Bock*, 3.3 – 3.9%
- *De luxe*, more than 4.4%
- *Bières spéciales*, more than 5.5%

Some **breweries** offer an intermediate category, *Light* with 2.8 – 3.2% alcohol. Shandy [*panaché*], a mixture of beer and lemonade contains up to 1.2% alcohol, and flavoured [*aromatisé*] beers containing fruit juice are of low alcohol content. For an overview of beer in France, see *La Bière et la Brasserie* by Claude Bourgeois (Paris, Presses Universitaires de France, 1998, 128 pages paperback, ISBN 2-130-48911-7).

*2004 consumption figures from *Brasseurs de France*.

Breweries [*Brasseries*]

Despite modest consumption, France is the fifth largest beer producing country in

Europe, with an annual production of nearly 1700 million litres, a tenth of it exported. There are 51 major breweries in the country, many with guided tours; the Kronenbourg brewery at Strasbourg is among the city's top ten tourist attractions. Additionally, there are some 200 micro-breweries, of two sorts: craft breweries [*brasseries artisanales*] appealing to local markets and producing 10,000 to 500,000 litres a year, and café breweries [*café-brasseries*], where beer is produced and sold on the spot. For further information, including links to the eight beer museums, collections of brewery paraphernalia and the like, contact the French Breweries Association [*Brasseurs de France*], 25 Boulevard Malesherbes, 75008 Paris, Tel: 01.42662927, *www.brasseurs-de-france.com*, *contact@brasseurs-de-france.com*, or, for brewery training and education, the French Institute of Brewing and Malting [*Institut Français des Boissons, de la Brasserie et de la Malterie*], 7 rue du bois de la Champelle, BP 267, 54512 Vandoeuvre Cedex, Tel: 03 83448800, *www.ifbm.fr* with pages in French and English.

Combating drugs [*Lutte contre la drogue*]

Four governmental agencies are involved in combating illegal drugs and drug addiction:

* DATIS, the abbreviation for *Drogues, alcool, tabac info service*, The Drug, Alcohol and Tobacco Information Service, a national help line with three numbers: 08 00231313 for drugs, 08 11913030 for alcohol and 08 11912020 for cannabis.

* INPES, the abbreviation for *Institut national de prévention et d'éducation pour la santé*, the **National Institute for Prevention and Health Education** (Chapter 22), *www.inpes.sante.fr*.

* OFDT, the abbreviation for *Observatoire français des drogues et des toxicomanies*, the French Monitoring Centre for Drugs and Drug Addiction, the national focal point for *Réseau européen d'information sur les drogues et les toxicomanies (REITOX)* coordinated by the European Monitoring Centre for Drugs and Drug Addiction (EMCDDA) and consequently dedicated to cooperation and networking of national and international resources, *www.ofdt.fr*.

* Toxibase, the national network of nine information and documentation centres dealing with the care, prevention and integration of persons suffering pharmacodependence, *www.toxibase.org*.

The four agencies have pooled their capabilities in an information portal supported by MILDT, the abbreviation for *Mission interministérielle de lute contre la drogue et la toxicomanie*, the Interdepartmental Mission for the Fight against Drugs and Drugs addiction, 7 rue Saint Georges, 75009 Paris, Tel: 01 44632050, *www.drogues.gouv.fr* in French and English.

Institut national des appellations d'origine (INAO)

The INAO, part of the Ministry of Agriculture, is responsible for regulating the use of place names and consequently is involved in identifying and maintaining a system of delimitation of geographic areas that may be associated with their produce. Its roots go back to 1905, with the enactment of a law giving the government the power to designate the boundaries of areas of noteworthy name. In 1935, the *Appellations d'Origine Contrôlée (AOC)* was clearly defined, and the INAO was founded with its decision-making body, the *Comité national des vins et eaux de vie*, empowered to put proposals to ministries. In 1990, the INAO remit was extended to dairy and other agricultural products. In 1992, a European Council regulation set up a system for protecting geographic names in two categories, Protected Designation of Origin (PDO) and Protected Geographic Indication (PGI). In 1994, the AOCs were designated as PDOs of France according to the EC regulations, and in 1999 the EC enacted a wine regulation including the rules for **Quality Wine Produced in Specified Regions (QWPSR)**. In less than 95 years, the French concept of the worth of a designated place of origin, an *appellation*, has become the practice for a wide range of comestibles across France and for wines across Europe. For further information, contact INAO at 51 rue d'Anjou, 75008 Paris, Tel: 01 53898000, *www.inao.gouv.fr* with pages in French and English.

Narcotics [*Stupéfiants*]

French is more precise than English in describing drugs, as it has two words for narcotic substances: *narcotiques*, medicinal drugs, and *stupéfiants*, recreational drugs as well as addictive medical drugs. The *stupéfiants* include the narcotics and psychotropic substances that are illegal in France as well as in all other countries adhering to the United Nations international drug control conventions, as monitored by the International Narcotics Control Board (INCB) [*Organe International de Contrôle des Stupéfiants (OICS)*], *www.incb.org*. The principal illegal *stupéfiants* are:

- narcotics, such as opium, morphine, codeine, thebaine, heroin, methadone and related drugs and substances
- depressants, such as barbiturates, methaqualone, meprobamate, benzodiazepines
- stimulants, such as cocaine, amphetamines and methamphetamines, anorectic drugs, and related substances
- cannabis, as in marijuana, herbal cannabis, cannabis resin, hashish, or hashish oil
- hallucinogens, such as LSD, mescaline and peyote, STP, DOB, MDA, MDMA, phencyclidine (PCP) and related substances.

Importing or smuggling *stupéfants* into the country is a customs offence punishable by fines or imprisonment, and their possession, use, delivery and sale are offences under criminal law. If you use prescription psychotherapeutic drugs for medical reasons and wish to take them with you to France, you must provide official documentation for their import: a **Schengen certificate** (Chapter 22) from an EU/EEA country, or a permit issued by an agency recognised by the **French Health Products Safety Agency** (Chapter 22) from other countries.

Narcotics Anonymous [*Narcotiques anonymes*]

Narcotics Anonymous is the international organisation that helps drug addicts cure themselves. In France, there is a head office in the greater Paris area at 1 bis rue Gutenberg, 93100 Montreuil Sous Bois, Tel: 01 48583846, and a regional office in Marseille at 1 rue Barbaroux, 13001 Marseille, Tel: 04 96120581, as well as a national website at *www.nafrance.org*.

National Association of Drug Addiction Interveners [*Association nationale des intervenants en toxicomanie (ANIT)*]

Founded in 1980, ANIT is the national forum for drug addiction interveners, the professionals who work with drug addicts and are concerned with all aspects of drug addiction. ANIT is concerned with the rights of drug addicts as persons in all aspects of decision making. It adheres to the concept that drug addiction cannot be isolated from its social context nor from the society in which it occurs. It works to this remit by acting as a central clearing house for publications and other information on drug addiction. It was one of the founding members of the Federation of European Professional Associations Working in the Field of Drug Abuse [*Fédération Européenne des Associations d'Intervenants en toxicomanie (ERIT)*], an initiative under the auspices of EU Public Health [*Santé Publique*]. With ten regional groups across the country, it has a head office in Paris at 9 passage Gatbois, 75012 Paris, Tel: 01 43437238, *www.anit.asso.fr*.

National committee against smoking [*Comité national contre le tabagisme (CNCT)*]

The CNCT is the principal anti-smoking organisation that works for smoke-free public and workplace environments, limiting promotion of tobacco, heightening awareness of the hazards of smoking, combating addiction and regulating tobacco and nicotine at the national level. It also is among the oldest organisations of its sort, founded in 1868 by Dr. Henry Blatin (1806-1869). It now has the status of a public agency and consequently is involved in national public awareness campaigns and in promoting legislation to curtail the damage of passive smoking. For further information, contact the head office at 31 av du Général Michel-Bizot, 75012 Paris, Tel: 01 55788510, *www.cnct.org*.

Non-smokers' rights association [*Droits des non-fumeurs (DNF)*]

DNF was founded in 1973 to promote the rights of non-smokers, an aim it still pursues through collecting research on the hazards of passive smoking, lobbying and otherwise working to influence public opinion. It has offices in almost all regions and a head office at 5 passage Thiéré, 75011 Paris, Tel: 01 42770656 and a website at *dnf.asso.fr* with services for non-smokers, including a guide to non-smoking restaurants (*Guide des restaurants non-fumeurs*) and an interactive locator map of the regional offices.

Quality Wine Produced in Specified Regions (QWPSR) [*Vins de qualité produits dans des régions déterminées (VQPRD)*]

The laws and regulations governing wine now conform to the European Council regulation on the common organisation of the market in wine across Europe*. Part of the regulations specify the rules for Quality Wine Produced in Specified Regions (QWSPR), which apply to wines, semi-sparkling wines, sparkling wines and liqueur wines. The word "quality" is used in the sense of "eminence": just as the production of a luxury car is more complex and selective than that of an ordinary car, a quality wine is defined in terms of restrictions applied to its area of production, the vine varieties, the cultivation methods, the wine-making methods, the minimum natural alcoholic strength, the yield per hectare and the analysis and assessment of organoleptic characteristics. Two French **wine categories** are QWSPR: *Appellation d'Origine Contrôlée (AOC)* and *Vin Délimité de Qualité Supérieure (VDQS)*.

*Council Regulation (EC) No. 1493/1999 of 17 May 1999, on the common organisation of the market in wine, amended several times, most recently 14 October 2003.

The smoking law [*La loi concernant le tabac*]

The smoking law, principally the Éven act (*La loi Évin*) effective 1 January 1993, and associated rulings and regulations are intended to limit the damage to health caused by the smoking, snuffing, sucking or chewing of tobacco products. The principal provisions are:

- Save for a few exceptions, such as the display windows of tobacco shops, advertising is banned, both direct – as for tobacco products, pipes, cigarette papers and cigarette rollers – and indirect, as for other products bearing the brand names of tobacco products.

- Mandatory health warnings on packaging as well as concise statements of the tar and nicotine yield of cigarettes.

- The minimum age for buying tobacco products is 16.

- Children younger than 16 cannot smoke in schools, and smoking is prohibited in schools with children younger than 16.
- Vending machine sale of tobacco products outside tobacco shops is prohibited.
- No smoking on public transport vehicles or in facilities for public use, including cinemas, theatres, and museums.
- Restaurants must be divided into smoking and non-smoking areas.

Tobacco (*Tabac*)

Tobacco has been monopolised since 1674. In 1786, the government took over control of the tobacco sector, and the first brands of cigarettes were sold in 1876. In 1926, the government set up *Service d'exploitation industrielle des tabacs (SEIT)*, which in 1959 was renamed *Société d'exploitation industrielle des tabacs et Allumettes (SEITA)*. In 1984, SEITA was privatised, with the government holding all shares. In 1995, SEITA was floated on the Paris Bourse and consequently no longer was completely controlled by the government. In 1999, SEITA merged with *Tabacalera* of Spain to form *ALTADIS*, an acronym for *Alliance du Tabac et de la Distribution*. ALTADIS now is the world's fourth largest tobacco company, with cigarette brands including *Ducados, Fortuna, Gauloises* and *Gitanes*. Its cigar operation is the world's largest, with a quarter of the global market, and is most known for brands including *Antonio y Cléopatra, Farias, Hav-a-Tampa* and *Montecristo*. In addition to manufacture of tobacco products, SEITA also licenses and controls the distribution of tobacco products in France. For further information, contact ALTADIS, Eloy Gonzalo 10, 28010 Madrid, Spain, Tel: +34 913609000, *www.altadis.com*.

Tobacco consumption [*Consommation de tabac*]

According to the most recent figures compiled by the **National institute for prevention and health education** (Chapter 22) in its "Health barometer" (*Baromètre santé*) statistics, among the population, 15-75 years old, smoking is declining, most among the young, 15-25 years old, and now a quarter of all women and more than a third of all men smoke regularly.

Vendanges

La vendange means mature wine grapes as well as the harvest of them. The plural, *les vendanges* means the time of the year at which the wine grape harvests take place, usually in September, but depending on the region and the maturity of the grapes, sometimes as early as late August and as late as early October. Accordingly, *vendange* is the root of *vendémiaire*, the name of the first month of the **Revolutionary calendar** (Chapter 30), corresponding to 22 September – 21

October. *Vendange* applies only to wine grapes and not to table grapes for eating or to raisin grapes. Today, most wine grapes are harvested by automatic agricultural machines known as *machines à vendanger*, but harvesting by hand is still done in some vineyards.

The first month of the Revolutionary calendar was named after the wine grape harvest.

Vocabulary [*Vocabulaire*]

The vocabularies of beer and wine drink are large; below are the most commonplace words in French and English.

French	English
Bière	**Beer**
à la pression	on draught
aromatisé	flavoured
bock	bock, but limited to 3.9% alcohol content
brasserie	brewery
de luxe	luxury, more than 4.4% alcohol content
de table	mild
houblon	hops
levure	brewers' yeast
light	light, up to 3.2% alcohol content
orge	barley
panaché	shandy (mix of beer and lemonade)
sans alcool	non-alcoholic
spéciales	strong, more than 5.5% alcohol content
Vin	**Wine**
blanc	white
brut	dry (often sparkling)
cave	winemaker's cellar, may or may not be underground
cave coopérative	winemaker's cooperative

cépage	grape variety
chai	wine and spirit storehouse
châteaux	estate, with or without a manor house
clos	walled vineyard
côte	coast, slope
cru	vineyard, in the sense of the plants grown
cuve	vat, tank
cuvée	vatful, vintage
délimitation de la zone de production	demarcation of the area of production
demi-sec	medium dry
domaine	estate
doux	sweet
eau-de-vie	spirits
encépagement	vine varieties
fermentation	fermentation
mis en bouteille	bottled
moûts de raisins	grape must
raisin	grape
rendement à l'hectare	yield per hectare
rouge	red
sec	dry
supérieur	0.5%-1% greater alcohol content
titre alcoométrique volumique minimal naturel	minimum natural alcoholic strength by volume
variétal	varietal
vignoble	vineyard
vinification	wine-making method
vins de liqueur	liqueur
vins mousseux	sparkling wines
vins pétillants	semi-sparkling wines

Wine categories [*Catégorie de vins*]

Wine is produced in four categories. There are two table wine categories:

- *Vin de Table* is everyday wine that may be produced from any variety of wine grapes anywhere in France, but by law cannot be subjected to chaptalisation (enhancing by adding calcium carbonate or sugar). It is the cheapest category, often used in cooking and accounting for about 30% of all wine sold.

- *Vin de Pays*, literally "wine of the country", is simple wine produced in a particular area or region – usually comprising one or more *Départements* – from specified grape varieties that may be stated on labels. Sometimes called "house wine" [*vin ouvert*], it is more expensive than *vin de table* and accounts for about a quarter of all wine sold.

and two categories of **Quality Wine Produced in Specified Regions (QWPSR)**, with ranking and registration administered by the *Institut National des Appellations d'Origine (INAO)*.

- *Vin Délimité de Qualité Supérieure (VDQS)* is wine produced under strict regulations on place of origin, permissible varieties of grapes, viticultural methods, yields per hectare of growing area, production methods and alcohol content achieved by natural means. As VDQS wines are made according to the same regulations as for AOC wines, the VDQS category sometimes is a step on the way to AOC, the highest category. Nonetheless, some wines remain VDQS, and together account for about 2% of all wine sold.

- *Appellation d'Origine Contrôlée (AOC)*, sometimes shortened to *Appellation Contrôlée (AC)* is a certification of geographical origin and characteristics that applies to wines as well as to dairy and other agricultural products. By law, it is illegal to produce and sell a product under one of the AOC designations if it does not comply with the relevant requirements of that designation. For wines, the AOC parameters of place of origin and grape variety are stated on labels as the hallmarks of the *appellation* involved.

The four wine categories sometimes are called "quality rankings", in which "quality" means "eminence" or "luxury", as for clothing, accessories and cars. The basic wine qualities related to health, purity and authenticity of origin are specified by laws administered by the **DGCCRF** (Chapter 27).

Wine guides [*Guides des vins*]

Of the innumerable guides to French wines, arguably the most authoritative is *Le vin – Gault Millau*, compiled each year by the publishers of the **Gault Millau Guide** (Chapter 47). The 2006 edition (1160 pages, 13×21 cm, ISBN 2-914913-11-7) lists the essentials of 1350 *domaines* and *châteaux* and descriptions of 16,800 wines.

14

Education, science and technology

France spends more on education than the average for OECD countries, nearly 6% of its gross domestic product (GDP)*. Across the country, more than 15 million people – a quarter of the population – are in schools or higher educational institutions.** The education system is similar to that of other European countries at the basic schooling levels but differs in higher education. There are three levels:

1. Primary and lower-secondary schools, compulsory for all.

2. Upper secondary schools, the first year compulsory until age 16, the remaining two of three years elective.

3. Higher education, selective, often by entrance examination, consisting of degree programmes at universities, university-level institutions and vocational training schools.

Two French designations use the same words as in English, but with different meanings:

- *Collège*, a lower secondary school, not as in English, an establishment of higher education, often part of a university.

- *Baccalauréat*, a diploma awarded after upper secondary school, not as in English, the degree of Bachelor awarded after three or four years of higher education.

France has long had a reputation for educational excellence. Indeed, the word "intellectual" is a French invention, brought in from Latin in the 13th century. Moreover, the teaching profession is highly regarded, at all levels; university students speak not of "going to college", but rather of *aller à la fac*, being at a faculty. Even the schools often have been ahead of their time. In the 19th century, the teaching of mathematics in secondary schools included calculation in a variety of number systems, including the octal system to base 8, the hexadecimal system to base 16 and the binary system to base 2, as well as conversions between the systems developed in 1798 by mathematician Adrien Marie Legendre (1752-1833).

In an educational reform implemented in 1898, number systems other than the commonplace decimal system to base 10 were dropped from school mathematics curriculum, as pragmatic educators argued that though theoretically interesting, they had no practical application. That decision was premature. In the 1940s, binary, octal and hexadecimal arithmetic became essential in the development of digital computers, and engineers and scientists sought out old French mathematics textbooks to learn what French secondary school pupils had been taught in the 19th century.

That mathematical excellence built upon the tradition of centuries arguably dating back to the work of Marin Mersenne (1588-1648), the French monk who in 1644 devised a method of identifying prime numbers that to this day are called "Mersenne numbers". Likewise, the roots of computer programming and open-source software can be

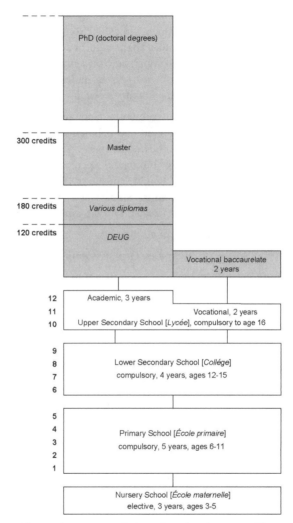

General structure of the educational system. The numbers at the left are the school years for primary and secondary schooling, and credits for higher education, shown shaded.

traced back to a single French invention, now more than two centuries old. In 1804, Joseph Marie Jacquard (1752-1834) developed an attachment for a loom that facilitated automatic control of the actions of weaving complex patterns. Aside from creating modern mechanical figure weaving, the Jacquard attachment was the first programmed device, as it was controlled by chains of punch cards. Moreover, in 1806, his invention was bought by the government and declared to be public property, which is the first known instance of open-source software.

Today, France spends about 2.2% of its GDP on research, more than average for the EU, half of it government funded*. Some high-profile research is on the leading edge of technologies that augur significant breakthroughs in the 21st century, such as a new generation of supersonic passenger aircraft due to fly in 2020, while much research is on more down-to-earth matters, such as land and forest use and water resources so vital to the country's leading agricultural sector.

Though educational excellence and research tradition and funding promote progress, curiosity remains the mainspring. Pierre Morvan, who lives in Brittany, has become a world-renowned expert on ground beetles and has contributed to the understanding of how biological species are formed. He has no formal higher education, but is self taught, and until 1987, when his work was recognised by a Rolex Award, his scientific studies and field trips to the Caucasus, Iran, Bhutan, Nepal and Tibet were financed by his job as a taxi driver.

*OECD in Figures, 2005.

**Including the overseas *Départements*, figures from *L'éducation nationale en chiffres, 2004-2005*.

Academic Ranking

Each year, the Shanghai Jiao Tong University ranks universities round the world and publishes a list of the top 500. Universities world-wide have come to accept the ranking as a reliable comparative index of academic performance. Not unexpectedly, the USA dominates the higher positions, though in the 2006 rankings, there are 26 European universities in the top 100, of which four are in France: *Université Pierre & Marie Curie* (Paris 06) ranked 45th, *Université Paris-Sud* 11 ranked 64th, *Université Louis Pasteur* Strassbourg ranked 96th and *École Normale Supérieure* (Paris) ranked 99th. Of the top 100 European Universities, 12 are in France. The complete rankings are available on the Shanghai Jiao Tong University website at *ed.sjtu.edu.cn/ranking.htm*, *ranking@sjtu.edu.cn*.

Academy [*Académie*]

In French, the name *Académie* has two principal meanings:

- a learned body, one of five Academies of the **Institut de France**
- an educational agency, one of the 36 administrative divisions of the educational system, 26 in metropolitan France including Corsica and nine overseas. Under the leadership of a *Recteur*, each *Académie* administers and manages the budgets of educational activities within its delimited area. For further information, including an interactive locator map of the *Académies* visit the **Education portal** website page at
  www.education.gouv.fr/systeme_educatif/academie/default.htm.

Adult education centres [*Groupement d'établissements publics d'enseignement (GRETA)*]

Across the country, more than 290 adult education centres in the GRETA network coordinate and administer the adult education programmes offered by 6500 educational institutions, mostly lower and upper secondary schools. Most of the programmes aim to enable adults already in the workforce to qualify for certificates and thereby for jobs in sectors requiring special skills, such as:

* accounting
* agricultural industries
* broadcasting (audiovisual)
* business
* civil engineering
* electrical and electronics industries
* health and social services, environment
* hotel trade and tourism
* industrial technologies
* information technology
* languages
* printing and graphic arts
* secretarial services and office automation
* shipbuilding.

For further information, visit the GRETA website with an interactive locator map of the 290 GRETA centres, at *www.education.gouv.fr/fp/greta.htm*.

Adult vocational and professional training and education association [*Association nationale pour la Formation Professionnelle des Adultes (AFPA)*]

AFPA, a principal agency of the Ministry of Social Affairs, Labour and Solidarity, has extensive facilities and services for training adults to promote their access to or return to work. It has a staff of more than 5000 teachers and instructors, 800 career advisers and 350 counselling engineers who provide services in guiding, training and validating for employment in France. Moreover, AFPA shares its expertise with European partners and is involved in the Equal, Interreg III and Leonardo pan-European programmes. It also supports international cooperation, principally by setting up training and skill assessment schemes in other countries. For further information, as well as for an interactive listing of AFPA services and contact addresses in all Regions, visit the website at *www.afpa.fr*.

Aerospace research [*Recherche aéronautique et spatiale*]

The French contributions to modern aerospace technologies are legend. The Sud-Aviation Caravelle, produced from 1955 to 1972, was the first commercially successful jet passenger aircraft and accordingly has been called "the DC-3 of the jet age". The Anglo-French Concorde, designed in the 1960s and in service for 25 years, from 1976 to 2000, was the first and to date only supersonic passenger aircraft. In 2005, Airbus, the French, German, British and Spanish consortium based in Toulouse, delivered 378 aircraft, against rival Boeing's 290, making it the world leader for the third consecutive year. Arianespace, the pan-European commercial space transportation company owned 60% by France and headquartered at Courcouronnes, 20 km southeast of Paris, is the world leader in satellite launching from a base in French Guiana [*Guyane*], using the Ariane launch vehicle, now the world's most powerful.

In June 2005, at the Paris Air Show, the French Aerospace Industries Association [*Groupement des Industries Françaises Aéronautiques et Spatiales (GIFAS)*] and the Society of Japanese Aerospace Companies (SJAC) entered an agreement to conduct research and develop a 300-passenger supersonic commercial aircraft scheduled for first flight in 2020. For further information on this project as well as on all other aerospace research, contact GIFAS at 8 rue Galilée, 75116 Paris, Tel: 01 44431700, *www.gifas.asso.fr* in French and English.

Allowance for school children [*Allocation de rentrée scolaire (ARS)*]

The *Allocation de Rentrée Scolaire (ARS)* is one of the means-tested **Family benefits** (Chapter 22) that is paid once a year by the **National Family Allowance Fund** (Chapter 22) for each child, age 3 to 18, attending school, in an apprenticeship or pursuing studies. It is set in late July and paid out in late August by the 123 local *Caisses d'allocations familiales (Caf)* across the country. For further information on ARS, contact the nearest Caf, listed in the **Yellow pages** (Chapter 31) or located by keying in your postcode in the dialogue box on the Caf website at *www.caf.fr*. As this book goes to press, the ARS is €263.28, and the means test is a net annual family income of €17,011 with one child, €20,937 with two children, €24,863 with three children and an additional €3,926 for each additional child.

Baccalaureate [*Baccalauréat*]

The *Baccalauréat* is a diploma awarded at the end of upper secondary [*Lycée*] studies as well as the examinations that students sit to qualify for it. It is similar to the British A-Levels and to the German *Abitur* and is the certification required to enter higher education or pursue a vocational career. Consequently, it differs from the Baccalaureate of English-speaking countries, which is the university degree of bachelor awarded after three or four years of higher education.

The *Baccalauréat* is awarded in various streams of studies. Until the 1994-95 academic year, there were eight principal streams, identified by letters A to H. In 1993, the designations were rearranged to be more descriptive, and there now are three principal streams, each subdivided:

General [*Général*]

- S: Scientific [*Scientifique*]

- L: Literary [*Littéraire*]

- ES: Economic and Social [*Économique et Sociale*]

Technological [*Technologique*]

- STG: Science and Ancillary Technologies [*Sciences et technologies de la gestion*]

- STI: Industrial Sciences and Technologies [*Sciences et technologies industrielles*]

- STL: Research Sciences and Technologies [*Sciences et technologies de laboratoire*]

- SMS: Health and Social Sciences and Techniques [*Sciences médico-sociales*]

- STPA: Food Industry Sciences and Technologies [*Sciences et technologies du produit agroalimentaire*]

- STAE: Agricultural and Environmental Sciences and Technologies [*Sciences et technologies de l'agronomie et de l'environnement*]

- TMD: Techniques of Music and Dance [*Techniques de la musique et de la danse*]

- Hotel and restaurant business. [*Hôtellerie – Restauration*]

- Vocational [*Professionnel*]

- More than 70 trades [*spécialités*], from *Aéronautique* (Aeronautics) to *Vente-marketing* (Sales and marketing).

Comprehensive, up-to-date information on the Baccalauréat is available at the **Education portal**, on page *www.education.gouv.fr/sec/baccalaureat/default.htm*

Bilingual Schools [*Écoles bilingues*]

There are numerous bilingual schools that offer instruction in French and other languages, both to assist foreign children who wish to integrate into the French school system and to provide mother-tongue instruction for children who will continue in the school systems of other countries. There are three principal options:

- French schools in which extra tutoring is provided for foreign pupils who are insufficiently proficient in French to follow a normal course of study.

- Bilingual schools offering instruction in French and in other languages.
- International schools operated by foreign-language communities or interest groups.

The *enfantsbilingues.com* portal provides a comprehensive overview of bilingual schooling across the country. The international public schools are shown on a locator map downloadable at *www.investinfrance.org/France/Living/Education/ map_international_public_schools_en.pdf*.

Bologna declaration [*Déclaration de Bologne*]

The Bologna declaration, so named because it was first signed by the Ministers of Education of 29 European countries meeting at the University of Bologna, Italy in 1999, puts forth a framework of three cycles of higher education – bachelor's, master's and doctoral degrees – aimed to harmonise academic hierarchies across Europe and thereby promote mobility between academic communities. France was one of the original 29 signatories, and more than 40 countries now are signatories and consequently members of the European higher education area. For further information, contact the Bologna Process Committee of the National Unions of Students in Europe (ESIB), head office at 17A Avenue de la toison d'Or, BE-1050 Brussels, Belgium, Tel: +32 2 5022362, *www.esib.org/BPC/welcome.html* or the Bologna Process Secretariat 2005-2007, Department for Education and Skills, Sanctuary Buildings, Great Smith Street, London, SW1P 3BT, UK, Tel: +44 0870 0002288, *www.dfes.gov.uk/bologna*.

Bullying and violence in schools [*Violences scolaires à l'école*]

As in other countries, school bullying and violence (SBV) are persistent social problems with which educators increasingly are concerned. In a landmark book, *Histoire de l'enseignement en France 1800-1967* (Paris, Armand Colin, 1968, republished 1991, 523 pages, ISBN 2-2003-1079-X), historian Antoine Prost (1933-) pointed out that violence in schools was hardly new, as it had entrenched historical roots. Though long viewed by sociologists as a minor problem*, school violence now is a matter of public concern and there have been many books on it, most recently *L'École et ses Violences* (Paris, Economica Editions, 2006, 181 page paperback, ISBN 2-71718-5158-5) by Jacques Pain, a professor of educational sciences at the *Université Paris X*. Accordingly, the **French Forum for Urban Safety** (Chapter 10) joined with similar forums in other countries in the VISIONARIES-NET project, which in 2006 launched the VISIONARY web portal on SBV at *www.bullying-in-school.info* that has become a principal clearing house for information in many languages as well as a forum for promoting means of dealing with SBV.

Tackling Violence in Schools: A Report from France, by Eric Debarbieux,

Catherine Blaya and Daniel Vidal, European Commission CONNECT Initiative UK-001, 2001.

Centre international d'études pédagogiques (CIEP)

Founded in 1946, the *Centre International d'Études Pédagogiques (CIEP)* – it uses that name in English – is concerned with French as a foreign language and foreign languages in France as well as with international cooperation in education and training. Among its many tasks are the administration of the **International Option Baccalaureate (OIB)** and the organisation of the **French proficiency examinations** (Chapter 28). CIEP has a staff of 200, a head office at Sèveres near Paris and an agency on Réunion Island. In addition to compiling and offering extensive documentation on languages, CIEP hosts conferences in its extensive facilities in the 19th century *Manufacture royale de porcelaine chateaux* and grounds. For further information, contact CIEP at 1 Avenue Léon Journault, 92310 Sèvres, Tel: 01 45076000, *www.ciep.fr* with pages in French, English and Spanish and a downloadable brochure in French, English or Chinese versions.

Concours

Entry into many sectors of public service is contingent upon qualification awarded by competitive examination [*concours*]. There are eight principal qualifications, seven for primary education and one for higher education:

- *CRPE*, an abbreviation for *Concours de recrutement des professeurs des écoles*, the State recruitment exam for teaching in primary education

- *CAPES*, an abbreviation for *Certificat d'aptitude au professorat de l'enseignement secondaire*, the State recruitment exam for teaching a mainstream subject in secondary education

- *CAPET*, an abbreviation for *Certificat d'aptitude au professorat de l'enseignement technique*, the State recruitment exam for teaching a technical subject in secondary education

- *CAPEPS*, an abbreviation for *Certificat d'aptitude au professorat d'éducation physique et sportive*, the State recruitment exam for teaching physical education and sports in secondary education

- *CAPLP*, an abbreviation for *Certificat d'aptitude au professorat de lycée professionnel*, the State recruitment exam for teaching in vocational upper secondary education

- *CPE*, an abbreviation for *Concours de recrutement de conseiller principal d'éducation*, the State recruitment exam for pastoral education counsellors

- *CAFEP*, an abbreviation for *Certificat d'aptitude aux fonctions d'enseignant dans les établissements d'enseignement privé du second degré sous contrat*, the State recruitment exam for teaching in private secondary education

- *Agrégation*, the certificate for teaching in higher education.

The number of candidates admitted to *concours* depends on the number of positions available. For further information as well as for the details of the *concours* to be held, see the two-volume special issue of the educational bulletin, *Bulletin Officiel*, published each year in mid May and available online at *www.education.gouv.fr/bo/default.htm*.

Distance education [*Enseignement à distance*]

Distance education started in 1939 with the founding of the National Centre for Distance Education [*Centre National d'Enseignement à Distance (CNED)*]. Today CNED is a public agency of the Ministry of Education and is the largest distance education operator in Europe, with 350,000 registered students, more than half of the total for France and more than a tenth of the total for Europe. CNED offerings include ordinary schooling, higher education and vocational training. Certificates and diplomas signifying the successful completion of CNED studies are awarded not by CNED but rather by the educational institutions with which it cooperates. For overviews, course catalogues and other information, contact CNED, BP 60200, 86980 Futuroscope Chasseneuil Cedix, Tel: 05 49499494, *www.cned.fr* with pages in French, English and Spanish.

The National Conservatory for Art and Craft [*Conservatoire National des Arts et métiers (CNAM)*] was founded in 1794 to preserve the arts and crafts of the old regime. Today, it is an institute of higher education that conducts research and offers degrees up to the level of engineer [*ingénieur*], physically from 150 centres across the country and in cooperation with 32 partner institutes of higher education in other countries. For further information, contact CNAM, 292 rue Saint-Martin, 75141 Paris Cedex 03, Tel: 01 40272000, *www.cnam.fr*.

The National Association for the Vocational Training of Adults [*Association nationale pour la Formation Professionnelle des Adultes (AFPA)*] is the principal education entity of the Ministry of Social Affairs, Labour and Solidarity. It guides and trains adults, principally unemployed people with no, or very few, qualifications. Its principal goal is to encourage trainees to access or return to employment. Its distance education division is the National Centre for Distance Education and Training [*Centre National d'Enseignement et de Formation A Distance (CNEFAD)*], 111 rue Henry Wilhelm, 68027 Colmar Cedex, Tel: 03 89217400, *www.di.afpa.fr*.

Distance education at the university level is provided by 35 universities amalgamated for the purpose in the Interuniversity Federation for Distance Education [*Fédération Interuniversitaire de l'Enseignement à Distance (FIED)*].

The degree options and the arrangements for study are similar to those of the distance education offered by open universities in other countries, such as the Netherlands and the UK. For further information, contact FIED at Domaine universitaire de la Bouloie, Bâtiment TD2, 25030 Besancon Cedex, Tel: 05 49499494, *www.telesup.univ-mrs.fr*, with links to member universities as well as to other organisations active in distance education.

Education in the arts [*Education artistique et culturelle*]

Across the country there are countless schools of art, cinema, dance, drama, entertainment, music and other genres of the arts and culture. For example, in music there are two national conservatories, one in Paris and one in Lyon, 36 national conservatories at the regional level [*Conservatoires nationaux de région (CNR)*], 105 national music schools [*Écoles nationales de musique (ENM)*] and myriad smaller schools at the municipal level. The best single source of information on all aspects of education in the arts is the Ministry of Culture and Communications website at *www.culture.gouv.fr*; click on *Infos pratiques*, then on *formation*, and then on one of nine sectors, such as on *Musique, danse, théâtre et spectacles* for an overview of programmes, requirements and schools of music, dance, theatre and the performing arts. The Ministry is located at 3 rue de Valolis, 75001 Paris, Tel: 01 40158000, and offers a broad selection of cultural information to the public, such as the *www.culture.fr* website in French, English and Spanish, with an interactive map of forthcoming events in the *Régions*.

Education portal [*Portail de l'éducation*]

The **Ministry of Youth, Education and Research** maintains a comprehensive portal at *www.education.fr* with concise, up-to-date information on education at all levels, from preschool through university. It includes the relevant details of primary and secondary schools and of higher education, including degrees, fields of study, curricula and graduation requirements. There are practical guides to admission and financial aid. Those wishing to pursue a career in teaching will find all relevant details, including the full texts of educational laws and regulations. There are links to more than 140 specialised websites as well as an onsite search engine. Most of the documentation is in French, but principal documents as well as the main site are also available in English, German and Spanish.

EduFrance

EduFrance is a public website dedicated to the international aspects of education and training in France with an emphasis on offerings to students coming from other countries. It provides extensive information on coming to and studying in France, as well as the details of the 180 educational institutions, including 71 universities, with which EduFrance cooperates and the offices that EduFrance has abroad, around the world. For further details, contact EduFrance at 173, boulevard Saint-Germain, 75006 Paris, Tel: 01 53633500, *www.edufrance.fr*, with pages in French, English, Spanish, Arabic, Bulgarian, Chinese, Korean, Greek, Indonesian, Japanese, Polish, Portuguese, Russian, Thai, Turkish and Vietnamese.

Égide

Égide is a non-profit organisation that manages governmental international cooperation initiatives. Its roots go back to 1960, when the Ministry of cooperation founded ASATOM, an organisation to arrange courses for overseas technicians. Its focus remains in the educational sector, but today it is an extensive organisation with a staff of more than 200 that deals with foreign students, scholarship holders, guests, academics and other high-level experts, as well as with managing conferences, exchange programmes and twinning projects between French agencies and their counterparts in other countries. Its head office is in Paris, and it has branches in Lyon, Marseille, Montpellier, Toulouse and Strasbourg, as well as smaller offices in 21 other towns in the country. It has copious databases and offers extensive information free on its website, in French and in English. The name Égide, adopted 1 January 2000, is the French word for "aegis" and comes from the classical Greek word for the breastplate worn by Zeus and by Athena, the goddess of wisdom and science, and consequently connotes protection of learning. Égide, 28 rue de la Grange aux Belles, 75010 Paris, Tel: 01 40405858, *www.egide.asso.fr*.

Enrolment in school [*Inscription a l'école*]

If you wish to enrol a child in school and already are in France, inquire at the nearest town hall [*Mairie*]. Depending on the size of the town and the way the *Mairie* is organised, the enrolment office may be called *service des écoles* or may be combined with other functions, such as *service des écoles, des jeunes et de l'information (SEJI)*. In cities, you may be directed to an *Inspection académique*. If you are abroad and seek information in advance, contact the **Academy** (regional educational agency) for the *Département* where you and your child will live. To enrol a child for the first time, you will need to furnish four items of information:

- the child's passport or birth certificate (translated if not already in French)
- proof of residence, such as a recent utility bill or rental contract
- immunisation record showing immunisation against diphtheria, polio, tuberculosis (BCG) and whooping cough
- *attestation d'assurance scolaire*, proof of **insurance** (Chapter 2).

Equivalency [*Équivalences*]

If you wish to transfer your vocational qualifications, education or training to France from another country in Europe, you may do so using a **Europass**. If you seek equivalency for education or experience gained in a country outside Europe, contact the **National Commission for Vocational Certification** for information on the procedures required.

If you seek equivalency of an academic diploma awarded in another country, contact the French institute of higher education where you intend to continue your studies, as France has no set procedure for assessing the equivalence of foreign and French diplomas. Nonetheless, there are *de facto* guidelines, ensured by the **Bologna declaration** and by the **European Credit Transfer System (ECTS)**. Further details are available in pages on the **Égide** website at *www.egide.asso.fr*.

Europass

Set up in December 2004, Europass is a joint initiative of the European Commission and the *Centre Européen pour le Développement de la Formation Professionnelle (CEDEFOP)* that aims to open doors to learning and working across Europe. A Europass makes skills and qualifications clearly and easily understood anywhere in Europe and thereby promotes mobility. A Europass consists of five documents:

- a Curriculum Vitae (CV) and a Language Passport that you can fill in yourself
- a Certificate Supplement, a Diploma Supplement and a Mobility statement that are filled in and issued by national authorised organisations.

Europasses are supported by a network of National Europass Centres; the French national centre website is at *www.europass-france.org*. For further information on Europass in 17 European languages, visit the CEDEFOP website at *europass.cedefop.eu.int*.

European Credit Transfer System (ECTS) [*Système européen de transfert d'unités de cours capitalisables*]

ECTS was developed in by the European Commission (EC) to provide consistent procedures that ensure recognition of academic qualifications transferred between countries. It now is used by more than 1000 colleges and universities across Europe and includes means of measuring and comparing learning, including uniform guidelines for academic credits, marks and recognition, including the Diploma Supplement (DS) document that can be attached to a diploma to provide a standardised description of the education that it certifies. For further information on ECTS, visit the portal at *www.ects.info*. The ECTS/DS national coordinator for France is Martine Froissart, Directeur du CESEM, Reims Management School, 59 rue Pierre Taittinger, BP 302, 51061 Reims Cedex, Tel: 03 26774580, *martine.froissart@reims-ms.fr*.

Eurydice

Eurydice is the Information Network on Education in Europe. Set up in 1980, it promotes the exchange and the compiling of accurate, comparable information on educational systems and on national educational policies and now involves more than 30 countries. The National Unit in France is maintained by the Ministry of Youth, Education, and Research (*Ministère de l'Éducation nationale, de l'Enseignement supérieur et de la Recherche, Direction de l'Évaluation et de la Prospective*), 61-65 rue Dutot, 75732 Paris Cedex 15, *www.education.gouv.fr*. The European Unit of the Network coordinates activities and supports comparative studies. For further information, contact the head office, Avenue Louise 240, B-1050 Brussels, Belgium, Tel: +32 26005353, Fax: +32 26005363, *www.eurydice.org*, *info@eurydice.org*.

Experience credit [*Validation des acquis de l'expérience (VAE)*]

The VAE permits skills gained through on-the-job experience to be considered equivalent to formal courses for attaining vocational certificates. If you seek certification and believe that your experience may count toward it, contact the nearest office of the **National Commission for Vocational Certification** for the details of VAE that apply to your profession.

Grandes écoles

Higher education takes place at public universities and other academic establishments known as *Grandes écoles*, literally "Great schools", but seldom translated into English. Unique to France, the concept of the *Grandes écoles* was initiated by Napoleon to ensure that the country's brightest young minds could be drawn to the government, the military and the engineering corps. The success of that aim is evident today, as many top-level positions in government as well as six in ten CEOs of the country's 100 biggest companies are *Grand école* graduates.

Admission to a *Grand école* is selective and entails successful completion of a two-year preparatory course, commonly called *Prépas*, after the baccalaureate of upper secondary school. There are 174 *Grandes écoles* in the country, of which four are said to be the "aces" in educating the elite of the country:

- *Hautes Etudes Commerciales – HEC*, a leading **Business school** founded in 1881 in Paris: HEC Campus, 1 rue de la Libération, 78351 Jouy en Josas Cedex, Tel: 01 39677000, *www.hec.fr*.

- *École Nationale d'Administration – ENA*, the national school of public administration founded in 1945 in Paris and now with a second campus in Strasbourg, ENA, 13 rue de l'Université, 75343 Paris Cedex, 01 49264545, *www.ena.fr*.

- *École Normale Supérieure – ENS*, originally a teacher training school founded in 1794 and now a broad scope academic institution offering curricula in the liberal arts and the sciences; ranked 31st in the top 100 universities in Europe in the 2005 **Academic ranking**: ENS, 45 rue d'Ulm, 75230 Paris Cedex 05, Tel: 01 44323000, *www.ens.fr.*

- *École Polytechnique – EP*, the most prestigious engineering *Grande école*, with curricula in the sciences, founded 1794 and renowned worldwide for having had many of the great names of science on its faculty or as students, including Ampère, Carnot and Poisson, ranked 83rd in the top 100 universities in Europe in the 2005 **Academic ranking**: EP, 98128 Palaiseau Cedex, Tel: 01 69333333, *www.polytechnique.fr.*

For a complete list of all *Grandes écoles* and details of the education they offer, in French and in English, contact *Conférence des Grandes Écoles*, 6 boulevard Saint-Michel, 75272 Paris Cedex 06, *www.cge.asso.fr.*

Higher education [*Enseignement supérieur*]

Higher education is offered by the *Grandes écoles* and by the **Universities,** mostly public but also some private. Public higher education is free, though small registration fees are required. Private higher education may require fees.

Institut de France

Established in 1795, Institut de France is one of the vanguards of the learned world. In 1867, historian and theorist Ernest Renan* observed that "The *Institut de France* is something unique to France. Several countries have academies that can rival our own as far as the renown of the individuals who comprise them and the significance of their work. However, only France has an institution wherein all the endeavours of the human mind may converge; where the poet, historian, critic, mathematician, physician, astronomer, naturalist, economist, jurist, sculptor, painter, and musician can all call one another 'colleague'."

The *Institut de France* comprises five *Académies*:

- The French Academy [*Académie française*], founded in 1635 and concerned with French language and culture
- The Academy of Inscriptions and Literature [*Académie des inscriptions et belles-lettres*], founded in 1663 and concerned with works of writing
- The Academy of Sciences [*Académie des sciences*], founded in 1666
- The Academy of the Fine Arts [*Académie des beaux-arts*], established in 1816 by merging three older Académies: the Academy of Painting and Sculpture, founded in 1648, the Academy of Music, founded in 1669, and the Academy of Architecture, founded in 1671

- The Academy of Ethics and Political Science [*Académie des sciences morales et politiques*], founded in 1795, abolished in 1803, and reinstated in 1832.

The Institut also has a Department of Education and a Publications Service. For further information on the institute and its five *Académies*, contact the principal facility at Château de Chantilly, Musée Condé, BP 70243, 60631 Chantilly, Tel: 03 44626262, *www.institut-de-france.fr*, with pages in French and summary pages in English and Italian.

*Ernest Renan (1823-1892), one of the leading intellectuals of his day, is most remembered for his famous essay, *Qu'est-ce qu'une nation?* ("What is a Nation?") of 1892, first presented as a lecture at the **Sorbonne**.

International Baccalaureate Organisation (IBO)
[*Organisation du baccalauréat International*]

The International Baccalaureate comprises three educational programmes established by the International Baccalaureate Organisation (IBO):

- Primary Years Programme (PYP) for pupils ages 3 to 12 years
- Middle Years Programme (MYP) for pupils ages 11 to 16 years
- Diploma Programme (DP) for pupils ages 16 to 19 years.

The three programmes form a continuous sequence, but each may be offered independently. Around the world, 1756 schools in 122 countries together offer IBO programmes. In France, there are 11 schools offering one or more of these programmes. For further information on and the addresses of these schools, visit the international IBO website at *www.ibo.org*, click on "Europe" in the "Around the World" map and then on "Countries in this Region" and select "France" to bring up a list of the schools. Contact the IBO head office for other information, International Baccalaureate Organization, Route des Morillons 15 Grand-Saconnex, CH-1218, Genève, Switzerland, Tel: +41 227917740, Fax: +41 227910277, *www.ibo.org*, *ibhq@ibo.org*.

International Option Baccalaureate
[*Option Internationale du baccalauréat (OIB)*]

The OIB is an international option of one of the three General **Baccalaureates** that is offered to foreign students at *Lycées* with foreign language programmes. It is a French diploma and consequently differs from the programme of the **International Baccalaureate Organisation**. Each year, about a thousand young people from other countries take the OIB examinations, organised and administered by the **Centre International d'Études Pédagogiques (CIEP)**. For further information, visit the OIB pages of the CIEP website at *www.ciep.fr/oib* in French, English and Spanish, with an online locator map of schools across the country that offer the OIB.

Ministry of Youth, Education and Research
[*Ministère de l'éducation nationale, de l'enseignement supérieur et de la recherche*]

The Ministry is responsible for all aspects of education, from preschool to the universities, as well as for research in the public sector. It publishes extensively, both in print and online via the **Education portal**. For further information, contact *Ministère de l'éducation nationale, de l'enseignement supérieur et de la recherche*, 110 rue de Grenelle, 75357 Paris SP 07, Tel: 01 55551010, *www.education.gouv.fr*. For an overview of education in figures, visit the website, click on *Ministère*, then on *publications* and then on *Les grands chiffres de l'éducation* to download the most recent edition of *L'éducation nationale en chiffres*.

Montessori schools [*Écoles Montessori*]

Montessori schools offer education based on the approaches developed by Maria Montessori (1870-1952), the first woman medical doctor in Italy. In her work in Rome at a free clinic for the children of the working class and the poor, she became convinced that intelligence is not rare and that most newly born children have a human potential that only needs to be developed. Accordingly, she evolved principles, practices and teaching methods aimed to elicit that inborn potential. The ideas spread, and there now are Montessori schools and foundations world-wide.

In France, across the country there are nursery, primary and secondary schools and an institute for training Montessori teachers, *L'Institut Supérieur Naria Montessori (ISSM)*; for further information, contact *L'Association Montessori France (AMF)*, 322 rue des Pyrénées, 75020 Paris, Tel: 01 43588472, *www.montessori-france.asso.fr*. Moreover, there is a teachers' association, *Montessori en France (MEF)* that organises activities and exchanges, provides background materials and acts as a clearing house for international teacher mobility: MEF, Artracing, 30 rue Edith Cavell, 92400 Courbevoie, Tel: 06 26125923 Monday-Friday 20-21 hours, *www.montessorienfrance.com*.

National Centre for Educational Information
[*Centre National de Documentation Pédagogique (CNDP)*]

The CNDP is a national teaching resource centre that has 30 regional centres [*Centres Régionaux de Documentation Pédagogique (CRDP)*], 170 media libraries [*médiathèques*] and 130 bookshops open to the public for sale of books and other documentation relevant to education. It supports the *SCÉRÉN* Internet portal that offers catalogues, brochures and other educational materials, most of which may be downloaded free. For further information, contact CNDP, 29 rue d'Ulm, 75230 Paris Cedex, Tel: 01 55436000, *www.cndp.fr*, with an interactive Regional Centre locator map at *www.cndp.fr/cndp_reseau/default.asp?rub=cndp_carte*

National Commission for Vocational Certification [*Commission nationale de la Certification Professionnelle (CNCP)*]

The CNCP was set up in 2002 as an interministerial, interprofessional agency concerned with vocational education and certification. Its three principal areas of activity are:

- maintaining the **National Register of Professional Certifications**
- supporting measures for **Experience credit**
- interacting with *Centre Européen pour le Développement de la Formation Professionnelle (CEDEFOP)* in internationalisation of vocational education and training, including support of the **Europass**

For further information, contact CNCP at 80 rue Lecourbe, 75015 Paris, Tel: 01 44383153, *www.cncp.gouv.fr* with a list of CNCP regional offices across the country and links to other national and international organisations.

National Office for Information on Education and Careers [*Office National d'Information sur les Enseignements et les Professions (ONISEP)*]

ONISEP develops and makes available comprehensive documentation about training, educational resources, employment and jobs across the country. It is concerned with education in the broad sense, vocational as well as academic. It offers numerous magazines and guides, available online or at its 28 offices in the *Régions*. For further information, contact the head office at 12 mail Barathelemy Thimonnier, BP 86, 74423 Marne La Vallee Cedex, Tel: 01 64803500, *www.onisep.fr* in French, with summary pages in English and Spanish and an interactive locator map of offices across the country.

National Register of Professional Certifications [*Répertoire National des Certifications Professionnelles (RNCP)*]

RNCP is a database of all vocational certifications, including certificates, diplomas and certificates of qualifications [*Certificats de Qualification Professionnelle (CQP)*], maintained by the **National Commission for Vocational Certification** on its website at *www.cncp.gouv.fr*. The database is searchable using numerous descriptors, such as level [*niveau*], vocational sector [*secteur d'activité*] and details of experience [*éléments de compétence acquise*] and has online tools to facilitate search regardless of whether you know or do not know the name of the title of a certification [*l'intitulé de la certification*].

Prépas

Prépas is the everyday contraction of *Les classes Préparatoires aux Grandes Écoles*

(CPGE), the two-year preparatory course taken after the **Baccalaureate** as part of the admission requirements to one of the *Grandes écoles*. Full information on the CPGE are available on the **Education portal** at *www.education.gouv.fr/sup/cpge.htm*.

Private schools [*Écoles privées*]

About 17% of primary and secondary school pupils attend private schools [*écoles privées*], as do about 14% of students in institutions of higher education. The costs of private schooling vary, principally according to whether a school offers the same curriculum as do public schools and consequently receives State support. There are two forms of contract for State-supported schools:

* Simple contracts [*contrats simples*], principally for elementary schools offering the same curricula as public schools.

* Contracts of association [*contrats d'association*], with more extensive requirements of equivalency with public schools.

All private schools, whether State supported or not, must meet minimum standards set by the Ministry of Education. An overview of private schooling and the regulations applying to it is available on the **Education portal** at *www. education.gouv.fr/systeme_educatif/enseignement_prive.htm*.

Four organisations provide information on private schooling:

* *Centre d'Information et de Documentation sur l'Enseignement privé (CIDE)*, 84 boulevard Saint-Michel, 75006 Paris, Tel: 01 53103320, *www.cide.fr*.

* *Centre National de Documentation sur l'Enseignement Privé (CNDEP)*, also called *Centre Fabert*, 20 rue Fabert, 75007 Paris, Tel: 01 4705 268, *www.fabert.com*.

* *Fédération Nationale de l'Enseignement Privé Laïque (FNEPL)*, 37 rue d'Amsterdam, 75008 Paris, Tel: 01 40230336, *www.fnepl.com*.

* *Office de Documentation et d'Information de l'Enseignement Privé (ODIEP)*, 45 avenue Georges Bernanos, 75005 Paris, Tel: 01 43299070, *www.odiep.com*.

Despite widespread acceptance of a proper State education for all, many middle-class families send their children to private schools, in part to ensure religious instruction not given in the secular public school system. As France is Catholic by tradition, many of the private schools are Catholic, like Lycée de Marcq, whilst some, like Lycée Ozar Hatorah, are Jewish. Thanks to State support, the costs of attending a private school are moderate, now slightly less than € 3000 a year.

Moreover, judging by the baccalaureate secondary-school leaving examination results, private schools increasingly outperform public schools. In March 2006, the *Le Figaro* newspaper analysed the results of the 2005 baccalauréat examinations given across the country and found of the 29 Lycées attaining a top ranking of 100% passing the examination, 28 were private and only one, the Lycée Henri IV in Paris, was public.

221

Research institutions [*Organismes de Recherche*]

Across the country, there are numerous public and private research institutions and groups, together with staff totalling 320,000, half of whom are research scientists. For further details, contact the Ministry of Research, 1 rue Descartes, 75231 Paris Cedex 05, Tel: 01 55559090, *www.recherche.gouv.fr*. The Deputy Ministry for Higher Education and Research [*Ministère délégué à l'Enseignement supérieur et à la Recherche*] publishes brochures and reports on all aspects of research and advanced technology, including overview brochures on the country's major research institutions, available in French and English editions, in printed form or in downloadable PDF files from the website at *www.recherche.gouv.fr/brochure/index.htm*.

School books and kits [*Livres et fournitures scolaire*]

Public schooling is free, and primary and lower secondary schools supply schoolbooks. However, parents are expected to equip their children with a reasonable kit of materials as well as sports shoes and clothing for school sports programmes and, from upper secondary school [*lycée*] on, all textbooks. Primary schools usually give out lists of recommended items in a child's school kit at the beginning of the school year [*la rentrée scolaire*]. A typical list might include:

- ballpoint pens, 3 [*3 stylos a bille*]
- coloured pencils in a bag [*une pochette de crayons de couleur*]
- diary [*un agenda*]
- exercise book [*un cahier de brouillon*]
- glue sticks, 2 [*deux bâtons de colle*]
- HB pencils, 2 [*2 crayons à papier*]
- marker board, wipeable, [*une ardoise et un chiffon*]
- napkin marked with child's name [*une serviette de table marquée au nom de l'enfant*]
- pencil case [*une trousse*]
- pencil sharpener [*un taille crayon*]
- plastic document holder [*un protège document*]
- plastic folders, 50 [*50 pochettes plastifiées*]
- ring binders, 2 [*grands classeurs*]
- rubber [*une gomme*]
- ruler, 20 cm long [*un double-décimètre*]
- schoolbag or satchel [*cartable*]
- smock or old shirt [*une blouse ou une vielle chemise*]

A low-income family may apply for means-tested **Allowance for school children**

(**ARS**) in order to afford the combined expenses of a proper school kit, **school dinners** and, for *lycée* onwards, books.

School dinners [*Restauration scolaire*]

France was among the first countries, if not the first, to serve proper meals in schools. In 1844, the mayor of Lannion in the *Département* of Côtes d'Armor (No. 22) created *Salle d'asile et d'hospitalité*, which provided meals to children of needy families. In 1849, several other *communes*, notably Paris, had established school meal programmes. In 1862, while in exile on the island of Guernsey, famed novelist Victor Hugo (1802-1885) financed hot meals for children at the local school. By 1898, 395 schools in Paris offered dinners for their pupils.

Today, across the country at midday, schools serve smaller versions of traditional French multi-course adult meals. The school day is arranged accordingly, allowing a break of at least an hour for the meal. Shorter breaks are considered barbaric, as are the vending machines and fast food services found in schools in some other countries. School meal services are supported, so meals are offered at low prices, and poor families and families with many children are given discounts. About half of the 12 million children in school eat their midday meal in the school canteen, and in the course of their schooling, eat some 2000 meals there. Consequently, parents are concerned, as school meals are essential in forming lifetime eating habits. So parents interact with school authorities and nutritionists to shape school meal policy. These and other facts about the school meal programmes are put forth in a brochure, *Votre enfant mange à la cantine*, published by the **National Consumer Institute** (Chapter 27) and downloadable from its conso.net website at *www.conso.net/securite_alimentaire_2002/brochure.htm*.

School system [*Système scolaire public*]

Most of the more than 12 million children in school attend free public schools, while 17% of them attend **private schools** that entail tuition costs. Schooling is compulsory from age 6 to 16, and the overall goal of the school system is to educate all children at least to the level of *Certificat d'Aptitude Professionnelle (CAP)*, the basic vocational certificate, and to educate 80% of them further, to the **Baccalauréat**. Save for some private schools operated by foreign communities or interest groups, all schools offer the national curriculum set forth by the Ministry of Education. The school system is typically European, with two levels, primary and secondary, and an additional optional pre-school level.

Pre-school education [*Enseignement préélémentaire*], also called "Nursery school" [*École maternelle*] is an optional offering to children aged two to five. More than a third of two-year-olds attend in *pré-maternelle* classes, and 99% of three-year-olds attend for the three years, comprising:

- *Petite section (PS)*, age 3
- *Moyenne section (MS)*, age 4
- *Grande section (GS)*, age 5.

The principal focus is on social skills and integrating children into a classroom environment; formal schooling begins in GS, when children are introduced to reading.

Primary education [*Enseignement élémentaire*], also called *École primaire*, is for children aged 6 to 11 in a programme of five successive years:

- *Cours préparatoire (CP)*, age 6
- *Cours élémentaire première année (CE1)*, age 7
- *Cours élémentaire deuxième année*, age 8
- *Cours moyen première année (CM1)*, age 9
- *Cours moyen deuxième année (CM2)*, age 10.

The principal focus is on basic skills in reading, writing and mathematics, to build a foundation for secondary school. Foreign language teaching often starts in primary school, and more than eight in ten CM2 level pupils now learn a foreign language. There are 26 hours of lessons per week and a midday lunch break of an hour and a half to two hours. Most schools offer **school dinners** during the break.

Secondary education [*Enseignement secondaire*] consists of lower secondary [*collège*] and upper secondary [*lycée*] schooling. The designation *collège* differs from that of the college of English-speaking countries, which is an establishment of higher education, often part of a university. There are four years of lower secondary [*collège*] schooling:

- *Sixième (6e)*, age 11
- *Cinquième (5e)*, age 12
- *Quatrième (4e)*, age 13
- *Troisième (3e)*, age 14.

The principal focus is on enabling pupils to manage their own time and studies. Foreign languages are taught. The last year concludes with the *Brevet des collèges* examination that qualifies pupils to enter *Lycée*. A pupil may then choose between two directions:

- general or technical *lycée*, to prepare for **higher education**
- vocational *lycée*, to prepare for entering the workforce.

There are 27 to 32 hours of classes per week, a midday lunch break of an hour and a half to two hours and two 15-minute breaks during the school day.

There are three years of upper secondary [*Lycée*] schooling:

- *Seconde (2de)*, age 15

- *Première (1ᵉ)*, age 16
- *Terminale (Term)*, age 17.

Schooling is compulsory to age 16, so pupils may leave after *Première* after two years. There are two types of *Lycées*:

- General or technological *Lycées* [*Lycées d'enseignement général et technologique*] that prepare pupils for the **Baccalauréat.**
- Vocational *Lycées* [*Lycées professionnels*] that offer 33 to 36 hours of classes a week to prepare pupils to the level of CAP, an abbreviation for *Certificat d'Aptitude Professionnelle*, a basic vocational certificate, and, with additional studies, to the level of BEP, an abbreviation for *Brevet d'Etudes Professionnelles*, a vocational proficiency certificate, or further to a vocational Baccalauréat.

School year [*Année de scolaire*]

The school year starts in early September and finishes in early July. In that period, there are 180 school days, for primary as well as secondary schools, seven and a half weeks of holidays – a week and a half in the autumn, two weeks at Christmas and two weeks in the spring, including Easter – as well as public holidays not included in school holidays, typically Armistice 1918 day, 11 November, Easter Monday and Ascension Day.

Sorbonne

La Sorbonne is the oldest and most famed institute of higher education in France, if not Europe. It was founded in 1257 as a theological college by Robert de Sorbon (1201-1274), a theologian who took his surname from his native village of Sorbon, now in the *Département* of Ardennes (No. 8). Today, it is a university, Paris IV, located in the *Quartier Latin*, at 47 rue des Écoles, 75007 Paris, Tel: 01 40462025, *www.sorbonne.fr*.

Steiner-Waldorf Schools [*Écoles Steiner-Waldorf*]

Steiner schools practice concepts put forth by Rudolf Steiner (1861-1925), the Austrian philosopher, scientist, artist and educator who inaugurated anthroposophy, the movement to develop cognition and the realisation of spiritual reality. The Steiner schools are part of the educational movement based on Rudolf Steiner's principles. In some countries, including France, the movement is known as Waldorf education, after the first such school founded in 1919 in Germany, for the children of the workers at the Waldorf-Asoria cigarette factory. There now are Steiner or Waldorf schools world-wide, there are anthroposophical societies in many countries and a world head office in Dornach, near Basel, Switzerland. In France, there are 900 schools [*écoles*] and 1600 nursery schools [*jardin d'enfants*]. For further information, contact *La Fédération des écoles Steiner-Waldorf en France*, 13 rue Gassendi, 75014 Paris, Tel: 01 43222451, *www.steiner-waldorf.org*, with an interactive locator map for schools and nursery schools across the country.

Student unions [*Syndicat étudiants*]

There are two student unions:

* Federation of General Students Associations [*Fédération des associations générales etudiantes (FAGE)*], an independent confederation of 1400 student associations; head office at 5 rue Frédérick Lemaitre, 75020 Paris, Tel: 01 40337070, *www.fage.asso.fr*
* National Union of Students in France [*Union nationale des étudiants de France (UNEF)*], associated with the **Unions** (Chapter 3), head office at 112 boulevard de la Villette, 75019 Paris, Tel: 01 42022555, *www.unef.fr*.

Both are full members of The National Unions of Students in Europe (ESIB), head office at 17A Avenue de la toison d'Or, BE-1050 Brussels, Belgium, Tel: +32 2 5022362, *www.esib.org* in English with an on-site machine translator to French, German, Italian, Spanish and Portuguese.

Teacher training faculty
[*Institut universitaire de formation des maîtres (IUFM)*]

The IFUMs are teacher training faculties attached to universities across the country and offering programmes that prepare prospective teachers for the **concours** recruitment examinations for seven certificates required to teach in primary and secondary schools. Present demographic trends suggest that from 2006 to 2015, France will lose more than half of its teachers, so the IFUMs are stepping up their programmes and accordingly by 2008 will become schools within the universities. For further details, contact Conférence des directeurs d'IUFM, Maison des universités, 103 boulevard Saint Michel, 75005 Paris, *www.iufm.education.fr* in French, English, German and Spanish and with an interactive locator map for IFUMs across the country.

Universities [*Universités*]

In the terms of the **Bologna declaration** that designates a reference architecture of higher education commonly called "3-5-8", the *Licence* corresponds to three, the *Maîtrise* or *Mastère* to 5 and the *Doctorat* to eight years of study. There are 89 public universities in the country. Their names, addresses and websites are in a list on the **Education portal** at at *www.education.gouv.fr/sup/univ.htm* under *Enseignement* *supérieur, Liste des universités*, as well as in the interactive locator map on the **Universities Network Committee** website at *www.amue.fr/Universites/Default.asp*.

Universities Network Committee
[*Comité Réseau des Universités (CRU)*]

The CRU is an academic consultative body to the Ministry of Education as well as a national and international forum for the academic community. It supports *La Maison des Universités*, the online portal at *www.cpu.fr*, with some pages in English and links to the organisations concerned with higher education, including:

- Conference of University Presidents [*Conférence des Présidents d'Université (CPU)*]
- Agency for Mutualisation of Higher Education [*Agence de Mutualisation des Universités (AMUE)*]
- Conference of Directors of Institutes for Teacher Instruction [*Conférence des Directeurs d'IFUM (CDIFUM)*]
- University Institute of France [*Institut Universitaire de France (IUF)*].

For further information, contact CRU, *Centre de Ressources Informatiques*, Campus de Beaulieu, 35042 Rennes Cedex, *www.cru.fr*.

Vocabulary [*Vocabulaire*]

The vocabulary of education is large in any language, and comparisons of educational terms, even across Europe, is an even larger field of study, as educational systems differ. Cooperation within the EU has prompted more uniform terminology and has resulted in comprehensive comparisons of terms between countries.

Educators may benefit from two **Eurydice** publications:

- European Educational Thesaurus (EET), an information resource in the 11 official languages of the EU that comprises sets of terms linked to one another by hierarchical or associative relationships.
- European Glossary on Education in four Volumes: Volume 1 on Examinations, Qualifications and Titles with 1000 national terms; Volume 2 on Educational Institutions with 670 national terms; Volume 3 on Teaching Staff with 600 national terms; and Volume 4 on Management, Monitoring and Support Staff with 500 national terms, all in English, French and German editions, with some volumes in other languages.

Both publications may be downloaded free from the website at *www.eurydice.org*, select the English, French or German site, click on Publications and then on Terminological tools.

Non-specialists may benefit more from the two downloadable glossaries of French educational terms compiled by **Égide**, one with definitions in French at *www. egide.asso.fr/fr/guide/comprendre/glossaire* and one with the same terms defined in English at *www.egide.asso.fr/uk/guide/comprendre/glossaire*.

Vocational studies [*Études professionnelles*]

Vocational studies usually start when a pupil elects the vocational line in secondary school. In chronological order, the four principal certifications are:

- CAP, an abbreviation for *Certificat d'Aptitude Professionnelle*, a basic vocational certificate usually taken by pupils leaving school at age 16 to pursue trades.

- BEP, an abbreviation for *Brevet d'Etudes Professionnelles*, a vocational proficiency certificate awarded after successful completion of upper secondary studies.

- BTS, an abbreviation for *Brevet de Technicien Supérieur*, a higher technician certificate in one of more than a 100 specialisations, usually taken at a *Lycée*.

- DUT, an abbreviation for *Diplôme Universitaire de Technologie*, a university diploma in technology awarded after successful completion of studies at a University Institute of Technology [*Institut Universitaire de Technologie (IUT)*]

For each school year, the **National Centre for Educational Information** publishes two comprehensive catalogues of schools and educational materials, available for free download at *www.cndp.fr/produits/*.

15

Electrical and electronic goods

As elsewhere in Europe, electrical and electronic goods classify into three broad categories, historically named after the prevailing colours of the goods when they were first made and sold:

* white goods [*produits blancs*], usually referred to as appliances [*électro-ménager*]: large domestic appliances such as refrigerators and washing machines

* brown goods [*produits bruns*], commonly referred to as audiovisual products [*appareils audiovisuels*]: smaller apparatus, usually for entertainment, such as radios and television sets.

* grey goods [*produits gris*], commonly called IT and office [*équipements informatiques et bureautiques*], though it also includes the increasingly large category of telecommunications equipment that like telecommunications itself, is broken down into three sectors: fixed line telephony [*téléphonie fixe*], broadband [*haut débit*] and mobile [*mobile*].

Today, the three designations, white, brown and grey, are trade terms, used mostly by professionals and lawmakers, while shops, advertisements and yellow page listings most often use the everyday descriptive terms.

In turnover, most white goods, brown goods and grey goods now are sold by chain stores that rely on volume sales of internationally traded brands to keep prices low, but speciality shops often are competitive pricewise and often offer more personalised service. Moreover, bargains can almost always be found in the frequent online and physical shop sales [*soldes*], clearances of overstock and remaindered goods [*déstockages*] and offerings of seconds [*produits de second choix*].

All electrical appliances are made for 220 V, 50 Hz **electricity** (Chapter 25), as is common across Europe. Appliances made for other electricity supplies, such as the 110 V, 60 Hz common in North America, will not work without transformers. And even with a transformer, an appliance with a motor, such as a refrigerator or washing machine, will run more slowly and may seriously overheat. Moreover, as electrical connection regulations differ, a 110 V appliance with a transformer may be dangerous in use on a 220 V mains. Consequently, it's wise to leave any 110 V 60 Hz appliances behind when you move. Competition is keen and sales are frequent, so in most cases, it's cheaper to leave any larger appliances behind and buy new when you arrive.

Brown goods [*Appareils audiovisuels*]

Shops selling brown goods usually are listed under *Télévision, vidéo: appareils et accessoires* in the Yellow Pages. The market is keenly competitive and sales are frequent, so prices fluctuate. If you buy a TV, you must either have a **TV licence** (Chapter 44) or submit payment for one upon first purchase. If you intend to bring in a TV from abroad, be sure that it complies with the European **TV standards** (Chapter 44).

Electrical goods marking
[*Marque de certification de produits électriques*]

Electrical goods are marked to indicate their compliance with regulations and directives. The most common marks and labels are shown on the next page.

Electric plugs [*Prises*]

The plugs for connecting electrical apparatus to mains outlets are similar to those most prevalent across Europe, with two round pins, 4.8 mm in diameter and 19 mm long, spaced 19 mm from each other. The two most common types are:

- Flat plug [*Fiche Male 6A*] developed by the International Electrotechnical Commission (IEC) and used in most European countries and consequently called the "Euro plug", as fitted on the cords of lamps and small appliances up to 500 W power consumptions, such as power supplies for computers and telecommunications devices.

- Earthed plug [*Fiche male 16A + T*] ("Male plug, 16 Ampere circuit with *Terre* Earthed contact") as fitted on the cords of appliances, power tools, larger entertainment apparatus and the like. Because goods increasingly are marketed across Europe, these plugs usually are made to fit both French outlets with a projecting earth pin and German *Schoko* outlets with earthing strips on either side, as used in many European countries. *Adapteurs Schoko* are available for cords not fitted with plugs so arranged.

For further information on plugs and the different types in use around the world, visit the IEC plug and socket zone website at *www.iec.ch/zone/plugsocket/ps_intro.htm*.

Mark or label	Meaning
	Certification of electrical safety by **LCIE** (Chapter 30); obligatory for all apparatus connected to mains. The round USE symbol, usually with a certification month and year and a reference number, dates from 1907 but is still in use; it usually is used together with the NF national standards symbol.
	Certification of safety according to LCIE and to German GS (*geprüfte Sicherheit*) standards; found on goods sold in France and in Germany.
	CE marking (Chapter 30) indicating compliance with the EU/EEA safety standards and radio noise standards; found on goods sold across Europe.
	The EU energy consumption marking from A (most efficient) to G (least efficient), usually on a self-adhering label or the packaging of a new appliance, including all white goods; mandatory by EU directive on goods sold across Europe.
	The Energy Star marking indicating compliance with guidelines for energy-efficient office equipment, computers and other electronics equipment; originally a US Environmental Protection Agency (EPA) mark, now an EU standard mark; further information on the Energy Star website at www.eu-energystar.org.

Electrical goods marking.

Grey goods [*Équipements informatiques et bureautiques*]

Grey goods include:

- Personal computers [*micro-ordinateurs*]
- Fixed line telephony [*téléphonie fixe*] apparatus, including telephones and telefaxes [*téléphones et télécopieurs*, or more popularly, *faxes*] as well as other devices that may be connected to telephone lines, such as modems and ISDN boards.
- Broadband [*haut débit*], both fixed line and mobile
- Mobile phones [*téléphones mobiles*, or more popularly, *portables*].

See Chapter 44 for further information on these four categories of goods.

In the Yellow pages, look for computers and accessories listed under *informatique: logiciels, progiciels* "Data processing: software, software packages" or *vente, maintenance de micro-informatique*, "Sale, maintenance of personal computers", for telephone equipment listed under *vente, location, entretien de téléphonie, péritéléphonie*, "Sale, rentals, maintenance of telephone equipment and peripherals", and for mobile phones and accessories listed under *téléphonie mobile, radiomessagerie, radiocommunications*, "Telephony mobile, radio messaging and communications".

An item of fixed-line equipment, such as a telephone or telefax terminal, bought in another country may be used only if it meets the requirements of the ARCEP, the **French Telecommunications Regulator** (Chapter 44). Equipment sold in EU/EEA countries usually will meet the requirements, but equipment sold elsewhere may not comply with the requirements and consequently may not function properly when connected.

The standard French telephone connection plug [*fiche téléphonique*] has six or eight contacts, divided three or four on either side of a rectangular strip, 32 mm long, that plugs into a corresponding jack [*prise téléphonique*]. Many adapters are available, such as to and from the RJ-11 four-wire and RJ-45 eight-wire connectors [*connecteurs*] widely used to interconnect computer and telecommunications equipment.

Transformers [*Transformateurs*]

In 126 countries round the world, including Europe, the mains electricity in homes is 220 to 240 Volt, 50 Hz; in France it is 230V, 50Hz. You will need a transformer to step down the 230V if you wish to bring in and use electrical or electronic apparatus made for the lower voltage mains of another country, such as the 110 Volt, 60 Hz used in Canada and the USA. Most larger radio and electronics shops carry the transformers, also called converters [*convertisseurs*]; two that offer online ordering are:

- Konnecto, 22 boulevard de la Paix, 92400 Courbevoie, Tel: 01 43343621, *www.konnectoo.com*

- Saint Quentin Radio, 6 rue de St Quentin, 75010 Paris, Tel: 01 40377074, *www.stquentin.net.*

Waste Electrical and Electronic Equipment (WEEE) [*Déchets d'équipements électriques et électroniques (DEEE)*]

Across Europe, waste electrical and electronic equipment are now discarded and recycled in compliance with EU directives*, made law in France effective 13 August 2005. For consumers, compliance with the WEEE [*DEEE*] law depends on whether the end-of-life equipment was bought before or after 13 August 2005:

- End users are responsible for proper disposal of equipment bought before 13 August 2005, which is classified as "Historic WEEE" [*Gisement Historique*]. Accordingly municipalities and refuse collection organisations provide various means of collecting WEEE.

- Distributors and importers are responsible for collecting and properly disposing of and recycling equipment bought after 13 August 2005, which should be marked, either on equipment or on its packaging, with the selective collection symbol of a crossed refuse bin. As this book goes to press, the facilities for WEEE return have yet to be standardised across the country but include return to shops and discarding in bins provided by refuse collection operators.

The WEEE regulations apply specifically to **white goods** [*électroménager*], **brown goods** [*appareils audiovisuels*] and **grey goods** [*équipements informatiques et bureautiques*] as well as to miscellaneous electrical and electronic equipment, such as power tools [*outillages*] and toys [*jouets*].

For further details on WEEE in France, contact Éco-Systèmes, 17, rue de l'Admiral Hamelin, 75783 Paris Cedex 16, *www.eco-systemes.fr* with links to all public, private and international organisations concerned with WEEE. For further information on WEEE across Europe, visit the WEEE Forum website at *www.weee-forum.org*.

* Two EU Directives: 2002/95/EC concerning RoHS, the abbreviation for "Restriction of the use of certain Hazardous Substances in electronic equipment" relevant to the manufacture of goods sold, and 2002/96/EC, the abbreviation for "Waste Electrical and Electronic Equipment, relevant to the disposal of end-of-life goods. Though arcane for most end users, these directive numbers are sometimes used in marketing goods. For instance, a manufacturer may advertise products that are "RoHS Compliant 2002/95/EC" to signify that they contain no hazardous substances.

White goods [*Électroménager*]

The complete home has an array of white goods, including a cooker/stove [*cuisinière*], sometimes with a separate oven [*four*], dishwasher [*lave-vaisselle*], freezer [*congélateur*], iron [*fer à repasser*], microwave oven [*four à micro-ondes*], refrigerator [*réfrigérateur*], tumble dryer [*séchuse*], vacuum cleaner [*aspirateur*], and washing machine [*machine à laver*]. Large appliances may or may not be included in housing sales or rentals, though they almost always are included in furnished rentals.

Shops selling white goods are listed under *Electroménager* in the Yellow Pages.

16
Emergencies

Many aspects of emergency services are like those of countries across Europe: there are four countrywide telephone numbers to call in emergencies – three for fixed line telephone and one for mobiles – to contact police, call firefighters or request medical services – and there are many helplines to call for counselling and support. However, the French medical emergency system differs markedly from equivalent systems of other countries, most notably English-speaking countries, in that Emergency Medical Assistance (EMA) often is initiated at the scene of an acute illness or accident, rather than after transport to a hospital emergency department.

Ambulances [*Ambulances*]

In the majority of countries, all vehicles designated for the care and conveyance of ill and injured people are considered to be ambulances. Not so in France, where the general term is "vehicle adapted to health care transport" [*véhicules adaptés au transport sanitaire*], and only two of the four classes [*catégories*] of vehicles it covers are "ambulances". The distinction is historic, as the first workable ambulances were devised in 1798 by French military surgeon Dominique Jean Larrey (1766-1842), who also pioneered treatment on the spot, sometimes performing more than a hundred amputations a day on the battlefield. Today, the four classes of vehicles are designated according to their principal service functions and are listed in the chart on the next page.

Emergency call stations [*Bornes d'urgence*]

Emergency call stations are located at intervals of 2 km along motorways [*autoroutes*], at tourist spots [*les sites touristiques*], at unguarded beaches [*les plages non surveillées*] and at construction sites [*les chantiers*], to provide free connection to the **emergency numbers** upon pressing a button and speaking into a microphone. Most call stations are orange, have the emergency call logo of a telephone receiver and the letters SOS and have an identification number used in calling to locate the station in reporting an emergency. The principal manufacturer

Class	Designation and principal service function	Vehicle and operator
A	Ambulance for rescue and emergency care [*Ambulance de Secours et de Soins d'Urgence (ASSU)*].	Larger vehicle in which personnel can stand and use on board medical equipment; fitted with flashing blue lights and three-tone horn for emergency vehicle priority in traffic; used by **Emergency Medical Assistance (EMA)** (Chapter 22) units.
B	Rescue and casualty assistance vehicle [*Véhicule de Secours et d'Assistance aux Victimes (VSAV)*] for first response, as dispatched by a **SAMU** call centre.	Vehicle similar to Class A except that emergency horn is two-tone; used by **Firefighters,** sometimes with the older designation of Vehicle for rescuing the asphyxiated and the injured [*Véhicules de Secours aux Asphyxiés et aux Blessés (VSAB)*].
C	Ambulance for transporting a lying patient.	Ordinary vehicle, such as a large estate or a van, in which accompanying paramedic can sit but not stand and accordingly not provide care in transport; fitted with flashing blue lights and three-tone horn for emergency vehicle priority in traffic; used by hospitals and by **private ambulance services**.
D	Light health care vehicle [*Véhicule Sanitaire Léger (VSL)*] for transport of a patient who can sit.	Ordinary car with no special equipment, no horns or blue lights and no emergency vehicle priority in traffic; used by **private ambulance services**.

Ambulance categories.

of the call stations used in France is Stramatel, ZI de Bel Air, 44850 le Cellier, Tel: 02 40254690. *www.stramatel.fr* with pages in French, English and German.

Emergency numbers [*Numéros d'urgence*]

Emergency telephone numbers that are active 24 hours a day [*Les services d'urgence fonctionnent 24H/24*] are widely published, in telephone directories, on public bulletin boards and on Internet sites. A call to 15 is answered by a **SAMU** doctor; a call to 17 is answered by the nearest police, which for 95% of the area of the country is a unit of the ***Gendarmerie*** (Chapter 11); a call to 18 is answered by the departmental dispatcher of the **Firefighters**; and a call to 112 from mobiles is answered by a dispatcher who will redirect to SAMU, the Police or the Firefighters.

When you call an emergency number, speak slowly, particularly if you have yet to speak French well or must speak in English. The efficiency of help provided depends on the accuracy of information you supply [*L'efficacité des secours dépend des informations données*] concerning:

- the exact address of the calamity or accident [*adresse précise du lieu du sinistre ou de l'accident*]
- situation and time of occurrence [*circonstances (ce qui est arrivé)*]
- what you have observed [*ce que vous constatez*]
- number and apparent condition of victims [*nombre et état apparent des victimes*]
- possible additional dangers [*éventualité d'un danger supplémentaire*]
- caller's contact phone number for further information [*numéro de téléphone de l'appelant pour obtenir des renseignements complémentaires*].

Remember, in calling:

- do not be the first one to hang up [*ne raccrochez jamais le premier*]
- do not call if you know that someone else already has called concerning the same incident [*n'appelez pas si vous savez que quelqu'un l'a déjà fait ou est déjà en relation avec un service d'urgence*]
- if your identity is requested for verification, your anonymity will be protected [*si les coordonnées du requérant sont demandées pour vérifications, son anonymat sera préservé*].

15 **SAMU**	17 **POLICE**	18 **POMPIER**
Medical emergencies [*Urgence médicale*]	Personal safety [*sécuritaire*]	Rescue and fire [*secoures aux personés*]
• distress [*détresses*] • major medical emergencies at home [*grandes urgences médicales à domicile*] • accidental injuries [*blessés par accident*] • sudden illness in public places [*malaises dans un lieu public*] • workplace accidents [*accidents du travail*]	• road accidents [*accidents de la route*] • public disorder [*troubles à l'ordre public*] • crimes [*infractions pénales*]	• fires [*incendies*] • road accidents [*accidents de la route*] • domestic accidents explosions, gas or toxic vapour leaks [*accidents domestiques, explosions, dégagement de gaz ou de vapeurs toxiques*] • persons in peril, drownings, floods [*personnes en péril, noyades, inondations*]
112 **European emergency number (from mobiles)**		

European emergency call number
[*Numéro d'appel d'urgence européenne*]

Across Europe, countries have implemented the universal, free emergency call number 112, in accordance with the European Council Universal Service Directive of 1998. In some countries, 112 now is the only emergency call number for fixed-line and mobile telephones, whilst in others, including France, it coexists with existing fixed-line numbers and consequently is intended primarily for emergency calls from mobile phones. For further information on 112 in Europe, visit the SOS 112 Europe website at *www.sos112.info* in English, with an interactive map that brings up information on emergency services in countries across Europe. For information on the advantages and use of 112, contact the European Emergency Number Association (EENA), 88 rue d'Aqueduc, B-1050 Brussels, Belgium, *www.eena.org* with pages in English.

Firefighters [*Corps du sapeurs-pompiers*]

As reflected in their name, the firefighters of France comprise one of the country's oldest public services. Created by decree in 1811 by Napoléon, the *sapeurs-pompiers* were army engineers [*sapeurs*] who manned pumps [*pompier*] to extinguish fires. Today, most of the more than 36,000 professional firefighters [*sapeurs-pompiers professionnels (SPP)*] are civilians, but two units are military: the Paris fire brigade [*Brigade des Sapeurs-Pompiers de Paris (BSPP)*] attached to the Army Engineers Corps, and the Marseilles marine fire battalion [*Bataillon des Marins-Pompiers de Marseille (BMPM)*] attached to the Navy. The professionals are augmented by a larger force of nearly 198,000 volunteers [*sapeurs-pompiers volontaires (SPV)*] who have other jobs and are paid as firefighters only in training and in operations. One in 12 civilian *sapeurs-pompiers* is a woman, and some 10,500 *sapeurs-pompiers* are qualified paramedics, pharmacists, nurses or veterinarians in the *Service de santé et de Secours Médical (SSSM)*.

In addition to fighting fires, the *sapeurs-pompiers* are the principal first responders to medical emergencies as well as to road accidents. In numbers of responses, these services outweigh their operations as firefighters: across the country in an average year, 60% of the 3.7 million responses of the *sapeurs-pompiers* are to medical emergencies. In everyday life, they are the most visible emergency service and consequently are highly regarded. The black uniform, with the words *sapeurs-pompiers* front and back on a red band around the chest of a pullover, is worn with pride, in villages, towns and cities. Children who aspire to grow up to be firefighters can start early: across the country, there are 820 sections of the junior firefighters [*Jeunes Sapeurs-Pompiers (JSP)*] that together have more than 25,000 members, 10 to 18 years old, who meet one or two days a week, on Wednesdays and Saturdays.

And aside from these professional services, the *sapeurs-pompiers* are socially active. The TV programme *Sam le pompier* is popular, and at Christmastime they take up a collection for their benevolent fund that supports the junior firefighters and finances Christmas parties with gifts for needy children.

The *sapeurs-pompiers* are organised under the fire and rescue services of the *Départements* [*Services Départementaux d'Incendie*]. As elsewhere in Europe, the *sapeurs-pompiers* vehicles are painted red and like police vehicles, are fitted with flashing blue lights and two-tone horns, to distinguish them from ambulances, which have three-tone horns.

For further information, contact *Fédération nationale des sapeurs-pompiers de France (FNSPF)*, 32 rue Bréguet, 75011 Paris, Tel: 01 49231818, *www.pompiers.fr* with extensive information for the public, including a downloadable lexicon [*lexique*] of firefighting and rescue terms.

Helplines [*Numéros d'assistance*]

Helplines are listed in printed telephone directories as well as by the various organisations supporting them. Many are ordinary telephone numbers, dialled and charged as are other calls. The principal national helplines listed below have distinctive numbers and are charged at lower rates. Three-digit numbers and **Freephone** (Chapter 44) numbers beginning with 0800 [*Nº Vert*] are at no cost to the caller. Numbers beginning with 810 [*Nº Azur*] and four-digit numbers are charged at local call rates. Numbers beginning with 0820 to 0825 [*Nº Indigo*] are charged at a low national call rate.

AIDS helpline [*SIDA info services*]	Tel: 08 00840800
Alcohol addiction helpline [*Alcool info-service*]	Tel: 08 11912020
Alcoholics Anonymous [*Alcooliques Anonymes*]	Tel: 08 20326833
Cancer information [*Écoute cancer*]	Tel: 08 10810821
Cannabis addiction helpline [*Cannabis info-service*]	Tel: 08 11912020
Contraception information [*Info contraception*]	Tel: 08 25089090
Drug addiction helpline [*Drogues info-service*]	Tel: 08 00231313
Hepatitis information [*Hépatites info services*]	Tel: 08 00845800
Lost or stolen Eurocard MasterCard	Tel: 08 00901387
Lost or stolen French chequebook	Tel: 0836683208
Lost or stolen Visa card	Tel: 08 36690880
Medical advice [*SOS Médecins*]	Tel: 08 20332424
Narcotics Anonymous [*Narcotiques Anonymes*]	Tel: 01 48583846
Public Services hotline [*Allô Service Public*]	Tel: 3939
Racial discrimination [*Discrimination raciale*]	Tel: 114
Red Cross [*Croix Rouge*]	Tel: 08 00858858

SOS Child abuse [*Allô enfance maltraitée*]	Tel: 119 or 08 00054141
SOS Drug/alcohol addiction [*Drogue tabac alcool info*]	Tel: 113
SOS Homeless in distress [*Accueil sans abris*]	Tel: 115 or 08 00306306
SOS violence against women [*SOS Viols*]	Tel: 08 00059595
Suicide crisis [*Suicide Écoute*]	Tel: 01 45394000
Violent crime victim hotline [*Aide aux victimes*]	Tel: 08 10098609
Youth health [*Fil santé jeunes*]	Tel: 08 00235236

Maritime rescue [*Sauvetage en mer*]

Maritime rescue is coordinated by and performed mostly by the National Maritime Rescue Society [*La Société Nationale de Sauvetage en Mer (SNSM)*], founded in 1967 by the amalgamation of *Société Centrale de Sauvetage des Naufragés*, founded in 1865, and *Hospitaliers Sauveteurs Bretons*, founded in 1873. Today, SNSM has 232 rescue stations along the coasts, of which 174 are staffed year-round, 24 hours a day, and 58 are staffed in summer, operating a modern fleet of lifeboats [*canots*], cutters [*vedettes*], hovercraft [*aéroglisseurs*] and inflatables [*pneumatiques*]. It also gives instruction in water safety and life saving and operates 28 training centres for beach lifeguards. As needed, its SNSM units coordinate operations with and supply services to the **Firefighters** and **SAMU**. Financed in part by governmental subsidy and in part by private donations, its services are free to the some 10,000 persons rescued each year. For further information, contact SNSM, 31 Cité d'Antin, 75009 Paris, Tel: 08 90711064, *www.snsm.net* with an interactive list of all stations, some with their own websites.

Meteorological warnings [*Vigilance Météo*]

Météo France continuously provides warnings of meteorological hazards, updated twice a day, at 06 and 16 hours, via a hotline telephone no. 3250 and online at *www.meteo.fr*. Hazards are ranked in four degrees of severity, shown by colours of the *Départements* on the online map of the country:

- **Red**: Extreme danger forecast, keep posted regularly.
- **Orange**: Danger forecast, keep posted.
- **Yellow**: Ordinary phenomenon, keep posted.
- **Green**: No unusual danger foreseen.

Clicking on a *Département* shown in orange or red on the online map will bring up the latest safety bulletins [*Cliquez sur un département orange ou rouge pour obtenir le bulletin de suivi*]. Seven icons are used to identify the nature of the hazards involved in orange or red severity warnings:

Violent winds [*Vent violent*]

 Avalanches [*Avalanches*]

 Heavy precipitation
[*Fortes précipitations*]

 Extreme cold [*Grand froid*]

 Lightning [*Orage*]

 Heat wave [*Canicule*]

 Snow/ice [*Neige/Verglas*]

For further information including the specifics of the meteorological hazards, see the Meteo France brochure, *Dangers météorologiques*, downloadable from the website at *www.meteo.fr*.

Mountain rescue [*Sauvetage en montagne*]

The *Gendarmerie* (Chapter 10) provide mountain rescue services year-round in the mountain areas of the country. In all, 260 *Gendarmes* are stationed in 15 high-mountain platoons [*Pelotons de gendarmerie de haute montagne (PGHM)*] at Chamonix, Briançon, Grenoble, Bourg St Maurice, Modane, Annecy, Jausiers, St-Sauveur-sur-Tinée, Pierrefite Nestalas, Bagnères-de-Luchon, Oloron-Ste-Marie, Savignac-les-Ormeaux, Osseja, Corte and St-Denis-de-La-Réunion, and five mountain platoons [*Pelotons de gendarmerie de montagne (PGM)*] at Xonrupt, Munster, Les Rousses, Murat and Le Mont Dore. For further information, contact the local *Gendarmerie* or visit the *Gendarmerie nationale* website at *www.defense.gouv.fr/sites/gendarmerie* and navigate to *Gendarme de montagne*.

Gendarme de montagne badge.

Poison Control Centres [*Centres antipoison*]

Across the country, there are ten Poison Control and Toxicology Centres [*Centres Antipoison et de Toxicovigilance*] that have helplines staffed 24 hours a day, seven days a week to give advice and refer to hospital when required.

Angers	02 41482121	Bordeaux	05 56964080

Lille	08 25812822	Lyon	04 72116911
Marseille	04 91752525	Nancy	03 83323636
Paris	01 40054848	Rennes	02 99592222
Strasbourg	03 88373737	Toulouse	05 61777447

Additionally, there are three Toxicology Centres [*Centres de Toxicovigilance*] that keep ordinary office hours:

Grenoble	04 76765646
Reims	03 26784136
Rouen	02 32888128

For further information, call one of the centres or visit the *Centres Antipoison et de Toxicovigilance* website at *www.centres-antipoison.net*, with extensive information on poisons and toxins and an interactive locator map of the centres as well as hospitals with poison control and toxicology units.

Private ambulance services [*Services ambulanciers*]

Private ambulance services are organised in each *Département* in an Urgent Health Transport Association [*Association Départementale des Transports Sanitaires d'Urgence (ADTSU)*] that in turn tenders their services to the 15 call centre staffed by **SAMU**. Consequently, when you call the medical emergency number 15, the duty doctor will evaluate the severity of your situation and if it is not acute, may choose to order a private ambulance for transport to a clinic or hospital.

The services offer patient transport in two classes of **Ambulance**: "class C" that can transport a lying patient and a sitting paramedic, is marked with the six-point star of life ambulance symbol, is fitted with ambulance warning horns and flashing blue lights and has emergency vehicle priority in traffic, and "class D" that is an ordinary car having no special equipment [*Véhicule Sanitaire Léger (VSL)*], for transport of a patient who can sit, and accordingly has neither ambulance horns nor blue lights and no emergency vehicle priority. All services have VSLs, and many have "class C" ambulances.

You may find services listed under *Ambulances* in the Yellow Pages. Particularly in smaller cities and towns, ambulance services may be combined with taxi services and the hire of funeral vehicles [*véhicules funéraires*] for use by undertakers [*pompes funèbres*], and so advertised in the Yellow pages, typically "Ambulances – VSL – Taxis – Pompes Funèbres". You also can find the names and addresses of ambulance services on the French Ambulance Operators Association [*Ambulanciers de France*] website at *www.ambulance.fr* with an interactive locator map of services in all *Départements*.

The costs of ambulance services are covered by health insurance. In general, services ordered by SAMU are debited directly without the patient being involved, whilst services ordered by doctors or hospitals may require patient involvement. In any case, it's wise to have your **Social security card** (Chapter 22) available if you are a resident of France, or its equivalent – your **European health insurance card** (Chapter 22) if you are a resident of an EU/EEA country, or proof of health insurance if you are a resident of a country outside Europe.

Blue star of life ambulance logo.

SAMU

SAMU, the abbreviation for *Service d'Aide Médicale d'Urgence*, is the national **Emergency Medical Assistance (EMA)** (Chapter 22) service. Its principal function is medical dispatch. Across the country, SAMU has 96 reception and dispatch call centres [*Centres de Réception et de Régulation des Appels (CRRA)*], one in each *Département*, staffed 24 hours a day by doctors and health care professionals to respond to calls to the medical emergency number 15.

When a call comes in to one of the *Centres 15*, the duty doctor evaluates the severity of the situation and accordingly responds by:

- offering medical advice on the phone
- sending a general practitioner doctor to the home
- ordering a private ambulance for transport to a clinic or hospital
- dispatching a fire brigade first response emergency ambulance to the scene of a road accident or other acute emergency
- dispatching a Hospital Mobile Intensive Care Unit (H-MICU) road vehicle or helicopter whenever rapid intervention is indicated.

In an average year, the *Centres 15* receive some 10 million calls, nearly 60% from individuals and more than 25% from **firefighters**.

SAMU has other duties, including managing the **Emergency preparedness** (Chapter 11) white plan and training emergency doctors. The Paris SAMU manages emergencies arising in the operation of the high-speed TGV trains and in the operation of Air France aircraft. The Toulouse SAMU manages emergencies at sea.

For further information, visit the SAMU website at *www.samu-de-france.com* and click on *Le SAMU c'est* to bring up overview pages in French, English or German.

Scuba diving accidents [*Accidents de plongée*]

Scuba diving is popular along the coasts, particularly along the Mediterranean coast where it is a year-round sport. Accordingly, the French Federation of Underwater Studies and Sports [*Fédération française d'études et de sports sous-marins (FFESSM)*] supports extensive safety measures, including cooperating with insurance companies and publishing accident procedure posters that are put up at diving ports and on board diving vessels. For further information, contact FFESSM, 24 Quai de Rive-Neuve, 13284 Marseille Cedex 07, Tel: 04 91339931, *www.ffessm.fr*.

Skiing accidents [*Accidents de ski*]

Each winter, some 7.6 million people take to the slopes in ski resorts across the country, and for each 1000 skier-days, there are 2.66 accidents. So, all resorts have rescue services. However, rescue is not free, so wise skiers, snowboarders and snowshoers buy ski accident insurance, which is inexpensive and usually can be bought along with a lift pass at a resort's cash desk. The largest company offering this type of insurance is *Carré Neige*, offered at 70 resorts, *Diot montagne assurance,* BP 19, 73701 Bourg-Saint-Maurice Cedex, *www.carreneige.com* in French and English. The victim of a snow sports accident requires treatment, so each winter, *Médecins de montagne (MDEM)* stations some 250 doctors at resorts across the country. For further information, contact MDEM, Maison des Parcs et de la Montagne, 256 rue de la République, 73000 Chambery, Tel : 04 79964350, *www.mdem.org*.

243

17
Family and children

The number of households in the country is growing, but the size of the average household is shrinking. Today, one home in three is a single-person household. The fertility rate is now 1.9 births per woman of child-bearing age, down from 2.5 in 1970. Marriages are also declining, as cohabitation becomes more widespread. Clearly, the family is not what it was in the middle of the last century.

Nonetheless, the rights of and provisions for families and children are more extensive than ever. And rights have been extended beyond the traditional definition of a family, to cohabitating couples and to same-sex registered partnerships. The home remains one of the principal strengths of the country.

Adoption [*L'adoption*]

A married couple may adopt a child, provided they have been married at least two years, or, if married less than two years, both spouses are 28 or older. There is no age requirement if one spouse of a couple wishes to adopt the other spouse's child. The adopting parents must be more than 15 years older than the child they wish to adopt, or ten years, if one spouse is adopting the other's child. For complete information on adoption requirements and procedures, contact:

- *La mission de l'adoption internationale (MAI)*, an agency of the Ministry of Foreign Affairs [*Ministère des affaires étrangères*], 224, boulevard Saint Germain, 75303 Paris 07 SP, Tel: 01 43179090, *www.diplomatie.fr/mai*.

- *Enfance & familles d'adoption*, a federation of 90 departmental associations, 221 rue La Fayette, 75010 Paris, Tel: 01 40055770, *www.adoptionefa.org*.

- *SOS Grossesse*, a family counselling service of the Local Department of Social Services [*Direction Départementales des affaires sanitaires et sociales (DDASS)*] of the city of Paris, 51 rue Jeanne d'Arc, 75013 Paris, Tel: 01 45845591, *www.sosgrossesse.org*, click on *L'adoption*.

Age-based rights [*Droits selon l'âge*]

A person is considered to be a minor [*mineur*] until age 18 and thereafter of age [*majeur*]. The term "adult" [*adulte*] implies physical, intellectual and psychological maturity but no longer is a legal demarcation. Rights begin before birth, as a parent may contract for life insurance for an unborn child [*enfant à naître*], and a conceived child [*enfant conçu*] may be designated an heir contingent upon being born alive and viable. From birth [*dès la naissance*], a child may be issued a **national identity number** (Chapter 38) and have a savings account. Thereafter, age-based rights relate to a person's last birthday:

- 2: attend nursery school [*école maternelle*]
- 6: start primary school [*école primaire*]
- 7: play football
- 12: be insured, take up boxing
- 13: consent to adoption; change name upon acquiring French nationality
- 14: drive a moped [*cyclomoteur*]; obtain a light aircraft licence; be arrested and punished for crime; choose own education; hunt if accompanied by a licensed hunter.
- 15: have own passport, consent to heterosexual or homosexual relations with person of same age or older
- 16: mandatory schooling ends; may buy alcoholic drink and tobacco in shops (but not be served in public), take up full-time work, file for declaration of nationality; make out a will; join a union; open a current account in a bank; drive a light motorcycle [*motocyclette légère*]; be a learner driver to practise for the car **driving licence** (Chapter 4)
- 18: hold a **driving licence** (Chapter 4), serve on a municipal council, marry (a law that permitted girls to marry at age 15 was annulled in 2005); be responsible for own affairs and finances; acquire French citizenship automatically
- 21: stand for election to a regional council
- 23: hold political office at national level
- 25: stand examination for a titled profession
- 35: be elected to the Senate
- 60: retire.

Au pair

Au pair, from the French for "equal to", designates a young person, usually a woman, living equally with the members of a family in a foreign country, usually with the goal of learning the language. In compliance with the pan-European agreements on au pair placement, an au pair in France must:

- be unmarried, 18 to 30 years old.
- stay for at least three to six months and no more than 18 months.

- have completed upper secondary school with commensurate capability in French.
- attend French language classes during the stay.

The responsibilities and rights of an au pair are set forth by the Ministry of Labour. Usually, an au pair combines child minding and light house work for no more than five hours a day, up to 30 hours a week, on a schedule that permits attending a French course. In return for work, an au pair is entitled to a private bedroom [*chambre de bonne*], board, health insurance coverage, and a monthly allowance to meet the costs of French language classes and pay for local transport.

If you are a young person wishing to be an au pair in France, or a family in France seeking an au pair, it's advisable to contact a French au pair agency, to ensure compliance with French as well as international rules and regulations. The principal agencies are listed by two organisations, one international and one French:

- International Au Pair Association, Bredgade 25H, 1260 Copenhagen K, Denmark, Tel: +45 33170066, *www.iapa.org* with pages in English, Dutch, French, German and Spanish, and, for France, a list of 10 au pair agencies.
- Union Française des Associations Au Pair, 13 rue Vavin, 75006 Paris, Tel: 01 43298001, *www.ufaap.org* in French and English, with an interactive agency locator map of the country.

Birth statistics [*Statistiques de naissance*]

Each year, some 760,000 babies are born in the country. The fertility rate, which is the average number of children born to a woman of child-bearing age, is declining slowly. In 1970, the average woman bore 2.5 children; by 2004, the average had fallen to 1.9.

Burial grounds [*Cimetières*]

There are some 60,000 burial grounds in the country. Graves in them are made available with four durations of non-transferable lease: temporary (15 year maximum), 30 years, 50 years and perpetual. Most burial grounds are secular and are administered by the offices of the mayors of municipalities. However, all people of faith have the right to burial in consecrated ground, so there are consecrated plots in public burial grounds as well as burial grounds for various faiths; contact the relevant clerics for details. Catholicism is historically and culturally the faith of France so there are many suitable Catholic burial grounds. Information on the burial grounds of the three leading minority faiths are available online: Jewish at *www.col.fr*, Muslim at *www.naros.info* and Protestant at *www.hugenots.info/cimetieres*.

Child minders [*Gardes d'enfants*]

Garde d'enfants is the general term for persons and facilities that mind infants and young children. In alphabetical order by their names in French, the specific terms are:

- *assistante maternelle*: a mother's helper, often a mother herself, who assists in the house in addition to child minding.

- *au pair*: a young person, 18 to 30 years old, most often a woman and often a foreigner, who lives in the home and performs general household chores as well as child minding, for five working hours a day.

- *baby sitter*: a part-time employee in the house who may be either a professional, hired from a baby sitting service or, for sporadic, short-term minding, usually a local girl, located upon recommendation by other parents or by reading a notice posted at a *crèche* or a local store.

- *crèche*: a nursery for infants and young children, two and a half months to three years old; usually arranged in one of three ways:

  - family *crèche* [*la crèche familiale*] in a home with a professional child minder hired for the purpose and with expenses shared by several families.

  - parental *crèche* [*la crèche parentale*] usually in a separate building rented or owned and managed by a parents' association, with a professional staff.

  - company *crèche* [*la crèche d'entreprise*] provided by a company for its employees and usually located at or near their workplaces and staffed by professionals.

- *garde partagée*: a cost-cutting approach entailing the sharing of child minding, usually by two families and usually entailing the hiring of a single *nounou* who stays in one home and also minds children from the other.

- *nounou*: a professional child-minder, the French equivalent of the British nanny; historically a live-in servant in the house, but now often part-time.

- *nourrice*: a professional child-minder, often registered [*nourrice agréée*] and often with nurse training; may be employed in a *crèche* or in a private home.

You can locate professionals either in the Yellow Pages, listed under *Garde d'enfants* or in online child minding centres, such as *Bébé Nounou* at *www.bebe-nounou.fr*. For the latest information on child minding and related matters, read *Famili* magazine (head office at 10 boulevard des Frères-Voisin, 92130 Issy-les-Moulineaux, Tel: 01 41468888) or visit its extensive website at *www.famili.fr*. For further information on the child minding professions as well as on relevant laws and regulations, contact the child minders' union, *Syndicat professionnel des assistants maternels et assistants familiaux (SPAMAF)*, Bât Cévennes, 19 bis rue Blaise Pascal, 78800 Houilles, Fax: 01 61049505, *www.assistante-maternelle.org*.

Children's games [*Jeux d'enfants*]

Most of the traditional children's games played throughout Europe, North America and elsewhere, are played in France. In alphabetical order of their names in English, the most popular games are:

- Cops and robbers or cops and thieves [*Les gendarmes et les voleurs*] play "police" hunt "robbers".

- Hide-and-seek [*Cache-cache*] one or more of the players hide, and the rest, at a given signal, set out to find them.

- Hopscotch [*La marelle*] a player hops on one foot and drives forward with it a flat stone, fragment of a slate or tile, etc., from one compartment to another of an oblong figure traced out on the ground, so as always to hop over or clear each scotch or line.

- Marbles [*Les billes*] a number of marbles are arranged in a ring or sometimes in a row, from which the players attempt to dislodge them by "shooting" a marble at them with the finger and thumb.

- Tag [*loup* or *chat*] a pursuer – the wolf [*loup*] or cat [*chat*] chases the other players, and anyone caught becomes the new pursuer. In the *chat perche* version, the pursued can climb something where they are "safe" from being caught.

- Tug of war [*Le tir à la corde*] a contest between two teams who haul at the opposite ends of a rope, each trying to drag the other over a line marked between them; played mostly at fairs [*kermesse*].

- *1, 2, 3 Soleil*, the equivalent of "What's the time Mr. Wolf" in English: one player, the leader, stands at a wall, back to the other players standing at the start about 20 metres from the wall. The leader starts counting aloud – *un, deux, trois* – and the other players run forward. When the leader shouts *Soleil!* and turns around, the other players must freeze in their tracks. A player caught moving must return to the start. The first player to reach the leader then becomes the leader of the next round.

Civil Union [*Le pacte civil de solidarité (PACS)*]

Established by law in 1999*, PACS protects the mutual interests of partners living together in same-sex or mixed sex couples. As for marriage, the minimum age is 18 and agreements are not available to persons already in another marriage or relationship. A PACS agreement entails specified responsibilities and rights, such as joint ownership of property. For further details, see the *Le Pacte Civil de Solidarité* brochure, one of the series on **Legal matters** published by the Ministry of Justice.

Loi no 99-944 du 15 novembre 1999 relative au pacte civil de solidarité

Children's rights [*Droits de l'enfant*]

The rights of children are ensured in several ways, in compliance with the United Nations Convention on the Rights of the Child [*Convention relative aux droits de l'enfant*] that specifies five groups of basic rights and freedoms: civil, political, financial, social and cultural. Two governmental websites provide copious information as well as links to ombudsmen [*Médiateurs*] and other governmental agencies supporting children's rights: *Défenseur des enfants* at *www.defenseurdesenfants.fr* and *Droits des jeunes* at *www.droitsdesjeunes.gouv.fr*. Moreover, compliance with the provisions of the Convention as well as other matters concerned are monitored and administered in France by the national UNICEF agency, 3 rue Duguay-Trouin, 75282 Paris Cedex 06, Tel: 01 44397777, *www.unicef.fr*.

Cohabitation [*Concubinage*]

Living together as a couple without being married or in a civil union is increasingly popular. Today, more than 2.5 million people cohabit, compared to less than half a million in 1975. About a fifth of the population between the ages of 20 and 49 are in cohabitant relationships, and four children in ten are born outside of marriage, compared to one in ten in 1970. A cohabiting couple can obtain a Certificate of cohabitation [*Certificat de concubinage ou attestations d'union libre*], provided that neither is married or in a civil union. In many cities and towns, the Certificate is available upon application at the city hall [*mairie*] and if not at the city hall, at the nearest magistrate's court [*tribunal d'instance*]. In some aspects of everyday life, such as joint bank accounts, discounts on travel tickets and family welfare benefits, a cohabiting couple enjoys the same advantage as a couple with the formal legal bond of marriage or civil union. However, in matters of greater legal consequence, such as inheritance and adoption, privileges differ.

Cremation [*Crémation*]

In 1886, the dominant Catholic Church forbade cremation, so it was little practised in France. The ban was lifted in 1963, but tradition persisted: in 1980, less than one per cent of the deceased were cremated. Today, it is more accepted: about a quarter of the deceased are cremated, and there are 116 crematoriums in the country. The rules for cremation are similar to those for burial with the addition of the requirement that the body does not contain any prosthetic devices with artificial radioactive sources. The ashes may be placed in an urn of metal, wood, granite or porcelain, and urns are most often stored in a columbarium (a sepulchral vault with recesses to accept urns), for a period of 10, 30 or 50 years. An urn also may be buried in a traditional grave or in a "garden of memory" [*jardin du souvenir*], or the ashes may be scattered outdoors, but not on a public road. For further information, contact the French Cremation Federation [*Fédédration française de crémation (FFC)*],

50 rue Rodier, BP 411-09, 75423 Paris, Tel: 01 45263307, *www.cremation-france-ffc-com* with an interactive crematorium locator map.

Death [*La mort*]

Each year, there are about 550,000 deaths in the country. The everyday perception of death is the classical definition of cessation of breathing and heartbeat, partly reinforced by a papal pronouncement of 1957*. However, from December 1996 on, brain death has been the legal definition* of the cessation of life. Moreover, the certificate of brain death [*Le certificat attestant la mort cérébrale*] must be signed by two doctors, one of whom preferably should be skilled in interpreting EEG.

If a death occurs in a public place, on a public road, street or highway, is violent or suspicious, is due to accident in a private place or is due to a workplace accident, the public prosecutor [*le procureur de la République*] may order a *post-mortem*, which the family cannot dispute. Otherwise, with the consent of the surviving family members and provided that while alive, the deceased specifically requested that an *post-mortem* not be performed, an *post-mortem* may be performed for medical or scientific reasons, such as to discover the true cause of a death.

*Pope Pius XII: "The prolongation of life", 24 November 1957.

**Le décret no 96-1041 du 2-12-1996 (art. R 671 du Code de la santé publique).*

The disabled [*Les handicapés*]

In France, an estimated 3.2 million people suffer disabilities of varying degree, due to impairment, illness, injury or age. Of the population 18 and older, half a million are "protected persons of age" [*les majeurs protégés*] who need assistance to cope with everyday life. The relevant welfare facilities are accordingly extensive: 2500 establishments with 127,000 places for children, 4300 establishments with 201,000 places for adults, and more than 40,000 jobs in sheltered workshops. For further information, contact Handroit, the principal organisation dealing with all aspects of the disabled, at route de Liverdy, 77170 Coubert, Tel: 01 64422044, *www.handroit.com*. For a comprehensive overview of the rules, regulations and facilities for protected persons, see the *Les majeurs protégés,* a 52-page monograph, one of the publications on **legal matters** available from the Ministry of Justice and downloadable from its publications website page at *www.justice.gouv.fr/publicat/fiches1.htm*.

Divorce [*Le divorce*]

Today, there are close to half as many divorces as marriages*. That trend is new. In 1972, there were 416,300 marriages and only 44,738 divorces. Divorce is granted on three grounds:

- mutual consent, either by joint request or by application of one partner accepted by the other.
- irretrievable breakdown of the marriage.
- grounds of fault entailing repeated violation of marital obligations.

For the complete details of the relevant procedures and legal requirements, see the *Le divorce* and *Les conséquences juridiques du divorce* brochures in the series on **Legal matters** published by the Ministry of Justice.

*Annuaire statistique de la France, édition 2006: Table B02-1: 276,000 marriages and 125,200 divorces in 2003.

Funeral directors [*Pompes funèbres*]

The provision of funeral services reflects events of the past century. In 1904, the municipalities were empowered by law to provide funerals as a public service, as up to then, only churches and consistories could arrange funerals and about 40% of the population was poor. The law was noble in intent but flawed in practice. The municipalities complied by partly or completely granting concessions for funeral services to private funeral directors or by permitting a free market for their services. Consequently, well-established companies obtained the most profitable concessions, principally in larger cities. The result was a virtual monopoly, as competing funeral directors in a municipality were obliged to be sub-contractors to the concessionaire. In effect, the market was restricted and choice was limited.

In 1986, several independent funeral directors challenged status quo by founding the French Funeral Freedom [*France Obsèques Liberté*] movement to lobby for an open market. The movement was successful, and by 1998 the old rulings were repealed and the market was opened to full competition. Today, there are more than 2,154 funeral directors in the country*, of which about 15% are under the aegis of the municipalities [*régie municipale des pompes funèbres*] and about 85% are independent of them. All are listed in the Yellow Pages under *Pompes funèbres*. Most of the funeral directors are independent operators, but there are several chains, of which the largest is *Pompes Funèbres Générales* with 546 agencies that can be located via an interactive map on its website at *www.pfg.fr*.

For further information, contact:

- *France obsèques liberté*, 120 chemin de Groslay, 93140 Bondy, Tel: 01 41551335, *www.obseques-liberte.com*.
- *Confédération des professionnels du funéraire et de la Marberie (CPFM)*, 14 rue des Fossés Saint-Marcel, 75005 Paris, Tel: 01 55433000, *www.cpfm.fr*.
- *Fédération française des pompes funèbres (FFPF)*, 40 rue des Aulnes, 92330 Sceaux, Tel: 01 46602424, *www.acom.fr/ffpf* with a locator map of members across the country.

- *Association française d'information funéraire (AFIF)*, 9 rue Chomel, 75007 Paris, Tel: 01 45449003, *www.afif.asso.fr* in French with selected pages in English, including comprehensive guidelines entitled "Choosing a funeral home".

*Le France des Services, edition 2004/2005, §2.13, INSEE, 2006.

Funerals [*Enterrements*]

A funeral may be a simple, secular ceremony held by a funeral director, or it may be a religious ceremony in a place of worship. The Catholic faith recognises the right of all baptised Christians to a religious funeral followed by burial or cremation and can perform a funeral in the absence of a body, such as after disappearance at sea. Protestant practices vary but usually entail ceremonies with the coffin in a church or chapel. In Judaism, there is no ceremony in the Synagogue, but psalms are read before transfer to a burial ground. In Islam, a body is ritually washed and prayers are held in the family residence and at the burial ground.

Gays and lesbians [*Les gays et lesbiennes*]

France has no laws prohibiting homosexuality, and the age of consent is 15 for both homosexual and heterosexual relations. Established in 1999, a **civil union** affords the same privileges as **marriage**. Many anti-discrimination laws and rulings apply to gays and lesbians. As in English, the word *gay*, sometimes spelled *gai*, is used to designate both all homosexuals as well as male homosexuals, as opposed to lesbians [*lesbiennes*]. The principal resources for gays and lesbians are:

- France Guide for the Gay Traveller, a publication of *Maison de France*, *www.franceguide.com/gay* in English.
- Pink TV, a gay TV channel distributed on cable, satellite and DSL, *www.pinktv.fr* in French and English.
- Gay Provence, a gay-friendly tourist guide, *www.gay-provence.org* in French, English, German and Spanish.
- Aides Fédération Nationale, a support organisation for people affected with HIV and AIDS, *www.aides.org* in French with pages in English.
- Syndicat National Entreprises Gaies (SNEG), a community resource network, *www.sneg.org*.
- Front Runners de Paris, a gay and lesbian jogging club in Paris, *www.frparis.free.fr* in French with pages in English.

Association Gay Lesbienne Handicap, a resource for handicapped homosexuals, *www.aglh.com*.

- Lesbian & Gay Hospitality Exchange International, an exchange resource based in Berlin, with contacts in France, *www.lghei.org* in German, English, French, Italian and Spanish.

Legal matters [*Questions de droit*]

One of the best ways to learn about an everyday legal matter is to read one of the many brochures and monographs published by the Ministry of Justice, as they are comprehensive, written in everyday language and are frequently updated to reflect the most recent legislation. The printed publications are free and are distributed across the country by various public service offices as well as sent upon written request to Ministère de la Justice, Service Central de l'Information et de la Communication, 13 place Vendôme, 75042 Paris Cedex 01. Online HTML and PDF files of the publications may be downloaded from the Ministry's website page for publications aimed at private persons at *www.justice.gouv.fr/publicat/fiches1.htm*.

Marriage [*Mariage*]

In France, as well as in Belgium and Switzerland, the churches no longer have civil functions, so church weddings are not legally recognised. Consequently, couples must be married at a civil ceremony, which takes place at the town hall [*Mairie*] and is conducted by the Mayor [*Maire*] or his/her Deputy [*Adjoint au maire*], regardless of whether they wish to have a religious wedding, which may be held days or weeks later. A cleric will require a certificate of civil marriage before performing a religious ceremony.

At least one of the persons to be married must have lived in the city or town for at least 40 days. Both must be at least 18 years old, not married or in a civil union and free of serious communicable disease. The minimum documentation required of each is proof of identity, such as a national ID card or passport, a birth certificate [*Extrait d'acte de naissance*] and a medical certificate [*Certificat médical*]. Additional documentation may be desired or required, such as a **prenuptial agreement** if signed and additional documentation if one of the persons is a foreigner. For further information on the civil ceremony, contact the *Mairie* in the town of your residence. For further information on the requirements for foreign citizens, contact the French embassy in your home country.

At least 10 days before the ceremony, the *Mairie* will post a marriage banns [*publication des bans*], which is a public notice that permits objection. After the civil ceremony, the couple will be given a Marriage certificate [*Attestation de mariage*] and a **Family record book** (Chapter 38).

The word "marriage" is used in many contexts; the principal usages, in alphabetical order by their equivalents in English, are:

annulled marriage	*mariage annulé*
annulment of marriage	*annulation du mariage*
arranged marriage	*mariage arrangé*
breakdown of marriage	*rupture du mariage*

child of a marriage, dependent child	*enfant à charge*
church or religious marriage	*mariage religieux*
civil marriage	*mariage civil*
common-law marriage	*union de fait*
dissolution of marriage	*dissolution du mariage*
invalid marriage	*mariage invalide*
marriage certificate	*extrait de mariage*
marriage contract	*contrat de mariage*
marriage in name only	*mariage fictif*
marriage of convenience	*mariage de convenance*
polygamous marriage	*mariage polygame*
proxy marriage	*mariage par procuration*
same-sex marriage	*mariage homosexuel*
trial marriage	*mariage à l'essai*

Names [*Noms*]

Upon marriage, a couple may take a common surname, usually the man's, hyphenate their surnames, or retain the surnames appearing on their birth certificates. Name changes as well as Gallicising of foreign names are permitted upon application to a county court [*tribunal de grande instance*]. Today there are more than a million surnames, many tied to specific parts of the country, and in 2005, a dictionary of them was published: *Dictionnaire historique des noms de famille*, by Marie-Odile Mergnac (Paris, Nouveau monde editions, 2005, 900 pages hardcover with a CD-ROM, ISBN 2-84736-128-6).

Polygamy [*Polygamie*]

Polygamy is illegal in France, particularly since the enactment of a law in August 1993 that specifically forbade polygamy for foreign nationals living in the country. Nonetheless, polygamy exists, particularly among people from the some 50 countries that permit it, and an estimated 180,000 people live in polygamous families. The situation is regarded to be a violation of human rights, particularly the rights of women. Consequently, on 9 March 2006, the **National Consultative Commission of Human Rights** (Chapter 27) issued a white paper giving an overview of polygamy and setting forth specific measures to curtail it. The paper, entitled *Avis sur la situation de la polygamie en France* can be downloaded from the Commission's website at *www.commission-droits-homme.fr*.

Prenuptial agreement [*Contrat de mariage*]

A prenuptial agreement is a legal contract entered by two people prior to marriage or civil union. It is used mostly in marriages and consequently usually is called a marriage contract [*contrat de mariage*]. The content of a marriage contract varies but most often includes specifications of the division of property and custody or children should the couple divorce. A contract may be drawn up by a lawyer, but most contracts are drawn up by **Notaries** (Chapter 29).

Rights and duties of parents [*L'obligation et l'autorité parentale*]

The rights and duties of parents are set forth in a succinct yet comprehensive brochure, *L'autorité parentale*, one of the many on **Legal matters** published by the Ministry of Justice, available in print from the distribution centre at 13 place Vendôme, 75042 Paris Cedex 01, or online at *www.joustice.gouv.fr*.

Youth Clubs [*Maisons des jeunes et de la culture*]

Founded in 1944, the *Maisons des jeunes et de la culture* offer social, sporting, cultural and educational events in most towns across the country. They are financed by the State, the municipalities and by two principal associations that coordinate their activities across the country as well as with similar youth clubs elsewhere in Europe:

* *Confédération des maisons des jeunes et de la* culture *de France (CMJCF)*, 168 bis rue Cardinet, 75017 Paris, Tel: 01 44852950, *www.mjc-cmjcf.asso.fr*, with 460,000 members and 3,700,000 users of the clubs.

* *Fédération française des maisons des jeunes et de la* culture *(FFMJC)*, 15 rue La Condamine, 75017 Paris, Tel: 01 44698225, *www.ffmjc.org*, with 600 associations, mostly in rural areas, and 1,500,000 users.

18
Farms, farming and gardening

France is a leader in agriculture. Farmlands comprise more than half the area of the country and a third of the farmland within the EU. Accordingly, agriculture accounts for nearly 22% of France's industrial turnover, well ahead of the aeronautical and automotive sectors. On the world scale, France is the second largest agricultural producer, after the USA. No wonder that the bucolic image stands strong, among the French themselves as well as among the foreign tourists who arrive in numbers that have made France the world's most popular tourist destination.

Yet the image is in part legend that has become decreasingly accurate. The number of farmers, particularly small farmers [*paysans*] is declining as is the number of farms they work. In their places are companies operating industrialised larger farms that together account for nearly half the farmed area of the country.

Nonetheless, the image is integral in the *éclat* of the country. Though only 3.6% of the workforce now is occupied in agriculture, two generations ago the figure was a third, so most families have some rural connections. Moreover, the French preference for good wine and food rests on a reverence for the *terroirs*, the earths that nurtured them. As President Chirac once remarked: "The farmers are the gardeners of our country and the guardians of our memory."

Mr. Chirac spoke in part of a tradition that also is changing, as gardening has become a popular leisure pursuit and 60% of households now have gardens. The *joie de vivre* of tending the *terroirs* now is commonplace.

Agribusiness [*Agro-alimentaire*]

Agribusiness comprises the processing and marketing of foodstuffs and the design and manufacture of the equipment and systems used in processing. The French agribusiness sector has a total annual turnover of 138 billion (in 2004), which ranks it number one in the country and number six in the world. Most companies in the sector are small and medium-sized enterprises (SMEs) of which more than half have fewer than 50 employees. Although agribusinesses are set up across the country, 28% are located in rural areas. For further information, contact the National Association of Food Industries [*Association Nationale des Industries Alimentaires (ANIA)*], 28 rue Leblanc, 75015 Paris, Tel: 01 53838600, *www.ania.net*.

Agricultural data [*Données agricoles*]

The Ministry of Agriculture and Fisheries Documentation and Information Centre [*Centre de documentation et d'information Agreste (CDIA)*] is the most comprehensive single source of data, statistics and studies on all aspects of the agricultural sector, including fisheries, forests, aquaculture and rural environments. Indeed, its everyday name, *AGRESTE*, an acronym formed from the keywords for its activities, *AGRicolE* and *STastiquE*, is a word connoting the entire rural environment, in the sense of being rustic [*champêtre*]. It publishes extensively, both in print and online, and supports other systems, such as agricultural databases, as described in its annual catalogue. For further information, contact CDIA, 251 rue de Vaugirard, 75732 Paris Cedex 15, Tel: 01 49558585, *agreste.agriculture.gouv.fr* in French with summaries in English.

Bienvenue à la ferme

Bienvenue à la ferme, literally "Farm welcome", is a network of farms that offer meals, bed and breakfast accommodations, campsites and farm familiarisation and educational programmes. Started in 1985 by the **Chambers of agriculture**, the network now has more than 1400 guest cottages and is supported by more than 5200 farmers. For further details, contact the head office of the Chambers of agriculture, APCA, 9 avenue George V, 75008 Paris, Tel: 01 53571144, *www.bienvenue-a-la-ferme.com* with a locator map of farms in the network and pages in French and in English.

Bienvenue à la ferme logo.

CEMAGREF

CEMAGREF, the acronym for *Centre national du machinisme agricole, du génie rural, des eaux et des forêts*, is the leading agricultural and environmental engineering research organisation, with facilities at nine locations across the country as well as on the island of Martinique. It conducts research in 25 fields, organised into four scientific departments:

- Aquatic environments and quality of discharges
- Land management
- Ecotechnologies and agrosystems
- Water resources, usages and risks

For 2004-2008, CEMAGREF has three scientific priorities:

- Hydrosystems and agriculture, to evolve a scientific basis for the integrated management of aquatic ecosystems.
- Natural risks, to understand natural hazards and develop appropriate protection strategies.
- Common scientific methods, to exploit and link the common stock of scientific methods for more efficient research.

For further information, contact the head office: Cemagref Antony, Parc de Touvoie, BP 44, 92163 Antony Cedex, Tel: 01 40966121, *www.cemagref.fr* with pages in French and English.

Certificates of quality and origin
[*Signe officiel de qualité et d'origine*]

Some 116,000 farms, one in three in the country, produce under one or more of the four certificates of quality and origin, administered by the Ministry of Agriculture and Fisheries*:

- *AOC*, the abbreviation for *Appelation d'Origine Contrôle* (Chapter 13), the oldest and most widespread, developed originally for wines and subsequently extended to dairy and other food products
- *Label Rouge* (Chapter 19), instituted in 1965 to designate high quality of a range of food products, now 400 in all; similar in concept to AOC.
- *CCP*, the abbreviation for **Certificate of Product Conformity** (Chapter 19), instituted in 1990 distinguish quality products, now more than 250.
- *AB*, the abbreviation for *Agriculture Biologique*, the production of **Organic foods** (Chapter 19) without the use of synthetic chemical products. Though the smallest of the four quality sectors, AB is growing rapidly.

* *Agreste Primeur,* no. 169, September 2005.

Chambers of agriculture [*Les Chambres d'Agriculture*]

The Chambers of agriculture [*Les Chambres d'Agriculture*] are the State administrative bodies that represent and serve the agricultural sector, via local Chambers, one in each *Département*. The ten members of a Chamber represent individuals and organisations and are elected for six-year terms. The Chambers have a permanent central organisation and head office, *Assemblée permanente des chambres d'agriculture (APCA)*, 9 avenue George V, 75008 Paris, Tel: 01 53571010, *paris.apca.chambagri.fr* with an interactive Chamber locator map and the *France des Saveurs* guide to local cuisines.

Common Agricultural Policy (CAP)
[*Politique Agricole Commune (PAC)*]

The Common Agricultural Policy (CAP) was introduced by the European Community in 1960, specifically to:

- provide a fair standard of living for farmers
- secure reasonable food prices for all
- stabilise markets
- increase productivity
- ensure regular food supplies.

It was structured to attain these goals by employing three principles:

- A single farm product market with uniform prices and free movement of agricultural goods within the EC
- Preference for EC members
- Relevant costs shared by all.

Despite these clear goals and guidelines, the CAP soon became the biggest policy concern within the EU as well as the most costly programme, accounting for nearly half the EU budget. From the 1980s onwards, the CAP clearly was in trouble: criticism of and resistance to it arose in most EU agricultural countries, notably France, the largest recipient of CAP subsidies by virtue of the size of its agricultural sector. Describing the CAP and the difficulties that now befall it would require a book larger than this, and indeed many books and reports have been written on CAP topics. Arguably the best starting point is an EU monograph entitled "The Common Agricultural Policy Explained" (EU, 33 pages, A4 format in PDF file, publication KE-62-04-276-EN-C, released in 2005) available online, in English and French editions, from the EU website; the link for the English edition is *europa.eu.int/comm/agriculture/publi/capexplained/cap_en.pdf*.

Farmers' unions [*Les syndicats des fermiers*]

There are many farmers' associations and unions; the four largest, in alphabetical order by their names, are:

- *Confédération Paysanne* ("Small farmers' confederation") was founded in 1987, principally to promote traditional farming as opposed to intensive, industrialised farming. In 2000-2005, José Bové, its colourful spokesman, became a popular hero by attacking globalisation and the CAP for industrialising agriculture and neglecting the small farmer. Head office: 81 avenue de la République, 93170 Bagnolet, Tel: 01 43620404, *www.confederationpaysanne.fr*.

- *Coordination rurale syndicat* ("Rural syndicate") was founded in 1999, as a result of a chain of events that began with the publication in 1991 of a manifesto against the **Common Agricultural Policy** [*Politique Agricole Commune (PAC)*]. Head office: 15 rue Paul Descomps, BP 590, 32022 Auch Cedex 9, Tel: 05 62601496, *www.coordinationrurale.fr*.

- *Fédération nationale des syndicats d'exploitants agricoles (FNSEA)* ("National Federation of Farmers' Unions") was founded in 1946 and is by far the largest farm organisation, claiming 70% of farmers as its members. It supports a wide range of farm-related publications and activities, including a comprehensive farm youth programme, *Le centre national des jeunes agriculteurs (CNJA)*. Head office: 11 rue de la Baume, 75008 Paris, Tel: 01 53834747, *www.fnsea.fr* with pages in French, English and Spanish.

- *Mouvement de défense des exploitants familiaux* ("National Confederation of Family Farmers' Unions") was founded in 1959 and is linked to left-leaning political parties and to an ideology formerly called rural communism. Head office: 14 Bd d'Aquitaine, BP 316, 16008 Angoulême Cedex, Tel: 05 45910049.

Farms and farmers [*Fermes et fermiers*]

Although more than 80% of the area of mainland France is rural, either farmland or forests, the people who work farms and forests comprise no more than 3.6% of the working population. And their numbers are diminishing: in the decade from 1993 to 2003, the number of farms in the country fell from 801,000 to 590,000. As the number of small farms, 35 hectares and less, fell more rapidly than the total, the number of large farms, 100 hectares and more, many owned by corporations, increased to cover nearly half the area farmed in the country.

That trend toward ever more industrialised farming has been the cause of much unrest among small farmers and was one of the triggers of the founding of *Confédération Paysanne*, now one of the four largest **Farmers' unions**. Another cause of unrest has been the trend, set in Brussels, of distributing 80% of farm subsidies to 20% of the farms. The result has been low wages in farming: the national annual average is less than €12,000 a year. On the social scale, farmers stand apart from most employees in the country. They often work twice as long as the 35-hour working week, and if they keep animals, they seldom, if ever, take holidays, because leaving the animals means hiring someone to tend them. Many fear that the low wages and long hours will cause ever more young people to leave farming. Nonetheless, it is the small farmers who are the trustees of the **terroir** (Chapter 5) that is so indelible in the national reverence for its farmlands and the traditions of those who work them.

Gardening professions [*Professions aux mains vertes*]

Professional gardeners [*jardineries*], nurserymen [*pépiniéristes*], horticulturists [*horticulteurs*], florists [*fleuristes*] and landscape gardeners [*paysagistes*] can be located under listings for the respective professions in the Yellow Pages. The *Annuaire des Fleuristes* website at *www.annuaire-fleuristes.com* has interactive locator maps for all these professions, for France, Belgium and Switzerland.

Gardening [*Jardinage*]

Despite Voltaire's advice that *il faut cultiver notre jardin* ("we must cultivate our gardens"), gardening traditionally has been a low-key, pragmatic pursuit, the cultivation of vegetables, or a matter for the elite, who could afford to hire professionals to plan and maintain resplendent estates. No more. Starting in the late 1990s, amateur gardening has bloomed. According to Promojardin, which promotes gardening, it is the fastest growing consumer sector, now with an annual turnover of more than €6 billion. For further information, contact Promojardin, 11 villa Brune, 75014 Paris, Tel: 01 45432525, *www.promojardin.fr*.

There are many triggers for the upsurge, of which the reduction of the working week to 35 hours in 2000 may be the most important. With less work and more leisure, gardening appeals as an inexpensive leisure pursuit. Six in ten households now have a garden, and many others have balconies where plants are cultivated. Garden centres and shops have spread across the country, to meet the burgeoning demand for garden plants and implements, and there are three major chains of them:
Gamm vert (*www.gammvert.fr*), Jardiland (*www.jardiland.fr*) and Truffaut (*www.truffaut.com*). The amateur gardeners' association, *Jardiniers de France*, has 3500 affiliated clubs and 130,000 members across the country; for information, contact the head office, 40 route d'Aulnoy, BP 559, 59308 Valenciennes Cedex, Tel: 08 26020313, *www.jardiniersdefrance.com* with an interactive club locator map.

Gîtes de France

As across Europe, people living in cities escape to the countryside on holidays. However, by tradition, such holidays used to be the luxury of the well-to-do, who could afford second homes or stays at resort hotels. That changed in 1950, when Émile Aubert (1906-1969), then a Senator for Alpes-de-Haute-Provence, reasoned that people in cities should enjoy the countryside at reasonable cost and that rural populations could derive much needed income from providing facilities that would, in part, help slow **rural exodus**. Hence he proposed that rural families offer *gîtes* ("holiday cottages") as holiday accommodations for urban families. The first *gîte rural* opened in 1951. In 1952, the Ministry of Agriculture approved the prototype, and set up grants for farmers for setting up *gîtes*, and the *Crédit agricole* and *Crédit hôtelier* accordingly granted loans at favourable rates. The idea spread rapidly, and today there are more than 56,000 *gîtes* in the country that together provide 35 million person-holiday days a year, in accommodations ranging from simple farm accommodations to wings of Renaissance *châteaux*, as listed in 11 national guides and three regional guides. Aside from being popular with French as well as people of other countries on holiday, the growing network of *gîtes* has helped preserve the cultural landscape, saving an estimated 100,000 buildings from ruin by neglect, so the concept has spread to other countries and resulted in the founding of EuroGîtes, website at *www.eurogites.com*. For further details, contact *Gîtes de France*, 59 rue Saint-Lazare, 75349 Paris Cedex 09, Tel: 01 49707575, *www.gites-de-franc.fr* in French, English and German, with an interactive locator map of *gîtes* across the country.

Gîtes de France logo that appears in publications and on signs.

Landscapists [*Paysagistes*]

Landscapists are professional gardeners skilled in landscaping parks, gardens, road works, business and industrial properties and the like. In France, there are more than 500 qualified landscapists, most with independent businesses listed under *Paysagistes* in the Yellow Pages. For further information on the profession and its practitioners across the country, contact *Fédération Française du Paysage*, 4 rue Hardy, 78000 Versailles, Tel: 01 30214745, *www.f-f-p.org*.

Pastoralism [*Pastoralisme*]

Historically, pastoralism is the practice of shepherds in tending their flocks or herds. In modern times, as opposed to livestock farming, pastoralism entails raising, tending and using animals fed principally by grazing on natural vegetation. In many countries, where livestock farming has been industrialised, pastoralism has all but died out. However it survives in many countries, in Europe in France, Italy, Norway, Romania, Spain, Sweden Switzerland and Turkey. It is most noticeable by its practice of transhumance, the seasonal movement of livestock that takes advantage of the differences in climate with elevation, with herds and flocks moving up to mountain pastures in summer and down to valleys or plains in winter.

In France, pastoralism is as old as agriculture. Unsurprisingly, there are specific words for it, including *transhumance*, borrowed by English and other languages, and *orri*, a shepherd's stone cabin, many of which remain in mountain areas. Indeed, mountains are essential to transhumance as it is practised in Europe, and in France, transhumance takes place today mostly in the Pyrénées but also in the Alps and the *Massif Centrale*. Every spring and autumn, there are transhumance movements of livestock in the farming regions to the northwest of Montpellier and Nîmes, two so large that they have become tourist attractions: from Jocelyne et François in Gard and from Michel et Mocelyne in Aveyron to the higher mountain regions of Lozère. For details, contact *La Gazette de Montpellier*, 13. place de la Comédie, 34000 Montpellier, Tel: 04 67067777, *www.gazettedemontpellier.fr* or *La Gazette de Nîmes*, 11. rue Régale, 3000 Nîmes, Tel: 04 66587777, *www.gazettedenimes.fr*. For information on pastoralism in France, contact *L'Association française de pastoralisme*, c/o CEMAGREF, 2 rue de la Papeterie, BP 76, 38400 Saint Martin d'Heres, *www.pastoralisme.org*.

Rural exodus and urbanisation [*L'exode rural à la urbanisation*]

As in other countries, the industrialisation of the 19th century triggered a shift in populations from rural districts to urban areas. By the early 20th century, the drift had dwindled and changed character, as immigrants from Italy, the Maghreb and Poland came to work in heavy industries and native rural French emigrated. The next exodus from rural areas started in 1945, after the Second World War, and was most noticeable in western regions of Anjou, Bretagne and Vendée, that had up to then retained a greater part of their rural populations. That drift also dwindled, and by 1975 was insignificant. Moreover, from the early 1990s onwards, the intertwining of town and country life, began and grew, particularly around cities, with the result that many people living in rural areas now commute to work in cities. For further details, browse the list of nearly 200 reports compiled by the **National Institute of Statistics and Economic Studies** (Chapter 42) available online at *www.insee.fr*.

Salon International de l'Agriculture (SIA)

The SIA is an agricultural show of respectable tradition. In 1870, for the first time, farm animals and products were shown together in Paris, when the first *Concours Général Agricole* was held at the Palais de l'Industrie on the Champs-Elysées. Breeding animals were added in the 1876 show, and wines followed in 1893. By 1963, the show had become a major event, and in 1964, the first international show was held. Now, in the 21st century, the annual show features more than a thousand exhibitors and attracts more than 600,000 visitors. For further details, contact SIA, Parc des expositions de la Porte de Versailles, 75015 Paris, Tel: 01 49096056, *www.salon-agriculture.com* in French and in English. As this book goes to press, the next SIA will be held 24 February-4 March 2007.

19
Food and eating

In food and eating, the venerable traveller's advice of "when in Rome, do as the Romans" remains your best advice. There are many cuisines in France, each evolved through the centuries by the people of a locality to meet their needs in their surroundings. These many styles combine to make France a gourmet's delight and, indeed, the subject of countless books dedicated to the subject: this chapter comprises only the elements common to all French cuisines.

Additives [*Additifs*]

Across Europe, food-labelling regulations require specification of the ingredients. This includes additives, specified according to uniform E-number codes that are independent of language: the same E-number means the same additive, regardless of the country of origin or sale of a product or the language on its label. Nonetheless, some food manufacturers designate additives by their chemical names rather than their E-numbers. Both types of labelling – chemical name and E-number – are permitted.

Chemical names and E-numbers sound modern, but many of them designate products long in use. For instance, E330 is citric acid, which originally came from lemon juice and has been used as a food additive since the 1890s, and ordinary baking powder is a blend of several E-number additives, principally E500 (bicarbonate of soda), E450 (tetrasodium diphosphate) and E341 (dicalcium phosphate). Scientists in the EU and the World Health Organisation (WHO) analyse each additive and set an Acceptable Daily Intake (ADI) for it. The ADI for an additive sets the maximum amount of it that a human can safely consume per day for an entire lifetime. For further information on additives and the latest list of E-numbers, contact the **European Food Information Council**.

Baby food [*Aliment pour bébé*]

Most food shops offer a selection of baby foods including at least two of the four leading brands:

- Blédina, the leading brand in France, head office at 383 rue Philippe Héron, BP 432, 69654 Villefranche-sur-Saône Cedex, *www.bledina.com*.

- Nestlé, the major international brand, head office in France at 7 bd Pierre Carle, BP 900 Noisel, 77446 Marne la Vallée Cedex 2, *www.bebe.nestle.fr*.

- Picot, formulas, drinks and cereals, head office at 189 Quai Lucien Lheureux, PB83, 62102 Calais Cedex, *www.picot.fr*.

- Vitagermine, Babybio and Kalibio brands of organic foods, head office at Avenue Ferdinand de Lesseps, Canéjan, 33612 Cestas Cedes, *www.vitagermine.com*.

For further information on a company's products, contact customer services at the head office postal address or visit its website.

Bread [*Le Pain*]

Most people eat bread at every meal. Nonetheless, the amount of bread consumed is modest, slightly less than 56 kg/year per resident, well below first-place Germans who consume more than 84 kg/year per resident*. Bread is classified in three categories according to the manner in which it is produced and sold:

- Traditional French bread [*pain de tradition française*] without additives, treatment or deep freezing, as produced and sold by more than 37,000 *boulangeries* across the country.

- Ordinary French bread [*pain courant français*] that can contain up to 14 additives including ascorbic acid and emulsifiers, as produced by larger bakeries.

- Prepackaged [*préemballé*] bread that may contain up to 14 additives and preservatives, as produced by industrial-scale bakeries.

The long, thin *baguette* weighing up to 250 gr remains most popular, though there are many other varieties made from a range of grains and cereals and some containing herbs, nuts or raisins.

In May each year, *La Fête du Pain* – the bread festival – is celebrated across the country; for information, visit the festival website at *www.fetedupain.com* with an interactive locator map of participating *boulangeries*.

*source: QUID 2006

Breakfast [*Petit déjeuner*]

By tradition, most people begin the day with a light meal, known in English as the *Continental breakfast*, to distinguish it from the far heavier variety traditionally, but rarely today, consumed in the British Isles as well as in many other countries outside Europe. As its name, *petit déjeuner* – "little lunch" – implies, it is modest, usually consisting of bread with butter and preserves or honey and a drink, milk or juice for children and coffee for adults. That said, traditions are changing, and cereals, fruit, toast and yoghurt are increasingly popular at breakfast time.

Cereals [*Céréales*]

France is the world's seventh biggest producer of cereals*. That ranking, along with the national affinity for bread and pastries, may explain why food shops and supermarkets offer a wide selection of flour [*farine*]. The principal varieties, alphabetically by their designations in French:

- *blé*: wholemeal flour
- *châtaigne*: chestnut flour
- *froment*: wheat flour
- *gâteaux*: cake flour
- *gruau*: fine wheat flour
- *lin*: linseed meal
- *maïs*: corn flour
- *manioc*: cassava flour
- *riz*: rice flour
- *sarrasin*: buckwheat flour
- *seigle*: rye flour
- *son*: bran flour

Flour is graded in relation to the degree of milling: a light flour (T45) is used for pastry, whilst wholemeal flour is designated T150. For further information on flour, contact Inter-Farine, 24 Chaussée du Vouldy, BP 23, 10001 Troyes, Tel: 03 25711910, *www.farine.com*.

*Source: The Economist Pocket World in Figures 2006, p. 47.

Certificate of product conformity [*Certification Conformité Produit (CCP)*]

The CCP is one of the four **Certificates of quality and origin** (Chapter 17). Instituted in 1990, it distinguishes quality products, now more than 250, that conform to European and French standards. For further information, contact the issuing organisation, Certipaq, 44 rue La Quintinie, 75015 Paris, Tel: 01 45309292, *www.certipaq.com*.

Cheese [*Fromage*]

From Roman times on, when Cantal and Roquefort cheeses were taken to Rome to be enjoyed by the wealthy, France has been renowned for its cheeses. Today, there are said to be more varieties of French cheeses than there are days in a year. Some 47 of them are certified according to the ***Appellation d'Origine Contrôlée (AOC)*** (Chapter 12), the same designation system as for fine wines: Abondance, Banon, Beaufort, Beurre Charentes-Poitou, Bleu d'Auvergne, Bleu de Gex Haut Jura, Bleu des Causses, Bleu du Vercors-Sassenage, Brie de Meaux, Brie de Melun, Brocciu, Camembert de Normandie, Cantal, Chabichou du Poitou, Chaource, Chavignol, Chevrotin, Comte, Crème d'Isigny, Epoisses, Fourme d'Ambert, Fourme de Montbrison, Laguiole, Langres, Livarot, Maroilles, Mont d'or, Morbier, Munster, Neufchâtel, Ossau-Iraty, Pelardon, Picodon, Pont l'Evêque, Pouligny-Saint-Pierre, Reblochon, Rocamadour, Roquefort, Saint-nectaire, Sainte-Maure de Touraine, Salers, Selles-sur-Cher, Tome des Bauges and Valençay. There are many books on cheeses, one on the AOC cheeses alone: *Fromages AOC de France* by Jean-Pierre Duval (Paris, Romain, 2004, 96 pages, 17 × 17 cm softcover, ISBN 2-8435-0141-5).

Coffee [*Café*]

Coffee is favoured at breakfast and after dinner. The two main varieties are:

- "Ordinary" coffee [*café*], most often roasted and ground from *caffea canephora* (*Robusta*) beans originally native to Africa and common in international-brand coffees as well as in instant coffee [*café soluble*]. It is the variety most sold in supermarkets and served in homes.

- Espresso coffee [*Expresso*], mostly roasted and ground from *coffea Arabica* beans, originally native to Ethiopia and having about half as much caffeine as robusta coffee. High quality robusta coffees are mixed in some espresso blends to provide a more foamy head, known by its name in Italian, *crema*. Espresso is the variety most served in restaurants.

Both varieties can be served black and drunk with or without sugar and are made in a variety of automatic and manual coffeemakers [*cafetière*]. Among the more popular coffeemakers in homes are the:

- Chambord "French press" coffeemakers, as those made by Bodum of Switzerland, *www.bodum.com*.

- Filter coffeemakers and filters of various types; as those made by Melitta of Germany, *www.melitta.de* and in France *www.melitta.fr*.

- Espresso coffeemakers, as those made by Bialetti of Italy, *www.bialetti.it*.

Both varieties are also served with heated milk, distinguished by specific names:

- *Café au lait*: ordinary coffee with warmed milk ('white coffee' in the UK)

- *Café crème*: espresso coffee with steamed milk.

The two names are sometimes muddled. In Italy, espresso is so much the norm that it is often served unless you specify another variety, such as *café americano*. That's only partly the case in France, as many restaurants offer both varieties and take orders literally: a *café au lait* usually is a small bowl of ordinary coffee and warmed milk, whilst a *café crème* is a cup of espresso with steamed milk. Confusingly, outside of France, the mix of espresso and steamed milk often is called *café au lait*, perhaps by similarity to the names of the same drink in Italian, *café latte,* and in Spanish, *café con leche*. A coffee bar in the UK that lists *café au lait*, *café latte*, and *café con leche* on its menu simply is offering the same preparation under three names. But *café au lait* in France is a different drink.

Cookery books [*Livres de cuisine*]

Cookery books abound, in bookshops, in book departments in hypermarkets and on shelves in supermarkets. Perhaps most popular is the new edition [*nouvelle édition*] of *Petit Larousse de la Cuisine* (Paris, Larousse, 2006, 1120 pages hardcover, ISBN 2-03-56054-0), the condensed version of *Larousse Gastronomique* (Paris, Larousse, 2000, 1215 pages hardcover, ISBN 2-03-560227-0), the world's most famous culinary reference work. More than 2500 recipes from *Larousse Gastronomique* have been collected and published in English in a four-volume set, Larousse Gastronomique Recipe Set (London, Hamlyn, 2004, 4 volumes, in all 1535 pages softcover, ISBN 0-600-61158-2).

Cuisine

What's known in other countries as "French cuisine" actually comprises the embellished dishes served by exclusive Paris restaurants. It is based on the regional cuisines of the northern part of the country but otherwise differs from the many regional cuisines, which divide into four groups:

- northeast, with dishes using sauerkraut and sausages, as in Germany
- northwest, with dishes using apples, butter and cream
- southeast, or Provençal, with dishes using herbs, olive oil and tomatoes
- southwest, with dishes using duck fat, foie gras and mushrooms.

Aside from the main four groups, there are many local cuisines, such as the Basque cuisine using chilli and tomatoes and the Loire Valley cuisine using freshwater fish. There are magazines that attempt to describe all the regional cuisines in detail, such as *Cuisine et Vins de France*, 10 boulevard des Frères Voisin, 92792 Issy-Les-Moulineaux Cedex 9, Tel: 01 41468888, *www.cuisineetvinsdefrance.com*, as well as many online references and shops, including Cuisine AZ at *www.cuisineaz.com* and Toutes les recettes at *www.toutesrecettes.com*.

That said, in French, *cuisine* is the everyday word for kitchen as well as for a specific manner or style of cooking. Consequently, the *cuisine* department of a white-goods shop sells cookers, refrigerators, freezers and kitchen appliances, and the *cuisine* department of a DIY shop sells kitchen furniture. The adjective *cuisiné* (with the final e being acute) simply means "cooked": a *plat cuisiné* is a ready-made dish as sold by a caterer [*traiteur*].

Cutlery [*Couverts*]

Knives and forks are used in the continental European manner. Throughout a meal, the fork is held in the left hand, the knife in the right. The knife is used to move food onto the fork and to cut one piece of food for each bite. At breakfast, a knife only may be used to butter bread, and fingers are used in eating many dishes, such as mussels or clams. However, at an ordinary meal, holding only the fork in the right hand and moving it to the left to hold meat or fish while cutting many pieces, as is the custom in some countries outside Europe, is considered bad manners. But it is acceptable in fast food restaurants when only a plastic fork is provided.

Desserts [*Desserts*]

A dessert usually is the last course of a dinner and often the last of a lunch. Accordingly, there are thousands of recipes for desserts, many parts of local cuisines. There are books about them, such as *Larousse des desserts* by Pierre Hermé (Paris, Larousse, 2002, 20 × 27 cm, 462 page paperback, ISBN 2-03-560272-6), as well as websites dedicated to them, such as Recette Dessert at *www.recette-dessert.com* and Tous les desserts at *www.touslesdesserts.com*.

Diabetic foods [*Aliments pour diabétiques*]

Most markets, supermarkets and hypermarkets offer selections of diabetic and dietetic foods. Three widely available brands are:

- *Gayelord Hauser* and *Vivis*, two brands of Distriborg Groupe, 217 Chemin du Grand Revoyet, 69561 Saint Genis Laval Cedex, *www.distriborg.com* in French and English.
- *Supplex*, the principal brand of Spécialités Supplex, 53 rue Pasteur, BP 50018, 72500 Château-du-Loir, Tel: 02 43440153, *www.supplex.fr* in French and English.

Eating and drinking places [*Restaurations*]

Each year, more than 250,000 eating places across the country together serve some 6.3 billion meals. Nearly half are **restaurants**; the other half consists of a variety of establishments:

- *Auberge*: an inn, usually in a rural district and consequently also called *auberge rural*. An *auberge* usually serves the traditional country fare of its locality. A farmhouse inn [*ferme-auberge*], as those of the **Gîtes de France** (Chapter 18) establishments, often will serve local dishes based on the produce of the farm.

- *Bar*: as elsewhere, a bar is dedicated to serving alcoholic drink and seldom serves food other than snacks or ready-made sandwiches. A *piano-bar* offers entertainment; a *bar américain* is a cocktail bar.

- *Bistro* or *bistrot*: an in-between designation that may be anything from a simple bar or pub to a full-service restaurant.

- *Brasserie*: a type of bar-restaurant, so named because it originated in Alsace, famed for its breweries [*brasseries*]. Most *brasseries* serve traditional French dishes in set-price [*prix fixe*] menus at reasonable prices.

- *Buffet* or *buvette*: a simple serving place, such as a counter or kiosk at a railway station offering snacks, ready-made sandwiches and drinks.

- *Café*: principally a serving place for coffee [*café*] and small dishes that go with it. Once the hubs of urban social circles, traditional *cafés* are declining in number, in step with changing lifestyles and in face of competition from newer eating and drinking places, particularly fast-food restaurants [*restaurations rapide*].

- *Café de routiers* or *restaurant de routiers*: a transport café along a major road or motorway offering no-frills fare.

- *Cafétéria*: a self-service restaurant [*restauration libre-service*], often found alongside a supermarket [*supermarché*] or a hypermarket [*hyermarché*]..

- *Crêperie*: a type of café specialising in crêpes and other sweets.

- *Pizzéria*: a restaurant specialising in pizzas and other Italian dishes, usually of a brand chain, including Pasta del Arte, Pizza Païe, Pizza Hut, Pizza Pino and Vesuvio.

- *Pub*: a *café* decorated in English style and offering more food service than a bar.

- *Restauration rapide*: a fast-food outlet, usually of a brand chain. Starting with the first in 1974, there now are more than 1000 McDonalds fast-food restaurants. Other major chains are Quick with 313 restaurants, Brioche dorée with 222, La Croissanterie with 104 and Relay with 97. Today, nearly one restaurant meal in seven is provided by a fast-food outlet.

- *Restauration enseignement*: a cafeteria or other food service in an educational institution. Together, these services provide about 1.1 billion meals a year, more than traditional restaurants that together provide 912 million meals.

- *Rôtisserie*: a restaurant specialising in roasted and grilled meats.

- *Salon de thé*: a tea room offering a variety of teas as well as small dishes, such as cakes, pastries, quiches and salads.

Eggs [*Œufs*]

As elsewhere in Europe, eggs are sold in cartons of six or twelve. In accordance with EU directives, there are two quality classes:

- A table eggs, fresh [*œufs frais*]
- B second-class eggs [*œufs de deuxième qualité*] that may be used in industry but, since June 2004, may not be sold as table eggs.

Table eggs are sold in four size categories:

- XL extra large [*très gros*], 73 gr. or more average weight
- L large [*gros*], 63-73 gr. average weight
- M medium [*moyen*], 53-63 gr. average weight
- S small [*petit*], less than 53 gr. average weight.

Egg durability [*date de durabilité*] should be stamped on the carton in the DD/MM/YY format, with the date indicated being no more than 28 days after the eggs were laid. This is customarily marked as the consume-by date [*A consommer de préférence avant le*]. Alternatively, a recommended date of sale [*date de vente recommandée*] no more than 21 days after the eggs were laid may be stated. The typical label on a half-dozen carton of large free-range eggs will be imprinted:

6
Œufs frais de poules élevées en plein air
63/73 g   AL

and will be stamped with the best-by date and a code designating the producer. Free-range eggs are labelled as above; organic eggs are additionally labelled *biologique*.

European Food Information Council (EUFIC) [*Le conseil européen de l'Information sur l'alimentation*]

The European Food Information Council (EUFIC) is a non-profit organisation that acts as a clearing house for information on the food sciences and related topics. Based in Brussels and supported by major food and beverage companies, it offers information for professionals and consumers in 12 sectors:

1. Adult Nutrition [*Nutrition de l'adulte*]
2. Children nutrition [*Nutrition de l'enfant*]
3. Obesity [*Obésité*]
4. Functional foods [*Aliments fonctionnels*]
5. Carbohydrates [*Glucides*]
6. Physical activity [*Activité physique*]
7. Food safety [*Sécurité alimentaire*]
8. Food allergy [*Allergie alimentaire*]

9. Food additives [*Additifs alimentaires*]

10. Agriculture [*Agriculture*]

11. Fats [*Graisses*]

12. Dental health [*Santé dentaire*]

EUFIC publishes a periodical four-page newsletter, Food Today, and issues reviews and leaflets on specific subjects. Several of its publications are compiled jointly with national and international organisations. For further information, contact EUFIC, 17 rue Guimard, 1040 Brussels, Belgium, Tel: +32 2 5068989, *www.eufic.org* in English, French, German, Italian, Portuguese and Spanish.

European quality marks [*Signes de qualité européennes*]

Three European quality marks are linked to the national regime of quality indications on foods and accordingly are affixed to food packaging:

- The *Appellation d'Origine Protégée* is a certification of origin that, like the **Appellation d'origine Contrôlée (AOC)** (Chapter 13) for wines, is legally regulated and recognised across Europe.

- The *Indication Géographique Protégée* is a certification of the use of geographically traditional or special methods of production. It also is subject to EC directives applicable to plant and animal products.

- The *Spécialité Traditionnelle Garantie* is used in transferring French quality rankings to the European level.

For further information, contact Certipaq, 44 rue La Quintinie, 75015 Paris, Tel: 01 45309292, *www.certipaq.com*.

Fish and shellfish [*Poissons, coquillages et crustacés*]

The culinary term for fish and shellfish is "fruits of the sea" [*fruits de mer*], though fishmongers [*poissonneries*] and departments in supermarkets use the more specific terms of fish [*poissons*], molluscs [*coquillages*] and crustaceans [*crustacés*]. About 40% of all products sold are fresh, 23% frozen, 20% chilled delicatessen and 18% tinned. In order of total household expenditures over a year, the most popular products are salmon [*saumon*], cod [*cabillaud*], oysters [*huitre*], mussels [*moule*], coley [*lieu*], monkfish [*baudroie, lotte*], Nile perch [*perche du Nil*], sole [*sole*], scallops [*coquille St. Jacques*], whiting [*merlan*], scampi [*langoustine*], sea bass [*bar*], sea bream [*dorade*] and tuna [*thon*]*. For further information on fish and shellfish, contact *Office national interprofessionnel des produits de la mer et de l'aquaculture (OFIMER)*, 76/78 rue de Reuilly, 75012 Paris, Tel: 01 53334700, *www.ofimer.fr* in French with selected pages in English, or order the OFIMER consumer guide, *Poissons, Coquillages, Crustacés, Le Petit Guide Alimentation & Santé*.

source OFIMER 2006 key figures

Food guide [*Guide des aliments*]

Doctors Jean-Michel Cohen and Patrick Serog have collected an enormous amount of information on the agricultural, botanical and nutritional characteristics of foods in a single volume, *Savoir manger, Le guide des aliments 2006-2007* (Paris, Éditions Fammarion, 2006, 968 pages softcover, ISBN 2-08-068755-7).

Food processing industries [*Industrie agroalimentaire*]

The national and international brands of processed foods in shops increasingly are the offerings of large national and international food processing conglomerates, of which the 11 leaders are:

- Bonduelle: salads and chilled foods, ready-to-serve dishes, frozen foods, tinned vegetables, preserves, *www.bonduelle.fr*.

- Danone: Actimel, Bio, Blédina baby food; Danone, Danonino and Vitalinéa dairy products; Aqua, Evian, Volvic and Wahala bottled water; Lu biscuits and cereals, *www.danone.fr*.

- Fleury Michon: hams and other prepared meats, cold cuts, ready-to-serve dishes, *www.fleurymichon.fr*.

- Groupe Bongrain: cheese and processed dairy foods, *www.bongrain.com*.

- Heinz: sauces, condiments and tinned goods, *www.heinz.fr*

- Kraft Foods: Côte d'Or, Daim, Milka, Suchard and Toblerone chocolate; Carte Noire, Grand Mère, Jacques Vabre, Maxwell House and Velours Noir coffee, *www.kraftfoods.fr*.

- Lactalis: dairy products, *www.lactalis.fr*.

- Mars: M&M, Mars, Snickers and Twix sweets; Whiskas and Pedigree pet foods; Uncle Ben's rice; Klix and Flavia drinks, *www.mars.com*.

- Nestlé: many brands, including Nescafé coffee and powdered coffee; Nestlé baby food; Maggi soups and sauces; and Herta cold cuts, *www.nestle.fr*.

- Pillsbury: the General Mills group with many brands in France, including Häagen Dazs ice cream, Green Giant (Géant Vert) tinned goods and Old El Paso tinned and convenience foods, *www.pillsbury.com*.

- Unilever: many brands, including Findus frozen foods; Knorr soups and sauces; and Lipton tea, as well as many brands of household and non-food products, *www.unilever.com*.

Food safety [*Sécurité des Aliments*]

The quality and safety of food is affected by the actions of all involved in the increasingly complex chain of production, processing, transport, distribution, sale and consumption. Put simply, the safety and quality of food is a shared responsibility from farm to fork. Accordingly, international and national agencies advise, monitor and conduct research on food safety. At the European Union level, the European Food Safety Authority (EFSA) [*Autorité Européenne de Sécurité des Aliments*] was established in 2002 as the central agency, with a head office at Largo N. Palli 5/A, I-43100 Parma, Italy, Tel: +39 0521036111, *www.efsa.eu.int* in English, French, German and Italian. The principal agency in France is *Agence Française de Sécurité Sanitaire des Aliments (AFSSA)*, 23, avenue du Général de Gaulle, BP 19, 94701 Maisons-Alfort Cedex, Tel: 01 49771350, *www.afssa.fr*.

Food supplements [*Compléments alimentaires*]

The definition, composition and labelling of food supplements is regulated in compliance with European Parliament Directive 2002/46/EC. For further information, contact AFSSA, the principal agency responsible for **Food safety**.

French Nutrition Institute
[*Institut français pour la nutrition (IFN)*]

Established in 1974, IFN is the principal research institute concerned with nutrition, the food sciences and the food industry. It conducts basic and applied research, supports nutritional research in the country, and awards two annual prizes, *Prix de la Recherche en Nutrition* and *Prix "jeune chercheur" Bernard Beaufrère*. For further information, contact IFN, 71 avenue Victor Hugo, 75116 Paris, Tel: 01 45009250, *www.ifn.asso.fr*.

Frogs' legs [*Cuisses de grenouilles*]

Frogs' legs is arguably the dish most identified with French cuisine. Whether the dish is typically French is debatable, as frogs' legs are considered a delicacy and there are recipes for them in the cuisines of many other countries, principally China, Lebanon, Spain and the South and Midwest of the USA. Three popular French recipes are:

* *Grenouilles à la Lyonnaise* brown the legs along with thinly sliced onions in hot butter and serve with parsley and vinegar sauce.

* *Grenouilles à la Meunière* season, flour and fry the legs in butter, then garnish with lemon juice, parsley and butter.

* *Grenouilles à la Provençale* fry the legs in olive oil, then garnish them with crushed garlic, chopped parsley, salt and pepper.

Frozen foods [*Surgelés*]

Supermarkets and hypermarkets offer selections of frozen foods, often of their own brands but also of international brands, of which the three leading are Findus, *www.croustibat.fr*, Knorr, *www.pourtoutvousdire.com* and Maggi, *www.nestle.fr*.

Fruits and vegetables [*Fruits et légumes*]

France is an importer as well as exporter of fruits and vegetables, so there is a broad selection in shops year-round. The fruits and vegetables in season [*fruits et légumes de saison*], as sold at markets and by roadside stands, as well as at lower in-season prices in food shops and supermarkets, are:

- January and February: apples, cabbage, chicory, clementines, leeks, lettuce, mandarins, nuts, oranges, turnips.
- March: chicory, carrots, oranges, radishes.
- April and May: artichokes, asparagus, carrots, new potatoes, turnips, peaches, peas, radishes, spinach.
- June: apricots, artichokes, asparagus, cherries, green beans, lettuce, carrots, new potatoes, peas, spinach, strawberries.
- July: almonds, artichokes, cherries, cucumbers, green beans, lettuce, melons, new carrots, new potatoes, peaches, peas, plums, raspberries, spinach, strawberries, tomatoes.
- August: artichokes, aubergines, broad beans, courgettes, cucumbers, currants, green beans, lettuce, melons, peaches, pears, peppers, plums, salsify, spinach, table grapes, tomatoes.
- September: apples, chestnuts, figs, pears, plums, table grapes.
- October: apples, artichokes, broad beans, chestnuts, figs, green beans, nuts, pears, potatoes, salsify, table grapes, tomatoes.
- November: apples, broad beans, cabbage, chestnuts, chicory, dates, kiwis, turnips, nuts, pears, peppers, spinach.
- December: apples, clementines, dates, grapefruit, mandarins, nuts, pears.

Gastronomy [*Gastronomie*]

Gastronomy, the art of fine dining, is the most prominent facet of *Art de vivre*, the art of living for which France is famed. The passion for it is long standing, reflected in the histories of its renowned restaurants. Opened in 1888, *L'Auberge de la Mère Poulard* is a scenic as well as culinary attraction at 50170 Le Mont-Saint-Michel, Tel: 02 33896868, *www.mere-poulard.com* in French, English and six other languages. *Maxim's* opened in 1893 near the Eiffel Tower at 3 rue Royale, 75008 Paris, Tel: 01 42652794, *www.maxims-de-paris.com* selectable in French or English.

Founded in 1895, the famed *Le Cordon Bleu* culinary academy now has 26 international schools in 15 countries; for further information, contact the head school at 8 rue Léon Delhomme, 75015 Paris, Tel: 01 48530396, *www. cordonbleu.edu* in English. Across the country, there are fine restaurants, listed in the **Gault Millau Guide** and in the **Michelin Guide** (Chapter 47).

Halal food [*Alimentation halal*]

Islamic dietary laws specify three categories of food:

- Halal: lawful and permitted for Muslims to consume according to dietary laws in the Koran.
- Haram: unlawful and prohibited for Muslims.
- Mushbooh: an Arabic term meaning "suspect" and consequently designating foods that Muslims should avoid.

There are many online guides to the availability of Halal meats as well as to the classifications of generally-available foods in France. In February 2006, a comprehensive reference book on Halal meat products was published by Dr. Ahmed Daoudi, *Les produits carnés halal: Charcuteries et préparations bouchères* (Vesoul, Éditeur Maé-Erti, 17 × 25 cm, 450 pages paperback, ISBN 2-913338-07-0), and there is a monthly printed and online Halal Magazine, 123/133 avenue Félix Faure, 75015 Paris, Tel: 08 92681215, *www.halalmagazine.com*.

Herbs and spices [*Herbes et épices*]

The extensive use of herbs and spices distinguishes the cuisines of the country from each other as well as from the cuisines of other countries. There are many guides to herbs and spices and their uses in various dishes, of which the two most popular are:

- *Herbier Gourmand* by François Couplan et. al. (Paris, Hachette, 2004, 20 × 27 cm, 215 pages hardcover, ISBN 2-01-2357983-8), a well-illustrated guide to the gastronomy of herbs and spices.
- *Larousse de la cuisine facile* (Paris, Larousse, July 2006, 19.2 × 26 cm, 320 pages softcover, ISBN 2-03-582352-8, also available on CD-ROM), a four-part guide to the skills and techniques of cooking, with an overview of herbs and spices in Part 1.

Ice cream [*Glace*]

Ice cream is said to have been first served in Italy in the mid 16th century, but records of it are uncertain. However, in 1674, French pharmacist Nicolas Lémery (1645-1715) described flavoured ices in *Recueil de curiosités rares et nouvelles des plus admirables effets de la nature*, so perhaps the history of ice cream in Europe is as much French as it is Italian.

Today, *Glace* on a menu or on a freezer display in a supermarket is the general term for both ice cream [*crème glacée*], containing cream, and for sorbet [*sorbet*], which is flavoured water ice. Eating focuses on quality as a part of cuisine, and there are books about and websites dedicated to the recipes for ice cream and sorbet dishes, such as *www.glaces.org* and *www.recettes-glace.com*. Consequently, in volume, consumption is modest, just 6 litres per resident per year, two-thirds as much as in Italy or the UK (9 litres/year) and less than a third as much as in the USA (22 litres/year)*.

*Source: QUID 2006.

Kosher food [*Alimentation kasher*]

Kashrut, the Jewish dietary laws, specify foods and their means of preparation, as set forth in the Torah. Foods meeting the requirements are termed Kosher [*Kasher*] and are so certified by a Rabbinate, in France often by the Grand Rabbinate of Paris. Kosher foods are offered by several firms, such as André Krief, 64 rue des Roches, 93100 Montreuil, Fax: 01 41585855, *www.rpjf.com* in French and English with online catalogue ordering. The European Bureau of Kosher Certification [*Bureau de certification Kosher Européen (BCKE)*] is in France at 60 rue Jean Claude Vivant, 69100 Villeurbanne, Tel: 06 07022679, *www.kosherlabel.com*.

Label rouge

Created in 1965, the *Label rouge* designates high quality in a range of food products. It is similar to the *Appellation d'origine contrôle (AOC)* (Chapter 13) for wines, but does not relate food products to their geographic origins. Foods in six categories are eligible for labelling:

- poultry and rabbit
- cooked and salted meats
- meats: bovine, veal, pork and lamb
- dairy products
- seafood and fish
- fruits and vegetables.

To find producers of *Label Rouge* products, visit the Ministry of Agriculture website at *www.agriculture.gouv.fr* and navigate to *Liste des Labels Rouges par régions*. For further information on *Label Rouge*, contact the association that maintains it, Centre de développement des Certifications des Qualités Agricoles et Alimentaires at 9 avenue George V, 75008 Paris, *www.label-rouge.org*.

White on red Label Rouge logo.

Lunch and dinner [*Déjeuner et dîner*]

By tradition, the main meal of the day was eaten at midday. The tradition remains in rural districts. In urbanised areas it is changing, though vestiges of it remain, most noticeably in the language – the word *repas*, from the old French *nourriture*, meaning "food", connotes the principal meal of the day – and in the closing of shops and offices for two hours or more at midday. Although snacks are increasingly common at lunchtime in cities, a proper lunch, even the typical **school dinner** (Chapter 14), has two or more courses. A dinner or a traditional midday *repas* may have three or four courses, beginning with a small *entrée*, such as a salad or pâté, continuing with a main dish [*plat principal*] of fish or meat, followed by cheese and then dessert.

Meals [*Repas*]

There are three or four meals a day: breakfast [*petit déjeuner*] in the morning, lunch [*déjeuner*] at midday, a late afternoon snack [*goûter*] mostly for pre-teen children and dinner [*dîner*] in the evening. By tradition, the two principal meals, lunch at 12.00-14.00 and dinner at 19.00-21.00, are times when the family prefer not to be disturbed, as often indicated by HR, the abbreviation for *heures des repas*, suffixed to a telephone number, indicating that you should not call then.

Measures in cooking [*Mesures de cuisine*]

Today, most measures in recipes and on food packaging are in metric units, but there are exceptions, particularly in traditional recipes. The most common descriptive dry and liquid measures are:

Dry measures:

French	English	Metric
pincée	pinch	3-5 gr salt or sugar
cuiller à café rase	level teaspoon	0.5 cl liquid, 5 gr salt or sugar, 3-5 gr flour
cuiller à soupe rase	level soupspoon	1.5 cl liquid, 15 gr sugar or flour
verre à moutarde ou verre à eau	mustard glass or water glass	18-20 cl liquid, 100 gr flour

Liquid measures:

French	English	Metric
verre à liqueur	liqueur glass	3 cl
verre à porto	port glass	6-7 cl
tasse à café	coffee cup	10 cl
petit pot de crème	small pot of cream	10 cl
tasse à thé	tea cup	15 cl
verre à bordeaux	wine glass	15 cl
pot de yaourt	yoghurt container	15 cl
verre à whisky	whisky glass	20-25 cl
tasse à déjeuner	soup cup	20-25 cl
grand pot de crème	large pot of cream	25 cl
grand bol à déjeuner	soup bowl	40 cl
bouteille de vin	wine bottle	75 cl

Meat [*Viande*]

Meat is considered a principal staple, so much so that the modern word for it, *viande* once meant "food", as it did in the Middle English *viand* and still does in the modern Spanish *viands*. Butchers [*boucheries*] and the meat departments of supermarkets offer selections of meats in three classes:

Red meat [*Viande rouge*]

- beef of two sorts, from a cow or bullock raised for meat [*bœuf*] or from a bovine animal not specifically raised for meat [*viande bovine*], both sorts in 30 or so cuts
- horse [*cheval*] in 12 cuts
- lamb [*agneau*] in 11 cuts
- mutton [*mouton*] in 11 cuts.

White meat [*Viande blanche*]

- pork [*porc*]
- poultry [*volaille*]
- rabbit [*lapin*]
- veal [*veau*] in 16 cuts.

Dark meat [*Viande noire*]

- game [*gibier*].

Milk, cream and yoghurt [*Lait, crème et yaourt*]

All milk sold in shops is pasteurised. Most milk also is sterilised [*stérilisé*] and packaged in aseptic containers for long shelf life [*longue conservation*] at room temperature and is stocked on ordinary shop shelves. Most shops also sell fresh [*frais*] milk that is not sterilised and is kept with other perishable foods in cooler displays. Screw caps and labels are colour coded to facilitate identification of products:

- Milk [*lait*]:
    - Red: whole milk [*lait entier*], 3.6% fat
    - Blue: semi-skimmed milk [*lait demi-écrémé*], 1.5% fat
    - Green: skimmed milk [*lait écrémé*], 0.1 – 0.2% fat
    - Pink: infants' milk [*lait de croissance*], for ages 10 months – 3 years
    - Light blue: children's milk [*lait 2e âge*], for ages 2 years and older
    - Light green: 80% lactose reduced milk [*80% de lactose en moins*]
    - White: goat's milk [*lait de chèvre*], 3.6% fat
- Cream [*crème*]:
    - Red: full cream [*crème entière*], 35% fat
    - Blue: half cream [*crème légère*], 10% fat
    - Green: light cream [*extra légère*], 5% fat
    - Blue: light cream [*extra légère*], 4% fat
    - White: crème fraîche, 30% fat
- Yoghurt [*yoghourt* or *yaourt*] is available in a variety of fat contents and flavourings. The three principal brands are Danone, *www.danoneconseils.com*, Nestlé, *www.nestle.fr* and Yoplait, *www.yoplait.be*.

Mushrooms [*Champignons*]

Mushrooms are essential in many of the country's cuisines and consequently are sold in almost all food shops and markets. The button mushroom [*Agaricus bisporus*, called *champignon de Paris*] is the most common variety, of which some 150,000 tons a year are produced, principally in Val-de-Loire. Hunting for wild mushrooms is a popular leisure pursuit, and there are several field guides as well as brochures distributed by pharmacies with colour illustrations of the edible and poisonous varieties. Pharmacies will also provide an identification service to establish whether picked wild mushrooms are edible or not. There are several reference books on mushrooms, most prominently *Larousse des champignons* (Paris, Larousse, August 2004, 21.5 × 28 cm, 408 pages hardcover, ISBN 2-03-560338-8).

Organic foods [*Agriculture biologique*]

Organic agriculture is well established. A law supporting it was passed in 1981, and the *AB Agriculture Biologique* logo affixed to foods was launched in 1985. Today, there are more than 11,000 farms that together cultivate 534,000 hectares of land dedicated to organic farming. Accordingly, the National Organic Agriculture Federation [*La Fédération Nationale d'Agriculture Biologique (FNAB)*] has member organisations across the country, in 78 *Départements*. For further information, contact Maison de la Bio – Agroparc, BP 1221, 84 911 Avignon Cedex 9 *www.fnab.org* and *www.agriculturebio.org* both with an interactive organic food information centre map of mainland France as well as the overseas territories.

Oven temperatures [*Température du four*]

In recipes and on prepared food packaging, oven temperatures are given in degrees Celsius and sometimes in gas oven marks (*thermostat*, may be abbreviated *therm*), which are the same as the British gas oven Regulo® marks. The conversions are:

Relative term	Gas oven mark	Degrees Celsius	Degrees Fahrenheit
very cool	0	95°	200°
or slow	1/4	110°	225°
	1/2	120°	250°
cool or slow	1	135°	275°
	2	150°	300°
warm or	3	165°	325°
moderate	4	175°	350°
moderately hot	5	190°	375°
hot	6	200°	400°
	7	220°	425°
very hot	8	230°	450°
extremely hot	9	245°	475°
	10	260°	500°

Fan-assisted oven [*four à chaleur tournante*] temperatures usually are about 20% lower. For instance, the oven temperatures stated for warming a frozen pizza typically are 225°C in an ordinary oven and 180°C in a fan-assisted oven.

Restaurants [*Restaurants*]

There are more than 120,000 restaurants in the country, one in six attached to a hotel and consequently known as a *hôtel-restaurant*. From small, family-run restaurants to the grand establishments of **gastronomy**, there's a restaurant for every taste and pocket. Save for the high-end establishments, most restaurants have a menu [*carte*] posted outside the main entrance, so you can browse before you go in. The typical *carte* will list a choice of multi-course meals [*menus*] at various prices, as well as individual dishes [*à la carte*]. Drinks [*boissons*] are additional, unless specifically included [*boisson comprise*] in a *menu*. Usually, you must ask for water and both ask and pay for bottled water. Most restaurants close for a day or a day and a half a week and will post that schedule at the main entrance, along with opening hours. In cities, most people take lunch from 13.00 onwards and dinner from 20.30-21.00 on. Restaurants are listed in the Yellow pages under *Restaurants* as well as in the principal guides, such as the **Gault Millau Guide** and the **Michelin Guide** (Chapter 47).

Sell-by date [*Date limite de vente*]

The sell-by-date, *date limite de vente (DLV)*, indicates the last date on which an item legally can be sold. It applies principally to foods. But as foods may be kept long after purchase, there are two varieties of the DLV applicable to all consumable items:

The consume-by date, *date limite de consommation (DLC)*, applies to perishable foods and is crucial, as eating spoiled food may constitute a health hazard. On packaging, the DLC usually is indicated by a statement, such as *A consommer jusqu'au* followed by a date – day and month only – or the date alone.

The best-by date, *date limite d'utilisation optimale (DLUO)*, applies to foods that keep well but deteriorate with time, such as coffee that loses its aroma, baby foods that lose their vitamin content and dry biscuits that lose their taste. On packaging, the DLUO usually is indicated by a statement, such as *A consommer de préférence avant le* followed by a date in three formats: day and month for items that keep up to three months, day, month and year for items that keep from three to 18 months, and year for products that keep more than 18 months.

For further information, contact *Direction Générale de la Concurrence de la Consommation et de la Répression des Fraudes (DGCCRF)*, 59 boulevard Vincent Auriol, 75703 Paris Cedex 13, Tel: 01 44871717, *www.finances.gouv.fr/DGCCRF*, with an interactive locator map of its 101 offices across the country.

Snack [*Goûter*]

Pre-teen children usually have a late afternoon snack of milk or juice, bread with honey or chocolate and sometimes fruit.

Snails [*Escargots*]

Snails were eaten by the Romans and remain a popular dish in countries that once were part of the Roman Empire, most prominently France, where *escargots* are served as an appetiser, and Portugal, where *caracós* are served as a snack. More than 100 species of snail are edible; the two native to France that are used in preparing *escargots* are the *Petit-Gris* (*Helix aspersa*), known as the common garden snail in English, and the *Bourgogne* (*Helix pomatia*).

Recipes call for removing the snails from their shells and then gutting and cooking them in garlic butter before pouring them back into the shells for serving, usually on a metal plate with indentations to hold the shells. In eating, tongs are used to hold the shells, and small forks are used for extracting the meat. Most supermarkets sell packets of snail shells, which can be reused, and snails for home preparation, and the kitchenware departments of hypermarkets offer kits of *escargot* serving plates, tongs and forks.

Wild snails once were the raw material for *escargots*, but they now are endangered, as over gathering has reduced their numbers, and mechanised agriculture has depleted their habitats. So most edible snails now are produced by snail farms, most abroad, as some 90% of the 40,000 tons of snails eaten each year in France are imported. Snail farming, known as *Héliciculture* in French as well as in English, is a burgeoning business for small farmers across Europe, and there are innumerable sources of information on it. One comprehensive snail farming website is *Passion Escargot*, *escargot.free.fr*, with pages in English.

Sodexho

Sodexho, originally an acronym for *Société d'Exploitation Hôtelière* (literally "company providing services used by hotels"), was founded in 1966 in Marseille and now is one of the world's largest food service companies with operations at more than 26,000 sites in 76 countries. Its core business is operating food services for public and private organisations, for schools and higher-education institutions and for conventions and other events. In France, it is the sector leader, operating more than 1400 cafeterias and other public food services. It also provides management services, such as for the accommodation on offshore oil platforms, and supports systems for service vouchers and cards. For further information, contact the Sodexho Alliance, 78180 St. Quentin-en-Yvelines, Tel: 01 30857500, *www.sodexho.com* selectable in French or English.

Vegetarian food [*Aliments pour végétariens*]

The abundant selection of vegetables in food shops and the prevalence of salads in the various cuisines should make it easy to be a vegetarian in France. There are an estimated one to two million vegetarians in the country, and there are several websites dedicated to vegetarianism, most prominently *www.vegelist.online.fr*. Some restaurants offer vegetarian dishes and, in Paris, there are 14 vegetarian restaurants. There are more than 40 vegetarian recipe books, and the Vegetarian Alliance [*Alliance Végétarienne*] provides advice, publishes a newsletter and other brochures, and offers memberships with discount advantages; for further information, contact the office at 11 bis rue Gallier, 77390 Chaumes en Brie, *www.vegetarisme.fr* in French with selected pages in English.

Vocabulary [*Vocabulaire*]

The vocabulary of food and eating is arguably larger in French than in any other European language. There are several printed guides in English to it, of which the most comprehensive is *Vincent's French Food Dictionary* by Charles Vincent (Petersfield, Hampshire, UK, 2004, Harriman House Publishing, 112 pages paperback, ISBN 1-89759-748-7). And there are many websites with French-English food glossaries, of which the most current is *www.beyond.fr*; click on "Food dictionaries".

Water [*Eau*]

Though tap **water** (Chapter 7) is safe to drink, bottled still and carbonated mineral waters remain popular. Six popular and widely-sold brands are:

- Badoit, a slightly carbonated water from the Loire Valley, *www.danone.com*
- Evian, a still water from Évian-les-Bains, a spa town on Lake Geneva, *www.evian.com*
- Perrier, a carbonated water from Languedoc, *www.perrier.com*
- Sémillanté, a still water from the Catalan area, *www.brasserie-milles.com*
- Vittel, a still water from Hautes-de-Seine, *www.vittel.com*
- Volvic, a still water from the Auvergne, *www.danone.com*.

20
Foreigners, immigrants and minorities

Like most countries in Europe, modern France covers an area once inhabited by many peoples and consequently always has had minorities. Moreover, France has a long history of immigration. The distinction between a minority considered part of the native population and a minority made up of immigrants is a matter for scholars, beyond the scope of this book.

In modern times, immigration began modestly: in 1851, only 1.1% of the population were foreigners or naturalised citizens. In the turmoil of Europe between the World Wars, that figure rose dramatically, to peak at nearly 7.5% in 1931. Today, nearly 10% of the population are foreigners or naturalised citizens. Counting children born in France to immigrant parents, the figure is nearly half again as large*.

Unlike the wave of immigrants of the 1930s that came mostly from other European countries, the immigrants of the last two generations have come mostly from outside Europe, principally from Maghreb, Africa and Asia. The country has accordingly been challenged and changed, and today one person in four in the country is of foreign descent. France has become, in the words of historian Jules Michelet (1798-1874) "the universal homeland" [*la patrie de l'universel*].

*****Census** (Chapter 42) figures.

Beur

The word *beur* comes from the **Verlan** (Chapter 28), in which it is a contraction of the inverted syllables of the word *arabe*, and refers to children born in France of North African immigrants. The *Beurs* and *Beurettes*, the feminine form of the word, are educated in the French school system but are Arabic of heritage and consequently find themselves between two cultures. In that in-between land, they have cultural identity, expressed in novels, such as *Zeida de nulle part*, a novel by Leïla Houari published in 1985, *Mémoires d'immigrés, l'héritage maghrébin*, a documentary film by Yamina Benguigui released in 1998, and singer Amine's combination of rhythm

285

and blues with funk and rock in 2003. And there's an independent *Beur TV* channel on cable and satellite, with a website at *beurtv.over-blog.com*.

Directorate of French nationals abroad and foreign nationals in France [*Direction des français à l'étranger et des étrangers en France (DFAE)*]

The heir to an old chancery service, since 1979 DFAE has had the dual role of serving both French nationals abroad and foreign nationals in France. For French nationals abroad, it is a comprehensive *Mairie*, responsible both for governing them and for defending their interests as expatriates. For foreign nationals in France, it is involved in defining and administering government policy, including defining asylum and advising on applications. It represents France in numerous international organisations and cooperates with the Office for the Protection of Refugees and Stateless Persons [*Office Français de Protection des Réfugiés et Apatrides (OFPRA)*] in **asylum** (Chapter 1) matters. Along with the Ministry of the Interior, it is responsible for issuing entry visas. For further information, contact DFAE, Service des étrangers en France, 244 bd. Saint-Germain, 75303 Paris 07 SP, Tel: 01 43178450, *www.france.diplomatie.fr* in French, English, German, Spanish, Arabic and Chinese; enter DFAE as a search keyword.

Embassies and consulates [*Ambassades et consulats*]

France maintains diplomatic relations with almost all countries both through their embassies and consulates in France and through French diplomatic entities abroad. The Ministry of Foreign Affairs [*Ministère des Affaires Étrangères*] maintains and continuously updates three lists:

- Embassies and consulates of other countries in France [*Représentations diplomatiques étrangères en France*]
- French embassies and consulates abroad [*Représentations diplomatiques françaises à l'étranger*]
- French permanent missions in international organisations (*Les représentations permanentes*)

For further details, contact the Ministry, 37 Quai d'Orsay, 75351 Paris, Tel: 01 43175353, *www.diplomatie.gouv.fr*, with pages in English, German and Spanish. Searchable versions of the lists are available online at *http://www.mfe.org/*; click on *Annuaires* to bring up a dialogue box with links to the lists.

Ethnic minorities [*Minorités ethniques*]

When applied to a group of people, minority is an elusive term. In many usages, it may mean the numerical majority, such as women in most countries. Consequently, sociologists often distinguish between dominant and subordinate groups. In turn, the subordinate groups may be defined by many characteristics, including ethnic origin, race, religion, gender, sexual preference, age or disability.

Sociological definitions aside, the most common perception of a minority in Europe is historical and applies to an ethnic group subordinate to the majority of the modern country. That definition is flawed because it does not include the immigrant minorities that have grown over the past hundred years. Nonetheless, it's culturally significant, and there are organisations that study the ethnic minorities and work for their rights, most prominently *Groupement pour les droits des minorités (GDM)*, 212 rue Saint-Martin, 75003 Paris, *gdm.eurominority.org/www/gdm* and Eurominority, 6 straed François Menez, 29000 Kemper, Tel: 06 68974108, *www.eurominority.org* in French, English, German, Italian, Russian and Spanish and online lists and links to ethnic minority groups across Europe. In May 2005, Yves Plasseraud of GDM published a comprehensive, illustrated atlas of minorities across Europe: *Atlas des minorités en Europe* (Paris, Éditions Autrement, 80 pages softcover, ISBN 2-74670-629-6).

The France of immigration [*La France de l'immigration*]

"It's impossible to work on immigration without being motivated by civic concerns, such as curbing racism and prejudice. Memory is also a means of exclusion. Making memory part of the collective memory may enable us to shift the border between 'them' and 'us'." So defines historian Gérard Noirel (1950-) his dedication to immigration, his topic of expertise, in addition to his post as the director of *L'école des hautes études en sciences sociales*, *www.ehess.fr*. From 1980 onwards, he has published more than 20 books dealing with various aspects of immigration and integration, at least one of which has become a popular reference: *Gens d'ici venus d'ailleurs, la France de l'immigration* (Paris, Éditions du Chêne, 2004, 296 pages hardcover, ISBN 2-84277-520-1).

French Expatriates Abroad Centre
[*Maison des Français de l'Étranger*]

As expatriates usually discover, being a citizen of a country does not ensure thorough knowledge of it. Indeed, most of the useful information about a country is of the same sort that the natives of it need, whether they reside at home or abroad. French expatriates abroad often need information on France, just as do foreigners who have taken up residence in the country. That said, the one public source of information on France that probably is most relevant for foreigners is maintained by the Ministry of Foreign Affairs [*Ministère des affaires étrangères*] as a service to French expatriates living abroad.

The French Expatriates Abroad Centre [*Maison des français de l'étranger (MFE)*] supports a comprehensive information service on matters abroad, employment, labour, citizenship and foreign affairs. For further details, contact MFE, 30-34 rue La Pérouse, 75775 Paris Cedex 16, Tel: 01 43176970, Fax: 01 43177003, *www.mfe.org*.

Harki

Harki, from the Arabic *Harka* meaning "band of warriors", was the name given to Muslim Algerians who fought on the French side during the Algerian war of independence from 1954 to 1962. An estimated 50,000 to 150,000 Harkis and their dependents were killed in action or by lynch mobs after the ceasefire in 1962. Against official government orders, around 90,000 Harkis found refuge in mainland France, only to be kept in internment camps. Concern for the plight of the Harkis, who had suffered for their loyalty to France, finally led to their being freed from the camps in the 1970s and 1980s. Recently, the government has acknowledged their sacrifices, and there are several associations that work for their further recognition, including LDH-Toulon at *www.ldh-toulon.net*, focused on human rights, a site by and for Harkis at *www.harki.fr*, and a general Harki information site at *www.harkis.info* with an on-site translator to English and other languages.

Illegal immigrants [*Les immigrés*]

There are believed to be about a million paperless [*sans-papiers*] immigrants in the country. As elsewhere in Europe, their presence is a matter of national concern, not least because they cannot work legally and consequently have no access to the **CAI** (Chapter 1) and other measures for legal immigrants, including health care and schooling. Humanitarian organisations are concerned with and books have focused on their plight, most notably a comprehensive overview of their situation in Belgium and France from 1990 on: Anatoine Pickels (editor), *À la lumière des sans-papiers* (Brussels, Éditions Complexe, 2001, 252 pages hardcover, ISBN 2-87027-825-X). France now is moving to address the problems of illegal immigration, and accordingly in October 2005, the Senate set up a Board of Inquiry on Illegal Immigration [*Commission d'enquête sur l'immigration clandestine*]; its reports are available on order from the Library of the Senate [*L'espace librairie du Sénat*] at *www.senat.fr*.

Immigration [*L'immigration*]

Of the population of about 60 million, four million people are immigrants. From the time the first **Census** (Chapter 42) was taken in 1801 until the mid 1970s, immigration was mostly from other countries in Europe. But today, the majority of immigrants come from former French colonies in North Africa, **Maghreb** (Chapter 9), from the former colonies in Asia – Cambodia, Laos and Vietnam – and from Africa.

Immigration and integration statistics research institute [*Observatoire des statistiques de l'immigration et de l'intégration (OSII)*]

Founded in 2004 by the High Council on Integration [*Haut conseil à l'intégration (HCI)*], OSII analyses statistical categories and integration indicators. It works together with the **National Institute of Statistics and Economic Studies** (Chapter 42), eight Ministries and three governmental agencies. It is the National Contact Point (NCP) for the European Migration Network, *www.european-migration-network.org*. For further information, contact OSII, 35 rue St. Dominique, 75007 Paris, Tel: 01 40567989.

Maghrébins

Some 1.3 million people from the former colonies of Algeria, Morocco and Tunisia, collectively called the **Maghreb** (Chapter 9) live and work in the country. Most came during the period of prosperity after the Second World War, *Les trente glorieuses*, to work in car factories and other industries, and live in the high-rise *grands ensembles* of the suburban **Banlieues** (Chapter 9) built to house them. Their children are known as the **Beurs**.

National Centre for Immigration History [*Cité nationale de l'histoire de l'immigration*]

In acknowledgement of the increasingly obvious trend that the French of today are the immigrants of yesterday, the National Centre for Immigration History is gradually taking over the Palais de la Porte Dorée in the 12th *arrondissement* in south-east Paris. Open to the public from the first quarter of 2007, the Centre is a national museum, a multimedia resource, an establishment for teaching and research and a venue for cultural and artistic programming. For further information, contact the Centre at its postal address, 4 rue René-Villermé, 75011 Paris, Tel: 01 40096919, *www.histoire-immigration.fr* in French with selected pages and documents in English.

News in English [*Nouvelles en anglais*]

Newsagents across the country sell national newspapers and magazines from round the world, many printed in France by electronic transfer of files from head offices elsewhere. So if you seek home country news in English, you may find it at a newsagent or on the Internet at a newspaper website. Moreover, there are innumerable publications for expatriates, in many languages, printed and online. A leading expatriate newspaper in English is a monthly, The Connexion, BP 25, 06480 La Colle sur Loup, Tel: 04 93321659, *www.connexionfrance.com*.

One of Europe's, if not the world's leading newspapers is the International Herald Tribune (IHT), edited and published in English from a head office in Paris and now with offices and publishing points round the world. The IHT is sold across the country by newsagents; for subscriptions and home delivery, contact IHT, 6 bis rue Graviers 92521 Neuilly Sur Seine Cedex, Tel: 01 41439361, 08 0044487827, *www.iht.com* in English.

21
Government, politics and administration

France is a representative democracy governed in a semi-presidential system based on the Constitution of the Fifth Republic. It has a bicameral legislature and a distinct separation of legislative, executive and judicial powers. It has a well-defined governmental hierarchy staffed by civil service professionals. Hence, the structure of its government has much in common with the structures of governments in other western democracies. Yet it differs from the parliamentary system, as in the UK, as well as from the presidential system, as in the USA. These matters are the subjects of the entries of this chapter. For clarity, the original name in French appears in the title of an entry whenever its meaning differs from that of its related name in English.

Assemblée nationale

The National Assembly [*Assemblée nationale*] is the lower of the two houses of Parliament. It was created on 17 June 1789 and through the years has had various forms and names, but in 1946 resumed its original name. As its name implies, it directly represents the citizenry, as its 577 deputies are directly elected by vote of citizens of age 18 and over in the country's 577 constituencies. A deputy must be at least 23 years old and to be elected must gain the absolute majority of more than half the votes cast in the first ballot or a relative majority of the greatest number of votes cast in a second ballot. Deputies are elected for five years, but the National Assembly may be dissolved sooner by the **President**.

The National Assembly passes laws, supervises Government policy, votes on budget and questions Ministers. Should the two houses of Parliament fail to agree on the passage of a law, the National Assembly has the upper hand. Constitutional Acts must be adopted by both houses and then by a three-fifths majority of all deputies and senators convened in Congress. For further information, contact the Assemblée nationale, Palais Bourbon, 126 rue de l'Université, 75 355 Paris 07 SP, Tel: 01 40636000, *www.assemblee-nationale-fr* in French, English, German, Italian and Spanish.

Chef-lieu

A *Chef-lieu* is an administrative centre. In a *Département*, it is the **Prefecture**, or capital city. In an *Arrondissement*, it is sub-prefecture [*sous-préfet*] that performs functions of the Prefecture at the local level. In a *Canton*, it usually is the most populous city with centralised services including police and courts. In a *commune*, it usually is the largest city or town that administers the smaller towns and villages of the *commune*.

Cohabitation

Cohabitation arises when the **President** and the **Prime minister** are from opposing political parties. It is a consequence of the semi-presidential system [*système semi-présidentiel*], which differs from the parliamentary system in that the president is popularly elected and differs from the presidential system in that the prime minister has executive responsibility. In cooperation with the Cabinet, the President is responsible for foreign policy, whilst the Prime Minister is responsible for domestic policy. Their cooperation, or cohabitation when they are from opposing parties, is essential for functioning of the executive branch of the government. The term cohabitation was coined in 1986 to describe the first instance of it, when François Mitterrand (*Parti socialiste*) was President and Jacques Chirac (*RPR*) was Prime Minister.

Conseil général

Each *Département* is administered by a *Conseil général* made up of elected representatives [*conseillers*], one from each *Canton*. Any resident of a *Département*, 21 years old or more, may stand for election; elections are held every six years, and a *conseiller* may serve two terms. The *Conseillers généraux* work together in the *Assemblée des Départements de France*, which supports inter-departmental activities and publishes the *Départements* magazine. For further information, contact the head office of the *Assemblée* at 6 rue Duguay-Trouin, 75006 Paris, Tel: 01 45496020, *www.departement.org*.

Conseil municipal

Each municipality [*commune*] elects a local council, whose members must be at least 18 years old and serve for six years and who from among them elect a mayor [*maire*]. The mayor is responsible for the administration of the municipality and is the local representative of the State, performing official acts such as marriages and supervising elections. The office of the mayor and the administrative headquarters of the *Conseil municipal* are in the town hall [*mairie*], also known as the *Hôtel de ville* in larger towns. Across the country, there are 497,188 members of *Conseils municipal*, and among them, 36,555 mayors*. For further information, contact the **Mayors' association**.   **Source: QUID 2006.*

Conseil régional

Each *Région* has an administrative Conseil consisting of representatives of its *Départements*, elected for six years. In turn, the *conseillers régionaux* appoint a President and an executive group. For further information, contact *Association des Régions de France (ARF)*, 282 bd St-Germain, 75007 Paris, *www.arf.asso.fr* with an interactive *Conseil* locator map.

Constitution

The present Constitution is usually called the Constitution of the Fifth Republic, as it replaced the Constitution of the Fourth Republic that went into force on 27 October 1946. Its preamble references the Declaration of the Rights of Man and the Citizen of 1789 and states that France is a secular, democratic republic that derives its sovereignty from the people. It sets forth the structure and administration of government and provides for its own amendment.

The complete text of the Constitution of 1 October 1958, as last amended 1 March 2005, is available in many printed versions and can be downloaded in a PDF file from the National Assembly website at *www.assemblee-nationale.fr/connaissance/constitution.asp* as well as in English, German, Italian and Spanish translations from the website.

Décentralisation

The role of the governmental organisations in Paris in administering the whole of the country has long been questioned. In 1982, a law was enacted to grant the municipalities, *Départements* and *Régions* greater autonomy [*loi relative aux droits et libertés des communes, des départements et des régions*]. The provisions of the law effectively redistributed decision-making closer to the points affected, a process that became known as *décentralisation*. An overview of the law and of the events that have taken place since it was enacted are available on the **Assemblée nationale** website at *www.assemblee-nationale.fr/histoire/decentralisation.asp*.

eGovernment

Government services increasingly are delivered electronically via the Internet, in step with the expansion of eGovernment in most countries. IDABC, an abbreviation for Interoperable Delivery of European eGovernment Services to Public Administrations, Businesses and Citizens, is the central clearing house for all related information in Europe. An overview of the measures now operational in France is available at *ec.europa.eu/idabc/en/chapter/395*.

Elections [*Élections*]

Citizens who are 18 or older and are registered on the electoral rolls [*listes électorales*] may vote in national and local elections as well as in European elections. Residents who are citizens of other EU countries may vote in local and European elections. Elections may be held in two rounds; if an absolute majority (more than half of the votes) is not obtained on the first round, a second is held. For most elections, the rounds are scheduled on successive Sundays, or for presidential elections, at intervals of two weeks between the Sundays. To vote, a voter appears at a polling place, presents a voter registration card [*carte d'électeur*] and identification, and in a private polling booth, chooses a slip with the name of the preferred candidate, places it in an envelope that in turn is placed in a polling box [*urne*]. For further information on the elections held in the country, visit the Ministry of the Interior website at *www.interieur.gouv.fr*, click on *Les élections* and then navigate to *Les modalités d'élection en France*.

Gouvernement

The word *gouvernement* has two meanings. In general, it means the entire apparatus of government, including the civil service, and consequently appears in the abbreviated form, *gouv* in website and email addresses. Nonetheless, when used alone, the word most often means the *Conseil des Ministres*, which is the Ministerial Government headed by the **Prime minister**. That *gouvernement* is responsible to the *Assemblée nationale*, which is empowered to censure it and thereby force the resignation of the *Conseil des Ministres*. In practice, this obliges the *gouvernement* to side politically with the majority of the *Assemblée*. For further information, contact the office of the Prime Minister at 57 rue de Varenne, 75007 – Paris, Tel: 01 42758000, *www.premier-ministre.gouv.fr* in French, English, German and Spanish; click on *Composition du gouvernement* to bring up a list of Ministers with their addresses and links to their websites.

Government portal [*Portail du gouvernement*]

Continuously updated, comprehensive information on the Government is available online at seven governmental portals [*Portails du Gouvernement*] managed by the **Government Information Service** (Chapter 31):

- The Prime Minister's website with overviews of the ministries and the office of the prime minister, *www.premier-ministre.gouv.fr/fr/* in English, German and Spanish as well as French
- Information Technologies, New Technologies, Government, Media Studies, Administration [*Technologies de l'Information, Nouvelles technologies, Gouvernement, Communication, Administration*], *www.internet.gouv.fr*

- Retirement, Pensions, Social Welfare [*Retraite, Protection sociale*], *www.retraites.gouv.fr*
- Retirement, Pensions, Social Welfare, Civil Service [*Retraite, Protection sociale, Fonction publique*] *www.fonction-publique.retraites.gouv.fr*
- State Reform, Multimedia, New Technologies [*Politiques publiques, Réforme de l'État, Multimédia, Nouvelles technologies*], *www.forum.gouv.fr*
- Information on Europe [*Information sur l'europe*], *www.europe.gouv.fr*
- Multimedia, New Technologies, Media Studies [*Multimédia, Nouvelles technologies, Communication*], *www.agora.gouv.fr*.

International Commission on Civil Status (ICCS) [*Commission Internationale de l'état civil (CIEC)*]

The ICCS is an intergovernmental European organisation, now with 16 member countries, including France. It deals with matters concerning the status of persons, the family and nationality and conducts studies and works aimed to harmonise the relevant rules of the member countries, such as for the **Family record book** (Chapter 38). For further information, contact CIEC, 3 place Arnold, 67000 Strasbourg, Tel: 03 88611862, *www.wanadoo.fr/ciec-sg* in French and English.

Mayors Association [*Association des maires de France (AMF)*]

Founded in 1907, the Mayors Association represents more than 35,000 local mayors and chairpersons of the mainland and overseas territories and consequently is the principal national organisation of local authorities. It acts principally to lobby for local issues at the national level and to provide the municipalities with the information and tools they need to conduct their affairs. But it also supports local implementations of national initiatives, such as the **Road Safety Houses** (Chapter 4) and the channelling of European Union information relevant to everyday life. For further information, contact the local town hall or the head office at 41 quai d'Orsay, 75343 Paris Cedex 07, Tel: 01 44181414, *www.amf.asso.fr* with pages in English and in German and an interactive list of its constituent departmental associations.

Ministries [*Ministères*]

The principal Ministries are listed below along with addresses and telephone numbers for further information. For an overview of all Ministries, visit the **Government portal**.

State Council [*Conseil d'état*]
Place Beauvau, 75800 Paris, Tel: 01 40208100, *www.conseil-etat.fr*

Ministry of the Interior and Regional Development [*Ministère de l'Intérieur et de l'Aménagement du Territoire*]
Place Beauvau, 75800 Paris, Tel: 01 49274927, *www.interieur.gouv.fr*

Ministry of Defence [*Ministère de la Défense*]
14 rue Saint-Dominique, 00450 Armées, Tel: 01 42193011, *www.defense.gouv.fr*

Ministry of Foreign Affairs [*Ministère des Affaires étrangères*]
37 Quai d'Orsay, 75351 Paris Cedex 07, Tel: 01 43175353,
www.diplomatie.gouv.fr/

Ministry of Employment, Social Cohesion and Housing [*Ministère de l'Emploi, de la Cohésion sociale et du Logement*]
127 rue de Grenelle, 75700 Paris, Tel: 01 44383838, *www.cohesionsociale.gouv.fr*

Ministry of the Economy, Finance and Industry [*Ministère de l'Economie, des Finances et de l'Industrie*]
139 rue de Bercy, 75572 – Paris – Cedex 12, Tel: 01 40040404,
www.minefi.gouv.fr

Ministry of National Education, Higher Education and Research [*Ministère de l'Education Nationale, de l'Enseignement supérieur et de la Recherche*]
110 rue de Grenelle, 75357 – Paris 07 SP, Tel: 01 55551010,
www.education.gouv.fr

Ministry of Transportation, Capital Works, Tourism and Maritime Affairs [*Ministère des Transports, de l'Equipement, du Tourisme et de la Mer*]
246 boulevard Saint-Germain, 75700 Paris, Tel: 01 40812122,
www.equipement.gouv.fr

Ministry of Health and Solidarity [*Ministère de la Santé et des Solidarités*]
8, avenue de Ségur, 75700 Paris, Tel: 01 40566000, *www.sante.gouv.fr*

Ministry of Agriculture and Fisheries [*Ministère de l'Agriculture et de la Pêche*]
78 rue de Varenne, 75700 Paris, Tel: 01 49554955, *www.agriculture.gouv.fr/*

Ministry of the Civil Service [*Ministère de la Fonction publique*]
72 rue de Varenne, 75700 Paris, Tel: 01 42758000, *www.fonction-publique.gouv.fr*

Ministry of Culture and Communications [*Ministère de la Culture et de la Communication*]
3 rue de Valois, 75100 Paris, Tel: 01 40158000, *www.culture.gouv.fr*

Ministry of Ecology and Sustainable Development [*Ministère de l'Ecologie et du Développement durable*]
20 avenue de Ségur, 75302 Paris 07 SP, Tel: 01.42192021,
www.ecologie.gouv.fr/sommaire.php3

Ministry of Overseas France [*Ministère de l'Outre-Mer*]
27 rue Oudinot, 75358 Paris 07 SP, Tel: 01 53692000, *www.outre-mer.gouv.fr*

Ministry of Small and Medium-Sized Enterprises, Trade, Small-Scale Industry and the Professions [*Ministère des petites et Moyennes Entreprises, du Commerce, de l'Artisanat et des Professions libérales*]
80 rue de Lille, 75700 Paris, Tel: 01 43192424, *www.pme.gouv.fr*

Ministry of Youth, Sports and Associations [*Ministère de la Jeunesse, des Sports et de Vie associative*]
95 avenue de France, 75650 Paris Cedex 13, Tel: 01 40459000, *www.jeunesse-sports.gouv.fr*.

Official geographic code [*Code officiel géographique*]

The *Code officiel géographique* is a system of numbers designating all municipalities, *cantons*, *arrondissements*, departments, regions and overseas territories as well as countries round the world. It is kept by INSEE, the **National Institute of Statistics and Economic Studies** (Chapter 42), and is widely used by public as well as private organisations. INSEE maintains an updated list of codes as well as a code search engine on its website at *www.insee.fr*; click on *Nomenclatures, définitions, méthodes*, then on *Nomenclatures*, and then on *Code officiel géographique* to access the latest list and the search engine for codes assigned on mainland France, or continue by clicking on *Pays et territoires étrangers* for the codes of countries abroad or on *Outre-mer* for the codes of French overseas departments and territories.

Organisation for Economic cooperation and Development (OECD) [*Organisation de coopération et de développement économiques (OCDE)*].

France is a member of as well as the host for the head facility of the Organisation for Economic cooperation and Development (OECD), which assists member countries to develop economic and social policies that promote sustained economic growth and financial stability. It has 30 member countries and active relationships with some 70 other countries and Non-Government Organisations (NGOs). Each year, the OECD publishes more than 500 books and periodicals, most in English and French, on matters including agriculture and fisheries; cities, regions and countryside; development cooperation; economics and long-term analysis; economies in transition; education, employment labour and social affairs; environmental affairs; financial, fiscal and enterprise affairs; public management; science, technology and industry; trade; transport. Further details are available from the OECD, 2 rue André-Pascal, 75775 Paris Cedex 16, Tel: 01 45248200, *www.oecd.org*.

Palais

In Paris, three magnificent palaces built before the *Révolution* by the nobility now house the executive and legislative branches of the government and are frequently mentioned in association with them:

- Palais Bourbon, a large residence built in 1722-1728 on the Left Bank and now housing *Assemblée national.*
- Palais de l'Élysée, built in 1718-1722 just off the Champs-Élysées and now the official residence of the **President**.
- Palais du Luxembourg, built from 1615 onwards at Jardin du Luxembourg and now the seat of the *Sénat.*

Though smaller and not built as a palace, *L'hôtel Matignon*, built in 1719-1723 at 57 rue de Varenne, ranks with them, as it is the official residence and office of the **Prime minister**. Hence, in everyday usage, *Matignon* is a synonym for the office of the Prime minister, much as is "Downing Street" in the UK.

Parité

The law of parity (no. 2000-493 of 6 June 2000) states that political parties shall put forth equal numbers of male and female candidates, in all elections, from municipal elections in *communes* with populations more than 3500 up to the European level. Parties standing for election but failing to put forth equal numbers of candidates are penalised through reduction of their public funding. For further information on parity and the results of it to date, visit the Ministry Delegate for Social Cohesion and Parity website at *www.femmes-egalite.gouv.fr*, click on *Parité et responsabilités* and then navigate to *Le bilan de la loi sur la parité.*

Political parties [*Partis politiques*]

In the first **Assemblée nationale** of the *Révolution*, as seen from the seat of the President, the left-wing parties sat to the left and the right-wing parties sat to the right. That seating convention persists to this day, and the principal parties are aligned accordingly.

The principal right-wing parties are:

- *Union pour un Mouvement Populaire (UMP)*, formed after the 2002 election from a merger of *Rassemblement pour la République (RPR), Démocratie libérale (DL)* and most of the former *Union pour la démocratie française (UDF)*, *www.u-m-p.org.*
- The part of UDF that did not merge to form UMP and now a grouping that enables centre-right parties to work together, *www.udf.org.*
- *Rassemblement pour la France (RPF), www.rpf.altranet.fr.*
- *Front national (FN), www.frontnational.com.*

And the principal left-wing parties are:

* *Parti socialiste (PS), www.parti-socialiste.fr.*
* *Parti communiste français (PCF) www.pcf.fr.*
* *Parti radical de gauche (PRG), www.planeteradicale.org.*

There also are parties apart from the left-right constellation:

* *Les verts*, the greens, *www.lesverts.fr.*
* *Génération écologie*, the environmentalists, *www.generation-ecologie.com.*

Prefecture [*Préfecture*]

The word *Préfecture* has three meanings:

* the capital city of a *Département*
* part of the Ministry of the Interior that has administrative agencies in each capital city
* the building in which such an agency is located.

There are 100 *Préfectures* in the country, each under the direction of a *Préfet*. Each *Préfecture* is responsible for managing the police and fire brigades within its jurisdiction as well as for providing numerous public services including issuing identity cards, passports, driving licences, car registrations, residence permits and work permits. The exception is Paris, itself a *Département*, which together with three adjoining smaller *Départements*, has a single *Préfecture* for law enforcement, the *Préfecture de police*. In some *Départements*, there are Sub-prefectures [*Sous-préfectures*] in the capital cities of *arrondissements* other that the departmental capital. The Ministry of the Interior supports an online interactive locator map of all the *Préfectures* at *http://www.interieur.gouv.fr/rubriques/c/c4_les_prefectures/c46_votre_prefecture*; clicking on a *Département* on the map or entering its number will bring up the addresses and telephone numbers of its *Préfecture* and *Sous-préfectures*.

President [*Président de la République*]

The President of the Republic is the head of State, elected for a term of five years. The office plays a leading role in the governing of the country, particularly in its foreign policy. One of the greater powers of the President is to choose the **Prime Minister**. However, that power is subject to political constraints. The *Assemblée nationale* holds the power to dismiss the Prime Minister's Government, so the President is obliged to name a Prime Minister acceptable to the *Assemblée* majority. Like politics can strengthen the role of the President, whilst opposing politics can result in **cohabitation** that diminishes presidential power. For further information, contact the office of the President, Palais de l'Elysée, 55 rue du Faubourg Saint-Honoré, 75008 Paris, *www.elysee.fr* in French, English, German and Spanish.

Prime Minister [*Premier ministre*]

The Prime Minister is appointed by the **President** and, as the head of the Ministerial Government [*Conseil des Ministres*], is responsible for government affairs and thereby for domestic policy. The position is sometimes seen as one in which a politician may gain stature to become a candidate for the presidency, but it is not without political risk. The responsibility of the position may result in the Prime Minister being blamed for governmental failings and consequently losing popularity.

In addition to its role in the Ministerial Government, the office of the Prime Minister is responsible for more than 20 national directorates, centres and services. For further information on the various activities, contact the office at 57 rue de Varenne, 75007 – Paris, Tel: 01 42758000, *www.premier-ministre.gouv.fr* in French, English, German and Spanish and with links to numerous other governmental websites.

Private-sector enterprises owned by the State [*Établissement public industriel et commercial (EPIC)*]

As elsewhere in Europe, in the 1990s, deregulation and privatisation led to the reorganisation of many government agencies as private-sector enterprises, most notably the railways. The principal State-owned private-sector enterprises are:

- *Électricité de France (EDF)*, the leader in electricity generation, distribution and supply, *www.edf.com* with pages in English.

- *Gaz de France (GDF)*, the leading natural gas supplier, *www.gazdefrance.com* with pages in English.

- *Institut Français de Recherche Pour l'Exploitation de la Mer (IFREMER)*, the Research Institute for Exploration of the Sea, *www.ifremer.fr* with pages in English.

- *Institut National de l'Audiovisuel (INA)*, the leading audiovisual archive and digital image databank, *www.ina.fr* with pages in English and Chinese.

- *Institut de Radioprotection et de Sûreté Nucléaire (IRSN)*, the institute for radiological protection and nuclear safety, *www.irsn.fr* with pages in English.

- *Institut National de la Consommation (INC)*, the national institute for consumer protection, *www.conso.net*.

- *Réseau de Transport d'Électricité (RTE)*, the operator of the high voltage public power transmission system, *www.rte-france.com* with pages in English.

- *Réseau Ferré de France (RFF)*, the railway infrastructure manager, *www.rff.fr* with pages in English.

- *Societé Nationale des Chemins de Fer (SNCF)*, the incumbent Train Operating Company (TOC), *www.sncf.com* with pages in Dutch, English, German, Italian and Spanish.

Quai d'Orsay

The Ministry of Foreign Affairs [*Ministère des Affaires étrangères*] is located at the Quay d'Orsay, so in everyday mention, as in newspapers and on TV, Quay d'Orsay means the Ministry as well as its activities.

Référendum

The **President** may call a referendum in which a single question is decided by being put to a general vote by the electorate comprising all registered voters in the country. Twelve referendums have been held since 1946, the last on 29 May 2005, when the voters rejected ratification of the European Constitution.

Republic [*République*]

A republic is a country in which the supreme power is held by representatives elected by the people, as opposed to one headed by a monarch. The ordinal numbering of republics in France reflects history, as each has been created by a constitution or a proclamation that set its republican form of government apart from that of its predecessor. Since the **Revolution,** there have been five republics and intervening periods of other forms of rule:

- 1792 First Republic established by constitution.
- 1804 First Empire established by Napoleon Bonaparte (Napoleon I).
- 1848 Second Republic established by revolution, under President Louis Napoleon Bonaparte (Napoleon II).
- 1852 Second Empire established through Coup d'Etat by Charles Louis Napoleon Bonaparte (Napoleon III).
- 1870 Franco-Prussian war results in fall of Napoleon III; Third Republic established.
- 1940 France invaded; Henri Philippe Pétain Chief of State.
- 1944 Provisional government led by Charles de Gaulle.
- 1946 Fourth Republic proclaimed after end of Second World War.
- 1958 Fifth Republic established by new constitution adopted by referendum.

Schengen area [*Espace Schengen*]

Schengen is the name of a small town in Luxembourg where, in June 1985, seven European Union countries signed a treaty to discontinue border checkpoints and controls. Since then, eight more countries have joined the treaty. The Schengen area is the territory of the 15 countries that now are members of the Schengen Agreement: Austria, Belgium, Denmark, Finland, France, Germany, Iceland, Italy,

Greece, Luxembourg, Netherlands, Norway, Portugal, Spain and Sweden. For further information on the Agreement, visit the EU website page at *europa.eu.int/scadplus/leg/en/lvb/l33020.htm*.

If you stay in France or one of the 14 other countries, you most likely will seldom see the effects of the Agreement. But when you travel between the countries, you will notice that you can cross borders without checks and, if you are a citizen of one of the 15 countries, without your passport, just your National Identification card. Britons take note: the UK did not sign the Schengen Agreement, so you will need a passport to enter France.

Visa requirements are harmonised among the 15 countries, so a visa issued by one country is valid in the other 14. Checks at borders between the Schengen area and non-Schengen countries are according to a common standard. All the countries have access to the Schengen Information System (SIS), which makes personal identity and other data available throughout the Schengen area. The police and courts of the 15 countries cooperate, particularly in combating drug-related crime. The Agreement does not require a common asylum and refugee policy, but the policies of the 15 countries have become more alike as a consequence of it.

As this book goes to press, the ten new countries that became members of the EU in May 2004 – Cyprus, Czech Republic, Estonia, Hungary, Latvia, Lithuania, Malta, Poland, Slovakia and Slovenia – have internal border controls that will remain in place until the European Council decides that they are to be fully operational in the Schengen Agreement.

Sénat

The Senate [*Sénat*] is the upper of the two houses of Parliament. The 321 *Sénateurs* are elected indirectly by some 150,000 local officials [*grands électeurs*], including city councillors, deputies of the ***Assemblée nationale*** and city and town mayors. Until September 2004, *Sénateurs* were elected for nine-year terms and thereafter for six-year terms. In 2010, their number will increase to 346, reflecting demographic changes in the country.

The *Sénat* has almost the same powers as the ***Assemblée nationale***. It also monitors and controls Government action by regularly publishing reports on topics of national and international interest. The *Président du Sénat* is empowered to assume the duties of the **President** of the Republic, should the latter be incapacitated.

For further information, contact the Sénat, Palais du Luxembourg, 15 rue de Vaugirard, 75291 Paris Cedex 06, Tel: 01 42342000, *www.senat.fr* with links to five dedicated topic sites and access to 160,000 brochures and papers, 4.5 million Internet pages, 3000 online Parliamentary reports and 5500 legislative files.

UNECE [*CEE-ONU*]

The United Nations Economic Commission for Europe [*Commission économique des Nations Unies pour l'Europe*] is a forum at which the countries of Europe, North America and central Asia cooperate on economic matters. France has been a member since 1947, and the impact of the UNECE on daily life in the country is most obvious in transport, environmental matters and international shipment of goods. For instance, cars and other motor vehicles conform to UNECE regulations, and **Periodic vehicle inspection** (Chapter 4) is in compliance with UNECE directives. Further details on UNECE matters in France are available in the publications and press releases of the Ministries involved. For complete information on the UNECE, contact its Information Office, Palais des Nations, CH-1211 Geneva 10, Switzerland, Tel: +41 22 9171234, *www.unece.org*, *info.ece@unece.org*.

22
Healthcare and social security

Total health spending in France exceeds 10% of the GDP, more than average for EU countries. The healthcare system is extensive, and the World Health Organisation has ranked it best in the world*. Total social security spending amounts to 29.9% of the GDP, more than in any other European country save Sweden**. Nonetheless, change is underway. From 2000 onwards, universal healthcare insurance has been the right as well as the obligation of all residents. It is equitable, as it provides free healthcare for the poorest tenth of the population, and it is fair as it permits free choice and interlinks with private-sector healthcare insurance providers. Healthcare is changing, in part in step with a 2003 Parliamentary report*** calling for hospital reorganisation.

* Source: World Health Report 2000, the year that it featured the health systems of the world; for the full report, as well as those of other years on other topics, visit *www.who.int/whr*.

** Source: France in Figures *[La France en brief]* 2005 edition p. 25.

*** *Rapport d'information, par la commission des affaires culturelles, familiales et sociales sur l'organisation interne de l'hôpital*, 19 March 2003.

ANAMEVA

ANAMEVA is the acronym for *Association nationale des médecines conseils de victimes d'accident avec dommage corporel*, the "National association of medical consultants for injured accident victims". Founded in 1985 in response to needs expressed by victim associations and lawyers, it aims to give accident victims access to freely-chosen medical opinion, independent of insurance companies and of Social Security. In practice, ANAMEVA advisers intervene to evaluate physical injury subject to compensation. Typical cases concern:

* road accidents [*accidents de la voie publique*]
* assault [*agressions*]
* natural disasters [*catastrophes naturelles*]

- third-party accidents, such as in hunting, construction, animal attacks, etc. [*accidents divers impliquant la responsabilité de tiers (accident de chasse, effondrement de construction, blessures par animaux, etc.)*]

- private-sector contracts (indemnities, work disability, etc.) [*contrats privés (crédits, incapacités de travail, etc.)*]

- disputes with Social Security, the handicapped commission or insurance companies [*contentieux avec la sécurité sociale, COTOREP ou mutuelles*]

- workplace accidents and diseases [*accidents du travail, maladies professionnelles*]

- work-related disability or incapacity [*invalidité, inaptitude au travail*]

- adult handicap compensation for medical or surgical malpractice, military pension rights for victims of terrorism, etc. [*allocation adulte handicapé dommages imputables à des soins médico-chirurgicaux dommages ouvrant droit à pension militaire dommages imputables à des actes de terrorisme, etc.*].

ANAMEVA supports a comprehensive website, with an interactive medical expert map updated twice a year, in April and October, and a continuously updated list of victim organisations and contacts, *www.anameva.com*.

BiblioInserm

BiblioInserm is the portal for bibliographic databases in biomedicine and the life sciences, including Embase, Pascal Biomed and Pascal SciTech as well as the giant PubMed database at *www.pubmed.gov* and its component Medline with 13 million references in 30 languages. These databases are used by medical and healthcare professionals to access research results and to keep updated on developments across the fields of medicine and the life sciences. It is supported by **Inserm** and maintained by the *Institut de l'Information Scientifique et Technique (INIST)*, a part of *Centre national de la recherché scientifique (CNRS)*, contact INSIT-CNRS, 2 Allée du Parc de Brabois, CS 10310, 54519 Vandoeuvre-lès-Nancy, Tel: 03 83504600, *www.inist.fr* ; click on *BiblioInserm* to bring up the opening page.

CCAS

Across the country there are Social Action Community Centres [*Centres Communal d'Action Social (CCAS)*] that provide social and legal assistance and care for the elderly, for the handicapped, for children, for families in difficulty and for the socially excluded. Larger communities will have several CCAS – Paris has 37 – whilst smaller communities may share a *Centre Intercommunal d'Action Social (CIAS)*. You can find the nearest CCAS by inquiring at the local Town hall [*Mairie*] or by looking it up under *Santé, action sociale* in the Yellow Pages. The CCAS and CIAS are joined in a network, the National Union of Social Action Community Centres [*Union national des centres communaux d'action sociale (UNCCAS)*], 6 rue

Faidherbe, BP 568, 59208 Tourcoing, Tel: 03 20280750, *www.unccas.org* in French with selected pages in English and German.

CLEISS

The Centre of European and International Liaisons for Social Security [*Centre des liaisons européennes et internationales de sécurité sociale (CLEISS)*] liaises between the Social Security organisations of France and their counterparts in other countries, as well as implements European Community (EC) regulations and bilateral or multilateral agreements. In fulfilling this role, CLEISS provides extensive information on social security in the country, including the most recent details of the **Social security ceiling** (Chapter 2) and of **Social security contributions** (Chapter 3) and consequently is the best single source of information on all matters related to social security. For further information as well as for documentation, contact CLEISS, 11 rue de la tour des Dames, 75436 Paris, Tel: 01 45263341, *www.cleiss.fr* in French, English, German, Italian, Portuguese and Spanish.

Contraception [*Contraception*]

Almost all contraceptive devices and procedures are available. The most common non-invasive contraceptives are the condom [*préservatif*], oral contraceptive pill [*la pilule*], mini-pill [*minipilule*] intrauterine device [*dispositif intra-utérin (DIU)*], contraceptive patch [*patch contraceptif*] and cervical cap [*cape cervicale*]. Vasectomy [*vasectomie*] is the most common surgical procedure. Condoms are the most readily available, as they are sold by pharmacies, in the *hygiene* departments of supermarkets and by vending machines attached to the outside walls of pharmacies as well as online, as from *Le roi de la capote* at *www. leroidelacapote.com*.

For further information, contact *Coordination des Associations pour le Droit à la Contraception (CADAC)*, 21ter rue Voltaire, 75011 Paris, Tel: 01 43563648, *www.cadac.org*.and/or *Mouvement français pour le planning familial (MFPF)*, 4 square Saint Irénée, 75011 Paris, Tel: 01 48072910, *www.planning-familial.org* in French with selected pages in English.

Crise de foie

Crise de foie, literally "liver crisis", is the popular name of a commonplace illness brought on by overeating or overdrinking. Doctors agree that it's misnamed, as it seldom is associated with biliousness or other liver maladies, but is a syndrome of stomach upset or indigestion. Rest and high fluid intake, as of herb tea or vegetable broth, is the recommended cure. Medicines that may be taken include antispasmodics, such as Primperan (Sanofi Aventis), Spasfon (Cephalon) and Vogalene (Schwarz Pharma), for stomach upsets, and analgesics for headaches.

Dentists [*Dentistes*]

There are more than 41,000 dentists in the country, a third of them women*. Though the word *dentiste* now is commonplace, the historic names of practitioners, *chirurgien-dentiste* in France and *médecin-dentiste* in Switzerland, are still used, particularly by professional associations. *Dentistes* now usually are listed in the Yellow Pages by their specialisations:

- *chirurgie*: dental surgery including extraction of teeth and treatment of the gums.
- *endodontie*: endodontics, the treatment of the dental pulp.
- *implantologie*: implantology, the implantation or attachment of artificial teeth.
- *odontologie conservatrice*: routine dentistry and dental hygiene.
- *parodontie*: periodontics, the treatment of the gums and tissues.
- *pédodontie*: pedodontics, the care and treatment of children's teeth.
- *prothèse*: prosthetics, the replacement of missing parts with artificial structures.

Most dentists are independent practitioners and may be either registered [*conventionné*] so their fees are mostly reimbursable by *Sécurité sociale* or completely private [*non conventionné*].

In the greater Paris area, **SOS dentaire** provides round-the-clock emergency dental services.

For further information on dentistry in France, contact the professional association, *l'Ordre National des Chirurgiens-dentistes*, 22 rue Emile Ménier, BP 2016, 75716 Paris Cedex. *www.ordre-chirurgiens-dentistes.fr*. There are several commercial websites dedicated to dentistry and dental care, the largest at *www.dentalespace.com*.

Source:INSEE Données Sociales, Édition 2006

Departmental Directorate for Health and Social Affairs [*Direction départementale des affaires sanitaires et sociales (DDASS)*]

The administration of healthcare and social affairs is decentralised into departmental directorates (DDASS), one in each of the Prefectures, and regional directorates (DRASS), one in each of the *Chefs-lieu* (Administrative centres) of the Regions. Their activities are coordinated with those of the *Agences régionales d'hospitalisation (ARH)* that provide hospital and clinic services. The DDASS, DRASS and ARH are listed in the Yellow Pages, usually under *Santé et des affaires sociales*, and full descriptions of their services and locations are available online at *www.sante.gouv.fr*, click on *Sites régionaux* and then on the DRASS or ARH interactive maps to locate the nearest offices.

Doctors [*Médecins*]

There are some 206,000 doctors in the country, nearly 40% of them women*. The two principal types of doctors are:

- *Médecin généraliste*, a general practitioner (GP) who may be consulted on any health matter. Your **Primary care physician** usually will be a GP.

- *Spécialiste*, a specialist in a particular medical field, whom you may consult upon referral from your Primary care physician. You also may see a specialist without a referral, but then the specialist's fee is not reimbursable from *Sécurité sociale*.

Doctors may work in **hospitals** or may be independent [*médecins libéraux*] with their own practices [*cabinets de consultation*]. An independent doctor may be a:

- *médecin conventionné*, a registered doctor whose fees are reimbursed by *Sécurité sociale*. By default, all independent doctors are registered unless they choose otherwise.

- *médecin conventionné honoraires libres*, a registered doctor whose private fees may be partly reimbursed by *Sécurité sociale*.

- *médecin non conventionné*, a private doctor whose fees are mostly not reimbursed by *Sécurité sociale*. Few doctors, about 9% of the total, are completely private.

The reimbursements by *Sécurité sociale* are according to *les tarifs conventionné*, which change with time and are available from registered doctors as well as from *Sécurité sociale* offices.

You can choose a primary care physician that suits your personal needs and situation. You can find doctors listed under *Médecins* in the Yellow Pages, by inquiring at a Pharmacy or at the nearest *Sécurité sociale* office. You also can find a doctor by entering the town name and *Département* number in the interactive doctor locator window under *Annuaire* in the opening page of *www.conseil-national.medecin.fr*, the website of *Ordre national des médecins*, the organisation responsible for registering and monitoring doctors, with a head office at 180 bd Haussmann, 75008 Paris, Tel: 01 53893200. For the latest information on fees, social security reimbursement and the like, contact AMeli, the **Health insurance portal**.

Most doctors keep office hours posted outside their offices. **SOS Médecins France** provides round-the-clock medical services and handles most of the calls to **SAMU** (Chapter 16) in which the services of a doctor are required.

Source: INSEE Données Sociales, Édition 2006

E forms [*Formulaires communautaires*]

Across the EEA countries, reciprocal healthcare and social security arrangements are attested by forms. If you are resident in another EEA country and visit France, you should have a **European Health Insurance Card**. If you take up residence in France, you will need one or more of the many E-Forms that transfer rights between countries; the most-used forms are listed below. For example, if you take up residence but are not employed, you will need form E106 if you are below retirement age and form E121 if you are retired. For further information, contact the national insurance and social security organisations of your home country.

For information on the forms and their use in France, visit the **CLEISS** website at *www.cleiss.fr/docs/textes/rgt_formulaires.html*. All the forms presently in use across the EEA are listed on the **Europa server** (Chapter 31) at *ec.europa.eu/employment_social/soc-prot/schemes/eform_en.htm*.

Sector	E-Form	English	Français
Healthcare [*Assurances maladie*]	E104	Certificate concerning the aggregation of periods of insurance, employment or residence	*Attestation concernant la totalisation des périodes d'assurance, d'emploi ou de résidence*
	E106	Certificate of entitlement to sickness and maternity insurance benefits in kind for persons residing in a country other than the competent country	*Attestation de droit aux prestations en nature de l'assurance maladie maternité dans le cas des personnes qui résident dans un autre pays que le pays compétent*
	E109	Certificate for the registration of members of the employed or self-employed person's family and the updating of lists	*Attestation pour l'inscription des membres de la famille du travailleur salarié ou non salarié et la tenue des inventaires*
	E119	Certificate concerning the entitlement of unemployed persons and the members of their family to sickness and maternity insurance benefits	*Attestation concernant le droit aux prestations en espèces des travailleurs en chômage et des membres de leur famille*
	E121	Certificate for the registration of pensioners and the updating of lists	*Attestation pour l'inscription des titulaires de pension ou de rente ou des membres de leur famille et la tenue des inventaires*

Sector	E-Form	English	Français
Pensions [*Pensions*]	E201	Certificate concerning the aggregation of periods of insurance or periods of residence	*Attestation concernant la totalisation des périodes d'assurance ou de résidence*
Unemployment [*Chômage*]	E301	Certificate concerning the periods to be taken into account for the granting of unemployment benefits	*Attestation concernant les périodes à prendre en compte pour l'octroi des prestations de chômage*
	E303	Certificate concerning retention of the right to unemployment benefits	*Attestation concernant le maintien du droit aux prestations de chômage*
Family benefits [*Prestations familiales*]	E401	Certificate concerning composition of a family for the purpose of the granting of family benefits	*Attestation concernant la composition de la famille en vue de l'octroi des prestations familiales*
	E402	Certificate of continuation of studies for the purpose of the granting of family benefits	*Attestation de poursuite d'études en vue de l'octroi des prestations familiales*

Emergency medical assistance (EMA) [*Services d'aide médicale urgente*]

Emergency medical assistance (EMA) differs from that provided in the majority of countries, where EMA is practiced mostly in hospital emergency departments, and ambulances function to bring in the victims of acute illness or injury. The French approach to EMA is that an acute illness or injury, such as a heart attack or a road accident, is best treated on the spot without the delay of ambulance transport to a hospital emergency department. So calls to the medical emergency number 15 are to call centres staffed by **SAMU** (Chapter 15) doctors and health care professionals.

Upon receiving a call, the duty doctor evaluates the severity of the situation and chooses appropriate response by offering advice on the phone, sending a doctor, sending an ambulance for transport to a clinic or hospital or, in an acute case, dispatching:

- a Hospital Mobile Intensive Care Unit [*Unités Mobiles Hospitalières (UMH)*] from a pre-hospital care unit [*Service Mobile d'Urgence et de Réanimation (SMUR)*], *or*

- a rescue and casualty assistance vehicle [*Véhicule de Secours et d'Assistance aux Victimes (VSAV)*], also known by the older designation, Vehicle for rescuing the asphyxiated and the injured [*Véhicules de Secours aux Asphyxiés et aux Blessés (VSAB)*] from the firefighters [*Sapeurs-pompiers*].

In Paris, the fire brigade [*Brigade des Sapeurs-Pompiers de Paris (BSPP)*] has special versions of these mobile units, including the *Premiers Secours Relevage (PSR)* version of the VSAB, the resuscitation ambulance [*ambulance de réanimation (AR)*] version of the UMH and a larger vehicle fitted for evacuation, the *Premiers Secours Évacuation (PSE)*.

Aside from initiating treatment when time is most critical, this approach also eases the task of hospital emergency departments, as patents arrive in a more stable condition than had they merely been brought in by ambulance.

European Health Insurance Card
[*Carte européenne d'assurance maladie*]

If you travel in Europe and are a citizen or permanent resident and member of the national insurance schemes of one of the 28 countries of the EEA, you should carry a European Health Insurance Card, which entitles you to treatment on a par with the residents of the other 27 countries. A card is valid only if you are a visitor; if you take up residence in another country, you must join its health insurance system. The cards replace the E111 series of forms that have become invalid after 1 January 2006 and include: E111 and E111B used by most travellers, E110 used by international haulage companies, E128 used by students and workers posted abroad and E119 used by unemployed people seeking work in another EEA country.

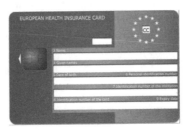

Front of generic card with microchip; Europa server images.

The cards are of uniform design and each carries the two-letter code for and explanatory text in the language of the issuing country. If you are a member of the health insurance scheme of another EEA country and settle in France, you should bring a card issued by the national health service of your home country, in order to have coverage until you obtain a French **Social Security Card** [*Carte d'assurance maladie*]; when you apply for that card, you also may apply for a French *Carte d'européenne d'assurance maladie*. For further details, contact the *Casse primaire*

311

d'assurance maladie (CPAM) in the *Département* where you live. For information on the international use and validity of the cards, contact **CLEISS**. For information on the cards and their use across Europe, visit the **Europa server** (Chapter 31) website and navigate to the card pages starting at *ec.europa.eu/employment_social/healthcard*.

Family benefits [*Prestations familiales*]

There are four categories of benefits intended to enable all families to raise and educate their children:

- General maintenance benefits:

  Family allowances [*Allocations familiales (AF)*], popularly called *allocs*, a monthly benefit paid after the birth of a second child.

  Family supplement [*Complément familial (CF)*], a means-tested benefit to persons assuming responsibility for three or more children, aged 3-21.

  Family support allowance [*Allocation de soutien familial (ASF)*] paid to a surviving spouse or single parent bringing up one or more orphaned children.

  Single parent allowance [*Allocation de parent isolé (API)*] provides a minimum family income to any parent who, following widowhood, separation or abandonment, is alone, being responsible for one or more children. It also is granted to single expectant mothers.

- Benefits associated with birth and adoption:

  Young child allowance [*Allocation pour jeune enfant (APJE)*], a means-tested benefit paid in two periods: from the fourth month of pregnancy until the child is three months old, and from the age of three months to the age of four years.

  Parental education allowance [*Allocation parentale d'éducation (APE)*] paid to families with two or more dependent children whenever one parent reduces working hours to care for the education of a child less than three years old.

  Adoption allowance [*Allocation d'adoption (AA)*], a means-tested benefit paid to families who adopt or who foster a child with a view to adoption.

- Special allowances:

  Special educational allowance [*Allocation d'éducation spéciale (AES)*] granted to parents responsible for a handicapped child.

  Family housing allowance [*Allocation de logement familiale (ALF)*] a means-tested allowance that offsets housing costs.

  Allowance for school children [*Allocation de rentrée scolaire (ARS)*], a means-tested benefit paid for each child, 3-18 years old and attending school, being an apprentice or pursuing studies.

  Parental presence allowance [*Allocation de présence parentale (APP)*] granted to a parent who interrupts work to care for an ill, injured or handicapped child in need of constant care.

- Childcare support:

  Family support for an approved maternal assistant [*Aide à la famille pour l'emploi d'une assistante maternelle agrée (AFEAMA)*] pays an employer's and employee's social security contributions associated with employing an assistant.

  Allowance for childcare at home [*Allocation de garde d'enfant à domicile (AGED)*] paid to working parents who employ a person to care for their children under the age of six.

The amounts of these allowances and their conditions change with time; for the latest details, visit the **Social security portal** or contact one of the *Caisse des allocations familiales (CAF)* listed under *Sécurité social* in the Yellow pages or found using the postcode locator under *Contact avec votre CAF* on the national website at *www.caf.fr*.

French Health Products Safety Agency [*Agence française de sécurité sanitaire des produits de santé (AFSSAPS)*]

The French Health Products Safety Agency is responsible for all measures that ensure the safety, quality and proper use of health products for human use, including:

- drugs and raw materials
- medical devices and in vitro diagnostic devices
- liable blood products or other biological products of human or animal origin, gene or cell therapy products and ancillary therapeutic products
- products for the upkeep or application of contact lenses, insecticides or similar products for human use, biocides
- cosmetics products, tattooing products, etc.

The Agency conducts benefit and risk assessments, performs laboratory controls, inspects production sites and test sites, and publishes extensively for professionals and the general public. Its principal facility is in Saint-Denis, and it also has laboratories in Montpellier and Lyon. Its website on health products attracts more than 9000 visitors a day and it has a mailing list of more than 13,000 subscribers. For further information, contact the head office at 143-147 bd Anatole-France, 93285 Saint-Denis Cedex, Tel: 01 55873000, *agmed.sante.gouv.fr* in French with selected pages and publications in English.

The French social security system [*Le régime français de sécurité sociale*]

Even within your home country, knowing where a matter sits within the hierarchy of the social security system is the first step to finding information on it. In the table below, the headings of the hierarchy of the French social security system are listed along with their official translations into English. The complete texts are available on the **CLEISS** website at *www.cleiss.fr* in French, English, German, Italian, Portuguese and Spanish.

French	English
INTRODUCTION	INTRODUCTION
Organisation, Financement, Étendue	Organisation, Financing, Scope and coverage
I – LES ASSURANCES SOCIALES	I – SOCIAL INSURANCE
A – Assurance maladie-maternité	A – Maternity / Sickness Insurance
B – Assurance invalidité	B – Disability Insurance
C – Assurance vieillesse	C – Old-Age Insurance
D – Assurance décès	D – Life Insurance
II – ASSURANCE ACCIDENTS DU TRAVAIL ET MALADIES PROFESSIONNELLES	II – INDUSTRIAL INJURIES AND OCCUPATIONAL DISEASES INSURANCE
Définition, Formalités, Réparation	Definition, Procedure, Compensation
A – Prestations dues en cas d'incapacité temporaire	A – Temporary Disability Benefits
B – Prestations dues en cas d'incapacité permanente: les rentes	B – Permanent Disability Benefits: Pensions
III – LES PRESTATIONS FAMILIALES	III. FAMILY ALLOWANCES
Méthode de calcul des prestations familiales	Method of calculation of Family Allowances
A – Prestations générales d'entretien	A – Basic Maintenance Benefits
Allocations familiales, Allocation forfaitaire, Complément familial, Allocation de soutien familial, Allocation de parent isolé	Family allowances, Flat-rate allowance, Family income supplement, Family Support Allowance, Single Parent's Allowance
B – Prestations d'entretien et d'accueil liées à la petite enfance	B – Benefits For The Maintenance And The Accommodation Of Infants
Prestation d'accueil du jeune enfant, Prime à la naissance ou à l'adoption, Allocation de base, Complément de libre choix d'activité, Complément de libre choix du mode de garde	Infant Accommodation Benefit, Birth or Adoption Grant, Basic Allowance, Supplement for free choice of working time, Supplement for free choice of custodial care

C – Prestations à affectation spéciale	C – Benefits For Special Purposes
Allocation d'éducation de l'enfant handicapé, Allocation de rentrée scolaire, Allocation de présence parentale, Allocation de logement familiale, Prime de déménagement	Special Education Allowance, Back-to-school Allowance, Parent's Attendance Allowance, Family Housing Allowance, Moving Bonus
IV – RETRAITES COMPLÉMENTAIRES	IV – SUPPLEMENTARY PENSIONS
Âge, Montant, Survivants	Age, Amount, Survivors
V – ASSURANCE CHÔMAGE	V – UNEMPLOYMENT INSURANCE
Organisation, Financement, Assujettissement, Prestation	Structural organisation, Financing, Liability, Benefits
ANNEXES	ANNEXES
• *Tableau récapitulatif des prestations familiales visées à l'article L 511-1 du Code de la sécurité sociale au 1er janvier 2006*	• Summary of family benefits falling under Section L 511-1 of the French Social Security Code as of 1 January 2006
• *Tableau récapitulatif des taux et plafond de cotisations de sécurité social et de chômage au 1er janvier 2006.*	• Summary of rates and ceilings of social security and unemployment contributions – as of 1 January 2006

Healthcare agency portal [*Portail des agences sanitaires*]

The healthcare agency portal at *www.sante.fr* provides information about and access to the websites of the Ministry of Health and Solidarity [*Ministre de la santé et des solidarité*] as well as its agencies, including the:

- Biomedicine Agency [*Agence de la biomédecine*]
- Food Safety Agency [*L'Agence française de sécurité sanitaire des aliments (AFSSA)*]
- French Agency for Environmental and Occupational Health Safety [*Agence française de sécurité sanitaire de l'environnement et du travail (AFSSET)*]
- French Health Products Safety Agency [*L'agence française de sécurité sanitaire des produits de santé (AFSSAPS)*]
- French National Blood Service [*Etablissement Français du Sang (EFS)*]
- Institute for Radiation Hygiene and Nuclear Safety [*Institut de Radioprotection et de Sûreté Nucléaire (IRSN)*]
- National Authority for Health [*Haute Autorité de Santé (HAS)*]
- National Institute for Prevention and Health Education [*Institut National de Prévention et d'Education pour la Santé (INPES)*]

- National Institute for Public Health Surveillance [*Institut de Veille Sanitaire (INVS)*]

- National School of Public Health [*Ecole nationale de la santé publique (ENSP)*].

Health insurance portal [*Assurance maladie en ligne (AMeli)*]

AMeli is the online portal provided by the national state health insurance office [*Caisse nationale d'assurance maladie (CNAM)*], the central agency that manages health insurance matters at national and local levels, through the *Caisse primaire d'assurance maladie (CPAM)* across the country. The AMeli portal is the best place to start looking for information on all aspects of health insurance, as well as social security matters via its links to other websites. For further information, contact AMeli, CNAM, 50 avenue du Professeur André Lemierre, 75986 Paris Cedex 20, Tel: 01 72601000, *www.ameli.fr* in French; under *Assuré*, click on "Foreign languages" to bring up links to extensive extracts in Arabic, English, Spanish and Portuguese.

Holiday vouchers [*Bons vacances*]

Holiday vouchers are a means-tested benefit paid to families with children up to age 16, to enable them to go on holiday or attend holiday camps, and are administered and paid in a manner similar to **family benefits**. For further information, contact the nearest *Caisse des allocations familiales (CAF)* listed under *Sécurité social* in the Yellow pages or found using the postcode locator under *Contact avec votre CAF* on the national website at *www.caf.fr*.

Hospitals [*Hôpitaux*]

According to the most recent figures*, in the country there are nearly 3000 public and private hospitals and clinics that together have more than 505,000 beds.

The public sector hospitals [*secteur publics (SPH)*] are fewer, one in three of the total, but larger, with 65% of all beds, in four principal types of facility:

- regional hospitals [*Centres hospitalier régional (CHR)*] and regional hospitals affiliated with universities (CHU)

- central hospitals [*Centre hospitalier (CH)*] not attached to the *Régions*

- local hospitals [*hospital local (HL)*]

- psychiatric hospitals [*centre hospitalier spécialise en psychiatrie (HP)*].

The private sector [*secteur privé*] healthcare facilities [*établissements de soins*] are more numerous, two in three of the total, but smaller, being mostly clinics and outpatient centres. Most of the facilities are **private clinics**, but there are many non-profit hospitals [*hôpitaux privés à but non lucratif*] operated by charities, such as the

Red Cross [*Croix-rouge*]. As in public sector hospitals, care in non-profit private sector hospitals is covered by *sécurité sociale*.

Hospitals and clinics are listed under *Hôpitaux* in the Yellow Pages. All the country's hospitals and clinics, public and private, are listed along with news on hospitalisation developments and trends, by the Regional Hospitalisation Agencies [*Agences Régionales de l'Hospitalisation*]; contact Direction de l'Hospitalisation et de l'Organisation des Soins, Ministère de la Santé et des Solidarités, 8 avenue de Ségur, 75350 Paris 07, *www.parhtage.sante.fr/re7/site.nsf* with an interactive hospital/clinic locator map.

* Source: INSEE, Annuaire Statistique de la France, Édition 2006, Tableau F.01-7.

Income support [*Revenu minimum d'insertion (RMI)*]

The RMI is an allowance intended to support poor families not entitled to unemployment benefits. It is means tested and is available to residents at least 25 years old and who have children but insufficient means of supporting them. It is not available to students or to trainees who are qualified and fit for work. The allowance provided depends on the number of children supported and on whether the applicant also must support a spouse. An RMI is available upon filling in and submitting an application [*Demande de RMI*] (Cerfa 12325*01). For further details, contact your local town hall [*mairie*].

Inserm

Inserm is the acronym for *Institut national de la santé et de la recherché médicale*, the "National Institute of Health and Medical Research". Founded in 1964, Inserm is the only public research body in the country that is completely dedicated to human health. It conducts basic, clinical, therapeutic, diagnostic and public health research in 360 laboratories, most associated with university hospitals or cancer treatment centres and that together have a total staff of more than 13,000 people, nearly half of whom are research scientists. It has become a leader in its field, having addressed public health issues and having contributed significantly to the sciences of biochemistry, immunohematology, cellular and molecular biology, genetics and new therapeutics. It has numerous publications in English as well as French, and it supports **BiblioInserm**, the French portal for the gigantic bibliographic databases in biomedicine and the life sciences. For further information, contact the head office at 101 rue de Tolbiac, 75654 Paris Cedex 13, Tel: 01 44236000, *www.inserm.fr* selectable in French or English.

Institut prévention accidents domestiques

As elsewhere, the home is a dangerous place: each year, more than a third of all accidents in which people are injured or killed happen in homes. On average, there is a serious accident in or around a home every four seconds, and each day, there are more than four times as many accidents in homes as on the road. Regrettably, small children, less than five years old, are most prone to home accidents, which worsens the overall picture. Despite these alarming figures, home accidents seldom are newsworthy. This lack of attention probably arises because people tend to regard their homes as havens, safer than the roads, workplaces, schools or sports.

The Institute for preventing home accidents [*Institut prévention accidents domestiques*] aims to make the home a safer place by publishing on safety matters, working with schools and citizen groups to heighten awareness of home safety, promoting measures for safety and making safety devices available at affordable prices. For further information, contact IPAD France, 19 Rue des Pimpelines, 27220 Saint Laurent des Bois, Tel: 02 32581334, *www.ipad.asso.fr* with lists of and links to public and private sector organisations concerned with safety.

Medical encyclopaedias [*Encyclopédies médicale*]

Medical guides and encyclopaedias are readily available, sold in book shops and on many newsagent and supermarket book section racks. Two popular encyclopaedias are:

- *Larousse Médical* (Paris, Larousse, 2006, 1219 pages, large-format 20 × 29 cm hardcover, ISBN 2-03-560425-7), a profusely-illustrated, comprehensive reference.

- *Petit Larousse de la Médecine* (Paris, Larousse, 2004, 1119 pages, 14 × 20 cm hardcover, ISBN 2-03-560325-0), an abridged version of the above book, with fewer illustrations.

Two popular encyclopaedic healthcare online sites are *Doctissimo* at *www.doctissimo.fr* and *Santeguerir* at *www.santeguerir.fr*.

Moving within the European Union
[*Déplacement à l'intérieur de l'Union européenne*]

The national social security systems of the member States of the European Union vary considerably. So, if you are resident in and accustomed to the social security system of one country, you will encounter differences in dealing with the social security system of another country, as may happen if you take up residence or are on a prolonged stay there. Consequently, the European Commission publications office has compiled a guideline brochure on the matter, entitled "The Community provisions on social security, Your rights when moving within the European Union" [*Vos droits de sécurité sociale quand vous vous déplacez à l'intérieur de l'Union européenne*] (2004 update, A4 format, 49 pages, English edition ISBN 92-894-8490-X, EC publication KE-64-04-0022-EN-C), available in all 11 official EU languages from the EC at Rue de la Loi 200, B-1049 Brussels, Belgium, and downloadable free from the website at *ec.europa.eu/employment_social*.

Mutual societies [*Mutuelles*]

One person in two in the country belongs to a mutualist society, which makes mutualism the country's largest social movement. Mutualism, the doctrine that mutual dependence is essential to individual and collective well-being, entails non-profit credit and voluntary association, principles first put forth by political theorist Pierre Joseph Proudhon (1809-1865). The first mutual societies were founded in the latter half of the 19th century, and in 1883 they met at Lyon and thereby took the first step to national recognition. In the early 20th century, that trend was formalised with the foundation of *Fédération national de la mutualité française (FNMF)*. Today, French Mutualism [*Mutualité française*] is a leading provider of **top-up insurance** and complementary healthcare [*complémentaire santé*] through its support of networks that together have 2000 offices and shops offering medical, paramedical and social services. For example, 540 **opticians** (Chapter 40) are *Mutualiste*, as are 400 dental clinics [*centres dentaires*], 300 retirement centres [*établissements et services pour personnes âgées*] and ten other categories of services. For further information, contact FNMF, 225 rue de Vaugirard, 75719 Paris Cedex 15, Tel: 01 40433030, *www.fnmf.fr*.

National Institute for Prevention and Health Education [*Institut national de prévention et d'éducation pour la santé (INPES)*]

Established in 2002, INPES works with the Ministry of Health and other government agencies to implement policies concerning prevention and health education within the general framework of public health policy. It does this in part by publishing extensively, releasing each year some 70 to 80 million documents for the general public as well as for healthcare and education professionals. It has a catalogue of some 230 references, including brochures, leaflets, posters, educational materials, stickers, books, CDs and audio cassettes. It has taken over publication of *La Sante de l'homme* ("Human Health"), a bimonthly magazine with a circulation of 11,000, now in its 60th year of publication and available in individual copies or upon annual subscription. For further information, contact INPES 42 bd de la Libération, 93203 Saint Denis Cedex, Tel: 01 49332390, *www.inpes.sante.fr* in French with selected pages in English and Spanish.

Obesity [*Obésité*]

Obesity is expanding in France, long held to be a country of people who ate well but stayed slim. Much has been written about the underlying causes, and there is a website dedicated to the topic at *www.obesite.com*. The cause most likely is that fast foods, fizzy drinks and frozen pizzas have gained at the expense of the traditional family meal. More than 40% of residents now are considered overweight, and more than 10% are obese*.

* Source: QUID 2006

Official rates [*Tarifs conventionnelles*]

The fees charged by most healthcare professionals are limited to ceilings [*tarifs conventionnelles*] set each year on 1 January. Among doctors there are some exceptions. Most doctors charge according to the official rates, they are said to be in *Secteur 1*, and their fees are approved for **reimbursement**. Some private doctors are in *Secteur 2* and charge higher authorised rates [*tarifs d'autorité*], most of which are not approved for reimbursement. The **Health insurance portal** keeps an updated list of the official rates at *www.ameli.fr/67/RUB/67/omb.html*.

Paternity leave [*Congé paternité*]

The father of a newborn baby is entitled to 11 consecutive days of leave, or 18 days in case of multiple births, regardless of the father's marital status and contingent only upon his living in France. If you are an expectant father and wish to take the paternity leave, you should apply a month in advance to your employer, in writing, stating the date or expected date of birth of the baby and enclosing a copy of your family book [*livret de famille*] or transcript of the birth register [*acte de naissance de l'enfant*] or medical certificated confirming the expected date of delivery [*acte de reconnaissance de l'enfant*]. For further information, visit the AMeli **Health insurance portal** at *www.ameli.fr*.

Pharmacies [*Pharmacies*]

Pharmacies (called "chemists" in the UK and "druggists" in Scotland and the USA) are identified by a green cross on a white background, sell prescription medicines, non-prescription medicines, and some cosmetics and toiletries [*parapharmacie*]. For every 100,000 people in the country, there are 38 pharmacies and more than 46 pharmacists*. Almost all pharmacies are owned and operated by their resident pharmacists; there are no pharmacy chains as in other countries.

A pharmacist [*pharmacien*] can supply a doctor's prescription [*ordonnance*], advise on the use of prescription and non-prescription medicines, give first aid and perform some simple tests, as for blood pressure. You must pay for all medicines, but are entitled to **reimbursement** for medicines bought on prescription. There are three reimbursement rates: 35% for ordinary medicines with a blue label [*vignette bleue*], 65% for vital medicines with a white label [*vignette blanche*] as well as for preparations compounded in the pharmacy [*préparations magistrales et produits de la pharmacopée*] and 100% for certain expensive yet essential medicines [*médicaments reconnus comme irremplaçables et particulièrement coûteux*].

Most pharmacies are closed on Sundays and public holidays, but for emergencies [*cas d'urgence*] there always is at least one duty pharmacy [*pharmacie de garde*] in or near a town that remains open out-of-hours; its address and phone number are published in local newspapers and posted on the doors of the closed pharmacies. You can find a pharmacy by looking under *Pharmacies* in the Yellow Pages or by keying in the postcode or name of your town in the online pharmacy locator on the *Ordre national des pharmaciens* website at *www.ordre.pharmacien.fr*, click on *Consultez l'annuaire des pharmaciens* and then on *Recherche par établissement* to bring up the locator dialogue window.

Supermarkets, hypermarkets and household shops [*drogueries*] usually offer smaller selections of non-prescription medicines as well as bandages, cosmetics and toiletries. Some online shops offer non-prescription medicines; the largest is *Pharmadiscount*, Pharmadiscount.com, 2 rue de Huningue, BP 140 68300 St Louis, Tel: 03 89676495, *www.pharmadiscount.com*.

* *Source: QUID 2006.*

Pharmacopoeia [*Pharmacopée*]

The national consolidated catalogue of pharmaceutical compounds marked in France, with directions for use, is entitled *Pharmacopée française*, compiled and published by the **French Health Products Safety Agency**. Once published on paper, from the present 10th edition of 2005 on, it is available only on CD-ROM, to facilitate frequent updates. A smaller companion to it, the List of Medicinal Plants [*Liste des plantes médicinales*] is still published on paper (Paris, Afssaps, 2005, 84 pages paperback, ISBN 3-2605009-594-5). Other pharmacopoeia are also available, including those published by the European Directorate for the Quality of Medicines as well as those covering the traditional medicines of other countries; the Amazon.fr online bookshop lists 115 pharmacopoeia titles.

Pregnancy [*Grossesse*]

Pregnant women are entitled to full coverage for antenatal, childbirth and postnatal care. Pregnancy test [*test de grossesse*] kits for home use are sold by pharmacies; two brands are *Clearblue* and *Révélatest*. If you test positive or otherwise suspect that you are pregnant, you should visit a doctor or a midwife [*sage-femme*] before the third month, to have your pregnancy confirmed. You then will be given a first antenatal examination [*premier examen prénatal*] form consisting of three pages. You then should send the first two blue pages to your nearest Family allowance fund [*Caisse d'allocations familiales (CAF)*] and the third pink page to your nearest Health insurance fund [*Casse d'assurance maladie*] to initiate social security and health insurance coverage. You will be sent a Guide to maternity and newborn care [*Guide de surveillance médicale de la mère et du nourrisson*]. From the day you file the antenatal examination forms through to the fifth month of your pregnancy, you will be reimbursed for medical expenses on the same basis as before you were pregnant. From the first day of the sixth month until 12 days following birth, you are entitled to 100% reimbursement, up to the limits set by social security.

After the first antenatal examination, you are entitled to at least six examinations by a doctor or a midwife:

- ultrasound scans: three or more if required by you or your baby's health condition, covered 70% up to the fifth month of pregnancy and 100% thereafter.

- genetic screening by amniocentesis and foetal serotype for risk pregnancies, against your doctor or midwife filing a *demande d'entente préalable* form with the Health insurance fund to provide full coverage.

- delivery preparation, eight optional sessions of physical preparation and information, fully covered.

Doctor's fees and hospital expenses for delivery, as for epidural anaesthesia, are fully covered up to the 12th day of your stay in hospital. If you are discharged from hospital within three to five days after giving birth, you are entitled to home health care up to the 12th day. A newborn baby will be screened for genetic illnesses, also fully covered. Within eight weeks of delivery, you may have a postnatal examination, fully covered, and, if needed, sessions with a physiotherapist [*masseur kinéstithérapeute*] for pelvic floor rehabilitation.

You are entitled to maternity leave from a job in two periods, antenatal leave before delivery and postnatal leave after delivery. The durations of these periods depends on the number of babies born and on the number of children already in your household:

Number of children in household before you give birth	Birth	Antenatal leave	Postnatal leave
none or one:	single	6 weeks	10 weeks
two or more:	single	8 weeks	18 weeks
0, 1, 2, 3 or more:	twins	12 weeks	22 weeks
	triplets or more	24 weeks	22 weeks

For complete health insurance details, in French or English, visit the **Health insurance portal** at *www.ameli.fr*.

If your pregnancy is unwanted, you may seek an abortion [*avortement*], called a voluntary termination of pregnancy [*interruption volontaire de grossesse (IVG)*]. If the pregnancy is unsafe, your doctor may prescribe a therapeutic abortion [*interruption médicale de grossesse (IMG)*]. In 1975, voluntary abortion [*IVG*] was made legal, initially for the first ten weeks of pregnancy, extended in 2001 to 12 weeks, and therapeutic abortion [*IMG*] permitted thereafter. In 1988, France was the first country to legalise the use of Mifepristone (also called RU-486, its name during early trials), a drug that induces abortion that is now estimated to be used in one in four abortions. For further information, contact *Coordination des Associations pour le Droit à la Contraception (CADAC)*, 21 ter rue Voltaire, 75011 Paris, Tel: 01 43563648, *www.cadac.org* and/or *Mouvement français pour le planning familial (MFPF)*, 4 square Saint Irénée, 75011 Paris, Tel: 01 48072910, *www.planning-familial.org* in French with selected pages in English.

Primary care physician [*Médecin traitant (MT)*]

From 1 July 2005 onwards, all residents age 16 or more who benefit from social security must choose a doctor as their primary care physician [*médecin traitant*]. The primary care physician then will be the doctor that you see most frequently, will keep your medical records, will advise you on healthcare and, when necessary, will refer you to other doctors. All visits to your primary care physician are reimbursable at a rate of at least 70%.

Any doctor may act as your primary care physician. Once a doctor agrees to be your primary care physician, you should fill in and sign a physician nomination form [*Déclaration de choix du médecin traitant*], have the doctor sign it, and then submit it to your nearest Health insurance fund [*Casse d'assurance maladie*]. If you move or for other reasons wish to change your primary care physician, or your doctor retires or dies, you must fill in and submit anew to nominate another doctor. If you live in a home for the elderly, you need not choose, as the primary care physician will be the doctor in attendance at the home.

For further information in French or English as well as for the nomination form, visit the **Health insurance portal** at *www.ameli.fr*.

Private clinics [*Cliniques privé*]

Across the country, there are some 1250 private clinics, in number amounting to about 40% of the overall spectrum of hospitals [*paysage hospitalier*] and together having about 100,000 beds. Most of the clinics offer surgical services, and 75% of the 6.5 million patients treated per year are ambulatory. The clinics range from single, independent units to chains, of which the largest is *Générale de santé*, with

162 clinics in France and 11 clinics abroad, in Italy and Switzerland. For further information, contact the head office at 96 Avenue d'Léna, 75016 Paris, Tel: 01 53231414, *www.generale-de-sante.fr* selectable in French or English, with an interactive clinic locator map. For further information on private hospitalisation and clinics across the country, contact *Fédération de l'Hospitalisation Privée*, 81 rue Monceau, 75008 Paris, Tel: 01 53835656, *www.fhp.fr* with an interactive clinic locator map.

Reimbursement [*Remboursement*]

For most minor healthcare expenditures, you pay the provider, such as a doctor or a pharmacy, and then apply for reimbursement to your nearest *Caisse primaire d'assurance maladie (CPAM)*. For major expenditures, such as hospitalisation, your CPAM or **Top-up insurance** provider will pay directly. Reimbursements are reckoned in percentage rates, applicable to the **official rates** for services and to the regulated ceiling prices for goods, such as medicines. The **Health insurance portal** keeps an updated list of the reimbursement rates [*taux de remboursement*] at *www.ameli.fr/229/DOC/1104/article.html*. Commonplace reimbursements from that list are given in the table below. The reimbursement rates are higher for some localities in Alsace-Moselle [*Régime d'Alsace-Moselle*] and for recipients of pension support [*Fonds spécial vieillesse (FSV)*]

Healthcare	*Soins*	Rate
Practitioner fees: doctors, dentists and midwives	*Honoraires des praticiens :* *médecins, chirurgiens-dentistes,* sages-femmes	70%
Auxiliary medical fees: nurses, physiotherapists, speech therapists, orthoptists,	*Honoraires des auxiliaires médicaux: infirmières, masseurs-kinésithérapeutes, orthophonistes, orthoptistes, pédicures-podologues, pedicurists-chiropodists*	60%
Medical lab, biological	*Actes de biologie*	60%
Hospitalisation	*Hospitalisation*	80%
Optics	*Optique*	65%
Orthopaedics	*Orthopédie*	65%
Medicines, blue label	*Médicaments à vignette bleue*	35%
Medicines, white label	*Médicaments à vignette blanche*	65%

Applications for reimbursement are made in one of two ways:

- traditional, paper-based: the practitioner or pharmacist gives you a partly filled-in healthcare statement [*feuille de soins*] that you complete and submit to the CPAM. The *feuille de soins* is a CERFA A4-sized form, brown on white, No. 1254*01 for professional services and No. 11389*03 for medicines and goods.

- automatic, electronic: you use your **Social security card** [*Carte d'assurance maladie*] and if you have **top-up insurance**, its "white card" [*Carte blanche*] to record payment and initiate reimbursement.

Schengen certificate [*Certificat de la convention de Schengen*]

If you travel to or from France and take a prescription medicine that may be classified as a narcotic, as are many hypnotics, sedatives and painkillers, you must be able to prove that the medicine is necessary for your own personal use, so it's best to keep the medicine in its original package that carries the prescription label of the pharmacy where you bought it. If you travel to or from countries inside EU/EFTA, you will need a Schengen certificate, the full name of which is "Certification to carry drugs and/or psychotropic substances for treatment purposes – Schengen Implementing Convention Article 75" [*Certificat pour le transport de stupéfiants et/ou de substances psychotropes à des fins thérapeutiques – Article 75 de la Convention d'application de l'Accord de Schengen*]. In France, as well as in most EU/EFTA countries, pharmacies issue the certificates. If you wish to know if a specific medicine is classified as a narcotic, ask at a pharmacy or, in France, the nearest **Departmental Directorate for Health and Social Affairs**. If your travel is to or from countries outside EU/EFTA you must carry the original prescription [*original de la prescription médicale*] and a permit for its international transport [*attestation de transport*]; for further details, contact the *Unité stupéfiants et psychotropes* of the **French Health Products Safety Agency.**

Social re-integration [*Réinsertion sociale*]

Across the country, there are numerous facilities for treating and re-integrating drug addicts into society, including:

- Lodging and re-integration centres [*Centres d'hébergement et de réinsertion sociale (CHRS)*], in 745 centres with 30,300 places, to be increased 32,100 places in 2007.
- Transitional housing [*Maisons relais*], in all 1799 places, to be increased by 600 places in 2007.
- Social housing [*Résidences sociales*], in all 480 residences that together accommodate 3300 people.

Contact the nearest **Departmental Directorate for Health and Social Affairs** for advice on facility availability. Further information on social reintegration in France is available online at *www.social.gouv.fr*. For information on drugs, drug addiction and treatment across Europe, contact the European Monitoring Centre for Drugs and Drug Addiction, Rua da Cruz da Santa Apolónia 23-25, P-1149045 Lisbon, Portugal, Tel: +351 218113021, *www.emcdda.europa.eu* in English.

Social security card [*Carte d'assuré social*]

The health insurance smart card [*Carte d'assurance maladie Vitale*], issued to all residents from age 16 on, is the social security card [*carte d'assuré social*] that is used for identification in all healthcare and social security matters. Each card has a unique 15-digit number that often is called the "Social security number" but actually is the **National identity number** (Chapter 38) of the cardholder. The Health Insurance Fund [*Casse primaire d'assurance maladie (CPAM)*] issues the cards from its offices across the country. You may apply for a card at the nearest CPAM office in the *Département* in which you live; you can find its address using the online locator on the health insurance website at *www.ameli.fr/84/cpam.html*.

Specimen social security card.

Social security contributions [*Contributions de sécurité sociale*]

If you are an employee of a French company or of a foreign company with a place of business in France, your employer will declare and pay your social security contributions. However, if you are self employed, you must attend to declaration and payment. Likewise, if you work in France as the employee of a foreign company that has no place of business in the country, its representative must declare and pay your social security contributions. Declaration and payment of contributions [*déclaration et paiement de contributions*] are easily done online on the Net-enterprises secure website at *www.net-entreprises.fr* in French; click on *Foreign companies* for selected pages in English; a helpline for the service is available Monday-Friday, 09:00-18:00 hours, Tel: 0820000516.

Social security portal [*Portail de la sécurité sociale*]]

The Social security portal at *www.securite-sociale.fr* is provided by the National Social Security Offices [*Caisses nationale de sécurité social*] in cooperation with the Social Security Administration [*Direction de la sécurité sociale (DSS)*]. The portal is the best place to start looking for information on all aspects of social security as well as by the offices involved – alphabetically by their abbreviations as used in official publications: ACOSS, CANAM, CANCAVA, CFE, CLEISS, CNAF, CNAMTS, CNAVTS, MSA, ORGANIC and UCANSS.

SOS Dentaire

In Paris there are two round-the-clock emergency dental services:

- *SOS Implants Dentaires*, 78 rue Roquette, 75011 Paris, Tel: 01 40218288

- *SOS Urgences Stomatologiques et Dentaires*, 87 bd Port Royal, 75013 Paris, Tel: 01 43363600 and 01 43375100.

SOS Médecins France

Founded in 1965, *SOS Médecins France* is the country's oldest and largest emergency medical service. Across the country, it handles some four million calls a year, including most of the calls to **SAMU** (Chapter 16) that require the services of a doctor. Across the country, it operates through 71 associations that together have a thousand emergency doctors. For emergency assistance, call the number of the nearest Association. For further information, contact the head office at 85 bd Port Royal, 75013 Paris, Tel: 08 20332424, *www.sosmedecins-france.fr* with pages in French and English and with an interactive Association locator map.

Top-up insurance [*Couverture complémentaire santé*]

The healthcare insurance system is mixed, with the generality of cover provided by the public system and top-up insurance provided by **mutual societies**, insurance companies and jointly-managed social protection funds. Companies with more than 50 employees usually negotiate top-up health insurance coverage for them, and individuals may buy top-up coverage from any of its many providers. Many of the top-up insurance polices are issued with a white card [*carte blanche*] of the same size and format as a bank payment card as well as the national **Social Security Card**, so *complémentaire santé* and *carte blanche* are synonymous in everyday usage. The purpose of top-up insurance is to provide coverage of the difference between the actual costs of healthcare and the **reimbursements** for them. Hence, together, a national *Carte d'assurance maladie* and a top-up insurance policy *carte blanche* provide full coverage. There are almost as many different packages of fees and coverage as there are companies providing top-up insurance, so it's wise to compare offerings before buying. Almost all insurance companies provide extensive information on *complémentaire santé*, both in print and online, and the approximately 43,000 professionals involved are affiliated in *Carte blanche santé*, a portal for top-up insurance, 38 rue La Bruyère, 75009 Paris, Tel: 01 53212425, *www.carteblanchesante.com*.

Universal Healthcare Insurance
[*Couverture maladie universelle (CMU)*]

In effect since January 2000, *Couverture maladie universelle (CMU)* ensures that all residents have adequate healthcare insurance and consequently have access to healthcare, regardless of their ability to pay. CMU is both a right and an obligation, as all residents are legally obliged to be members of the national health insurance system. In practice, this means that a resident must be a member of the local Health Insurance Office [*Caisse primaire d'assurance maladie (CPAM)*].

For most people, CMU covers an average of 75% of medical expenses, through a scheme of **reimbursement** against outlays according to **official rates**. A resident may buy **top-up** insurance and thereby be covered 100%.

Upon application to a local CPAM, low-income families are eligible for increased coverage percentages. CMU provides the six million most disadvantaged people in the country with free **top-up insurance** so they enjoy free healthcare. Moreover, it provides basic health insurance for some 150,000 people not covered by older schemes, either because they were ineligible or more often because they were unable to assert their eligibility.

For further information on CMU, contact your local CPAM or visit the **Health insurance portal** at *www.ameli.fr*.

URSSAF

The *Union de recouvrement des cotisations de sécurité et d'allocations familiales (URSSAF)* is the entity of the social security system that collects funds, controls contributions and deals with legal matters. Its long name is seldom used in French and even less used in English, though a rough translation might be "State social contribution collection organisation". It is a quasi-public organisation, as it is under the aegis of the Ministry of Labour and the Ministry of Social Affairs but is administered by representatives of the government, public and private sector employers and the unions.

Funds collected by URSSAF are turned over to its sibling organisation, *Agence centrale des organismes de sécurité sociale (ACOSS)* that in turn redistributes funds to various disbursement offices [*caisses*] for payment of social security benefits to individuals. The four principal disbursement offices are:

* *Caisse nationale d'assurance malade des travailleurs salaries (CNAMTS)* that serves salaried employees.
* *Caisses d'assurance maladies régionales (CMR)* which are under the *Caisse nationale d'assurance maladie des professions indépendantes (CANAM)* that serve self-employed persons.
* *Caisses primaires d'assurance maladie (CPAM)* that deals with reimbursements for healthcare.

- *Caisses d'allocations familiales (CAF)* that provides family income support.

URSSAF has 103 agencies across the country, with addresses and telecoms numbers in an interactive list on its website at *www.urssaf.fr*, and a head office together with ACOSS at 65 boulevard Richard Lenoir, 75536 Paris Cedex 11, Tel: 01 49233000.

Vocabulary [*Vocabulaire*]

The vocabulary of healthcare social security is extensive and only partly covered in bilingual dictionaries. Fortunately, comprehensive glossaries are available:

- for social security terms, **CLEISS** publishes updated bilingual glossaries, from English, German, Italian, Portuguese and Spanish into French, available on its website at *www.cleiss.fr*, click on *Documents* and then on *Glossaries*.

- for healthcare terms, there is a convenient printed bilingual *Glossary of Medical, Health and Pharmacy Terms*, compiled by Alan S. Lindsey (Surrey, Hadley Pager Info, 2003, 210 pages, 14.5 × 21 cm softcover, ISBN 1-872739-12-1).

The many organisations and measures involved in healthcare and social security often are mentioned only by their abbreviations. The fifty or so most prevalent are listed below along with their full names in French and the equivalents in English.

Abbreviation	for:	equivalent in English
AA	*Allocation d'adoption*	Adoption allowance, a means-tested support for adoption
ACOSS	*Agence centrale des organismes de sécurité sociale*	State social funds disbursement organisation, pays out funds collected by URSSAF
AES	*Allocation d'éducation spéciale*	Special educational allowance, support for parents of a handicapped child
AF	*Allocations familiales*	Family Allowance, a monthly benefit paid after birth of second child
AFEAMA	*Aide à la famille pour l'emploi d'un assistante maternelle agrée*	Family support for a maternal assistant employed in the home
AGED	*Allocation de garde d'enfant à domicile*	Allowance for childcare at home, offsets child minder wages paid by working parents
AGIRC	*Association générale des institutions de retraite des cadres*	Confederation of executive pension funds

Abbreviation	for:	equivalent in English
ALF	*Allocation de logement familiale*	Family housing allowance, means-tested support of housing costs
API	*Allocation de parent isolé*	Single Parent Allowance, support for a single, divorced, abandoned or widowed parent
APE	*Allocation parentale d'éducation*	Parental education allowance, compensation for wages lost in educating young children
APJE	*Allocation pour jeune enfant*	Young child allowance, means-tested benefit for parents of small children
APP	*Allocation de présence parentale*	Parental presence allowance, support for a parent caring for a handicapped child
ARH	*Agence régionale d'hospitalisation*	Regional Hospitalisation Services Agency
ARRCO	*Association des régimes de retraites complémentaires*	Confederation of complementary retirement insurance schemes
ARS	*Allocation de rentrée scolaire*	Allowance for school children, means-tested benefit for families with school-age children
ASF	*Allocation de soutien familial*	Family Support Allowance, paid to surviving or single parent bringing up orphaned children
CAF	*Caisse des allocations familiales*	Family allowances fund, local office deals with all allowances and benefits
CANAM	*Caisse nationale d'assurance maladie des professions indépendants*	National pension fund for self-employed professionals
CANCAVA	*Caisse nationale d'assurance vieillesse des artisans*	National pension fund for self-employed craftsmen
CCAS	*Centre communal d'action social*	Social Action Community Centre, aid to the underprivileged
CF	*Complément familial*	Family Supplement, a means-tested benefit for parents of many children
CFE	*Caisse des français de l'étranger*	Social security office for French citizens abroad

Abbreviation	for:	equivalent in English
CGSS	*Caisse générale de sécurité sociale*	General social security fund
CH	*Centre hospitalier*	Central Hospital not affiliated with a *Région*
CHR	*Centre hospitalier régional*	Regional Hospital
CHRS	*Centre d'hébergement et de réinsertion sociale*	Lodging and Re-integration Centre for drug addicts
CHU	*Centre hospitalier universitaire*	University Hospital
CIRDD	*Centre d'information et de ressources sur la drogue et les dépendance*	Drug and Dependence Information and Resource Centre
CMAF	*Caisse maritime d'allocations familiales*	Maritime family allowance fund, disburses AF to families of seamen
CMU	*Couverture maladie universelle*	Universal health cover
CNAF	*Caisse nationale d'allocations familiales*	National family allowance fund, disburses AF
CNAM	*Caisse nationale d'assurance malade*	National health insurance office
CNAMTS	*Caisse nationale d'assurance malade des travailleurs salaries*	National health insurance office for salaried workers
CNAV	*Caisse nationale d'assurance vieillisse*	National retirement insurance fund
CNAVPL	*Casse nationale d'assurance vieillesse des professions libérales*	National retirement insurance fund for independent professionals
CNAVTS	*Caisse nationale d'assurance vieillisse des travailleurs salaries*	National retirement insurance fund for salaried workers
CPAM	*Caisse primaire d'assurance maladie*	Local Health Insurance Office, deals with all medical matters
CRDS	*Contribution au remboursement de la dette sociale*	Tax introduced in 1996 to help pay off deficit in the social security budget
CRRA	*Centre de réception et de régulation des appels*	SAMU Reception and Dispatch Call Centres, one in each *Département*
CSG	*Cotisation sociale généralise*	Supplementary social security contribution to aid the underprivileged

Abbreviation	for:	equivalent in English
DDASS	*Direction départementale des affaires sanitaires et sociales*	Departmental Directorate for Health and Social Affairs
DRASS	*Direction régionale des affaires sanitaires et sociales*	Regional Directorate for Health and Social Affairs
DSS	*Direction de la sécurité sociale*	National Social Security Administration
FSV	*Fonds spécial vieillesse*	Pension support funds
GRICA	*Groupement de recherche et d'intervention sur les conduites addictives*	Addiction Research and Intervention Group
HL	*Hôpital local*	Local Hospital
HP	*Centre hospitalier spécialise en psychiatrie*	Psychiatric Hospital
MSA	*Mutualité sociale agricole*	Farm mutual pension fund
MT	*Médecin traitant*	Primary care physician
ORGANIC	*Caisse d'assurance vieillesse, invalidité et décès des non salariés de l'industrie et du commerce*	Pension, disability and life insurance fund for the self-employed in industry and commerce
SAMU	*Service d'aide médicale d'urgence*	National Emergency Medical Assistance Service
SPH	*Secteur publics hospitalier*	Public Sector Hospitals
UCANSS	*Union des Caisses Nationales de Sécurité Sociale*	Social security worker's union
URSSAF	*Union de recouvrement des cotisations de sécurité et d'allocations familiales*	State social security collection organisation, deals with self-employed people

23
Historical overview

Historical timeline [*Chronologie de l'histoire*]

The principal dates in the history of France are listed below. For brevity, Kings other than the first and last and Presidents before the Second World War are not listed.

30000-12000 BC	First human habitation.
57-62 BC	Under Julius Caesar, Roman Army conquers Gaul.
406-406	Barbarians invade Gaul.
751	First royal house, Mérovingien, created; rules until 768.
800	Charlemagne becomes emperor of the Occident.
885-886	Vikings besiege Paris.
1095	First Crusade.
1135-1144	Gothic art begun in Paris region.
Late 12th century	Legend of Tristian et Yseut first written down.
1230-1275	Novel *De la rose* changes ideals of courtesy.
1269	Philosopher Pierre Pèlerin de Maricourt explores magnetism and invents compass.
1300-1314	Polyphonic music evolved.
1309	Pope Clemit V takes up residence at Avignon, initiating 70 years of French papacy.
1314	*L'ordre des Templiers* founded.
1337	War against Great Britain (Hundred years war).
1344	Museum built on site of former residence of Abbots of Cluny; now most known example of medieval civil architecture in Paris.
1378-1417	Great Schism of the Occident.
1415	Defeat on 25 October by forces of Henry V at battle of Azincourt.

1431	Jean d'Arc burned at the stake 30 May.
1450	First passion play.
1453	Hundred Years War ends.
1529	*Collège de France* founded.
1539	French made official language.
1555	Nostradamus publishes Les Prophéties, discussed to this day.
1624	Cardinal de Richelieu appointed minister and evolves concept of nation-state.
1635	*L'Académie française* founded by Richelieu.
1641	René Descartes evolves Cartesian philosophy.
1666-1671	Molière evolves modern drama.
1673	Performance of first opera, *Cadmus et Hermione* by Lully.
1685	Edict of Nantes revoked.
1719	John Law, an expatriate Scot, creates first modern financial services.
1737	Pierre Simon Fournier devises first point system for sizes of type.
1748	Political science defined as a discipline of study.
1751-1772	First encyclopaedia published.
1772-1789	Antoine Laurent Lavoisier founds modern chemistry.
1774-1792	Reign of Louis XVI.
1789	*Révolution* starts 14 July.
1793	First Republic declared 24 June.
1793	First public museum, the Louvre.
1795	Metric system of measurement made obligatory.
1801	Xavier Bichat founds modern anatomy.
1804-1814	Napoleon I Emperor.
1809	Jean Baptiste Lamarck proposes a theory of evolution.
1815	Defeat at Waterloo.
1816-1826	Joseph Niépce originates photographic process.
1830	Algeria conquered; colonial empire begins.
1830-1848	Reign of Louis-Philippe I, last King.
1830-1857	Gustave Flaubert and Henri Beyle Stendhal write first novels mirroring society.
1835-1840	Charles Alexis de Tocqueville advocates liberalism in government.

1841-1863	Hector Berlioz initiates romantic music.
1848	Second Republic declared 4 November.
1861-1869	P. & E. Michaux invent bicycle with pedals.
1862	Louis Pasteur evolves theory of infection.
1870-1871	War against Germany.
1870	Third Republic declared 4 September.
1871-1893	Émile Zola evolves naturalism as genre of literature.
1874-1886	Impressionist movement in art.
1881	Compulsory secular primary school education initiated.
1884	Edouard Delmare-Debouteville patents world's first car.
1887-1889	Eiffel Tower built.
1894-1906	Dreyfus affair.
1896	H Becquerel discovers radioactivity.
1902	Claude Debussy writes first comic opera.
1904	*Entente Cordiale* agreement ends hostilities between France and Great Britain.
1914-1918	First World War.
1924-1930	Surrealism in art.
1938-1948	Jean Paul Sartre evolves existentialism.
1939-1945	Second World War.
1945-1973	*Les trente glorieuses* post-war prosperity period.
1946	Fourth Republic declared 13 October.
1946	Jacques Heim and Louis Reard design first bikini bathing suit.
1946-1954	War in Indochina.
1947	Dior creates New Look.
1954-1962	Algerian War of Independence.
1955-1972	Production of the Caravelle, first commercially successful jet passenger aircraft.
1955-1975	Three million *logements sociaux* built in the *banlieues*
1958	Fifth Republic declared 4 October.
1959	Age for leaving compulsory schooling raised to 16.
1959-1962	Charles de Gaulle President.
1968	Student uprisings in May.
1969–1974	Georges Pompidou President.
1970	Death of Charles De Gaulle.

1974-1981	Valéry Giscard d'Estaing President.
1976-2000	Anglo-French Concorde, first and to date only supersonic passenger aircraft in service.
1981	*Train à Grand Vitesse (TGV)* enters service; capable of speeds up to 320 km/h.
1981-1995	François Mitterand President.
1983	Luc Montagnier discovers human immunodeficiency virus (HIV).
1995-	Jacques Chirac President.

24
Holidays and feasts

Each year, there are ten public holidays, eight on fixed dates and two on variable dates related to the date of Easter Sunday, which is the first Sunday after the first full moon after the vernal equinox [*équinoxe de printemps*]. In addition to the public holidays, there are about 14 weeks of school holidays, six during the school year and eight in summer. Employed persons are entitled to five weeks of annual holiday, of which four may be taken together between 1 May and 31 October. By tradition, August is the peak holiday month, as it is after the school summer holiday begins in early July and before **Rentrée** (Chapter 5), when school resumes in September.

Indeed, holidays are so much a part of the lifestyle that there are schemes aimed to enable everyone to enjoy holiday travel, activities and entertainment, regardless of means, most prominently the **Holiday savings** (Chapter 2) supported by many employers and holiday vouchers [*Les bons vacances*] offered by the **National family allowance fund** (Chapter 22) to low-income families.

Fixed holidays [*Fêtes fixes*]

The fixed holidays consist of both traditional Catholic feasts and secular national holidays:

- 1 January, New Year's Day [*Jour de l'an*], a public holiday, traditionally celebrated with family meals.
- 6 January, Twelfth Night [*Fête des rois*], not a public holiday, but celebrated in homes and workplaces by serving of the traditional *galette des rois*, a rich pastry that contains a *fève*, or "bean" as was originally used. Today, the *fève* is a ceramic or plastic figure, and the person who finds the *fève* in their portion, wears a cardboard crown for the rest of the celebration.
- 2 February, Candlemas [*Chandeleur*], not a public holiday but celebrated in Christian churches, privately celebrated by eating *crêpes*.
- 14 February, St. Valentine's Day [*Saint Valentin*], not a public holiday, but cause for celebrating romantic relationships with gifts.

- 1 April, April Fool's Day [*Le premier avril*], not a public holiday, but a day for tricks on others, which, when performed, are announced by calling out *poisson d'avril!* ("April fish!").

- 1 May, International Labour Day [*Fête du travail*], a public holiday, often the time for political speeches and union demonstrations.

- 8 May, Victory Day [*Fête de la victoire*], a public holiday commemorating the victory in Europe that ended the Second World War.

- 23 or 24 June, Midsummer Day [*Feux de la Saint Jean*], not a public holiday, but an occasion for evening public gatherings, often with bonfires and fireworks.

- 14 July, Bastille Day [*Fête nationale*], a public holiday commemorating the events that triggered the *Révolution* of 1789, celebrated with parades, fireworks and public gatherings.

- 15 August, Assumption [*Assomption*], a public holiday, celebrated in Christian churches, but otherwise only by people busy with their summer holidays.

- 1 November, All Saints Day [*La Toussaint*], a public holiday, in the Christian church to commemorate saints, and in families to remember deceased relatives and friends, often by taking flowers to cemeteries.

- 11 November, Armistice Day [*L'Armistice*], a public holiday commemorating the end of the First World War in 1918 and a day of remembrance for all who have fallen in defence of the country. In Paris, the President lays a wreath on the tomb of the unknown soldier beneath the *Arc de Triomphe*, and across the country, in cities and towns, parades with war veterans are held.

- 8 December, Feast of the Immaculate Conception [*Fête de l'immaculée conception*], not a public holiday, but celebrated particularly in Lyon, where it is known as *Fête de la lumière*, commemorating the intervention by the Virgin Mary believed to have prevented the plague from reaching the city in the Middle Ages.

- 24 December, Christmas Eve [*Veille de Noël*], not a public holiday, but traditionally the day when the Christian faithful attend Midnight Mass [*Messe de minuit*] and on which most people exchange presents and families gather for the Christmas Eve meal [*le réveillon*].

- 25 December, Christmas Day [*Noël*], a public holiday, by tradition celebrated by family gatherings.

- 26 December, Day after Christmas [*Saint Étienne*], not a public holiday, but celebrated in the *Départements* of Bas-Rhin, Haut-Rhin and Moselle.

- 31 December, New Year's Eve [*Saint-Sylvestre*], not a public holiday, but usually a cause for celebrations focusing on good food and drink.

Movable feasts [*Fêtes mobile*]

The movable feasts principally are those of the Catholic Church:

- Shrove Tuesday [*Mardi gras*], not a public holiday; the last day of carnival and the day before Ash Wednesday when Lent starts. By tradition, *crêpes* are eaten at supper.
- Good Friday [*Vendredi saint*], not a public holiday in most of the country but partly so in the *Départements* of Bas-Rhin, Haut-Rhin and Moselle, and celebrated in Christian churches across the country.
- Easter [*Pâques*], both Sunday [*Dimanche de Pâques*] and Monday [*Lundi de Pâques*] are public holidays, celebrated in churches and by family gatherings, often with events for children, featuring treasure hunts for hidden sweets or chocolate eggs.
- Ascension Day [*Ascension*], 40 days after Easter Sunday, usually on a Thursday, a public holiday celebrated principally in churches.
- Whitsun [*Pentecôte*], the seventh Sunday and Monday after Easter, not a public holiday but since 2005, an allowable free day without pay.
- Mother's Day [*Fête des Mères*], the Sunday after Whitsun, honouring mothers and celebrated with family gatherings.
- Father's Day [*Fête des Pères*], the Sunday two weeks after Mother's Day, honouring fathers and again celebrated with family gatherings.

School holidays [*Vacances scolaires*]

School holidays are fixed across the country. The autumn, Christmas and summer holidays are the same for all schools:

- Autumn: Late October and early November: Thursday of week 43 to Sunday of Week 44
- Christmas: Christmas Day to 2 January
- Summer: Early July to early September: Wednesday of week 27 to Sunday of Week 35.

Zone	Académies	Winter holiday usually	Spring holiday usually
A	Caen, Clermont-Ferrand, Grenoble, Lyon, Montpellier, Nancy-Metz, Nantes, Rennes, Toulouse	Weeks 8 & 9	Weeks 17 & 18
B	Aix-Marseille, Amiens, Besançon, Dijon, Lille, Limoges, Nice, Orléans-Tours, Poitiers, Reims, Rouen, Strasbourg	Weeks 7 & 8	Weeks 16 & 17
C	Bordeaux, Créteil, Paris, Versailles	Weeks 6 & 7	Weeks 15 & 16

In the mainland including Corsica, there are 26 *Académies*, listed below with the Départements that they comprise.

Académie	*Départements*, numbers in parentheses
Aix –Marseille	Alpes-de-Haute-Provence (04), Hautes-Alpes (05), Bouches-du-Rhône (13), Vaucluse (84)
Amiens	Aisne (02), Oise (60), Somme (80)
Besançon	Doubs (25), Jura (39), Haute-Saône (70), Territoire de Belfort (90)
Bordeaux	Dordogne (24), Gironde (33), Landes (40), Lot-et-Garonne (47), Pyrénées-Atlantiques (64)
Caen	Calvados (14), Manche (50), Orne (61)
Clermont-Ferrand	Allier (03), Cantal (15), Haute-Loire (43), Puy-de-Dôme (63)
Corse	Haute-Corse (2A), Corse-du-Sud (2B)
Créteil	Seine-et-Marne (77). Seine-Saint-Denis (93), Val-de-Marne (94)
Dijon	Cote d'Or (21), Nièvre (58), Saône-et-Loire (71), Yonne (89)
Grenoble	Ardèche (07), Drome (26), Isère (38), Savoie (73), Haute-Savoie (74)
Lille	Nord (59), Pas-de-Calais (62)
Limoges	Corrèze (19), Creuse (23), Haute-Vienne (87)
Lyon	Ain (01), Loire (42), Rhône (69)
Montpellier	Aude (11), Gard (30), Hérault (34), Lozère (48), Pyrénées-Orientales (66)
Nancy-Metz	Meurthe-et-Moselle (54), Meuse (55), Moselle (57), Vosges (88)
Nantes	Loire-Atlantique (44). Maine-et-Loire (49), Mayenne (53), Sarthe (72), Vendée (85)
Nice	Alpes-Maritimes (06), Var (83)
Orléans-Tours	Cher (18), Eure-et-Loir (28), Indre (36), Indre-et-Loire (37), Loir-et-Cher (41), Loiret (45)
Paris	Paris (75)
Poitiers	Charente (16), Charente-Maritime (17), Deux-Sèvres (79), Vienne (86)
Reims	Ardennes (08), Aube (10), Marne (51), Haute-Marne (52)
Rennes	Côtes-d'Armor (22), Finistère (29), Ille-et-Vilaine (35), Morbihan (56)
Rouen	Eure(27).Seine-Maritime (76)
Strasbourg	Bas-Rhin (67), Haut-Rhin (68)
Toulouse	Ariège (09), Aveyron (12), Haute-Garonne (31), Gers (32), Lot (46), Hautes-Pyrénées (65), Tarn (81), Tarn-et-Garonne (82)
Versailles	Yvelines (78), Essonne (91), Hauts-de-Seine (92), Val-d'Oise (95)

Moreover, there are four overseas *Académies*, covering Guadeloupe, Guyane, Martinique and Réunion.

25
Housekeeping

As elsewhere in Europe, traditional housework [*travaux ménagers*] is increasingly mechanised. Of all homes in the country, 99% have refrigerators, 80% have freezers, 92% have washing machines, 44% have dishwashers, and 74% have microwave ovens*. Suitable, then, that the word housekeeping in English translates to the French *économie domestique*, which back translates to "home economics", the skill of managing a home. With few exceptions, that skill is easily transferable between European countries. So, this chapter is about how you may discover the similarities and deal with the differences of housekeeping in France.

Source: INSEE 2004.

Alarm systems [*Systèmes d'alarme*]

Two types of alarm systems are used in homes: personal alarms used by individuals to summon aid and condition alarms that are activated by incidents, such as fire or burglary.

Personal alarms provide a user, usually an elderly or disabled person, with automatic or manually-activated means of notifying a monitoring centre should aid be needed. The various systems classify as *téléassistance*, because they communicate via fixed telephone lines or wireless telecommunications to remote centres that send assistance. Providers of personal alarm systems are listed under *Télésurveillance* in the Yellow Pages. Two leading providers are:

- *AXA Assistance*, an insurance company, 12 bis Boulevard des Frères Voisin, 92798 Issy-Les-Moulineaux, Cedex 9, Tel: 01 55924150, *www.axa-assistance.fr*
- *Attendo Systems*, Village d'entreprises, Harfleur 2000, BP 28 Rond-Point Harfleur, 71201 Le Creusot Cedex, Tel: 03 85730505, *www.attendo.fr*.

A condition alarm may be either a stand-alone alarm [*alarme*] that sounds upon activation or a proximity system [*sécurité proximité*] connected to one of the **Security services** (Chapter 10). Companies involved are listed in the Yellow Pages under *Alarmes* or under *Télésurveillance*. Four leading providers are:

- *123 Alarme*, makers of the *Pack Alarme* DIY kits for stand-alone alarms,

628 Allée de la Marine Royale, Le Suffren A, 06210 Mandelieu, Tel: 08 05855500, *www.123alarme.fr*.

- *Comodo*, a leading maker of home security, personal alarms and other alarm systems, 7125 route de l'Aveyron, 82000 Montauban, Tel: 05 63313040, *www.comodoalarm.com* in French with selected pages in English.

- *Daitem*, a principal supplier of home and business alarm systems, 246 rue du pré de l'Orme, 38926 Crolles Cedex, Tel: 08 00414000, *www.daitem.fr*.

- *Securitas*, suppliers of the *Aroundio* condition alarms, 1 Centrale Parc, Avenue Sully Prud'homme, 92990 Châtenay Malabry, *www.aroundio.fr*.

Avoiding junk mail [*Comment éviter la publicité*]

As elsewhere, unwanted advertising and other junk mail has become an annoyance for homeowners as well as an environmental problem, because in the course of a year, 42 kg of it accumulates in the average letter box. You can stop junk mail by placing a "No junk mail" sticker on your letter box, as distributors are obliged to heed it. You can make and affix your own sticker; *Pas de Publicité S.V.P.* is a phrase commonly used. Or you can affix a green *StoPub* sticker launched October 2005 by **France Nature Environment** (Chapter 7). It is available free at town halls (*mairies*) or download and print out a copy from *http://www.preventiondechets.fr/campagne/sp_fne.gif*. The StoPub sticker is preferable, as it is recognised and includes a statement permitting delivery of municipal information. If your letter box is outside, the free sticker from the town hall is best, as it is made of weatherproof plastic.

StoPub sticker, full size 3.5 cm diameter.

Beds and bedding [*Lits et literie*]

Bedding is similar to that used elsewhere in Europe. Various qualities of mattresses [*matelas*] of foam or with innersprings are available. Adult mattress sizes are to prevailing European standards, 180 cm and 200 cm in length and 90 cm, 140 cm, 160 cm and 180 cm in width. Longer lengths are available on order. There are various children's sizes, in lengths up to 120 cm and widths up to 75 cm. Sheets [*draps*] are made to fit the standard beds, both in traditional flat and fitted [*drap-housse*] sizes. Upper sheets and blankets [*couvertures*] are commonplace, but duvets [*couettes*] are in widespread use. Duvets and pillows [*oreillers*] are available with down [*édredon*] or synthetic [*synthétique*]. By weight, traditional down is warmest and most expensive, although some synthetic fills are nearly as warm.

Bedding shops [*literies*] as well as the bedding departments of supermarkets and hypermarkets [*linge de la maison*] offer many brands. The leading French brands of sheets, pillowcases and duvet covers are Boutons, Sissi, Sonate and Troubador. The leading brands of duvets are Dodo for synthetic-fill products, *www.dodo.fr*, and Pyrenex for down fill products, *www.pyrenex.com* in French and English. As for mattresses, the sizes are mostly standardised:

- duvets: 140 × 200 cm and 200 × 200 cm single and 220 × 240 cm double and 240 × 260 cm kingsize
- pillows: 60 × 60 cm and 65 × 65 cm square and 45 × 70 cm and 50 × 70 cm rectangular.

Caretaking and maintenance [*Gardiennage et entretien*]

Caretaking [*gardiennage*], the watching over a property while the occupant is away, now is almost always associated with security and surveillance services, so companies offering it will be listed in the Yellow Pages under *Surveillance, gardiennage, protection*. Buildings jointly owned [*copropriétés*], such as blocks of private-ownership apartments, may engage a *gardiennage* service that accordingly watches over the apartments of all residents. Routine building maintenance [*entretien*] is provided by companies that principally offer commercial cleaning [*nettoyage*] or domestic cleaning [*ménage*] and listed under these headings in the Yellow Pages.

CNMIS

CNMIS is the abbreviation for *Comité National Malveillance Incendie Sécurité*, the organisation concerned with providing information to consumers and professionals on the certifications of fire safety and electronic security products according to French and European regulations and standards. A CNMIS label on a product indicates that it complies with the standards applicable to it. For further information, contact CNMIS, 8 place Boulnois, 75017 Paris, Tel: 01 53890040, *www.cnmis.org* in French with extracts in English and German.

Colours [*Couleurs*]

Several colour systems are in use for commercial products, including paints and varnishes. The international Natural Colour System, originally developed in Sweden and now used by about 1000 companies in 60 countries, including France, is prevalent. In it, colours are designated in a Colour Atlas [*Atlas des couleurs*] based on the way humans perceive six pure colours. In all, there are 1950 colours in the most recent 2005-2006 edition of the atlas. NCS is not related to other colour systems, such as Munsell in Japan and the USA and Pantone, as used in graphic arts, but the NCS Colour Centre in the UK offers cross references between the colour systems, 71 Ancastle Green, Henley on Thames, Oxfordshire RG9 1TS, UK, Tel: +44 1491411717, Fax: +44 1491411231, *www.ncscolour.co.uk*, *info@ ncscolour.co.uk*. For further information on NCS, contact the NCS Colour Centre, 14, rue de la Beaune, 93181 MONTREUIL CEDEX, Tel: 01 56933740, Fax: 01 56933749, *http://www.color-3c.com/*, *color-3c@color-3c.com*.

Major paint manufacturers, such as Ripolin and Dulux Valentine, have charts of their proprietary colour selections [*Nuancier*]. For further information, contact Ripolin, BP 43, 80110 MOREUIL, Tel: 03 22353889, *www.ripolin.tm.fr* or Dulux Valentine Service Conseil, 92607 ASNIÈRES CEDEX, Tel: 01 46883232, *www.duluxvalentine.com*.

The paint and varnish departments of many **DIY shops** (Chapter 40) have a dispensing system that can mix colours according to international systems, such as NCS, or manufacturer selections, such as Ripolin.

Dish washing [*Faire le vaisselle*]

In traditional hand dish washing, you use a dishcloth [*lavette*] or more likely a small, square biodegradable dishwashing sponge [*éponge*] usually sold in mixes of various colours in five-packs, and dish washing liquid detergent [*détergent pour lave-vaisselle*], and afterwards dry using a tea towel [*torchon de cuisine*]. If you use a dish washer [*lave-vaisselle*], you will use dish washer powder [*poudre pour lave-vaisselle*] or tablets [*doses pour laive-vaisselle*].

DIY [*Bricoler*]

France is a country of do-it-yourself (DIY) enthusiasts, so much so that in French there is a verb specifically for the pursuit, *bricoler*, and a shop that sells DIY goods is a *bricolage*. Even the smallest *bricolage* offers a selection of timber and panels in pre-cut sizes, tile and wood flooring, hardware, plumbing supplies, paints and varnishes, flat-pack kitchen and bath furniture and the like, lighting and electrical wiring and supplies, tools and power tools, outdoor furniture, roofing and masonry supplies. The larger **DIY shops** (Chapter 40) have sufficient selections of goods to put up an entire house.

Domestic help [*Aide à domicile*]

Informal domestic help exists and is made known as it is elsewhere, by word-of-mouth and by neighbourhood contact, as when local schoolgirls put notes in nearby mailboxes offering to mind children and do housecleaning for pocket money. Two organisations, ADMR and Particulieremploi, are involved in organised domestic help.

- ADMR, the abbreviation for *Association du service à domicile*, is the older of the two. It was founded in 1945, initially to provide assistance to needy rural families. Today it is a network, with local associations across the country, in the major municipalities of all *Départements*. Each ADMR association is managed by a team of volunteers familiar with the locality. In each case where domestic help is provided, they coordinate the efforts of other volunteers and people hired in to best benefit the recipient of the help. ADMR offers minimum services to the general public [*tous publics*] and more extensive services to families [*familles*], elderly persons [*personnes âgées*] and handicapped persons [*personnes handicapées*]. For further information, contact the nearest ADMR office, listed under *Aide à domicile* in the Yellow Pages, or the head office at 184A rue du Faubourg Saint-Denis, 75484 Paris Cedex 10, Tel: 01 44655555, *www.admr.org* with an interactive local ADMR association locator map.

- Particulieremploi, literally "Individual employment", is the younger. Born of the age of computerisation, it is an online service that was activated on 1 January 2006. Its principal aim is to bring together people who seek and people who provide domestic help in an easy and straightforward manner that minimises paperwork. It does this by maintaining seeker and provider databases and supporting online access to them round the clock. It also arranges payments via a third-party service that takes care of transactions and issues payment vouchers called *CESU*, the abbreviation for *Cheque emploi service universel*. The CESU issued in each case depends on the service involved and on the support of it, as by social security. For further information on *Particulieremploi*, contact the information office at 65 rue de Sèvres, 92100 Boulogne, Tel: 01 46051257, *www.particulieremploi.fr*. For further information on CESU, contact *Centre national du Chèque emploi service universel*, 3 avenue Émile Loubet, 42961 Saint-Etienne Cedex 9, Tel: 08 20868584, *www.cesu.urssaf.fr*.

EDF-GDF

EDF-GDF is the abbreviation for Électricité de France-Gaz de France, the everyday name of the combined utilities that distribute electricity and gas. The name of the joint company is EDF Gaz de France Distribution, abbreviated EGD. However, EDF and GDF are separate companies. Further information on the companies is available, in French and in English on their websites at *www.edf.com* and *www.gazdefrance.com*.

EDF is one of the world's largest producers of electrical energy, supplying more than a fifth of the electricity consumption of the EU countries. Nearly three-quarters of EDF's total production is in nuclear power plants, of which there are more in France than in any other European country. Hydroelectric power accounts for slightly more than 16% of the total, thermal power for less than 10% and renewable energy about 0.1%. GDF is one of Europe's leading transporters and distributors of natural gas, 95% of it imported, principally by pipeline from Algeria, the Netherlands, Norway and Russia. Overall, gas supplies 15% of the **energy** (Chapter 7) consumed in the country. As this book goes to press, EDF and GDF have a monopoly, but that may change after 1 July 2007, when the energy market is deregulated and opened in accordance with EU directives.

Electricity [*Electricité*]

As elsewhere in Europe, the electricity supply to homes is 230 Volt, 50 Hz alternating current [*courant alternatif*]. Technically it is called *basse tension (BT)*, "low voltage", to distinguish it from *haute tension (HT)*, "high voltage", as used in electric transmission lines, and from *très basse tension (TBT)*, "very low voltage", as used in vehicles and by many electronic devices, and the regulations concerning it are worded accordingly. Electric energy consumption in kilowatt-hours (kWh) is measured by a meter, installed in a cabinet outside or fitted in the distribution box inside, and EDF sends bills up to six times a year.

Fire extinguishers [*Extincteurs*]

Of the many types of fire extinguishers, the best for home use is the dry-powder type [*extincteur poudre*], which is a pressurised container that discharges a chemical powder to put out a fire. These extinguishers are rated according to the class of fire that they are made to combat:

- Class A – ordinary combustible materials: wood, paper, rubber, etc. [*combustibles ordinaires: bois, papier, caoutchouc, etc.*]
- Class B – flammable liquids: gas, oil, grease, etc. [*liquides inflammables: gaz, huile, graisse, etc.*]
- Class C – electrical fires: live electrical equipment, household appliances, televisions, etc. [*équipements électriques sous tension, appareils ménagers, télévisions, etc.*].

Almost all extinguishers for home use are rated for all three classes of fires and accordingly are labelled "ABC". As across continental Europe, fire extinguishers are painted signal red and the ABC class for home are made to European Standard EN3 and are available in several sizes by weight of dry powder content, from 1 kg up to 9 kg. Fire protection experts recommend that a kitchen also be fitted with a fire blanket in a wall-mount case [*couverture anti-feu à fixer au mur*], from which the flame-retardant blanket can be quickly pulled out to cover a cooker or oven fire.

Perhaps the best sources of information on home fire protection are the ProtectionIncendie online shop at *www.protectionincendie.com* as well as its parent company, Comodo, a leading maker of home security, personal alarms and other alarm systems, 7125 route de l'Aveyron, 82000 Montauban, Tel: 05 63313040, *www.comodoalarm.com*, click on *Alarme Incendie* on the opening page.

Furniture [*Meubles*]

Furniture is mostly of two sorts, period [*style*] and contemporary [*contemporains*], and furniture shops are designated accordingly in the Yellow Pages. Period furniture is so named because its styles are those of periods of the past, in chronological order including Medieval, Renaissance, Henry II, Louis XIII, Louis XIV, Regency, Louis XV, Transition, Louis XVI, Directoire, Empire, Restoration, Louis-Philippe, Napoléon III, Art nouveau and Art deco. Contemporary furniture now is mostly flat-pack, as sold by **Home furnishing shops** (Chapter 40), such as IKEA, But and Fly, and increasingly by **DIY shops** (Chapter 40). **Second-hand shops** (Chapter 40), listed in the Yellow Pages under *Dépôt-vente*, usually with the specification *meubles*, often offer nearly-new furniture at reasonable prices.

Hardware [*Quincaillerie*]

There are some 3300 hardware shops in the country, 60% of them larger **DIY shops** (Chapter 40)*. But the traditional hardware shop remains, listed under *Quincaillerie, détail* in the Yellow Pages. In addition to offering selections of hardware, tools and household goods, these shops often offer special services, such as rapid key cutting [*service clés minute*], lock repairs [*dépannage en serrurerie*], replacement of floor tiles [*remplacement de carreaux*] and after-sales service [*service après-vente (SAV)*].

* *Source: QUID 2006.*

Heating [*Chauffage*]

Today, of all homes, one in three is heated by electricity, nearly as many by gas, and only one in six by oil*. Electric heating is mostly by wall-mounted convection panels [*convecteurs*] or radiators [*radiateurs*] or by ceiling or high-wall mount radiant heaters [*rayonnants*]. Gas is mostly used in central heating [*chauffage central*]. Water is heated by gas or electricity, in a larger tank unit [*chauffe-eau*], 75-200 litres, that provides hot water for the entire house, or in tankless instantaneous heaters [*chaudières*] that provide hot water where it is used, as in a kitchen or bath, at rates up to 20 litres/minute. The nine companies of the Atlantic Group together dominate the home heating sector; for further information, contact Groupe Atlantic, 44 boulevard des Etats-Unis, BP 65, 85002 La Roche Sur Yon, Tel: 02 51443434, *www.groupe-atlantic.com*. Heating goods and services suppliers and shops are listed under *Chauffage* in the Yellow Pages; **DIY shops** (Chapter 40) sell selections of electric heaters.

Source: Science &, Les économies d'énergie, Oct. 2004.

Housecleaning [*Ménage*]

Housecleaning is done as it is across Europe, using a vacuum cleaner [*aspirateur*], brooms [*balais*], dusters [*chiffons à poussière*], sponges [*éponges*] and squeegees [*raclettes*]. Dry and wet mop systems are popular, particularly for use on tiled floors. Supermarkets and hypermarkets offer proprietary house brands and some international brands, of which Vileda is the most popular; for information, contact Vileda, rue du Fosse Blanc – Batiment A3, 92238 Gennevilliers, Tedl: 01 41322232, *www.vileda.com* in many languages; select France on the opening page to enter the French website.

Interior decoration [*Décoration*]

Since the *marchand-merciers* decorated the homes of the wealthy of 18th century Paris, interior decoration has been an essential element of the well-appointed home. Today in France, there are more than 10,000 independent interior decorators [*décorateurs*], most offering a range of services, including painting [*peinture*] and many also involved in general building work [*entreprise générale*]. Interior decorators are listed under *Décorateurs* in the Yellow Pages as well as in online listings, such as *www.decorateurs.enligne-fr.com* with a dialogue window for finding *décorateurs* by postcode. **DIY shops** (Chapter 40) offer selections of *décoration* products for the DIY enthusiast [*bricoleur, bricoleuse*], and at least one company, Initiatives Décoration, specialises in them and provides guides to their use, including a DVD sold by DIY shops; head office at 20 avenue André Dulin, BP 30027, 17301 Rochefort Cedex, Tel: 05 46888800, *www.initiativesdecoration.com* selectable in French, English, Spanish or Italian.

Laundry [*Laverie*]

Most laundry is done at home, using a washing machine [*machine à laver*] and often a dryer [*séchoir*]. Accordingly, supermarkets offer ample selections of washing powders [*lessive*] and liquids and fabric softeners [*assouplissant*]. Travellers or people who have no machines at home often use coin-operated laundries [*laveries automatique*], which can be found in cities and in towns that welcome people on holiday. Commercial laundries [*blanchisseries*] sometimes offer other services, including ironing [*repassage*]. In the Yellow Pages, laundries and self-service laundries are listed under *laveries, blanchisseries en libre-service*. Dry-cleaners [*teinturerie*], now most often called *Pressings* because they both clean and press clothing, are listed in the Yellow Pages under that term.

Light bulbs [*Lumière*]

The commonplace light bulbs include general lighting service (GLS) incandescent light bulbs [*lampes à incandescence classique*], tubular fluorescent lamps [*tubes fluorescent*], compact fluorescent lamps [*tubes fluorescent compactes*] and tungsten-halogen lamps [*lamps à incandescence aux halogènes*]. Most are made for 230 V fixtures, whilst the tungsten-halogen lamps are made for 12 V as well as 230 V fixtures.

GLS light bulbs are by far the most commonly used and are made with two sizes of standard "Edison screw" bases, the 14 mm diameter E14 and the 27 mm diameter E27, and the 22 mm diameter B22 bayonet base. Some soft light fixtures use long incandescent tubes, such as those in bathrooms [*tube salle de bain*], with 7 mm diameter S19 contacts on either end.

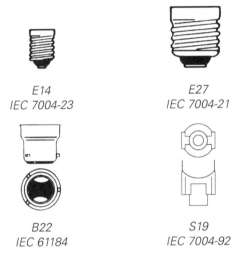

E14
IEC 7004-23

E27
IEC 7004-21

B22
IEC 61184

S19
IEC 7004-92

Light bulb contacts.

There are four leading varieties: standard [*standard*] and globe [*globe*] with an E27 base or B22 base, and candle [*flamme*] and round-bulb [*sphérique*] with an E14 base, all with either frosted [*blanc*] or clear [*claire*] glass. Compact fluorescent lamps are also fitted with E27, E14 or B22 bases. Tubular fluorescent lamps and tungsten-halogen lamps have pin contacts that plug into their respective standard fixtures. Bulbs are sold in supermarkets and food shops, as well as in lighting shops and **DIY shops** (Chapter 40), in small cartons and blister packs, usually with one or two bulbs. Packaging labelling varies, but usually includes the light bulb type along with voltage (230 V or 12 V), strength in Watts, glass type (frosted or clear) and base type, and specification of the socket which the bulb fits. All light bulbs of current manufacture also have **CE Marking** (Chapter 30). Most brands marketed internationally in Europe are widely available.

Light switches [*Interrupteurs*]

Light switches are similar to those fitted across Europe. Lights that might inadvertently be left on when not needed often are fitted with automatic turn-off. Switches for lights in hallways and stairways in apartment blocks often are fitted with auto turn-off after two to four minutes, and the switches have small red LED lamps so you can find them in the dark. Like street lighting, outdoor lighting on buildings usually is controlled by photocells arranged to turn on at dusk and turn off at dawn.

Mailboxes [*Boîtes aux lettres*]

Most mailboxes are metal, usually galvanised steel, with a hinged access door fitted with a cylinder lock and a flap closer over the letter slot, and powder coated in green, black, white, brown, ivory or grey. Dimensions are not standardised, but range from 27 to 32 cm height, 30 to 40 cm width and 8 to 40 cm depth. There are various fixings, including wall mount, post attachment and flush in wall. There are individual models [*individuelles*] as well as multi-box bays [*collectives*] as used for blocks of flats. **DIY shops** (Chapter 40) usually offer selections of brands, models and colours. The two leading manufacturers are Decayeux, 24 rue Jules Guesde, BP 27, 80210 Feuquières-en-Vimeu, Tel: 03 22253481. *www.decayeux.com* in French with a link to the subsidiary DAD UK website, and Renz, rue des Forgerons, 57915 Woustviller, Tel: 03 87989800, *www.boitesalettres.com*.

Municipal charges [*Charges municipales*]

Municipal charges, as for rubbish collection [*ramassage d'ordures*], street sweeping [*balayage*] and other local services, are paid by **Direct local taxes** (Chapter 43).

Paint and varnish [*Peinture et vernis*]

France is a major producer of paints and varnishes, with an annual production of about 1.1 million tons a year*. Four leading brands of household paints and varnishes, as sold in **DIY shops** (Chapter 40) are:

- Dulux Valentine, interior and exterior paints, customer service [*service conseil*] at 92607 Asnières Cedex, Tel: 01 46883232, *www.duluxvalentine.com*.

- Ripolin, interior and exterior paints, head office at BP 43, 80110 Moreuil, Tel: 03 22353889, *www.ripolin.tm.fr*

- Servais, finishing, protection and decoration products for wood, furniture and fittings, head office at 407 rue St Gabriel. Z.I. d'Amilly, 45200 Montargis, Tel: 02 38950404, *www.servais-sa.fr* in French and English.

- V33, paints and anti-rust treatments for outdoor metalwork and furniture, head office at BP 1, 39210 Domblans, Tel: 03 84350000, *www.v33.com*.

For a more complete listing of paint and varnish manufacturers, contact *Office des Prix du Bâtiment,* 14 rue de l'Aire, 34070 Montpellier, Tel: 08 99707034, *www.batitel.com.*

* *Source" QUID 2006.*

Rentals of white and brown goods
[*Location appareils ménager et télévision*]

Kitchen appliances as well as televisions, radios, audio systems and the like can be rented from companies listed in the Yellow Pages under *Locations.* Moreover, there are websites dedicated to rentals; one, *Loca-club* at *www.loca-club.com* indexes links to rental shops across the country.

Sewing and alterations [*Couture et retouches*]

The tradition of sewing is strong; indeed, the original meaning of *couture,* a synonym for fashion, is needlework, a sense in which it still is used. Many related terms in English have French origins, most notably crochet and embroidery. Even the smallest of towns have shops offering sewing, alterations and related services. A vocabulary useful for finding the shops in the Yellow Pages:

bonneterie	hosiery shop
broderie	embroidery
confection	clothing
confection sur mesures	bespoke clothing
couture	needlework
crochet	crochet
repassage	ironing
mercerie	haberdasher's shop
retouches	alterations
tricot	knitting

Sizes [*Tailles*]

Most furnishings are now made in sizes based on modules, so that items of different manufacture will work together. For instance, **beds and bedding** are in standard sizes, so mattresses will fit frames, sheets will fit mattresses, pillowcases will fit pillows, and so on. Likewise, other furnishings that must work together are of standard dimensions. Kitchen counters are 60 cm deep and 85 cm above the floor, and the cabinets under them are fitted with 14 cm long adjustable legs for fine regulation of height. Most kitchen appliances, such as cookers, dishwashers and refrigerators, are 60 cm deep and 60 cm wide, and half-width models are 60 cm deep and 30 cm wide. Doorframes are 194 cm, 204 cm or 214 cm high by 63 cm, 73 cm, 83 cm or

103 cm wide. Window frames are sized in a similar matrix of multiples of 10 cm, but vary widely, according to the age of the building and its exterior architecture.

Smoke alarms [*Détecteurs de fumées*]

Smoke detectors for home use are stand-alone units that upon detecting smoke sound alarms, so in full they are known as *détecteurs autonomes avertisseurs de fumées (DAAF)*, usually shortened to *détecteurs de fumées*. They are of two types:

- ionisation alarms [*détecteurs ionique*] are the cheapest and most readily available. They are best at detecting flaming fires that burn fiercely, such as when oil ignites on a kitchen cooker. They can be triggered by air contaminants other than smoke, so they can go off accidentally, as when you are cooking.

- optical alarms [*détecteurs optiques*] are more expensive and better at detecting slow-burning fires, such as overheated electrical wiring and smouldering foam-filled furniture. They are less likely to go off accidentally and consequently are best for smaller homes on one level.

Both flaming fires and slow-burning fires start in homes, so it's best to have at least one of each type of alarm. If it's impractical to have two alarms, as in a small studio apartment, it's safer to have one alarm than none at all. If your home has gas heating or a gas cooker, it's also wise to fit a combustible gas alarm [*détecteur de gaz*] or a carbon monoxide alarm [*détecteur de monoxide de carbone*].

These alarms are easy to install and are sold by **DIY shops** (Chapter 40) and by shops selling **white goods** (Chapter 14) as well as by online shops; one online shop, *www.protectionincendie.com* specialises in smoke alarms and fire extinguishers and the like. From 1 May 2006 on, standards for DAAF alarms are harmonised across Europe. The relevant French standard is NF EN 14606, and conformance to it usually is indicated by a **CNMIS** label attached to a smoke alarm or its packaging.

Each year in France there are about 250,000 fires in homes in which some 10,000 people are injured and 800 die. According to safety experts, that high rate reflects the rarity of smoke alarms. Arguably because they are not required by law or fire regulations, smoke alarms are fitted in only 1% of homes, compared to 48% in the UK, 85% in the USA and 97% in Norway, countries that have mandatory smoke alarm laws and regulations and thereby lowered their fire accident rates. Consequently, in October 2005, **CEPR** (Chapter 33) supported a private bill proposal to the *Assemblée nationale* calling for mandatory smoke alarm legislation*. The proposal was accepted, and the new law most likely will take effect within five years of its first official publication, that is, by 2011. Until then, even though legally not required, fitting a smoke alarm is wise, as statistics show that it halves the risk of death in a home fire.

* Facts and figures quoted from Parliamentary proceedings: *Assemblée nationale, compte rendu intégral, Première séance de jeudi 13 octobre 2005, Détecteurs de Fumée.*

Toilets [*Toilettes*]

As common in western countries, most homes as well as public toilet facilities have flush toilets with seats, of various designs, including the traditional bowl with a rear cistern [*WC à réservoir attenant*] and wall-mount bowls [*cuvettes suspendues*]. However, some homes and public facilities, particularly those in rural areas and along motorways, have squat toilets, called "Turkish basins" [*toilettes turques*] as the design is believed to have originated in Turkey. The basic toilet consists of a ceramic or stainless steel inlay in the floor near a wall or in a stall, with raised footrests on which the user squats above a bowl depression, facing the door of the stall, and flushing is by a water jet. Many users prefer squat toilets, and operators of public facilities often favour them, as they are easier to clean and less subject to vandalism than toilets with seats. So, several makers of sanitaryware offer squat toilets, including Porcher, *www.porcher.com*, Blinox, *www.blinox.fr* and Sanitec, *www.sanitec.fr*.

Ceramic squat toilet; Porcher catalogue photo.

Tradespeople [*Ouvriers*]

The principal trades that you may encounter in keeping house or owning a property are briefly described in Chapter 45. Whenever you hire labour, you should verify that the persons or their company are properly registered. Do this by looking for the 14-digit SIRET or nine-digit SIREN number in company advertising or other papers or by consulting the **SIRENE database** (Chapter 38), in which all properly registered tradespeople are listed with their numbers. Hiring only properly registered tradesmen ensures that you don't employ those on the black economy and provides you with a means of recourse should you wish to lodge complaint about work done.

Waste [*Déchets*]

Each year, the average resident discards about 540 kg of waste*. So source sorting [*tri des déchets à la source*] and recycling [*recyclage*] now are commonplace, in part to reduce the amount of waste dumped in landfills [*enfouissement*]. Typically, a municipality will set out pairs of waste bins, one for ordinary rubbish [*poubelle* *traditionnelle*] and one of another colour for recyclable materials including plastic bottles [*bouteilles en plastique*], paperboard cartons [*briques cartonnées*], metal containers [*boîtes métalliques*], cardboard boxes, and newspapers and magazines [*cartonnettes, journaux, magazines*], each labelled with its weekday of collection. Elsewhere in town there will be special containers for glass [*conteneur spécial verre*]. Other waste can be taken to the nearest waste collection centre [*déchetterie*], usually listed under *Déchets des ménages* in the Yellow Pages. You may need to get a card from the *Mairie* permitting you to access the local *déchetterie*.

* Source: Valmag.

Waste water [*Eaux usées*]

Almost all cities, towns and villages have sewerage consisting of main sewers, also called mains drainage, which are larger-diameter sewers into which building sewers drain. These systems are in service in 60% of the country's municipalities that together serve 93% of the population of the country. Some 80% of the sewerage systems, which serve 89% of the population, connect to treatment plants [*stations d'épuration*], some of which are gigantic: the station at Achères northeast of Paris is the world's second largest, treating more than two million cubic metres of sewage a day*.

The remaining mostly rural 7% of the population have various smaller, often individual sewage systems, principally of two types:

- septic tank [*fosse septique*]: a tank, embedded in earth, into which sewage drains and is allowed to decompose. Water discharges from the tank to a drainage field, but sludge from settled solids remain in the tank.

- septic treatment system [*fosse toutes eaux*]: a small sewage treatment system similar to but more advanced than a septic tank. In it, sewage flows are subjected to bacterial treatment in the tank and in a following tile bed or tank, so their action produces foam that blocks oxygen and enhances anaerobic processes in the tank.

Both systems require maintenance and emptying of accumulated sludge at least once a year, as provided by specialists listed under *Fosses septiques et accessoires* in the Yellow Pages. Starting 31 December 2005, all such facilities not connected to municipal sewage systems are subject to periodic inspection by a municipal or inter-communal authority, *Service public de l'assainissement non collectif (SPANC)*.

* Source of figures: QUID 2006.

Water softeners [*Adoucisseurs*]

All freshwater contains minerals, principally calcium. Though the water is safe to drink, if the calcium content is sufficiently high, the water is said to be "hard", a term coined in the early 18th century to designate water that made the skin rough, as opposed to "soft" water that made the skin smooth. Hard water has two principal drawbacks. Firstly, it reacts with soaps and detergents, which both degrades their cleaning abilities and leaves precipitates, from spotting on dishes and glassware to the familiar bathtub ring. Secondly, the calcium precipitates as a solid that adheres to and with time clogs the surfaces of pipes and water heaters, degrading efficiency and shortening the life of hot water heaters, dishwashers and washing machines. These drawbacks can be overcome by installing a water softener, which is a device that uses an electrochemical reaction to soften water.

The level of hardness of the water determines whether a water softener is useful. In France, the level of hardness is expressed as *titre hydrotimétrique (TH)*, which is measured in degrees, written °F, not to be confused with degrees Fahrenheit. One °F is equal to 10 milligrams of calcium carbonate per litre of water, which numerically is equal to ten parts per million (ppm). Relative hardness is ranked by °F:

- 0°-10°F   very soft [*très douce*]
- 10°-20°F   soft [*douce*]
- 20°-30°F   moderately hard [*moyennement dure*]
- 30°-40°F   hard [*dure*]
- over 40°F   very hard [*très dure*]

Across the country, the water ranges from very soft in the far western *Départements* on the Atlantic coast to hard in the northern *Départements* south of the Belgian border. Water softeners are considered useful whenever hardness exceeds 20°-25°F, which geographically is the case for the greater part of the land area of the country. You may inquire at your local town hall [*Mairie*] for the exact *TH* of the water of your town. For further information on water softeners and related products as well as on the 800 shops selling them, contact the largest supplier, *Centre Pilote Eau Douce (CPED)*, 14 rue du Petit Albi, BP 38400, 95805 Cergy Pontoise Cedex, Tel: 08 10741040, *www.cped.fr*.

26
Housing

The 29.3 million dwellings in the country, more than 80% are main homes and 10% second homes; the remainder are vacant. More than half of all residents own their homes, and nearly 60% of all dwellings are detached houses. Modern conveniences, such as an inside toilet and bath, are increasingly prevalent: only 3% of all homes lack them, compared to 11% in 1984. The average family spends more than a fifth of its disposable income on housing. Housing is considered a basic right, so there are schemes to provide and support housing for people who otherwise cannot afford it. Likewise, in step with growing awareness of home safety and environmental impact, there are schemes to encourage fire safety and to support environmental efficiency and noise abatement in homes.

Advertisements [*Annonces*]

Most **Estate agents** belong to associations or groups that publish free A4-format gazettes as well as online catalogues listing the offerings of their members. The major Paris daily newspapers, particularly *Le Figaro*, publish advertisements of housing for rent and sale, as do local newspapers for the areas they serve. Two online and printed newspapers are dedicated to housing advertisements:

- Particulier à Particulier, a real estate group with a head office in Paris and 11 agencies elsewhere in the country, a weekly magazine as well as a continuously updated website; 40 rue du docteur Roux, 75724 Paris, Tel: 01 40563960, *www.pap.fr* in French, English, German, Portuguese and Spanish.
- FUSAC, the abbreviation for France USA Contacts, a biweekly free magazine for English-speaking expatriates in the greater Paris area, 26 rue Benard, 75014 Paris, Tel: 01 56535454, *www.fusac.fr* selectable in French or English.

ANAH

ANAH is the abbreviation for *Agence Nationale pour l'Amélioration de l'Habitat*, the "National Agency for Housing Improvement". Through its delegations in the *Départements*, ANAH encourages and financially supports housing improvements in three categories: energy efficiency, noise abatement and accommodation for the physically handicapped. There are four principal requirements for support: the residence must be at least 15 years old; the applicant(s) must have lived there for at least nine years; the improvement work must be done by professionals; and ANAH approval must be obtained before work starts. For further information, contact the nearest ANAH office or the head office at 8 avenue de l'Opéra, 75001 Paris, *www.anah.fr* with an online departmental office locator map.

Apartment size [*Tailles d'appartement*]

Apartment sizes are stated in total square metres of living space as well as in number of main rooms exclusive of kitchen, bath and wc. The number of main rooms is identified by the prefix letter T, originally an abbreviation of *Type*, designating an apartment, or F, a letter arbitrarily selected to differ from T, designating a house. However, today, T sometimes is used in describing houses and F in describing apartments. As an example, a 50 square-metre T2 apartment most likely will have a bedroom, an open kitchen, dining and living room, a bath and a wc.

Architects [*Architectes*]

You may hire an architect to design and supervise the completion of building work. If the net internal area [*surface hors œuvre nette (SHON)*] (one of the measures of **space** in a building) to be built is less than 170 square metres, you may design and supervise the work yourself. However, if it is 170 square metres or more, you must hire an architect for the task. That said, regardless of the area to be built, it's wise to hire an architect, who will be familiar with building practices and with attending to the paperwork involved. There are two classifications of architect:

- *Architecte diplômé*, a chartered architect who is a graduate of an approved school of architecture and therefore will use the suffix title DPLG, the abbreviation for *Diplôme par le gouvernement architecte*. A DPLG architect's office often is called a Consultancy [*Cabinet d'Etudes*].
- *Agrée en architecture*, a building professional who has architectural skills but is not a graduate of a school of architecture.

Both classifications usually are listed together in the Yellow Pages under *Architectes et agrées en architecture*. Most chartered architects are members of *Conseil National de l'Ordre des Architectes*, 9 rue Borromée 75015 Paris, Tel: 01 56586700, *www.architectes.org* ; click on *Votre Région* and then on *l'annuaire des architectes* to bring up a locator window for member architects across the country.

Building code [*Code de la construction et de l'habitation*]

All building is governed by the Building code, which in two parts sets forth the laws and general rules [*Dispositions générales*] and the specific regulations [*Partie réglementaire*]. Both are available on the official **Legal information** (Chapter 31) website at *www.legifrance.gouv.fr*. They also are available in book form, with supplementary explanations for readers not expert in codification practices. The most recent edition is the 13th, published in April 2006: *Code de la construction et de l'habitation 2006*, by Jean-Philippe Brouant (Paris, Dalloz-Sirey, 2006, 1498 pages, 14 × 20 cm hardcover, ISBN 2-2470-6659-3). Moreover, building codes across Europe are changing, in step with the Eurocodes that are bringing about harmonisation of building designs and construction practices. ICAB, a company specialising in software for civil engineering and construction, has made the Eurocodes available along with ancillary computer-aided-design (CAD) tools. For further information, contact ICAB, 2 rue Jolly, 31400 Toulouse, Tel: 05 62260606, *www.icab.fr* selectable in French or English.

Building permit [*Permis de construire*]

A building permit is an authorisation to put up a building, issued by a municipality and subject to the **building code** as well as to local regulations, such as those of an Architectural and urban heritage protection zone [*Zone de protection du patrimoine architectural et urbain (ZPPU)*]. You may apply for a building permit at the office of the mayor [*maire de la commune*], which will give notice within 15 working days via registered post.

Buying or selling a home [*Achat ou vente d'une maison*]

The details of buying and selling a home include several steps and procedures, some that are required in all transactions and some that depend on the type of property as well as by its location in the country. No brief overview in this chapter could provide the essentials of all varieties of transactions. Fortunately, two regularly-updated, authoritative guides in English do just that:

- *Make Yourself at Home in France*, published by *Chambre de Commerce Française de Grande-Bretagne*, 21 Dartmouth Street, London SW1H 9BP, Tel: +44 20 73047071, 2003 edition: 208 pages softcover, ISBN 0-9541776-4-9.

- *Buying or selling a home*, published by *Notaires de France*, the national organisation of **Notaries** (Chapter 29), available in print from Notaries or downloadable online from the organisation's website at *www.notaires.fr*.

Certificate of conformance [*Certificat de conformité*]

A certificate of conformance for a new building is issued by the municipality upon completion of construction according to the relevant **building permit** and in compliance with attachments to it.

Conveyancing [*Rédaction des actes de cession*]

Conveyancing is the branch of law concerned with the drawing of deeds and with the transference of property from one person to another. The word is a verbal substantive that comes from an archaic word in French. In English, a conveyancer is a person offering professional services in conveyancing. Today in France, only **Notaries** (Chapter 29) may offer services in conveyancing, so almost all property transactions are handled by them. In most cases, a seller or seller's agent will elect a *Notaire*, which also will be used by the buyer, but a seller and a buyer may also have different *Notaires*.

Energy efficiency and noise abatement
[*Économie d'énergie et amélioration acoustique*]

As elsewhere, much energy is wasted in homes, and many people are beset by noise from nearby airports and roads. So the Environment and Energy Management Agency, **ADEME** (Chapter 7), provides extensive information on and offers financial support for home improvements for energy efficiency and noise abatement. For further information, contact one of the ADEME *Espace Info-Energie (EIE)* offices; the ADEME website has an interactive office locator map at *www.ademe.fr*, click on *Espaces info Energie* under *Espace Particuliers* to open the map window. For the details of support, including tax breaks and **ANAH** subsidies, see *Les aides financières habitat*, ADEME's 36-page brochure on the topic, downloadable in a PDF from the website at *www.ademe.fr*, click on *Agir* under *Espace Particuliers*, then on *Aides financières* and then on *Télécharger le guide* to download the file.

Estate agents [*Agents immobilières*]

Across the country there are nearly 79,000 estate agents working in nearly 28,000 estate agencies*, most listed under *agences immobiliers* in the Yellow Pages. The estate agencies increasingly are affiliated in networks, of which the three largest are *FNAIM*, which also is a professional association with 9300 member agencies, *www.fnaim.fr*, *ORPI*, with 900 agencies, *www.orpi.com* and *Century 21* with 685 agencies, *www.century21.fr*, each with an online locator map of its agencies across the country. In addition to these networks, which have physical agencies, printed gazettes and online listings, there are many online agencies, of which the three largest are Explorimmo at *www.explorimmo.com*, ImmoStreet at *www.immostreet.com* and SeLoger at *www.seloger.com*.

Estate agents are regulated by law and carry indemnity insurance. Larger agents will have financial guarantees so they can handle financial transactions. Agent fees, which average from 5% to 10% of a selling price, might be paid by the seller, the buyer or in some cases shared by seller and buyer. So before proceeding with any transaction, make sure who is responsible for paying fees. Once an agreement has been reached for a transaction, an agent usually will send all documentation of the agreement to a *Notaire* for **conveyancing**, the formal transfer of a property from one person to another.

For further information on the rules, regulations and professional practices of estate agents, contact one of the professional associations, of which the three largest are:

- *FNAIM*, the abbreviation for *Fédération nationale de l'immobilier*, 129 rue St. Honoré, 75008 Paris, Tel: 01 44207700, *www.fnaim.fr*.

- *SNPI*, the abbreviation for *Syndicat national des professionnels immobiliers*, 26 avenue Victor Hugo, 75116 Paris, Tel: 01 53649191, *www.snpi.com* with pages in French, English, Chinese, German and Spanish.

- *UNPI*, the abbreviation for *Union de la propriété immobilière*, 11 auqi Anatole France, 75007 Paris, Tel: 01 44113242, *www.unpi.org*.

* *Source: INSEE*

Fire protection [*Protection contre l'incendie*]

In 2004, the government initiated *Campagne nationale de prévention des incendies domestiques*, a public awareness campaign aimed to help stem the alarming rate of home fires that each year injured people, claimed lives and destroyed property. One outcome of the resulting heightened awareness was the drafting of a new law that will make **smoke alarms** (Chapter 25) obligatory in homes. Another outcome was that *Groupement technique français contre l'incendie (GTFI)* and the Brussels-based European Flame Retardants Association (EFRA) pooled their knowledge bases to make information on fire protection more readily available to professionals and to the general public. As a result, GTFI now acts as a clearing house for fire protection technologies and offers a broad range of extracts, brochures and leaflets in everyday language. For further information, contact, GTFI, 10 rue du Débarcadère, 75852 Paris Cedex 17, Tel: 01 40551313, *www.gtfi.org* in French with selected pages in English.

HLM

HLM is the abbreviation for *habitation à loyer modéré*, the prevalent form of public housing. Usually an HLM is an apartment in an estate, offered to rent with an option to buy after renting for at least five years. HLMs are built and managed by public agencies, by cooperatives and by private organisations supported by State loans. Throughout the country, there are more than 2.1 million HLMs that together house 17% of the population. For further information, contact the national federation of HLM organisations, *L'union sociale pour l'habitat*, 14 rue Lord Byron, 75008 Paris, *www.union-habitat.org* with links to HLM organisations across the country.

Housing information portal
[*Portail pour information sur logement*]

The Ministry of Employment, Social Cohesion and Housing supports an Internet portal with comprehensive coverage of the rules, regulations and practices concerning housing as well as providing free downloadable publications, at *www.cohesionsociale.gouv.fr*, click on *Logement* to access the portal.

Housing support services [*Aides personnelles au logement*]

The Directorate for Town Planning and Construction [*Direction générale de l'urbanisme et de la construction*], the Ministry of Employment, Social Cohesion and Housing [*Ministère de l'emploi, de la cohésion sociale et du logement*], the National Family Allowance Fund [*Caisse national d'allocations familiales (CNAF)*] and the Farm Mutual Pension Fund [*Mutualité sociale agricole (MSA)*] together offer a variety of housing support services, now described in a single 72-page, A4 format guide entitled *Eléments de calcul des ides personnelles au logement*, published December 2005 and downloadable from the **Housing information portal** at *www.cohesionsociale.gouv.fr*.

Rooms [*Pièces*]

In an apartment or house, the number [*décompte*] of rooms [*pièces*]:

- includes the principal rooms and the kitchen if it is larger than 12 square metres as well as detached rooms occupied by the members of a household, but
- excludes ancillary rooms, such as a kitchen smaller than 12 square metres, corridors, baths, toilets, utility rooms and the like.

Space [*Surface*]

The area of a house or an apartment is measured in three ways:

- Living space [*surface habitable*]: the total area of all rooms excluding walls, partitions, halls, stairwells, openings for doors and windows, unfinished attics, basements, cellars, garages or parts of a dwelling with ceiling height less than 180 cm. The area of the living space is the figure stated in applications for loans.
- Gross floor area [*surface hors œuvre brute (SHOB)*]: the total area of all floors within the perimeter of the exterior walls, including the ground floor and all other floors, mezzanines, galleries, lofts, basements, verandas and terraces, but excluding inaccessible terraces. The SHOB is used principally in building documentation.
- Net internal area [*surface hors œuvre nette (SHON)*]: the SHOB minus areas with ceiling height less than 180 cm, boiler rooms less than 5 square metres, roofless areas of first floor and above, roof terraces and spaces for vehicle

parking. For buildings completed according to regulations effective from 1989 onwards that require additional insulation in walls, after these deductions have been made, an additional 5% is deducted to compensate for the increased wall thickness. The SHON is used in local tax assessment as well as in statutory matters, such as the requirement that an architect be responsible for building work having a SHON of 170 square metres or more.

Town planning certificate [*Certificat d'urbanisme*]

All cities, towns and villages have a town plan that among other matters sets forth the taxation of land areas and the types and configurations of buildings that may be built on available land. So, you must consult the town plan if you have land or contemplate buying land and wish to put up a building on it. This is easily accomplished by filing an application for a Town Planning Certificate [*Certificat d'urbanisme*], which is an official extract of the plan pertaining to a specific property, valid for one year from its date of issue. There are two types of certificate:

- Planning rights of the property [*droit de l'urbanisme applicable au terrain*]: information on the regulations according to planning and zoning as well as on taxes and on prior rights, as for public roads.

- Clarification concerning the property [*précision concernant la propriété*]: a reiteration of the planning rights of the property and an appraisal of the conformance of the intended building with the town plan.

You may file an application for a town planning certificate at the office of the mayor [*maire de la commune*], which will give notice within two months. Once you have a town planning certificate that says you may build on a specific piece of land, you may apply for a **building permit** and once it is granted, start building. For any contemplated building, the town planning certificate is a sensible first step, both because it's free and because it allows you time to plan work properly, without wasting effort, as might happen should you design a building that conflicts with the town plan and consequently cannot be built.

Vocabulary [*Vocabulaire*]

Notaires de France supports a comprehensive lexicon of housing and property terms, in French and in English with definitions, on its website at *www.notaires.fr*. Catalogue listings and advertisements of houses and apartments for sale or rent use abbreviations, of which the most common are:

ag. s'abst. for *agences s'abstenir*	no agencies
c.c. for *chauffage central*	central heating
centr.ville for *centre ville*	centrally located
env. for *environ*	approximately
imméd for *immédiatement*	available now

jard. for *jardin*	garden
lib. for *libre*	free from
ll for *lavage-linge*	washing machine
mais. bourg. for *maison bourgeoise*	large family house
mais. indiv. for *maison individuelle*	detached house
mais. gard. for *maison de gardien*	caretaker's house
p. for *pièce*	room(s)
park for *parking*	parking space
part. for *particulier*	private seller
prest. lux. for *prestations luxueuses*	luxuriously appointed
prox. for *à proximité de*	near
px. à déb. for *prix à débattre*	price negotiable
quart. for *quartier*	neighbourhood
rés. for *résidence*	apartment building(s)
sdb for *salle de bains*	bathroom
sde for *salle d'eau*	shower cubicle
tb for *très belle*	delightful
terr. for *terrain*	garden, plot
tt cft for *tout confort*	all modern conveniences
urgt for *urgent*	urgently

27
Human rights and consumer rights

The rights of the individual are enshrined in the motto of the *Révolution*: *Liberté, Egalité, Fraternité*. Fittingly, the European Court of Human Rights in Strasbourg is located on a street named after a French judge who was a pioneer in international human rights. Across the country, nearly 20 public and private organisations are dedicated to consumer protection and safety, and a joint French and German consumer affairs agency has become a driving force in international consumer protection.

Anti-discrimination and equality authority [*Haute Autorité de Lutte contre les Discriminations et pour l'Égalité*]

The Anti-discrimination and equality authority [*Haute Autorité de Lutte contre les Discriminations et pour l'Égalité (HALDÉ)*] is an independent authority that acts as a watchdog as well as a clearing house for all matters relevant to discrimination on the bases of age, handicap, sex, sexual orientation, origin, physical appearance, religion, political beliefs or trade union activities. Set up in December 2004 as the successor to research groups, it supports a wide range of activities to promote equality, initiate reforms and provide expertise to organisations, agencies and the public.

Organisations or persons subjected to discrimination may contact HALDÉ by post at its head office at 11 rue Saint Georges, 75009 Paris, or by telephone on its help line, 08 10005000, 09:00 – 19:00, Monday-Friday. Further information is available on the HALDÉ website at *www.halde.fr*, with links to other French and international organisations concerned with combating discrimination.

Consumer Safety Commission
[*Commission de la sécurité des consommateurs (CSC)*]

The CSC is an independent government agency tasked with ensuring consumer safety in the use of products and services. It acts by conducting inquiries into and tests of dangerous products or services, by publishing recommendations and by issuing warnings to consumers, as in TV flashes. It also offers advice to consumers faced with dangerous products or services. For further information, contact CSC, Cité Martignac, 111 rue de Grenelle, 75353 Paris 07 SP, Tel: 01 43195668, *www.securiteconso.org* in French and English.

Directorate General for Competition, Consumer Affairs and the Suppression of Fraud [*Direction générale de la concurrence de la consommation et de la répression des fraudes (DGCCRF)*]

DGCCRF is the governmental watchdog, tasked with monitoring and enforcing competition and consumer protection rules. Across the country, it has offices where consumers may obtain information, request advice or lodge formal complaints. It publishes practical brochures [*fiches pratiques*] on all matters of interest to consumers, in print and downloadable from its website. Moreover, it supports an online glossary of consumer and everyday terms [*les mots de la conso et de la vie quotidienne*]. For further information, contact DGCCRF, 59 bd Vincent-Auriol, Télédoc 071, 75703 Paris Cedex 13, Tel: 01 44871717, *www.finances.gouv.fr/DGCCRF* with an interactive regional office locator map.

Ethnic equality [*Égalité ethnique*]

Ethnic equality means that people of all ethnic backgrounds shall have equal rights in all sectors of society. It is widespread, and international as well as national organisations are dedicated to promoting it.

In France, the principal organisation is the Fund for Action and Support of Integration and for Combating Discrimination [*Fonds d'Action et de soutien pour l'intégration et la lutte contre les discriminations (FASILD)*] that liaises with other government agencies, promotes anti-discrimination and anti-racism in programmes offered by its local offices, is actively involved in integration activities and is involved in the **National centre for immigration history** (Chapter 31). For further information, contact FASILD, 209 rue de Bercy, 75585 Paris Cedex 12, Tel: 01 40027701, *www.fasid.fr* with an interactive map for locating its offices across the country. At the international level, FASILD interacts with The European Commission against Racism and Intolerance (ECRI) [*Commission européenne contre le racisme et l'intolérance*] based in Strasbourg, and the European Monitoring Centre on Racism and Xenophobia (EUMC) [*Observatoire européen des phénomènes racistes et la xénophobie*] based in Vienna.

European Consumer Centre France
[*Centre européen des consommateurs France*]

Established in 1993 upon the launching of the European single market, the European Consumer Centre France is half of the unique bi-national entity; the other half is the equivalent organisation for Germany. The two organisations share a head facility at Kehl in Germany, near Strasbourg, and work to:

* inform and advise consumers on their rights in Europe, the actions entailed in obtaining out-of-court settlements and the mediation mechanisms available.
* reach out-of-court settlements on cross-border consumer disputes.
* promote mediation and conciliation.
* raise consumer awareness and understanding on consumer issues.

For further information, contact ECC, Rehfusplatz 11, D-77694 Kehl, Germany, Tel: +49 7851991480, *www.euroinfo-kehl.com* in French, German and English.

Gender equality [*Égalité des sexes*]

Gender equality means that women and men shall have equal rights in all sectors of society. It's a widespread and recognised principle, promoted by the United Nations, the OECD and other national and international organisations. In France, many measures have furthered gender equality, most recently the Charter for Equality between Men and Women [*La charte de l'égalité – pour l'égalité des hommes et des femmes*] of 8 March 2004 and the founding in December 2004 of the **Anti-discrimination and equality authority**.

Two national agencies, each with a countrywide network of offices, are dedicated to gender equality measures:

* The regional Offices for Women's Rights and Equality [*Délégations régionale aux droits des femmes et à l'égalité (DRDFE)*] that monitor adherence to regulations, act as contacts on relevant matters and enable local measures for professional training. Head office: 10-16, rue Brancion, 75015 Paris, Tel: 01 40566000, *www.social.gouv.fr*.
* The 119 public Information Centres on Women's Rights [*Centres d'Information sur les Droits des Femmes (CIDF)*] offer direct aid and advice, under the direction of a central agency, the National Information and Documentation Centre for Women and Families [*Centre National d'Information et de Documentation des Femmes et des Familles (CNIDF)*], 7, rue de Jura, 75013 Paris; CNIDF is administrative and has no services for the public, so queries should be directed to the CIDF centres that can be located on the interactive map at *www.infofemmes.com*.

National consultative commission of human rights
[*Commission nationale consultative des droits de l'homme*]

The connection between universal human rights and lasting peace has long been recognised. In the words of jurist and judge René Cassin, "For as long as human rights are violated somewhere in the world, there will be no peace on this planet" [*Il n'y aura pas de pais sur cette planète tant que les droits de l'homme seront violés en quelque partie du monde*]. For Judge Cassin, those words were based on actions: from 1924 to 1938, he was the French delegate to the League of Nations; he was among the first to join General de Gaulle and the government-in-exile in London during the Second World War; he was one of the authors of the Universal Declaration of Human Rights, and he was a member and then the president (1965-1968) of the European Court of Human Rights. Fittingly, the Court building in Strasbourg is located on Rue René Cassin. Equally fitting, the National consultative commission of human rights [*Commission nationale consultative des droits de l'homme (CNCDH)*] now supports a broad range of human rights activities at the national and international levels, and each year commemorates Judge Cassin's pioneering activities in the award of the Médaille René Cassin for achievements in human rights. For further information on CNCDH and its activities, contact the head office at 25 rue Saint-Dominique, 75007 Paris, Tel: 01 42757713, *www.commission-droits-homme.fr*.

National consumer institute
[*Institut national de la consommation (INC)*]

The National Consumers Institute [*Institut national de la consommation (INC)*] is an information and testing centre for consumer associations and for consumers. With a head office in Paris and consumer service centres across the country, it communicates its findings via its own publications and the media in general and maintains an extensive documentation centre open to consumer groups. Its information services for consumers include:

- *Consomag*, a television programme broadcast four times a week on the France 2 and France 3 channels.
- *60 Millions de consommateurs*, a no-advertising magazine available by subscription and sold by newsagents across the country.
- the magazine website at *www.60millions-mag.com* with free downloadable information and interactive links, such as to test Internet connection speeds.

For further information, contact INC, 80 rue Lecourbe, 75732 Paris Cedex 15, Tel: 01 45662020, *www.conso.net* with an interactive consumer service centre locator map and links to 18 consumer organisations across the country.

National Federation of Consumers
[*Union fédérale des consommateurs*]

The National Federation of Consumers is a non-profit association of 172 local associations that together have more than 105,000 members. It is one of the founding members of *Bureau Européen des Unions de Consommateurs (BEUC)* based in Brussels and acts as the office for International Consumer Research and Testing (ICRT). Under the abbreviated name, "What to choose" [*Que choisir*], it publishes consumer magazines and supports online portals on consumer and environmental matters. For further information, contact the head office at 233 boulevard Voltaire, 75011 Paris, Tel: 01 43485548, *www.quechoisir.org*.

28

Language

In 1539, at his *château* at Villers-Cotterêts northeast of Paris, King Francis I issued an edict that made French the official language of the country. The edict was observed by government functionaries and the judiciary, but not as much by the citizenry. In 1804, when Napoleon became emperor, half the population spoke regional languages but neither spoke nor understood French.

The situation today differs. Save for recent immigrants, French is spoken and understood by all citizens, and regional languages are used by about a tenth of the population. Additionally, Belgium, Canada, Côte d'Ivoire, Switzerland and 47 other countries have French as an official language. French is one of two working languages of the United Nations and of the International Olympic Committee, the only international language for postal services and the main language of the African Union. Francophone, the linguistic term meaning French-speaking, has become a global concept.

In part that rests on a long-standing esteem for language and linguistics. Founded in 1635, the French Academy [*Académie française*] remains unique in the world of languages. One of the great names in linguistics is Jean-François Champollion (1790-1832), who began research in ancient Egyptian writing while still at the Lycée in Grenoble and in 1823 announced his full decipherment of hieroglyphs, a feat long believed to be nigh impossible.

Respect for language starts early. The International Phonetic Alphabet, born in 1886 at a meeting held in Paris, now is used worldwide in dictionaries, textbooks and language courses, and in France, also in primary school language books.

Abbreviations [*Abréviations*]

As in other languages, abbreviations abound in French, particularly in the terminology of government and administration and in the professional fields. The abbreviations most often seen in everyday life are listed below along with their uses.

A for *Autoroute*, Motorway, on road signs and maps.

AB for *Agriculture Biologique*, Organic Foods, on food labels.

CCP for *Compte chèque postal*, current account with La Banque Postal, part of La Poste.

D for *Route Départementale*, Deparmental Road, on road signs and maps.

E for *Route Européenne*, E-Road, on road signs and maps.

F, an arbitrarily selected letter chosen to differ from **T** in designations of number of principal rooms of a dwelling; originally applied to houses as opposed to apartments, but now also applied to apartments.

GIC for *Grand invalide civil*, Disabled Civilian, on reserved parking spaces and car stickers.

GIG for *Grand invalide de guerre* Disabled War Veteran, on reserved parking spaces and car stickers.

HR for *Heures des repas*, at mealtimes, in advertisments and notices.

HT for *Hors Taxes*, exclusive of VAT, on statements of prices.

ISO for *Organisation internationale de normalisation*, International Organisation for Standardisation, in statements of standards conformance on goods and for services.

N for *Route nationale*, National Highway, on road signs and maps.

NF for *Norme française*, French Standard, in statements of conformance to standards.

PCV for *Paiement contre verification*, reverse charge call, in notice of availability at **public payphones** (Chapter 44), in hotels and the like.

RIB for *Relevé d'identité bancaire*, Bank Account Particulars, as used in direct debiting.

RSTP for *Réponds s'il te plait*, informal form of RSVP.

RSVP for *Répondez s'il vous plait*, as used in English, a polite request for a reply.

SARL for *Société à responsabilité limitée*, Limited Company, suffixed or prefixed to names of limited companies.

SVP for *S'il vous plait*, idiom "if you please", in signs and in letters and notes.

T for *Tailles*, Size, as on clothing labels.

T for *Type*, prefix for designation of number of principal rooms in an apartment; a T3 apartment has three rooms, exclusive of kitchen, bathroom and WC.

TIP for *Titre interbancaire de paiement*, Interbank payment order, remittance slip on an invoice.

TTC for *Toutes taxes comprises*, inclusive of VAT, on statements of prices.

TVA for *Taxe sur la valeur ajoutée*, Value-Added Tax (VAT), on statements of prices.

YC or **y c.**, for *y compris*, including, in accounts, statistics and business statements.

ZA for *Zone d'activités*, Business Park, on road signs, usually after name of town or city that the Park serves.

ZAC for *Zone d'aménagement concerté*, Urban development zone, on signs and in publications.

ZPPAU for *Zone de protection du patrimoine architectural et urbain*, Architectural and urban heritage protection zone, in municipal building regulations and city plans.

Académie française

Académie française, one of the five *Académies* of **Institut de France** (Chapter 14), is a scholarly body founded in 1634 by Cardinal Richelieu. Today, it acts principally to monitor developments in the French language. Its rulings on usage, recorded in *Dictionnaire de l'Académie française*, are sometimes not taken seriously by the general public. Its 40 members, selected on the strength of their contributions to scholarship or literature, are elected for life and known therefore as *Les immortels*. For further information, contact Institut de France, Château de Chantilly, Musée Condé, BP 70243, 60631 Chantilly, Tel: 03 44626262, *www.institut-de-france.fr* in French with summary pages in English.

Alphabet [*L'alphabet*]

Like English, French uses the Latin alphabet of 26 letters. However, certain accented letters also appear in modified versions or with punctuation, principally as a guide to pronunciation. They appear on the French **Keyboard** (Chapter 27). If you have an English keyboard, you can enter the accented letters using special keystrokes:

- On PCs, enter the ANSI and/or ASCII code of an accented letter by holding down the ALT key and keying in a code on the right-hand number pad with the Num Lock toggle on.

- On Macs, use the Option key in a sequence.

See chart on the next page.

Argot [*Argot*]

Argot, originally a French word that has come into English and other languages, is the jargon or slang of a particular group. University students have developed one of the more extensive argots. Some samples:

- *argo*: preparatory classes for the *Écoles agronomiques*.

- *bica*: fourth-year student.

Accent	Letter	PC: ALT + code		Mac: Option key sequence
		ANSI code	ASCII code	
acute [l'accent aigu]	é	0233	130	Option + e, e
	É	0201	144	Option + e, Shift + e
grave [l'accent grave]	à	0224	133	Option + `, a
	À	0192		Option + `, Shift + a
	è	0232	138	Option + `, e
	È	0200		Option + `, Shift + e
	ù	0249	151	Option + `, u
	Ù	0217		Option + `, Shift + u
circumflex [l'accent circonflexe]	â	0226	131	Option + i, a
	Â	0194		Option + i, Shift + a
	ê	0234	136	Option + i, e
		0202		Option + i, Shift + e
cedilla [la cédille]	ç	0231	135	Option + c
	Ç	0199	128	Shift + Option + c
dieresis [le tréma]	ë	0235	137	Option + u, e
	Ë	0203		Option + u, Shift + e
	ï	0239	139	Option + u, i
	Ï	0207		Option + u, Shift + i

Accent key strokes.

- *bizuth*: first-year-student.

- *carré*: second-year student.

- *cube*: third-year student.

- *khâgne*: preparatory classes in the humanities for entrance to *École normal supérieure*. *Hypokhâgne* is the first-year class attended by *hypokhâgneux*, and *khâgne* is the second-year class attended by *khâgneaux*.

- *prépa*: intensive two-year post-baccalauréat course of study to prepare for competitive entrance examinations for admission to the *Grandés écoles*.

- *taupe*: preparatory classes in mathematics and the sciences for entrance to a *Grandé école*. *Hypotaupe* is the first-year class attended by *hypotaupins*, and *taupe* is the second-year class attended by *taupins*.

- *véto*: preparatory classes for the *Écoles vétérinarires*.

Common European Framework of Reference for Languages
[*Cadre européen commun de référence pour les langues*]

The Common European Framework of Reference for Languages, often abbreviated CEF, is a guideline compiled by the Council of Europe and used since 1996 to describe the proficiencies of learners of foreign languages across Europe. The CEF sets concise standards to be attained at successive stages of learning, which, when tested by examination, provide validation of language qualifications. In order of ascending capability, the first four CEF levels are:

- A1: General familiarity, able to understand and express oneself on simple topics related to everyday situations.

- A2: Ideas and feelings, able to understand and express feelings, intentions, opinions and points of view.

- B1: Written comprehension, able to understand published texts on general topics and write about them.

- B2: Oral comprehension, able to understand and take part in spoken discussion.

The complete CEF guideline may be downloaded from the Council of Europe website and is available in print in English from Cambridge University Press (published February 2001, 276 pages paperback, ISBN 0-521-00531-0). For further information on CEF, contact Language Policy Division, Council of Europe, Avenue de l'Europe, 67075 Strasbourg Cedex, Tel: 03 88412000, *www.coe.int* selectable in EU languages.

Today, most courses in French as a second language follow CEF guidelines and aim for successful passing of **French proficiency examinations**.

Francophonie

Francophonie, a word coined in 1871 by geographer Onésime Reclus (1837-1916), means the world of 56 countries where French is spoken as the official language or is the language of culture. Some 500 million people live in the 56 countries, but only 120 million of them are native French speakers. Nonetheless, the impact of *Francophonie* is considerable, not least because the global **TV5** (Chapter 44) channel is the world's second largest. For further information, contact *Organisation Internationale de la Francophonie (OIF)*, 28 rue de Bourgogne, 75007 Paris, Tel: 01 44111250, *www.francophonie.org*.

Franglais

Franglais is a corrupted version of French due either to indiscriminate use of English words and phrases in French or to intentional or unintentional mixings of English and French. Its roots are old, but it bloomed in full after the Second World War as American neologisms became commonplace. Linguists were aghast; in 1964, René

Étiemble (1909-2002), a professor of comparative languages at the Sorbonne, attacked the burgeoning pidgin mix in a book that became a best seller and still is in print: *Parlez-vous franglais?* (Paris, 1991 latest edition, Editions Flammarion, 436 page paperback, ISBN 2-070-32635-7).

French proficiency examinations
[*Examens d'évaluation de français*]

The Ministry of National Education [*Ministère de l'éducation nationale*] offers two types of French language proficiency examinations:

- *Test de connaissance du français (TCF)*: a written and oral test of language skill usually taken to assess capabilities; successful passing is signified by a certificate valid for two years.

- *Diplôme d'études de langue française (DELF)* and *Diplôme approfondi de langue française (DALF)*: formal examinations in conformance with the **Common European Framework of Reference for Languages**; successful passing is signified by an educational diploma valid for life. From 2005 on, an introductory level diploma examination, *Diplôme initial de langue française (DILF)* also has been offered.

For further information on TCF, DELF, DALF and DILF, contact **Centre International d'Etudes Pédagogiques (CIEP)** (Chapter 13), *www.ciep.fr*.

The Chamber of Commerce and Industry of Paris [*Chambre de commerce et d'industrie de Paris (CCIP)*] offers language training programmes and examinations, including:

- *Test d'évaluation de français (TEF)*, an objective measure of proficiency offered by 300 centres round the world.

- *Examens de français de la CCIP (FAP)*, a range of general examinations, including the DELF and DALF, and specific examinations for the professions, taken each year by more than 8000 applicants.

For further information, contact CCIP, 28 rue de l'Abbé-Grégorie, 75279 Paris, *www.fda.ccip.fr*.

ILO Thesaurus [*Thesaurus BIT*])

If you know a work-related term in English or Spanish and fail to find the equivalent term in French – or the other way round – the best reference to consult is the International Labour Organisation (ILO) Thesaurus, a compilation of more than 4000 terms relating to the world of work. Every term is presented in English, French, and Spanish. Many of the terms are followed by definitions or explanatory notes. Alphabetical indexes are available in the three languages and include all terms as well as many variants. The thesaurus is broken down into 19 subject categories, each of which is sub-divided. The ILO Thesaurus is online at *www.ilo.org/public/english/support/lib/thes/about.htm*, and printed editions of the indexes may be requested from the ILO Library at *inform@ilo.org*.

International Phonetic Alphabet (IPA)
[*Alphabet phonétique international*]

The International Phonetic Alphabet comprises letters and letter-like symbols to represent spoken sounds. Its roots are French: in 1886, a group of British and French language teachers met in Paris to promote the use of phonetic notation in schools to aid children in learning language. Under the leadership of French linguist Paul Édouard Passy (1859-1940), the group founded an association and named it *Dhi Fonètik Tîcerz' Asóciécon (FTA)*. In 1889, the name was changed to *L'Association Phonétique des Professeurs de Langues Vivantes (AP)*, and, in 1897 it was changed to its present form, *L'Association Phonétique Internationale (API)*, or, in English, the "International Phonetic Association (IPA)". Today, the IPA promotes scholarly study of phonetics and its applications and supports the International Phonetic Alphabet (IPA), now used worldwide. In France, the IPA is in widespread use; the first sentence in a popular first-year language book for 7 and 8 year-old children* reads:

"*Le son [ʃ] s'écrit presque toujours **ch**.*"

So, from primary school on, the IPA is part of language studies. For further information on the IPA and links to other websites offering ancillary services, including replication of symbols on PCs and Macs, visit the International Phonetic Association website at *www.arts.gla.ac.uk/IPA*. Until 2007, the Secretary of the IPA Council is Dr. Katherina Nicolaidis, Aristotle University of Thessoloniki, Thessaloniki 54124, Greece, *knicol@enl.auth.gr*. The French member of the IPA Council is Prof. Cécile Foureron, Institut de Linguistique et Phonétique Générales et Appliquées – ILGPA, Université de la Sorbonne nouvelle, 19 rue des Bernardins, 75008 Paris, *Cecile.fougeron@univ-paris3.fr*.

* *BLED, Orthographe, Grammaire, Conjugaison, 7/8 ans, CE1*, Paris, Hachette Éducation, 2003, 64 page paperback, ISBN 2-01-16-9018-8.

Language learning [*Apprentissage des langues*]

Being able to understand and communicate in more than one language is a desirable skill for anyone travelling or residing outside their home country in Europe. A recent Eurobarometer report* showed that half the citizens of the EU countries can hold a conversation in at least one language other than their mother tongue. Foreign-tongue fluency varies, from a record 99% of Luxembourgers to lows in Spain, Italy and Portugal (36% each), the UK (30%) and Hungary (29%). In France, the figure is 45%.

Reciprocal proficiencies vary. For example, 34% of the residents of France speak English, but only 14% of the residents of the UK speak French. As these figures imply, for living in France, learning the language is essential, and English speakers will most often need to learn. That said, despite much shared history of their countries of origin, French and English differ noticeably, principally because they belong to different subfamilies of the Indo-European family of languages: French is Italic, whilst English is Germanic. So for English speakers with no previous experience in Italic languages, learning French may be demanding. Even professed experts in England err; of the form masters who taught French at exclusive schools in England, Paris-born author W. Somerset Maugham (1874-1965) remarked that "since they knew the grammar as well as any Frenchman, it seemed unimportant that none of them could have got a cup of coffee in the restaurant at Boulogne unless the waiter had known a little English" (*Of Human Bondage*, Chapter 15).

Fortunately, language learning is more accessible and effective than in author Maugham's school days. For comprehensive overviews and specific details visit the Europa Server website at *www.europa.int* in 20 languages, and click on "Languages" to enter the language and language learning subsite.

* *Europeans and Languages*, Eurobarometer report 237-Wave 63.4, published September 2005.

Learning French [*Apprendre le français*]

Probably the best way to learn French is to attend a course taught by a qualified native French speaker in a programme meeting the requirements of the Ministry of Education as suited to enable learners to sit the **French proficiency examinations**. To find courses taught round the world, contact:

- *Alliance Française*, founded in 1883 and thereby the oldest organisation for teaching French as a second language, now with more than a thousand associations in 30 countries, head office at 101 bd Raspail, 75270 Paris Cedex 06, Tel: 01 42849000, *www.alliancefr.org* in French and English and with an interactive locator map of associations round the world.

- *Centres culturel français*, the cultural centres abroad, in capitals with French Embassies as well as in some cities with Consulates; many have libraries open to the public and offer courses and lectures in French language and culture; for further details, contact the French embassy in your country.

To find courses taught in France [*Français-langue-étrangère (FLE)*], contact:

- *Agence de Promotion du FLE*, a network of 43 language centres in France, head office at 17 bis avenue Professeur Grasset, 34093 Montpellier Cedex 5, *www.fle.fr* in French, English, German and Spanish.

- **EduFrance** (Chapter 14), *www.edufrance.com* selectable in 15 languages, with an interactive locator map of programmes of French studies across the country.

- Europa Pages, an online directory of native language courses in France, Germany, Spain, Ireland and the UK at *www.europa-pages.com*, an interactive course locator map of the courses in each country.

- *SOUFFLE*, an association of 19 language schools and universities across the country, head office: Espace Charlotte, 83260 La Crau, Tel: 08 70407434, *www.souffle.asso.fr* selectable in 9 languages.

Numbers [*Nombres*]

Numbers are written in the convention of continental European languages: the decimal symbol is the comma and the three-figure group separator is a space or a dot. So the figure one million, two hundred and thirty-four thousand, five hundred and sixty seven and eighty-nine hundredths is written 1 234 567,89 or 1.234.567,89.

There are disparities in the ways cardinal numbers in the 70s, 80s and 90s are spelled and spoken in France and in other French speaking countries:

No.	spelled and spoken in France and in Canada	spelled and spoken in Belgium and in parts of Switzerland, mainly Geneva *canton*	spelled and spoken in other French-speaking countries (and in other parts of Switzerland)
70	*soixante-dix*	*septante*	*septante*
71	*soixante et onze*	*septante et un*	*septante et un*
72, etc.	*soixante-douze*, etc.	*septante-deux*, etc.	*septante-deux*, etc.
80	*quatre-vingts*	*quatre-vingts*	*huitante*
81	*quatre-vingt-un*	*quatre-vingt-un*	*huitante et un*
82 etc.	*quatre-vingt-deux*, etc.	*quatre-vingt-deux*, etc.	*huitante-deux*, etc.
90	*quatre-vingt dix*	*nonante*	*nonante*
91	*quatre-vingt-onze*	*nonante et un*	*nonante et un*
92, etc.	*quatre-vingt-douze*, etc.	*nonante-deux* etc.	*nonante-deux*, etc.

Old French [*Le vieux français*]

A landmark reference on the evolution of French is *Dictionnaire de l'ancienne langue française et de tous ses dialectes du IXe au XVe siècle* compiled by Frédéric Godefroy (1826-1897) and published in Paris in ten volumes from 1891 to 1902. Aside from being essential for scholars of the medieval language, it's the principal reference for the etymologies of English words that have roots in French, a Louvre of the language. Today, there are two editions of it: a facsimile printed edition (Geneva, M. Slatkine & Fils, 1982, ISBN 2-05-100443-9) and an electronic database version published on CD-ROM (Paris, Honoré Champion Éditeur, Champion

Electronique, 2002, ISBN 2-7454-0824-6). Both are expensive, but access to them, as well as to the original edition, is made available to registered users of principal academic libraries in France, Canada and the UK, such as the Sorbonne library online access at *bibliotheque.paris4.sorbonne.fr/aiecat/signets/cat12.htm*. For further information, contact M. Slatkine & Fils, 5 rue des Chaudronniers, 1211 Genève 3, Switzerland, Tel: +41 223100476, *www.slatkine.ch* or Honoré Champion Éditeur, 3, rue Corneille, 75006 Paris, Tel: 01 46340729, *www.honorechampion.com*.

Regional languages [*Langues régionales*]

Though French is the official language, some 76 regional languages are spoken on mainland France and DOM-TOM. The principal six regional languages of the mainland are:

- Alsatian, the Germanic language of Alsace, in the northeast, on the border with Germany and Switzerland.

- Basque, the language of the people that has since prehistoric times inhabited the Basque region in the Pyrenees mountains in France and Spain. An estimated two million people live in the region and speak the language.

- Breton, the ancient Celtic language of Bretagne, related to Cornish, Gaelic, Irish and Welsh.

- Catalan, a language spoken by a quarter of the people in Spain and by people in the Pyrénées-Orientales *Département* in southwestern France.

- Corsican, the language of *La Corse*, the island off the southeast coast of the mainland.

- Occitan, the ancient language of southern France, *Langue d'Oc*, from which the *Région* of Languedoc-Roussillon takes the first part of its name. It is spoken by an estimated four million people in 32 *Départements*.

The regional languages are taught in some schools, and some parts of a Baccalauréat may be taken in Breton, Catalan or Corsican. For further information on regional languages, contact *Institut national de la langue française (INaLF)* at the Paris A delegation of the National Centre for Scientific Research [*Centre national de la recherche scientifique (CNRS)*], 27 rue Paul Bert, 94204 Ivry-sur-Seine Cedex, Tel: 01 49604040, *www.cnrs.fr*.

Register [*Registre*]

All languages have differing levels of usage: the way a matter is discussed in Parliament differs from the way the same matter is discussed in the street. In linguistics, the differing levels of usage are known as registers, each of which designates usage in degree of formality, choice of vocabulary and pronunciation, all related to the social context of a situation. In French, there are five recognised registers:

Register	Registre	Example in French	Equivalent in English
Cultivated, literary	français cultivé/ littéraire	réprimander	reprimand
Standard	français courant	attraper	tell off
Daily	français familier	enguirlander	tell off
Familiar	français populaire	enguirlander	bawl out
Vulgar	français vulgaire	engueuler	bawl out

The first three registers occur in both the written and spoken language, while the last two usually are spoken only. Most native speakers shift between the registers, depending on the social situation, as a chat at the breakfast table shouldn't sound like a university lecture.

Sousveillance

The import of English words into French – **Franglais** – may be commonplace, but nowadays there is a flow the other way. In the mid 1960s, *disco* entered English via the colloquial American contraction of *discothèque*, then a French neologism after *bibliothèque*. In the early 1970s, English took up *hypermarket*, anglicised from *hypermarché* coined in 1968 by magazine publisher Jacques Pictet (1908-1991) to describe the giant market malls then being put up in France. The most recent import is *sousveillance*, a French play on the word surveillance by extracting its first three letters as the word *sur*, meaning above, and replacing them with its antonym, *sous*, meaning below. The surveillance cameras in malls and public places watch from above, so sousveillance is watching from below. It takes place whenever the watched become the watchers, as when individuals use digital cameras, phone cameras and, now, purpose-built wireless webcam video camera pendants to record events in which they participate. And it's a burgeoning subculture, much discussed by academic groups and in blogs. As this book goes to press, the word seems headed for the mainstream and may soon appear in dictionaries. There's French precedence for that. In the 1790s, the word surveillance came into English in reports of the events of the decade following the *Révolution*.

Swearwords [*Jurons*]

As in all languages, many words voiced in anger or in confrontations are not in ordinary dictionaries, perhaps because lexicographers find them too rude to include. If you have not grown up with the swearwords of the language, you may find that sector of the vocabulary incomprehensible. Luckily, there are comprehensive dictionaries of swearwords, which, even if you never utter any of them, are a colourful guide to the meanderings of the language through the years.

In 1979, a serious dictionary of insults in French, *Dictionnaire des injures* ("Dictionary of insults"), compiled by Robert Édouard, was published by Tchou of Paris. It was a large book, appreciated mostly by language scholars. In 2004, it was reprinted in paperback in two volumes, edited by Michel Carassou: *Dictionnaire des injures* (Editions 10/18, 509 pages paperback, ISBN 2-264-03975-2) with the words, and *Traité d'injurologie* ("Treatise of injuriousness") (Editions 10/18, 333 pages paperback, ISBN 2-264-039734-4) with the thematic index and explanatory material.

Also in 2004, Presses universitaires de France, a publisher of scholarly works, released *Dictionnaire des jurons* ("Dictionary of swearwords") by Pierre Enckell (800 pages hardcover, ISBN 2-13-053933-5), an overview of swearing in France from 1600 to the present day, with 750 entries of various degrees of obscenity, and including an anthology and a bibliography.

Translation software [*Logiciel de tranduction*]

Automatic translation by computer has yet to equal translation by a capable person, but today's translation software indeed will help you understand a text in a language that you don't read well. Two French software houses offer translation software that is widely used across the country:

- *Softissimo* offers the Collins bilingual electronic dictionaries and the Reverso translation software that may be tested free at *www.reverso.net*. Head office: 33 avenue Mozart, 75016 Paris, Tel: 01 56752525, *www.softissimo.com*.

- *Systran*, with many online solutions, including those powering automatic translation on Internet sites, such as Babel Fish at *babelfish. altavista.com/translate.dyn*, as well as desktop products; head office: Paroi Nord – La Grande Arche, 1 Parvis de la Défense, 92044 Paris La Défense Cedex, Tel: 01 825801080, *www.systransoft.com*.

Translators [*Traducteurs*]

There are several thousand translators in the country, most associated with one of three associations, all of which have lists of translators and translation agencies:

- Translators' French Society [*Société française des traducteurs*] and the National Union of Professional Translators [*Syndicat national des traducteurs professionnels en France (SFT)*], 22 rue des Martyrs, 75009 Paris, Tel: 01 48784332, *www.sft.fr*.

- French Literary Translators' Association [*Association des traducteurs littéraires de France (ATLF)*], 99 rue de Vaugirard, 75006 Paris, Tel: 01 45492644, *www.atlf.fr*.

- International centre for drama translation [*Centre international de la traduction théâtrale*], Maison Antoine Vitez, 2733 av. Albert Einstein, Domaine de Grammont, 34000 Montpellier, Tel: 04 67224305, *www.maisonhantoinevitez.fr*, *contact@maisonantoinevitez.fr*.

Many translators and translation agencies offer specialised services, such as in law or medicine. Registered translators [*traducteurs agréés*] offer services approved by governmental agencies, as required in official applications.

Transliteration [*Transcription*]

The Romanised (Latin alphabet) spellings in French of words originally written in other alphabets are similar to those of English. For instance, transliteration from Chinese uses the Pinyin (from Chinese; literally "spell-sound") system adopted internationally in 1979. The Cyrillic alphabet, used in writing Russian as well as Bulgarian, Serbian, Ukrainian and other languages of the former USSR, is the most widespread non-Latin alphabet of Europe. Transliterations from the Russian are listed here. The French transliteration norm differs slightly from the International Standards Organisation (ISO9, 1996) norm for scientific works and from the British norm, as indicated in the table. As a consequence of the differences, transliterations differ: the composer Шостакович is *Chostakovitch* in French, but Shostakovich in English.

Russian letter	Transliteration ISO Scientific	British	French
А а	a	a	a
Б б	b	b	b
В в	v	v	v
Г г	g	g	g, gu
Д д	d	d	d
Е е	e	e/ye	ié
Ё ё	ë		e, yo
Ж ж	z	zh	j
З з	z	z	z
И и	i	i	i, ï
Й й	j	i	ï
К к	k	k	k
Л л	l	l	l
М м	m	m	m
Н н	n	n	n, ne
О о	o	o	o
П п	p	p	p
Р р	r	r	r
С с	s	s	ss
Т т	t	t	t
У у	u	u	ou
Ф ф	f	f	f
Х х	h	kh	kh
Ц ц	c	ts	ts
Ч ч	č	ch	tch
Ш ш	š	sh	ch
Щ щ	šč	shch	chtch
Ъ ъ	"	not transliterated	
Ы ы	y	y	y
Ь ь	'	not transliterated	
Э э	é	e	é
Ю ю	ju	yu	ïou, iou
Я я	ja	ya	ïa, ia

Russian Transliteration letter ISO Scientific British French.

Verlan

Verlan, or "backslang" in English, is a form of slang in which words are coined by reversing the order of syllables of ordinary words. For instance, the word *verlan* is formed from *l'envers* ("the other side") by reversing its syllables to *vers-l'en*, which in turn is contracted to *verlan*. In the late 1930s, *verlan* was born in the spoken slang of the *banlieues* and remained there until the 1970s and 1980s, when it surfaced in pop songs. In the 1990s, it was further popularised by rap singers and then, after the turn of the millennium, it became part of the lingo of SMS messaging on mobile phones. For definitions of contemporary *verlan*, visit the slang website at *argot.abaabaa.com*.

29
Law, lawyers and courts

The word "justice" came into English and other languages from the Old French *jostise* or *justice*, from the Latin *justitia*, meaning righteousness, uprightness or equity. In more modern times, the *Révolution* brought in 1789 the Declaration of the Rights of Man and of the Citizen that defined individual and collective rights that still have constitutional validity, and in 1804 the Napoleonic code that underpins the legal systems of France and many other countries. As a whole, the judiciary of today resembles that of other western countries. In some respects, its practices are found elsewhere, such as lawyers being principally of one of two sorts, as barristers and solicitors in the UK. However, at least in one respect, the judiciary is unique to France: it has two parallel court systems, the judicial and the administrative, each with a clearly defined remit.

Barristers [*Avocats*]

Avocats are lawyers who may plead in the courts of the country; they are comparable to **barristers** in the UK. According to the most recent Ministry of Justice figures, more than 42,600 *Avocats* practise at 181 bars [*barreaux*], more than 17,000 of them in Paris, more than 1800 in Lyon and more than 1600 in Nanterre. Most offer their services as independent consultants and are listed under *Avocats* in the Yellow Pages. For further information on the profession, contact *Conseil national des barreaux*, 22 rue de Londres, 75009 Paris, Tel: 01 53308560, *www.cnb.avocat.fr*.

Court systems [*Ordres de juridiction*]

The judiciary is divided into two parallel court systems [*ordres de juridiction*]: the judicial courts [*tribunaux judiciaires*] that deal with almost all civil and criminal cases, except when the State or a State entity is involved, and the administrative courts [*tribunaux administratifs*] that are part of the executive branch and handle administrative disputes. Each system consists of a number of courts.

The judicial system consists of 11 types of permanent court*:

- 1 Supreme court [*Cour de cassation*]

- 35 Courts of appeal [*Cours d'appel*]
- 2 Higher appellate courts [*Tribunaux supérieurs d'appel*]
- 181 County courts [*Tribunaux de grande instance*]
- 5 Courts of first instance [*Tribunaux de première instance*]
- 154 Juvenile courts [*Tribunaux pour enfants*]
- 116 Social security tribunals [*Tribunaux des affaires de sécurité sociale*]
- 476 Magistrate's courts and police courts [*Tribunaux d'instance et tribunaux de police*]
- 271 Industrial arbitration courts [*Conseils de prud'hommes*]
- 6 Labour relations tribunals [*Tribunaux du travail*]
- 185 Commercial courts [*Tribunaux de commerce*].

In each *Département*, there also is a non-permanent criminal court [*Cour d'assises*] in which the most serious crimes are tried by jury.

The administrative system consists of three types of permanent court*:

- 1 Council of State, the system's supreme court [*Conseil d'état*] that also is the legal counsel for the government.
- 8 Courts of administrative appeal [*Cours administratives d'appel*]
- 36 Civil service courts [*Tribunaux administratifs*].

For further information, contact the **Ministry of Justice** or any of the courts. Complete overviews are available online at *www.justice.gouv.fr/justorg/justorg.htm*.

* Latest figures, released October 2005 and published in the Ministry of Justice annual overview, *Les chiffres-clés de la Justice*.

Declaration of the Rights of Man and of the Citizen [*Déclaration des Droits de l'homme et du Citoyen*]

Adopted in August 1789, The Declaration of the Rights of Man and of the Citizen [*Déclaration des Droits de l'homme et du Citoyen*] is a principal document of the *Révolution* that defines individual and collective rights. Its roots go back to the *Magna Carta* of 1215, and it is based in part on the declaration of human rights in the Declaration of Independence of the United States of 4 July 1776 and on the Virginia Declaration of Rights of June 1776, which in turn was based on the English Bill of Rights of 1689.

The *Déclaration* is short, consisting of 17 brief articles. The first sentence states that "Men are born and remain free and equal in rights" [*Les hommes naissent et demeurent libres et égaux en droits*]. The principles of the *Déclaration* have constitutional validity in France and since have influenced later national and international conventions on human rights.

Great Seal of the French Republic
[*Grand sceau de la République Française*]

The title, Keeper of the Seals [*Garde des Sceaux*] refers to the Minister of Justice, who is empowered to impress the Great Seal of the Republic on the principal documents of the country. The seal was made during the First Republic by Jacques-Jean Barre (1793-1855), chief engraver of the Mint of Paris, and was finished in September 1848. Since then, it has been used to seal constitutions and constitutional amendments, most recently the constitution of the Fifth Republic in 1958 and thereafter the amendments to it.

Law [*Droit*]

As in many countries, law is divided into private law [*droit privé*] and public law [*droit public*].

- Private law includes all rules, regulations and acts relating to persons and principally comprises civil law [*droit civil*] and criminal law [*droit pénal*].
- Public law deals mostly with administration law [*droit administratif*] and constitutional law [*droit constitutionnel*].

In some cases, the distinction between private and public is unclear, so in most everyday legal situations, laws are spoken of as being civil, criminal or administrative.

For the texts of laws and regulations, some in translations to other languages see **Legifrance** (Chapter 31) website or the online legal encyclopaedia of the laws of France, Europe and countries elsewhere at *www.lexinter.net*. For interpretations and summaries of laws, contact **France Pratique** (Chapter 31) or the French law student portal at *jurisforum.free.fr*.

Legal aid [*Aide juridique*]

State-funded legal aid [*aide juridique*] is of two types:

- *Aide juridictionnelle*: partial or total State-funded legal aid for representation and litigation, provided by private lawyers reimbursed for their services.
- *Accès au droit*, literally "access to the law" provides assistance in all legal matters except litigation and in matters not involving appearance in court, as in drafting wills.

Aide juridictionnelle is available subject to a means test by one of the *Bureaux d'Aide Juridictionnelle (BAJ)* located at the *Tribunaux de grand instance*, of which there are 175 in the country. They are listed under *Administration de la justice et autorités judiciaires* in the Yellow Pages and can also be found by keying a postcode into the locator window on the Ministry of Justice website at *www.justice. gouv.fr/region/consult.php*.

Accès au droit is managed by the *Conseils Départementaux de l'Accès au Droit (CDADs)*, of which there are 42 in the country. They are listed under *Administration de la justice et autorités judiciaires* in the Yellow Pages and can also be found on the CDAD locator map at *www.justice.gouv.fr/region/mjdanten.htm*.

Across the country, there are Legal Advice Centres [*Maisons de la Justice et du Droit*] that act as points of contact for and guidance in accessing the legal system. There are 117 Centres attached to 27 Courts of Appeal. You can find the nearest Centre listed under *Administration de la justice et autorités judiciaires* in the Yellow Pages or in the Ministry of Justice online list at *www.justice.gouv.fr/ville/mjd.htm*.

Legal information [*Information légale*]

Your legal rights [*Vos droits*], the various legal procedures [*procédures*] in which you may be involved, the legal institutions [*institutions*] that may deal with them, the various entities [*acteurs*] that may be involved in legal matters and other publications [*autres*] relating to French and international law are set forth in easily-understood brochures and guides published by the **Ministry of Justice** and downloadable from the Ministry website page at *www.justice.gouv.fr/publicat/fiches1.htm*. Other information on legal matters is available from three organisations described in Chapter 31: **Legifrance** for laws and regulations online, **Forms online** for all governmental forms you might need in legal matters, and explanation of laws [*droits*] part of **France Pratique**, an information portal.

Legal professions [*Professions judiciaires*]

As in the UK and some other countries, the legal profession is divided into two principal disciplines that sometimes are confused with each other and in many instances overlap in practice.

- *Avocats* may plead in the courts of the country; they are comparable to **barristers** in the UK.

- *Avoués* mediate conflicts and may appear and speak in lower courts; they are comparable to **solicitors** in the UK. *Notaires* are solicitors who offer general legal services; they are comparable to general **notaries** in the UK.

By analogy to the medical profession, *avoués* and *notaires* are general practitioners, whilst *avocats* are specialists. *Huissiers* are a third profession, equivalent to bailiffs in the UK and usually professionally attached to the jurisdiction of a court of appeal [*Cour d'appel*].

Ministry of justice [*Ministère de la justice*]

The Ministry of justice [*Ministère de la justice*] is the judiciary of the country, and the Minister of Justice [*Ministre de la justice*] is an important member of the Cabinet [*Conseil des ministres*].

The Ministry is divided into six divisions:

- Judiciary services [*Direction des Services Judiciaires (DSJ)*]
- Civil affairs and the seal [*Direction des Affaires Civiles et du Sceau (DACS)*]
- Criminal affairs and pardons [*Direction des affaires criminelles et des grâces (DACG)*]
- Penitentiary administration [*Direction de l'Administration Pénitentiaire (DAP)*]
- General administration and facilities [*Direction de l'Administration Générale et de l'Equipement (DAGE)*
- Legal protection of juveniles [*Direction de la Protection Judiciaire de la Jeunesse (DPJJ)*]

and three services:

- Access to rights under national and local law [*Service de l'Accès au Droit et à la Justice et de la Politique de la ville (SADJPV)*]
- European and international affairs [*Service des Affaires Européennes et Internationales (SAEI)*]
- Information and communication [*Service central de l'Information et de la Communication (SCICOM)*].

In addition to its principal judicial activities, the Ministry provides a comprehensive range of publications on legal matters, in everyday language, intended for the public and available from the Law Courts [*Palais de justice*], the Departmental Councils for Access to Legal Assistance [*Conseils départemental de l'accès au droit (CDAD)*] and the Legal Advice Centres [*Maisons de justice et du droit (MJD)*] across the country, listed under *Administration de la justice et autorités judiciaires* in the Yellow Pages and catalogued in interactive locator maps on the Ministry website.

The headquarters of the Ministry are at *Hôtel de Bourvallais*, a magnificent palace in Paris that has housed it continuously for more than 250 years. Finished in the early 18th century, the palace is a landmark in the city; its history and the details of its many restorations are put forth in an illustrated, 27-page full colour brochure published by and available free from the Ministry, in print or downloadable from its website.

For further information, contact the Ministry *Service Central de l'Information et de la Communication*, 13 place Vendôme, 75042 Paris Cedex 01, Tel: 01 44776115, *www.justice.gouv.fr*.

Napoleonic code [*Code Napoléon*]

On 21 March 1804, a new French civil code [*Code civil des Français*] entered into force. As it had been drawn up at the behest of Napoléon I, in 1807 it was named *Code Napoléon*. Its principal intent was to reform the legal system in compliance with the principles of the Revolution and to provide a basis for uniform law across the country. As such, it was the first civil legal code in Europe, and it influenced the drafting of similar codes in other countries. Today, it still underpins the legal system of France as well as of many other countries.

Notaries [*Notaires*]

Notaires are solicitors who deal with everyday legal affairs, including family [*famille*], housing [*logement*], estate [*patrimoine*] and business [*entreprise*] matters. Typically, two notaries will have an office with a staff trained in attending to formalities, such as those of conveyancing, which comprises the documentation, record keeping and financial transactions entailed in buying and selling property. According to the latest figures released by *Congrès des Notaires de France*, there are more than 8000 notaries in the country. They offer services in more than 4500 practices that together have staffs totalling more than 45,600. Each year, the notaries and their staffs provide services to 20 million people, so they are the legal professionals that people in everyday life most frequently encounter. You can find them listed under *Notaires* in the Yellow Pages or by visiting the *Notaires de France* website at *www.notaires.fr* in French and English and clicking on *Rechercher un Notaire*, or "Find a *Notaire*" on the English version of the site. That brings up a dialogue window for finding a *Notaire* by name, postcode or *Département* and also offers selection according to foreign language spoken in the office: German, English, Spanish, Greek, Italian, Dutch or Portuguese. For further information on *Notaires* and their services as well as for pamphlets and brochures on various legal matters, in French and in English, visit the website or contact a notary. The head office of *Notaires de France* is at 41 Rue Liège, 75008 Paris.

Solicitors [*Avoués*]

Avoués are lawyers who represent clients in civil and commercial matters at courts of appeal [*cours d'appel*]. Accordingly, their practices usually are relevant to a particular court; for instance, the *Pages Jaunes* online Yellow Pages list nearly 80 *avoués* who offer their services at the Paris Court of Appeal. For further information on the profession, contact *Chambre nationale des avoués près les cours d'appel*, 3 Avenue de l'Opéra, 75001 Paris, Tel: 01 47031870, *www.chambre-nationale-avoues.fr*.

Vocabulary [*Vocabulaire*]

As in any language, the legal vocabulary is extensive and often difficult to understand for persons not trained in law. Fortunately, the **Ministry of Justice** publishes an excellent 81-page guide to it, *Les 200 mots clés*. As its title – "The 200 keywords" – implies, it provides clear, easily-understood explanations of the 200 most-used legal terms, with many diagrams illustrating legal procedures and the organisation of the courts. It's available in print from the Ministry and online on the Ministry website at *www.justice.gouv.fr/publicat/fiches1.htm*, click on *Autres* and then on the title to download a PDF file.

30
Measurements and standards

France is a world leader in metrology, the science of measurement, as well as in standards, which are specifications of design and performance. The *Révolution* triggered that lead. In 1793, the metre was adopted as the unit of length, defined as one ten millionth of the distance from the pole to the equator. Within two years, that definition was found to be imprecise, and a standard metre bar was made. Since then, there have been improved metre bars and a standard kilogramme, kept at the International Bureau of Weights and Measures [*Bureau International des poids et mesures (BIPM)*] at Sèvres near Paris. In 1960, an atomic standard replaced the metre bar as the international reference, but the kilogramme of 1889 remains the world standard. Today, the principal task of BIPM is to ensure worldwide uniformity of measurements and conformance to the international system of units, through a diplomatic treaty, *Convention du Mètre*, between 51 nations.

AFNOR

The principal standards organisation, founded in 1926, is *L'Association française de normalisation (AFNOR)*, 11 avenue Francis de Pressensé, 93571 Saint-Denis La laine Cedex, Tél: 01 41628000, Fax: 01 49179000, *www.afnor.fr*, with selectable pages in English. Almost all French standards may be bought online on the website; click on *Normes en ligne*. The organisation concerned with quality assurance and third-party certification, *Association française d'assurance qualité (AFAQ)*, *www.afaq.org*, now is part of the AFNOR Group and operates internationally as AFAQ-AFNOR International.

French standard mark.

CE marking [*Marquage CE*]

The EU and EEA countries have an agreement, *Conformité européenne* (European Conformity), on safety standards and performance requirements on a wide range of goods. The CE mark on sub-assemblies or finished goods is a declaration by its manufacturer that it meets all applicable standards and accordingly can be sold in EU and EEA countries. It is not equivalent to a guarantee, which must be separately stated. In France, CE marking is administered by **AFNOR**.

Century [*Siècle*]

The centennial year is counted as the last of a century, so the present 21st century began on 1st January 2001 and will end on 31st December 2100. Spoken mention of a century is by its ordinal number, and written mention uses Roman Numerals. The 20th century is spoken *le vingtième siècle* and written *le XXe siècle*.

Dates [*Dates*]

There are three ways of writing dates: French alphanumeric, French numeric and ISO numeric. The usual French alphanumeric format is DD. MMMM CCYY (DD = day numerical, MMMM = month spelled out, CCYY = century and year numerical), with the first D dropped if it is zero; 3rd August 2006 is written:

3 août 2006

Dates are also written numerically, such as 03/08/2006, with slash or dot separators.

The ISO 8601 numeric standard is used throughout the EU and EEA and is favoured in business and government. The full format is CCYY-MM-DD, so 3rd August 2006 is written:

2006-08-03

It can be shortened to YY-MM-DD:

06-08-03

The ISO recommends the full format, as it prevents misinterpretation of dates for the years 2000 to 2031.

European Committee for Standardisation [*Comité européen de normalisation (CEN)*]

CEN promotes voluntary technical standards across Europe. Goods and services complying with CEN standards may carry the blue and yellow CEN Keymark. For further information, contact CEN, 36 rue de Stassart, B-1050 Brussels, Belgium, Tel: + 32 2 5500811, Fax: + 32 2 5500819, *www.cenorm.be*, *infodesk@cenorm.be*.

Identification cards [*Cartes d'identification*]

Identification card sizes are according to the **ISO** 7810* standard that specifies card sizes and physical characteristics.

Size number	Dimensions in millimetres	Use(s)
ID-000	25 × 15, rounded corners, one bevelled	SIM cards, processed with ID-1 cards and having a relief area around perimeter to permit removal without tools
ID-1	85.60 × 53.98, corners	rounded Payment cards, driving licences (from 2007 in France)
ID-2	105 × 74, A7 paper format	Folded size of present (2006) French driving licence; personal ID cards in some countries
ID-3	125 × 88. B7 paper format	Passports and visas

* Identification cards – Physical characteristics [*Cartes d'identification – Caractéristiques physiques*], ISO/IEC 7810:2003

ISO – International Organisation for Standardisation [*Organisation international de normalisation*]

The International Organisation for Standardisation, the world's leading developer and publisher of standards, is a network of the national standards institutes of 153 countries, with one member per country; **AFNOR** is the member in France. The abbreviation of the name of the organisation might differ by language, such as IOS in English and OIN in French. So the official name is ISO, derived from the Greek word *isos*, meaning "equal". From 1947 to the present day, ISO has published more than 15,000 international standards, most pertaining to technical matters, but increasingly many having social and economic impact. For further details, contact AFNOR in France or the ISO General Secretariat, 1 rue de Varembré, Case postale 56, CH-1211 Geneva 20, Switzerland, Tel: +41 227490111, Fax: +41 227333430, *www.iso.org*, in English and in French.

ISO 9000, ISO 14000

ISO 9000 and ISO 14000 are voluntary international standards on quality and on environmental impact. Companies certified according to one or more of these ISO standards often so state in their advertisements, such as "our quality management system is certified to ISO 9001". Certified French companies are listed by AFAQ online at *www.afaq.org*.

LCIE [*LCIE*]

LCIE, the abbreviation for *Laboratoire central des industries électriques* was founded in 1882, the year after the Electricity World Fair was held in Paris. Initially, LCIE was concerned with electrical measurements and testing, and with time other services were added. In 1996, it was privatised as a limited company, and now offers a wide range of services in measurements, testing and certification, including issuing the NF mark on behalf of **AFNOR**. For further information, contact the head office at 33 avenue du Général Leclerc, 92260 Fontenay-aux-Roses, Tel: 01 40956060, *www.lcie.com*, with pages in English.

National Metrology and Test Laboratory [*Laboratoire national de métrologie et d'essais*]

Metrology, the scientific study of measurements, is centralised in *Laboratoire National de métrologie et d'essais (LNE)*, which harmonises the work of all national laboratories in measurements, testing, certification and training. For further information, contact LNE, 1 rue Gaston Boissier, 75724 Paris Cedex 15, Tel: 01 40433700, Fax 01 40433737, *www.lne.fr* with pages in English, *info@lne.fr*.

Paper [*Papier*]

Trimmed paper sizes are according to the **ISO** 216* standard that numbers sheet sizes, starting with A0 for a sheet of one square metre in area. Each successive size in the series is half the area of the preceding size and has a long side that is the same length as the short side of the preceding size. A "B series", based on a 1.414 square metre sheet (size B0) is used principally in the printing industry to provide sizes between those of the A series. The ratio of the long side to the short side of the sheets of the A and B series is always 1.414 (square root of 2). There is also a "C series" for envelopes to suit papers of the A and B series. The most common A series sizes are listed over the page.

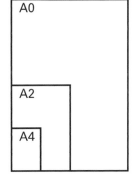

A Series paper sizes.

Size number	Dimensions in millimetres
A0	841 × 1189
A1	594 × 841
A2	420 × 594
A3	297 × 420
A4	210 × 297
A5	148 × 210
A6	105 × 148
A7	74 × 105
A8	52 × 74
A9	37 × 52
A10	26 × 37

Tabloid newspapers are about A3 size, and many magazines and ordinary letter paper are A4 size. The prevalent standard for loose leaf binders and accordingly for the holes punched in A4 sheets to be put in them ISO 838, which specifies two holes in a paper sheet, located 80 mm from each other and 12 mm in from the edge of the sheet.

* Writing paper and certain classes of printed matter – Trimmed A and B series [*Papiers d'écriture et certaines catégories d'imprimés – Formats Séries A et B*) ISO 216:1975.

Revolutionary calendar [*Le calendrier républicain*]

In October 1793, the National Convention of the French Republic instituted a calendar based on reason rather than on tradition. It started on Saturday, 22 September 1792, the day after the establishment of the Republic and the day of the autumn equinox. It became effective on Sunday, 24 November 1793 and was used until Tuesday, 31 December 1805, as Napoleonic edict replaced it with the Gregorian calendar effective 1 January 1806. The Revolutionary calendar was again used briefly, 6-23 May 1871, but not since then.

The Revolutionary Calendar divided the year into 12 months of 30 days each, followed by five days (six in leap years) not assigned to months. National Convention deputy Philippe Fabre d'Églantine (1750-1794) named the months:

1. *Vendémiaire* ("Vintage")

2. *Brummaire* ("Fog")

3. *Frimaire* ("Sleet")

4. *Nivôse* ("Snow")

5. *Pluvoiôse* ("Rain")

6. *Ventôse* ("Wind")

7. *Germinal* ("Seed")

8. *Floréal* ("Blossom")

9. *Prairial* ("Pasture")

10. *Messidor* ("Harvest")

11. *Thermidor* ("Heat")

12. *Fructidor* ("Fruit").

Each of the 12 months was divided into three decades (*decades*), with the days named by their ordinal positions in the decade:

1. *Primidi*

2. *Duodi*

3. *Tridi*

4. *Quartidi*

5. *Quintidi*

6. *Sextidi*

7. *Septidi*

8. *Octidi*

9. *Nonidi*

10. *Decadi*.

The tenth day, *Decadi*, was declared the day of rest.

The five (six in leap years) unassigned days were declared holidays (*sansculottides*) and were named for precepts of the Revolution:

1. *Jour de la Vertu* ("Virtue Day")

2. *Jour du Génie* ("Genius Day")

3. *Jour du Labour* ("Labour Day")

4. *Jour de la Raison* ("Reason Day")

5. *Jour de la Récompense* ("Reward Day")

6. *Jour de la Révolution* ("Revolution Day") in leap years.

Further details on the Revolutionary Calendar are available in many calendrical references; perhaps the most comprehensive is Chapter 15 of "Calendrical Calculations: The Millennium Edition" (Cambridge University Press, 2001, ISBN 0-521-77752-6). There are many online calculators for converting French Revolutionary to Gregorian Calendar dates; among the simplest is a table at the Genealogical website at *www.guide-genealogie.com/guide/calendrier_republicain.html*.

SI – International System of Units
[*Système international d'unités*]

As the principal initiator of the metric system in the latter half of the 19th century, France uses the International System of Units, known by its international abbreviation SI. In the system, there are seven base units: the metre, the kilogramme, the second, the ampere, the Kelvin, the mole, and the candela. From them, other units are formed by combining base units. The SI is not fixed, but continually evolves to meet ever newer needs for measurement. For overview brochures and reports or for further information on SI, contact the international bureau of weights and measures, BIPM, Pavillion de Breteuil, 92312 Sèvres Cedex, Tel: 01 45077070, Fax: 01 45342121, *www.bipm.fr*, with a complete duplicate site in English.

Temperature [*Température*]

The Celsius scale common throughout Europe is used. Named after Swedish astronomer Anders Celsius (1701–1744), its zero is the freezing point and its 100 degrees is the boiling point of distilled water at sea level. Until 1948, it also was known as the "centigrade" (meaning one-hundred degree; same word in French and English) scale.

Time of day [*Heure du jour*]

The time of day is stated in the 24-hour custom, from 01 to 24. Specific times may be written with a dot or a colon between the hour and minutes, but most often are written with the letter "h" following the hour: a sign on a shop may announce its opening hours as "9h à 19h30". But in everyday speech, the 12-hour clock is used. The equivalents of am and pm of English are *du matin* and *l'après midi*. An evening hour may be so described: "10 in the evening" is *10 heures du soir*. Telephone time announcements [*horloge parlante par téléphone*] accurate to 1/50 second are supported by The Observatory of Paris, the official timekeeper of the country, at Tel: 3669. This "speaking clock" answers some 200 thousand calls a day. A graphic online service based on it is available online at *www.horlogeparlante.com*, with pages selectable in 12 languages and time zones selectable for countries on six continents.

Time zone and summer time [*Fuseau horaire et heure d'été*]

France is in the Central European time zone, written GMT + 1, meaning one hour ahead of Greenwich Mean Time (GMT), also called UTC for Universal Coordinated Time. The EU practice for summer time is followed: clocks are advanced one hour at 02.00 hours on the last Sunday in March, and turned back one hour at 03:00 hours on the last Sunday in October.

UTAC

UTAC, an abbreviation of *L'Union technique de l'automobile, du motocycle et du cycle*, is principally a testing agency, most widely known within the country as the panoply organisation for **Periodic vehicle inspection** (Chapter 4) and as the national vehicle type and equipment approval tests in conformance with EU directives. However, it also is an international standards certification organisation and a prominent contributor of expertise to European and international bodies on vehicles and automotive equipment, particularly on their safety aspects. It has supplied testing and other services to countries abroad, including Argentina, Australia, Brazil, Canada, Saudi Arabia and the USA. For further information, contact the head facility, UTAC, BP 20212, 91311 Montihéry Cedex. Tel: 01 69801700, *www.utac.com*, *infos@utac.com*.

Weeks [*Semaines*]

The business week and the calendar week both begin on Monday and end on Sunday. In business and government and on office and school calendars, the weeks of the year are consecutively numbered, from 01 to 52 or 53, with week 01 being the one that includes the first Thursday of the year. This means that "Week 01" of the year starts with a Monday between 29 December and 4 January, and that the last week of the year ends on a Sunday between 28 December and 3 January. Though the country officially is secular, the names of Catholic Saints associated with days are indicated for all days save for national holidays.

31
Media, information and documentation

In 1982, with the launch of **Minitel** (Chapter 44), France became the first country ever to make information available to the public by electronic means. Since then, the government has expanded its electronic services to the public to a degree that in 2004 the country ranked first among large European countries in electronic government*. With digital telephone lines and broadband available across the country, France ranks sixth in the world in number of Internet hosts, yet compared to its population a comparatively lower 22nd. The figures for books are similar: seventh in the world in total sales, yet 26th in sales per capita. Nonetheless, France is a country of readers, ranking eighth in the world in time spent reading** and even in small towns, there are one or more newsagents.

That situation is due in part to having an extensive public library system and the world's fifth largest library, outdone in number of volumes kept only by libraries in more populous countries. Moreover, though merely 26th in the world** in per-capita newspaper sales, the press in France plays a central role in cultural life, revered as the fourth estate [*le quatrième pouvoir*].

According to a survey conducted by Cap Gemini Ernst & Young.

** *The Economist Pocket World in Figures 2006, pages 92, 93 and 94.*

ADELE

As its name implies, ADELE, an acronym for *Administration électronique*, makes administrative services available online to the general public, businesses and local governments at *adele.service-public.fr*. For the general public, the website offers extensive information in four categories: family [*ma famille*], work [*mon travail*], civil responsibility [*ma vie de citoyen*] and leisure [*mes loisirs*]. Its two online brochures, one on affairs of the individual [*Les services en ligne pour les particuliers*] and one on local administration [*Les services en ligne pour les collectivités locales*] comprise a succinct overview of everyday matters. Since its start in 2004, ADELE has become one of the country's most-used online services. In 2004, nearly four million taxpayers filed their tax returns online, and by 2006, more than twice as many are expected to file online.

Advertising [*Publicité*]

Advertising has long been prominent, in part because some of its techniques evolved in the innovative cultural sector. Henri Toulouse-Lautrec's 1891 poster painting for the **Moulin Rouge** (Chapter 11) is a classic, as is the 1935 poster for the *Normandie* transatlantic liner and the first posters designed to be seen by people in fast-moving vehicles, created by Cassandre, the pseudonym of Adolphe Jean Marie Mouron (1901-1968). Today, three of the world's largest advertising companies are French:

- Publicis Groupe, fourth largest in the world, with offices in 196 cities in 104 countries round the world, and a headquarters complex at 133 Avenue des Champs Elysées, 75008 Paris, Tel: 01 44437000, *www.publicis.com* in French and English.

- Havas, sixth largest in the world, with offices in 77 countries and a headquarters at 2 allée de Longchamp, 92281 Suresnes Cedex, Tel: 01 58479000, *www.havas.fr* in French and English.

- JC Decaux, the outdoor advertising specialist that is first in the world in street furniture and in airport advertising, with operations in 40 countries and a headquarters at 17 rue Soyer, 92523 Neuilly-sur-Seine Cedex, Tel: 01 30797979, *www.jcdecaux.com* in French and English.

For further information on advertising, including contacts with more than 200 advertising agencies, contact the Association of French Advertising Agencies [*Association des Agences Conseils en Communication*], 40 Boulevard Malesherbes, 75008 Paris, Tel: 01 47421342, *www.aacc.fr* in French and English.

AFP

Agence France-Presse, abbreviated AFP and not translated, is the world's oldest and today third largest news agency, behind the Associated Press and Reuters. Founded in 1832 by publisher Charles-Louis Havas (1783-1858) as *Agence Havas*, AFP today has a headquarters in Paris, five regional centres and journalists in 165 countries that together each day produce about half a million words of text, a thousand photos and 50 news graphics. For further information, contact AFP, 11-15 place de la Bourse, 75002 Paris, Tel: 01 40414646, *www.afp.com* in Arabic, English, French, German, Portuguese, Spanish and Russian.

Books [*Livres*]

In overall sales of books, France ranks seventh in the world*. Today, there are more than 270 major publishers, of which the largest, Hachette Livre, ranks fifth in the world as well as second in both Great Britain and Spain. **Bookshops** (Chapter 40) sell hardcover [*relié*], paperback [*broché*], cardboard article [*cartonné*] (paperback with a hard cover) and small, pocket-sized paperbacks [*livres de poche*], and **newsagents** sell mostly paperbacks. Increasingly, supermarkets and hypermarkets have book departments. For further information on books, contact the National Book Centre [*Centre national du livre*], Hôtel d'Avejan, 53 rue de Verneuil, 75343 Paris Cedex 07, Tel: 01 49546868, *www.centrenationaldulivre.fr*.

*The Economist Pocket World in Figures 2006, p. 92.

CDU

CDU, the abbreviation for *Centre de documentation de l'urbanisme*, "the national centre for documentation on urban planning", collects, processes, distributes and archives documentation in urban planning, development and housing. In addition to being a resource for professionals, it interacts with similar organisations and documentation centres in other countries and has a large library that is a part of the National Library [*Bibliothèque nationale de France*] and is open to the public. It supports national, and interfaces with international, online multilingual thesauruses and glossaries and consequently is the best single reference for definitions and translations of words and phrases concerning housing, towns and cities. For further information, contact CDU, Arche Sud, 92055 Défense Cedex, Tel: 01 40811178, *www.urbanisme.equipement.gouv.fr/CDU* in French with key topics in English and Spanish.

CFC

CFC, the abbreviation for *Centre français d'exploitation de droit de Copie*, is the national Reproduction Rights Organisation (RRO) that administers rights for photocopying and other secondary uses of printed and published copyrighted works. Understandably, CFC actively promotes public respect for the rights of authors, in part through language. The CFC motto is *Photocopier oui, photocopiller non*. The first word is the transitive verb, to photocopy, whilst the second is a neologism, formed from *photocopie* and *piller*, meaning to plunder or steal. The equivalent noun is *photocopillage*, used in caveats on books, usually with *tue de livre* to convey the message that illegal photocopying kills books.

Among CFC's tasks is the collection and distribution to authors of royalties accrued from the photocopying of their copyrighted works. In 2004, the last year for which figures are available as this book goes to press, CFC collected and distributed 2.4 million Euros to authors. For further information, contact CFC, 20 rue des Grands-Augustins, 75006 Paris, Tel: 01 44074770, *www.cfcopies.com*. CFC is the French member of the International Federation of Reproduction Rights Organisations

(IFRRO), rue du Prince Royal 87, B-1050 Brussels, Belgium, Tel: +32 2 5510899, *www.ifrro.org*.

CIRA

CIRA, the acronym for *Centres interministériels de renseignements administratifs*, "Inter-ministerial Centres for Administrative Information", is a telephone information service of the office of the Prime Minister. Centres across the country provide callers, who may remain anonymous, with expertise on:

- banking and insurance [*banques et assurances*].

- business and customs [*commerce et douanes*]: import, export, indirect taxes.

- civil service [*fonction publique*]: recruitment, careers, pensions.

- courts [*justice*]: civil and criminal procedure, succession, rights of the family.

- education [*enseignement*]: scholarships and aid, diplomas, exams.

- environment and agriculture [*environnement et agriculture*]: pollution, neighbourhoods, rural rights.

- healthcare and social security [*affaires sociales, santé et sécurité sociale*]: social security, health insurance, pensions, services, welfare.

- housing and urbanism [*logement et urbanisme*]: leases, co-ownership, town planning regulations.

- inland affairs [*intérieur*]: registry offices and steps, relations with officials, local authorities, rights of associations.

- tax offices [*trésor public*]: income tax, TV licence, property tax.

- work and employment [*travail et emploi*]: labour law, collective agreements, hiring and dismissal.

The **Public service portal** supports telephone access to CIRA via its *Allô Service-Public* number, 3939 (€0.12/min), Monday-Friday 08.00-19.00 and Saturday 09.00-13.00. The nine centres are located in cities across the country: Bordeaux, Tel: 05 56115656; Lille, Tel: 03 20494949; Marseille, Tel: 04 91262525; Metz, Tel: 03 87319191; Paris, Tel: 01.40011101; Rennes, Tel: 02 99870000; Lyon, Toulouse and Limoges, Tel: 08 36681626.

Comics [*Bande dessinée*]

Bande dessinée, usually abbreviated *BD*, plays a notable cultural role in the country. Though bilingual dictionaries often translate *band dessinée* to "comic strip", the BD is not simply entertainment for children and youth, but a popular literature form, that among **the arts** (Chapter 11) now is recognised as the ninth art [*neuvième art*], with its own cultural website at *www.neuvieme-art.net* and its own impact on the language: an avid follower of BDs is a *bédéphile* and a BD library is a *bédéthèque*. The BD is a graphic novel, and each year, it is celebrated at the **International Comics Festival** (Chapter 32), and Franco-Belgian comic characters have become household names across Europe and round the world. Oldest and perhaps most famous is Tintin, first published in 1930s in Brussels, the birthplace of its creator, Georges Remi (1907-1983), who wrote under the penname of Hergé. To date, Tintin has been sold in 200 million copies with translations from the original French into 38 languages and has become the subject of many books, including a history, *Tintin, le rêve et la réalité* (Paris, Moulinsart, 2001, 205 page paperback, ISBN 2-9302-8458-7). Another French BD originating in Belgium, Lucky Luke, created in 1947 by Morris, the pseudonym of Maurice de Bévère (1923-2001), went quickly from its original French into other languages round the world. Perhaps most popular today is a world bestseller, Astérix, a French BD named for its principal character, a cunning little Gallic warrior of ca. 50 BC, was created in 1959 by writer René Goscinny (1926-1977) and illustrator Albert Uderzo (1927-   ). Astérix has been translated into more than a hundred languages and dialects, including Latin and Ancient Greek, with a Dutch website dedicated to its global popularity at *www.asterix-oblelix.nl*, its own official website, *www.asterix.com* in French, English, Dutch, German and Spanish, and an amusement park near Paris, *Parc Asterix*, *www.parcasterix.fr*. BDs have become collectors' items, sold by second-hand book shops and websites, such as *www.bdtheque.com*.

A Tintin history and a best-selling Astérix book.

Documentation française

The Government Documentation Centre [*Documentation française*], part of the office of the Prime Minister, is the principal clearing house for all printed and online information on the government and civil service. Head office: 29-31 quai Voltaire, 75344 Paris Cedex 07, Tel: 01 40157000, *www.ladocumentationfrancaise.fr*. Its principal online services for the public are the **Public service portal** and the *Vie Publique* portal that supports access to public record databases, including documentation of policies, public speeches, selected themes, chronologies of the past 30 years, libraries of public reports and current events, *www.viepublique.fr*.

Encyclopaedias [*Encyclopédies*]

The benchmark encyclopaedia is *Larousse*, published almost continuously since a publishing house by that name was founded in Paris by Pierre Larousse (1817-1875). Today, Larousse publishes a variety of single-volume printed encyclopaedias under the *Petit Larousse* title as well as comprehensive electronic CD/DVD disk encyclopaedias that have replaced the former multi-volume printed editions. Further details at *www.larousse.fr*.

The single-volume *Quid* (Chapter 47), an annual encyclopaedia and reference launched in 1963 by Dominique and Michèle Frémy, has become a best-seller, with an annual sales of more than 400,000 copies. It is available in print and online by subscription at *www.quid.fr*.

The online *Wikipedia*, an open, free, multilingual encyclopaedia launched on the Internet in 2003, has a selectable French version with some 200.000 articles. Visit *www.wikipedia.org* and select *Français* on the opening page.

Europa server [*Europa serveur*]

The European Union (EU) and its Institutions have extensive presence on the Internet, accessible via a central portal, the Europa Server of the European Commission (EC) at *www.europa.eu* in 20 languages selectable on the opening page.

European Union publications
[*Publications des communautés européennes*]

Abundant information published by the European Union is available on the Internet at *europa.eu.int* and even more is available as conventional publications on paper, catalogued, stocked and sold in France by *Journal officiel*, 26 rue Desaix, 75727 Paris Cedex 15, Tel: 01 40587979, click on *Publications de l'Union européenne* on the opening page of *www.Journal-officiel.gouv.fr*, *info@journal-officiel.gouv.fr*.

Foreign trade advisors
[*Conseillers du commerce extérieur (CCE)*]

Starting in 1898, a network of private sector executives has shared the expertise of its members in advising public and private sector organisations on international trade. These *Conseillers du Commerce Extérieur (CCEs)* are appointed by the Prime Minister for three years and now number some 3600, of which 1600 are in offices across France and 2000 are in offices around the world. The CCEs provide information on international markets and advise small- and medium-sized companies in international trade. For further information, contact the National Committee of French Foreign Trade Advisors [*Comité National Conseillers du*

Commerce Extérieur de la France (CNCCEF)], 22 avenue Franklin Roosevelt, BP 303, 75365 Paris Cedex 08, Tel: 01 53839292, *www.cnccef.org*, *cnccef@cnccef.org*.

Forms online [*Formulaires en ligne*]

Most governmental forms that you may need to fill in have been made available online by the Centre for recording and revision of administrative forms [*Centre d'enregistrement et de révision des formulaires administratifs (CERFA)*]. Forms used in private life [*pour particuliers*] and in professional matters (*pour professionnels*) that are identified by a CERFA number may be downloaded from the official website at *www.service-public.fr/formulaires*. The *Ministère des Transports, de l'Équipement, du Tourisme et de la Mer* has made more than 150 forms in its principal fields of responsibility – lodgings and residences, town planning, nautical affairs, tourism and transport, including the applications for driving licences and vehicle registration documents – available online at *www2.equipement.gouv.fr/formulaires*.

France pratique

France pratique is an information portal on law [*droits*], money matters [*argent*], education [*education*] and health and well-being [*forme/sante*] at *www.pratique.fr*. It offers free access to online texts written for the general public and to online ordering of books and periodicals published by Editions Prat in these fields. It is a division of the French part of Reed Business Information, a business sector of the multinational Reed Elsevier Group PLC, a professional communications and publishing company. The headquarters of the French company are at 2 rue Maurice Hartmann, BP 62, 92133 Issy-Les-Moulineaux Cedex, Tel: 01 46294629, *www.reedbusiness.fr*.

Freedom of the press [*Liberté de la presse*]

In the annual Worldwide Press Freedom Index compiled by **Reporters Without Borders** (Chapter 33) and published in October each year, France ranks relatively low compared to many other European countries, in 30th place out of the 167 countries listed in 2005. The slip, from 19th place in 2004, is largely due to searches of media offices, interrogation of journalists and the designation of new press offences. For further information, visit the RSF website at *www.rsf.org*.

French Publishers' Association
[*Syndicat national de l'édition (SNE)*]

SNE is the national book publishing trade association that represents more than 400 publishers and other book enterprises. It represents the French publishing sector as a member of both the Federation of European Publishers (FEP) and the International Publishers Association (IPA). It supports numerous book shows and fairs, including the annual **Book fair, Paris** (Chapter 11) and the May Art Book Festival [*Mai du livre d'art*]. For further information, contact SNE, 115 bd Saint Germain, 75006 Paris, Tel: 01 44414050, *www.sne.fr* in French with selected pages in English.

Government Information Service
[*Service d'information du gouvernement*]

The Government Information Service is a department of the Prime Ministry, 19 rue de Constantine, 75007 Paris, Tel: 01 42758000, *www.premier-ministre.gouv.fr*, with pages in French, English and German. It provides information at the top levels of government and administration.

ISBN

The International Standard Book Number (ISBN) identifies all published books and usually appears on the back cover along with a bar code. For books published by 31 December 2006, the ISBN consists of ten digits, of which the first comprise the group identifier, which designates a country, a region or an area comprising many countries or regions in which a language is spoken. The English Area has Group Identifier 0 or 1. The French Area – France, Luxembourg and the French-speaking regions of Belgium, Canada and Switzerland – has Group Identifier 2. For books published from 1 January 2007 on, the ISBN consists of 13 digits, of which the first three are the 978 bar code for books, so the first five digits of books published in France 978-2. Books published in 2005 and 2006 that may remain in print after 1 January 2007 may have both the older ten-digit and newer 13-digit ISBNs. For further details, visit the International ISBN Agency website at *www.isbn-international.org/index.html* with pages in English, French and Spanish.

ITU Standard Phonetic Alphabet
[*Alphabet phonétique ITU normalisé*]

The ITU Standard Phonetic Alphabet comprises code words for letters that have long been used in voice communications by telephone and radio and now are standardised by the International Telecommunications Union (ITU). The code words are pronounced nearly alike in English, French and many other languages, and consequently are used round the world. Typically, a speaker will spell a word, such as an unfamiliar surname, using the code words, to ensure comprehension by the listener.

A	Alfa	H	Hotel	O	Oscar	V	Victor
B	Bravo	I	India	P	Papa	W	Whiskey
C	Charlie	J	Juliet	Q	Quebec	X	X-Ray
D	Delta	K	Kilo	R	Romeo	Y	Yankee
E	Echo	L	Lima	S	Sierra	Z	Zulu
F	Foxtrot	M	Mike	T	Tango		
G	Golf	N	November	U	Uniform		

In the name of the Alphabet, the word "phonetic" is used in the sense of "articulatory", as it means giving voice to symbols that customarily are written. The customary sense, as in the **International Phonetic Alphabet** (Chapter 28), is the converse: "phonetic" means the use of symbols to represent spoken sounds.

Label France

Label France is a quarterly, full-colour news magazine distributed by the Diplomatic Service to foreign opinion-shapers round the world, in ten language versions: French, Arabic, Chinese, English, German, Italian, Japanese, Portuguese, Russian and Spanish, with an average press run of 150,000 copies. The typical issue has 50 pages and features articles as well as regular sections, written by freelance writers and extracted from leading French news publications. In addition to the printed version, it is available online with a searchable database of more than a thousand articles and a thousand photographs. Contact: Direction de la Communication et de l'Information (DCI), 37 quai d'Orsay, 75007 Paris, Tel: 01 43175238, *www.diplomatie.gouv.fr/label_france*.

Legal information [*Legifrance*]

Legifrance is the official website that publishes legislation, codes, rules, regulations and other legal information. It has links to Celex, the legal information system of the European Union that is an online repository and search facility for legal documentation across the EU. Legifrance supports searches of all French legislation by topic and by theme, and provides access to translations of key codes and acts into English, German and French. It is maintained by the Government's General Secretariat [*Secrétariat général du gouvernement (SGG)*] under the office of the Prime Minister. For further information, contact SGG, 57 rue de Varenne, 75700 Paris, Tel: 01 42758000, *www.legifrance.gouv.fr*.

Libraries [*Bibliothèques*]

There are an estimated 4000 public and private libraries in the country. The giant among them is the French National Library [*Bibliothèque national de France (BNF)*], which in number of volumes kept, more than 13 million, ranks fifth in the world, along with the Library at Novossibirisk and the Harvard Library in the USA*. It has several facilities and many physical and online services, including databases of books, periodicals, manuscripts and other documents kept in libraries across the country. For further information, contact the main BNF at quai François-Mauriac, 75013 Paris, Tel: 01 53795959, *www.bnf.fr*. Second largest is Public Reference Library [*Bibliothèque publique d'information (BPI)*] at the Pompidou Centre in Paris, with 14 km of book shelves, 2200 seats and 400 computer terminals, contact BPI, 75197 Pasris Cedex 04, Tel: 01 44781233, *www.bpi.fr*. Away from Paris, there are:

* 98 *Bibliothèque Départementale de Prêt (BDP)*, one in each *Département* plus 65 annexes and 159 library buses [*Bibliobus*].

* More than 3000 *Bibliothèque municipale, Bibliothèque intercommunale* and *Bibliothèques municipales à vocation régionale (BMVR)*.

For further information on these libraries including their addresses, visit the Ministry of Culture library and media library portal at *www.culture.fr/ Groups/bibliotheques_et_mediatheques/home*. The best single source of information on libraries is the National School of Library and Information Science [*École nationale supérieure des sciences de l'information et des bibliothèques (ENSSIB)*], 17-21 boulevard du 11 novembre 1918, 69623 Villeurbanne Cedex, Tel: 04 72444343, *www.enssib.fr* in French with onsite translation to English and other languages.

QUID 2006, p. 545.

Maps and guides [*Cartes et guides*]

Maps and guides are sold by bookshops, newsagents, supermarkets and hypermarkets across the country. There are two principal producers of maps, one public and one private, and two private producers of guides.

The **National Geographic Institute** (Chapter 7) produces a full range of paper and electronic maps and map products. Its maps for general public use include road maps [*routes*], aeronautical maps [*aéronautique*], town and urban street maps [*plans* *de ville, villes et agglomérations*], walking and hiking maps [*promenades et randonnées*], outdoor recreation maps [*loisirs de plein air*], tourist maps of France [*tourisme France*] and tourist maps of other countries [*tourisme étranger*]. Headquarters: 136 bis rue de Grenelle, 75700 Paris 07 SP, Tel: 01 43988000, *www.ign.fr.*

Michelin produces paper and electronic maps and map products as well as guides, including the famed Guide Michelin books, for France as well as for other countries. Its ViaMichelin division designs, develops and markets digital travel assistance products and services. For a catalogue of its road and street maps and Green Guide books, visit the online shop on the ViaMichelin website at *www.shop.viamichelin.fr*, select French as the language, and then click on *Cartes et Guides Michelin* to bring up the catalogue of *Cartes et guides papier*. Head office: place des carnes-Dechaux, 63040 Clermont-Fd, *www.michelin.com.* Route planning services are also available at *www.viamichelin.com.*

Mappy, a subsidiary of Orange, which is part of France Telecom, is a supplier of online and electronic maps, itinerary calculators, tourist information and the like, with a website in 12 languages. Mappy, 47 rue de Charonne, 75011 Paris, *www.mappy.com* .

The tourism division of the Hachette publishing group produces a range of guidebooks including the Routard guides for various parts of the country as well as for tourist destinations elsewhere. A complete overview is available online at *www.routard.com.* The head office of Hachette Tourisme is at 43 quai de Grenelle, 75905 Paris Cedex 15, Tel: 01 43923000, *www.hachette.com.*

Nautical charts [*Cartes marines*]

There are two types of nautical charts. The national Hydrographic and Oceanographic Service [*Service hydrographique et océanographique de la marine (SHOM)*], an agency of the Ministry of Defence, publishes charts and other conventional and electronic navigation aids, principally for seagoing ships sailing national and international waters. Contact: SHOM, BP 30316, 29603 Brest Cedex, *www.shom.fr. Editions Grafocarte* publishes the *Navicarte* series of nautical charts for coastal waters, river navigation charts, trilingual (French, English and German) river navigation pilots, tide tables, tidal current lists and other aids, principally for coastal and inshore navigation, as by smaller commercial ships and for recreational boating and yachting. *Navicarte* products are sold by bookshops and nautical supply shops and also may be ordered online from the publisher at *www.navicarte.fr*, in French or in English.

Newspapers [*Journaux*]

In figures, France ranks a modest 26th in the world in newspaper sales*. However, it has one of the world's greater selections of magazines, most glossy and in full colour. The principal daily newspapers [*quotidiens*] are:

- L'Équipe, sports, published in Paris since 1946, 369,000 circulation, *www.lequipe.fr*
- L'Humanité, communist, published in Saint-Denis since 1904, 55,000 circulation, *www.humanite.presse.fr*
- La Croix, catholic, published in Paris since 1880, 98,000 circulation, *www.la-croix.com*
- Le Figaro, nearly moderate, published in Paris since 1826, 360,000 circulation, *www.lefigaro.fr*
- Le Libération, left-leaning national, published in Paris since 1973, 146,000 circulation, *www.liberation.fr*
- Le Monde, most respected national, published in Paris since 1944, 371,000 circulation, *www.lemonde.fr*; has a monthly supplement, Le Monde Diplomatique, focus on global issues, published in 19 languages round the world, 300,000 circulation, *www.monde-diplomatique.fr*
- Le Parisien, published just north of Paris at Saint-Ouen since 1944, *www.leparisien.com*
- Ouest-France, popular western regional paper published in Rennes since 1944, now in 41 local editions with a combined 781,000 circulation, *www.ouest-france.fr*.

The principal weekly magazines [*hebdomadaires*] are:

- L'Express, current affairs, published in Paris since 1953, 435,000 circulation, *www.lexpress.fr*
- Le Canard enchaîné, satirical, published in Paris since 1915, 400,000 circulation, *www.canardenchaine.com*
- Le Nouvel Observateur, current affairs, published in Paris since 1964, 544,000 circulation, *permanent.nouvelobs.com*.
- Paris Match, current affairs, published in Paris since 1949, 625,000 circulation, *www.parismatch.com*.

For further information on the press in general, contact the French National Press Federation [*Fédération national de la presse française (FNPF)*], 13 rue La Fayette, 75009 Paris, Tel: 01 53209050, *www.portail-presse.com*. For subscriptions, contact the individual newspapers and magazines or the ViaPresse central agency that carries 4000 titles and offers 300 on subscription at *www.viapresse.com*, or, for professional publications, its affiliate *www.viapressepro.com*.

*The Economist Pocket World in Figures 2006, pp 92-93.

Official gazette [*Journal officiel*]

The *journal officiel de la République française*, commonly shortened to *Journal officiel (JO)*, is the gazette that publishes public records, legal codes, laws, regulations, administrative rulings, records of commercial enterprise registration and an official bulletin of notices of public works contracts [*Bulletin officiel des annonces des marchés publics (BOAMP)*]. It is published in a printed edition and since June 2004, an online edition. Head office: Direction des journaux officials – JO, 26 rue Desaix, 75727 Paris Cedex 15, Tel: 01 40587979, *www.journal-officiel.gouv.fr*.

Pornography [*Pornographie*]

As elsewhere, pornography exists, in print, on screen and online. According to the National Library catalogue list of serial publications at *bibliographienationale.bnf.fr/Series/P12_05.H/cadre778-1.html*, there are ten French pornographic and erotic magazines. The Marc Dorcel film studio specialises in "adult" feature films for the international market and has an Internet site at *www.dorcel.com* with pages in French and English. AB Sat offers a pornographic TV channel via satellite and cable, XXL, *www.xxltv.fr*. And as elsewhere, pornography has long been an imbroglio in public debate. Opposition builds on considerations of civil life [*laïque*] and secularism [*laïcité*] integrated into the protection of minors. Books have been written on it, and contemporary philosopher Ruwen Ogien, the director of the National Centre for Scientific Research (CNRS) pondered it in *Penser la pornographie* (Paris, Presses Universitaires de France, 2003, 176 pages paperback, ISBN 2-1305-3867-3). Indisputably, though, sex sells. In 2001, author Catherine Millet (1948-) published a semi-autobiographical book, *La vie sexuelle de Catherine M.* that became a bestseller and was translated into 33 languages. Now in paperback in France (Paris, Seuil, 2002, 233 pages paperback, ISBN 2-0205-55130-6) as well as in English in the UK, under the title *The Sexual Life of Catherine M.* (London, 2003, Corgi Adult, 224 pages paperback, ISBN 0-552-77172-4), the book has to date sold more than 2.5 million copies.

Press distribution [*Distribution de presse*]

Distribution of newspapers and other periodicals started in 1789 and at first was a postal monopoly. In 1852, Louis Christophe François Hachette (1800-1864), who had founded the Hachette publishing house in 1826, developed an independent distribution system for books, newspapers and periodicals. By 1897, the system had grown to serve some 8000 customers in France and Algeria. Today, there are three press distribution systems, two of them related to the original Hachette system.

- *Nouvelles messageries de la presse parisienne (NMPP)* was founded in 1947. It now commands about 85% of domestic distribution, and its SEDDIF subsidiary is involved in retail outlets, principally **Newsagents** (Chapter 40), it is owned 49% by Hachette and 51% by five press cooperatives. Head office: 52 rue Jacques Hillairet, 75612 Paris Cedex 12, *www.nmpp.fr*, *mailnmpp@nmpp.fr*.

- *Messageries lyonnaises de presse (MLP)* was founded in 1945. It now commands about 15% of domestic distribution and since 1999 has been building a chain of retail outlets. Head office: PO Box 59, 38329 Saint-Quentin-Fallaver Cedex, Tel: 04 74821414, *www.mlp.fr*.

- *Hachette Distribution Services (HDS)*, part of the Lagardère media and high-technology group, operates the largest international network of media and entertainment stores, some 22 brand chains in all, and is the leader in international press distribution. Head office: 2 rue Lord Byron, 75008 Paris, Tel: 01 42990700, *www.hachette-distribution-services.com*.

Public service portal [*Service-public*]

Service-public is the official portal to the public sector. Its information resources include an on-site search engine, a civil service directory, a public web sites directory, access to laws and official reports, a guide to individual rights and procedures, on-line forms, on-line performance of procedures, a guide to working in the civil service, extensive information for businesses and the professions, news and an online question-and-answer service. In all, it provides access to 5000 French and foreign public websites, 11,000 government services, 13,000 government officials, 2400 information sheets, 1200 questions and answers and 600 downloadable forms. All pages are in French, but key pages, including the home page, directories and guidelines, also are in English, German and Spanish, selectable on the home page at *www.service-public.fr*. The portal's *Allô Service-Public* call centre, Tel: 3939 (€0.12/min), Monday-Friday 08.00-19.00 and Saturday 09.00-13.00, offers user support and provides access to services on the site. A similar site for EU-related information was launched in May 2006 as a joint effort between the French government and the European Commission, *www.touteleurope.fr*.

Science & Décision

Science & Décision is a website created in 2002 at the initiative of the scientific community of the country. It aims to enable decision makers and the general public to more readily understand the scientific matters that increasingly affect daily life. It does this by publishing online overviews of scientific topics of current interest in everyday language in question-and-answer format, a few a year. The first in December 2002 was on mad cow disease [*la vache folle*], and, as this book goes to press, the most recent in June 2006 was on cell cultures and cloning [*cellules souches et clonage*]; other topics have included biotechnology, energy and the Internet. For further information, contact Science & Décision, c/o Infobiogen, 523 place des Terrases, Immeuble Evry II, 91000 Evry, Tel: 01 60873723, *www.science-decision.net*.

Society factbook [*Données sociales*]

The Society factbook [*Données sociales*], published by INSEE, the **National Institute of Statistics and Economic Studies** (Chapter 42) is a compendium on the society of France, as indicated by its subtitle, *La société française*. From *Académie* to *Zus*, in eight chapters it provides in-depth analyses and figures on population and families [*population, famille*], education and training [*éducation, formation*], employment [*emploi*], work and professions [*conditions de travail et relations professionnelles*], income and property [*revenues et patrimoine*], housing [*logement*], healthcare and social security [*santé et protection sociale*] and everyday life [*vie sociale*]. Its 70 articles are written by the experts of 14 specialist agencies and consequently provide authoritative information beyond that customarily found in statistical abstracts. The succinct texts are augmented by many clear charts and histograms in colour, and there are numerous historical and international comparisons. It's the definitive single-volume reference on the society of the country: *Données sociales la société française*, Paris, Statistique Publique, May 2006, 667 pages, 19 × 26 cm paperback, ISBN 2-11-068371-6, €37.00.

Trade portals [*Portails des sites Internet*]

The two principal trade portals are governmental. The Ministry of Economy, Finance and Industry has extensive trade information on its website, maintained by its head office at 139, rue de Bercy, 75572 Paris Cedex 12, Tel: 01 40040404, *www.minefi.gouv.fr*, *dircom-cnt@direcom.finances.gouv.fr*. In 2003, *UBIFRANCE*, the agency for international business joined with *l'Usine Nouvelle*, a business weekly magazine to form a business-to-business (B2B) website, maintained by a webmaster at the UBFRANCE head office, 14 avenue d'Eylau, 75116 Paris Cedex, Tel: 01 44345091, *www.firmafrance.com*, *contact@firmafrance.com*.

Yellow pages [*Pages jaunes*]

Pages jaunes is the trademark for a classified telephone directory or part of a directory printed on yellow paper and alphabetically listing organisations and businesses by the categories of goods and services offered. The trademark is held by a company of the same name, owned 54% by **France Télécom** (Chapter 44). But there are other publishers whose directories also have classified sections printed on yellow paper. In addition to printed directories, *Pages jaunes* are available by phoning Tel: 118008 and online at *www.pagesjaunes.fr* with pages in English. The principal sections of the website, selectable at tabs in its taskbar, are:

- Yellow Pages [*Pages Jaunes*], the classified directory
- White Pages [*Pages Blanches*], an alphabetical directory
- Reverse Search [*Recherche à proximité*], number to subscriber search, at a fee
- World Directories [*Annuaires du monde*], links to directories worldwide.

Most users visit the website to look up a business, so the default opening page is *Pages jaunes*, which is centred on a search entry form with five fields.

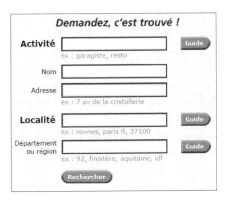

Search entry form.

The most direct way to search is to key in the classification of business [*Activité*], city or town [*Localité*] and *Département* or *Région* and then click on *Rechercher* to bring up the list of businesses. Like all search engines, the *Pages jaunes* search is intolerant of typing errors. So unless you are certain about spellings and key in words correctly, it's best to click on the *Guide* buttons to bring up list boxes in which you can scroll to the correct words to enter in the fields. Should a search fail even though your entries in the fields are correct, try a synonym in the *Activité* field. For example, a search for **Driving schools** (Chapter 4) with *Écoles de Conduite* in the *Activité* field will fail, because the *Pages jaunes* database recognises only the synonym, *Auto-écoles*, which, when entered, results in a successful search.

Other yellow page directory publishers include Findexa, a subsidiary of the Texas Pacific Group that has operations in 11 countries in Europe. In France it has three businesses that together publish some 40 regional yellow page directories.

- *Elitel*, part of *Bégécom*, the short name of *Annuaires téléphoniques de Bretagne (ATB)*, that publishes 15 directories in the southern and western parts of the country and supports online access to them at *www.begecom.fr*.
- *L'Annuaire Soleil* that publishes 14 directories [*bottins*] for regions surrounding Paris and supports online access to them at *www.annuaire-soleil.com/bottin/*.
- *Annuaire Phone Edition (APE)* that publishes 12 local directories, at present with no website.

There are five other major directory publishers:

- *ABC France*, part of the Bonnier International Group, offers business-to-business directories, principally online at *www.abc-d.fr*.

- *Eurédit*, based in Paris but owned by Seat Pagine Gaille of Italy, publishes the Europages business-to-business, Europe-wide directories on paper and CD-ROM and with a website at *www.europages.fr*, selectable in 25 languages.

- *Infobel*, the tradename of the online service of *Kapitol* of Belgium, offers information and services for some 184 countries. In France, it offers CD-ROMs and online services, accessible by clicking on France on its website at *www.infobel.com* in six selectable languages.

- *Kompass*, a subsidiary of Orange, part of France Télécom, offers business-to-business information on more than 70 countries via printed directories, the Internet and CD-ROMs. In France, *Kompass* publishes 19 regional directories that are available online at *www.kompass.fr*.

- *1bis.com,* an online company owned by Plainfax, a multimedia map publisher. The website at *www.1bis.com* offers directory and map services.

Youth Information Centres
[Centre information et documentation jeunesse (CIDJ)]

Across the country, there are more than 1600 contact places where young people may go to find information on youth issues and information on careers and studies. For further information as well as the addresses and telecommunications numbers of the regional, local and mobile offices and other contact points, contact CIDJ, 101 quai Branly, 75015 – Paris, Tel: 01 44491200 and 08 25090630 (Monday-Friday 10:00-12:00 and 13:00-18:00), *www.cidj.com* with an interactive contact point locator map.

32
Museums, exhibitions and festivals

Museums, exhibitions and festivals abound in cities and towns across the country; hardly a town is without one, and Paris alone has several hundred. Describing them all would require a book many times as large as this one. So in this chapter, the more famous of them are described along with principal names, addresses and websites that provide access to the venues and events across the country.

Art galleries [*Galeries d'art*]

In cities and towns across the country, there are innumerable art galleries that exhibit and sell works of art. The larger galleries usually are listed under *Galeries d'art* in the Yellow pages, and in most cities, there are gallery associations with websites featuring their members, such as *Association des galeries* in Paris, with 125 venues and a website at *www.associastiondesgaleries.org*.

Cannes film festival [*Festival de Cannes*]

Each year since 1946, a film festival has been held at Cannes, a resort on the *Côte d'Azur* of the Mediterranean coast in the southeast part of the country. Held in May, it now is one of the world's leading festivals and perhaps the one with the most facets, from a programme aimed to discover and promote new talent from round the world to the Golden Palm [*Palme d'Or*] award for the best feature film. For further information, contact *Association Française du Festival International du Film*, 3 rue Amélie 75007 Paris, Tel: 01 53596100, *www.festival-cannes.org* selectable in French and English.

Centre Georges Pompidou

Also known as *Centre Beaubourg* after the district where it stands, the Pompidou Centre is the largest exhibition centre in Paris. The escalators in clear tubes and multicoloured ventilation pipes on its exterior made it controversial when it opened in 1977, but it now is a popular landmark that each year draws more than 800,000 visitors to a wide range of musical events, contemporary art exhibitions and cinema, as well as to special programmes for children and young people. For further information, see the well illustrated visitor's guide, in French, English, German, Italian, Spanish, Japanese and Mandarin Chinese editions, on sale at the Centre or available by online order, or contact the centre at 75191 Paris Cedex 04, Tel: 01 44781233, *www.cnac-gp.fr* selectable in French, English and Spanish, with online sales of tickets.

Festivals

There are innumerable festivals throughout the year, most in spring and summer. Eight that are popular and have international appeal are:

- Avignon for theatre, July, Bureau du Festival d'Avignon, Cloître Saint-Louis, 20 rue du portail Boquier, 84 000 Avignon, Tel: 04 90276650, *www.festival-avignon.com* in French and English.
- Aix en Provence for opera, July, 11 rue Gaston de Saporta, 13100 Aix-en-Provence, Tel: 04 42173434, *www.festival-aix.com* in French and English.
- *Carnaval de Chalon-sur-Saône* for street music and performances, February-March, Salle Marcel Sembat, Place Mathias, 71100 Chalon-Sur-Saône, Tel: 03 85430839, *www.carnavaldechalon.com* in French and English.
- *Chorégies d'Orange* for opera, July and August, BP 205, 84107 Orange Cedex, Tel: 04 90342424, *www.choregies.asso.fr* in French, English and German.
- *Festival européen de la photo de nu*, Arles, May, Office de Tourisme, Accueil, bd des Lices, 13200 Arles, *www.fepn-arles.com*.
- *Festival interceltique de Lorient* for Celtic music and dance from round the world, 10 days in August, 8 rue Nayel, 56 100 Lorient, Tel: 02 97212429, *www.festival-interceltique.com*.
- *Francofolies la Rochelle* for **Chanson Française** (Chapter 11), mid July, 6 rue de la Désirée, 17042 La Rochelle Cedex, Tel: 05 46505577, *www.francofolies.fr*
- *Jazz à Vienne,* late June and early July, Vienne Action Culturelle, Acédémie jazz à Vienne, 21 rue des Célestes, 38200 Vienne, Tel: 08 92702007, *www.jazzavienne.com*.

Fête de la musique

On the summer solstice, 21 June of each year since 1982, *Fête de la Musique* is celebrated across the country. Unlike most music festivals, it is free to the public and open to both amateur and professional musicians, who perform for free. Started in France, it has become an international event, with Fêtes in 250 cities in 100 countries round the world, where performances of all varieties of music are given outdoors to large crowds. For further information, contact *Coordination générale de la Fête de la Musique,* 30 rue René Boulanger, 75010 Paris, Tel: 01 40039470, *fetedelamusique.culture.fr* in French and English.

International Comics Festival
[*Festival international de la bande dessinée*]

Each year since 1974, the International Comics Festival is held in Angoulême, in the *Département* of Charente (No. 16), a paper-making centre since the 14th century. Now held over four days in January, the Festival has become famous for the Comics Prizes, awarded in six categories and announced the first evening at the awards ceremony held at the Théâtre d'Angoulême. For further information, contact the head office, International Comics Festival, 71 rue Hergé, 16000 Angoulême, Tel: 05 45978650, *www.bdangouleme.com* in French and English, *info@ bdangouleme.com.*

Museums [*Musées*]

There are 33 **National museums**, several hundred Departemental museums and innumerable municipal and private museums, most listed under *Musées* in the Yellow Pages.

National museums [*Musées nationaux*]

There are 33 National museums across the country, including the **Louvre Museum** (Chapter 11) in Paris. They are administered by the *Direction des musées de France (DMF)*, a directorate of the Ministry of Culture. For a complete list, contact DMF at 6 rue des Pyramides, 75001 Paris, Tel: 01 40158000, *www.culture.gouv.fr/culture/dmf* with a list of the museums and their addresses. For the dates and descriptions of special events, visit the **Culture portal** (Chapter 11) at *www.culture.fr* with pages in French, English and Spanish.

Paris Motor Show [*Mondial de l'Automobile*]

The Paris Motor Show is held every two years in late September at Paris Expo, Porte de Versailles. It is the world's largest and oldest automobile show, founded in 1898 by automobile pioneer Albert de Dion (1856-1946). Arranged by the International

Organisation of Motor Vehicle Manufacturers (*Organisation Internationale des Constructeurs d'Automobiles*) it features world premieres of new models, makes, technologies and concepts, and has become a major media attraction that draws more than 1.4 million visitors. Comprehensive information, in French and in English, is available from the head office at 22 avenue Franklin Roosevelt, 75008 Paris, Tel: 01 56882240, *www.mondial-automobile.com*, *info@amcpromotion.com*.

Quai Branly

Opened in June 2006 by President Jacques Chirac, *Musée du Quai Branly* is the largest new museum built in Paris since **Centre Georges Pompidou** opened in 1977. Its architecture is modernist French, but its focus is elsewhere, as it is dedicated to the cultures of non-European civilisations, with collections of some 300,000 works from Africa, Asia, Oceania and the Americas. In addition to its role as a museum, it has physical and computerised research facilities and offers a range of publications, both for scholars and for the general public. For further information, contact the museum at 37 Quai Branly, portail Debilly, 75007 Paris, Tel: 01 56617000, *www.quaibranly.fr* in French, English and Spanish.

33
Non-government organisations

Non-government organisations (NGOs) abound, most likely because of the widespread respect for freedom of expression. Some are branches of international NGOs, but several that were founded in France have gone the other way and become international, most notably the *sans frontiers* ("Without Borders") organisations, as for medical doctors, founded in 1971, and for media reporters, founded in 1985. Another reason for the prominence of NGOs is that their non-profit status has long been recognised. On 1 July 1901, a law concerning articles of association [*Loi relative au contrat d'association*] specifically set forth the requirements for non-profit [*non lucratif*] status. So, today, a non-profit organisation will describe itself as complying with that law, usually with a statement such as: *cette organisation, à but non lucratif régie par la loi du 1er juillet 1901...* Save for well-known international NGOs founded in other countries as well as in France, the prominent NGOs described in this chapter are in alphabetical order according to their names in French, which, in some cases, are used untranslated in other languages.

Amnesty International

In 1971, just a decade after Amnesty International was founded in the UK, *Amnesty International section française* was founded in Paris by concerned opinion leaders including philosopher Vladimir Jankélévitch (1903-1985) and famed judge René Cassin (1887-1976), who in 1968 had received the Nobel Peace Prize for drafting the Universal Declaration of Human Rights that had been adopted by the United Nations in 1948. Today, *Amnesty International section française* has 380 groups across the country and a head office at 72-76 Bd de la Villette, 75940 Paris Cedex 19, Tel: 01 53386565, *www.amnesty.fr* with an interactive group locator map.

ATTAC

ATTAC, the abbreviation for *Association pour la Taxation des Transactions pour l'Aide aux Citoyens* was created in December 1998 at an international meeting in Paris, as an activist organisation calling for taxation of currency speculation. However, it now addresses a broader range of issues including control of financial markets, fair but not unrestricted free trade, conservation of public goods such as air and water and services including health and social services, curtailment of tax evasion, sustainable globalisation and cancellation of the debts of developing countries. Consequently, it now translates its name to "International movement for democratic control of financial markets and their institutions". It has affiliated organisations in 37 countries in addition to having 30,000 members in 215 local committees and a head office in France at 66 rue Marceau, 93100 Montreuil, Tel: 01 41581740, *www.attac.org* in French, English, German, Italian and Spanish and with links to the 38 national websites.

Avocats sans frontières (ASF)

ASF was founded in 1992 in Brussels by lawyers, barristers and magistrates concerned with preserving justice by making professional legal services available to all, regardless of ability to pay. ASF France was founded almost simultaneously. The concept spread to other countries, including in 2000 the USA where it is called Lawyers Without Borders (LWOB), though there is no connection between the organisations. For further information on ASF France, contact the head office at 35 rue Ozenne, 31000 Toulouse, Tel: 05 34311783, *avocats.france.free.fr*.

CEPR

CEPR is the abbreviation for *Centre européen de prévention des risques*, the European Risk Prevention Centre, founded in 1997 by the network of European mutual insurance companies and partly supported by the municipality of Niort, in which it is located. As its name implies, CEPR focuses on risk prevention, principally in five sectors: homes [*risques domestiques*], road traffic [*risques routiers*], workplaces [*risques en entreprise*], natural hazards [*risques naturels*] and foods [*risques alimentaires*]. It conducts studies, publishes white papers and public information materials, holds annual colloquia and works to influence decision makers, public and private, on safety and risks. For further information, contact CEPR, 18 rue Marcel Paul, 79000 Niort, Tel: 05 49046677, *www.cepr.fr*.

Comité contre l'esclavage moderne (CCEM)

With the support of the Daphné Programme of the European Commission (EC), CCEM works to combat domestic slavery and trafficking in France and worldwide. It monitors abuses, collects statistics and publishes reports and a newsletter. For further information, contact the head office at 31 rue des Lilas, 75019 Paris, Tel: 01 44528890, *www.ccem-antislavery.org*.

ELISA

ELISA, the acronym for *Equipe Légère d'Intervention de Secours Aéroportée*, was founded in the late 1990s by **Firefighters** and **SAMU** (Chapter 15) professionals as a benevolent organisation to make use of their professional expertise in providing post-disaster rescue services, principally by helicopter. It specialises in nimble, rapid response by trained crews of up to six specialists, selected to cope with the demands of a rescue mission. To date, it has had many missions across France and as far abroad as South America and Indonesia. For further details, contact the head office at 649, rue de la République, 07350 Cruas, *www.elisa-urgence.org*.

Emmaüs

Emmaüs is a movement that provides aid to the underprivileged at home and abroad. Founded in 1954 by Henri Grouès (1912-), a popular Catholic priest known by the honorary title of Abbé Pierre, Emmaüs is a Biblical name, the village in which according to Luke 24:13, Jesus appeared on the day of resurrection. Today in France, Emmaüs has centres across the country, run by volunteers who collect and sell used furniture and other items to support the organisation. And it is an international organisation with 323 member groups in 50 countries. For further information, contact the head office at 183 bis rue Vaillant Couturier, BP 91, 94143 Alfortville Cedex, Tel: 01 48932950, *www.emmaus-international.org* in French, English and Spanish.

European Council on Refugees and Exiles
[*Conseil européen sur les réfugiés et les exilés*]

The European Council on Refugees and Exiles (ECRE) is the coordinating organisation for 74 national NGOs dealing with refugees in 29 countries across Europe. Its extensive publications include reports on countries, and it supports the European Legal Network on Asylum (ELENA). Its secretariat is in London, at 103 Worship Street, London EC2A 2DF, UK, Tel: +44 20 73777556, *www.ecre.org*, *ecre@ecre.org*. There are four ECRE member organisations in France:

- *CIMADE*, 176 rue de Grenelle, 75007 Paris, Tel: 01 44186050, *www.cimade.org*, *sg@cimade.org*

- *Forum Réfugiés*, B.P. 1054, 69612 Villeurbanne Cedex, Tel: 04 78037445, *www.forumrefugies.org*, *europe@forumrefugies.org*.

- *France Terre d'Asile*, 25 rue Ganneron, 75018 Paris, Tel: 01 53043996, *www.ftda.net*, *international@france-terre-asile.org*

- *Secours Catholique*, 106 rue du Bac, 75341 Paris, Tel: 01 45497300, *www.secours-catholique.asso.fr*, *jean-haffner@secours-catholique.asso.fr*.

European Forum for Urban Safety

Founded in 1987 by Parliamentarian Gilbert Bonnemaison, the European Forum for Urban Safety (EFUS) [*Forum européen pour la sécurité urbaine (FESU)*] is a network of local authorities that work together to strengthen crime reduction policies and promote the role of their streetwise experience in shaping European policies. Today, in addition to France, EFUS has national forums in Belgium, Italy, Luxembourg and Spain and links with cities in Africa and South America as well as with the International Centre for Crime Prevention based in Montreal, Canada. For further information, contact the international head office at 38 rue Liancourt, 75014 Paris, Tel: 01 40644900, *www.fesu.org* in French, English, German, Polish and Spanish.

Fondation Danielle Mitterrand – France Libertés

Founded in 1986 by Danielle Mitterrand (née Gouze, 1924-), then the wife and now the widow of President François Mitterrand (1916-1996), the Foundation is dedicated to personal and collective freedoms in the face of ever more powerful national and international interests. One of its ongoing campaigns, for instance, is the human right to access to adequate water, in face of France being home to three of the world's four largest private water management companies. For further information on the Foundation and its activities around the globe, contact the head office at 22 rue de Milan, 75009 Paris, Tel: 01 53251040, *www.france-libertes.fr*.

Fondation de France

Established in 1969, *Fondation de France* raises and distributes funds to support worthy endeavours in culture, the environment, healthcare, scientific research and solidarity with a particular focus on combating poverty and aiding the underprivileged. It provides expertise to aid individuals and organisations set up and manage charitable foundations. In 1989, it joined with six other leading European foundations to establish the European Foundation Centre (EFC). In 1997, it initiated the *Observatoire de la Fondation de France* that now compiles statistics and publishes reports on philanthropy, in part to heighten public awareness of the role of foundations and the importance of their grants. For further information, contact the head office at 40 avenue Hoche, 75008 Paris, Tel: 01 44213100, *www.fdf.org*. For information on the role of foundations and individual and corporate philanthropy across Europe, contact the European Foundation Centre, 51 rue de la Concorde, 1050 Brussels, Belgium, Tel: +32 2 5128938, *www.efc.be* in English.

Forum des droits sur l'internet

Founded in 2000, *Forum des droits sur l'internet*, sometimes translated to the Internet Rights Forum, is an independent, private body, supported by the government, with the remit of critically examining online and electronic activities with an eye to their impact on civil rights. It is unique in Europe, and though it has no legally binding powers, it often is consulted by government agencies. It publishes regular reports and white papers, most in French but many in English, and its website is in French and English. Head office: 6 rue Déodat de Séverac, 75017 Paris, Tel: 01 44013800, *www.foruminternet.org*.

GISTI

GISTI is the acronym for *Groupe d'information et de soutien des immigrés*, an organisation that provides information and support to immigrants, and, through its knowledge of French and international immigration law, defends foreigners, offers training and publications and takes part in public debate on migration policy. It publishes *Plein Droit*, a quarterly journal on French and European migration policies and it acts as a continuously updated clearing house of information on organisations and activities relevant to immigration. For further information, contact the head office at 3 Villa Marcès, 75011 Paris, Tel: 01 43148484, *www.gisti.org* in French, English and German.

Groupe de secours catastrophe français (GSCF)

The GSCF is a volunteer organisation set up in 1999 by professional **Firefighters** (Chapter 16) to make their skills more widely available in rescue operations across the country and around the world as well as to heighten public awareness of hazards and the means to cope with them. To date, GSCF has provided rescue services to more than 500 disasters on four continents. For further information, contact the head office at 30 rue des Victoires, BP 80222, 59654 Villeneuve d'Ascq Cedex, Tel: 03 20477415, *www.gscf.fr* in French with online videos in French and English.

International Federation of Little Brothers of the Poor
[*Fédération internationale des petits frères des pauvres*]

As its name implies, the Federation is dedicated to aiding the poorest of the poor: the impoverished elderly. It was founded in 1946 by Armand Marquiset (1900-1981), a man born to wealth who became one of the country's leading philanthropists. In the aftermath of the Second World War, he was appalled by the plight of the elderly poor who, as his mentor, the Abbot of Audouin had remarked, were the great victims of the war. He responded personally, starting in a poor district of Paris, carrying meals that he had cooked himself, often up six flights of stairs to attic rooms where the forgotten elderly lived, no longer capable of fending for themselves. Soon he was joined by young volunteers, and aided by funds that he cajoled from his wealthy friends, *Les petits frères des pauvres* grew. Today, it is an international federation of independent benevolent organisations in eight countries aside from France, in Canada, Germany, Ireland, Mexico, Poland, Spain, Switzerland and the USA. For further details, contact the executive office at 64 avenue Parmentier, 75011 Paris, Tel: 01 47007968, *www.petitsfreres.org* selectable in the languages of the nine countries.

Human rights league [*Ligue des droits de l'homme*]

Ligue des droits de l'homme (LDH) was founded in 1894, in the aftermath of the political scandal of the **Dreyfus affair** (Chapter 5) and consequently is the oldest human rights organisation in the country. In 1922, it was one of the founding members of the International Federation on Human Rights [*Fédération internationale des lignes des droits de l'Homme (FIDH)*] that now has 141 member organisations round the globe, *www.fidh.org*. LDH has activities across the country and a head office at 138 rue Marcadet, 75018 Paris, Tel: 01 56555100, *www.ldh-france.org*, with a locator for groups across the country.

Ligue des droits de l'Homme (LDH)

LDH is one of the 141 human rights organisations in 110 countries that belong to the International Federation for Human Rights [*Fédération internationale des droits de l'homme (FIDH)*] that was founded in 1922 and has its head office in Paris. LDH acts to promote human rights in France and works closely with FIDH in global human rights incentives. Accordingly, it has a comprehensive range of publications, including the annual survey of human rights in France; as this book goes to press, the most recent edition is *L'état des droits de l'Homme en France Édition 2006* (Paris, Éditions La Découverte, April 2006, paperback, ISBN 2-7071-4867-9). For further information, contact LDH at 138 rue Marcadet, 75018 Paris, Tel: 01 56555100, *www.ldh-france.org*. For international information, contact FIDH at 17 Passage de la main d'or, 75011 Paris, *www.fidh.org* in French, English, Spanish and Arabic.

Médecins sans frontières

Founded in 1971 by a small group of French doctors, *Médecins sans frontières* is known around the world for its projects in war-torn areas and in developing countries. It is mostly known by its name in French or by the abbreviation MSF, though in some countries, such as the USA, it goes under the name Doctors Without Borders. Today, MSF provides health care and training to populations in more than 70 countries and each year recruits more than 3000 doctors and other healthcare professionals to staff projects. In 1999, it was awarded the Nobel Peace Prize in recognition of its members' efforts to provide medical care in acute crises as well as its role in heightening international awareness of potential human disasters. For further information, contact the French head office at 8 rue Saint Sabin, 75011 Paris,

Tel: 01 40212929, *www.msf.fr* or the international operations headquarters at Rue de Lausanne 78, CP 116, 1211 Geneva 21, Switzerland, Tel: +41 22 8498488, *www.msf.org* with links to MSF websites in other languages in 22 countries.

Médecins du monde

In 1979, doctor, diplomat and politician Bernard Kouchner (1939-), the co-founder of **Médecins sans frontières** left the organisation due to a conflict of opinion with its chairman, Claude Malhuret, and together with 15 other doctors, in 1980 founded a similar organisation, *Médecins du monde*. Today, the two organisations provide similar responses to emergencies and often work in the field in the same countries. Known as "Doctors of the World" in English, *Médecins du monde* now has delegations in 11 countries in addition to France and is active in speaking out against impeded access to healthcare and violations of human rights and dignity. For further information, contact the international head office at 62 rue Marcadet, 75018 Paris, Tel: 01 44921414, *www.mdm-international.org* in French and English.

Mémoire 2000

Mémoire 2000 is a human rights organisation that, as its name implies, is dedicated to building on past memories to benefit the present millennium. It works to bridge the memory gap between generations and thereby counterbalance the ills brought about by the tendency of each generation to repeat the mistakes of the previous generation. It does this in principle by enabling the adults of today to look back at our collective memory and transmit the essential components of it on to the adults of tomorrow. In practice, it takes its message of anti-racism and tolerance to the young of today through films, sessions in schools that each year are attended by thousands of pupils, and by field trips, such as to second world war concentration camps. For further details, contact the head office at 55 avenue Marceau, 75116 Paris, Tel: 01 40477348, *www.memoire2000.asso.fr* in French and English.

MRAP

MRAP, the abbreviation for *Mouvement contre le Racisme et pour l'Amitié entre les Peuples*, was founded in 1949 specifically to combat discrimination and racism. Today, it offers a broad range of publications, including books, brochures, reports, postcards and CDs on themes related to racism. It is an activist at the national level, lobbying in 2006 against the amendments of the immigration law [*Code de l'entrée et du séjour des étrangers et du droit d'asile (CESEDA)*], collecting signatures on petitions opposing it, under the motto of "Against disposable immigrants" [*uni(e)s contre une immigration jetable*] linked to the familiar circular prohibitive road sign. For further information, contact the head office at 43 boulevard Magenta, 75010 Paris, Tel: 01 53389999, *www.mrap.asso.fr* in French with downloadable documents in English and other languages.

Privacy International

In 1990, more than a hundred human rights organisations and privacy experts from 40 countries, including three from France, linked to found Privacy International (PI), a watchdog on surveillance and privacy intrusions by governments and corporations. PI is based in London and has affiliates in 18 countries. It now is most known for the annual Big Brother Awards, named after the oppressive head of state in George Orwell's *1984* and given in recognition of persons and organisations that have done the most to threaten personal privacy.

Each year since 2000, the Big Brother Awards France (BBA-F) ceremony is held in early February and features several categories of awards for public and private intrusiveness during the previous year as well as occasional special recognitions, such as the Lifetime Menace Award. The ceremony also includes the award of the Voltaire Prize in recognition of the most significant effort in combating threats to privacy. Each year, there are more than 30 nominations for the awards, which are decided by a jury comprising academics, magistrates, lawyers, journalists, software and media advocates, writers and artists. For further information, contact the PI headquarters at 6-8 Armwell Street, London, EC1R 1UQ, UK, Tel: +44 7947 778247, *www.privacyinternational.org* in English. For information on BBA-F, visit its website *www.bigbrotherawards.eu.org* in French and English.

Red Cross [*Croix-rouge française*]

Croix-Rouge française is one of the 16 oldest national Red Cross organisations, as it resulted from the inception meeting held in August 1864 in Geneva, where the international organisation now has its headquarters. Today, *Croix-Rouge Française* has delegations in all 100 mainland and DOM *Départements*, 1045 local delegations and 559 other establishments across the country. For further information, contact the head office at 98 rue Didot, 75694 Paris Cedex 14, Tel: 01 44431100, *www.croix-rouge.fr* with an interactive delegation locator map.

Reporters sans frontières

Since it was founded in 1985, *Reporters sans frontières*, or Reporters Without Borders as it is known in English, has become widely recognised as the world voice of press freedom. Today, it has a permanent staff based in Paris, sections in ten countries, a network of partner organisations on all continents and more than 110 correspondents worldwide. Each year, it publishes the Press Freedom Index, agitates for the release of journalists imprisoned around the world and compiles reports as well as freedom of expression publications, such as the "Handbook for Bloggers and Cyber-Dissidents" released in 2006 in French, English, Russian Arabic, Chinese and Persian editions for free download from its website. For further information, contact the international head office at 5 rue Geoffroy-Marie, 75009 Paris, Tel: 01 44838484, *www.rsf.org* selectable in French, English and Spanish.

Restos du Cœur

Restos du Cœur, literally "Restaurants of the Heart", is a countrywide organisation dedicated to serve meals to the poor and the homeless, particularly in winter. It was founded in September 1985 by Coluche, the stage name of Michel Gérard Joseph Colucci, a popular comedian of Italian heritage, born in 1944 in Paris. He knew well the need, as he once had quipped: *Quand j'étais petit à la maison, le plus dur c'était la fin du mois. Surtout les trente derniers jours.* ("At home when I was little, it was hardest toward the end of the month, especially the last thirty days.") The public responded with support, and today there are 113 *Restos du Cœur* associations with together 2500 serving points across the country that each year serve more than 600,000 people. *Restos du Cœur* may be the most successful grassroots charity ever, though regrettably founder Coluche didn't live to see its success, as he died in a motorcycle accident in June 1986. For further information on *Restos du Cœur*, including details of the benefits that may be realised from even small contributions, contact the head office at 8 rue Athènes, 75009 Paris, Tel: 01 53322323, *www.restosducoeur.org*.

The Salvation Army [*Armée du salut*]

Founded in 1865 in London, the Salvation Army is an integral part of the Christian Church, though distinctive in its administration and practice. Today, it is active in 109 countries and conducts its affairs in more than 140 languages. In France, the

Armée du salut was founded in 1881 and now has 1500 officers and 145 centres across the country. Each year, it serves more than 100,000 street meals, accommodates 160,000 people in its emergency shelters and receives 74,000 people in its day-care centres. For further information, contact the Foundation at 60 rue Frères Flavien 75976 Paris Cedex 30, Tel: 43622500, *www.armeedusalut.fr* with an interactive centre locator map.

Samusocial

Samusocial is the abbreviation of *Services Ambulatoires d'Urgence Sociale*, an organisation founded in 1993 in Paris to provide medical, psychological and social support to the increasing numbers of homeless people living on the streets. It operates by providing access to healthcare facilities and shelters and by having roving teams that are on duty around the clock. The concept soon evolved to be national, and today there are *Samusocial* units in sixty cities in 40 *Départements*. In 1998, *Samusocial* International was founded so cities elsewhere could benefit from *Samusocial* experience in France. Aside from France, there now are *Samusocial* units in 11 countries. For further information, contact *Samusocial* International, 35 avenue Courteline, 75012 Paris, *www.samu-social-international.com* in French and English.

Secouristes Sans Frontières (SSF)

SSF was founded in 1985 to make French search and rescue and emergency medical expertise and facilities available worldwide on short-term missions of up to 15 days duration. In general, missions are staffed by qualified rescue workers and paramedics from units across the country, but also may include emergency medical doctors and nurses, such as when field hospitals are set up. To date, it has sent missions to aid the victims of earthquakes, floods and cyclones on four continents. For further information, contact SSF, 5 Avenue Victor Hugo, 94160 Saint Mande, Tel: 01 41749468, *www.ssf-france.org*, with an interactive group locator map.

SSAÉ

Founded in 1932, SSAÉ, the abbreviation for *Service social d'aide aux émigrants*, aims to help individuals and families with personal or social problems resulting from migration across borders. It has six district agencies, offices in 44 Departments and a head office in Paris at 58A, rue du Dessours-des-berges, 75013 Paris, Tel: 01 40779400, *www.ssae.net*, *comm.@ssae.asso.fr*. It is affiliated with the International Social Service (ISS), an organisation created in the aftermath of the First World War that now has offices in more than 100 countries and a head office at 32 quai du Seujet, 1201 Geneva, Switzerland, Tel: +41 229067700, *www.iss-ssi.org*, *irc-cir@iss-ssi.org*.

34
Orders, societies and associations

Except for children of less than school age, almost every resident belongs to one or more non-professional organisations. A third of the population belong to associations that are so much a part of everyday life that there is a government agency dedicated to them. There are more than 25 clubs of national or international rank, and brief descriptions of the historical and present orders of the country take up 17 pages in a reference encyclopaedia. Listing, or even naming them all is beyond the scope of this book. So, this chapter provides the details of the principal international orders, societies and associations to which many new residents belong before moving to the country or seek after arrival, as well as the orders famed in the culture of the country.

Conseil national de la vie associative (CNVA)

Associations are prominent in the life of the country: some 20 million people, age 14 and over are members of an association, and together, the associations employ 1.6 million people. Accordingly, under the office of the Prime Minister, there is an agency dedicated to dealing with associations, *Conseil national de la vie associative (CNVA)*, 62 bd de la Tour-Maubourg, 75007 Paris, Tel: 01 53597256, *www.associations.gouv.fr* with an interactive locator map of agencies across the country and links to related resources.

Croix Bleue

Founded in 1877 in Switzerland, The Blue Cross [*La Croix Bleue*] is a temperance organisation with Sections across Europe, the first in France in 1883. Today in France, *La Croix Bleue* has 110 units in 12 *Régions* with some 2300 members. For further information, contact the head office at 189 rue Belliard, 75018 Paris, Tel: 01 42283737, *www.croixbleue.fr*.

Druidism [*Druidisme*]

The Druids were the priestly class of the ancient polytheistic Celtic societies that existed in the British Isles and Western Europe north of the Alps. They are believed to have survived until the 7th century in Ireland, Flanders and the low countries. In the 18th century, Druidism experienced a revival in England and Wales and in the 19th century in France, with the establishment of a *Gorsedd* ("throne" or "high seat") in Brittany [*Le Gorsedd de Bretagne*]. Today, the historic Druidic sites in Brittany have grouped together in *Bretagne des druides et des mégalithes*, *www.bretagne-celtic.com* selectable in French and English. Moreover, there are some 40 Druidism societies in France, an information centre at 43 rue Saint Michel, 29120 Brasparts and an annual holiday, *Gorsedd digor*, the third Sunday of July. For further information, contact the World-Wide Celtic Creed [*Kredenn Geltiek Hollvedel*], c/o Alain Le Goff, Bothuan, 29450 Commana, *analgow@bzh.net*.

A druidic symbol.

Freemasonry [*Franc-maçonnerie*]

In 1721, the first Masonic organisation was founded in France, and today there are regular and traditional as well as liberal orders [*obédiences*], nine in all: *Grand Orient de France, Grande Loge de France, Fédération Française du Droit Humain, Grande Loge Féminine de France, Grande Loge Traditionnelle et Symbolique Opéra, Grande Loge Féminine de Memphis-Misraïm, Loge Nationale Française, Grande Loge Mixte Universelle,* and *Grande Loge Mixte de France*. Though the reasons for there being nine orders are rooted in a history of differences of opinion, starting in 2001, the orders have an inter-order organisation, *Franc-maçonnerie française*, *www.fm-fr.org* selectable in French or English with information on the history and current activities of Masonry in France as well as links to and information on the nine orders.

Gay and lesbian associations [*Associations gaies et lesbiennes*]

There are nearly 900 gay and lesbian associations in the country. They are linked to each other in The Gay and Lesbian Families [*Gais & Lesbiennes Branchés (GLB)*] that serves as a clearing house for information across the country, including maintaining a continually updated calendar of gay and lesbian events. For further information, contact GLB at 32 rue de l'Orangerie, 78000 Versailles, *www.france.qrd.org* with an alphabetical directory of associations.

Kiwanis International

Kiwanis International is a service organisation with the mission of aiding the children of the world. It was founded in 1915 in Detroit in the USA and now has 250 clubs in France and Monaco. For further information, contact Kiwanis France-Monaco, 45 rue Pasteur, 10350 Marigny Le Chatel, *www.kiwanis.fr*.

Légion d'honneur

The *Légion d'honneur* was instituted in 1802 by Napoléon Bonaparte to recognise military exploits and today is an honour conferred upon men and women, French or foreign, for outstanding achievement in civilian or military life. It has five grades of distinction, from the basic knight [*chevalier*] to the highest, grand cross [*grand-croix*]. It is awarded by the President, who is the grand master [*grand maître*]. It has a national museum [*Musée de la Légion d'honneur et des ordres de chevalerie*] with an extensive library and exhibitions at 2 rue de la Légion d'honneur, 75007 Paris, Tel: 01 40628425, *www.legiondhonneur.fr*.

Lions Clubs

The Lions Club is a community-based service club founded in 1917 in the USA and now the world's largest club of its sort. The first Lions Club in France was founded in 1948, and there are now more than 1200 Lions Clubs with 31,500 members in the country. For further information, contact Lions Clubs de France, 295 rue Saint Jacques, 75005 Paris, Tel: 01 46341410, *www.lions-france.org* with an interactive Club locator map.

Ordre national du mérite

The National order of merit [*Ordre national du mérite*] was founded in 1963 by President Charles de Gaulle to replace the many orders previously awarded by the Ministries and to create an official recognition more easily awarded than the prestigious *Légion d'honneur*. Like the *Légion d'honneur*, it may be awarded to men and women and has five grades of distinction, from the basic knight [*chevalier*] to the highest, grand cross [*grand-croix*]. It is awarded by the President, who is the grand master [*grand maître*]. It has a national association of members, *Association nationale des membres de l'ordre national du mérite (ANMONM)*, Hôtel National des Invalides, 129 rue de Grenelle, 75700 Paris, Tel: 01 47057592, *www.anmnom.com* with a list of local associations in all *Départements*.

Rotary Clubs

The Rotary Club is a non-partisan, non-sectarian service club founded in 1905 in Chicago and then named Rotary because its meetings were rotated between the offices of the members of the club. The first Rotary Club in France was founded in 1921, and there are now more than 1000 Rotary Clubs with nearly 35,000 members in the country. For further information, contact Rotary International District 1660, 40 bd Émile Augier, 75116 Paris, Tel: 01 45032620, *www.rotary1660.org* with an interactive Club locator map.

Scouting [*Scoutisme*]

In 1907, the Boy Scout movement was founded in England, and just four years later, the first was formed in France. Today, there are five Scout organisations. For more information, contact *Fédération du scoutisme français*, 64 rue de la Glacière, 75013 Paris, Tel: 01 43370357, *www.scoutisme.fr* with overviews of scouting in the country as well as the details of the five member organisations:

- Boy scouts and Guides of France [*Scouts et Guides de France*], *http://www.scoutsetguides.fr/*
- Boy scouts Muslims of France [*Scouts Musulmans de France*], *http://www.scouts-mf.org*
- Girl guides and Scouts Israelites of France [*Eclaireuses et Eclaireurs Israélites de France*], *http://www.eeif.org*
- Girl guides and Scouts of France [*Eclaireuses et Eclaireurs de France*], *http://www.eedf.asso.fr*
- Girl guides and Scouts Unionists of France [*Eclaireuses et Eclaireurs Unionistes de France*], *http://www.eeudf.org*.

Youth hostels [*Auberges de jeunesse*]

The French link of the International Youth Hostel Federation (IYHF) is *Fédération unie des auberges de jeunesse (FUAJ)*, which now has 160 hostels in towns, rural districts, mountain areas and the seaside. Most of the hostels have smaller rooms with 4 to 6 beds, and in all they offer 17,000 beds. For further information, contact FUAJ at 27 rue Pajol, 75018 Paris, Tel: 01 44898727, *www.fuaj.org* selectable in French or English and with an interactive hostel locator map.

35
Pets and animals

Pets are kept, and wild animals roam the forests and mountains, much as elsewhere in Europe. Likewise, concern for animals is widespread and long standing. In July 1850, General and Parliamentarian Jacques de Grammont (1796-1862) successfully put through a new law that made persons guilty of maltreatment of animals in public [*les personnes ayant fait subir publiquement des mauvais traitements aux animaux*], punishable by fines or imprisonment.

Save for the endangered species, there are few estimates of the numbers of wild animals. Pets are another matter, as animal welfare association data show a national population of 8.1 million dogs, 9 million cats, 7 million birds, 27.3 million fish and 2 million rodents. Clearly, pets are popular: three magazines and one TV show are devoted to them. Nonetheless, each year, about 1,000,000 dogs and some 80,000 cats are abandoned or became feral strays, and all the animal welfare associations have animal shelters and active adoption programmes to find new homes for animals. Unquestionably, if you want a pet in France, you need not go far to find one.

Cats [*Chats*]

Cats must be the easiest of all pets to find. One may appear on your doorstep, as there are an estimated 80,000 abandoned and stray cats across the country. You can check the notice board at your local supermarket, as there always are cats and kittens looking for a new home. Or inquire at the nearest *SPA* shelter, *www.spa.assoc.fr* or at a website listed on one of the **portals**. Check the rules for **pet import** if you wish to bring a cat with you to France. If you're interested in pedigree cats, contact the official pedigree registry, *Livre Officiel des Origines Félines (LOOF)*, 5 rue Regnault, 93697 Patin Cedex, Tel: 01 417103335, *loof.asso.fr*, which has international liaison with The International Cat Association (TICA). For an overview of breeds [*les races*], breeders [*éleveurs*], shelters [*refuges*], shows [*expos*] and other matters concerning cats, visit *www.felichats.com* with an interactive breeder locator map.

Dogs [*Chiens*]

Dogs are popular pets, particularly in rural districts and in smaller cities and towns. Finding a dog is fairly simple, as at any one time, there are about 100,000 lost, stray and abandoned dogs in the country, many of which are picked up by an animal welfare association; to adopt, check at the nearest SPA shelter, *www.spa.assoc.fr* or at a website listed on one of the **portals**. Check the rules for **pet import** if you wish to bring a dog with you to France. If you're interested in one of the some 100 pedigrees of dogs registered in the country, contact the pedigree registry, *Société centrale canine (SCC)*, 185 avenue Jean Jaurès, 93535 Aubervilliers Cedex, Tel: 01 49375400, *www.scc.asso.fr* with an interactive regional society locator map and list as well as lists of links to the associations for the individual breeds [*Associations des races*] and to the major organisations [*sites institutionnels*] concerned with shows, grooming, training and other matters concerning dogs and their breeding.

Dogs allowed, Dogs prohibited [*Chien autorisé, chien interdit*]

Owners are legally responsible for their dogs and consequently for any damage done by them. A dog should be identified by a tattoo and by the name of its owner on its collar. In cities and urban areas, dogs should be kept on a leash. Otherwise, in cities, dogs are allowed:

- in city parks if on a leash
- at undeveloped bathing places along coasts
- at municipal campsites if on a leash or in a basket
- if small and carried in a basket, on buses, underground trains and trains
- if large, on trains at a charge, if on a leash and muzzled
- in some hotels; check in advance
- in most restaurants if on a leash
- if less than 5 kg, as hand baggage on airplanes if carried in a basket, subject to specified conditions
- if more than 5 kg, as baggage on airplanes if in a carrier and against a fee

and prohibited:

- in public gardens
- in public places where *Interdit Aux Chiens* or pictorial signs are posted
- at developed beaches
- if large, on buses and underground trains
- in food shops
- in public service venues, such as post offices and city halls.

Dog droppings [*Déjections canines*]

Dog droppings are a prevalent nuisance on city and town streets and pavements. Odd statistics are put forth on them, such as the 200,000 dogs in Paris leaving some 16 tons of droppings on the city's streets every day, and at least one recent humorous book focuses on them, *A Year in the Merde* by Stephen Clarke (London, Black Swan, 2005, 383 page paperback, ISBN 0-552-77296-8). However, the nuisance is subsiding, thanks to two dog dropping pick-up kits made in France and given away free to users from dispensers with pictorial instructions, increasingly common in public places across the country.

- The "dropping tongs" (*Pince à crotte*®) kit consists of biodegradable cardboard tongs and a robust paper bag for disposing of the picked-up droppings and soiled tongs into marked refuse bins. For further details, contact Societé Compofac, 5 rue de l'Admiral-Courbet, 94700 Maisons-Alfort, Tel: 01 43530465, *www.compofac.fr* with pages in English, Spanish and German as well as French, *pac@compofac.fr*.

- The "doggie-neat" [*Toutounet*] kit is a plastic bag, 22 × 30 cm, large enough to insert a hand to grasp the droppings and then turn inside-out and tie to seal for disposal in marked refuse bins. For further details, contact Sepra, 42720 La Benisson, Dieu, Tel: 04 77666666, *www.toutounet-ville-propre.com*, *separa@wanadoo.fr*.

Fondation 30 millions d'amis

Fondation 30 millions d'amis is a charity dedicated to protecting the welfare of lost, stray and abandoned pets and to promoting animal rights. It takes its name from a popular TV show on animals, launched in 1976 by media journalist Jean-Pierre Hutin (1931-), and today has 240 animal shelters across the country and acts as a clearing house for animal welfare information. For further information, contact the head office at 40 cours Albert, 75402 Paris Cedex 08, Tel: 01 56590444, *www.30millionsdamis.fr*.

French Animal Rights League
[*Fondation ligue française des droits de l'animal*]

Founded in 1977, the French Animal Rights League conducts research in and lobbies for animal rights, in part by publicly objecting to cruelty to animals in bull fighting, circuses, fishing, hunting and zoos, as well as in animal experiments. It has numerous publications and each year awards a biology prize for developing research methods that do not require animal experiments, named for one of the League's founders, physicist Alfred Kastler (1902-1984), the winner of the 1966 Nobel Prize in Physics. For further information, contact the League at its headquarters, 39 rue Claude Bernard, 75005 Paris, *www.animal-rights.org* in French and English.

Guide dogs [*Chiens guides*]

Across the country, guide dogs for the blind are made available by associations affiliated with the French Federation of Guide Dog Associations [*La Fédération Française des Associations Chiens guides d'aveugles (FFAC)*] which also coordinates:

- ten guide dog schools for the blind [*Écoles de chiens guides d'aveugles*]
- a breeding and selection centre [*Centre National d'Elevage (CESECAH)*] that provides the schools with puppies to be trained
- the association of guide dog users [*Association Nationale des Maîtres de Chiens Guides d'Aveugles (ANMCGA)*].

If you wish to bring a guide dog into the country, it will be subject to the same **pet import** regulations as for other dogs. If you need a guide dog in France or seek further information on the dogs and their training, contact the FFAC head office at 71 rue de Bagnolet, 75012 Paris, Tel: 01 44648989, *www.chiensguides.fr* in French and English.

Magazines [*Revues*]

Three magazines are dedicated solely to pets and animals. One, *Animaux Magazine*, with ten issues a year, is published by the SPA, office at 39 Boulevard Berthier, 75847 Paris Cedex 17, Tel: 01 43809706, *www.spa.asso.fr/abonnement.asp*. Two are commercial magazines, *30 Millions d'amis* with eleven issues a year and *Mon Animal*, a monthly, available at newsagents or by online subscription, such as offered by *www.viapresse.com*.

Pet import [*Importation d'animaux de compagnie*]

You may import any breed of cat or any breed of dog other than Staffordshire terrier, American Staffordshire Terrier, Mastiff or Tosa not pedigreed in France. Breeds of dogs which resemble these prohibited breeds must be accompanied by an original pedigree certificate and ID-number that proves the animal's breed.

The import of dogs, cats and ferrets, the most common pets as well as the most likely rabies carriers, is subject to rules that comply with those of the EU and the EEA. In all cases, the owner, or the owner's appointed representative, must accompany the pet(s) upon import. Up to five animals may be imported as family pets. Import of more than five animals is regarded to be commercial and is subject to separate regulations. Otherwise, the rules vary according to the country of last residence of the pet(s).

Import from EU countries and from low-rabies-risk countries* outside the EU is permitted provided you adhere to five rules:

1. Identification: the animal must be identified by a microchip (transponder) to ISO Standards 11784 Annex A or 11785 (if it is to another standard, you must supply

a reader for it). Until 3 July 2011, a clearly readable tattoo is allowable, except for Ireland, Malta and the UK, which already require the transponder.

2. Vaccination against rabies: the animal must have been vaccinated against rabies according to World Health Organisation (WHO) guidelines, and a blood sample for confirmation of antibody titre must have been taken not earlier than 120 days and not later than 365 days after the last vaccination.

3. *Enchinococcus* treatment: dogs and cats must have had a tapeworm (*enchinococcus*) treatment no more than 10 days before being imported.

4. Pet passport or Veterinary Certificate: a pet coming from an EU/EEA country must be accompanied by an EU Pet Passport issued by a vet in the country of origin (the EU does not issue the passports). A pet coming from another country* must be accompanied by a Veterinary Certificate in English or French, certified by the country's Health Authority.

5. Customs control: upon clearing customs with an animal, go through the red zone with the animal and its documentation.

Import from countries not considered low-rabies-risk is permitted, following the first four of the five rules listed above, with an extended fifth and an additional sixth rule:

5. Customs control: the border vet must be notified at least 48 hours prior to import, and you must have written confirmation that the notice has been received. Upon clearing customs with an animal, go through the red zone with the animal and its documentation, including the vet's confirmation of your request.

6. Quarantine: after you have cleared customs with an animal, it will be taken into quarantine for at least four months, followed by two months of "home quarantine" isolated from other animals.

For further information in general, visit the European Commission animal health and welfare website at *europa.eu.int/comm/food/animal/liveanimals/pets/index_en.htm* or for information specific to France, visit websites of the Ministry of Foreign Affairs at *www.france.diplomatie.fr* with pages in English, German and Spanish, or the National Association of Veterinarians [*Ordre national des vétérinaires*] at *www.veterinaire.fr*.

The EU Pet Passport, full size 10 × 15.2 cm; general English language version shown.

* According to EC Regulation 425/2005 of 15 March 2005: Ascension Island (AC), United Arab Emirates (AE), Antigua and Barbuda (AG), Netherlands Antilles (AN), Australia (AU), Aruba (AW), Barbados (BB), Bahrain (BH), Bermuda (BM), Canada (CA), Chile (CL), Fiji (FJ), Falkland Islands (FK), Hong Kong (HK), Croatia (HR), Jamaica (JM), Japan (JP), Saint Kitts and Nevis (KN), Cayman Islands (KY), Montserrat (MS), Mauritius (MU), New Caledonia (NC), New Zealand (NZ), French Polynesia (PF), Saint Pierre et Miquelon (PM), Russian Federation (RU), Singapore (SG), Saint Helena (SH), Taiwan (TW), United States of America (US), Saint Vincent and the Grenadines (VC), Vanuatu (VU), Wallis and Futuna (WF), Mayotte (YT)

Portals [*Sites portails*]

Innumerable websites are devoted to pets and animals. The three most comprehensive are:

* *Animaux-Online*, a panoply portal with sections for cats [*chat*], dogs [*chien*], horses [*cheval*], birds [*oiseau*], other animals [*autre*] and newer species of pets [*nac*, the abbreviation for *nouveaux animaux de compagnie*] including reptiles, rats and spiders, and links to breeders [*éleveurs*] and other organisations as well as to advertisements and subscriptions, *www.animaux-online.com*.

* *French toutou*, literally "French doggie", a clearing house for information on dogs as well as an online shop for dog supplies, 30 rue Edith Cavell, 92411 Courbevoie Cedex, Tel: 08 92701092, *www.frenchtoutou.com*.

* *French matou*, literally "French tom", the sibling of *French toutou* and a clearing house for information on cats as well as an online shop for cat supplies, 30 rue Edith Cavell, 92411 Courbevoie Cedex, Tel: 08 92701092, *www.frenchmatou.com*.

Society for the Prevention of Cruelty to Animals [*Société protectrice des animaux (SPA)*]

The Society for the Prevention of Cruelty to Animals was founded by Doctor Étienne Pariset (1770-1847) in 1845, just 21 years after the Society for Prevention of Cruelty to Animals (SPCA), the world's first animal protection organisation, was founded in 1824 in London (the R prefix for Royal came in 1840, after Queen Victoria endorsed the SPCA.)

Today, the SPA is one of the country's larger charities, with 53,000 members, 3000 supporters and a staff of 455. In addition to playing an active role in promoting and enforcing animal welfare legislation, the SPA operates 58 animal shelters that each year put up 45,000 animals for adoption and in cooperation with **Samusocial** (Chapter 33) operates 12 clinics [*dispensaires*] across the country to help homeless women with pets. It publishes a newsletter, *La lettre de la SPA*, and the *Animaux* *magazine*, and it arranges numerous activities across the country. For further information, contact the head office: 39 Boulevard Berthier, 75847 Paris Cedex 17, Tel: 01 43804066, *www.spa.asso.fr*.

Vets [*Vétérinaires*]

There are more than 18,000 vets in the country, more than 10,000 of them in private practice, listed under *Vétérinaires praticiens* in the Yellow Pages. There are two associations of vets that can supply further information on veterinaries and other matters concerning animal health:

- *Ordre des Vétérinaires,* 34 rue Bréguet, 75011 Paris, Tel: 01 47001227, *www.veterinaire.fr*.
- *Syndicat national des vétérinaires d'exercice libéral (SNVEL)*, 10 place Léon Blum, 75011 Paris, Tel: 01 44933000, *www.snvel.fr* with links to national and international veterinary organisations, and *www.vetpro.fr*, a members' website with information for the public.

Wildlife [*Faune*]

In the country there are 123 species of mammals, 357 species of birds, 38 species of reptiles, 38 species of amphibians, 428 species of fish and cyclostomes, 34,600 species of insects, 1400 species of molluscs, 250 species of marine invertebrates and 2500 species of crustaceans*. Many species are endangered, such as in the case of mammals, brown bears, lynx, mink, otters, seals and porpoises. The government is concerned, as is the public, though sometimes the two clash. Early in 2006, the Ministry of Environment feared that the only bears remaining in the country, a stand of a dozen or so animals roaming the Pyrenees, would soon disappear if nothing was done. Accordingly, bears were imported and turned loose to build up the genetic pool and save the stand from extinction. Local sheep farmers understandably were annoyed and there were anti-bear protests. But the farmers soon realised that the government understands the risks, as it pays compensation for livestock losses. Polls taken across the country indicated that 72% of the population supported building up the bears, and even in the Pyrenees, some 58% were in favour.

For overviews of wildlife and the French strategy for biodiversity, contact the Ministry for National Development and Environment [*Ministère de l'écologie et du développement durable*], 20 av. de Ségur, 75302 Paris Cedex 07, Tel: 01 42192021, *www.ecologie.gouv.fr* in French, English, German and Spanish.

QUID 2006, p. 172.

36
Post and courier

The Post is the oldest public service in the country. Its roots go back to 1477, when King Louis XI set up a military courier service to carry his correspondence. In 1672, the first general domestic and international postal services were initiated and Secretary of State François de Louvois (1641-1691) was appointed Secretary-General of the Posts. The service spread, and by the time of the *Révolution* in 1789, there were 1300 post offices across the country. Less than a century later, the Post embraced the instantaneous communication offered by the telegraph and in 1879, the ministry of *Postes et Télégraphes* was founded. Likewise, in 1921, it expanded to include telephony, and became the ministry of *Postes, Télégraphes et Téléphones (PTT)*. As elsewhere in Europe in the mid 20th century, the PTT became synonymous with the burgeoning communications sector and came to mean the Ministry as well as the services it offered. Consequently, even after the Ministry changed its name to *Postes et Télécommunications* in 1960 to reflect changes in communications technologies, the abbreviation PTT was retained. But in 1991, in step with the privatisation of governmental services, the PTT ceased to exist and *La Poste* was split off as a private-sector enterprise owned by the State.

Starting in the 1980s, private-sector courier services began competing with the Post, at first in international and then in domestic services. Today, parcels as well as documents are carried both by *La Poste* and by private-sector courier services, particularly in urban areas and internationally.

Address format [*Format d'adresse*]

Addressing has been standardised since 1997*, to ease and speed handling of mail within the country and to comply with international addressing standards. Though older conventions of writing addresses persist, postal and courier services recommend adherence to the standard, as an item with an address in non-standard format may be delayed or returned. The **National Address Management Service** states that an address shall have:

* Information in order, starting with the name and/or company name and finishing with the addressee's locality.

- No more than six lines, or seven for international mail. Blank lines must be deleted.
- No more than 38 characters per line, including spaces. There must be spaces between all words.
- No punctuation marks, underlining or words printed in italic in the "street number and name" line; no coma after the street number.
- A last line in capital letters, and preferably also the 4th, 5th and 6th lines.
- Left justification.

and illustrates the requirement with the following sample of a letter correctly addressed:

Line Information	Example
1. address identification	Monsieur Jean DELHOURME
2. additional delivery point information	Chez Mireille Copeau Appartement 2
3. additional geographical information	Entrée A Bâtiment Jonquille
4. street number and name	25 RUE DE L EGLISE
5. place name or service	CAUDOS
6. postcode and destination locality	33380 MIOS

The above example is for a private residence. If Monsieur Jean DELHOURME has a small user [*CIDEX*] code, it will appear on line 2. If he has a PO Box [*Boîte postale (BP)*], it will appear on line 5. If he has a large user [*CEDEX*] code, it will appear on line 6, or on line 5 if its location differs from that of the destination locality on line 6.

Spécifications postales – Adresse postale, mai 1997, AFNOR XP Z10-011, published by and available in print and online from **AFNOR** (Chapter 30).

Courier services [*Courrier*]

Courier services and accordingly the way they are listed in the Yellow Pages divide into two categories: parcel couriers [*Courrier, colis*], principally the **postal services** and the various varieties of delivery and collection services [*Courses et livraisons*], which includes almost all private-sector courier and messenger services. The principal courier services are, in alphabetical order:

- Chronopost, a subsidiary of the La Poste postal services, *www.fr.chronopost.com* in French and English.
- DHL, founded in the USA but now part of Deutsche Post in Europe, in France it has 300 sites in 125 cities and towns, *www.dhl.fr*.

- Sernam, a French logistics road transport service founded in 1970, now with 55 local branches across the country, *www.sernam.fr* in French and English.

- TAT Express, a French courier founded in 1976, now with 34 agencies and six transit centres across the country, *www.tatexpress.com* with an interactive agency locator map.

- TNT, founded in Australia, in France it has 120 sites, *www.tnt.com* in English; select France to access French site.

- UPS, based in the USA and operating in countries around the world, *www.ups.com* in English; navigate to France to bring up lists of locations in Paris, Annecy, Grenoble, Le Mans, Nice and Rennes.

Courrier international

Courrier international is the La Poste dedicated first-class priority international service in three categories, all using postage prepaid packaging of distinctive design and standard international format:

- *Envelope internationale*, E65 size (11 × 22 cm) business format, sold individually or in packets of ten at a discount. Valid for the countries of the world.

- *Postexport*, packaging of five types in four weight classes: C4 size (23 × 32.4 cm, for A4 size paper) paperboard envelopes for 100 gr and 500 gr weight classes, B4 size (25 × 35.3) Tyvek (polyethylene fibre) envelopes for 1 kg and 2 kg weight classes and cartons for 2 kg weight class. Colour-coded in three price classes according to countries served: blue for the EU and Switzerland, red for Europe outside the EU and for Africa, and green for the rest of the world.

- *Postexport premier*, two envelope formats for express, tracked delivery to ten European countries: Denmark, Finland, Germany, Great Britain, Ireland, the Netherlands, Portugal, Spain, Sweden and Switzerland.

For further information, inquire at any post office or visit the Courrier International website at *www.laposte.fr/courrierinternational* in French with selected topics in English for clients abroad.

National Address Management Service
[*Service national de l'adresse (SNA)*]

SNA has a staff of more than 100 experts concerned with all aspects of addressing. It is principally concerned with maintaining a national database of addresses and to implementing solutions for minimising returns due to relocations. But it also supports numerous services useful to businesses and the general public, including the standardised **address format** and an online **postcode** finder. Further information as well as most services are available online at *www.laposte.fr/sna* in French and English and with an interactive operational centre (COA) locator map.

PO Boxes, Large and small user postcodes
[*Boîte postale, CEDEX et CIDEX*]

Geographical addresses remain most common, but addressing options are available:

- Post Office Box [*Boîte postale*], delivery to a box at a post office, written BP followed by the number of the box, with the postcode indicating the post office where the box is located.

- Large user postcode [*Courrier d'entreprise à distribution exceptionnelle (CEDEX)*] for corporate users, with an assigned unique postcode, and written CEDEX, in large cities with a two-digit suffix indicating the *arrondissement*.

- Small user postcode [*Courrier individuel à distribution exceptionnelle (CIDEX)*] for groups of users, usually in rural areas or at holiday venues, to designate joint delivery to one point.

SNA, the **National Address Management Service** illustrates the correct ways for addressing these services by example of a hypothetical Monsieur Durand at Libourne:

Addressing:	For:
M DURAND 12 AVENUE DES FLEURS 33500 LIBOURNE	Mr. Durand's private residence at a geographical address.
DURAND SA BP 25 33506 LIBOURNE CEDEX	Mr. Durand's company that has a postal address.
DURAND SA 12 AVENUE DES FLEURS BP 25 33506 LIBOURNE CEDEX	Mr. Durand's company with both postal and physical addresses.
DURAND SA 12 AVENUE DES FLEURS BP 25 CHAMPS SUR MARNE 77453 MARNE LA VALLEE CEDEX 2	The company with a physical address but with a postal address in another municipality

Postage [*Tarifs postaux*]

Post offices as well as **Tobacconists** (Chapter 40) sell postage stamps [*timbres postaux*]. Many post offices have a vending machine [*distributeur automatique*] for postage franks [*affranchissement*] fitted with a scale on top for weighing items to be posted and with operating instructions selectable in French, English, German, Italian or Spanish.

Postal services [*Poste*]

La Poste, the national postal service, has 17,000 outlets across the country, more than 3900 of them in larger buildings that it owns. The principal postal services offered to the public are:

* First-class letters [*Le courrier lettre*]
* Second-class letters [*Le courrier économique*]
* Registered letters [*Le courrier recommandé*]
* Prepaid envelopes [*Prêt-à-poster*]
* Parcels [*Colis*, trade named *Colissimo*]
* Express Courier [*Chronopost*]
* Banking [*Banque Postale*], from 1 January 2006 a separate service.

As this book goes to press, *La Poste* has begun an extensive modernisation programme called *Cap Qualité Courier* and has redesigned many aspects of its services, including its familiar blue-on-yellow logo. For further details on *La Poste*, select one of the many brochures offered on racks in post offices or visit the website at *www.laposte.fr*.

Old logo, 1984-2005.   New logo, 2006- .

Post-boxes [*Boîtes aux lettres*]

Large, yellow post-boxes with blue lettering, with slots into which letters are posted, are at all post offices and are fixed to walls and pillars in cities and towns across the country. A post-box will have a small sign affixed listing the times at which it is cleared. From top to bottom, a typical sign reads:

Sign wording	English translation
Heures Des Levées	Hours of collection
Jours ouvrables	Working days
Semaine	Weekdays
Samedi	Saturdays
Dimanches et Jours Fériés	Sundays and public holidays
Bureau Le Plus Proche	Closest Post Office

Times are stated to the nearest half hour. For instance, *Semaine 14H30* means that the box is cleared at 14.30 on weekdays.

Postcodes [*Codes postaux*]

A postcode comprises five digits, of which the leading digits are the *Département* number, the first two for the 96 mainland *Départements* and the first three for the four overseas DOMs. The three principal series of postcodes are:

- for most cities, towns and rural districts:

  DDCC0

  where DD is the *Département* number, CC is the *Canton* number, and the last digit is a zero.

- or the three largest cities, Lyon, Marseille and Paris:

  DD0AA

  where DD is the *Département*: 69 for Lyon, 13 for Marseille and 75 for Paris, the third digit is zero, and AA is the *arrondissement* number

- for large users (CEDEX):

  DDLLL

  where DD is the *Département* and LLL is the CEDEX number

Many postcode finders are available on the Internet, some public and some private, available upon subscription. Arguably the best two are free, as they are supported by the *La Poste* database, which always is the most up-to-date:

- *La Poste*: *www.laposte.fr*, click on *ENTRÉ* under *PARTICULIER*, then on *OUTILS PRATIQUES* and finally on *Trouvez un code postal, un code cedex ou une commune* to bring up the postcode dialogue box.
- *SNA*: *www.laposte.fr/sna*, click on *SERVICES EN LIGNE* and then on *Trouver un code postal* to bring up the postcode dialogue box.

In France, if you lack Internet access, inquire at a post office, as all have online terminals.

PostEurop

PostEurop is the abbreviation for the Association of European Public Postal Operators [*Association des Opérateurs Postaux Publics Européens*]. It was founded in 1993 by 26 public postal operators that until then had been members of the European Conference of Postal and Telecommunications Administrations [*Conférence Européenne des Administrations des Postes et des Télécommunications (CEPT)*], an organisation that had been founded in 1959 to coordinate the activities of governmental post and telecommunications monopolies. In the wave of deregulation then sweeping across Europe, post and telecommunications were split off as private sector enterprises. Each sector continued cooperation in a new organisation, PostEurop for post and **ETNO** (Chapter 44) for telecommunications, and the CEPT became concerned with policy making and regulation only. Today, PostEurop has 43 members and works to support and enhance sustainable postal service across Europe. For further information, contact the head office at Av. du Bourget 44, 1130 Brussels, Belgium, Tel: +32 2 7247280, *www.posteurop.org* selectable in French or English.

Principal postal prices [*Principaux tarifs*]

Postal prices are set one or more times a year. Complete lists of them are available at post offices and online at *www.laposte.fr*. The prices for letters can be downloaded in PDF files. First click on *Entrée* under *Particulier*, then on *Envoyez recevez du courrier*, then on *Les tarifs* and then select the brochure from the list of four for the mainland [*métropolitaine*] and three overseas *Départements*. A similar navigation sequence, clicking on *Envoyez recevez des colis* leads to pages listing the various parcel rates.

Track and trace [*Suivi des envois*]

All carriers of letters and packages labelled with barcodes offer online track and trace. *La Poste* offers several track and trace services; for an overview with links to the services, visit *www.laposte.fr*, click on *PARTICULIER*, then on *PROFITEZ DE NOS SERVICES EN LIGNE* and finally in the drop-down menu, on *Suivi des envois* to bring up the overview page. Most of the courier services offer track and trace via a dialogue window on the opening page of their websites.

Universal Postal Union [*Union Postale Universelle*]

Established in 1874, the Universal Postal Union (UPU) is the principal forum for cooperation between postal services round the world. Today, some 190 countries are members of the UPU, and its many published reports and references provide authoritative overviews as well as details useful in comparing postal services. For further information, contact Universal Postal Union, International Bureau, Case postale 13, 3000 Berne 15, Switzerland, Tel: +41 313503111, *www.upu.int* selectable in French or English.

Vocabulary [*Vocabulaire*]

Today, postal services are international, and their comprehensive vocabularies similar, though many terms differ from those customarily found in general purpose multilingual dictionaries, perhaps because the principal postal services around the world evolved nationally before they became international. Fortunately, the **Universal Postal Union** offers a multilingual glossary in five languages: English, French, German, Portuguese and Spanish:

- in print, as the "Multilingual Vocabulary of the International Postal Service", now with Supplement 1 "Marketing of the Postal Service" and Supplement 2 "Information Technology, Telematics and Electronic Mail"

- online, the TERMPOST glossary at *www.upu.int*.

Though no longer in print, the *Vocabulaire polyglotte du service postal international* (Bern, UPU, 1992, ISSN 0252-9467) covers three more languages, Arabic, Chinese and Russian, and remains a much-used reference. The La Poste **Courrier International** service supports an online French-English glossary on its website at *www.laposte.fr/courrier.international*, click on *Particulier*, then on *Informations pratiques* and then on *Traducteur postal* to bring up the glossary window.

37
Prices

As in any country, prices change continuously. So a price mentioned in this book can be valid at press time (late 2006) but soon may be outdated. Consequently, the prices mentioned in the other chapters of this book are few and are of the sort most likely to stay fixed for a year or more, such as governmental fees. Everyday prices that vary more rapidly can be estimated from the measures and trends outlined in this chapter.

Consumer price index [*Indice des prix à la consommation*]

The consumer price index (CPI) of a country is an economic indicator that measures the changes over time in the prices of consumer goods and services. CPIs are referenced to a base year in which the prices of a range of product groups each are assigned a value of 100, meaning 100%. In a later year, the prices of the same groups are again observed and changes are expressed relative to the base year. So CPIs are used to track changes in the prices of goods and services bought by households. Utility charges, as for water, and value-added-tax (VAT) are included, but investments, as in housing, are excluded. Consequently, housing prices are often expressed in separate indexes.

The first CPI in France was referenced to the 1914 base year and covered mostly food. With time, the prices of services and of manufactured goods were added. By 1990, the sixth-generation CPI covered 265 groups and reflected price data collected in all cities and towns with a population of more than 2000. In 1999, the seventh-generation CPI was launched and referenced on the 1998 base year. It is the CPI used today, so all present mentions of the consumer price index mean prices relative to 1998.

INSEE, the **National Institute of Statistics and Economic Studies** (Chapter 42) compiles and publishes three CPIs covering metropolitan France and the DOMs. For April 2006, the latest available as this book goes to press, they are:

Coverage	CPI, April 2006
All households, all items	114.16
All households, all items except tobacco	113.02
Urban households headed by a manual or clerical payroll worker, all items except tobacco	112.90

For the latest CPI, visit the INSEE website at *www.insee.fr*. On the opening page, select French or English, and then click on Consumer price index [*Indice des prix à la consommation*] in the list under Main Indicators [*Les grands indicateurs*].

Inflation [*Inflation*]

In economics, inflation in a country means an increase in prices or in its money supply. In everyday life, price inflation is most relevant, as it is linked to the **Consumer Price Index** and directly indicates decreases in the purchasing power of money. The **National Institute of Statistics and Economic Studies** (Chapter 42) compiles data on and regularly issues reports on inflation in France as does **EUROSTAT** (Chapter 42) for all of Europe. EUROSTAT now bases its inflation figures on the year 2005.

As this book goes to press, the most recent EUROSTAT inflation figure for the Euro area was 2.4% at the end of April 2006. The figure for France was 2.0%, which indicates that prices rose less rapidly in France than elsewhere in the Euro area. For the most recent figures, visit the EUROSTAT website at *epp.eurostat.cec.eu.int*.

Price levels [*Niveaux des prix*]

Prices have climbed through the years. But, as shown in the table below, wages have gone up more, so the time worked to buy essentials has gone down.

Price levels in Euros, 1980-2003*

Item	1980	1990	1995	2003
1 kg beef	8.08	13.97	14.90	17.09
1 kg bread	1.02	1.91	2.34	2.84
1 litre super petrol	0.52	0.84	0.90	1.11
Minimum hourly wage	2.13	4.77	6.41	7.61
National budget expenditure, billions	88.4	195.4	262.3	280.1

*France in Figures [*La France En Bref*] 2005.

Prices of housing [*Prix des logements*]

As elsewhere in Europe, the housing market is changing. Home ownership, long viewed as unimportant as in many other countries, is on the upswing, and more than 55% of all residents own their homes. The number of persons per household is declining and now is 2.4, down from 2.8 in 1978, which favours apartments over houses. Second homes are becoming more popular and now account for more than a tenth of all housing.*

And, as elsewhere, prices vary widely. For ten larger cities in 2003-2004, average dwelling prices ranged from €126,000 in Lille to €335,000 in Nice. The prices of apartments vary the most, by location and size. For example, in late 2004 in Paris, apartment prices ranged from €3614 per square metre in the 20th *Arrondissement* to €7045 per square metre in the 6th *Arrondissement*, and in Saint-Tropez a record €14,340 per square metre was paid for a third-floor apartment with a view of the port.**

These price levels reflect the global housing price bubble that analysts recently have predicted may leak or burst. But as this book goes to press (late 2006), *The Economist,* which updates global house price indicators four times a year, reckoned that housing prices had gone up 14.2% over a year earlier, the fourth highest rate among the developed countries tracked.

*France in Figures [*La France en Bref*] 2005 and *Annuaire Statistique de la France*, tables E02-1 to 10.

**Conseils par des notariés de France*, March 2005, No. 336, pp. 7-9.

***The Economist, print edition, December 8th 2005.

Purchasing power parity [*Parité du pouvoir d'achat*]

Purchasing power parity (PPP) is a concept that equates the buying power of various currencies. Its main principle is that exchange rates should move toward levels which equalise the prices of goods and services, no matter where they are bought. But prices vary. So PPPs are computed to examine their differences. The strength of the PPP concept is that it permits currencies to be compared with each other. Its drawback has been that the PPP is difficult to calculate. Goods differ from country to country, as do the ways of providing services.

There's one increasingly popular exception to that rule. In 1986, *The Economist,* the renowned British weekly finance and news magazine, instituted a light-hearted guide to PPP by selecting a simple collection – or "basket" as economists call it – of goods consisting of a Big Mac hamburger. The Big Mac is uniform and is produced in more than 100 countries. Its price reflects the costs of local goods – the ingredients – and services – the preparation and serving. The Big Mac PPP is based on the price of a Big Mac averaged over four cities in the USA, its home country. It signals whether each currency is over-valued or under-valued against the US dollar.

The Big Mac PPP index has become a regular annual feature in a spring or early summer issue of *The Economist*, in the print edition with an abbreviated list of countries surveyed and online at *www.economist.com* with the complete list of countries.

As this book goes to press, the latest index was published 25 May 2006. The average price of a Big Mac in four American cities then was $3.10 (including tax). The cheapest was in China ($1.31), the most expensive in Norway ($7.05). This meant that the Chinese Yuan was the world's most undervalued currency (by −58%), the Norwegian Krone its most overvalued (by +127%). The average for the Euro area was $3.77, (+22%), just slightly more than Britain, $3.65 (+18%), which implies that if you are accustomed to British prices, you will find the EU area, which includes France, only slightly more expensive.

Relative prices [*Prix relative*]

Upon visiting or settling in France, you may find some goods and services expensive [*cher*] and others inexpensive [*pas cher*]. For example, if you come from a country where alcoholic drink is heavily taxed, as in Scandinavia, you will find wine in France cheap. If you come from a country where motor fuels are negligibly taxed, such as the USA, you will find petrol in France expensive. Such findings relate to your previous experience of wages and prices and will change with time as your perceptions adjust to living and working in France. That said, wealth, wages and prices [*fortune, salaries et prix*] are of principal concern to anyone living in the country, which perhaps is why they comprise one of the first chapters in QUID, the popular family reference annual (pp 47-63, 2006 edition, ISBN 2-2210448X, *www.quid.fr*).

38

Registrations and certificates

Numerous registrations and certificates are required in everyday affairs. All residents need a National Identity Number, and citizens may have a National identity card. If you marry or enter a civil union, you will have a Family book. If you are self-employed or found a company, you must register at one of the Company procedures centres. If you are an inventor or you create works deserving of protection, you will be interested in patents or copyright. If you come from abroad or wish to extend the validity of French documents to other countries, you will need an *Apostille*. These matters are the topics of this chapter. Otherwise, if you are a foreigner, you may need a **Residence Permit** (Chapter 2) or a **Work Permit** (Chapter 2). All residents need a **Social Security card** (Chapter 22). If you drive a motor vehicle, you need a **Driving licence** (Chapter 4). If you enter civil contracts or buy property, **Notaries** (Chapter 29) are your points of contact for the relevant paperwork.

Apostille [*Apostille*]

An Apostille – from the French word for "commendatory note" – is a simplified certification of public and notarised documents used in the 84 countries that are signatories to the Hague Convention of 5 October 1961* that abolished the former and often complex requirements involved in legalising foreign documents. In practice, an Apostille usually is affixed by a government agency of the country in which an original legally valid document was issued to give it international validity. Typically, an Apostille may be affixed to a marriage certificate, a birth certificate, a will, a company registration certificate, a notarised form or an approved copy of a passport or other official document, to ensure validity of the document in France. Likewise, an Apostille may be affixed to a French document to ensure its validity elsewhere.

Apostilles usually are issued by an administrative or judicial agency of the government of a country. Notaries as well as embassies will have the relevant details. In some countries, private-sector document legalisation services offer apostilles by post against a set fee; in the UK, one such company is Apostille.biz, Tel: 0800 3287994, *www.apostille.biz*.

In France, apostilles are issued at no charge by judicial offices. In Paris, there is an office dedicated to them: Palais de Justice, Service Apostille, Salle des pas perdus (Kiosque accueil), 6, boulevard du Palais, 75001 Paris, Tel: 01 44325137.

Outside Paris, apostilles are issued by the public services [*Le service civil*] at the offices of the General Prosecuters [*Les Procureurs généraux*] or the Courts of Appeal [*Cours d'appel*]. Each Department has an assigned Court of Appeal, and some Courts serve several Departments. For instance, the Court of Appeal at Montpellier serves the Department of Hérault (34), in which the city is located, as well as the Department of Aveyron (12) to the north and the Departments of Aude (11) and Pyrénées-Orientales (66) to the south.

*For the full text of the Convention and the current list of countries that are signatories to it, visit the Hague Conference on Private International Law website at *hcch.e-vision.nl*.

Cadastre

A cadastre is a public register of the extent, value and ownership of real property. The word, in English as well as French, comes from the Latin *capitastrum*, a unit into which the Roman Provinces were divided for territorial taxation. That same purpose was furthered in 1807 by Napoléon when the properties of the country were made subject to registry in cadastres. Today, the cadastre of a town or *canton* is the reference for assessment of **Property tax** (Chapter 43). A registration sheet in a cadastre usually includes a map, in scale 1:5000 for rural areas and 1:500 for urban areas. The cadastres of the country now are being digitised and made available in central databases. For further information on cadastres and their uses, contact *Commission nationale de l'information et des libertés (CNIL)*, 8 rue Vivienne, CS 30223, 75083 Paris, Tel: 01 53732222, *www.cnil.fr*. For information on historical cadastres, contact the Sarthe archive that keeps them, 9 rue Christian-Pineau, 72016 Le Mans Cedex 2, Tel: 02 43547474, *www.archives.sarthe.com* with an interactive *canton* cadastre locator map.

Company procedures centres
[*Centres de formalités des entreprises (CFE)*]

Businesses of all sorts, from self-employed persons to large corporations, must be registered with various governmental agencies, not least for tax purposes. The government agencies responsible vary according to the size and nature of the business, but collectively all are known as Company procedures centres [*Centres de formalités des entreprises (CFE)*], and all centres may be located in the national network, *Réseau CFE*. For further information as well as for a list of the centres, contact Réseau CFE, 18 boulevard Adolphe Pinard, 75675 Paris Cedex 14, Tel : 01 41176611, *www.sirene.tm.fr/annuaire.cfe*.

Copyright [*Droit d'auteur*]

Intellectual property rights have long been a matter of concern. In 1878, author Victor Hugo founded the French Association for the International Protection of Authors' Rights [*Association Française pour la Protection Internationale du Droit d'Auteur (FPIDA)*], 82 rue du Faubourg Saint-Honoré 75008 Paris, *www.afpida.org*. Today, many organisations, some affiliated with FPIDA, are concerned with intellectual property rights. In alphabetical order by their common abbreviations, the six largest are:

- *ADAGP, Société française de gestion collective des droits d'auteur dans les arts visuels*, 11 rue Berryer, 75008 Paris, Tel: 01 43590979, *www.adagp.fr* in French and English.

- *CSDM, Chambre Syndicale des Éditeurs de Musique*, 62 rue Blanche, 75009 Paris, Tel: 01 48740929, *www.csdem.org*.

- *SACD, Société des Auteurs et Compositeurs Dramatiques*, 11 Bis Rue Ballu, 75 442 Paris, Cedex 09, Tel: 01 40234444, *www.sacd.fr* in French and English and with links to SACD organisations in Belgium and Canada.

- *SACEM, Société des Auteurs, Compositeurs et Éditeurs de Musique*, 225 av. Charles de Gaulle, 92528 Neuilly-sur-Seine Cedex, Tel: 01 47154715, *www.sacem.fr*.

- *SAIF, Société des Auteurs des arts visuels et de l'Image Fixe*, Maison des Photographes, 121 rue Vieille du Temple, 75003 Paris, Tel: 01 44610782, *saif.free.fr*.

- *SCAM, Société Civile des Auteurs Multimedia*, 5 avenue Vélasquez, 75008 Paris, Tel: 01 56695858, *www.scam.fr* in French and English.

Family record book [*Livret de famille*]

In many continental European countries, when a couple marries, they are given a family record booklet in which details, including births, marriages and deaths, are recorded. The booklets conform to the **International Commission on Civil Status** (Chapter 21) norm and are commonplace in Belgium, France, the Netherlands, Spain and Switzerland. The French book, *Livret de famille*, is issued according to five definitions of a family:

- a married couple [*le livret de famille des époux*]
- the mother of an illegitimate child [*le livret de famille de la mère d'un enfant naturel*]
- the father of an illegitimate child [*le livret de famille du père d'un enfant naturel*]
- the father and mother of an illegitimate child [*le livret de famille commun du père et de la mère d'un enfant naturel*]
- the father and mother of an adopted child [*le livret de famille du père ou de la mère d'un enfant adopté*]

For further information, contact the city hall [*Mairie*] having jurisdiction over the place where you live.

National identification card [*Carte nationale d'identité*]

The present national identity card, introduced in 1987, is a non-mandatory, secure form of identification offered to citizens. It carries the portrait photo and signature of the bearer, is valid for ten years and may be used instead of a passport for cross-border travel within the **Schengen Area** (Chapter 21). For further information and application materials, contact the nearest town hall [*Mairie*] or **Prefecture** (Chapter 21).

In February 2005, the Ministry of the Interior proposed a new mandatory secure electronic national identification card [*Identité nationale électronique sécurisée (INES)*] that included biometric data and could be remotely read without physical contact. Civil libertarians voiced concerns about the proposal and six human rights groups, including the **Human rights league** (Chapter 33), protested and formed an Internet coalition against the proposal, ironically named with the INES, though meaning *Inepte, Nocif, Effrayant, Scélérat* ("Inept, Noxious, Dreadful, Villainous"). Consequently, the **Internet rights forum** (Chapter 33) was asked to study the matter. In a report submitted in mid June 2005, it concluded that the proposal was flawed and that further study was needed. As this book goes to press, the proposed new card remains postponed.

France is hardly alone in having a proposed biometric data card protested by civil rights groups. According to information compiled by Privacy International, the human rights watchdog group of more than a hundred experts and organisations in 40 countries, including France, such difficulties are increasingly commonplace. For further details, contact the head office: 6-8 Armwell Street, Clerkenwell, London CD1R 1UQ, UK, *www.privacyinternational.org*, *privacyint@privacy.org*.

National Identity Number [*Numéro national d'identité*]

Each resident is assigned a unique identity number [*numéro national d'identité (NNI)*] that is used in dealings with government agencies. It is popularly called the "Social security number" [*Numéro de sécurité sociale*] because that is the most commonplace application of it.

But the number itself only designates an entry in a register [*numéro d'inscription au répertoire – NIR*] called the National Identification Register of Private Individuals [*Répertoire National d'Identification des Personnes Physiques (RNIPP)*] that is maintained by the **National Institute of Statistics and Economic Studies (INSEE)** (Chapter 42). The Register of persons born on the mainland, on Crete, or in the Overseas Departments (DOM) is maintained at the Nantes Regional Office of INSEE, and the Register of persons born in Overseas Territories (TOM) or abroad is maintained by the **National Old-Age Insurance Fund** (Chapter 21) on delegation of authority from INSEE. Because INSEE is responsible for the database, the NIR sometimes is called an "INSEE-number", though that name can mislead, as INSEE neither deals with the public nor assigns NIRs.

The NIR consists of 15 digits in the format:

G	YY	MM	DDPPP	NNN	CC
Gender	Year of birth	Month of birth	Birthplace	Sequence	Check digits
1 for male 2 for female	last two digits	two digits, 01 - 12	five digits: DD = department PPP = place	three digits to distinguish people born on same day at same place	two digits

The birthplace is coded according to *COG*, the **Official geographic code** (Chapter 20): DD is the department number, 01 – 96 or 99 for persons born abroad, and PPP is the place – city, town or rural district – of birth, or a three-digit country COG country code for persons born abroad. For instance, for a person born in Great Britain, where this book is published, the birthplace code is 99132.

If you are not born in France or are not French, upon taking up residence, you may apply for an NNI at *SANDIA* (*Service administratif national d'immatriculation des assurés*), part of the National Old-Age Insurance Fund [*Caisse nationale d'assurance vieillesse (CNAV)*] at 15 avenue Louis Jouhanneau, BP 266, 37002 Tours Cedex, Tel: 02 47887407.

Patents [*Brevets*]

Patents, inventions, designs and the like may be registered with the National Patent Office [*Institut national de la propriété industrielle (INPI)*], that has a head office in Paris and regional offices in 12 other cities across the country. For further information, contact INPI, 26 bis, rue de Saint Petersbourg, 75008 Paris Cedex 08, Tel: 08 25838587, *www.inpi.fr* with an interactive regional office locator map. INPI acts as the French portal for the European Patent Office (EPO), Erhardstr. 27, D-80469 München, Germany, Tel: +49 8923990, *www.european-patent-office.org* in English, French and German.

SIRENE database [*SIRENE base de données*]

All registered businesses and public bodies are assigned a registry number held in the SIRENE database maintained by the **National Institute of Statistics and Economic Studies** (Chapter 42). First implemented in the late 1970s, SIRENE is an acronym for *Système Informatique pour le Répertoire des Entreprises et des*

Etablissements, literally "Computer system for the register of enterprises and local units (establishments)". The database builders had a sense of humour, as they contracted by twisting the rules of accents in French to make the acronym read in capitals like the word *sirène*, which means "mermaid". The SIRENE number identifies the registered entity, which may be a person, a legal person such as a business, or a public body. It consists of nine digits, of which the last is a check digit. The digits have no significance, save for the numbers for public bodies that begin with 1 or 2.

As a registered entity may operate at more than one location, the SIRENE number is suffixed by an internal classification number [*Numéro Interne de Classement (NIC)*] that consists of four digits plus a check digit. The combination of the SIRENE number and the NIC is known as the SIRET, the 14-digit number that uniquely identifies a registered business or public body and facilitates finding information on it. For complete information on SIRENE and SIRET, visit the database portal at *www.sirene.tm.fr* or inquire at one of the **Company procedures centres**.

39
Retirement

As in other developed countries, the number of retired persons is increasing as the population ages. By 2010, one person of working age in four will be over 50, twice as many as today, and by 2050, more than half the population over 20 years old could be retired*.

The retirement milieu of today has its roots in the enactment in 1910 of the *Retraites ouvrières et paysannes* law that set up collective insurance and thereby initiated pension policy. With time, the policy shaped the perception of a third age of life that follows the first two, youth and working. By the 1970s, the third age had come to designate an active period of life, in which people could pursue traditional leisure time activities, engage in self-improvement or continue contributing to their professions or to society in general. They became seniors [*les séniors*], people active in life but older than others. One indication of the changed perception of the retired was the foundation of third age clubs, such as the *Clubs des aînés ruraux* that now have more than 800,000 members across the country. Another indication was a marked upswing in interest among the elderly for continued education and professional activities. Some of the French initiatives founded then have gone well beyond the borders of the country. Started in Toulouse in 1973, the Universities of the Third Age [*Universités du troisième âge*], a programme of low-cost education for the elderly, now has been taken up by other countries. Started in 1974, French Senior Volunteers now provides engineering, scientific and management volunteer consultant expertise round the globe.

*Ageing and employment policies [*Vieillissement et politiques de l'emploi*] OECD report, 2005, ISBN 92-64-00886-1, downloadable online from *www.oecd.org*.

CLEIRPPA

CLEIRPPA, the abbreviation for *Centre de liaison, d'étude, d'information et de recherche sur les problèmes des personnes âgées* ("Cooperative centre for studies, information and research on the problems of the elderly"), is a non-government organisation that acts a coordinating body and clearing house for 16 national organisations. It publishes a newsletter, brochures and monographs, both for professionals and for the general public, and it supports studies and also provides expertise to public agencies. For further information, contact CLEIRPPA, 86 avenue de Saint-Quen, 75018 Paris, Tel: 01 40254960, *www.cleirppa.asso.fr*.

EURAG

EURAG, an acronym from its name in German, *Europäische Arbeitsgemeinschaft*, is the European Federation of the Elderly, a not-for-profit, apolitical, non-sectarian organisation founded in 1962. Through its member organisations in 33 European Countries, including several in France, EURAG aims to promote the quality of life of senior citizens. It acts at the international level by putting proposals and motions before international organisations. It holds congresses and regularly publishes news of interest to senior citizens. For further information, contact the secretariat, Wielandgasse 9, A-8010 Graz, Austria, Tel: +43 316 814608, *www.eurag-europe.org* selectable in English, French, German and Italian.

FIAPA

FIAPA, the abbreviation for *Fédération Internationale des Associations de Personnes Agées* ("International Federation of Associations for Elderly People") was founded in 1980 in Paris by Belgian, French, Italian and Spanish national associations for the elderly. The concept spread, and now FIAPA has 150 member associations or federations in 60 countries on five continents.

FIAPA acts as a clearing house for information and regularly publishes reports and booklets on matters of concern for the elderly. At the international level, FIAPA now has either consultative or participative status in major international organisations, including the Council of Europe, the European Union (EU) and the World Health Organisation (WHO). For further information, contact the head office at 10 rue Chauchat, 75009 Paris, Tel: 01 44568431, *www.fiapa.org* in French, English and Spanish.

French Senior Volunteers [*Professionnels Seniors Bénévoles*]

French Senior Volunteers is an association of recently retired professional engineers, scientists and managers who choose to continue doing what they do best by volunteering their expertise to solve problems for clients that otherwise might not be able to afford the services of consultants. Founded in 1974 as *Echanges consultations techniques internationaux (ECTI)* to provide expertise to developing countries, the association is principally concerned with contributing to economic, cultural and social development; to creating jobs and maintaining employment; and to assisting developing countries in setting up a market economy. On assignments, which may be no longer than ten days, the ECTI consultant receives no salary, and the client is charged only for the consultant's direct travel and subsistence expenses plus a means-tested contribution to ECTI's general expenses. Today, ECTI has its headquarters in Paris, 53 regional offices across France and 54 representatives in other countries. For further details, contact ECTI, 101-109 rue Jean Jaurès, 92300 Levallois-Perret, Tel: 01 41403600, *www.ecti-vsf.org* selectable in French, English, Spanish or Chinese, with an interactive office locator map of France and a representative locator map of the world.

Housing and care for senior citizens
[*Hébergement des personnes âgées*]

There are various public and private provisions for housing and care for senior citizens that depend in part on the age and health of a person. They divide into six categories:

- Retirement homes [*Maisons de retraite*] for able and disabled persons who can manage on their own but need some attention and nursing care.

- Care homes [*Maisons de retraite avec "section de cure médicale"*] for persons who cannot look after themselves but have no need to be hospitalised.

- Sheltered housing [*Foyers logements*], usually complexes of flats or small houses, similar to local authority housing. The residents look after themselves and may by assisted by home help or community care services.

- Shared residences [*Résidences service*], usually comprising apartments of three or four rooms and with medical surveillance and shared services.

- Retirement villages [*Villages retraite*], usually comprising detached houses [*pavilions*] in rural areas.

- Long term facilities [*Centres et unités de long séjour*] for persons requiring constant medical care. Some facilities are specialised, such as in caring for dementia patients.

There are three approaches to finding housing and care provisions:

- Local: inquire at the *Mairie* of the city or town where you live or at the *Conseil général* of the *Canton*. These offices are listed in the Yellow Pages under *Administrations régionales, départementales et locales*. Some cities and *Cantons* have a *Conseil de la vie sociale d'une maison de retraite* dedicated to the matter.

- Departemental: inquire at the *Direction départementale des affaires sanitaires et sociales (DDASS)* listed in the Yellow Pages under *Administrations de la santé et des affaires sociales* and online at *www.sante.gouv.fr*, click on *Le Ministère* and then on the *Les DRASS et DDASS* link to bring up an interactive locator map.

- Private sources: there are many online websites that offer private facilities as well as portals that offer overviews and catalogues of public and private facilities across the country; the two most comprehensive are *www.maisons-retraite.com* with a selectable directory of facilities and *annuaire.agevillage.com* with an interactive facility selector map.

Pension system [*Système de retraite*]

Though compulsory, the pension system is not directly managed by the State, but by social partners [*partenaires sociaux*] that represent people who contribute to and benefit from the system. So pensions are managed not by public agencies, but by private social security [*sécurité sociale*] insurance funds that by law provide a public service. These compulsory pensions may be augmented by voluntary supplementary pensions [*retraite complémentaire*] offered by some companies and by some employment sectors.

The dominant part of the compulsory sector is *le régime général* that covers about 60% of the population. In it, a national organisation, *Caisse Nationale d'Assurance Vieillesse CNAV)* manages pensions paid out by the 16 *Caisse Régionale d'Assurance Maladie (CRAM)* that also deal with health insurance; for further information, visit the CNAV website at *www.cnav.fr* with an interactive CRAM locator map. There are nine other parts of the sector:

- Civil service [*Régime des fonctionnaires civils et militaires de l'Etat*]
- Local government [*Régime des collectivités locales*]
- Employment sectors [*Régimes spéciaux d'entreprise et assimilés*]
- Navy [*Régime des marins*]
- French citizens abroad [*Régime des français à l'étranger*]
- Students [*Régime des étudiants*]
- Parliament [*Régime spécifique des assemblées*]
- Agriculture [*Régime agricole*]
- Self-employed, non-farm [*Régime des non salaries non agricoles*].

The pension system is fragmented and involves 38 agencies and organisations. Moreover, it is being reformed, in part to stay abreast of the changing needs of an ever older population. For an overview of the system after the most recent pension reform of 21 August 2003, contact *Espace-retraite*, Tel: 08 25809879, *www.espaceretraite.tm.fr* and from it download the *Réforme des retraites* brochure.

Portals [*Sites portails*]

Innumerable websites offer information on topics related to retirement. Two of them are comprehensive portals, one public one private, each covering a broad variety of topics and providing links to other websites:

- *Personnes âgées, www.personnes-agees.gouv.fr*, supported by the *Ministère délègue aux personnes âgées*, 8 avenue Ségur, 75007 Paris, Tel: 01 40566000.
- *AgeVillage, www.agevillage.com*, supported by Eternis SA, 32 rue de l'Échiquier, 75010 Paris, Tel: 01 42466803.

Universities of the third age [*Universités du troisième âge*]

First offered at the University of Toulouse in 1973, a University of the third age, often abbreviated U3A, comprises activities tailored for the elderly that are offered by an academic institution. The idea caught on and spread across Europe and to other continents: today there are U3A programmes in Europe, Asia, North America and South America, the most extensive in France, with 16 academic institutions. The programmes differ, as do the peoples of the countries, but all have in common the aim to prolong learning through a wide range of activities and studies that build on an individual's lifetime of experience. For further information on U3A activities and academic institutions offering them round the world, contact *Association Internationale des Universités du Troisième Âge (AIUTA)*, 1 rue Augustine Variot, 92245 Malakaff Cedex, Tel: 01 46731213, *www.aiuta.asso.fr* in French with selected pages in English, Italian and Spanish and an interactive academic institution locator map.

40
Shopping

The roots of the word "shopping" go back to the old French *eschoppe*, which in modern French is *échoppe*, a lean-to booth or cobbler's stall. Yet the French contributions to modern shopping go beyond the word. The concept of luxury goods is a French invention, as is the word "luxury", from the old French *luxurie*, and today the world's leading luxury goods conglomerate is LVMH of Paris. Likewise, the word "hypermarket" is the Anglicisation of *hypermarché*, a word coined in 1968 to describe a huge supermarket that sells a great variety of goods in addition to food, and today a French food and non-food retailer, Carrefour, is second largest in the world.

As elsewhere, supermarkets and hypermarkets loom large in the food sector, together each year accounting for 87% of the total turnover in foods and related items. Yet across the country, small food shops outnumber supermarkets and hypermarkets. Including tobacconists, they outnumber the super and hypermarkets 12 to one. Though the big shops account for the lion's share of sales each year, the small shops still reflect the shopping habits of France, so much so that hypermarkets will have departments named after the sorts of small shops that they supplant – *boucherie, boulangerie, charcuterie, chocolaterie, fromagerie, poissonnerie, traiteur* and so on.

In non-foods the picture is more mixed. There are large department stores and supermarket-sized DIY shops, but small and medium-sized shops prevail, many in chains but nonetheless independent. In all, there are nearly a third of a million of them across the country.

Antiques [*Antiquités*]

There are some 40,000 antique shops [*antiquaires*] and their kindred bric-a-brac shops [*brocanteurs*], a quarter of them in the greater Paris area. The shops are listed in the Yellow pages under *Antiquités* and under *Brocante* as well as by the professional associations: *Syndicat national des antiquaires (SNA)*, to which 400 of the most exclusive dealers belong, office at 17 boulevard Malesherbes, 75008 Paris, Tel: 01 44517474, *www.franceantiq.fr* in French and English, and *Syndicat national du commerce de l'antique, de l'occasion et des galeries d'art moderne et contemporain (SNCAO)*, to which some 4800 dealers belong, office at 18 rue de Provence, 75009 Paris, Tel: 01 47708878, *www.sncao-syndicat.com.*

Baby clothing and goods
[*Vêtements pour bébés et articles de puériculture*]

Baby clothing and goods are sold by supermarkets, hypermarkets and speciality shops across the country. Pampers is the leading brand of nappies [*couches*] and baby care [*hygiène bébé*] products, *www.pampers.com*, click on *France* to access the French site. The leading speciality chains are New Baby, 10 rue Nicolas Appert, 75011 Paris, Tel: 01 43574300, *www.newbaby-nb.com* with an interactive locator map of 124 shops across the country, and Natalys, 18, avenue du Général Gallieni, BP 714, 92007 Nanterre Cedex, *www.natalys.fr* in French and English and with an interactive locator map of shops across the country. For the names of items in French and English, see the well-illustrated Natalys printed and online catalogues.

Boats [*Bateaux de plaisance*]

Boating is popular; there are an estimated 840,000 pleasure boats in the country, and there are numerous **marinas** (Chapter 41), mostly along the Atlantic and Mediterranean coasts and in Ile de France. In the Yellow Pages, boats [*bateaux*], boating supplies [*accastillage*] and related goods and services are listed under *Bateaux de plaisance, accessoires, vente, réparation*. A magazine, *Mag Nautic*, available free from stands in harbour towns and otherwise on subscription, lists new and used boats for sale, boating supplies, repairs, service and the like; it is published by the H3S Group, BP 165, 13322 Marseille Cedex 16, Tel: 04 91091760, *www.mag-nautic.fr*. Since 1960, in early December each year, the Paris International Boat Show [*Salon nautique de Paris*] attracts more than a quarter of a million visitors to the venue at Paris Expo, Porte de Versailles; for further information, visit the show website at *www.salonnautiqueparis.com.*

Bookshops [*Libraires*]

France ranks seventh in the world in overall book sales*, and each year some 40,000 new titles are published. Understandably, there are many bookshops listed in the Yellow Pages under *Libraires* as well as in the interactive shop locator map at *www.bief.org*, the website of BIEF, the portal for the French book industry in France as well as abroad. There are several bookshop chains; the largest is FNAC, a chain of 69 shops in 56 cities, that in addition to books also sell music, photographic and computer equipment, in addition to operating a booking service for cultural events; head office at 67 Bd du Général Leclerc, 92612 Clichy Cedex, *www.fnac.com* in French with pages in English and other languages for markets and affiliate operations abroad. There are many online bookshops; the largest is *www.amazon.fr*.

* *Source: Economist Pocket World in Figures 2006, p. 92*

Clothing [*Habillement*]

In overall clothing sales, France is third in the world*. Understandably, the garment industry is large, and there are many brands, sold by shops listed in the Yellow Pages under *Vêtements* as well as by the clothing departments of hypermarkets and supermarkets. Clothing is classified as it is elsewhere: men's [*homme*], women's [*femme*], children's [*enfants*], ready-to-wear [*prêt-à-porter*], styles [*confection*] and fashion [*mode*]. Many of the brands have their own chains of shops; an incomplete listing of brand-name shops, many with online order services and all with interactive shop locator maps or dialogue windows on their websites:

- Aigle, outdoor sports clothing for men, women and children, 61 shops, *www.aigle.com* in French and English.
- Armand Thierry, men's and women's ready-to-wear, 250 shops, *www.armandthiery.fr* in French and English.
- Brice, men's ready-to-wear, 214 shops and 23 corners in department stores, *www.brice.fr*.
- Camaïeu, women's ready-to-wear, 70 shops, *www.camaieu.com* in French and English.
- Caroll, women's ready-to-wear, 280 shops, *www.caroll.fr* in French and English.
- Celio, men's ready-to-wear, 240 shops, *www.celio.com* in French, English, Dutch, Italian and Spanish.
- Gap, men's and women's ready-to-wear, 33 shops, *www.gap.com*, select France.
- H&M, men's, women's and children's ready-to-wear, 76 shops, *www.hm.com* select France.
- Jennyfer, women's fashions, 300 shops, *www.jennyfer.com* in French, English, Italian and Spanish.
- Jerem, ready-to-wear for tall and large men, 11 shops, *www.toofashion.com*.
- Jules, men's clothing, 200 shops, *www.jules.fr*.
- Kiabi, men's, women's and children's ready-to-wear, 122 shops, *www.jules.fr*.
- Kookaï, women's ready-to-wear, 128 shops, *www.kookai.fr* in French and English.
- La Halle aux Vêtements, men's, women's and children's ready-to-wear, 300 shops, *www.lahalle.com*.
- New Man, men's, women's and children's styles, 57 shops, *www.newman.fr*.
- Promod, women's ready-to-wear, 151 shops, *www.promod.com* in French, English and German.

- Zara, men's, women's and children's fashions. 52 shops, *www.zara.fr*.

* *Source: QUID 2006.*

Computers and software [*Ordinateurs et logiciels*]

Computers, software and associated products are sold by speciality shops listed under *Informatique* in the Yellow Pages as well as by the *Ordinateurs* and *Logiciels* departments of hypermarkets. Shops selling subsystems and components for building computers are listed under *Informatique: matériel et fournitures* in the Yellow Pages. Several chains of them have online and physical shops, such as Cybertek, 130 Rue Achard, ZA Achard, Bâtiment U, 33300 Bordeaux, Tel: 08 90710237, *www.cybertek.fr* with an interactive locator map of the 24 physical shops.

Department stores [*Grands magasins*]

The department store is a French invention. The first opened in 1852 in Paris, when Aristide (1810-1877) and Marguerite (1816-1887) Boucicaut founded *Le Bon Marché*, a drapery and dry-goods shop. In 1869, the shop was the first to display goods with price tags, and in 1871 it was the first to publish a mail order catalogue. Today it is among the leading department stores that include:

- BHV, the abbreviation for Bazar de l'Hôtel de Ville, founded in 1855 and now with 9 stores in the Paris area and 6 elsewhere in the country; main store at 55 rue de la Verrerie, 75004 Paris, Tel: 01 42749000, *www.bhv.fr* with an interactive store locator map.
- Le Bon Marché, the descendant of the first shop, 24 rue Sèvres, 75007 Paris, Tel: 01 44398050, *www.lebonmarche.fr* selectable in French or English.
- Galleries Lafayette, now the country's largest department store chain, with 422 stores and 56 affiliates, main store at 40 Boulevard Haussmann, 75009 Paris, Tel: 01 42823456, *www.gallerieslafayette.com* in French, English and nine other languages and with an interactive shop locator map.
- PRP, the abbreviation for Pinaut-Printemps-Redoute, specialising in luxury goods, 10 avenue Hoche, 75381 Paris Cedex 08, Tel: 01 45646100, *www.ppr.com* in French and English.
- Samaritaine, founded in 1869 and now the largest shop in Paris, at 17-19 rue de la Monnaie, 75001 Paris, Tel: 08 00010015, *www.lasamaritaine.com*.

Discount stores [*Solderies*]

Discount stores that began selling out-of-range products have evolved to low-price non-food retailers [*produits non-alimentaires premier pris*]. Most are listed in the Yellow Pages under *Discount, stocks, dégriffés*, "Discount, overstocks, off-label".

Many of the stores are organised in smaller and sometimes regional chains, such as *Bazarland*, with outlets in 13 *Départements* across the country, *www.bazarland.fr* and *ID Stock* with 11 outlets in the northeastern part of the country, *www.idstock.com*. The largest is *GiFi* with more than 300 outlets across the country as well as shops in Belgium, Italy and Spain, *www.gifi.fr* in French and English.

DIY shops [*Bricolages*]

As the DIY designation implies, the typical *bricolage* sells a broad selection of hardware, building and decorating supplies, tools and the like. There are *Bricolage* departments in supermarkets and hypermarkets, and there are smaller *bricolage* shops in smaller towns and villages. But the trend is toward larger shops that rival supermarkets in size and usually are located in suburban areas around cities, with large car parks serving malls. Most *bricolages* are in chains, of which the largest are:

- Brico depôt, with 64 shops, *www.bricodepot.com*.
- Bricomarché, with 460 shops, *www.bricomarche.com*.
- Briconautes, with 109 shops, *www.les-broconautes.com*.
- Bricorama, with 90 shops, *www.bricorama.fr*.
- Castorama, with 101 shops, *www.castorama.fr*.
- Catena, with 101 shops, *www.catena.fr*.
- Gedimat, with 215 shops, *www.gedimat.fr*.
- Leroy Merlin, with 95 shops, *www.leroymerlin.fr*.
- Logimarché, with 40 shops, *www.logimarche.com*.
- Mr. Bricolage, with 381 shops, *www.mr-bricolage.fr*.
- Weldom, with 263 shops, *www.weldom.com*.

Factory shops [*Magasins d'usine*]

The many factory shops across the country are mostly individual enterprises; there are several Internet guides to them, such as *www.magasinsusine.free.fr*.

Feminine hygiene [*Hygiène féminine*]

Feminine hygiene products are sold by pharmacies, supermarkets and hypermarkets. The chain supermarkets and hypermarkets usually have their own brands as well as major national and international brands, of which the three leading are Nana, *www.nana.fr*, Tampax, *www.tampax.com* and Vania, *www.vania.com*.

Flea markets [*Marchés aux puces*]

Across the country, there are many flea markets selling art objects, decorations, furniture, jewellery, paintings, porcelain and the like. One of the larger is *Marché aux puces des Salins*, geographically in the middle of the country, at La Pardieu, BP 6, 63064 Clermont-Ferrand Cedex 1, Tel: 04 73283122, *www.puces63.com*. The oldest, largest and most famed is *Les Puces de Paris Saint-Ouen*, with extensive exhibition sites and regular publications, contact *Association Développement et Promotion des Puces de Paris Saint-Ouen (ADPPPSO)*, 140 rue des Rosiers, 93400 Saint-Ouen, Tel: 01 40123258, *www.parispuces.com* selectable in French or English.

Florists [*Fleuristes*]

By per-capita expenditure, France is a modest ninth in Europe in the use of flowers. But that ranking may be deceptive, as domestic production of flowers is high, and there are 12,000 florists in the country, listed in the Yellow Pages under *Fleuristes*. Many florists offer online ordering, and the international Interflora network offers online ordering with rapid delivery across the country as well as abroad, *www.interflora.fr*. By numbers sold, the 12 most favoured flowers are roses [*roses*], chrysanthemums [*chrysanthèmes*], carnations [*œillets*], tulips [*tulipes*], lilies [*lis*], gerberas [*gerberas*], lilies of the valley [*muguets*], freesias [*freesias*], orchids [*orchidées*], iris [*iris*], mimosa [*mimosa*] and anemones [*anémones*]*. Flowers usually are welcome, save when a "no flowers by request" [*ni fleurs ni couronnes*] notice is given.

* Source of rankings: QUID 2006

Greetings cards [*Cartes vœux*]

Almost all newsagents, bookshops and many supermarkets have racks of greetings cards. As elsewhere in Europe, there are six principal varieties, usually labelled on the display racks: *Anniversaire* (Birthday), *Bonnes fêtes* (Happy holiday) including *Noël* at Christmas, *Correspondance* (Notes), *Mariage* (Wedding), *Naissance* (Birth) and *Deuil* (Condolence). The four principal publishers are *Céline Carterie*, *Chromovogué, Editions Cely* and *Groupe Leconte*. The *Celine Carterie* website at *www.celine-carterie.fr* has an attractive clickable display of its collection that includes all the various varieties of greetings cards.

Hard discount

Across Europe, a hard discount is a mini-supermarket that specialises in low prices. Though the words are English, the term "hard discount" was coined in the 1930s in France to describe the concept then first tried for *prix uniques* shops. Since then, the French equivalent, *maxidiscompte*, was suggested but never gained popular usage.

Today, "hard discount" appears in French texts in advertisements, on Internet sites and on walls of shops.

A hard discount cuts prices principally by minimising costs. The typical hard discount is located in a low-rent area, away from higher-cost shops and almost always with ample car parking. It sells lesser-known brands, sometimes its own, and offers limited selections. Compared to a conventional supermarket of the same size, it will be run by fewer people. Goods are seldom placed on shelves, but usually are left in their shipping cartons, which are on shelves or on pallets on the floor. The bulk of the business is in long shelf life, non-fresh foods, though shops seeking to offer single-stop shopping may have a smaller fresh-food section offering fruits, vegetables, meats and bread. Today, the four leading hard discounters are:

- Aldi, the German chain of 7000 hard discount shops in 12 countries, including 700 in France, *www.aldi.fr*.

- Ed, part of the giant Carrefour retailing group, with 804 shops, including 100 in the Paris area, *www.ed-fr.com*.

- Lidl, the German giant of hard discount, with 1200 shops in France, *www.lidl.fr*.

- Netto, part of the Mousquetaires group, with more than 360 shops, *www.netto.fr*.

Hearing aids [*Appareils acoustique*]

Hearing is tested and hearing aids sold and serviced by specialists, listed in the Yellow Pages under *Audioprothésistes*. The leading brands of hearing aids are Beltone, Bravissimo and Medel. Most hearing aid specialists are organised in chains, of which the six leading are:

- Amplifon, with 190 shops, *www.amplifon.fr*.
- Audika, with 360 shops, *www.audika.com*.
- Audio 2000, with 135 shops, *www.audio2000.fr*.
- Audition Conseil France, with 230 shops, *www.auditionconseil.fr*.
- Audition Mutualiste, with 192 shops, *www.fnmf.fr*, click on *Complémentaire santé* and then on *2000 établissements*.
- Audition Santé, with 300 shops, *www.auditionsante.fr*.
- Entendre, with 200 shops, *www.entendre.fr*.

For further information on specialists, shops, and hearing products, visit the trade portal at *www.franceaudition.com*.

Home furnishings [*Mobilier de la maison/fourniture maison*]

Home furnishings increasingly are sold by international chains, of which the three largest are:

- BUT, offering furniture [*ameublement*], appliances [*électroménager*], audio and video [*image & son*] and information technology [*nouveaux médias*] products in 230 shops across the country as well as shops abroad; head office at 1 avenue Spinoza, 77437 Marne la Vallée Cedex 2, Tel: 01 64612626, *www.but.fr* with an interactive shop locator map.

- FLY, specialising in styles for the young, 130 shops across the country as well as 20 abroad in Canada, Spain and Switzerland; head office at BP 52458, 68944 Mulhouse Cedex 9, Tel: 03 89623606, *www.flymeubles.com* with an interactive shop locator map.

- IKEA, the giant, Swedish-based global chain with home furnishings hypermarkets in 36 countries on four continents including 20 in France; head office at BP 002, 91005 Evry Cedex, Tel: 08 10808808, *www.ikea.com*, click on *France* to access the French site.

Household shops [*Drogueries*]

Across the country, there are some 1760 household (or hardware) shops [*Drogueries*], more than 90 of them in the greater Paris area. There are several chains of shops; the largest is *Schlecker* of Germany that has 75% of the *drogueries* in that country and shops across Europe, including France, with 64 shops, *www.schlecker.fr* with a shop locator dialogue window.

Hypermarket navigation [*Plan hypermarché*]

Many hypermarkets and supermarkets have signs as well as maps to guide shoppers to goods displayed. A typical hypermarket map is shown below. The equivalents in English of its location identifiers are:

Location identifier	Equivalent in English
Accueil	Customer Service Centre
Animalerie	Pet Supplies
Auto	Care Parts & Accessories
Bagagerie	Luggage
Beauté Santé	Cosmetics and Health Supplies
Boucherie	Butcher, fresh meats
Boulangerie	Bakery
Bricolage	DIY & Hardware
Cabines d'essayage	Fitting Rooms
Caisses	Checkouts
Charcuterie	Sausages & Processed Meats

Droguerie	Hardware
Electroménager	White Goods (Appliances)
Enfant / Bébé	Infants/Babies
Entrée Alimentaire	Foods Entrance
Entrée Principale	Main Entrance
Epicerie Salée / Sucrée	Delicatessen, Snacks/Sweets
Fromages	Cheeses
Fruits & Légumes	Fruits & Vegetables
Habillement Femme	Women's Clothing
Habillement Homme	Men's Clothing
Jardin	Garden
Jouet	Toys
La Cave Boissons	Wine Cellar
Lait	Milk
Lingerie Bijouterie	Lingerie, Jewellery
Livres / bd Musiques	Books, Recordings, Music
Maroquinerie	Leather Goods
Ménage	Housekeeping Supplies
Meubles	Furniture
Micro informatique	Personal Computers & Ancillaries
Parapharmacie	Medical Supplies, Toiletries and Vitamins
Pâtisserie	Pastry & Cakes
Photo	Photography
Poissonnerie	Fish
Puériculture	Child Care
Saisonnier	Seasonal Goods
Self Discount	Low price bulk and pick & mix products
Son/Photo	Audio/Photo
Sport	Sport
Stands Traiteur	Catering Stands
Surgelés	Frozen Foods
Téléphone	Telephone / Telecoms
Télévision	Television
Textile de la Maison	Bedclothes & Household Linen
Toilettes	Toilets

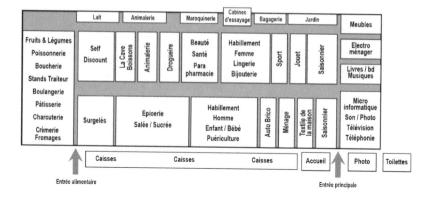

Typical locator map (shop shown is Auchan hypermarket at Avenue d'Espagne, Perpignan, renovated July 2005; original in colour; black/white replication by permission).

Large retailers [*Grands détaillants*]

Though the general public views big business and globalisation with suspicion, France is home to many big, internationally-successful companies, particularly in the food sector. One company, Carrefour, is the world's second-largest retailer, after Wal-Mart of the USA. Five other retailers are large by any measure, and all have subsidiaries operating under other names as well as affiliates and operations in other countries. The six are:

- Auchan, with 120 hypermarkets, 400 *ATAC* fresh-food shops, on-line ordering and 4 fresh-food halls in the Paris area, *www.auchan.fr*.

- Carrefour, with 216 hypermarkets, 2376 supermarkets, 4934 hard discounts, 2699 convenience stores and 203 cash-and-carry, *www.carrefour.com* selectable in French or English.

- Casino, with 121 hypermarkets, 341 supermarkets, 2145 mini-supermarkets under the Casino name and 4368 shops under other names, *www.groupe-casino.fr* in French and English.

- E. Leclerc, with 391 hypermarkets, 131 supermarkets and 39 speciality shops, *www.e-leclerc.com*.

- Les Mousquetaires, with 2139 local food stores, 360 hard discounts, 74 restaurants and 837 non-food speciality shops, in all operating under 10 names, *www.mousquetaires.com* in French and English.

- Systeme U, a cooperative with 52 hypermarkets, 676 supermarkets and 148 food shops, *www.magasins-u.com* in French and English.

472

Luxury goods [*Luxe*]

Luxury goods are almost synonymous with *Louis Vuitton Moët Hennessy (LVMH)*, the Paris-based holding company that is the world's largest luxury goods conglomerate. The 50 or so companies of the conglomerate manage prestigious brands in wines and spirits, watches and jewellery, fashion and leather goods, retailing, and perfume. Several of the brands are a century or more old, including Château d'Yquem wines from 1593, Moët & Chandon wines and spirits from 1743, Hennessy wines and spirits from 1765, Louis Vuitton leather goods from 1853 and Le Bon Marché, the world's first department store, from 1852. For further information, contact LVMH, 22 avenue Montaigne, 75008 Paris, Tel: 01 44132222, *www.lvmh.com* selectable in French, English, Chinese or Japanese and with links to the individual brand websites.

Markets [*Marchés*]

In almost all cities, towns and villages, open-air markets [*marchés découverts*] are held in public squares one to three times a week, and in larger cities, there are covered markets [*marchés couverts*] that keep more regular shop hours. In Paris there are more than 60, so many that the city hall [*Mairie de Paris*] supports a regularly updated guide to them, *Les marchés parisiens*, on its website at *www.paris.fr*. Some markets specialise in fruits and vegetables [*Les marchés fruits et légumes*] and some in specialised wares [*Les marchés spécialisés*], while many, particularly the weekly markets in small towns, will feature a wide range of goods from local vendors, including foods, clothing, hardware, books and collectables. Outside of Paris, the best way to find market times and locations is to inquire at the town hall or ask your neighbours.

Newsagents [*Magasins de presse*]

Even smaller towns have one or more newsagents, not because the population are avid readers – France ranks 26th among countries in per-capita newspaper sales and in book turnover – but because many newsagents often fulfil other functions, including selling books, stationery, sundries and tobacco products, which are not sold in supermarkets or food shops, as well as operating online **gambling** (Chapter 16) in the national lottery and in off-track betting on horse races. Many newsagents are local ventures, and there are four chains, all subsidiaries of **press distribution** (Chapter 31) companies:

- Maison de la presse, a subsidiary of SEDDIF, part of the NMPP, with 629 shops and a website at *www.maisondelapresse.tm.fr* that has an interactive shop locator map.

- Mag presse, an independent franchising subsidiary of SEDDIF, part of NMPP, with 934 shops and a website at *www.magpresse.com* that has an interactive shop locator map.

- Relay, part of Hachette Distribution Services, with 1100 shops in 14 countries, principally at airports and railway stations and a website at *www.relay.com* that has an interactive shop locator map.

Opening hours [*Heurs d'ouverture*]

Most shops are closed at lunch time, typically 12.00-14.00 as well as all day one day a week, and will accordingly post a notice on or beside the door. A typical sign, as on a *boulangerie* might read:

Ouvert
7h – 12h, 14h – 19h
Fermé le Mercredi
toute la journée

which means that the shop is open from 07.00 to 19.00 hours but closed midday from 12.00 to 14.00 hours and is closed all day Wednesday.

Shops not closed at midday will so proclaim on their signage, such as: *Non-stop de 9h à 19h30*. Round-the-clock opening, as self-serve petrol stations, will have signs saying so, as *Ouvert 7/7, 24/24*.

Opticians [*Opticiens*]

There are some 13,600 opticians in the country, most qualified both as a dispensing optician [*opticien-lunetier*] and as an ophthalmic optician [*opticien optométriste*]. Most opticians are in private practices of one or a few professionals, listed in the Yellow Pages under *Opticiens* and in the postcode locator under *Opticiens* on the trade portal at *www.kifekoi.org*. The opticians in chains are also listed on the chain websites in postcode locators or interactive maps. The five largest chains are:

- ATOL, with 600 shops, *www.opticiens-atol.com*.
- Lissac, with 188 shops, *www.lissac.com*.
- Optic 2000, with 1050 shops and 188 affiliates, *www.optic2000.fr*.
- Opticiens Krys, a cooperative with 800 shops, *www.krys.com*.
- Opticiens Mutualiste, with 540 shops, *www.fnmf.fr*, click on *Complémentaire santé* and then on *2000 établissements*.

For further information on the trade, contact *Union des opticiens*, 45 rue de Lancry, 75010 Paris, Tel: 01 42060731, *www.udo.org*.

Sales [*Soldes*]

By tradition, shops across the country hold sales twice a year, in mid January and in late July or early August. Otherwise, shops may hold overstock [*déstockage*] sales at any time of the year. Sales are regulated by law and all discounts must be on goods at ordinary prices, not special lines offered for the sale period only.

Second-hand shops [*Dépôts ventes*]

There still are many traditional second-hand shops [*vendeurs d'objets d'occasion*] and bric-a-brac shops [*brocante*], listed in the Yellow Pages under *Brocante* and *Dépôts vente*. But in the ever more rapid pace of the computer age, they are being eclipsed by the increasing numbers of computerised online and physical auction and second-hand shops [*magasins de troc et de dépôts ventes*]. The largest of the new breed of second-hand shop is Cash Converters, the franchiser founded in 1984 in Australia that now has 600 shops worldwide, including 70 in France, of which 10 are in the Paris area, head office at 33 rue des Vanesses, BP 50332 Villepinte, 95941 Roissy Charles-de Gaulle Cedex, Tel: 01 48171166, *www.cashconverters.fr* with an interactive shop locator map. Similar second-hand shop franchise chains include Tonton Cash, Troc de l'île and La Trocante.

Shoes [*Chaussures*]

The average resident buys six pairs of shoes a year, but domestic production is equivalent to about one pair a year per resident*. So most shoes are imported. Accordingly, there are many brands, sold by shops listed in the Yellow Pages under *Chaussures* as well as by the shoe departments of hypermarkets and supermarkets. Shoes are classified as they are elsewhere: men's [*homme*], women's [*femme*], children's [*enfants*], sport [*sport*] and fashion [*mode*]. Some of the brands have their own chains of shops, and several chains sell many brands; an incomplete listing of shops, all with interactive shop locator maps or dialogue windows on their websites:

- Bata, men's, women's and children's fashion shoes, 200 shops, *www.bata.fr*.
- Chaussland, men's, women's and children's shoes, 84 shops, *www.lahalleauxchaussures.com*.
- Jef, men's, women's and children's shoes and *Plante Jef* young styles, 8 shops *www.jefchaussures.com*.
- Kickers, teen style shoes, *www.kickers.fr*
- La Halle aux Chaussures, men's, women's and children's shoes, 500 shops, *www.lahalleauxchaussures.com*.
- Orcade-Minelli, men's, women's and children's fashion shoes, 130 shops, *www.minelli.fr*.

- Paraboot, men's, women's and children's shoes, 20 shops, *www.paraboot.com* in French, English and Japanese.
- J.M. Weston, handmade men's shoes and riding boots, 21 shops, *www.jmweston.com* in French, English and Japanese.
- San Marina, men's and women's shoes, about 100 shops, *www.sanmarina.fr*.

*Source: QUID 2006

Small food shops [*Petits magasins d'alimentation*]

Each year, the hypermarkets, supermarkets and hard discounters together take in more than eight in ten Euros spent on food, but across the country, they are out numbered 12 to one by the small shops, more than 62,000 in all*. Mostly, they are neighbourhood shops, each dealing in one of the traditional specialties, including:

Boucherie, a butcher selling fresh beef, lamb, pork, poultry and sometimes game.

Boulangerie, a bakery, usually open from early in the morning, selling fresh-baked breads.

Charcuterie, originally a pork butcher, but now a delicatessen selling cooked meats, sausages, salads and the like.

Chocolaterie, a maker and seller of bon-bons and other chocolate sweets.

Confisserie, a sweet shop.

Épicerie, a grocer's shop.

Fromagerie, a cheese shop.

Fruits et légumes frais, a fresh fruit and vegetable shop.

Pâtisserie, a pastry shop.

Poissonnerie, a fish shop.

Produits fermiers, a farm products stand, usually along a road.

Traiteur, a caterer selling ready-to-eat dishes.

* *Source: INSEE Informations Rapides no. 361, December 2005.*

Sports goods [*Sports articles et vêtements*]

Across the country, there are nearly 2500 large sports goods shops, some the size of supermarkets and most in chains. The five largest, each with physical shops and online services, including interactive shop locator maps, are:

- Décathlon, a global enterprise with shops in 14 countries including 218 in France, *www.decathlon.fr*.

- Go Sport, with 326 shops as well as shops in Belgium and Poland, *www.go-sport.fr*.
- Intersport, the world's largest sports goods chain with 486 shops in France, *www.go-sport.fr*.
- Mondial Pêche, with 42 fishing equipment shops, *www.mondial-peche.fr*
- Sport 2000, the world's second largest sports good chain with 3200 shops, of which 400 are in France, *www.sport2000.fr*.

Supermarkets and hypermarkets [*Supermarché et hypermarché*]

In May 1957, the country's first supermarket opened in the 17th *Arrondissement* in Paris. Named the *Bardou*, it had a floor area of 400 square metres, large for the day. By today's standards, it was small, though its area remains as the lower mark of the statutory definition of a supermarket as being a self-serve shop with a floor area of 400 to 2500 square metres. In June 1963, Carrefour opened the first 2500 square metre supermarket in Sainte-Geneviève-des-Bois, a Paris suburb. Other equally large supermarkets followed. In 1968, magazine publisher Jacques Pictet coined the term *hypermarché* to distinguish the big stores from their smaller counterparts. The hypermarket also grew; today the largest Carrefour hypermarkets have a floor area of more than 20,000 square metres, twice the size of an international-standard football pitch. Yet, like the first supermarket that brought low-price competition to food retailing, today the minimalistic **hard discounts** are the low-price competitors to supermarkets and hypermarkets. Accordingly, the **large retailers** now have supermarkets, hypermarkets and hard discounts. One result of the profusion of trade names and shop types has been that there's an online guide to them all, *France Supermarchée* at *www.france-supermarche.info*.

Tattooing and body piercing [*Tatouage et piercing*]

Each year, about 20,000 people are tattooed and five times as many pierced, so they may wear jewellery attached to body parts*. Tattooing studios are listed in the Yellow Pages under *Tatouage*, and most of them also perform piercing. There are many websites devoted to tattooing and piercing, such as *www.tatouagedoc.net* and *www.tattoo-passion.com*.

* Source of figures: QUID 2006

Tobacconists [*Buralistes*]

Across the country, there are more than 31,000 tobacconists [*buralistes*] whose shops are the only sellers of tobacco products and consequently are commonly known and listed in the Yellow Pages as *bureaux de tabac*. One tobacconist in three also is a **newsagent** (Chapter 31), and all sell postage stamps and **revenue stamps** (Chapter 43) as well as sundries. **Tobacco consumption** (Chapter 13) is declining, so starting in 2005, the tobacconists have been reorganising and diversifying to offer a wider range of goods, including CDs, DVDs and phone cards. Most tobacconist shops are identified by a vertical orange sign, which, because it resembles a carrot, is according to urban myth said to commemorate raw carrots once put in tobacco to keep it moist. Though amusing, that explanation has no basis in historical fact*, as the sign merely replicates the shape of the small rolls of tobacco as it originally was sold. For further information on the tobacconist trade, contact *Confédération des Débitants de Tabac de France*, 75 rue d'Amsterdam, 75008 Paris, Tel: 01 53211000, *www.buralistes.fr*.

C'est Beau Mais c'est Faux, by Patrice Louis, Paris, Editions Arléa, 2000 hardcover ISBN 2-86959-490-9 and 2003 softcover ISBN 2-86959-605-7.

Many tobacconists display both newsagent and tobacconist signs.
Marianne Hadler photo.

Toys [*Jouets*]

Children's toys are much in demand: in Europe, France ranks second after the UK in toy sales, with more than 21% of the annual € 17 billion market. The toy departments of hypermarkets account for nearly half and toy speciality shops for nearly a third of all toys sold. International brands are sold across the country: Toys R US has 42 shops, 12 of them in Ile-de-France; for information and shop locations, contact Service Relation Clientèle, 2 rue Thomas Edison, 91044 Evry Cedex, *www.toysrus.fr*; Hasbro has numerous outlets in all *Départements*; contact the customer service centre at Savoie Technolac, 73370 Le Bourget du Lac,

Tel: 04 79964848, *www.hasbro.fr*. One of the world's leading manufacturers of toys is French: Smoby, with operations in 90 countries; contact SMOBY, BP 7, 39170 Lavans les Saint-Claude, Tel: 03 84413800, *www.smobymajorette.fr* in French, English, Dutch, German, Italian and Spanish. The affection for toys is widespread. Another leading manufacturer is Jouéclub, *www.joueclub.com*. The Barbie doll has a fan club, *Club des amies de Barbie www.mesbarbies.com* with more than 250,000 members, and there are numerous Barbie websites. And tradition stands strong: wooden *Jouets Dejou*, produced from 1937 to 1985, are coveted collectors' items.

Vide grenier

In towns and villages across the country, the *vide grenier* is a popular used goods sales event that takes place at regular or irregular intervals, up to several times a year. In translation it means "emptying the garage", and indeed a *vide grenier* resembles the car boot sale of the UK, the *vente de garage* of Québec and flea markets everywhere. A *vide grenier* usually is held along a closed-off street or in a town park. Ordinary townspeople will use it to rid themselves of unwanted household items, and local second-hand dealers will offer overstocks. So a *vide grenier* offers the opportunity to buy household goods and clothing at knock-down prices, and there usually are buyers aplenty. The *vide greniers* have become so popular that they now are tourist attractions, and many local tourist information offices have joined to market them via a website at *www.vide-greniers.org* with an interactive *vide grenier* locator map that brings up venues and dates of the events.

White and brown goods shops [*Electroménagers*]

Most hypermarkets as well as some home furnishings shops sell white goods – kitchen appliances – and brown goods – TVs, radios, audio systems and the like. Moreover, there are nearly 1500 shops specialising in white and brown goods, many in chains, of which the three with the most outlets are *COPRA* with 600 shops, *www.copra.fr*, *Darty* with 203 shops, *www.darty.com* and *Expert*, the world's largest chain with 3200 shops in Europe, 220 of them in France, *www.expert.fr*.

41
Sport and leisure

Sport and leisure may be the most international facets of the culture, as reflected in the multinational names of the most popular sports, such as football, golf and tennis, as well as that of the most popular card game, bridge. And numerous French terms have been taken into other languages. The first probably was *trapeze*, the apparatus invented by performer Jules Léotard (1837-1869), whose surname also became international as the term for the close-fitting, one-piece garment worn by acrobats and dancers. One of the more recent is *pétanque*, the game of bowls that originated in the southern part of the country and now is an international sport. And on the international scene, the name of the country is associated with excellence in many sports and games. *Tour de France* arguably is the world's most famed bicycle race, the Chamonix Guides were the first to offer professional mountaineering services, the French Open is one of the four Grand Slam tournaments of world tennis, and France ranks seventh in the world in chess. Understandable, then, that almost all residents pursue one or more hobbies and one in every two practises a sport regularly.

Aeronautical sports [*Aéronautique*]

In the country, there are some 45,000 licensed private pilots affiliated with 585 aeronautical sports clubs operating from 400 airfields, and each year there are various meets and competitions, such as the 2006 World Championships in Precision Flying. For further information, contact *Fédération française aéronautique (FFA)*, 155 avenue de Wagram, 75017 Paris, Tel: 01 44299200, *www.ff-aero.fr*.

Amateur radio [*Radioamateur*]

Amateur radio call signs begin with the country identifier F. The many amateur radio clubs of the country are affiliated in two national organisations: *Association national union des radio-clubs et des radioamateurs (URC)*, 25 allé des Princes, 95440 Ecouen, *www.urc.asso.fr* and *Réseau des émetteurs français (REF)*, 32 rue de Suède, BP 77429, 37074 Tours Cedex 2, Tel: 02 47418873, *www.ref-union.org* in French and English.

Basketball [*Basket-ball*]

With nearly 450,000 players in 16 major and innumerable smaller clubs for men and women, basketball is the country's fifth most popular sport. For further information as well as links to the clubs, contact *Fédération française de basket-ball*, 117 rue du Chateau des Rentiers, 75013 Paris, Tel: 01 53942500, *www.basketfrance.com*.

Boating, sailing, windsurfing and surfboarding [*Nautisme, voile, glisse, windsurf*]

There are an estimated 840,000 pleasure boats in the country, and there are numerous **marinas**, mostly along the Atlantic and Mediterranean coasts and in Ile de France. Likewise, sailing, windsurfing and surfboarding are popular. Accordingly, many organisations are dedicated to these sports; a selection:

- Motor-powered boating, *Portail du nautisme, www.nautisme.com*.
- Sailing, *Le monde de la voile*, *www.sail-online.fr* and *Fédération française de voile, www.ffv.fr*.
- Surfboarding, *Portail des sports de glisse*, *www.agoride.com* and *Surf*, *www.surfsession.com*.
- Windsurfing, *Wind surf journal*, *www.windsurfjournal.com*.

Boules [*Pétanque*]

Boules, a type of lawn bowls, is played across the country, using metal balls and a jack [*cochonnet*]. It can be played anywhere, on any flat ground and has become the country's leading outdoor recreation, with an estimated 17 million participants. In cities, towns and villages, boules playing areas [*terrains de boules*] are set aside in parks, and there now are some covered halls for the game [*boulodromes couverts*]. It also has become a competitive sport, with hundreds of clubs organised in 22 leagues that together have nearly half a million players.

The roots of the game are believed to be in a pastime of the nobility in ancient Greece and Rome. It came to France well before the *Révolution* and long was a royal recreation. The first Boules association was founded in 1850 in Lyon, and today the *Fédération française de pétanque et jeu provençal (FFPJP)* is by membership the fourth largest sports association in the country. The sport has become international, and there are Pétanque associations in more than 20 countries as well as an international federation, *Confédération Mondiale des Sports de Boules* with its head office in Monaco. Each year, there are national and international meets, and world championships are held every other year, with divisions for men, women and juniors. For further information, contact FFPJP, 13 rue Trigance, 13002 Marseille, Tel: 04 91140580, *www.petanque.fr* or visit the Internet portal for the game at *www.petanque.com*.

Canoe and kayak [*Canoë et kayak*]

Along the many inland waterways, canoeing and kayaking are principal recreations and many clubs, as well as regional organisations, provide maps and guides as well as rentals and instruction. Competitive kayaking is a major sport, with more than 230,000 registered competitors, both for white water and sea kayaking. For further information, contact *Fédération française canoë-kayak (FFCK)*, 87 Quai de la Marne, BP 58, 94344 Joinville le Point, Tel: 01 45110850, *www.ffck.org* or visit the canoeing and kayaking portal at *www.eauxvives.org*.

Card games [*Jeux de cartes*]

All European and some American card games are played, most with international names. Bridge is by far the most popular, and there are innumerable bridge clubs and tournaments. For further information, contact *Fédération française de bridge*, 20-21 quai Carnot, 92210 Saint-Cloud, Tel: 01 55573800, *www.ffbridge.asso.fr*. Other popular games include the combination games [*jeux de combinaisons*] such as Rummy [*rami*] and Canasta; casino or gambling card games [*jeux de casino ou de hasard*] such as Baccarat, Blackjack and Poker; solitaire (or patience) games [*jeux solitaires (ou patiences)*] such as FreeCell, Klondike and Solitaire; shedding games [*jeux de défausse*] such as Mao, and accumulating games [*jeux d'accumulation*] such as Bataille and Snap. The four suits are:

- ♠ *pique* ("spades")
- ♣ *trèfle* ("clubs")
- ♥ *cœur* ("hearts")
- ♦ *carreau* ("diamonds")

Grimaud, made by *Groupe France Cartes*, Europe's leading manufacturer of board games, is the most sold brand of playing cards; for information, contact *France Cartes*, 49 rue Alexandre 1er, BP 49, 54130 Saint-Max, Tel: 03 83213232, *www.france-cartes.fr* in French and English with an online shop selling all products. For an overview of card playing and its history in France, visit *Musée français de la carte à jouer*, 16 rue Auguste-Gerrais, 92130 Issy-les-Moulineaux, *www.issy-com/statiques/musee* in French and English.

Chess [*Échecs*]

Across the country, parks often have permanent chess tables, which attest to the widespread popularity of the game. More than 53,000 people take the game seriously, belonging to 920 chess clubs that participate in various tournaments*. France has 29 Grand Masters and 70 International Masters and ranks seventh in the world by average rating of its top ten players**. The international focus is of long standing: from the mid 18th to the mid 19th century, all four unofficial world champions were French. In 1924, the World Chess Federation [*Fédération internationale des échecs (FIDE)*] was founded in Paris, *www.fide.com* selectable in French or English. For further information as well as for online purchase of chess sets and paraphernalia, contact *Fédération française des échecs (FFE)*, 3 Place Jean Jaures, BP 2022, 34024 Montpellier Cedex 1, Tel: 04 67600221, *www.echecs.asso.fr*.

*Source: FFE

**Source: FIDE rankings 2006

Colonies de vacances

The *Colonies de vacances* are holiday camps and centres for children, 6 to 18 years old. Colloquially known as *Les colos*, they are largely subsidised by the State and offer recreational and educational activities in day camps as well as camps with overnight lodging. For further information, contact one of the **Youth Information Centres** (Chapter 31) or visit the online *colo* portal at *www.lescolos.com*.

Cyber-Budget

Launched in June 2006, *Cyber-Budget* is an online game supported by the government to heighten public awareness of budgetary matters using the very real numbers of the budget of the country, about 300 billion Euros a year. Players deal not only with figures but also with the constraints underlying them, such as deficit and economic growth. The game is free and can be played by anyone at *www.cyber-budget.fr*.

Cycling [*Cyclisme*]

By numbers of participants, fewer than 100,000 registered cyclists, competitive cycling is not among the top ten sports of the country. But as the annual **Tour de France** attests, it is a national fascination, and across the country there are cycle meets year-round. Recreational cycling, particularly on a mountain bike [*Vélo tour terrain (VTT)*] is popular and posted *Parcours VTT* cycle tracks abound. For further information, contact *Fédération Française de Cyclisme*, Bat. Jean Monnet, 5 rue de Rome, 93561 Rosny Sous Bois, Tel: 01 49356900, *www.ffc.fr* or visit the cycling club portal at *www.cyclisme-info.com*.

ENSA

ENSA is the abbreviation for *École national de ski et d'alpinisme*, the world famed academy of skiing and mountaineering. Founded in 1937, it is located in Chamonix, venue in 1924 of the first Olympic Winter Games (OWG), in the valley below Mont

Blanc, highest and in 1820 first climbed of the Alpine summits. Legendary names in mountaineering, among them Gaston Rébuffat (1921-1985) have been on the staff, and today ENSA offers a broad range of curricula for Alpine ski instructors, mountain guides, ski patrollers and climbing instructors as well as for other snow sports specialists. For further information, contact ENSA, 35 rue du Bouchet, BP 24, 74401 Chamonix, Tel: 04 50553030, *www.ensa-jeunesse-sports.fr* in French, English, German and Spanish.

Equestrianism [*Equitation*]

Equestrianism ranks high among the sports of the country. Indeed, the name of the most known of the three Olympic equestrian disciplines, dressage, the training of a horse in deportment and obedience, comes from the French verb *dresser*, meaning to drill, train. The *École nationale d'équitation (ENE)* at Saumur in *Département* 49 is among the world's oldest equestrian academies, founded in 1814, and its teaching staff, the *Cadre Noir* equestrian display team is a living legend in the sport; for further information, contact ENE, BP 207, 49411 Saumur Cedex, Tel: 02 41535055, *www.cadrenoir.fr* selectable in French or English. For further information on the competitive equestrian disciplines, contact *Fédération d'équitation*, 81-83 avenue Edouard Vaillant, 95217 Boulogne-Billancourt Cedex, Tel: 01 58175817, *www.ffe.com*. For information on recreational as well as competitive riding, visit the equestrian portal at *www.1cheval.com* in French and English. The *L'Eperon* equestrian magazine publishes an annual guide to the sport, *L'Annuaire du cheval* that can be ordered online from its website at *www.cavadeos.com*.

Fishing [*Pêche*]

With 250,000 km of rivers [*fleuves*], tributaries [*rivières*], streams and brooks [*ruisseaux*] and canals [*canaux*], lakes [*lacs*] covering 50,000 hectares and 4800 km of coast [*littoral*]*, France is a fishing paradise. Understandably, some three million people fish, 10,000 of them competitively**. Two annual authorisations are required for all sports fishing, in public or private waters:

- a rod licence [*taxe piscicole*] valid across the country and relevant to the licence holder – children up to 16 pay less and the disabled are exempted – as well as contingent on the fishing to be done – fishing for some species, such as salmon at sea, is at a surcharge.

- a fishing permit [*carte de pêche*] valid for the permit holder in one or more designated areas and issued in five categories, from temporary holiday permits to year-round permits.

In practice, both authorisations are sold by the 4200 *Associations agrées pour la pêche et la protection du milieu aquatique (AAPPMA)* that are organised in 93 departmental federations that in turn are members of the *Union nationale pour la pêche en France et la protection du milieu aquatique (UMPF)*, 17 rue Bergère, 75009 Paris, Tel: 01 48249600, *www.umpf.fr* with an interactive association locator map. AAPPMA also has a website at *www.assopeche.com* with an interactive postcode association locator.

Two agencies regulate sports fishing:

- *Conseil supérieur de la pêche (CSP)* administers and monitors fishing and its related environmental aspects; head office at 16 avenue Louison Bobet, 94132 Fontenay-sous-Bois Cedex, Tel: 01 45143600, *www.csp.environnement.gouv.fr* in French and English.

- *Directions régionales et départementales des affaires maritimes* administers and regulates sports fishing as well as commercial fishing along the coasts, contact *www.mer.equipement.gouv.fr*, click on *Administration* and then on *Services de proximité* to bring up an interactive Directorate locator map.

* Source of figures: UMPF

** Source of figures: QUID 2006

Football

As elsewhere in Europe, football is by far the leading competitive sport, with more than two million players in teams across the country. The national team, known as *Les Bleus* from the blue strip on their jerseys, are the sixth most successful in the FIFA World Cup, placing first in 1998, second in 2006, third in 1958 and 1986 and fourth in 1982. Innumerable books, magazines and websites are devoted to football, such as the round-the-clock fans portal at *www.football365.fr* and the national team supporters portal at *www.bleus2006.com*. For further information on football in France, contact *Fédération française de football*, 60 bis avenue d'Iéna, 75783 Paris Cedex 16, Tel: 01 44317300, *www.fff.fr*; for information on international football, visit the *Fédération international de football association (FIFA)* website at *www.fifa.com* selectable in French, English, German or Spanish.

Francoplaque

Around the world, number plate collecting is popular among car buffs. It's most common in the USA and Canada, where plates are replaced frequently, often every two years, but less common in Europe, where plates may be fixed to a car for its lifetime. Nonetheless, number plate collecting has an avid following, particularly in France, where *Francoplaque* has a virtual museum of more than 30,000 number plates, online at *plaque.free.fr* in French and English, a site that now has more than 25,000 visitors a month.

Gambling [*Jeu d'argent*]

Gambling is a State-controlled monopoly available in two forms:

- *Loto* the national lottery [*loterie nationale*] with two draws a week broadcast live on TV on Wednesday and Saturday evenings, *www.loto.fr*.

- *PMU* the abbreviation for *Pari Mutuel Urbain*, off-track horse race betting on a Tote system, *www.pmu.fr* in French and English.

Across the country, **Tobacconists** (Chapter 40) have betting slips, online terminals and free brochures well as *PMUMag* a free magazine.

Golf

Scotland is regarded to be the home of modern golf, as the first course opened there in 1854 at Saint Andrews. But the French tradition is almost as venerable, as the first course opened just two years later, in 1856 at Pau in the Pyrènes Atlantiques *Département*. Today, there are more than 350 golf courses in the country, and there are some 350,000 registered players, which makes golf the country's ninth most popular sport. Arguably the best guide to golf in Europe is the bilingual English and French *Europe's Top 1000 Golf Courses* (Paris, Peugeot Golf Guide, 2006-2007 edition, 15 × 24 cm, 1326 pages hardcover, ISBN 2-952-4849-0-2). For further information on golf in the country, contact *Fédération française de golf*, 68 rue Anatole France, 92309 Levallois Perret Cedex, Tel: 01 41497700, *www.ffgolf.org* or visit the golf portal at *www.francegolf.fr* in French and English.

Gymnastics [*Gymnastique*]

Gymnastics is the fourth most popular sport in the country, with 1619 clubs that together have nearly a quarter of a million qualified gymnasts, 80% of them women. The clubs specialise in the seven disciplines governed by the *Fédération internationale de gymnastique (FIG)*:

- Men's artistic gymnastics (MAG) [*Gymnastique artistique masculine*]

- Women's artistic gymnastics (WAG) [*Gymnastique artistique féminine*]
- Rhythmic gymnastics (RG) [*Gymnastique rythmique*]
- Trampolining (TRA) [*Trampoline*]
- Sports acrobatics (ACRO) [*Gymnastique acrobatique*]
- Sports aerobics (AER) [*Gymnastique aérobic*]
- General gymnastics (GG) [*Gymnastique forme et loisirs*].

For further information, contact *Fédération française de gymnastique*, 7 ter Cour des Petites Ecurie, 75010 Paris, Tel: 01 48012448, *www.ffgym.com* with an interactive club locator and online subscription to the two national magazines of the sport, *Le Gymnaste Magazine* and *Gym Technic*.

Hash House Harriers

The Hash House Harriers (HHH) is an informal running club, founded in 1938 by British colonial officials serving in Malaysia. The name came from the byname of their lodgings, the "Hash House" for its monotonous food, and from the form of the meets in which a hare was given a head start to mark a trail and was followed by a pack of harriers. Only the hare knew the destination, which most often was a pub or a tub of beer. The HHH recipe of combining sport and socialising spread, and at last count, there are some 1800 HHHs in cities around the world. Originally for men only, the HHHs now have gatherings for women. And the finale of a gathering always is a social activity, known as a Down Down or an On In, at which beer usually is the beverage; indeed HHH has been described as a "drinking club with a running problem". The organisation of HHH is completely informal and local, and HHH groups may form or be disbanded at any time. There are no HHH offices, but there are some websites, which today provide the principle means of contact. At last estimate, there are seven HHH groups in France: Canigou (Perpignan and Prades), Grenoble, Lorient, Paris, Riviera (*Département* 06), Toulouse and Without Clue (western Paris).

Hiking and walking [*Randonnée et promenade*]

Across the country, there are an estimated quarter million footpaths and hiking trails for public use. Of these, some 180,000 km are marked and maintained by *Fédération française de la randonnée pédestre (FFR)* and its member organisations. There are three categories of trails and paths, all clearly marked with paint strips on rocks, cairns and tablets:

- *GR*, the abbreviation for *Grand Randonnée*, a long-distance trail in the national network totalling 60,000 km. GR are marked with white and red stripes, and the longest is GR® 10, from the Mediterranean Sea to the Atlantic Ocean via the Pyrenees Mountain Range.

- *GR Pays*, the abbreviation for *Grand Randonnée de Pays*, independent loops marked with yellow and red stripes. Two popular GR Pays are GR® 1 and 11, *La ceinture verte de l'Ile de France*, a 600 km loop around Paris, and GR® 13, *Tour du Morvan les grands lacs* offering hikes of one to three days.

- *PR*, the abbreviation for *Promenade et Randonnée*, a shorter distance hiking and walking trail or path, suitable for strolls of an hour up to hikes of six hours. The PR® are marked with yellow stripes.

All are shown on topographic maps [*topo*] of various scales. The *GR* are shown on hiking maps [*cartes de randonnées*] in scale 1:50,000 (1 cm on the map equals 500 m in terrain) and are issued in series for individual GR. For example, the trans-Pyrenees GR® 10 is covered by a series of 11 maps, from the first, *Pays Basque Ouest* on the Atlantic coast, to the eleventh, *Roussillon* on the Mediterranean coast. The *cartes de randonnées* are published by *Rando éditions*, part of the **National geographic institute** (Chapter 7) and sold by newsagents and bookshops as well as by FFR.

You may walk and hike along the trails and paths on your own, as they are free of charge. But if you are new to an area, you will enjoy the experience more if you join the local hiking and walking association, most of which have regular programmes of walks and hikes guided by experienced members. You can find the local association by asking people you meet along trails or by contacting the nearest FFR departmental council. For further information, contact *Centre d'information de la randonnée pédestre*, 14 rue Riquet, 75019 Paris, Tel: 01 44899393, *www.ffrandonnee.fr* with an interactive regional and departmental council locator map and online sales of guidebooks and maps.

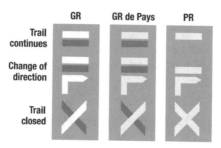

White and red GR, yellow and red GR de Pays and yellow PR trail markings. Diagram courtesy of FFR.

Historic vehicle clubs [*Clubs de véhicules historiques*]

There are 125 clubs for historic cars, trucks and motorcycles, dedicated to particular marques, countries of manufacture or vehicle purpose. Most of the clubs have membership magazines and many publish retro owners' manuals, workshop manuals and the like and offer access to used and new parts. For contact details or for an overview of historic vehicles, contact *Fédération française des véhicules d'époque (FFVE)*, 91 rue de Paris, BP 50603, 35006 Rennes Cedex, Tel: 02 23201414, *www.ffve.org*. For equivalent information at the international level, contact *Fédération internationale des véhicules anciens (FIVA)*, which was founded in 1966 in France and now has its head office in the UK at 30 St. Peter's Street, Duxford, Cambridgeshire, CB2 4RP, UK, Tel: +44 1223 573550, *www.ffva.org* selectable in French or English.

Hunting [*Chasse*]

Hunting is widely practised, particularly in rural areas. A licence [*permis de chasse*] is required and is issued for a year (1 July to 30 June) or for various shorter periods, by application which should be filled in, submitted and paid to the local tax office [*Trésor*] or the local hunting association. There are more than 1.5 million licensed hunters and an estimated 700,000 hunting dogs in the country. Access to private lands varies across the country, as does the hunting season, which usually is from late September to late February.

Hunting is mostly for birds, for wood-dwelling game including red deer, roe deer, and boar, and for wood and field game, including fox, hare and rabbit. Wood and field hunting is mostly with hounds and is done both on horseback [*la vénerie à cheval*] with larger packs of 40-80 hounds and on foot with small packs of 10-30 hounds of smaller breeds. By practice, hunting divides into three sectors:

- Ordinary hunting, on foot or on horseback. Some hunters use dogs that they have bred and trained, but the trend now is toward belonging to and using the dogs of a cooperative hunting dog association [*société de chasse*].
- *Déterrage*, literally "underground", the hunting on foot or on horseback of game that dwells underground, principally fox and badger. The hounds are of small size, usually of terrier or dachshund breeds, and there are an estimated 1750 underground-hunting packs.
- *Vénerie*, also called *chasse à courre*, the pursuit of game by large packs of dogs followed by mounted hunters who use no firearms. The practice is similar to that of the English fox hunt, but other game also are hunted, including boar, hare, rabbit, red deer and roe deer.

Two organisations are involved in the administration, regulation and organisation of hunting:

- *ONCFS*, the abbreviation for *Office national de la chasse et de la faune sauvage*, the governmental agency that issues hunting licences, monitors hunting and its impact on the environment, conducts research and publishes relevant brochures and papers. For further information, contact ONCFS at either of its two offices, 85 bis avenue de Wagram, BP 236, 75822 Paris Cedex 17, Tel: 01 44151717, or rue de Saint Thibaud, St Benoit, 78160 Auffargis, Tel: 01 30466000, *www.oncfs.gouv.fr*.

- *FNC*, the abbreviation for *Fédération nationale des chasseurs*, the national federation of local hunting associations, 13 rue du Général Leclerc, 92136 Issy Les Moulineau Cedex, Tel: 01 41096510, *www.unfdc.com* with an interactive local association locator map and online ordering of numerous publications.

Other organisations of interest to hunters include:

- *Maison de la chasse et de la nature*, a foundation, resource centre with a library of 3300 works, permanent art exhibitions in Paris and a retreat 90 km east of Reims, *www.chassenature.org*.

- *Chasse-enligne*, a website design house specialising in hunting, *www.chasse-enligne.com*.

- *Chassons.com*, a portal for hunting and related matters, such as travel and taxidermy, *www.chassons.com*.

- *CPNT*, the abbreviation for *Chasse – Pêche – Nature – Traditions*, a single-issue political party representing the interests of hunters and fishermen at the national level, *www.cpnt.asso.fr*.

- *Ligue ROC*, a conservationist group principally concerned with hunting, *www.roc.asso.fr*.

- *Parlons chasse*, a portal and online shop, *www.parlonschasse.com*.

Marinas [*Ports de plaisance*]

Along the coasts and inland waterways, there are more than 400 marinas, listed in the Yellow Pages under *Ports de plaisance* as well as under *Bateaux, hivernage* for winter storage facilities. For further information, contact:

- *Annuaire nautisme*, an annual guide to marinas, boat clubs, boats and motors, equipment and services, *Les éditions de Chabassol*, 16-18 bd de Lagny, Bussy St. Georges, 77600 Marne-la-Vallée Cedex 3, Tel: 01 64766490, *www.nautisme.com* with an interactive marina locator map.

- *Fédération française de ports de plaisance (FFPP)*, 17 rue Henri Bocquillon, 75015 Paris, Tel: 01 433352626, *www.ffports-plaisance.com* or *Euromarina*, the pan-European organisation for which FFPP is the secretariat, *www. euromarina.org* selectable in French or English.

Martial arts [*Arts martiaux*]

With more than 5000 clubs that together have 560,000 members, judo is the third most popular sport in the country. For further information on it, as well as on jujitsu, kendo and associated disciplines, contact *Fédération française de judo-jujitsu kendo et disciplines associées*, 21-25 avenue de la Pte de Châtillon, 75014 Paris, Tel: 01 40521616, *www.ffjudo.com*. By numbers, Karate is slightly less than half as popular, but nonetheless has clubs across the country, in all *Départements*. For further information, contact *Fédération française de karaté et disciplines associées*, 122 rue de la Tombe Issoire, 75014 Paris, Tel: 01 43954200, *www.ffkarate.fr*. Both organisations publish magazines and guides to the sport and support online services including interactive club locator maps.

Ministry for Youth, Sports and Voluntary Associations
[*Ministère de la jeunesse des sports et de la vie associative*]

The Ministry is the best single source of information on sport in the country, including overviews of statistics and finances, addresses of amateur and professional sports organisations and numerous other publications on national and international sports events. The Ministry has a head office in Paris as well as 105 decentralised services and 30 public services across the country. For details, contact *L'administration centrale, Ministère de la jeunesse, des sports et de la vie associative* 95 avenue de France, 75650 Paris Cedex 13, Tel: 01 40459000, *www.jeunesse-sports.gouv.fr*.

Mountaineering [*Alpinisme*]

The first mountain climbing in France is the reported ascent on 26 April 1336 of Mont Ventoux (1912 m) in the Baronnies massif by scholar Francesco Pétrarca (1304-1374), his brother and two servants. Though the report, in a letter to a friend, has been questioned, it dates the start of a fascination for the peaks of the country. With time, progressively higher peaks were climbed, culminating on 8 August 1786 with the first ascent of Mont Blanc (4808 m), the highest in the Alps, by guide Jacques Balmat (1762-1834) and doctor Michel Paccard (1757-1827). In the annals of mountaineering, that signalled the start of the golden age of the sport. Mountain guiding became a profession, first in 1821, with the founding of *Compagnie des guides de Chamonix*. Clubs were founded, in the UK in 1857, Switzerland in 1863, and, belatedly, in France in 1874. And one by one, the formidable peaks were climbed, perhaps most famously the Matterhorn in Switzerland in 1877 by Englishman Edward Whymper (1840-1911). In 1938, **ENSA**, the first national academy of mountaineering, was founded in Chamonix. By the 1950s, the summits of the Alps had been climbed and climbed again, and the frontier of mountaineering interest turned elsewhere, to the eight-thousanders, the 14 peaks of the Himalaya over 8000 m in elevation. Again, French climbers were first, on 3 June 1950, when Maurice Herzog (1919-) and Lous Lachenal (1921-1955) reached the summit of Annapurna (8091 m). One month short of five years later, countrymen Jean Couzy (1923-1958) and Lionel Terray (1921-1965) were first on Makalu (8463 m), so one in seven of the eight-thousanders were conquered by French climbers.

Today, 240 clubs and their 89,000 members practise traditional mountaineering and are affiliated in the *Fédération française des clubs alpins et de montagne (FFCAM)*, the present name of *Club alpin français* founded in 1874. Chamonix remains the hub of the sport. Its peaks and needles continue to challenge, and the *Compagnie des guides de Chamonix* has 200 licensed guides as well as a guide training school that welcomes aspiring guides from round the world. In 1988, the *Centre national d'instruction de ski et d'alpinisme de la Gendarmerie (CNISAG)* set up in Chamonix, thereby making it a major centre for both civilian and military mountaineering training.

In 1942, *Fédération française de la montagne et de l'escalade (FFME)* was founded to augment traditional mountaineering by organising expeditions and extending activities. Early on, it mounted the 1950 Annapurna expedition, and today it is the central clearing house for 1150 clubs active in mountaineering, rock climbing, mountain skiing and ski touring, snowshoeing and *canyoning*, the French neologism for sports practised in canyons, including climbing, whitewater rafting, kayaking and swimming (hydrospeed).

For further information, contact:

- *Compagnie des guides de Chamonix*, 190 place de l'Eglise, 74400 Chamonix, Tel: 04 50530088, *www.chamonix-guides.com* in French and English.
- *Fédération française des clubs alpins et de montagne (FFCAM)*, 24 avenue de Laumière, 75019 Paris, Tel: 01 53728700, *www.ffcam.fr* with interactive cabin and club locator maps.
- *Fédération française de la montagne et de l'escalade (FFME)*, 8-10 quai de la Marne, 75019 Paris, Tel : 01 40187550, *www.ffme.fr* with an interactive club locator map.

Probably the most famed badge in mountaineering.

National and Regional Parks [*Parcs nationaux et régionaux*]

There are seven National Parks, one on Guadeloupe and six on the mainland: *Les Pyrénées* in the mountain chain on the Spanish border, *Cévennes* in the south central part of the country, *Port-Cros* on an island in the Mediterranean, and *Les Ecerins*, *Le Mercantour* and *La Vanoise* in the Alps. Together they total more than 2% of the area of the country and each year attract some seven million visitors. For park addresses and descriptions, visit the *Parcs nationaux de France* website at *www.parcsnational-fr.com* in French, English, German, Italian and Spanish.

There are 44 Regional Parks, two on Guyane, two on Martinique, one on Corse and 39 on the mainland. One of the more stunning attractions is the Great Dune at Pyla, adjacent to the *Landes de Gascogne* Regional Park on the Atlantic coast, Europe's highest sand dune that affords magnificent vistas of the ocean and has become a starting point for hang gliding, itself a major attraction with its own website, *www.dune-pyla.com* in French and English. For park addresses, descriptions and images, contact *Fédération des parcs naturels régionaux de France*, 9 rue Christiani, 75018 Paris, Tel: 01 44908620, *www.parcs-naturels-regionaux.fr*.

National Institute for Sports and Physical Education Training [*Institut national du sport et de l'éducation physique (INSEP)*]

INSEP is the national institute for education in, research on and information concerning top-level sports. Originally founded in 1852 upon decree of Louis Napoléon Bonaparte as an academy for civil servants and the military, *École normale de gymnastique civile et militaire*, it now is a multipurpose institution that offers numerous services to the general public, including sales of publications, DVDs and CDs and access to a comprehensive library. For further information, contact INSEP, 11 av du Tremblay, 75012 Paris, Tel: 01 41744100, *www.insep.fr*.

Orienteering [*Course d'orientation*]

Orienteering is a competitive event entailing running, cross-country skiing or offroad cycling in varied, often wooded terrain, using a map and compass to find control points not known to the competitor in advance, but indicated on the map and in terrain flagged with square orange-and-white markers. There are individual as well as relay events over various distances for men, women and juniors. The sport originated in Scandinavia in the latter half of the 19th century and spread from there to other countries, including France. Today there are orienteering clubs across the country, and there are more than 100 permanent orienteering centres [*Espaces sports d'orientation (ESO)*] with fixed courses and control points to facilitate practice of skills. Across the country each year, there are numerous local, national and international meets, in October 2006 including the finale of the Orienteering World Cup. For further information, contact *Fédération Française de Course d'Orientation (FFCO)*, 15 Passage des Mauxins, 75019 Paris, Tel: 01 47971191, *www.ffco.asso.fr*.

Outdoor multisport [*Multi-sport-nature*]

Outdoor multisport is a sport discipline in which competitors race in continuous series of dissimilar events, switching without rest between them. It differs from the multisport disciplines of the Olympics, such as pentathlon and decathlon, in which the events are not continuous but are held with hours or sometimes days between them.

Most outdoor multisport meets combine two to five events, including cross-country running [*course à pied*], orienteering [*course d'orientation*], offroad cycling [*VTT*], canoe and kayak [*canoe et kayak*], rock climbing [*escalade*], inline skating [*roller*], swimming [*natation*] and archery [*tir à l'arc*]. Triathlon, combining cycling, running and swimming, is one of the classic outdoor multisport events.

Outdoor multisport gained popularity in the late 1980s and early 1990s. The turning point came in 1992, when Bruno Pomart, formerly a sports instructor for *RAID*, the acronym for *Recherche, assistance, intervention, dissuasion*, a multidisciplinary elite unit of the **National police** (Chapter 10) founded an outdoor multisport organisation and used the RAID acronym in its name to connote plurality of events: *Association RAID adventure organisation*. The name appealed and soon Raid became the more common term; today *Raid nature* and *Raid sportif* are the most-used terms.

Across the country each year, there are innumerable Raid events, such as *Rando-Raid SFR* named for its lead event, walking, and its sponsor, SFR, *www.randoraid.com*. For further information on the ever greater spectrum of Raid events and activities, contact *Association RAID adventure*, 13 rue Charles de Gaulle, 91400 Orsay, Tel: 01 69418437, *www.raid-adventure.org*.

Pelote

Pelote, or *pilota* in Basque and Catalan, is the name of a variety of court sports played with a ball, using a hand, a racket or wicker basket to propel it against a wall or over a net to an opposing player. In the Basque region it is the most popular sport and therefore is most often called *Pelote Basque*. It is played informally as well as by clubs, of which there are 335 that together have nearly 20,000 regular players. Across the country, meets are held each year, and the sport has spread from Spain and France to other countries on all continents. For further information, contact *Fédération française de pelote basque*, Trinquet Moderne, BP 816, 64108 Bayonne, *www.ffpb.net* with interactive club locator maps for France and countries elsewhere.

Roller

Le roller, roller skating on inline skates, is a major recreation, with an estimated five million practitioners across the country. It also is a family of competitive events, including races, figures and dancing, hockey, acrobatics and touring. Free inline skating is practised as is skateboarding, in acrobatic manoeuvres, mostly on city streets, but also in competition using ramps and rails made for the purpose. For further information, contact *Fédération française de roller*, 6 Bd Franklin Roosevelt, BP 33, 33034 Bordeaux Cedex, Tel: 05 56336565, *www.ffrs.asso.fr*.

Rugby

Rugby is the tenth most popular sport in the country, with 1630 clubs and nearly a quarter of a million players*. Each year, there are innumerable rugby matches, from the local level up, and France regularly competes in the six nations cup against England, Ireland, Scotland, Wales and Italy, the only other continental European country in which rugby is taken seriously. Across the country, there are 38 levels of competition, and beach rugby, touch rugby and women's rugby are fast-growing sports. For further information, contact *Fédération française de rugby*, 9 rue de Liège, 75009 Paris, Tel: 0153211515, *www.ffr.fr* with an interactive club locator map, or visit the commercial rugby portal at *www.rugbyrama.com*.

* *Source: FFR, 31 May 2006.*

Sailing [*Voile*]

Sailing is a popular recreation as well as a keen competitive sport. Across the country, there are 1,087 sailing clubs that together have 276,644 qualified sailors*. Sailing and sailboats divide into six broad classes: habitable sailing boat [*habitable*], dinghy [*dériveur*], keelboat [*quillard*], catamaran, windsurfer [*planche à voile*] and radio-controlled sailing [*voile radio commande (VRC)*] in the international one-metre (IOM) class. For further information, contact *Fédération française de voile*, 17 rue Henri Bocquillon, 75015 Paris, Tel: 01 40603700, *www.ffvoile.org* with an interactive club locator map.

* *Source: QUID 2006*

Skiing [*Ski*]

By any measure, France is among the world leaders in skiing. Though the ways of compiling figures vary, France vies with Switzerland and Austria in the extent of its ski resorts. Europe's highest ski lift is the gondola to the upper station just below Aiguille du Midi at 3777 m elevation, nearly two and a half vertical kilometres above the base station in Chamonix at 1316 m elevation. From that station, skiers can depart on runs down the *Vallée Blanche*, the world's longest continuous downhill ski slope. *Le 3842*, the restaurant at Aiguille du Midi, is Europe's highest. Three Olympic Winter Games (OWG) have been held in France – the first in Chamonix in 1924, the tenth in Grenoble in 1968, and the 16th in Albertville in 1992 – more than in any other country in Europe. Two French companies are world leaders in their ski business sectors: Poma in ski lifts and Rossignol in skis and skiing equipment. All the snow sport disciplines are practised, from the traditional competitive Nordic and Alpine events to freestyle, acrobatics, Telemark and snowboarding. For further information, contact:

- *Ski France International*, the official website of the French ski resorts at *www.ski-ride.france.com* selectable in French or English.

- *Fédération française de ski (FFS)*, the governing body for competitive snow sports, 50 rue des Marquisats, BP 2451, 74011 Annecy Cedex, Tel: 04 50514034, *www.ffs.fr*.

- *Fédération française de la montagne et de l'escalade (FFME)*, an organisation involved in mountain skiing and ski touring, *www.ffme.fr*.

- Rossignol, the leading ski and ski gear maker, *www.rossignol.com* selectable in French or English.

- Poma, the leading manufacturer of ski lifts and other cable transportation systems, *www.poma.net* selectable in French or English.

Sports media [*Médias sports*]

The sports media is extensive; a selection of its leaders includes:

- *L'Equipe*, a daily newspaper founded in 1946, now with a circulation of 370,000, 4 rue Rouget de Lisle, 92130 Issy Les Moulineaux, Tel: 01 40932020, *www.lequipe.fr*.

- *Eurosport*, the pan-European television network founded in 1989 that provides broadcast, satellite and cable TV sports in 19 languages, 3 rue Gaston et René Caudron, 92798 Issy-les-Moulineaux Cedex 9, Tel: 01 40938000, *www.eurosport.fr* selectable in French, English, German, Italian, Spanish, Russian or Chinese.

- *Sport.fr*, a sports media portal founded in 1997 and now providing access to present and past coverage of 100 sports, 24 hours a day, Groupe Sport.fr, 32 boulevard Paul Vaillant Courier, 93108 Montreuil Cedex, Tel: 01 48519040, *www.sport.fr*.

- *Sport24.com*, an Internet sports news channel subsidiary of the *Le Figaro* newspaper that provides sports news round-the-clock, 14 boulevard Haussmann, 75009 Paris, Tel: 01 75554159, *www.sport24.com*.

Stamp collecting [*Philatélie*]

Accurate figures are not kept, but stamp collecting probably is the country's most practised indoor hobby. The many dealers are listed in the Yellow Pages under *Philatélie* and *La Poste* has an extensive philatelic service at *www.laposte.fr* under *Philatélie* in French and English. For 22 years, from 1961 to 1983, the ORTF television network featured *Télé-Philatélie*, a regular programme on stamp collecting. The European Academy of Philately [*Académie européenne de philatélie (AEP)*] is at *Musée de la Poste*, 34 bd de Vaugirard, 75015 Paris, *www.aephil.net* selectable in French or English.

Swimming [*Natation*]

Swimming is a popular recreation along the many beaches [*plages*] and in many public and private swimming pools [*piscines*], and more than 210,000 competitive swimmers are members of clubs across the country. For further information, contact *Fédération française de natation*, 148 avenue Gambetta, 75980 Paris Cedex 20, Tel: 01 40311770, *www.ffnatation.fr* with an interactive club locator map.

Tennis

Tennis is the country's leading individual sport and the most popular sport among women. Each year, some 380,000 players take to the country's 33,500 tennis courts, and there are more than 8600 tennis clubs, from smaller local clubs to RCF in Paris with more than 5300 members*. The French Open, officially the Roland Garros Tournament, held over two weeks in late May and early June, is the second of the four Grand Slam tournaments (the other three are the Australian Open, Wimbledon and the US Open); for further information, visit the tournament website at *www.rolandgarros.com* selectable in French, English or Spanish. For further information on tennis in general, contact *Fédération française de tennis (FFT)*, Stade Roland Garros, 2 avenue Gordon Bennet, 75016 Paris, Tel: 01 47434800, *www.fft.fr*.

* *Source: FFT*

Roland Garros tournament logo, by permission of FFT.

Theme parks [*Parcs d'attractions et de loisirs*]

Across the country, there are innumerable amusement and recreational parks featuring animals, cultural attractions, fictional characters, scientific topics and numerous other themes. For a complete overview as well as for online ordering of tickets to the larger parks, visit the European Infoparks website at *www.infoparks.com* selectable in French, English, Dutch, German, Italian or Spanish.

Tour de France

Tour de France probably is the world's most famed cycle race, watched from the roadside by 15 million spectators and viewed on TV by many more round the globe.

It consists of 21 stages on as many days, 11 on the flat, seven in mountains and four pure time trials. The route differs each year, but the finish is always around 14 July on Champs-Élysées in Paris. It was inaugurated in 1903, and now is put on by the largest sports organiser in France, Amaury Sport Organisation (ASO), 2 rue Rouget de L'Isle, 92130 Issy Les Moulineaux, Tel: 01 41331400, *www.aso.fr* in French and English. For information on the event itself as well as for online purchase of souvenirs, visit the official website at *www.letour.fr* in French and English.

Underwater sports [*Sports sous-marins*]

Underwater sports are practised along the coasts in great variety, including skin diving [*plongée*], scuba diving [*plongée en scaphandre*], underwater hockey [*hockey subaquitaine*] and deep-sea fishing [*pêche sous-marine*]. Accordingly, along all coasts there are clubs and schools dedicated to the sports. For further information, contact *Fédération française d'études et de sports sous-marins (FFESSM)*, 24 quai de Rive-Neuve, 13284 Marseille, Cedex 07, Tel: 08 20000457, *www.ffessm.fr* with a postcode club locator window and links to governmental organisations that certify practitioners and regulate the sports.

University sports [*Sport universitaire*]

Sports in higher-education are organised by associations [*les associations sportives des établissements d'enseignement supérieur*] as well as by clubs [*les clubs universitaires*]. The various associations and clubs compete with each other, and each year there are national cups [*Coupes de France*]. For further information, contact the sport association or club of your institute of higher education or the *Fédération française du sport universitaire (FF Sport U)*, 108 avenue de Fontainebleau, 94270 Le Kremlin-Bicêtre, Tel: 01 58682275, *www.sport-u.com*.

Venues [*Sites*]

There are innumerable sports grounds, pitches, halls and stadiums across the country. The four largest venues are:

- *La stade vélodrome,* a 35,000 seat stadium that is the home of the Marseille sport club, Boulevard Michelet, 13008 Marseille, *www.marseillais-du-monde.org* in French and English.

- *Parc des Princes*, a 45,000 seat stadium built in 1972, principally as a home for the Paris Saint-Germain football club, 24 rue du Commandant Guilbaud, *www.psg.fr*.

- *Paris-Bercy*, a 17,000 seat enclosed stadium, 8 Boulevard de Bercy, 75012 Paris, *www.bercy.fr*.

- *Stade de France*, an 80,000 seat stadium built for the 1998 World Cup in football, when France was host nation, *Consortium Stade de France*, 93216 Saint Denis La Plaine Cedex, Tel: 08 92700900, *www.stadedefrance* in French and English.

Whitewater sports [*Sports d'eau vive*]

In the Alps and the Pyrenees there are ten canyons that offer innumerable challenges in whitewater rafting, kayaking, swimming (hydrospeed) and climbing. For their locations and descriptions, visit the *Fédération française de la montagne et de l'escalade (FFME)* website at *www.ffme.fr*, click on *Disciplines*, then on *Canyonisme* and then on *Carte de France des canyons* to bring up the interactive map. The *Fédération française de canoe-kayak* lists whitewater clubs and competitive events on its website at *www.ffck.org*. Several organisations offer whitewater adventure trips and guiding; the largest is *Coureurs de Rivières*, Vulmix, Bourg St Maurice, 73700 Les Arcs, Tel: 06 11222622, *www.coureurs-rivieres.com* in French and English.

499

42
Statistics, analyses and polls

As elsewhere, the statistics of the country are a collection of its historical and current facts and figures along with analyses and interpretations of them. Historically, the world's first statistics analysis is attributed to John Graunt of England, in "Natural and Political Observations Made Upon the Bills of Mortality", published in 1662. The compilation of statistics in France began in 1801, and a governmental statistics agency, the predecessor of *Institute national de la statique et des études économiques*, was established in 1833. Private sector organisations provide various analyses of the country as well as polling of the population.

Census [*Recensement*]

The first census was taken in 1801. Thereafter, general censuses [*Recensements généraux*] were taken at five year intervals, save for the years of the first and second world wars, until 1946, and thereafter at irregular intervals until 2004. From 2004 onwards, a partial census is taken each year [*recensement permanent*], and results are published as averages over five years. Census data are published each year in *Annuaire statistique de la France* and are available online on the INSEE website at *www.insee.fr*.

The Economist Intelligence Unit (EIU)

As its name implies, The Economist Intelligence Unit (EIU) is the country, industry and management analysis service of *The Economist*, the weekly magazine (though it still calls itself a "newspaper") first published in 1843 and now the only truly independent global economic and political news and analysis source. The EIU Country Reports are updated monthly for 117 countries, including France and are available on subscription or by single issue purchase. In addition to the Country Report France, EIU offers more than 40 continuously updated reports on various aspects of the economy, business and politics of France. EIU has more than 40 offices worldwide; its headquarters are in London with regional centres in Hong Kong, Vienna and New York. For further details, contact the London headquarters, 15 Regent Street London SW1Y 4LR, UK, Tel: + 44 (0) 20 78301007, Fax: + 44 (0) 20 78301023, *www.eiu.com* with pages in English only, *london@eiu.com*.

Euromonitor

Euromonitor International is a global consumer market intelligence company with a staff of more than 600 analysts and consultants and offices in London, Chicago, Singapore, Shanghai and Vilnius. It publishes and sells in-depth reports and books by market sector and by country and provides free overview summaries at its online Press Centre. At present, it offers several hundred market sector reports on France. For further details, contact the London office, Euromonitor International, 60-61 Britton Street, London EC1M 5UX, UK, Tel: + 44 (020) 72518024, Fax: +44 (020) 7608 3149, *www.euromonitor.com* with pages in English only, *info@ euromonitor.com*.

EUROSTAT

Eurostat is the statistical office of the European Communities that keeps and publishes extensive statistics on all EEA countries, in all some 300 million items of statistical information. The "Eurostat yearbook" is the single best reference to statistics across Europe, and Eurostat's many theme pocketbooks make comparative statistical data meaningful and understandable. All Eurostat data and publications are available free of charge online from its website at *europa.eu.int/comm/eurostat*, and printed editions are sold by the Eurostat Datashop in Paris at the INSEE Info Service (IIS), 195 Rue de Bercy, 75012 Paris. For general queries on Eurostat, contact the Press Office, BECH Building, L-2920 Luxembourg, Tel: +352 430133444, Fax: +352 430135349.

National Institute of Statistics and Economic Studies [*Institut National de la Statistique et des Études Économiques – INSEE*]

INSEE, a General Directorate of the Ministry of the Economy, Finance and Industry (MINEFI), is the national statistics compilation, analysis and publication agency. Its work is carried out in four directorates: the Demographic and Social Statistics Directorate [*Direction des Statistiques Démographiques et Sociales (DSDS)*], the Business Statistics Directorate [*Direction des Statistiques d'Entreprise (DSE)*], the Statistical Coordination and International Relations Directorate [*Direction de la Coordination Statistique et des Relations Internationales (DCSR)*] and the Dissemination and Regional Action Directorate [*Direction de la Diffusion et de l'Action Régionale (DDAR)*].

The operations of the Demographic and Social statistics Directorate are the most widely known in everyday life and consist principally of:

- Taking population, household and dwelling census
- Maintaining the National Identification Register of Private Individuals [*Répertoire National d'Identification des Personnes Physiques (RNIPP)*]
- Keeping voter registration records

- Compiling the consumer price index
- Conducting household surveys
- Extracting data from administrative records on households, employment and income
- Conducting surveys of enterprise and local government bodies.

The INSEE head office is in Paris at 18 Boulevard Adolphe Pinard, 75014 Paris, and it has offices in the administrative capitals (*chefs-lieux*) of the 22 Regions as well as 2 Regional offices overseas. The INSEE Info service (IIS) operates a bookshop and reference room at 195 Rue de Bercy, 75012 Paris. For further information, call Tel: 08 25889452, Mondays to Fridays, 09.00-17.00, or for current statistics, the voice server at 08 92680760. The extensive website at *www.insee.fr*, with pages in English, supports links to other sites and supports online ordering of INSEE publications, such as *La France en Bref / France in Figures*, an overview summary brochure for the public, published every two years.

OECD Statistics [*Statistique OECD*]

The **OECD** (Chapter 20), of which France is a member, compiles myriad statistics into publications that are available online and may be ordered from its online bookshop at *www.oecd.org*.

Opinion polls [*Sondages d'opinion*]

As elsewhere, opinion polls attempt to assess national or selected sector opinion on matters by putting questions to samples of the population by telephone, personal interview or filling out forms. The **National Institute for Statistics and Economic Studies** conducts polls for governmental purposes, and several market research institutes conduct polls. The leading private-sector institutes with website pages in English are:

- *CSA*, with a head office in Paris and regional offices specialising in local affairs, 2 rue Choiseul, 75002 Paris, Tel: 01 44944000, *www.csa-fr.com*.
- Gallup polling in France is conducted by the UK office of the Gallup Organisation, founded in 1935 by pioneering pollster Dr. George Gallup: The Gallup Organisation Ltd., Drapers Court, Kingston Hall Road, Kingston-upon-Thames, Surrey, KT1 2BG, UK, Tel: +44 20 89397000, Fax: +44 20 89397039, *www.gallup.com*.
- *Ipsos*, founded in 1975 in France and now with operations round the world, 35 rue du Val de Marne, 75628 Paris Cedex 13, Tel: 01 41989999, *www.ispos.com* and *www.ispos.fr* with pages in English.

UN Statistics Division

The United Nations Statistics Division compiles statistics from many international sources into global overviews, including the *Statistical Yearbook* in printed and CD versions and the *World Statistics Pocketbook* (printed only), as well as yearbooks on selected sectors. The Commodity Trade Statistics Database (UN Comtrade) of statistics by countries and other updates are available online at *unstats.un.org/unsd* (site in English only). For ordering printed publications or for further information, contact the Sales Section, Palais des Nations, CH-1211 Geneva 10, Switzerland, Fax: +41 229170027, *unpubli@unog.ch*.

43
Taxes, duties and excise

The total tax revenue – the sum of direct and indirect taxes, duties and excise – amounts to 44.0% of the Gross Domestic Product (GDP), higher than the EU average (40.6%) and the OECD average (36.3%), but lower than first-place Sweden (50.2%) and three other countries – Denmark, Belgium and Finland*. Nonetheless, some taxes are lower than in other countries: the French Value Added Tax (*TVA*) is 19.6%, twelfth highest in Europe, after the Scandinavian countries and Hungary in first place with VATs of 25%. Income taxes are structured as they are elsewhere in Europe, and there is a wealth tax, first introduced in 1981 as a tax on great wealth [*impôt sur les grandes fortunes*] and now known as a "tax of solidarity on wealth" [*impôt de solidarité sur la fortune (ISF)*]

* *OECD in Figures*, OECD Observer 2005, Supplement 1, pp. 38-39.

Avoidance of double taxation [*À éviter les doubles imposition*]

France has signed conventions for the avoidance of double taxation with more than 100 countries. For example, with the UK a convention pertaining to income tax was signed on 22 May 1968 and a convention pertaining to succession duty was signed on 21 June 1963. For a complete list of the countries with which conventions have been signed, see the Annexes to **French taxation**.

Customs [*Douane*]

Upon import, **VAT** is charged on goods bought outside the EU, but not on goods bought in another EU country, on which VAT already has been paid. Customs duty [*droits de douane*] is charged on some goods; for example, the duty charged on musical instruments [*instruments de musique*] varies from 2.7% to 4.0%. A list of customs duties is available from the 40 Regional Customs Directorates [*Direction régionale des douanes*] listed under *Administrations de l'économie et des finances* in the Yellow Pages, or online on the customs website at *www.douane.gouv.fr*; click on *Voyageurs, estimez les droits et taxes à payer à la douane sur vos achats à l'étranger* under *Particuliers* on the opening page.

French taxation [*Fiscalité française*]

As in most countries, taxation, one of the responsibilities of the Ministry of Economy, Finance and Industry [*Ministère de l'économie des finances et de l'industrie*], is complex and there are many experts who interpret tax laws and regulations. Fortunately for the public, the Ministry regularly publishes a brochure that provides an overview of taxation in easily-understood language, in French (entitled *La fiscalité française*) and English (entitled "French Taxation") editions. Both contain the disclaimer that "This paper offers a brief overview of French taxation. It should in no event be construed as the official doctrine of the department by which it has been drafted." [*Ce document est une présentation synthétique de la fiscalité française. En aucun cas il ne constitue la doctrine officielle des services qui l'ont rédigé.*], but nonetheless probably is the most authoritative, up-to-date reference available in everyday language. The most recent editions as this book goes to press were published 1 April 2005 and comprise 16 theme chapters in four parts on the principal sectors of taxation: income taxes, taxes on expenditure, property taxes and local direct taxes. The brochures are available in print from the tax offices in the *Départements* listed under *Impôts* under the *Administrations de l'économie et des finances* in the Yellow Pages or locatable online at *www.impots.gouv.fr*, and they may be downloaded online from that website; click first on *Documentation* and then on *Impôts pratiques* to bring up the page from which the French and English versions may be downloaded.

Income tax [*Impôt sur le revenu*]

In legal language, income taxation depends on the country in which you are domiciled [*domiciliés*], or in everyday language, on the country of your permanent residence in a tax year. If you are domiciled in France, you are taxed on your total income from French and foreign sources. If you are not domiciled in France, you are taxed only on income from French sources. With a few exceptions, all income, whatever its source, is added together to arrive at an overall net income to which a single tax scale applies. The seven principal sources of income subject to taxation are:

- Business profits [*bénéfices industriels et commerciaux*]
- Professional profits [*bénéfices non commerciaux*]
- Agricultural profits [*bénéfices agricoles*]
- Real property income [*revenus fonciers*]
- Wages and salaries, pensions and annuities [*traitements, salaires, pensions et rentes viagères*]
- Income from transferable securities [*revenus mobiliers*]
- Capital gains [*gains en capital*].

The tax for a household is assessed according to an income splitting system [*technique du quotient familial*]. In it, the taxable incomes of all members of a **tax household** first are added together and then the sum is split up into a number of parts equal to the number of contributing members of the household. Each part then is assessed a portion of the taxable income [*fraction du revenu imposable*] of the household. For the 2006 tax year, the tax rate per part is:

Net income per part	Tax rate
up to €5,515	0%
€5,516 - €11,000	5.5%
€11,001 - €24,431	14%
€24,432 - €65,500	30%
€65,501 or more	40%

As in most countries, the income tax system is complex and can be confusing if you are not accustomed to it. Chapter 2 of Part One of **French taxation**, available in French and English editions, provides an excellent overview. For specific details, there are many printed and online sources, public and private. Perhaps the best two, one public and one private, are:

• the **Public service portal** (Chapter 31) at *www.service-public.fr*; click on *Impôt, taxe et douane* on the opening page and then on *Impôt sur le revenu* to bring up a comprehensive list of online documents, downloadable tax forms and on-site tools, including a tax calculator.

• *Syndicat National Unifié des Impôts (SNUI)* publishes an annual tax guide, *Guide pratique du contribuable* as well as tax sector guides and other tax-related publications; contact SNUI, 80 rue Monteruil, 75011 Paris, Tel: 01 44646444, *www.leguideducontribuable.com*.

Indirect taxes and similar charges (excise)
[*Contributions indirectes et réglementaires (accises)*]

Excise taxes are levied on:

• spirits and alcoholic beverages, mostly based on hectolitre pure alcohol content

• mineral oil products on the domestic market, *taxe intérieure sur les produits pétroliers (TIPP)*, and, in the overseas *Départements*, a *taxe spéciale de consommation (TSC)* on petrol and diesel

• tobacco

• entertainment, based on the receipts to most sports events, on gambling clubs and houses and on slot machines in public places

- precious metals

- polluting activities, *taxe générale sur les activités polluantes (TGAP)*.

On 1 January 1993, the excise taxes on alcoholic drink, mineral oil products and tobacco were for the most part harmonised with EC directives. The other excise taxes are determined by national rules. For further information on these taxes and charges, see Chapter 2 of Part Two of **French taxation**.

Local direct taxes [*Impôts locaux*]

Local direct taxes [*Impôts locaux*] are the oldest taxes in the country; they replaced the State's direct taxes of 1791 and in 1917 were transferred to territorial authorities. Save for a business tax [*taxe professionnelle*], they are assessed on land registry rental value [*valeur locative cadastrale*] as recorded in a **Cadastre** (Chapter 31). The land registry rental value is an assumed yield of a property [*revenue cadastral*] as determined by the authorities, not a rent reflecting prevailing market conditions.

The State collects local taxes for appropriation to territorial authorities – the *Régions*, the *Départements*, the municipalities [*communes*] and the inter-communal cooperation establishments [*établissements publics de coopération communale*]. Within limits set by the State, tax rates are determined by the territorial assemblies – *Conseils régional, Conseils général* and *Conseils municipal* – in working out the annual budget and reflect the income anticipated from tax appropriation. The four main taxes are: a real property tax on developed land [*taxe foncière les propriétés bâties*], a real property tax on undeveloped land [*taxe foncière les propriétés non bâties*], a residence tax [*taxe d'habitation*] and a business tax [*taxe professionnelle*]. The taxes are levied on 1 January, and usually are billed later in the year. The two land taxes are billed together [*taxes foncières*], so a private residence will receive two tax bills and a business may receive three.

The real property tax on developed land [*taxe foncière les propriétés bâties*] is levied on all buildings save those on public properties [*propriétés publiques*] and active farm buildings [*bâtiments ruraux*]. The tax is assessed at a rate applicable to 50% of the *revenue cadastral* of the property. New buildings less than two years old are exempt from the tax. Proportional tax relief for a principal residence is granted for low-income families, elderly persons and handicapped persons.

The real property tax on undeveloped land [*taxe foncière les propriétés non bâties*] is levied on all land save public properties [*propriétés publiques*] and active farms. The tax is assessed at a rate applicable to 80% of the *revenue cadastral* of the property.

The residence tax [*taxe d'habitation*] is levied on principal as well as secondary residences that are not used for industrial or commercial purposes. It is based on the *revenue cadastral* of the principal building and its outbuildings, such as gardens, garages, private parking spaces and the like. The tax is assessed at a rate set by the relevant local authority and usually is billed together with the **TV licence** (Chapter 44). For a private residence, it is the largest local tax. Means-tested full or partial tax relief for a principal residence is granted for low-income families, elderly persons and handicapped persons.

The business tax [*taxe professionnelle*] is levied on businesses, be they corporate or individual. It is assessed at a rate set by the relevant local authority on the basis of 80% of the value of equipment and movable property available to the taxpayer in the previous tax year. The tax reform of 2006, in force from 2008 on, will rebase the tax on 80% of the added value of the business [*valeur ajoutée*] and 20% on the land tax [*foncière*].

Further information on these taxes is available at the *France pratique* and **Public service portal** websites described in Chapter 31. For specific figures and details, contact the local tax office [*Trésor public*].

Revenue stamps [*Timbres fiscaux*]

Revenue stamps are adhesive labels used to pay some taxes, fees and fines. Historically, they were first used in the 17th and 18th centuries and predate postage stamps, which were first issued in 1840. Today, they are sold by **Tobacconists** (Chapter 12) in two series:

- Ordinary series in denominations of 1, 2, 5, 8, 10, 20, 30 and 90 Euros affixed to documents principally to pay fees, such as on applications for passports, university admission and the like.
- Special series of two stamps, one larger for payment and one smaller as a receipt, both with the same serial number, in denominations of 4, 11, 22, 35, 45, 68, 90 and 135 Euros used principally to pay traffic and parking fines.

Use of the revenue stamps is straightforward. For instance, an application requiring the payment of a 30 Euro fee will include an instruction to affix: *un timbre fiscal d'un montant de 30,00 € (les timbres fiscaux sont vendus dans les bureaux de tabac)*.

The only problem you may encounter in using the stamps is that the regulations concerning some fees have not yet been updated to reflect the change of currency from the Franc to the Euro. As this book goes to press in late 2006, for example, a university application form might request a revenue stamp fee payment of 33.54 Euros, which is simply the fee of Fr. 220 valid at 31 December 1998 when the currency was changed divided by 6.55957, the exchange rate then fixed between the Franc and the Euro. Of course, with time all fees will be to the Euro base, but until then the simplest solution is to round off a peculiar fee to the next highest whole Euro figure, in this case by buying one 30 Euro and two 2 Euro revenue stamps. For further information on *Timbres fiscaux*, see *Bulletin Officiel des Impôts, No 232 du 31 décembre 2001*, available from *Direction générale des impôts*, catalogue number

12B-1-01, downloadable from *alize.finances.gouv.fr/dgiboi/boi2001/boi.htm*, click first on "12R Recouvrement" and then on "Division B Ecritures compatables" to bring up the link to the document.

Ordinary series violet 8€ and orange 30€ stamps.

Special series green on orange 45€ stamp and receipt pair.

Tax household [*Foyer fiscal*]

The tax household [*foyer fiscal*] is an entity used in calculating **income tax** and **wealth tax**. It is similar but not identical to the household, an entity used in statistics, and to the home, in the everyday as well as sociological sense.

In short, the tax household consists of a person or persons living together at a place that is their normal, permanent residence. Typical tax households consist of:

* one person: unmarried, widowed or divorced
* two or more people: a married couple with dependent minor children
* two people: a same-sex couple after the first year of their civil union (*PACS*)
* one person of a cohabiting couple, save for **wealth tax**, in which the couple count as two
* several persons: a community of monks or nuns living together under religious vows.

A married couple does not comprise a tax household if the spouses:

* do not live under the same roof and have separate possessions
* are legally separated and authorised to have separate residences
* have different incomes, and one has left the marital home.

As a rule, children of age [*majeurs*] who earn income are taxed separately. However, a child earning income may be included in a tax household provided that he/she is

- less than 21 years old
- a student less than 25 years old
- disabled, of any age.

VAT [*TVA*]

TVA is the abbreviation for *Taxe sur la valeur ajoutée,* the country's value-added tax (VAT). It is a general consumption tax that is charged on all goods delivered and all services provided in France and is charged at three rates, last set 1 April 2000:

- 19.6% standard rate applicable to all transactions not subject to another rate
- 5.5% reduced rate for most food and agricultural products, certain types of animal feed, medical drugs not reimbursed by social security, books and some services, including public transport. Since 15 September 1999, the 5.5% rate also applies to works on dwellings more than two years old
- 2.1% special rate applicable to press publications and to medical drugs reimbursed by social security.

Most prices are stated inclusive of VAT [*Toutes Taxes Comprises (TTC)*], but some are stated exclusive of VAT [*Hors Taxes (HT)*]. For further information on VAT, see Chapter 1 of Part Two of **French taxation**.

Vocabulary (*Vocabulaire*)

For a Glossary [*Lexique*] of taxation terms, see the **French taxation** brochure; each term listed in the English edition is followed by the equivalent French term in parentheses, so it's a small but useful bilingual dictionary on taxation.

Wealth tax [*Impôt de solidarité sur la fortune (ISF)*]

Each **tax household** is subject to a wealth tax [*Impôt de solidarité sur la fortune (ISF)*] whenever its combined assets – cash, furniture, property and securities – exceed a threshold set each year on 1 January. The threshold for 2006 is €750,000. If you are domiciled in France, the wealth tax applies to your worldwide assets. If you are not domiciled in France, the wealth tax applies only to your assets in France. Several types of assets are excluded from ISF, including professional assets [*biens professionnels*], antiques and works of art [*objets d'antiquité, d'art ou tout simplement de collection*] and pension capitalisation [*valeurs de capitalisation des pensions de retraites*]. The wealth tax for the tax year starting 1 January 2006 is:

Combined assets	Wealth tax rate
less than € 750,000	0%
€ 750,000 - € 1,200,000	0.55%
€ 1,200,000 - € 2,380,000	0.76%
€ 2,380,000 - € 3,730,000	0.00%
€ 3,730,000 - € 7,140,000	1.30%
€ 7,140,000 - € 15,530,000	1.65%
more than € 15,530,000	1.80%

As its name implies, the wealth tax is aimed at the rich. However, due to the property boom, more than 330,000 tax households now pay it.

For complete information on the wealth tax, visit the tax website at *www.impots.gouv.fr*; click on *Particuliers* on the opening page, then on *Vos impôts* to activate a drop-down list, and in it click on *Impôt de Solidarité sur la Fortune* to bring up a page of links to relevant documentation.

44

Telecommunications, broadcasting and the Internet

By most measures, the telecommunications, broadcasting and Internet sectors in France are thriving in an increasingly competitive market. The country's telecommunication market is the third largest in Europe, after Germany and the UK. France Télévision's TV5 is the second largest global television network. Though Internet penetration is slightly lower than average across Europe, overall data communications may place the country on top, as the Minitel system was implemented and in widespread use ten years before the Internet became available to the public.

Alternative operators [*Opérateurs alternatifs*]

As in telecommunications across Europe, an alternative operator is a private-sector company that after deregulation entered the market to compete with the incumbent company, usually a former government monopoly. In France, that means companies that compete with France Télécom, that up to 1988 was a governmental monopoly, the *Direction Générale des Télécommunications*, a division of the Ministry of Posts and Telecommunications. In 1990, France Télécom gained autonomy, and as at 1 January 1998, it relinquished its monopoly of the telecommunications market. Consequently, starting in the late 1990s, numerous alternative operators entered the market to compete with the incumbent France Télécom, usually by offering lower prices and different packages of services. Today, the six most prominent for fixed-line services are:

- 3U Telecom, 12 Avenue de l'Arche, 92419 Courbevoie Cedex, Tel: 08 05101645, 08 05111645, *www.3u.net*.

- Cegetel, Quartier Valmy, Espace 21, Bât 5, 50 Place de l'Ellipse, 92985 Paris la Défense, *www.cegetel.fr*.

- One.Tel, 8 rue l'Evèque, 75008 Paris, Tel: 01 73502600, 01 73502001, *www.onetel.fr*.
- Primus Télécommunications, 3-5 rue Maurice Ravel, 92300 Levallois-Perret, Tel: 08 00333999, *www.primustel.fr*.
- TELE2 France, 14 rue des Fréres Caudron, BP 103, 78143 Vélizy Cedex, Tel: 01 39454444, *www.tele2.fr*.
- Tiscali Telecom, 10 rue Fructidor, 75017 Paris, Tel: 08 92955000, *www.telecom.tiscali.fr*.

There are other alternative operators for mobile telephony and for broadband. A complete list of all alternative operators is available on the *ART* website.

ART

ART is the abbreviation for *Autorité de Régulation des Télécommunications*, the national telecommunications regulator and a principal agency of *Autorité de Régulation des Communications électroniques et des Postes (ARCEP)*. Today, with widespread telecommunications, ART has become so recognised that its name seldom appears in full; a typical mention of ... *l'ART* ... means "the telecommunications regulations". ART also serves as panoply for related agencies, including:

- *Conseil supérieur de l'audiovisuel (CSA)*, the broadcasting regulator, Tour Mirabeau, 39-43 Quai André-Citroën, 75739 Paris Cedex 15, *www.csa.fr* in French, English, German and Spanish.
- *Agence nationale des fréquences (ANFR)*, the radio frequency allocation agency, 78 Avenue du general de Gaulle, 94704 Maisons-Alfort, Tel: 01 45187272, *www.anfr.fr* in French and English and with links to six regional sites.

ART publishes on all aspects of telecommunications policy and practice and maintains updated databases, such as of all telecommunications operators. Consequently, it is the best starting point for all matters concerning telecommunications, broadcasting and the Internet. For further information, contact the consumer services office, *Unité Consommateurs*, 7 square Max Hymans, 75730 Paris Cedex 15, Tel: 01 40477000, *www.art-telecom.fr* in French, English and German.

Broadband [*Haut débit*]

Broadband designates a high data speed connection to the **Internet** that operates at a data throughput greater than that available on an analogue line with a modem (up to 56 kbit/s) or on a digital line, such as an ISDN [*RNIS*] at 64 or 128 kbit/s. As this book goes to press, the number of high-speed connections is growing at a rate of more than 40% a year and there now are 10.5 million in the country*. More than nine out of ten broadband connections are implemented via fixed telephone lines, and the remainder are via cable. Links to all major broadband suppliers with data on current service status are available at *www.grenouille.com*.

*High-speed Internet observatory, 1ˢᵗ Quarter 2006 figures, downloadable from
ART.

Enquiries and information [*Renseignements*]

Enquiries and information are offered via six-digit telephone numbers starting with
118, at charges depending on the service offered. As this book goes to press, 57
services are available; for the most recent listing, visit the 118 services website at
www.appel118.fr. Four are pure directory enquiry services, most with reverse search
(number to subscriber name and address) functions, at varying costs stated by their
operators.

- *France Télécom* offers national directory white and yellow page enquiry via
  number 118008 from fixed telephone lines and 118712 from mobiles; the service
  previously was available via short code 12, which was deactivated on 3 April
  2006. The numbers of subscribers to alternative fixed and mobile operators are
  included. International enquiry is offered via number 118712, though the older
  short code 3212 may still be used. Online enquires are supported by the
  company's services for the **Yellow pages** (Chapter 31).

- *Annu* offers white and yellow page enquiry services via short code 3217 as well
  as online at *www.annu.com* with pages in Catalan, English, German and Italian.

- *IntraCall Centre* offers national and international enquiry services via short code
  3211; further details are available online at *www.3211.com*.

- *Scoot* offers yellow pages directory enquiry via short code 3200 as well as online
  at *www.scoot.fr*.

ETNO

ETNO is the abbreviation for the European Telecommunication Network Operators'
Association. It was founded in 1993 by 26 public postal operators that until then had
been members of the European Conference of Postal and Telecommunications
Administrations [*Conférence Européenne des Administrations des Postes et des
Télécommunications (CEPT)*], an organisation that had been founded in 1959 to
coordinate the activities of governmental post and telecommunications monopolies.
In the wave of deregulation then sweeping across Europe, post and
telecommunications were split off as private sector enterprises. Each sector
continued cooperation in a new organisation, ETNO for telecommunications and
PostEurop (Chapter 36) for post, and the CEPT became concerned with policy
making and regulation only. Today, ETNO has 40 members, including **France
telecom**, and works to support and enhance telecommunications across Europe. For
further information, contact the head office at Avenue Louise 54, 1050 Brussels,
Belgium, Tel: +32 2 2193242, *www.etno.be* in English.

European Computer Driving Licence – ECDL
[*Passeport de Compétences Informatique Européen*]

The European Computer Driving Licence is an internationally recognised standard of information technology proficiency available in 138 countries and in 32 languages. It is available to applicants who pass one theoretical and six practical tests, as given at authorised test centres. Worldwide, more than 5 million persons have qualified. The ECDL is managed by the ECDL Foundation, which is supported by the EU Commission and has its head office in Dublin, ECDL Foundation Ltd., Third Floor, Portview House, Thorncastle Street, Dublin 4, Ireland, Tel: +353 16306000, Fax: +353 16306001, *www.ecdl.com*, *info@ecdl.com*. The ECDL Foundation was established by the Council of European Professional Informatics Societies (CEPIS), *www.cepis.org*. As it spread beyond Europe, it became known also as the International Computer Driving Licence (ICDL). The French ECDL organisation is *Passeport de Compétences Informatique Européen*, Attention Jean-Claude Syre, Ophira 2, Place Bermond, Sophia Antipolis, 06560 Valbonne, Tel: 04 93001800, Fax: 04 93001801, *www.pcie.tm.fr*, *jean-claude.syre@pcie.tm.fr*.

Fixed-line telephony [*Téléphonie fixe*]

Fixed-line telephony is the modern term for traditional telephony via wires, to distinguish it from mobile telephony. In France, there are about 34 million fixed-line telephone connections to subscribers. About a third of all subscriber lines are digital, as analogue lines are converted to digital and new digital lines are installed. The digital subscriber line (DSL) technology is based on the Integrated Services Digital Network (ISDN) [*Réseau numérique à intégration de services (RNIS)*] hierarchy employed in telecommunications across Europe. Fixed lines supporting **broadband** are increasing in number, but some other services are declining. Since 2004, subscribers have spent more on calls via **mobile telephony** than on calls via fixed-line telephony, and the number of public payphones and the money spent calling from them are falling at a rate of about 10% a year*.

*ART Annual Report 2004.

France Télécom

France Télécom is the country's principal, and until the deregulation of the 1990s, only, supplier of telecommunications services. Until 1988, it was a government monopoly, the *Direction Générale des Télécommunications*, but from 1 January 1998, a private-sector enterprise in a competitive market. Today, it is the world's fifth largest telecommunications company in terms of revenue*. Its principal offerings to consumers are:

- Fixed-line telephony under its own name, for which it now has 33 million customers in France and 16 million in other countries.

- Mobile telephony under the Orange tradename, for which it has 22 million customers in France and 62 million in other countries.

- Broadband Internet access under the Orange tradename (Wanadoo before 1 June 2006), for which it has six million customers in France and as many in other countries.

For fixed line telephony and broadband Internet access, contact a **Telecoms installer**; for mobile telephony, contact a shop selling mobile phones. For general information on France Télécom, contact the headquarters of the company at 6 place d'Alleray, 75505 Paris Cedex 15, Tel: 01 44442222, *www.francetelecom.fr* in French and English with links to many other websites.

* *The Economist Business Miscellany 2005*, page 9.

Freephone and shared-cost numbers
[*Numéros libre appel et services à valeur ajoutée*]

Calls dialled to numbers starting with 08 are "geographically non-specific" and can be made from anywhere in the country at special rates, varying from zero. The principal services are:

Initial four digits of number	Common name, as used in advertising number	Designation, charge to the caller
0800 and 0805	Green number [*Numéro vert*]	Freephone, no charge.
0810 and 0811	Azure number [*Numéro azur*]	Shared cost, local rate.
0820 - 0826	Indigo number [*Numéro indigo*]	Shared cost, low rate.
0890 - 0899	Black number [*Numéro noir*]	Premium rate, higher charge.

Some organisations can be dialled free from abroad using a Universal International Freephone Number (UNIFN) that is the same in more than 40 countries supporting the service; further details are available from the International Inbound Services Forum, *www.iis-forum.com*. For further information on these and other numbers, see the Numbering Plan [*Plan de numérotation*] available from **ART**.

Information technology vocabulary
[*Vocabulaire des technologies de l'information*]

The terminology of information technology is extensive. The commonplace terms, as used in home computing, are listed below. For a complete list, see the ISO/IEC 2382 series of norms published by the **International Organisation for Standardisation** (Chapter 30).

blog	*blogue*	Internet user	*internaute*
broadband	*haut débit*	keyboard	*clavier*
browser	*logiciel de navigation*	laser printer	*imprimante laser*
dot matrix printer	*imprimante matricielle*	mouse	*souris*
email	*courrier électronique, email*	mouse mat	*tapis de souris*
		operating system	*système d'exploitation*
high definition	*haute definition*	portal	*portail*
ink-jet printer	*imprimante à jet d'encre*	printer	*imprimante*
interface	*interface*	programs (for PC/Mac)	*logiciels PC/Mac*
Internet	*Internet*	scanner	*scanner*
Internet access	*accès Internet*	screen	*écran*
Internet kiosk	*borne d'accès public à Internet*	webmaster	*webmaster*
		web service	*web service*
Internet Service Provider (ISP)	*fournisseur d'accès l'Internet*	website	*site web, site Internet*
		web space	*espace web*

Internet

There are an estimated 22 million Internet users and about 13 million Internet subscriptions in France. Internet access is available upon subscription via all **fixed line telephony** connections as well as at drop-in Internet Cafés, listed along with Internet Service Providers (ISPs) under *fournisseurs d'accès Internet* in the Yellow Pages or online at *www.cybercafes.com*, select France on the map or in the dialogue window. Of the more than 60 ISPs, in alphabetical order, the five largest are:

- AOL, *www.aol.fr*.
- ClubInternet, *www.club-internet.fr*.
- Noos, *www.noos.fr*.
- Orange (the **France Télécom** subsidiary named Wanadoo until 1 June 2006), *www.orange.fr*.
- Tiscali, *www.telecom.tiscali.fr*.

Many magazines feature regular Internet sections and there is one magazine dedicated to it, *Linternaute* at *www.linternaute.com*.

The best single source of information on the Internet in France is the government agency dedicated to Internet matters and through its *Internet Accompagné* incentive, to promoting the Internet, easing access to it and supporting the creation of new jobs that it affords, contact *Délégation Internet*, Tel: 3939, *www.delegation.internet.gouv.fr*.

Internet telephony [*Téléphonie Internet*]

As in other countries, Internet telephony (also known as VOIP) – the routing of voice conversations over the Internet at costs far lower than those of conventional telephone connections – is growing rapidly. The leading Internet Telephony Service Providers (ITSPs), such as Skype, *www.skype.com/intl/fr*, offer services, as do the French Internet access providers, most prominently Orange, *www.orange.fr*. The most usual connection uses a computer connected to the Internet, but there also are many Internet phone terminals, such as the BeWAN PhoneBox, *www.bewan.fr*.

Keyboard [*Clavier*]

Like the English "QWERTY" keyboard, the keyboard (*clavier*) used in France and surrounding countries is popularly named after the first six letters in the upper row of letter keys, "AZERTY". It differs from the QWERTY keyboard in that A and Q are interchanged, W and Z are interchanged, M is moved to the right of L (where the colon and semicolon key is on the US and UK layout), there's an extra key to the right of the left shift key, and accented French letters are included in the upper row of number keys. Further information on the French keyboard is available on the IBM website at *www-306.ibm.com/software/globalization/topics/keyboards/physical.jsp#France*.

French AZERTY keyboard layout, from IBM website.

Keypad [*Clavier numérique*]

The international standard keypad with four rows of three keys each, is used on all telephone instruments, mobile telephones and fax terminals, as well as on other devices for keying in numbers, such as cashpoints and point-of-sale (POS) terminals in shops. The number keys do not have letters, as do the keys of the North American keypads. The keypads of some models of telefax terminals and digital telephone instruments have letters to facilitate keying in information for alphanumeric display, but because these letters are not used for dialling, their arrangement may or may not agree with that of the North American keyboard. So if you call a number in North America that is listed by its letters only, you will need to know the letter positions on the standard keypad. They are: ABC on 2, DEF on 3, GHI on 4, JKL on 5, MNO on 6, PRS on 7, TUV on 8 and WXY on 9; there is no Q or Z. Mobile phones have letters at these locations as well as Q on 7 and Z on 9.

Minitel

Minitel is a data communications system that works over ordinary telephone lines. Launched in 1982 by the government agency that became **France Télécom**, it predates the commercial Internet by a decade and consequently is considered to be the world's first successful data communication system available to the public. Historians of the cyber age point to Minitel as the trigger of the high level of electronic access that has made France a leader in **eGovernment** (Chapter 21).

Minitel originally was implemented as a cost-cutting measure, to provide telephone subscribers with online access to continuously updated telephone directory databases instead of periodically sending out costly printed directories. In return for a free Minitel terminal, a telephone subscriber would receive only the printed yellow page directory, with its advertising, but not the alphabetical white page directory, which was free via the terminal. With time, other services were added, including mail-order retailing, airline and rail travel ticketing, information distribution and message boards. Today, more than 13,000 services are available at Minitel terminals, and the system can be accessed from computers connected to the Internet as well as from mobile phones. With the rise of the **Internet**, the demise of Minitel has been predicted several times. Though use has declined, Minitel remains one of the most popular data communication systems in the country, perhaps because compared to the Internet, Minitel is simple to use. Addresses are four-digit telephone numbers, operation is always the same, and, as the system is closed, it is not subject to the data communications viruses that plague the Internet. Several models of Minitel terminal are available, sold by physical and online telecommunications equipment shops. For further information, visit a shop or contact Minitel at *www.minitel.fr*.

Mobile [*Mobile*]

There are nearly eight mobile phones for every ten people in the country. Understandably, mobiles are most popular in urban areas, such as Ile-de-France where there are 13% more mobiles than people, and less popular in rural areas, such as Franche-Comté, where there are fewer than six mobiles for every ten people*. There are three mobile phone networks, each covering more than 95% of the area of the country:

- Bouygues, Tel: 01 39267500, *www.bouygestelecom.fr*.
- Orange, the **France Télécom** mobile network, Tel: 01 55222222, *www.orange.fr*.

- SFR, Tel: 01 71070707, *www.sfr.fr*.

There also are several **Alternative operators;** for their addresses as well as for other information on mobile phone networks, contact *Association française des opérateurs mobiles (AFOM)*, *www.afom.fr*. All mobile networks use the digital GSM standard, the world's most popular, and operate in two frequency bands, 900 MHz and 1800 MHz. Consequently, most of the mobile phones sold are "dual-band". Some other countries, principally in North and South America, use a third band at 1900 MHz, so a mobile used there must be a "tri-band" [*tri-bande*] model.

* First quarter 2006 figures released by **ART**.

Phonecards [*Cartes téléphoniques*]

Phonecards are prepaid telephone cards that resemble credit cards and are used in fixed and mobile phones with an international standard **keypad** that has asterisk (*) and hash mark (#) keys. There are three varieties, all widely available, sold by newsagents, telecoms shops, post offices and many other shops:

- prepaid smart cards that may be used in any of the 150,000 France Télécom public payphones across the country. The cards are sold with 50 or 120 message units.

- fixed-line telephone cards that may be used in any of the 35 countries supporting the service. This is a simple card of a type first used in 1974-76 in Italy and now common round the world. A card has a specified amount of prepaid call time, which you activate by scraping off a latex film to reveal a Personal Identity Number (PIN) code, just as you scrape the latex film off the play area of a lottery scratch card. Calls are placed by dialling a freephone number and then keying in the PIN to get the dialling tone to place the call. Most cards are valid only to specified countries, usually listed on their reverse sides or in attachments to them. The leading card is Kertel, *www.kertel.com*; its freephone number is 3003.

- cash cards for mobile phone services. A card has a specified amount of prepaid call charge, ranging from €10 to €100. You scrape off a latex film to reveal a payment confirmation code, which you enter in a voice prompt sequence upon calling the mobile operator's account recharge number. The cards are sold for the services of the principal mobile operators and feature progressive bonuses. For instance, an Orange card costing €30 has an extra €5 of call time, whilst one costing three times as much, €90, has seven times as much extra time, €35.

The faces of phone cards feature various artwork and photographs, and collecting them has become a world-wide hobby, with websites, clubs and auctions.

Radio broadcasting [*Radiodiffusion*]

In 1921, regular radio broadcasting began, with transmissions from the Eiffel Tower. In 1923, radio broadcasting was made a State monopoly, and Radio France was born. Through the years, it has been organised in various ways, as part of *Radio-Télévision Française (RTF)* in 1959 and as part of *Office de Radiodiffusion et de Télévision Française (ORTF)* in 1964. In 1974, ORTF was disbanded, and in 1982, television and radio broadcasting were privatised. Today, more than 450 stations broadcast radio programmes, most in the FM band. Radio France remains the largest broadcaster, with numerous national and international stations and programmes via conventional radio broadcasting as well as Web Radio and podcasting of programmes via the Internet for recording on MP3 players. For further information, contact Radio France, 116 avenue du Président-Kennedy. 75786 Paris Cedex 16, Tel: 01 42302222, *www.radiofrance.fr*.

Telecommunications numbers [*Numéros du téléphone*]

Almost all telephone numbers, including those for telefax terminals and computers connected to access Internet servers, have eight digits plus a two-digit dialling code [*Indicatif*]. There are four exceptions:

- two-digit emergency numbers: 17 for Police [*Police*], 18 for fire [*Pompier*], and 15 for ambulance [*SAMU*].

- three-digit helplines [*services d'urgence*] starting with 1, as 113 for Drugs, Tobacco and Alcohol information.

- four-digit short numbers [*numéros courts*] for accessing various services, in format 3NNN, where the first digit always is 3.

- six-digit subscriber numbers [*numéro de l'abonné*] for the overseas departments [*Département d'outre mer*], abbreviated *DOM* in telephone directories, and overseas territories [*Territoire d'outre-mer*], abbreviated *TOM*, with four- or five-digit prefixes [*faites précéder*].

The eight digits of most numbers are usually written in groups of two digits: NN NN NN NN plus the dialling code prefix [*indicatif*] that always begins with a zero.

Indicatif	Départements
01	91 Essonne, 92 Haut de Seine, 75 Paris, 77 Seine et Marne, 93 Seine St Denis, 94 Val de Marne, 95 Val d'Oise, 78 Yvelines
02	14 Calvados, 18 Cher, 22 Côtes d'Armor, 27 Eure, 28 Eure et Loire, 29 Finistère, 35 Ille et Vilaine, 36 Indre, 37 Indre et Loire, 41 Loir et Cher, 44 Loire Atlantique, 45 Loiret, 49 Maine et Loire, 50 Manche, 53 Mayenne, 56 Morbihan, 61 Orne, 72 Sarthe, 76 Seine Maritime, 85 Vendée

03	02 Aisne, 08 Ardennes, 10 Aube, 67 Bas Rhin, 21 Côte d'Or, 25 Doubs, 68 Haut Rhin, 52 Haut Marne, 70 Haute Saône, 39 Jura, 51 Marne, 54 Meurthe et Moselle, 55 Meuse, 57 Moselle, 58 Nièvre, 59 Nord, 60 Oise, 62 Pas de Calais, 71 Saône et Loire, 80 Somme, 90 Territoire de Belfort, 88 Vosges, 89 Yonne
04	01 Ain, 03 Allier, 04 Alpes de Haute Provence, 06 Alpes Maritimes, 07 Ardèche, 11 Aude, 13 Bouche du Rhône, 15 Cantal, 2A Corse du Sud, 26 Drôme, 30 Gard, 2B Haute Corse, 43 Haute Loire, 74 Haute Savoie, 05 Hautes Alpes, 34 Hérault, 38 Isère, 45 Loire, 48 Lozère, 63 Puy de Dôme, 66 Pyrénées Orientales, 69 Rhône, 73 Savoie, 83 Var, 84 Vaucluse
05	09 Ariège, 12 Aveyron, 16 Charente, 17 Charente Maritime, 19 Corrèze, 23 Creuse, 79 Deux Sèvres, 24 Dordogne, 32 Gers, 33 Gironde, 31 Haute Garonne, 87 Haute Vienne, 65 Hautes Pyrénées, 40 Landes, 46 Lot, 47 Lot et Garonne, 64 Pyrénées Atlantiques, 81 Tarn, 82 Tarn et Garonne, 86 Vienne

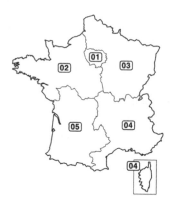

Telephone dialling codes.

For calls to overseas Departments and territories (*Pour téléphoner vers les DOM-TOM*) having six-digit subscriber numbers, dial four or five digit prefixes:

Overseas Department (*Département d'outremer, DOM*)	Prefix	Overseas Territory (*Territorie d'outre-mer, TOM*)	Prefix
Guadeloupe	0590	St. Pierre et Miquelon	0508
Guyan	0594	Nouvelle Calédonie	00 + 687
Martinique	0596	Polynésie Française	00 + 689
Réunion	0262	Wallis et Futuna	00 + 681
Mayotte	0269		

Telecoms installers [*Installateurs télécoms*]

Across the country, there are 1100 companies expert in Information and Communications Technology (ICT) [*Technologies de l'information et de la communication (TIC)*] that offer various mixes of professional services and do-it-yourself (DIY) installation kits to implement fixed-line telecommunications services in homes and businesses. Only they are authorised to connect physically to the telephone lines, whilst anyone may buy devices that connect via a plug [*fiche téléphonique*] to the telephone jack [*prise téléphonique*] provided by an installer. You may find an installer listed under *Télécommunications, Installateurs* in the Yellow Pages or by query to *Fédération Interprofessionnelle de la Communication d'Entreprise (FICOME)*, 32 rue de Ponthieu, 75008 Paris, Tel: 01 56436200, *www.ficome.fr*; click on *Recherche* to bring up an interactive company locator list.

Telefax terminals [*Télécopieurs physiques*]

Any fixed or mobile telephone connection may also be used for telefax (fax) communications. Telefax terminals communicate using one of four Groups, which are protocols, or rules for transmission. The older Group 1, which transmitted a page in about six minutes, and Group 2, which transmitted a page in about three minutes, are obsolete and no longer available. Group 3, which transmits a page in about one minute via an ordinary fixed line, now is the most used. Group 4, which transmits a page in a few seconds via a digital line, is now replacing Group 3, though terminals for it are more expensive. Telefax terminals are sold by telecoms shops and installers as well as by most electronics goods shops. Though still popular, fax use is declining, as email and other electronic messaging services are growing.

Television [*Télévision*]

France ranks 22nd in the world in TV ownership, with 95.9 colour TVs per 100 households, and 12th in TV viewing, with the average viewer spending 17.3 hours per week in front of the set*. Originally a governmental public service, television accordingly has evolved to a mix of public and private broadcasters offering programmes by cable, satellite and the Internet, as well as traditional broadcasting, now called *terrestrial* to distinguish it from satellite broadcasting. Describing it all would require a book almost as large as this one, updated frequently to keep abreast of the continually changing television scene. And indeed there is just such a book, an annual that is simply named *Télévision* with the appended year of issue, published in Paris by Editions Dixit, serial publication ISSN 0988-1042, sold by newsagents and book shops across the country.

*Figures quoted from The Economist Pocket World in Figures, 2006 edition, pages 90 and 94.

TÉLÉVISION 06

Organigrammes des chaînes
Câble et satellite
Bouquets numériques
Web TV
Organismes publics
Marchés et festivals
Presse

DIXIT

2006 edition of Télévision, 288 pages, ISBN 2-84481-108-6, €30.

TV5

TV5, France Télévision's international satellite and cable broadcaster, is the second-largest global television network, after MTV and ahead of CNN, available to 158 million households and 3.2 million hotel rooms worldwide. In all, TV5 has eight channels, each dedicated to a geographic area of the globe. Programming is general-interest and translated subtitles are supported in ten languages. Check with your local cable or satellite programme provider for accessibility details. For further information, visit the website at *www.tv5.org* with pages in English.

TV/FM connectors [*TV/FM fiches*]

As elsewhere in Europe and round the world, TV and FM aerials are connected by cables, and apartments in blocks and houses with cable TV now are fitted with one or more aerial entry boxes, often recessed in walls behind white faceplates. The plug, or "male" end of a cable fits a socket on a TV, and the socket, or "female" end of it fits a plug on the entry box. FM radios are connected with identical cables the other way round, with the socket end of the cable fitting the radio and the plug end fitting the entry box, which keeps TVs and radios from being wrongly connected.

Radio and TV shops make cables to any length, but most are ready-made in lengths from 1 to 5 metres and are sold in blister packs on racks, as in the non-food sections of supermarkets. The connectors fitted on radios, TVs, entry boxes and cables may be either of two incompatible sizes, an older 9 mm diameter [*ancienne norme française*] or a newer 9.52 mm diameter [*nouvelle norme*]. Unfortunately, connector size isn't always marked, so it's easy to buy the wrong cable. Fortunately, adaptors between 9 mm and 9.52 mm connectors are available and usually are sold in blister packs hanging on displays along with cables.

TV licence [*Redevance audiovisuelle*]

As elsewhere in Europe, TV owners are required to pay an annual licence fee, presently (2006) €116 for the mainland and €74 for the Overseas Departments. Once you are registered for *Redevance audiovisuelle*, you will be billed for it, together with property tax if you own a principal or second residence with a TV [*la taxe d'habitation qui occupe une résidence principale ou secondaire équipée*]. If you are not registered with a licence and buy a new television set, the shop where you purchase it will submit a licence application for you along with notification of sale of the set. If you buy a used television set or bring one into the country, you should apply for a licence to the nearest Regional Licence Centre (*Centre Régional de la Redevance Audiovisuelle*). The Centres are listed online at the government services portal, Service-Public, *www.service-public.fr*; key in *Redevance audiovisuelle* as a searchword to navigate to the relevant pages.

45
Trades

Craftspeople [*artisans*] practise their trades and are regulated as they are in other countries. More than 70 trades are recognised in France; those of interest to homeowners are described in the entries of this chapter, under slightly inconsistent headings that reflect the way the crafts are listed in directories, such as the Yellow Pages. As in English, *plombiers* (plumbers) are listed, but not their work, *plomberie* (plumbing); whilst *maçonnerie* (masonry) is listed but not the craftsman, *maçons* (masons) who work at it.

Builder [*Entreprise de bâtiment*]

A general builder is an *entreprise de bâtiment*, and the person owning the company is an *entrepreneur en bâtiment*. The companies are listed in the Yellow Pages under *Bâtiment (entreprises)*. A masonry company is a *maçonnerie*, and one that offers general building is a *maçonnerie de bâtiment* or a *maçonnerie générale*. Buildings of metal (rather than masonry) may involve the services of *constructeurs*, the trade sector principally concerned with mechanical works, including ships, machines and metal structures.

Carpentry [*Charpenterie*]

By tradition, carpentry [*charpenterie*] means structural carpentry in wood [*charpentes en bois*], and is so listed in the Yellow Pages to distinguish it from **metal carpentry**.

Electricians [*Électriciens*]

There are many electrical trades, so most companies offering the services of electricians are listed under *Électricité générale* in the Yellow Pages. The traditional trades of installing and repairing [*installation et dépannage*] are offered as specialisations, including electrical heating [*chauffage électrique*], air conditioning [*climatisation*] and electronics [*électronique*].

526

Joineries [*Menuisiers*]

Joiners are carpenters who make furniture, light woodwork and the like. Historically, their trade is the oldest in the country, as it was first recognised in 1467. Joinery principally means working with wood only, whilst cabinet making [*ébénisterie*] entails working with wood as well as other materials, such as inlays in cabinets.

Locksmiths [*Serruriers*]

Most locksmiths are listed under *Serrurerie* in the Yellow Pages, but in many cases, locksmith services are part of a metalworking shop, listed under *Métallerie*. Locksmiths cut keys, as do specialist key cutting shops [*Clés, reproduction*].

Masonry [*Maçonnerie*]

Masons [*maçons*] traditionally have worked with stone. However, most masons now work with more modern materials, and those who work with stone are called stone masons [*tailleurs de pierres*]. Tilers [*carreleurs*] work with tiled floors and walls [*carrelage*] and with paving and flagging [*dallage*].

Metal carpentry [*Charpentes métalliques*]

Metal carpentry is mostly involved with setting up metal buildings, though it also includes architectural metalwork. Consequently, many firms offer both metal carpentry [*charpentes métalliques*] and metalwork [*métallerie*].

Metalwork [*Métallerie*]

A *métallerie* usually performs sheet metal and architectural metalwork, as opposed to general work with mechanical devices [*mécanique générale*]. Often, a shop will offer both metalworking and **locksmith** services.

Painting [*Peinture*]

Most painting companies offer interior and exterior [*intérieure et extérieure*] work including waterproofing and other treatments and consequently are listed in the Yellow Pages under *Peinture, revêtements*. Specialist decorative painting is listed under *Peintre-décorateur*.

Plumbers [*Plombiers*]

In addition to traditional installation and repairs [*installations et dépannages*], most plumbers offer work in central heating [*chauffage central*], air conditioning [*climatisation*] and bath and toilet fitting [*sanitaire*].

Roofers [*Couvreurs*]

Roofers sometimes are known by their historical names related to the metals used, copper [*chaudronnerie*], lead [*plomberie*] and zinc [*zinguerie*], but most now deal with all roofing metals.

Shoe repairing [*Cordonniers*]

There are a few traditional shoemakers [*cordonnerie*], but most shops by that name offer repairs of footwear and other leather goods.

Tapestry [*Tapisserie*]

Tradesmen who hang tapestries or paper walls are listed under *Tapissiers-décorateurs*, while those who upholster furniture are listed under *Tapissiers-fournitures*.

Vocational qualification [*Qualification professionnelle*]

Vocational qualification, or trade certification, is an assurance that a person has the knowledge, skills and abilities to perform a trade. People become qualified through various combinations of formal and non-formal learning that are increasingly international, in step with the harmonisation of qualifications across Europe.

Today, most people start in the trades with a minimum of formal learning, after completing the requirements for a basic vocational certificate [*CAP*] at age 16 or the vocational proficiency certificate [*BEP*] upon completion of the upper secondary part of **Vocational studies** (Chapter 14) and then may work as an apprentice under the supervision of a qualified craftsman. In most cases, apprentices aged 16 to 25 also undergo further training at a vocational training centre [*Centre de formation d'apprentis (CFA)*]. There are many CFAs in all *Départements*; the greatest number in the Ile-de-France *Région*, with a website at *www.cfarif.net*.

A certification body, *Chambre de métiers et de l'artisanat (CMA)*, offers certifications, supports certification programmes and acts as a clearing house for information on training and certification. There are CMAs in all *Départements*; for further information, contact the national office, *Assemblée Permanente des Chambres de métiers* at 12 avenue Marceau, 75008 Paris, Tel: 01 44431000, *www.apcm.com*.

The **National Commission for Vocational Certification** (Chapter 14) maintains a national register of some 15,000 vocational qualifications [*Répertoire national des certifications professionnelles*], oversees the continuous updating of requirements for qualifications in step with changes in education and the labour market and advises educational and certifying organisations.

46
Travel and transport

France is among the world leaders in travel and transport. In terms of passengers served each year, Air France is the world's sixth biggest airline and the Charles de Gaulle airport near Paris the world's eighth busiest. French passenger train use ranks fourth in the world, and the TGV high speed trains are the fastest in Europe and the second fastest in the world*. One of the world's leading aerospace companies is EADS, a French-German joint venture, and the world's most read professional railway magazine is *La Vie du Rail*. French hotels and restaurants are a subject in themselves, so much so that there are books dedicated to them.

* Rankings quoted from *The Economist Business Miscellany*, 2005 edition.

Airlines [*Compagnies aériennes*]

Among the airlines of the world, Air France is a giant. After its takeover of KLM of the Netherlands in May 2004, the merged Air France-KLM is the world's largest airline in operating revenues as well as Europe's largest and the world's third largest in total passenger-kilometres per year. It operates a fleet of 378 aircraft (as at 31 December 2005) and serves 225 destinations in 88 countries. It is a member of the Sky Team Alliance that includes eight other large carriers: Aeroflot, Aeroméxico, Alitalia, Continental Airlines, CSA Czech Airlines, Delta Air Lines, Korean Air and Northwest Airlines. It is based at the Roissy Charles-de-Gaulle hub and in France has secondary hubs at the Orly and Lyon-Saint-Exupéry airports. For further information, contact Air France, 45 rue de Paris, 95747 Roissy CDG Cedex, *www.airfrance.com* with selectable sites and languages. Though Air France dominates, 15 other French carriers offer domestic and international services. In alphabetical order with their websites (most in two or more languages) they are:

- Aigle Azur, with scheduled and charter services between mainland France and Algeria, *www.aigle-azur.fr*.
- Air Austral, a local carrier based on Réunion, *www.air-austral.com*.
- Aircalin, a local carrier based on Nouvelle-Calédonie, *www.aircalin.com*.
- Air Caraïbes, a local carrier based on Guadeloupe, *www.aircaraibes.com*.

- Airlinair, a regional carrier based at Paris Orly, *www.airlinair.com*.
- Air Tahiti, a local carrier based in French Polynesia, *www.airtahiti.aero*.
- Air Tahiti Nui, an international and regional carrier based in French Polynesia, *www.airtahitinui.com*.
- Air Turquoise, a local carrier based at Bordeaux, *www.airturquoise.com*.
- Blue Line, a charter carrier, *www.flyblueline.com*.
- Brit Air, a local carrier based in Normandy offering services to the UK, *www.britair.com*.
- Corsairfly, a tourism carrier based at Paris Orly, *www.corsairfly.com*.
- Europe Airpost, a subsidiary of La Poste, principally a freight carrier but also with passenger services to the Maghreb, *www.europeairpost.fr*.
- Régional, a regional carrier and a subsidiary of Air France based at Clermont-Ferrand, *www.regional.com*.
- Star Airlines, a tourism carrier based at Roissy Charles de Gaulle hub, *www.star-airlines.fr*.
- Twin Jet, a low-cost carrier serving destinations in France as well as Jersey and Geneva, *www.twinjet.net*.

Airports [*Aéroports*]

Every year, more than 140 airports serve more than 130 million domestic and international scheduled airline flight passengers on the mainland and nearly 10 million in the overseas *Départements**. The six principal international airports are Lyon Saint Exupery, Marseille Provence, Nice Côte d'Azur, Strasbourg, and Paris Orly and Rossy Charles de Gaulle, the third busiest airport in Europe**. As this book goes to press, the international airports are expanding in step with increased traffic and new airports are planned. Service and facilities are uniformly of high quality; in June 2006, the Toulouse Blagnac airport won the annual Airports Council International award for the best in Europe in the 5 to 10 million passengers a year category (further information at *www.aci-europe.org*). For further information on all commercial airports in the country, contact *Union des aéroports français*, 28 rue Desaix, 75015 Paris, Tel: 01 40659868, *www.aeroport.fr* with drop-down list linking to data pages for the airports, and for airports in the Paris area, contact *Aéroports de Paris*, *www.aeroportsdeparis.fr* in French and English.

*2005 figures released by *Union des aéroports français*

**The Economist Pocket World in Figures 2006*, page 72.

Avenir Transports

Created in 1995, *Avenir Transports* is appropriately named – "Future transport" in translation – as it is a multidisciplinary body that brings together governmental agencies and public and private transport actors to coordinate and shape public transport policy. It fulfils this role through three principal activities: acting as a centre for meeting and debate [*Centre de rencontres et de débats*], for publishing and documentation [*Centre de publication et de documentation*] and for research [*Centre de recherches*]. For further information, contact the head office at BP 11 Paris Palais Bourbon, 75355 Paris 07 SP, *www.avenir-transports.org* in French and English with links to agencies and to principal public and private operators in the transport sector.

Bed and breakfast [*Chambres d'hôtes*]

Bed and breakfast (B & B) accommodation abounds across the country, particularly in rural areas, though there are many in cities, usually listed under *Gîtes ruraux, chambres d'hôtes* in the Yellow Pages. The **Gîtes de France** and **Bienvenue à la ferme** (Chapter 18) networks offer extensive choices. Two independent networks, Chambres d'hôtes at *www.chambresdhotes.com* and Innkeepers Exchange [*Échanges entre aubergistes*] at *www.innkeepers-exchange.com* also offer extensive listings. For further information on B & B and other rural tourism offerings, contact *Conférence Permanente du Tourisme Rural*, 23 place de Catalogne, 75685 Paris Cedex 14, Tel: 01 70399606, *www.cp-tourisme-rural.fr*.

Boat travel [*Voyage de bateau*]

There are many ferry services, most prominently across The Channel [*La Manche*] and from southern ports across the Mediterranean to ports in Europe and North Africa. Five principal services are:

- Brittany Ferries, car and passenger ferries between northwestern ports and ports on the southern coasts of the UK and Ireland, Tel: 08 25828828, *www.brittany-ferries.fr* in French and English.

- Emeraude Ferries, car and passenger between northwestern ports and Jersey, *www.emeraudeferries.com* in French and English.

- Société de Navigation de Normandie (Hugo Express), passenger catamarans between northwestern ports and the Channel Islands, Tel: 02 33610888.

- Société nationale maritime méditerranée ferry Corse (SNCM), car and passenger ferries between French ports and ports in Algeria, Corsica, Sardinia and Tunisia, Tel: 08 25888088, *www.sncm.fr* in French, English, German and Italian.

- Compagnie Tunisienne de Navigation, car and passenger ferry connections to Tunisia, Tel: +216 7134177, *www.ctn.com* in French, English and Arabic.

The French part of AFerry, the UK-based global distribution system (GDS) for ferry information and bookings, provides what may be the best single overview of international ferry connections to and from France, *www.aferry.fr*.

Many companies offer houseboats and other boats for hire on canals and other inland waters; the French Nautical Industries Federation [*Fédération des industries nautiques*] provides a directory of them on its website at *www.france-nautic.com* in French and English. *Voies navigables de France (VNF)* is a central clearing house and source for information on inland waterways, with a head office at 175 rue Ludovic Boutleux, 62408 Béthune, *www.vnf.fr* in French and English. The VNF affiliate of Paris, *Port autonome de Paris*, regularly updates and publishes a comprehensive, clearly and profusely illustrated recreational boating manual and guide to the Seine waterways, entitled *Guide du plaisancier*, in print and online; contact the office at 2 quai de Grenelle, 75732 Paris Cedex 15, Tel: 01 40582742, *www.paris-ports.fr*.

Bus travel [*Voyage d'autobus*]

Although *autobus* is the commonplace term, the language and vehicle regulations distinguish between two varieties of bus:

- *autobus*: a bus primarily for urban and suburban transport involving frequent stops and journeys of varying duration by many passengers in the course of a day. The doors are wide and arranged for rapid entry and exit, and newer buses are arranged to accommodate handicapped vehicles. Articulated buses up to 18 metres long may carry as many as 160 passengers.

- *autocar*: a bus (coach) primarily for inter-urban and tourist travel involving few stops and journeys of longer duration by as many passengers as can be accommodated by its seats. The buses usually have underfloor compartments for stowing baggage, newer buses are fitted with reclining seats and those for long-distance travel have onboard toilets.

In the Yellow Pages you can find bus services listed under *Transports routiers* for the urban and suburban transport variety, and under *Autocars* for the inter-urban and distance travel variety. Most *autobus* services are operated by the larger municipalities, and most *autocar* services operate within the *Départements*, but there are many exceptions, as in semi-rural districts where an *autocar* service will serve both towns and the roads between them. The few national bus services belong to international operations; the leader is Eurolines, with a head office at 22 rue Malmaison, 93170 Bagnolet, Tel: 08 92899091, *www.eurolines.fr* with an interactive services locator map of Europe.

Trans'Bus, a comprehensive online encyclopaedia of the country's bus and urban transport services compiled by Olivier Meyer, offers all you might want to know about buses, from their routes and services to their builders and technologies, at *www.transbus.org* with an interactive bus service locator map.

Camping and caravanning [*Camping et caravaning*]

Camping and caravanning are popular, particularly in the southwestern part of the country, in Languedoc-Roussillon, where there are 779 camping and caravanning campsites with, in all, 120,222 spaces, and in Bretagne, where there are 755 sites with a total of 90,040 spaces. In the country as a whole, there are 8,174 sites with together 934,642 spaces. The related services, including camper and caravan sales and service, are accordingly widespread. For further information, contact *Fédération française de camping et de caravaning (FFCC)*, 7 rue de Rivoli, 75004 Paris, Tel: 01 42727021, *www.ffcc.fr* with an interactive club locator map and links to other websites. There are two comprehensive annual camping and caravanning guides, both published in February of each year: the FFCC's *Guide officiel Camping et Caravaning* (2006 edition ISBN 2-9024-1765-9) and the Michelin *Camping France selection* (2006 edition ISBN 2-06-711628-2).

Containers [*Conteneurs*]

Containers are large, rectangular metal receptacles that can be loaded onto ships, railway goods wagons and trucks. There are three standard lengths: 20-foot (6.1 m), 40-foot (12.2 m) and 45-foot (13.7 m). The capacity of a container as well as of all terminals and conveyances handling containers is expressed in twenty-foot equivalent units (TEU), describing the capacity of a standard 20-foot container, 20 ft long, 8 ft wide and 8.5 ft high, about 39 cubic metres. So a 20-foot container is called "1TEU" and a 40-foot container "2TEU". The purpose-built ships that carry containers are called "lo-lo" (for "lift-on, lift-off"). There are many specialised container ports [*port à conteneurs*] in the country, and extensive land transport container facilities [*transport par conteneurs*], including rail [*train à conteneurs*] and road [*camion à conteneurs*]. **Removals** (Chapter 1) companies use mostly 20-foot containers that can be manoeuvred in cities. For further information on international container standards applicable in France, contact *Bureau International des Containers (BIC) et du Transport Intermodal*, 167, rue de Courcelles, 75017 Paris, Tel: 01 47660390, *www.bic-code.org*, *bic@bic-code.org*.

Cycling [*Cyclisme*]

For every thousand people in the country, there are 367 bicycles, more than in many countries in Europe, but fewer than in the Netherlands, where there are more bicycles than people. That difference underscores the role of the bicycle being more for recreation and sport than for basic transportation. The first cycle club was founded in 1890; across the country there are innumerable cycling clubs of all sorts; competitive cycling is a major sport, highlighted each year by the **Tour de France** (Chapter 46), the world's most famous cycle race. The five principle varieties of bicycle [*vélo*] are:

- *bicyclette*, an ordinary bicycle, basically for transportation, usually with few or no gears.

- *vélo enfant* or *vélo junior*, a children's bicycle, usually a smaller version of one of the full-sized adult varieties.

- *vélo tous chemins (VTC)*, a hybrid bicycle with more gears than an ordinary bicycle and with calliper or disk brakes, intended for recreational bicycle touring.

- *vélo tout terrain (VTT)*, a mountain or offroad bicycle, with sturdy tyres and a wide gear range, now (2006) the most popular variety among young people.

- *vélo de course*, a racing bicycle, with a light frame and narrow tyres, intended for riding on paved surfaces only.

For further information on cycling, contact *Fédération française de cyclotourisme (FFCT)*, 12 rue Louis Bertrand, 94207 Ivry-sur-Seine Cedex, Tel: 01 56208888, *www.ffct.org* with links to other cycling organisations and an interactive cycle club and cycling event locator map.

Discount travel [*Voyage à prix réduits*]

Most travel and transport companies offer a variety of discounts, principally linked to age. SNCF, the train operating company, offers a variety of discounts. The simplest is *Les tarifs découverte* that offers 25% discounts to people travelling together and are valid at any time, contingent upon available seats. SNCF also offers three discount cards:

- *Carte 12/25*, a youth card offering discounts of up to 50% on SNCF and associated trains and 25% on AVIS rental cars.

- *Carte escapades 26/59 ans*, an adult journey card offering discounts of up to 40% on trains.

- *Carte senior*, a card for people over 60, offering 25% discounts on all trains and up to 50% on some trains.

For further information, inquire at a railway station or contact SNCF, Tel: 3635, *www.voyages-sncf.com*.

Duty-free allowance
[*Quantité autorisée marchandises hors taxes*]

The principal duty-free allowances for travellers entering from other countries are listed below. However, as this book goes to press, the EU is expanding and its duty-free rules are changing; for the latest details, visit the Customs website at *www.douane.gouv.fr*, click on *Particuliers* and select the relevant publication.

	Arriving from EU country	Arriving from country outside EU
Cigarettes	800 cigarettes	200 cigarettes
Wine	90 litres	2 litres
Spirits	10 litres	1 litre

Helicopter services [*Services en hélicoptère*]

Eurocopter, a division of The European Aeronautic Defence and Space Company (EADS), a French-German conglomerate, is the world's leading producer of helicopters. Accordingly, helicopters are in prevalent use in the country: more than 800 are in service, nearly 600 of them in commercial passenger services, listed under *Transports aériens* in the Yellow Pages. The largest passenger service in the country is Heli-Paris, 102 avenue Champs Elysées, 75008 Paris, Tel: 08 25826006, *www.heliparis.com* in French and English.

Hotels [*Hôtels*]

In the country there are more than 18,000 hotels, two in three of them in hotel chains and one in three independent. Hotels are listed in the Yellow Pages under *Hôtels*, and those with extensive restaurant offerings are listed under *Hôtels-restaurants*. There are many guides to hotels; arguably the best are the **Gault Millau Guide** and the **Michelin Guide** (Chapter 47).

InterRail

Since InterRail was created in 1972, nearly seven million people have travelled on railways in Europe using inexpensive passes. InterRail divides the 30 countries of Europe and North Africa into eight zones, designated A–H, and there are three types of passes: one zone for 16 days, two zones for 22 days or all of Europe for one month, at three prices according to age: up to 12 years old, up to 26 years old and 26 years old or more. Further information is available in the InterRail brochure available at 350 SNCF railway stations across France or on the international website at *www.interrailnet.com* selectable in English, French, German, Italian or Spanish.

La Vie du Rail

Founded in 1938, *La Vie du Rail*, literally "Railway Life", is a printed and online book, magazine and multimedia publisher specialising in rail travel topics. In all its regional editions, the *La Vie du Rail* weekly magazine has a readership of 600,000, making it the world's most read railway publication. A monthly magazine, *Rail and Transport International*, is a leader in English professional rail publications. The company offers a broad range of publications and videos for the public as well as for railway professionals. For further information, contact the head office at 11 rue de Milan, 75009 Paris, Tel: 01 49701200, *www.laviedurail.com* in French and English.

Public transport [*Transport public*]

Cities and towns across the country have public transport systems suiting their sizes and populations; see **Transport atlas** for maps of the larger services. Many of the services are in networks, of which the six largest are, in alphabetical order:

- AGIR, with principal services in La Rochelle, Marseille, Pointers and Troyes, *www.agir-transport.asso.fr*.

- Keolis, a subsidiary of SNCF, with principal services in Lille, Lyon, Tours and Rennes, *www.keolis.fr* in French and English.

- RATP, the abbreviation for Régie Autonome des Transports Parisiens, in Paris and its suburbs, *www.ratp.fr* in French, English and German.

- SNCF across the country, *www.sncf.fr* in French and English.

- Transdev, with principal services in Grenoble, Nantes, Nantes, Montpellier and Strasbourg, *www.transdev.fr* click on French flag to bring up French site in French and English.

- Veolia Transport, with principal services in Bordeaux, Nancy, Rouen and Toulon, *www.veolia.fr* in French, English and Spanish; click on *Transport*.

For further information on public transport systems across the country, contact *Union des transports publics*, 9 rue Aumale, 75009 Paris, Tel: 01 48746351, *www.utp.fr* or *Groupement des Autorités Responsables de Transport (GART)*, 22 rue de Palestro, 75002 Paris, Tel: 01 40411819, *www.gart.org*.

Rail travel [*Voyage de train*]

SNCF, the abbreviation for Société nationale des chemins de fer français was founded in 1938 by a merger of several companies then operating rail services. In 1997, SNCF was split into operations, which it retained as a train operating company (TOC), and infrastructure that is owned, operated and maintained by the **Railway infrastructure manager**. The average person in France travels 1,203 km per year by rail, ranking SNCF fourth in the world behind first-place Japan, where the figure is 1,803 km per person per year*. The principal rail services are:

- TGV, the abbreviation for *train à grande vitesse*, the high-speed service that includes the Eurostar services to Belgium and Great Britain, Thalys services to Belgium the Netherlands and Germany, Lyria services to Switzerland and Aresia services to Italy, *www.tgv.com* selectable in French, English, Dutch, German, Italian or Spanish. Services are described by iDTGV, the Internet TGV portal at *www.idtgv.com* in French and English.

- Corail Téoz, express intercity services (not including TGV), *www.corailteoz.com*.

- TER, the acronym for *Transport express régional*, medium-distance services within the *Régions*, *www.ter-sncf.com*.

- Transilien, urban and suburban services centred on Paris in the Île-de-France *Département*, *www.transilien.com*.

- Fret SNCF, the goods transport and logistics service, *www.fret.sncf.com* in French and English.

SNCF supports three public information websites:

- InfoLignes, a train and services directory, *www.infolignes.com* with an interactive map of the country centred at Paris and divided into four sectors, north, east, west and south-east.

- Voyages-sncf, the online schedule and booking service, *www.voyages-sncf.com* selectable in French, English, German, Italian or Spanish.

- Sncf-com, the website on the company itself, with links to its other websites, *www.sncf.com* selectable in French, English, German, Italian or Spanish.

For further information, visit the websites listed above or physically visit the nearest SNCF station, listed under *Transports ferroviaires* in the Yellow Pages. See the **Transport atlas** for maps of rail services.

*The Economist Pocket World in Figures 2006, page 73.

Railway infrastructure manager
[*Gestionnaire des infrastructures ferroviaires*]

In 1997, in response to the initial EU Railway directive*, SNCF, the state railway monopoly, was split in two parts, operations – retained by SNCF – and infrastructure, the responsibility of a new company, Réseau Ferré de France (RFF), a **Private sector enterprise owned by the State** (Chapter 21). As in other countries in Europe, the division of responsibilities is clear: SNCF is a train operating company (TOC), and RFF owns, operates, maintains and manages the rail network, which consists of 32,888 km of line, of which 28,918 km are in use. More than half the lines in use are double track or wider and more than half are electrified. In all, 1,547 km are high-speed lines (HSL). For further information on RFF, contact the head office: 92, avenue de France, 75648 Paris Cedex 13, Tel: 01 53943000, *www.rff.fr*, with key pages in English.

*Number 91/440/EEC of 29 July 1991.

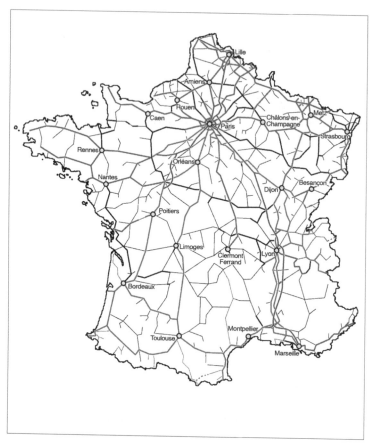

Principal rail lines.

Taxis [*Taxis*]

Across the country, there are some 45,000 taxis, many owned by their drivers. You can order a taxi by calling the dispatcher number listed under *Taxis* in the Yellow Pages. There are several taxi chains; the largest is *Taxis G7*, with services in 50 cities, Tel: 08 25007007. In smaller cities and towns, taxi services often are combined with **private ambulance services** (Chapter 15). In urban areas, you can go to the nearest taxi rank [*stationnement de taxi*] or hail a taxi on the street. A taxi is fitted with a roof lamp, which when lit indicates that the taxi is available for hire. Most taxis are saloon and estate cars and will take up to three passengers; extra passengers or additional baggage can be carried at surcharges upon advance booking. For further information on taxis, contact *Fédération nationale des artisans du taxi*, 45 rue Armand Carrel, 75019 Paris, Tel: 01 44522350, *www.artisan-taxi.com*.

Transport atlas [*Atlas des transports*]

The Transport atlas [*Atlas des transports*] presents 33 maps of rail services, 25 maps of urban metro and tram services, information on 225 urban transport systems, plans of 40 principal railway stations, a variety of local details and, from 2007, information on bus services. It is updated in a new edition every two years and is published by Moviken, a digital cartography group that publishes a variety of maps and map products, head office at Cité Descartes – Polytechnicum de Marne-la-Vallée, 23 rue Alfred Nobel, 77420 Champs-sur-Marne, Tel: 01 60330303, *www.itineraires-et-territoires.com*. The Transport atlas and other specialised transport map products may be ordered online from the *Itinéraires & Territoires* subsidiary at *www.itineraires-et-territoires.com*. The company also supports *itransports.fr*, an online local map and route locator service at *www.itransports.fr*.

Transport Authorities Organisation [*Groupement des Autorités Organisatrices de Transport (GART)*]

GART is the national organisation for the public transport authorities of 177 urban areas, 58 *Départements* and 19 *Régions*. Its principal goals are to promote public transport as well as other alternatives to travelling by car. It acts as a central clearing house for financial, legal, technical and social aspects of public transport, and it compiles statistics and offers a broad range of publications to the public. For further information, contact GART, 22 rue de Palestro, 75002 Paris, Tel: 01 40411819, *www.gart.org*, *gart@gart.org*.

Vocabulary [*Vocabulaire*] The vocabulary of travel and transport is large, as it is in any language. There are two online sources of terminology:

- GART, the public transport organisation, *www.gart.org*, click on *Transports publics en france* and then on *Lexique des transports publics*.
- Train-Rail, an interactive railway encyclopaedia at *www.train-rail.com*.

47
Useful books

In addition to the books and other publications mentioned in the previous 46 chapters, at least ten references may be useful to new as well as established residents.

Driving Licences in the EU and in the EEA

Driving Licences in the European Union and in the European Economic Area (Luxembourg, 2000, Office for Official Publications of the European Communities, 190 pages with gatefold covers, A4 format, spiral bound, ISBN 92-828-9537-8).

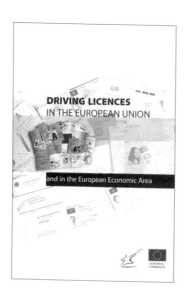

This book consists of colour reproductions of the driving licences of all EU/EEA countries valid from the mid 1950s until it was published in 2000, along with uniform explanations of them in English. For instance, for France there are seven versions of the *Permis de conduire*, from the one valid until 1954 to the last paper version valid from 1 March 1999 onwards. Though the effects of the European Commission driving licence directive that entered into force on 1 July 1996 are clearly evident in the similarity of national licences issued after that date, older licences differ, and some differences remain. So this is the best single reference for comparing the familiar – a driving licence that you may hold – with the less familiar – a driving licence issued in France or in another country.

Gault Millau Guide

Gault Millau Guide, 2006 edition, ISBN 2-914913-15-X.

In 1972, culinary critics Henri Gault (1929-2000) and Christian Millau (1929-) started a culinary movement, *La nouvelle cuisine* as well as a Guide to the restaurants of France, based in part on the success of a monthly magazine, *Le Nouveau Guide* launched three years earlier. The Guide ranks restaurants on a score of 1 to 20, and like the **Michelin Guide**, it is influential in the culinary world of France. Gault Millau also publishes guides for Austria, Germany and Switzerland as well as wine guides and a monthly magazine. Head office: 5, rue Madame de Sanzillon, 92586 Cichy Cedex, Tel: 08 92701169, *www.guides-gaultmillau.fr*.

Healthcare in France, Complementary Health Insurance in France

Healthcare in France, A Guide for Expatriates and its ancillary *Complementary Health Insurance in France*, both in A4 format, available on order from the head office in southern France at Les Ecureuils, Rte de la Motte, 83800 Figanieres, Tel: 04 94851550, *pjowen@rivieramail.com*, *www.expathealthdirect.co.uk* in English.

Expatriates from the UK often find the health insurance system of France confusing, principally because like the systems of other continental European countries, it is outwardly similar to, but in principle and practice differs from, the National Health Service. In 1998, Peter Owen, an expatriate Englishman who in 1993 had moved to France after 20 years in the British Army, sought a remedy to that frequent problem. He founded Expathealthdirect Ltd. specifically to advise fellow expatriates on healthcare in France. In addition to its advisory services, the company now publishes guides and two or three times each year updates them.

Lexicon [*Lexique*]

Le Petit Larousse (Paris, Larousse, 2006 most recent edition, 1856 pages, ISBN 2-035302064-4) and *Larousse super major* (Paris, Larousse, 2004, 1375 pages hardcover, ISBN 2-03532166-2).

The two disillusioned former schoolteachers could not have envisioned the outcome then, but in 1851 when they met, Pierre Larousse (1817-1875) and Augustin Boyer (1821-1896) formed a partnership that initially published children's books and with the years became one of the benchmarks of European lexicography. Today, *Le Petit Larousse,* now more than a century old, is the *de facto* standard desk dictionary and encyclopaedia, in homes and offices across the country. Its simplified sibling, *Larousse super major*, compiled for children in the last year of primary school and the first year of secondary school, is nearly as popular and also is appreciated by new residents learning the language.

Michelin Guide

Michelin Hôtels & Restaurants 2006 (Clermont-Ferrand, 2005, 2062 pages, 12 × 20 cm hardcover, ISBN 2-06-711569-3).

The famed Michelin Guide, published almost every year since it first appeared in 1900 and now probably the world's most famed restaurant guide.

OECD in Figures

OECD in Figures 2005 (Paris, OECD, 6 October 2005, 98 pages, ISBN 9264013059) available from the OECD bookshop at *www.OECDbookshop.org*.

This handy pocket data book is published in October each year, in English and in French versions, in printed editions stocked by the OECD bookshop and in free downloadable PDF files. It provides key data on all OECD countries, contains numerous comparative tables and graphs and has links to downloadable spread sheets underlying each.

Starting a business in France

Starting a Business in France by Richard Whiting (Oxford, HowToBooks, 2006, 160 pages paperback, ISBN 1-84528-123-3).

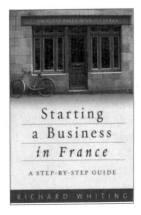

Starting a business in any country can be daunting, more so if you are unfamiliar with the relevant regulations and procedures. If you contemplate starting a business in France, you may benefit from *Starting a Business in France*, a DIY guide that in 12 chapters walks you through all you need to know, including what not to do.

Statistics [*Statistique*]

Annuaire Statistique de la France 2006, 560 pages plus 44 pages indexes and directories, 21.5 × 30.5 cm hardcover, ISBN 2-11-068365-1.

For all matters that can be expressed in figures, *Annuaire Statistique de la France,* the definitive A–Z compilation for the country is the best single source. Each annual edition includes the comprehensive statistics for previous years up to two years before the cover date, organised in 18 sectors and 41 thematic chapters, and is published by the INSEE regional facility in Marseille.

What

Quid 2006, Robert Laffont, 2178 pages, 19 × 28 cm hardcover, ISBN 2-22110448X.

Quid – from the Latin meaning "What" in the sense of underlying meaning – is a single-volume thematic encyclopaedia published annually since 1963. It now is a best-selling home reference, with some 2.5 million titbits of information, in large format – just slightly smaller than A4 – 5.2 cm thick, weighing more than 2.4 kg.

Don't get caught out when making regular foreign currency transfers

Even once you have bought your property in France you need to make sure that you don't forget about foreign exchange. It's highly likely that you'll need to make regular foreign currency transfers from the UK whether for mortgage payments, maintenance expenditure or transferring pensions or salaries, and you may not realise that using your bank to arrange these transfers isn't always the best option. Low exchange rates, high fees and commission charges all eat away at your money and mean that each time you use your bank you lose out. However, by using Currencies Direct's Overseas Regular Transfer Plan you can get more of your money time after time.

Exchange Rates
Your bank is likely to only offer you a tourist rate of exchange due to the small amounts being transferred. However, Currencies Direct is able to offer you a commercial rate of exchange regardless of the amount that you wish to transfer.

Transfer Charges
Most banks will typically charge between £10 and £40 for every monthly transfer. Currencies Direct is able to offer free transfers, which will save you a considerable amount of money over time.

Commission Charges
When made through a bank transfers are usually liable for a commission charge of around 2%. By using Currencies Direct you can avoid commission charges altogether.

How does it work?
It is very easy to use Currencies Direct. The first thing you need to do is open an account with them. Once this is done all you need to do is set up a direct debit with your bank and confirm with Currencies Direct how much money you would like to send and how often (monthly or quarterly). They will then take the money from your account on a specified day and once they have received the cleared funds transfer it to France at the best possible rate available.

Information provided by Currencies Direct.
Website: *www.currenciesdirect.com*
Email: *info@currenciesdirect.com*
Tel: 0845 389 1729

Index – English

Index – French